LIVES *of* *the* SAINTS

Also by Richard P. McBrien

Catholicism

The HarperCollins Encyclopedia of Catholicism (general editor)

The Lives of the Popes: The Pontiffs from St. Peter to Benedict XVI

The Pocket Guide to the Popes

The Pocket Guide to the Saints

LIVES *of* *the* SAINTS

From Mary and St. Francis of Assisi to John XXIII and Mother Teresa

RICHARD P. MCBRIEN

HarperOne
An Imprint of HarperCollins*Publishers*

Photo and art credits appear on p. 645 and consitute a continuation of this copyright page.

HarperCollins books may be purchased for educational, business, or sales promotional use. For information please write: Special Markets Department, HarperCollins Publishers, 10 East 53rd Street, New York, NY 10022.

HarperCollins books may be purchased for educational, business, or sales promotional use. For information please write: Special Markets Department, HarperCollins Publishers, 10 East 53rd Street, New York, NY 10022.

HarperCollins Web site: http://www.harpercollins.com

FIRST HARPERCOLLINS PAPERBACK EDITION PUBLISHED IN 2003

Designed by Jessica Shatan

Library of Congress Cataloging-in-Publication Data is available upon request.
ISBN 978–0–06–123283–1

09 10 11 12 13 RRD(H) 10 9 8 7 6 5 4 3 2

Contents

Preface

THIS BOOK CAME ABOUT AS THE RESULT OF A SUGGESTION FROM MY publisher, Stephen Hanselman, and my editor, John Loudon, to consider doing something on the saints similar in nature to my previous book *Lives of the Popes: The Pontiffs from St. Peter to John Paul II*, published in the fall of 1997.

As was the case with my book on the popes, the great bulk of this volume consists of biographical sketches of varying lengths (Part IV). The biographies are of the saints who appear on the General Roman Calendar, which contains the list of feast days celebrated throughout the Roman Catholic Church, as well as of the many other saints whose feasts are celebrated by various countries, religious orders, or other Christian denominations, particularly the Greek and Russian Orthodox Churches, the churches of the Anglican Communion, especially the Church of England and the Episcopal Church in the United States of America (USA), and the churches of the Lutheran World Federation, especially the Evangelical Lutheran Church in America. In addition there are references to holy persons not yet recognized as saints, including even non-Christians. Other features include a time line that integrates some of the Church's most important saints with the major events of church and world history; three introductory chapters (Parts I–III) explaining in some detail the meaning of sanctity, its varieties of expression, and the process by which saints are proclaimed and canonized; an epilogue (Part V) that recapitulates the history of the Church in relation to some of the key saints who helped to shape its life and mission in each of its centuries of existence, distinguishes the saints by categories, and proposes a list of twenty of the Church's most representative saints; a series of tables (Part VI), including lists of (1) feast days, (2) patron saints, (3) places and their patrons, (4) groups and causes with their corresponding patrons, (5) saints with their distinctive emblems in art and iconography, (6) saintly "firsts," and (7) a chart that compares Pope John Paul II's canonizations and beatifications with those of his predecessors; notes; a glossary of terms; a select and annotated bibliography of popular and scholarly resources; and an index of personal names and subjects.

I must make the same disclaimer here that I made in the preface to *Lives of the Popes*. This is not a work of primary or original historical scholarship. Indeed, most historians would require a lifetime of research to master the biographies of only one or two major saints and of the periods in which they lived. This book is the work of a theologian, not of a historian, and more specifically of an ecclesiologist, whose task is to reflect on the lives of the saints and on the process of canonization in the light of the nature, mission, and history of the Church as a whole. What do the saints tell us, individually and collectively, not only about the character of Christian discipleship, but about the meaning of human existence itself? And what does the action of the Church in proclaiming or canonizing various types of Christians as saints disclose about the fundamental religious values of the Church itself?

The originality of this book consists, first, in the overall concept and structure of the book; second, in the biographical material selected from the vast body of secondary literature as both theologically and historically pertinent and potentially interesting to nonspecialist readers; third, in the theological interpretations of sanctity, spirituality, and the canonization process; fourth, in the ecumenical and liturgical emphases employed throughout the book; and fifth, in the various features that are designed to expand and complement readers' understanding of and appreciation for the individual saints and the Church's own communal call to holiness.

Is the book a reference work, a book to be read as any other, from beginning to end, or a devotional resource, to be used for daily reflections on the lives of the saints? It is all three. Many readers will undoubtedly look first to see if their own favorite saints are mentioned and what is said about them. Then they may skip from month to month, perusing the biographies at random. It is my strong hope that readers who are immediately drawn to the Lives section of the book will not neglect for long the first three chapters and the Epilogue, because without them the biographical profiles are just so many disconnected vignettes of famous and not-so-famous religious figures from the distant and recent past.

Indeed, there is no more basic question for a Christian (or any individual human being, for that matter) to address than the question of sanctity. In what does a fully human life consist? What does it mean not only to be "good," but to be "really good," even outstandingly so? And what role does a global and multicultural community such as the Church have in inspiring others to live up to such standards of human behavior, and what responsibility does it have to live up to those standards itself?

In this regard, I am reminded of some powerful lines in the document "Justice in the World," of the Third World Synod of Bishops, meeting in Rome in 1971: "While the Church is bound to give witness to justice, it recognizes that anyone who ventures to speak to people about justice must first be just in their eyes" (III.2). Also cogent are these words of Pope Paul VI in his apostolic exhortation "On Evangelization in the Modern World" *(Evangelii nuntiandi)*, released in December 1975: "Modern men and women listen more willingly to witnesses than to teachers, and if they do listen to teachers, it is because they are witnesses" (n. 41). Both statements underscore the crucial point that religious people, more than any others, have a special obligation to practice what they preach. Indeed, no accusation against adherents of a religious faith is more devastating than that they say one thing, but do another. Meditation on the saints and on the Church's own communal call to holiness are important correctives to such tendencies. They remind us that it is humanly possible to practice what we preach, but that it also requires great and persistent effort as well as heroic virtue.

Readers can see for themselves what sources I found most useful in the completion of this project. They are listed, with pertinent comments, in the Select Bibliography toward the end of this book. I should like to single out for special praise the new twelve-volume *Butler's Lives of the Saints: New Full Edition*, edited by Paul Burns and published by The Liturgical Press, Collegeville, Minnesota, in conjunction with Burns & Oates in England. It is the most comprehensive treatment of the saints in the English language. The advantage of this book, however, is that the vast amount of biographical material that one finds in *Butler's Lives of the Saints* and in similar multivolume resources has been digested, synthesized, and compressed into a single volume. Moreover, the material is given a broader theological and historical context.

I could not have completed the book without help and encouragement from colleagues and friends. At the risk of leaving some of them out, I shall mention here just a few. My temporary graduate assistant, Edward Hahnenberg, a doctoral candidate in theology at the University of Notre Dame, did much of the preliminary research, identifying and evaluating resources as well as creating lists and charts that proved to be invaluable time-savers in the actual writing of the book. Two friends gave me helpfully critical assessments of the drafts: Thomas F. O'Meara, O.P., William K. Warren Professor of Theology at Notre Dame and a world-class expert on Thomas Aquinas and the theology of grace, and Beverly M. Brazauskas, who brought to the task long years of experience in teaching, religious education, and pastoral ministry. She also assisted, as she has with some of my previous books, in the preparation of the indexes. My longtime personal assistant, Donna Shearer, kept the rest of my commitments in order and on track as I focused almost single-mindedly on this project over the course of many months, but she also directly contributed in several ways to the completion of the book itself. My colleague Lawrence S. Cunningham, also a professor of theology at Notre Dame, is, as far as I am concerned, this country's leading expert on the saints. His advice, his ready availability for questions, and his generosity in making resources available to me out of his own personal library were especially valuable. My former graduate assistant Sally Vance-Trembath, who is currently writing her dissertation under my direction, was also generous in tracking down sources in the library and in making herself available for *ad hoc* assignments. I could not have completed the work as quickly as I did without the advantage of a fully funded sabbatical leave from my regular teaching responsibilities at Notre Dame. For that I am grateful to the university, and in particular to the chair of the theology department, John Cavadini, and to the dean of the College of Arts and Letters, Mark Roche. Finally, I am deeply appreciative of the support, encouragement, and guidance I have received from the people at Harper San Francisco: Stephen Hanselman, the publisher; John Loudon, executive editor; Terri Leonard, managing editor; Kris Ashley, assistant to John Loudon; Ann Moru, copy editor; and everyone else connected with the production of this book.

Since I have never read a book review that blamed any or all of those who assisted the author in writing the work, perhaps it is time to put to rest the custom of ending a preface with an acknowledgment that, in spite of all the external help, the deficiencies are the sole responsibility of the author. Those who are quick to criticize the work of other people should remember that even the heroically virtuous saints had their imperfections. This is a book about those who were, before all else, human. As someone whispered to St. Augustine while he strolled in his garden, "*Tolle, lege.*" Pick it up and read it. My fondest hope is that readers' investment of time and energy will be amply repaid.

RICHARD P. MCBRIEN
University of Notre Dame
May 2001

Time Line: The Saints in History

Church and Its Saints

1–100

The Blessed Virgin Mary and *Joseph* raise Jesus to manhood

Peter, the other apostles, and *Mary Magdalene* witness to the Resurrection

Christianity spreads through missionary activity

Peter preaches to the Jews; *Paul,* to the Gentiles; they are martyred in Rome (ca. 64 and ca. 62–67, respectively)

Persecutions by Nero (ca. 64), Domitian (ca. 81–ca. 96), and Trajan (ca. 98–117)

100

The Church interacts with secular philosophy: *Justin* and the other Apologists

Irenaeus opposes early heresies (Gnosticism, Docetism) that deny the humanity of Christ

Martyrdoms continue: *Polycarp*

200

Persecutions by Decius (249–51) and Valerian (257–58)

Age of martyrs: *Pope Sixtus II, Lawrence, Agatha, Cyprian of Carthage*

Period of imperial toleration (258–ca. 300)

300

Persecution by Diocletian (303–13)

The Edict of Constantine (313)

The First Council of Nicaea (325): *Athanasius,* the leading spokesman against Arianism

First Council of Constantinople (381): *Basil the Great, Gregory Nazianzen,* and *Gregory of Nyssa*

Monasticism takes root: *Anthony of Egypt, Pachomius, Paul the Hermit, Hilarion, Martin of Tours*

Conversion of *Augustine* by *Ambrose* (387)

400

Doctrinal controversies continue

Dawn of biblical studies: *Jerome* (d. 420)

Augustine of Hippo (d. 430) opposes Pelagianism

Council of Ephesus (431) opposes Nestorianism

Patrick's mission to Ireland (ca. 431)

Council of Chalcedon (451) opposes Monophysitism: *Pope Leo the Great, Cyril of Alexandria*

500

Benedict of Nursia founds Monte Cassino (ca. 525)

Monasticism takes root in Ireland: *Columba of Iona, Brigid of Kildare, Ita of Killeedy, Columban*

Gregory the Great (d. 604): first monk-pope, virtual civil ruler of Rome

Mission to Britain (597): *Augustine of Canterbury*

600

Tribal migrations throughout Europe; Muslim invasions in North Africa

Scholar-monks and scholar-bishops preserve Christian culture: *Isidore of Seville, Benedict Biscop, Cuthbert*

700

Merovingian dynasty yields to the Carolingians

Mission to the Germans (719): *Boniface, Chrodegang of Metz, Walburga*

Iconoclasm controversy (ca. 725–842); Second Council of Nicaea (787)

Preservation of Christian culture continues: *Venerable Bede, John Damascene*

800

Charlemagne is crowned Holy Roman emperor (800)

Reform of Benedictine monasteries in France: *Benedict of Aniane*

Cyril and *Methodius:* mission to the Slavs (ca. 862)

St. Peter's Basilica plundered by Muslim pirates (846)

Pope Nicholas I excommunicates Patriarch Photius of Constantinople (863)

900

Papacy sinks to moral depths; dominated by Roman families

Monastery of Cluny founded (909)

Christianity expands into Hungary (ca. 942), Poland (966), and Russia (ca. 988): *Adalbert of Prague, Vladimir of Kiev*

First papal canonization: *Ulrich of Augsburg* (993)

1000

The Church consolidates its missionary gains in Europe and England: *Stanislaus of Kraków, Anselm of Canterbury*

East-West Schism (1054)

Gregory VII (1073–85): reformer pope; claimed authority over whole Church

Bruno founds Carthusians (1084)

Roman Curia established (1089)

First Crusade (1096–99)

Robert of Molesmes and *Stephen Harding* found Cistercians (1098)

1100

Bernard of Clairvaux founds Cistercian abbey of Clairvaux (1114)

Norbert founds Premonstratensians (1120)

Second Crusade (1146–48)

Carmelites founded (ca. 1154)

Thomas Becket martyred in Canterbury Cathedral (1170)

Third Crusade (1189–92)

1200

Fourth through Seventh Crusades (1202–54)

Francis of Assisi founds the Franciscans (1209); *Dominic* founds the Dominicans (1215)

New mendicant orders produce major theologians and preachers: *Thomas Aquinas, Albert the Great, Bonaventure, Peter of Verona, Anthony of Padua*

Gregory IX establishes Papal Inquisition (1233)

The first Scottish saint to be canonized: *Margaret of Scotland* (1250)

Augustinian Hermits founded (1256)

Innocent V (1276): first Dominican pope

Women mystics: *Mechthilde of Magdeburg* (d. 1282)

Nicholas IV (1288–92): first Franciscan pope

Celestine V (1294): first hermit-pope; resigned after five months

1300

Avignon papacy (1309–77) opposed by *Catherine of Siena, Bridget of Sweden*, foundress of Brigittines

The first pope to be formally canonized: *Celestine V* (1313)

Great Western Schism (1378–1417), also opposed by *Catherine of Siena*

East and West alike venerate *Sergius of Radonezh* (ca. 1315–92)

1400

Council of Constance (1414–18) ends Great Western Schism

A century of great preachers: *Bernardino of Siena, Vincent Ferrer*

And of great women saints: *Frances of Rome, Joan of Arc*

Spanish Inquisition established (1479)

1500

Leo X (1513–21) excommunicates Martin Luther (1517); Reformation begins

English Reformation begins (1534)

Ignatius of Loyola founds Society of Jesus (1534)

Jesuit missions to India and Japan (1542–45, 1548–49): *Francis Xavier, Paul Miki*

Counter-Reformation and Catholic Reformation

Council of Trent (1545–63)

Theological and pastoral renewal: *Robert Bellarmine, Peter Canisius, Charles Borromeo*

Other new orders founded: *Philip Neri*, Oratorians; *Francis of Paolo,* Minims; *Camillus de Lellis,* Camillians; *Anthony Mary Zaccaria,* Barnabites; *Jerome Emiliani*, Somascan Fathers; *Angela Merici,* Ursulines; *Peter of Alcántara,* Alcantarines; *John of God,* Brothers Hospitallers

Pius V excommunicates Queen Elizabeth (1570); English Catholics are martyred: *Thomas More, John Fisher, Edmund Campion*

Roman catacombs discovered (1578)

Sixtus V (1585–90) reorganizes Roman Curia in present form

1600

Baroque Catholicism (ca. 1580–ca. 1750)

Jesuit missionary Matteo Ricci admitted to Peking (1601)

Galileo imprisoned (1633)

Lay apostolate and lay spirituality emerge: *Francis de Sales*

New orders for the sake of the poor and education: *Vincent de Paul,* Vincentians; *Louise de Marillac,* Sisters of Charity; *Jane Frances de Chantal,* Visitation Sisters; *John Eudes,* Congregation of Jesus and Mary; *Joseph Calasanz,* Piarists

Mission to North America: *Isaac Jogues and companions*

Mission to Latin America: *Peter Claver, Martin de Porres, Rose of Lima*

Devotion to the Sacred Heart: *Margaret Mary Alacoque*

First canonized saint of the Americas: *Rose of Lima* (1671)

1700

Still more orders founded: *Paul of the Cross,* Passionists; *Louis Grignion de Montfort,* Montfort Fathers and Daughters of Wisdom; *John Baptist de La Salle,* Brothers of the Christian Schools; *Alphonsus Liguori,* Redemptorists

Clement XIV suppresses the Jesuits (1773)

1800

Catholic Romanticism

Pius VII reinstates the Jesuits (1814)

New religious orders: *Anthony Claret,* Claretians; *John Bosco,* Salesians; *Elizabeth Ann Seton,* Daughters of Charity of St. Joseph; *Julia Billiart,* Sisters of Notre Dame de Namur; *Peter Julian Eymard,* Blessed Sacrament Fathers

Continued missionary expansion: *Andrew Kim Taegõn and companions* (Korea), *Andrew Dung-Lac and companions* (Vietnam), *Charles Lwanga and companions* (black Africa)

First Eastern saint to be formally canonized by the Roman Catholic Church: *Josephat* (1867)

First Vatican Council (1869–70)

1900

Delayed influence of nineteenth-century saints: *Theresa of the Child Jesus (Little Flower), Bernadette of Soubirous, Maria Goretti, John Vianney*

First American citizen canonized: *Frances Xavier Cabrini* (1946)

John XXIII convenes Second Vatican Council (1962–65)

First women Doctors of the Church: *Teresa of Ávila, Catherine of Siena* (1970)

First American-born saint: *Elizabeth Ann Seton* (1975)

The first Filipino saint: *Lawrence Ruiz* (1987)

First Canadian-born saint: *Mary Margaret d'Youville* (1990)

First Australian-born saint: *Mary MacKillop* (1995)

First saints connected with the Holocaust: *Maximilian Maria Kolbe* (1982), *Teresa Benedicta of the Cross (Edith Stein)* (1998)

2000

First Chinese saints: *the martyrs of China* (2000)

Secular History

1–100

Roman emperors: Tiberius (14–37), Caligula (37–41), Claudius (41–54), Nero (54–68), Domitian (ca. 81–ca. 96)

100

Roman emperors: Trajan (ca. 98–117), Antoninus Pius (138–61), Marcus Aurelius (161–80), Septimus Severus (193–211)

200

Roman emperors: Decius (249–51), Gallus (251–53), Valerian (253–60), Gallienus (260–68), Diocletian (284–305)

Partition of Roman Empire into East and West (285)

300

Constantine the Great (306–37): sole emperor

Seat of Roman Empire moved to Constantinople (331)

Empire splits again into West and East (340)

Barbarian migrations begin (ca. 375–ca. 568)

Theodosius the Great (392–95): last ruler of united empire

400

Barbarian migrations continue

Visigoths invade Italy (401)

Alaric captures and sacks Rome (410)

Vandals sack Rome (455)

End of Western Roman emperors (476)

Theodoric founds Ostrogoth kingdom of Italy (493)

Clovis, king of the Franks, converts to Christianity (496)

500

Justinian the Great (527–65)

Rome and Naples annexed to Byzantium (553)

Lombards drive Byzantines from northern Italy (565)

600

Muhammad (570–632)

Barbarian migrations end in western Europe (ca. 600)

Arabs conquer Jerusalem (637) and destroy Carthage (697)

700

Christianity in North Africa exterminated by Muslims (by 700)

Charlemagne becomes sole ruler of Frankish kingdom (771)

800

Charlemagne crowned first Carolingian emperor (800)

Arabs sack Rome (846) and conquer Sicily (878)

Emperor Basil recaptures Italy from the Arabs (880)

900

Arabs expelled from central Italy (916)

Otto I crowned Holy Roman emperor (962)

Otto II crowned Holy Roman emperor (967)

Otto III crowned Holy Roman emperor (996)

1000

Muslims sack the Church of the Holy Sepulchre in Jerusalem (1009)

Battle of Hastings (1066)

Henry IV excommunicated by *Gregory VII* (1076)

Henry IV imprisons *Gregory VII* (1084)

Crusaders capture Jerusalem (1099)

1100

Henry V crowned Holy Roman emperor (1111)

Lothar III crowned Holy Roman emperor (1133)

Frederick Barbarossa crowned Holy Roman emperor (1155)

Thomas Becket murdered in Canterbury Cathedral (1170)

1200

Crusaders capture Constantinople, establish Latin empire (1204)

England and Ireland become papal fiefs (1213)

Magna Carta (1215)

Marco Polo to China (1271–95)

Crusades formally end (1291)

1300

Black Death in Europe (1347–49)

Byzantines lose last possession in Asia Minor to Turks (1390)

1400

Constantine XI Palaeologus, last Byzantine emperor (1448–53)

Fall of Constantinople to Turks (1453)

Gutenberg Bible (1456)

Lorenzo de' Medici rules Florence (1469–92)

Moorish kingdom ends in Spain (1492)

Christopher Columbus discovers America (1492)

Alexander VI divides New World between Spain and Portugal (1493)

1500

Explorers: Vasco da Gama (1469–1524), Ferdinand Magellan (1480–1521), Francis Drake (1540–96)

Michelangelo (1475–1564)

Copernican theory (1512)

Mary succeeds Edward VI (1553)

Elizabeth I succeeds Mary (1558)

Gregorian calendar adopted (1582)

Defeat of the Spanish Armada (1588)

1600

First African slaves brought to North America (1619)

Peter Minuit buys island of Manhattan for $24 (1626)

Harvard College founded (1636)

Isaac Newton (1642–1727)

Peace of Westphalia (1648)

1700

American Declaration of Independence (1776)

U.S. Constitution (1788)

George Washington, first U.S. president (1789–97)

French Revolution (1789)

Rosetta Stone found in Egypt (1799)

1800

Napoleon crowned king of Italy (1805), annexes Papal States (1809), defeated at Waterloo (1815)

Holy Roman Empire ends (1806)

Charles Darwin (1809–82)

Karl Marx (1818–83)

Communist Manifesto (1848)

Italy proclaimed a kingdom (1861)

American Civil War (1861–65)

U.S. Emancipation Proclamation (1863)

Dominion of Canada established (1867)

Kulturkampf in Prussia (1871)

1900

Sigmund Freud (1856–1939)

Commonwealth of Australia established (1901)

New Zealand attains Dominion status (1907)

World War I (1914–18)

Russian Revolution (1917)

Irish Free State established (1922)

Frank D. Roosevelt elected U.S. president (1932)

Adolf Hitler, German chancellor (1933)

Spanish Civil War (1936–39)

World War II (1939–45)

United Nations charter (1945)

Cold War (1945–89)

Republic of Ireland established (1949)

John F. Kennedy assassinated (1963)

Vietnam War (1965–73)

Communism collapses (1989)

PART I

WHO IS A SAINT?

THE VENERATION OF SAINTS HAS BEEN AN INTEGRAL PART OF the Church's life practically ever since the death of its first martyr, Stephen [December 26].[1] Most Christians (and many non-Christians as well) are named after saints, as are some major and mid-sized cities in the United States, for example, St. Louis, St. Augustine, St. Paul, San Francisco, San Jose, San Juan, Santa Anna, Santa Barbara, San Bernardino, and San Antonio. The most famous golf course in the world is named after St. Andrew [November 30], and one of the world's most beloved mythical characters, Santa Claus, after St. Nicholas [December 6].

In 1955, however, Karl Rahner (d. 1984), the leading Catholic theologian of the twentieth century, noted the absence of any serious treatment of the saints in contemporary theology. "It is a strange thing," he wrote, "but if one takes a glance at an average modern dogmatic theology, one will find it necessary to look in a great many different places for the doctrine of the Saints of the holy Church and of their veneration."[2] Twenty-five years later, the situation remained essentially unchanged. Lawrence Cunningham, a well-established expert on the saints and spirituality, found no evidence in 1980 "that theologians are doing much serious reflection on the relevance or even the meaning of the saint in the Christian tradition."[3]

The saints were nevertheless an important part of the devotional life of Catholics during this period. Parents were carefully instructed to choose a saint's name for their newborn infants; otherwise, the priest would not baptize them. Boys and girls were expected to select a saint's name for Confirmation. Catholics of all ages routinely prayed to St. Anthony of Padua [June 13] to find lost articles or to St. Jude [October 28] in the face of seemingly hopeless situations. There were popular novenas to St. Anne [July 26], the Little Flower (St. Theresa of the Child Jesus) [October 1], the Miraculous Medal (a devotion promoted by St. Catherine Labouré [November 28]), and St. Jude. Children and adults alike wore medals imprinted with the images of St. Joseph [March 19], St. Benedict of Nursia [July 11], and St. Christopher [July 25]. The last was such a popular item in automobiles that it was a matter of widespread concern, even anxiety, for many Catholics (and some non-Catholics too) when Christopher was dropped from the liturgical calendar in 1969. Saints were also the subjects of colorful stained-glass windows in churches and of statues, medieval and modern. National or ethnic parishes were readily identified by their patron saints, for example, Anne (French), Anthony of Padua (Italian), Boniface [June 5] (German), Casimir [March 4] (Lithuanian or Polish), Cyril and Methodius [February 14] (Polish), Martin de Porres [November 3] (African American), Our Lady of Guadalupe [December 12] (Hispanic), Our Lady of Mount Carmel [July 16] (Italian), and Stanislaus [April 11] (Polish).

Since 1980 the saints and spirituality have moved closer to the center of theological as well as devotional attention.[4] The reasons vary and are perhaps too complex to pinpoint. However, the increased interest in narrative and storytelling and the heightened value of experience as a *locus* (Lat., "source") of theological understanding would have to be counted among the leading factors.[5] It may also be a matter of the delayed impact of the Second Vatican Council (1962–65), which clearly shifted the emphasis from the saints as miracle workers to the saints as models.[6] "No devotion to the saints is more acceptable to God," the great Christian humanist Erasmus [see July 12] once wrote, "than the imitation of their virtues. . . . Do you want to honor St. Francis? Then give away your wealth to the poor, restrain your evil impulses, and see in everyone you meet the image of Christ."[7]

The Saints as "Holy Ones"

Saints are holy people. Because God alone is holy, to be a saint is to participate in, and to be an image of, the holiness of God. "Be holy, for I, the Lord, your God, am holy" (Lev. 19:2). Persons, however, cannot make themselves holy. Only God can do that. The biblical notion of holiness, rooted in the Old Testament, involves a "being set apart" by God from what is profane in order to belong in a new and special way to God. This setting apart, or consecration, can apply not only to persons, such as priests and religious, but also to places, like a temple or land, or to things, like commandments or a chalice, or to communities, like Israel ("a holy nation" [Exod. 19:6]) or the Church ("one, *holy*, catholic, and apostolic Church").[8]

For Jesus, nothing is more precious than the Kingdom, or Reign, of God, which is the healing and renewing power and presence of God on our behalf. "Instead, seek his kingdom, and these other things will be given you besides" (Luke 12:31). Like a person who finds a hidden treasure in a field or a merchant who discovers a precious pearl, one must be prepared to give up everything else in order to possess the Kingdom (Matt. 13:44–46). But it is promised only to those with a certain outlook and way of life, as expressed in the Beatitudes (Matt. 5:3–12), and to those who see and respond to Christ in the hungry, the thirsty, the naked, the homeless, and the prisoner (Matt. 25:31–46). To the scribe who grasped the meaning of the two great commandments—love of God and of neighbor—Jesus said: "You are not far from the kingdom of God" (Mark 12:34). For Jesus, the Reign of God—and, therefore, a life of holiness—is open in principle to everyone.

To share in the holiness of God is to share in the very life of God. Holiness, therefore, is a state of being that is the practical equivalent of grace, God's self-gift. To be in the "state of grace" is to be permeated and transformed by the presence of God. Saints are persons in whom the grace of God, won for us by Christ, has fully triumphed over sin—which is not to say that the saints were without sin. Jesus alone was without sin (John 8:46; 14:30; 2 Cor. 5:21; 1 Pet. 2:22; Heb. 4:15), and only he could be called "the Holy One of God" (John 6:69).

The term "holy" (Gk. *hagios*) was applied to the disciples of Christ even during their earthly lives. First Peter 1:15–16 explicitly cites Leviticus 11:44 (". . . you shall make and keep yourselves holy, because I am holy") and 19:2 ("Be holy, for I, the Lord, your God, am holy") and applies these texts to Christians. St. Paul [June 29] addresses those to whom he writes as "holy ones" (Rom. 1:7; 15:25; 1 Cor. 1:2; 2 Cor. 1:1; Eph. 1:1; Phil. 1:1). Gradually the "holy ones" became more commonly referred to as the "saints."

Categories of Saints

In the Catholic tradition, there are at least four possible applications of the word "saints": (1) all those who have been sanctified, or made holy, by the grace of Christ, whether they are living or dead, Catholic or non-Catholic, Christian or non-Christian, people of explicit religious faith or none; (2) those who, having been sanctified by Christ on earth, have entered into the joy of eternal life; (3) biblical figures in the time before Christ who lived by the Spirit of God and who became luminous examples of holiness; and (4) those whom the Church, either through popular acclaim or formal canonization, has declared to be members of the Church triumphant (i.e., those already in the company of God, the angels, and the saints in heaven) and who are commemorated and invoked in the Church's public worship and in private prayer.[9]

The Church attests to that broadly inclusive tradition each year in its celebration of the feast of All Saints [November 1]. Grace, which is the sanctifying presence of God in an individual person, is available to everyone. Every human person is oriented toward God and possesses the radical capacity to receive the grace of God. Human existence, therefore, is graced existence. We are alive by a principle, namely, the grace of God, that transcends us. We are fully human, and yet, by the grace of God, we have the capacity to become more than that, namely, to become partakers of the divine life itself and to share ultimately in God's eternal glory.[10] To participate in God's grace and glory is to be a saint in the fullest sense of the word.

Given the broader, catholic understanding of sanctity, this book acknowledges the witness to sanctity of (1) those Catholics who have not yet either been popularly acclaimed or formally canonized, such as Dorothy Day [November 29], Mother Teresa of Calcutta [September 5], and Archbishop Oscar Romero, of El Salvador [March 24]; (2) non-Catholic Christians whose sanctity has been recognized and liturgically celebrated by other churches, such as the seventeenth-century Anglican priest-poets George Herbert [February 27] and John Donne [March 31], the fourteenth-century abbot Sergius of Radonezh [September 25], regarded by some as the Francis of Assisi [October 4] of Russian Orthodoxy, and the German Lutheran Dietrich Bonhoeffer [April 9], executed by the Nazis toward the end of World War II; (3) Jews, such as the ancient prophets of Israel and a twentieth-century prophet who wrote eloquently about them, the Hasidic rabbi Abraham Heschel [December 23]; and (4) other non-Christians, such as the Hindu holy man of India, Mohandas Gandhi [January 30].[11] The principal focus of the book, however, remains on those to whom the title "saint" has traditionally applied: (5) those who were acclaimed as saints within the undivided Church of the first Christian millennium, such as Peter and Paul [June 29], Agnes [January 21] and Agatha [February 5], and (6) those who were formally canonized by the Catholic Church during the second Christian millennium, such as Catherine of Siena [April 29] and Francis Xavier [December 3], and those who are now among the canonized saints of the third Christian millennium, such as Mother Katharine Drexel [March 3].

Types of Christian Saints

In the beginning, Jesus' disciples were considered "saints" and were addressed as such by St. Paul in his Letters, or Epistles, to the various churches of the first century. The first saints in a more restricted sense of the word were the *martyrs,* who had died for the faith and whose reward was believed to have been immediate transition to eternal life with Christ. The earliest mention of a memorial cult at the burial site of a martyr is in the *Martyrdom of Polycarp* (18:1–3), written in the middle of the second century. The cult involved veneration of the site, pilgrimages to it, adoption of the martyr as the patron saint of the local church or town, and a belief in the martyr's power to perform miracles on behalf of the living.[12] From the reign of Constantine in the early fourth century and with the end of the intermittent periods of persecution, the cult of saints (the so-called red martyrs) was extended to *confessors* (the so-called white martyrs, and not to be confused with priests who administer the sacrament of Penance), namely, those who suffered imprisonment, torture, expropriation of property, hard labor, and/or exile for the faith but who did not directly suffer the martyrdom of death; to *ascetics,* especially those, such as monks, hermits, and holy women who lived a life of celibacy or virginity;[13] to *wise teachers,* including theologians and spiritual writers; to pastorally effective *church leaders,* including bishops, outstanding members of the diocesan and religious clergy, and the founders and foundresses of religious orders; and to *those who cared for the sick and the poor.*[14]

The Veneration of Saints

A Brief History

The two kinds of martyrs—"red" and "white" alike—were honored on the anniversary of their deaths, as the day of their birth to a new life in heaven. Churches were named after them and placed under their patronage. Special prayers to them were added to the Mass and readings about them were inserted into the Liturgy of the Hours, or Divine Office. Eastern churches venerated their images, while Western churches venerated their relics.[15] Biographies of various saints—some historically reliable and others less so or not at all—were composed and became more familiar to people than the Scriptures themselves, contributing to the shaping the Catholic imagination of the Middle Ages.

Although Augustine [August 28] warned the faithful in Hippo to "worship God alone," he also exhorted them to "honor the saints," and specifically the martyrs (*Sermo* 273.9). He was only confirming what was already a common feature of worship and devotional life in North Africa at the time (early fifth century). However, by the end of the patristic era (ca. eighth century) it was a constant challenge for church leaders and theologians to keep the veneration of saints, angels, and the Blessed Virgin Mary in line with the central truth of Christian faith: that Jesus Christ is the one Mediator between God and humanity (1 Tim. 2:5). In 787 the Second Council of Nicaea insisted that God alone is worthy of our worship and adoration (Gk. *latria*); by contrast, the saints are to be given our respect and honor (Gk. *dulia*). Later theology proposed that Mary, however, is worthy of *hyperdulia,* a "higher" form of veneration, but far short of adoration or worship.[16]

In the West, pilgrimages to the shrines of particular saints were matters of local pride and profit. The cult of relics—many of which were sold, traded, falsified, stolen, and fought over—became increasingly important after the fall of the Roman Empire, especially in northern Europe, because many areas did not have their own local martyrs and shrines. The practice of the "translation," or transfer, of relics from tombs to churches throughout the Christian world became more common at this time, when the Church was encouraging the veneration of relics among the newly evangelized in order to help solidify their faith and to prevent any relapse into the worship of idols. Popes were often generous with the relics of saints buried in Roman cemeteries. In the twelfth century the Crusaders expropriated some of the East's most revered relics and took them back to various churches in the West, thereby enhancing the prestige of those churches.

Monastic piety also gave prominence to saints as founders and foundresses, patrons and patronesses, and intercessors and protectors. The sanctoral cycle in the liturgy grew rapidly. Local bishops gradually took control of the process from the fifth century. They would not allow a saint's name to be added to the calendar unless they were given a written account of the candidate's life (Lat. *vita*) and miracles. These accounts were read aloud in the presence of the bishop.[17] Upon approval of the bishop or local synod, the body was exhumed and transferred to an altar, an act that was the equivalent of canonization. The saint was assigned a feast day and the name was added to the local calendar. As the veneration of certain saints spread beyond the limits of a given diocese or country and also beyond the control of the local bishops and abbots, efforts were made to contain abuses, especially in the proliferation of shrines, relics, and devotional practices. The papacy eventually intervened, but the first papal canonization did not take place until 993, when Ulrich of Augsburg [July 4] was formally proclaimed a saint by Pope John XV. Almost two hundred years later (ca. 1170) Pope Alexander III, in a letter to the king of Sweden, insisted that no one should be venerated as a saint without the authority of the church of Rome. When this letter was included in the *Decretals* of Pope Gregory IX in 1234, it became part of the general law of the Church in the West, namely, that only the pope could canonize a saint.[18] The process acquired the character of a legal trial during the Avignon papacy (1309–77), when the Roman Curia became more streamlined in its operations. A distinction also emerged soon thereafter between those who were papally canonized (known as the *sancti* [Lat., "saints"]) and those who were venerated locally or by a religious order (known as *beati* [Lat., "blessed"]). Although the two categories continue to exist today, the basis for the distinction has changed. Those who have been beatified are now assigned a feast day and may be venerated by the universal Church.

The cult of saints took a major turn in the late Middle Ages as the ordinary faithful became more and more concerned with the question of life after death. Pope Benedict XII issued a constitution, *Benedictus Deus* (Lat., "Blessed God"), in 1336 teaching that the saints see God "in an intuitive vision face to face" (what is known as the Beatific Vision), and the Council of Florence reaffirmed this doctrine in 1439. Because of the saints' close proximity to God in heaven, they were increasingly viewed as powerful sources of spiritual and material favors. By the time of the Reformation in the sixteenth century the notion of a "treasury of merits" had also taken hold in the Church. The Church believed that it had title to a wealth of spiritual benefits earned by the good works and sufferings of the saints and the Blessed Virgin Mary as well as of Christ himself. These merits could be applied, in the form of indulgences, to each individual, living or dead, to cancel his or her temporal punishments due to sin in the state of purgatory. The Reformers, particularly Martin Luther, strongly objected to the cult of saints (and their relics) on the grounds that it detracted from Christ's role as the one Mediator between God and humanity. The Council of Trent (1545–63) rejected the Reformers' stance and encouraged Catholics to invoke the saints as sources of grace from God through Christ, who alone is our Redeemer.

In the Baroque period of the sixteenth and seventeenth centuries, devotions outside of Mass and the Divine Office, such as novenas in honor of the saints, pilgrimages to their shrines, and prayers to the saints in quest of some temporal or spiritual advantage, became increasingly popular. The celebration of the Mass became more theatrical and increasingly remote from the ordinary experience of the laity.[19] The new extraliturgical devotions filled in the spiritual gap. They appealed to the people's senses (few could read) and were in the vernacular (few could understand Latin). They provided tangible ways of making the grace of God vivid and concrete. The faithful learned the stories of their own local saints from art and sermons. Canonizations of new saints and devotions to them increased significantly, especially in Italy, Spain, and France, and continued at a vigorous pace until the Second Vatican Council.

Theological Reflections

The veneration, or cult, of saints belongs to the very essence of the Church, which is not only one, catholic, and apostolic, but also holy. As Karl Rahner pointed out, if the Church, understood as the people of God, lacked saints, it would not be what it was meant to be, namely, the corporate embodiment, or sacrament, of the victory of God's grace in human history and in the actual lives of real human persons.[20] Sanctity, or holiness, would be nothing more than an abstract ideal that is never achieved.

The saints confirm us in the hope that holiness is an achievable goal; they manifest holiness in the concrete texture of ordinary human existence. They live in history, are shaped by it, and, in turn, often shape it as well. Consequently, they function as "the initiators and the creative models of the holiness which happens to be right for, and is the task of, their particular age. They create a new style; they prove that a certain form of life and activity is a really genuine possibility; they show experimentally that one can be a Christian even in 'this' way; they make such a type of person believable as a Christian type."[21] But not only is sanctity possible in the concrete; there are also many ways in which it can be realized in individual persons, as we shall point out in greater detail in the next part. There is no one way to be holy, even as a Christian. Each disciple of Christ is a unique creation of God, and each period and place in the history of the Church is different from all other periods and places. The grace of Christ triumphs in this particular fashion, in this particular individual, in this particular time and place. The grace of Christ may also triumph in another fashion, in another individual, in another time and place.

"The Church, by canonization," Rahner continues, "confirms [the saints'] word, not so much or even principally in order to honor the saints, but because she thus finds her own task, her own nature, in so far as it has to be realized precisely here and now and then continuously maintained as thus realized."[22] In other words, by the action of the Church what is time-conditioned assumes permanent validity.

The Second Vatican Council taught that we should look to the saints not only as examples of Christian discipleship and sources of spiritual and material benefits, but also as fonts of strength in the practice of communal charity toward others. At the same time, the council called for the removal or correction of "any abuses, excesses, or defects which may have crept in here and there, and so restore all things that Christ and God be more fully praised." The Church, it declared, must "teach the faithful, therefore, that the authentic cult of the saints does not consist so much in a multiplicity of external acts, but rather in a more intense practice" of the love of Christ for all (Dogmatic Constitution on the Church, n. 51).

Accordingly, when the Church canonizes a saint, it affirms that God's redemption in Christ has actually and already happened in the case of this particular individual, that the Spirit has permeated and transformed this person, that their sins have been taken away, and that they bask now in God's eternal light. In the case of the saint, the grace of Christ is more than a possibility; it is a permanent reality. It is a reality, however, not only for individuals, but also for the whole community of disciples. The Church itself is called to be holy (Dogmatic Constitution on the Church, n. 39). It becomes thereby "the light of the nations" and "a sign and instrument . . . of communion with God and the unity of the entire human race" (n. 1).

Thus, the model by which we are to understand our relationship with the saints is no longer that of supplicant and benefactor, but one of communion and solidarity. Saints are fellow disciples in the community of disciples, and Mary is the disciple par excellence. The saints are not situated *between* us and Christ; they are *with* us, *in* Christ, as sisters and brothers with whom we share a common humanity, a common faith, a common ecclesial community, and a common destiny.

The Saints as Sacraments

The cult of saints is rooted in Catholicism's sacramental conviction that the infinite, invisible God is present and redemptively active in the finite, visible, human realities of this world, and especially in human persons who embody and practice the goodness and love of God.[23] Men and women, young and old alike, who have "heroically" responded to God's loving presence are saints, canonized or not. The full company of saints, both living and dead, is known as the communion of saints, and the Church is its core.

At the heart of this distinctively Catholic sacramental perspective is the belief that God's presence and redemptive activity have been supremely—and uniquely—embodied in the person of Jesus Christ, whose "mystical body" and "fundamental sacrament" the Church is.[24] Because the Church is the sacrament of Christ, it is called to manifest in its own life, its members, its ministries, and its structural operations the holiness of the one who alone can be called "the Holy One of God." As such, the Church is, as noted above, "a sign and instrument . . . of communion with God and of the unity of the entire human race" (Dogmatic Constitution on the Church, n. 1).

The principle of sacramentality takes form in these lines from the Letter to the Hebrews regarding the pedagogical and supportive role that holy people of the past play in the lives of those still on the way: "Therefore, since we are surrounded by so great a cloud of witnesses, let us rid ourselves of every burden and sin that clings to us and persevere in running the race that lies before us while keeping our eyes fixed on Jesus, the leader and perfecter of faith" (12:1–2). We look to the saints, therefore, as exemplars and models, "a cloud of witnesses." St. Paul was even more to the point—almost brazenly so—in his First

Letter to the Corinthians. To those who wondered how they could pattern their lives on Christ's when they did not know him, Paul wrote: "Be imitators of me, as I am of Christ" (11:1; see also 4:16; Phil. 3:17; 2 Thess. 3:7, 9). The Church lifts its saints before the world for this same purpose: to provide models and examples of discipleship. Imitate them, in whom the grace of Christ has triumphed, the Church assures us, and you will be imitating Christ himself.

The Second Vatican Council built upon these biblical foundations: "When we look at the lives of those women and men who have faithfully followed Christ, we are inspired anew to seek the city which is to come (see Heb. 13:14; 11:10), while at the same time we are taught about the safest path by which, through a changing world and in keeping with each one's state of life and condition, we will be able to arrive at perfect union with Christ, which is holiness. In the lives of those companions of ours in the human condition who are more perfectly transformed into the image of Christ (see 2 Cor. 3:18) God shows, vividly, to humanity his presence and his face. He speaks to us in them and offers us a sign of his Kingdom, to which we are powerfully attracted, so great a cloud of witnesses are we given (see Heb. 12:1) and such an affirmation of the truth of the gospel." (Dogmatic Constitution on the Church, n. 50).

The Saints and Ecumenism

The cult of saints is not peculiar to Catholicism alone, even if it is one of its distinctive characteristics.[25] The saints are also commemorated on the liturgical calendars of the Greek and Russian Orthodox churches and in the other churches of Eastern Christianity; in the Church of England, the Episcopal Church in the United States of America (hereafter, USA), and in other churches within the Anglican Communion; and in the Evangelical Lutheran Church in America and in Canada and in the other churches of the Lutheran World Federation.[26] Indeed, in referring to the many martyrs of the twentieth century, Catholic and non-Catholic alike, in his 1994 apostolic letter *Tertio Millennio Adveniente* (Lat., "As the Third Millennium Draws Near"), Pope John Paul II urged that "local churches should do everything possible to ensure . . . the memory of those who have suffered martyrdom." This action, he continued, "cannot fail to have an ecumenical character and expression. Perhaps the most convincing form of ecumenism is the ecumenism of the saints and of the martyrs. The *communio sanctorum* [Lat., "communion of saints"] speaks louder than the things which divide us" (n. 37).[27] On May 7, 2000, the pope held an ecumenical jubilee prayer service in the Roman Colosseum. In preparation for the ceremony the Vatican had collected over twelve thousand names of twentieth-century martyrs, Catholics and other Christians alike. More than two dozen leaders from nineteen Christian churches joined the pope in reading testimonies from a representative group of sixteen Catholic, Orthodox, Anglican, and Protestant victims of Nazism, Communism, dictatorships, civil wars, and religious intolerance. "The precious heritage which these courageous witnesses have passed down to us," John Paul II said on that occasion, "is a patrimony shared by all the churches and ecclesial communities."[28]

The Healthiness of Saints

Saints are holy people—people who have, on balance, lived their lives in conformity with the gospel. The words "on balance" are crucial here, because it is not the case that saints neither committed sins nor had any personal faults and weaknesses. The saints were as human as any of us, but they somehow managed to rise above the standard of ordinary human behavior and manifest heroic virtue when it counted most.

In canonizing a saint, the Church declares the person to be in heaven, that is, to have achieved salvation. The word "salvation" is derived from the Latin word *salus,* which means "health." To be saved, that is, to become a saint, means that one has been brought to the fullness of human health, to have been made whole. Indeed, holiness *is* wholeness,[29] albeit transcendently so. We are made holy by reason of the indwelling of the Holy Spirit, whose presence becomes manifest in acts of mercy, kindness, humility, meekness, and patience (Col. 3:12; Gal. 5:22; Rom. 6:22). The holy person is a person of integrity, that is, one who leads a whole life in which belief and practice converge, even in the face of death.

The saint is hopeful rather than despairing, loving rather than mean-spirited, courageous rather than weak, and has a passion for justice. In years past, these characteristics were readily recognized and called virtues, that is, "powers" by which a life of Christian discipleship, indeed a fully human life, is possible. There were, traditionally, the theological virtues of faith, hope, and love (1 Cor. 13:13), and the cardinal, or moral, virtues of prudence, justice, temperance, and fortitude, rooted in the *Nicomachean Ethics* of the Greek philosopher Aristotle (d. 322 B.C.) and developed by such early Christian theologians as Gregory the Great [September 3] and Augustine [August 28], and later by Thomas Aquinas [January 28]. Today, however, there are other virtues as well, such as stewardship of the environment, truthfulness even at the risk of reprisals, mercy and compassion, forgiveness, gratitude, and humility (not of the supine, doormat kind, but of an honest recognition of one's relationship to God and to others).[30]

By contrast, the life of the Spirit is not visibly present in the unholy, or the unhealthy. They tend instead to be self-righteous, judgmental, unforgiving, resentful, vindictive, grim, rigid and authoritarian, punitive, controlling, obsessive, gratified by the humiliation and misfortunes of those of whom they disapprove, burdened with guilt, ill at ease in the presence of others, especially those of the opposite gender, and wracked by fear of their own sexuality and of the human love and intimacy it expresses. In its extreme manifestations, unhealthiness generates cruelty and violence.[31]

On occasion, men and women with one or more of these unhealthy traits have been raised up by the Church as models of Christian discipleship. The message conveyed in the beatification and canonization processes, therefore, has sometimes been misleading, and the "cloud of witnesses" has become instead an impenetrable fog.

Confusion and even resentment can also be created when the great majority of officially recognized saints happen to be white, celibate European males, ordained and/or religiously professed, or white, celibate (or widowed) European females. Members of the worldwide Church may wonder if the response to the universal call to holiness is generally more difficult or less efficacious among people of color, among Asians and Africans, among the poor, and among married people.[32] Indeed, if the great majority of recognized saints had never expressed love for another human being in sexual intimacy, or if they manifested a disdain and contempt for such intimacy, what message would that send to the world and to the Church regarding the sanctity of marriage and the sacramental and cocreative character of human sexuality? Pope John Paul II himself called attention to this problem in the same apostolic letter cited above:

> In particular, there is a need to foster the recognition of the heroic virtues of men and women who have lived their Christian vocation in marriage. Precisely because we are convinced of the abundant fruits of holiness in the married state, we need to find the most appropriate means for discerning them and proposing them to the whole Church as a model and encouragement for other Christian spouses (n. 37).

There have been far more married people than monks and virgins who have been luminous examples of Christian discipleship. When the ratio of the one to the other is reflected in the canonization process itself, the Church will have achieved the balance that so many of its members have called for.

In Memory of Women

Some years ago, a New Testament scholar, Elisabeth Schüssler Fiorenza, exposed the pattern of inattention to the stories of women in the Bible on the part of male exegetes and biblical theologians. In a groundbreaking book, *In Memory of Her*, she called for a reconstruction and reclaiming of early Christian history as the history of women as well as of men.[33] In a similar fashion, Elizabeth Johnson has argued that "women's history of holiness has been largely erased from the collective memory of the church" and that "even when they are remembered, exemplary women's lives are interpreted as models of virtue that support the male-dominated status quo and cast women into submission."[34]

It is not only that far fewer women have been recognized as saints than men,[35] but also that women saints do not have as significant a place as men in the Church's liturgical and devotional life. Thus, only forty-one commemorations on the General Roman Calendar or the Proper Calendar for the (Roman Catholic) Dioceses of the U.S.A. are of women saints, and twelve of these commemorations are Marian-related. There are roughly fifty-two liturgical celebrations of male saints in the rank of "obligatory memorial," compared with twenty-three for female saints, of which five are Marian. Finally, there are sixty-six "optional memorials" for male saints and only thirteen for female saints, of which three are Marian. As one liturgical writer has observed, "If one excludes the various celebrations in honor of Marian titles, apparitions, or dogmas, the names and stories of other concrete women are heard with relative infrequency in Catholic liturgical assemblies."[36] Moreover, in the present sanctoral calendar the images of women tend to revolve around the titles of virgin, martyr, and religious. By far the greatest number of commemorated women are categorized as virgins. The few exceptions on the General Roman Calendar are Elizabeth of Portugal [July 4]; Mary Magdalene [July 22]; Anne, who is paired with her husband, Joachim [July 26]; Martha [July 29]; Monica [August 27]; and Margaret of Scotland [November 16].

Some writers have been justifiably critical of "the subtle ways in which the tradition has destroyed and continues to destroy the memory of women," pointing in particular to the reduction to bracketed, and therefore optional, status of the women who were traditionally mentioned in the Roman Canon of the Mass: Felicity and Perpetua [March 7], Agatha, Lucy [December 13], Agnes, and Anastasia [December 22 (in the East), December 25 (in the Roman liturgical tradition)].[37] Given the practice of most presiders when using the First Eucharistic Prayer, the names of women have effectively been obliterated from the central prayer of the Mass.

To be sure, the problem is not peculiar to Roman Catholicism. *Lesser Feasts and Fasts*[38] of the Episcopal Church in the USA, for example, contains 127 celebrations honoring men in comparison to 18 celebrations commemorating women. Of these 18, 3 are Marian-related. Thus, women comprise about 12 percent of the Episcopal sanctoral calendar. Based on a very rough estimate of the multitude of saints celebrated and commemorated on the Russian Orthodox calendar, the percentage of women saints is about the same as one finds in the Episcopal calendar. In the *Lutheran Book of Worship*,[39] women comprise about 15 percent of the sanctoral cycle.

The task of reconstruction and reclamation, therefore, is not only historical and theological, but also liturgical. The stories of women saints need to be recognized and proclaimed and then appropriately celebrated. The Church must teach through its worship that sanctity is gender-blind.

The Communion of Saints

The article on the "communion of saints" was first found in the Apostles' Creed at the end of the fifth century and was used much earlier in the East, though not as part of the creed. The doctrine was understood in the first instance as a communion of grace among all Christians who participate in the blessings of salvation and in the communion of God's holy people. Although this community of salvation was also understood to encompass the whole Church, the formal term "communion of saints" only gradually came to apply principally to the communion between the heavenly Church and the earthly Church. More recently still, the term has come to apply as well to the exchange of graces and spiritual benefits between individuals on earth, on the one hand, and the saints in heaven and the souls in purgatory, on the other. Together they represent what are known as the Church militant, the Church triumphant, and the Church suffering.

A fundamental biblical and theological meaning is grounded in the noun "communion" (Gk. *koinonia*). The Church is, first and foremost, a communion of disciples called by the Father, in Christ, through the power of the Holy Spirit (Heb. 2:14–17; Rom. 5:8–10; 8:3, 32–35; John 1:14; especially 2 Cor. 13:13). It is a communion that is not broken by death. Indeed, it flourishes for all eternity.

The doctrine of the communion of saints is affirmed in the Second Vatican Council's Dogmatic Constitution on the Church (and reaffirmed in *The Catechism of the Catholic Church*)[40]: "All, indeed, who are of Christ and who have his Spirit form one church and in Christ are joined together (Eph. 4:16). So it is that the union of the wayfarers with the brothers and sisters who sleep in the peace of Christ is no way interrupted; but on the contrary . . . this union is reinforced by an exchange of spiritual goods." Those in heaven, because of their close union with Christ, "consolidate the holiness of the whole church, add to the nobility of the worship that the church offers to God here on earth, and in many ways help in a greater building up of the church (1 Cor. 12:12–27)" (n. 49). They intercede for those of us still on earth and place their merits at our disposal.

When Christ appears at the end of history and the glorious resurrection of the dead occurs, "the glory of God will light up the heavenly city and the Lamb will be its lamp (see Rev. 21:23)" (n. 51). At that supreme moment, the charity of the whole Church will be manifested in adoration of God and of the Lamb who was slain, and all will proclaim with one voice: "To the one who sits on the throne and to the Lamb be blessing and honor, glory and might, forever and ever!" (Rev. 5:13).

Saints are individuals, but not just individuals. They are integral members of the Church and, as such, manifest its corporate holiness. They bear within themselves the hope and the assurance that the Church, which is called to be holy, will, in fact, achieve that end.[41]

That hope is succinctly expressed in the words of the First Eucharistic Prayer: "For ourselves, too, we ask some share in the fellowship of your apostles and martyrs, with John the Baptist, Stephen, Matthias, Barnabas, Ignatius, Alexander, Marcellinus, Peter, Felicity, Perpetua, Agatha, Lucy, Agnes, Cecilia, Anastasia, and all the saints. Though we are sinners, we trust in your mercy and love. Do not consider what we truly deserve, but grant us your forgiveness."

PART II

SAINTS AND SPIRITUALITIES

Saints are holy people who live a life of discipleship "according to the Spirit" (Rom. 8:5). Their particular vision and style of saintly life is a called a *spirituality*. When that saintly vision and style attracts disciples and imitators, not only in the lifetime of the saint, but well beyond, it becomes a *school of spirituality*.

Because each saint is a unique embodiment of the grace of God, there are, in principle, as many spiritualities as there are saints. But, in fact, many of the saints are more alike than different from one another. Accordingly, there are fewer spiritualities than there are saints. Moreover, because relatively few saints attract a following of disciples and imitators beyond their own lifetimes, there are far fewer schools of spirituality than there are spiritualities.

What Is Christian Spirituality?

Just as there are non-Christian as well as Christian saints, so there are non-Christian as well as Christian spiritualities. Mohandas Gandhi [January 30] was a Hindu saint. His style of life was his spirituality. To the extent that he had disciples and imitators beyond his own lifetime, he inspired a Gandhian school of Hindu spirituality characterized by asceticism and nonviolence.

Our focus in this book, however, is on Christian sanctity and Christian spirituality, and more particularly still on the saints and spiritualities of the Catholic tradition, ecumenically understood.

"For those who live according to the flesh set their minds on the things of the flesh," St. Paul [June 29] wrote, "but those who live according to the Spirit, set their minds on the things of the Spirit" (Rom. 8:5). To be "spiritual" means to know and to live according to the knowledge that there is more to life than meets the eye. The "more than" is the sacred, the holy, the transcendent, the supernatural, the divine. Insofar as the "more than" enters into and impacts the realm of human experience, it is called the Holy Spirit. To be "open to the Spirit" is to accept explicitly who we are, namely, creatures of God made into the image and likeness of God, and who we are destined to become and then to direct our lives accordingly, in response to God's grace within us.

Christian spirituality, therefore, has to do with a way of being Christian, that is, of being a disciple of Christ. Christian spirituality is rooted in the life of the triune God, centered on Jesus Christ, animated by the Holy Spirit, lived out within the Church and the wider world, and oriented always to the coming of God's Reign in all its fullness at the end of human history.

Christian spirituality is *visionary* in that it involves a new way of seeing reality and of seeing through things to their spiritual core, of thus "interpreting spiritual things to those who are spiritual" (1 Cor. 2:13). As such, it is also essentially *sacramental,* because every created reality is imbued, to one degree or another, with the hidden presence of God. Christian spirituality is also *relational,* because discipleship is lived in a community of disciples, namely, the Church. Finally, Christian spirituality is *transformational.* The spiritual Christian is consciously in touch with the presence of the Spirit as the power that heals, reconciles, renews, gives life, bestows peace, sustains hope, brings joy, and creates unity. In a word, the Spirit "transforms" whatever it touches and penetrates.

There is not, and never has been, a single Christian spirituality, nor a single Catholic spirituality, as the historical survey below should make clear.

Schools of Christian Spirituality

When the spiritual vision and lifestyle of a particular saint attract disciples and imitators, not only in the saint's lifetime, but well beyond, it becomes a *school* of spirituality. More often than not, the school is centered in a religious order, but it may also be identified with a particular country and culture or even with a particular movement within the Church, such as the Devotio Moderna, a fourteenth-century northern European lay movement, or the more recent liberationist and feminist movements. Schools of spirituality may also be identified with particular devotions, such as that to the Sacred Heart of Jesus. Given the broadly interfaith and ecumenical character of sanctity and spirituality, schools of spirituality may also be associated with particular religious traditions outside of Catholicism itself.

Schools of spirituality associated with religious orders include Augustinian, Benedictine, Camaldolese, Carmelite, Carthusian, Cistercian, Dominican, Franciscan, Ignatian, and Salesian. Schools of spirituality associated with countries, regions, or cultures include African, African American, American, Celtic, Eastern (Asian), Egyptian Desert Fathers, French, Hispanic, Hispanic American, and Native American. Schools of spirituality associated with non-Catholic and non-Christian religious traditions include Anglican, Anglo-Catholic, Islamic, Jewish, oriental Christian, Orthodox and non-Orthodox alike, and various denominational traditions within Protestantism. There are other categories as well, for example, eco-feminist, feminist, holistic, lay, and New Age.[1]

The principal characteristics of a school of Christian spirituality are (1) the introduction of a new and/or distinctive way of living the gospel relative to a particular moment in the history of the Church, as in the case of Francis and the Franciscans; (2) the production of various teachings, writings, customs, communal forms of life, institutions (e.g., Rules), and exemplary figures (beyond the school's original inspiration), as in the case of Ignatius of Loyola and the Jesuits; (3) the generation of distinctive styles of prayer, worship, community life, and apostolic activities, as in the case of Benedict and the Benedictines, Dominic and the Dominicans, and Francis de Sales and the lay apostolate; and (4) the reshaping and/or intensification of the spiritualities of many other individuals and communities beyond the original group—for decades, even centuries, beyond the original inspiration.[2]

The saints who have generated schools of spirituality, of varying degrees of scope, intensity, and longevity, include Anthony of Egypt [January 17], Augustine of Hippo [August 28], Basil the Great [January 2], Benedict of Nursia [July 11], Bernard of Clairvaux [August 20], Brigid of Kildare [February 1], Bruno [October 6], Clare of Assisi

[August 11], Columban [November 23], Dominic [August 8], Francis de Sales [January 24], Francis of Assisi [October 4], Hildegard of Bingen [September 17], Ignatius of Loyola [July 31], Ita of Killeedy [January 15], Jane Frances de Chantal [December 12], John Bosco [January 31], John of the Cross [December 14], John Vianney [August 4], Joseph [March 19], Louis Grignion de Montfort [April 28], Margaret Mary Alacoque [October 16], the Blessed Virgin Mary, Norbert [June 6], Paul of the Cross [October 19], Paul the Hermit [January 15], Philip Neri [May 26], Teresa of Ávila [October 15], Theresa of the Child Jesus [October 1], and Vincent de Paul [September 27], among others.[3]

A Brief History of Christian Spirituality

What follows is the story, told in highly schematic fashion, of the evolution of Christian spirituality (and of its many different forms) from the time of Jesus himself, through the Second Vatican Council of the mid-twentieth century, down to the present day.[4] What this historical survey should make unmistakably clear is the richly diverse and pluralistic character of Christian spirituality. In a word, Christian spirituality is catholic.

The First Seven Centuries

Christian spirituality as such began to take shape with Jesus' proclamation of the Kingdom of God (Mark 1:15) and the gathering of his first disciples around him (Matt. 4:18–22).

The first thing the Lord did when he appeared to his disciples after the Resurrection was to breathe the Holy Spirit upon them (John 20:19–23). Thereafter, the life of discipleship was to be lived within "the community of the disciples" (Acts 6:2).

If sanctity and spirituality have to do essentially with our union with God in Christ through the Holy Spirit, *martyrdom,* as we have already seen in the first part, provided in the earliest centuries of the Church an ideal means to such union. Martyrdom's importance was rooted in its close connection with Christ's own death and resurrection. To be put to death for the faith, that is, to be martyred (literally, to become a "witness"), was to experience ahead of schedule the final eschatological event. These were the so-called red martyrs.

After the Roman imperial persecutions had ended early in the fourth century, Christians wondered if the complete union with God in Christ offered by martyrdom was accessible in any other way. Origen (d. ca. 254) proposed that a life of complete self-sacrifice was a kind of unbloody martyrdom, and Clement of Alexandria (d. ca. 215) noted that every death is a true martyrdom provided one approaches it with the proper dispositions. Those who suffered in any way for the faith, whether by self-imposed ascetical practices, as in the case of the hermits and virgins, or by hardships meted out by others were considered unbloody, or "white," martyrs. They were called "confessors."

Monasticism—and the monastic spiritualities and schools of spirituality (Benedictine, Carthusian, Cistercian) that developed from it—had its roots in the New Testament, where some early Christians embraced celibacy "for the sake of the kingdom" (Matt. 19:12) and in postapostolic Syria, where ascetics, inspired by Luke's Gospel (9:60), sought to imitate the poor, homeless, and celibate Jesus. Most sources locate the beginnings of monasticism in Egypt, where it developed first as flight from persecution and later as a rejection of the Constantinian embrace of the Church in 312. Under the leadership of Anthony of Egypt and others, individual Christians went into the desert (Gk. *erēmia*, thus the word "hermit") to confront the devil, to come to terms with all the dark forces that war against the spirit, and to find simplicity of life in order to focus more sharply on the demands of the gospel. Some forms of asceticism were severe. In Syria, for example, various hermits used iron chains to punish themselves; others exposed themselves heedlessly to the elements. Gradually the hermits were joined by others, and a transition was made from the solitary form of monastic existence *(anchoritism)* to a modified community existence *(cenobitism).* Almost from the beginning, therefore, monastic life was looked upon as a continuation of apostolic life: perseverance together in prayer, in the community of goods, and in the breaking of the bread (Acts 2:42). The practice of consecrating virgins also developed at this time as yet another way of achieving fuller union with Christ.

Two or three generations passed before a spiritual theology emerged from the new monastic movement. According to the Neoplatonic schema of Pseudo-Dionysius (d. ca. 500)—probably a Syrian monk who identified himself with Dionysius the Areopagite, mentioned in Acts 17:34—the soul finds union with God only in going beyond itself, by rejecting all particular knowledge and allowing itself to be absorbed totally in the knowledge of God, whose love overflows in a stream of self-communicating goodness in creation. Thus, the spiritual life is divided into three stages: purification (the *purgative* way), meditation on the word of God (the *illuminative* way), and union with God (the *unitive* way).

Augustine was himself dependent upon this monastic spirituality as developed and practiced in the East, but he subtly revised it in a more psychological direction. Spiritual discernment does not bring us knowledge of God in Christ so much as *self*-knowledge in the light of Christ, the interior teacher of wisdom. On the other hand, it was also Augustine who wrote in the *City of God* that "no man must be so committed to contemplation as, in his contemplation, to give no thought to his neighbor's needs, nor so absorbed in action as to dispense with the contemplation of God" (29.19). It was John Cassian [July 23], however, who translated the purer form of Eastern monasticism to the West. The monk is not to seek anything beyond the Kingdom of God, and only purity of heart will open the mystery of the Kingdom to him. Christian life is one of constant prayer wholly inspired by the gospel.

One of the greatest spiritual authorities in the entire history of Church was Benedict of Nursia, author of the famous Rule of Benedict and generally regarded as the patriarch of Western monasticism. In composing his Rule for the monks of Monte Cassino, he drew freely from earlier monastic rules, both for individual, anchoritic spirituality and for communal, cenobitic spirituality. Augustine, Basil, and Pachomius [May 9] were among Benedict's sources. Marked by prudence and humanity, the Rule leads by observance and obedience to the perfect following of Christ. It speaks of the divine presence as "everywhere and . . . in every place," but especially in the monastic liturgy of the Divine Office (19:1–2). The basic asceticism is in the common life. Everything is centered on the needs of others (34), and much attention is paid to interpersonal relations. The person in whom Benedict most concentrates the divine presence, however, is the superior of the monastery, the abbot, through whom the will of God is mediated. He insists, at the same time, that God is to be met in the least likely circumstances and in the most unprepossessing persons (53:21).

Another key spiritual leader and writer of the time was Pope Gregory the Great [September 3], an adept popularizer of doctrine and an influential author on matters of faith and piety. His works are the first major sources of material on the lives of the saints, including Benedict, whose Rule he observed and whose cult he promoted. One of Gregory's books, *Regulae Pastoralis* (Lat., [Book of] "Pastoral Care"), had almost as much impact on the Church well into the Middle Ages as did Augustine's *City of God*. It was a practical treatise on the spirituality and ministerial skills required of bishops and of all who have the care of souls. The social disruptions created by the so-called barbarian invasions disclosed the fragile character of much of the Christianization that had occurred thus far.[5] Gregory's simple, straightforward style was particularly appealing because it was reassuring, and the type of monastic life his work advocated and celebrated proved to be one of the mainstays of the Church and of society generally for the next several centuries.

The Middle Ages: Eighth Through Fourteenth Centuries

From the time of Gregory the Great until the middle of the eighth century, monks generally maintained the ascetical ideal and gave an example of Christian life for all, laity, clergy, and bishops alike. Under the new Germanic influence, however, a certain externalism inserted itself into Christian spirituality: devotions to the cross, relics, and tombs of the saints; various forms of penance; the encouragement of confession of sins, and so forth. But Carolingian piety, reflected in the works of Benedict of Aniane [February 12] and Rabanus Maurus [February 4], was also marked by a deep reverence for the Bible and a love of the liturgy—both abiding preoccupations of Christian monks.

By the tenth and eleventh centuries, various monasteries began to develop loose federations, and these gave rise to congregations of monasteries and eventually to religious orders. The monastic ideal was spread ever more widely throughout the Christian world. Austerity characterized penitential practice even among the laity. Long pilgrimages and self-flagellation were common means of making reparation for sin or for curbing one's unruly appetites. Contemplative prayer too was presented as the standard that all Christians should meet. John of Fécamp (d. 1079), one of the most widely read spiritual writers of the time, recommended quiet, meditative reading to induce unimpeded and undistracted thoughts about God.

The new Cistercian order, founded in 1098 as a community of observant, renewed followers of the Rule of Benedict, accentuated the mystical element in Christian spirituality. Its principal proponents, Bernard of Clairvaux and William of St. Thierry (d. 1148), regarded the soul as being the image of God because of the gift of free will. But sin marred that image. Only by a contemplative life that conforms oneself to the Word of God can the individual soul be restored to its intended perfection, for Christ is the interior Lover who pursues and embraces the soul in a union of intimate love.

The stress on the contemplative life over dialectics (i.e., critical theology) continued into the twelfth century in the Parisian monastery of St. Victor, whose members, known as the Victorines, included some of the best-known writers of the period: Hugh of St. Victor (d. 1141), Richard of St. Victor (d. 1173), and others.[6] Richard's work would later be simplified by the English Augustinian Walter Hilton [March 24] and Hilton's, in turn, carried forward by Julian of Norwich [May 8], an anchoress and mystic who lived outside the walls of St. Julian's Church in Norwich, England.

But there also appeared at this time another, more idealistic spiritual movement urging radical poverty and an end to all formalism and legalism. Accordingly, by the end of the thirteenth century many laypersons were criticizing the existing social conditions, especially in the new urban centers of Europe, as well as the lives of the clergy and hierarchy. Extreme forms of this new purist tendency were to be found in Waldensianism and Albigensianism. But there were also more mainstream attempts to confront the same social conditions, abuses, and pastoral problems. The rise of the mendicant orders in the thirteenth century—Franciscans and Dominicans—built on the work of the many groups in the twelfth century who sought to engage in the *vita apostolica* (Lat., "apostolic life," i.e., life in imitation of Jesus and the apostles) and popular preaching. The new orders brought a more realistic, but no less serious, approach to poverty and service, because they were closer to the lives of ordinary people than were the monastic orders. They also produced their own schools of spirituality, rooted in the spiritual wisdom and genius of their founders.

Dominic provided his new Order of Preachers with an ideal that combined the best of monasticism with the best of the apostolic life. One of his spiritual sons, Thomas Aquinas [January 28], would produce an oft-cited formula on the interrelationship between the two: neither contemplation alone nor action alone is the highest form of Christian life; rather, it is contemplation in action, that is, a sharing with others the fruits of the contemplative life. As with other medieval theologians, Thomas's spirituality was one with his speculative theology.

Francis of Assisi, on the other hand, stressed imitation of the life of Christ in all its simplicity and poverty. God is reflected in the sun, the moon, and the stars, and indeed in all of the things of creation (the principle of sacramentality again). As with the Dominicans, it took another great theologian to systematize, and thereby give wider circulation to,

Francis's basic insight. Bonaventure [July 15], who saw the whole of creation as a mirror reflecting the power, wisdom, and goodness of God, identified three elements in the Franciscan way of life: (1) following Christ through the evangelical counsels, especially poverty (the other counsels are chastity and obedience); (2) laboring for the salvation of souls by preaching and hearing confessions; and (3) contemplation.

Another alternative to the traditional structures of monastic life was provided by the Beguines (and their male counterparts, the Beghards), who emerged toward the end of the twelfth century in Germany, the Low Countries, and France. They began as a group of single women living with parents or separately in tenements, with no rule of life. Their main apostolic purpose was service to the sick and needy. Their social views and sympathies led to a perception among church authorities that they were allied with the Spiritual Franciscans, a schismatic group that was eventually condemned by Pope John XXII (1316–34), and so they came under scrutiny and censure.

At the beginning of the fourteenth century a new current of spirituality took root in the Rhineland and the Low Countries and in England. A century earlier the works of Pseudo-Dionysius had been translated into the vernacular and made the subject of an extended commentary. Because the author was commonly associated in people's minds with Paul's convert, the Areopagite mentioned in Acts 17:34, his newly translated writings were accorded a quasi-apostolic authority throughout the Middle Ages. (They had already been translated into Latin in the ninth century by Duns Scotus Erigena.) The writings had particular influence on Meister Eckhart (d. ca. 1328), John Tauler (d. 1361), and Henry Suso [January 23], three German Dominican mystics, and on Jan von Ruysbroeck (d. 1381), a Flemish canon regular of St. Augustine. Their common concern was the soul's union with God, which reached its zenith in contemplation. Such union is impossible, however, apart from complete abandonment of, and detachment from, all creatures and worldly realities. This orientation was most pronounced in *The Cloud of Unknowing*, composed by an anonymous English author. The same stress on the interior life was to be found in Hildegard of Bingen and Hedwig [October 16].

Other spiritual writers, firmly committed to a life of prayer and penance, saw more clearly the pastoral implications and effects of their contemplative life. Catherine of Siena [April 29] was concerned with the reform of the Church, but insisted that her prayers and penances did more for the Church than her public acts did. Yet she advocated theological study, reformed religious life, and worked against papal corruption and endemic warfare.

The same concern for ecclesiastical renewal in the Low Countries stimulated the formation of a lay group, the Brethren of the Common Life, founded by Gerard Groote [August 20]. The movement's spirituality was known as the Devotio Moderna. Its one great product, written probably by Thomas à Kempis [July 24], was *The Imitation of Christ*, which laid great stress on the inner life of the individual and encouraged methodical meditation, especially on the life and Passion of Christ.

There was, however, a lack of intellectual and theological substance in much popular piety of the time, and it brought with it many serious problems: superstition (e.g., the belief that one could be saved from blindness by gazing on the Communion host), ignorance of the Bible, fascination with reports of visions, exaggeration of the value of relics, emotionalism, inordinate fears of the afterlife and of God's judgment, and devotional excesses unrelated to the central mysteries of Christian faith.

The Postmedieval Period

Although Protestantism rejected contemporary medieval spirituality's emotionalism, superstition, and inordinate reverence for such material objects as relics, it did not at the same time reject its individualism. Martin Luther (1483–1546) [February 18] stressed the uniqueness of the Christian believer's relationship with God and the realm of personal conscience (*sola fides*, Lat., "faith alone"). His recourse to the Word of God in Sacred Scripture (*sola Scriptura*, Lat., "Scripture alone") only underlined his concern for finding a direct approach to Christ, one in which the individual is illumined by the interior witness of the Holy Spirit (*sola gratia*, Lat., "grace alone"). Although it was not always obvious in the midst of medieval excesses, it *is* a matter of Catholic principle that the believer's relationship with God is a mediated relationship, mediated not only, or even primarily, through the biblical Word, but in and through the community of faith in which that Word is proclaimed.

Although various Christian humanists were sympathetic toward the contemporary emphasis on mysticism, they were strongly committed to the general restoration of Christian life itself, so much corrupted then by the worst of the Renaissance spirit. Love for classical antiquity and an optimistic view of human nature were characteristic of this so-called devout humanism, and the spiritual writings of Erasmus [July 12] are representative of it. In spite of his clashes with Luther on free will and his fidelity to the Catholic Church, he was subjected to censure and censorship before and after his death.

The same emphasis on the unity of prayer and action is found in one of the classics of Christian spirituality, the *Spiritual Exercises* of Ignatius of Loyola, a work that reflected the Baroque period's emphasis on personal conversion and method in prayer. Ignatius's spirituality—and the school that emerged from it—was marked by dialectical parallels between the medieval concepts of contemplation and action, on the one hand, and between flight from the world and acceptance of the world, on the other. Contemplation is adherence to the God who transcends this world. Action is the fulfillment of one's duty within the world, consistent with one's own individuality. Hence the Ignatian formula, which originated with the first circle of his followers: "*in actione contemplativus*" (Lat., "contemplative in action"). Ignatius's affirmation of the world, therefore, is not a naive optimism. It springs, rather, from a true grasp of the Cross: at once a judgment upon sin and a proclamation of our liberation from it. On the other hand, his profoundly positive evaluation of the contingencies of history puts him at the head of a whole new spiritual tradition—so much so, in fact, that the great Jesuit theologian Karl Rahner was convinced that the Holy Spirit raised up in Ignatius an original, creative reinterpretation of the Christian life.

"Work as if everything depended upon you, but pray as if everything depended upon God" is another well-known Ignatian formula. Although this is not the exact wording, it is close enough to the sense of the original, which says, in effect, that we should trust in God in such a way that we never forget to cooperate with God, and yet at the same time we should cooperate with God in such a way as to remain always aware that it is God alone who is at work. We are always at a distance, therefore, from God and even from our own deeds. We are at a distance from God, who is never revealed except in works carried out with the cooperation of secondary causes (i.e., free human beings); and we are at a distance from our deeds, which must never be taken as something of final value in themselves. The Christian must look to Christ, in whom alone the divine-human interaction is fully realized, and seek to imitate him. This is the core of Ignatian spirituality.[7]

The four hundred years from 1560 to 1960, the eve of Vatican II, formed another major period in Catholic history. After the shock of the Reformation, the Catholic Church underwent a major renewal, propelled by the Council of Trent (1545–63) and inspired by saints like Ignatius of Loyola. Spirituality, joined by art, affirmed and defended everything the Protestants attacked: devotion to Mary and the saints, images, and sacraments. This was especially the case with the Baroque period, in which individuals and groups proclaimed ways in which Jesus' incarnation was extended into people's lives and cultures. The period's art dramatically, and even emotionally, depicted the life of Christ and that of Mary and Joseph. The emotional element was also prominent in the biographies of saints, in sermons, in pastoral work at the parish level, and in foreign missions. The Christian life becomes manifest in extraordinary rather than ordinary events: dramatic conversions, visions, stigmata, and ecstasies.

The authentically mystical way, present in Ignatius, continued to flourish, however, especially in Spain. For Teresa of Ávila prayer consisted essentially in an exchange of love with God, but in the context of life in the Church. From our side, the signs of our love for God are manifested in the practice of the virtues, especially in love of neighbor, leaving to God the communication of grace whenever and however God wishes.[8] John of the Cross, one of Teresa's companions in her work of reform within the Carmelite order, is regarded by many as the greatest of the mystical writers.[9] His writings were at once poetic and speculative, drawing not only upon personal spiritual experience but upon Sacred Scripture and the classical authors as well. They detail the processes of spiritual purification, through trials and temptations and through deliberate detachment from external things, and they try to explain the life of union with God—a union brought about through the prayer of gifted contemplation. These great Carmelites employed not only an autobiographical method, but also a kind of developmental psychology, pointing out that we move progressively in life to even higher stages of prayer. Together they created the Carmelite school of spirituality.

Although Spanish spirituality after John of the Cross became increasingly theoretical and scientific, Italian spirituality was more practical. Reform of the Church, renewal of the interior life, and the improvement of priestly ministry were matters of immediate interest. These priorities are reflected in the works of Catherine of Genoa [September 15], Charles Borromeo [November 4], and Philip Neri.

In France developments in spirituality were centered on the life of Christ and the saints, especially mystics and missionaries, who were not only models for life, but also objects of liturgy and celebration.

Great directors of the spiritual life, such as Francis de Sales, Madame Acarie [April 18], also known as Mary of the Incarnation, and Pierre de Bérulle (d. 1629) developed personal approaches to the life of prayer. Among the other great figures of this period was John Eudes [August 19], an Oratorian priest, who developed a theology of the Sacred Hearts of Jesus and Mary, perhaps in response to the coldness of Jansenism. He chose the heart as a symbol of the overflowing love of God, most fully expressed in the Incarnation. Devotion to the Sacred Heart of Jesus received new impetus from Margaret Mary Alacoque [October 16], who reported having had visions of Jesus in which he revealed to her his human and divine love through the image of a heart resting on a throne of flames and surrounded by a crown of thorns. Encountering skepticism from the other sisters in her community, she found support from her Jesuit confessor Claude La Colombière [February 15].

This was also the time in France of theological controversy surrounding the whole issue of nature and grace. Some argued that human nature was so powerless that we can do absolutely nothing to advance our salvation (the Quietism of Madame Guyon [d. 1717]). Others insisted on the evil of the flesh and of all human desires and pleasures, urging a life of total abnegation, self-denial, and even repression (Jansenism). Against the Quietists, Jacques Bossuet (d. 1704) taught that abandonment of the soul to God should actually induce the soul to apply itself more deliberately to its religious exercises and to other Christian duties. Meanwhile, Francis de Sales and Jane Frances de Chantal sought to bring Christian piety out of the monasteries and convents into the world of the average layperson by showing the connection between Christian life and everyday occupations and by emphasizing—against the Jansenists—the joy of Christian existence.[10] A similar orientation appears in Italy in the writings of Alphonsus Liguori [August 1].

The spirit of the French school of spirituality, shorn of its excesses, is perhaps best expressed by Jean Jacques Olier (d. 1657), founder of the Sulpicians: "Christianity consists in these three points . . . to look upon Jesus, to unite oneself to Jesus, and to act in Jesus. The first leads us to respect and to religion; the second to union and to identification with Him; the third, to an activity no longer solitary, but joined to the virtue of Jesus Christ, which we have drawn upon ourselves by prayer. The first is called adoration; the second, communion; the third, cooperation."[11]

In the early eighteenth century the devotion to the Sacred Heart spread rapidly through France and to other countries such as Poland. Although Pope Clement XIII (d. 1769) approved the devotion in 1765, its great success came in the nineteenth century, when Margaret Mary Alacoque was beatified (1864) and Pope Pius IX extended the liturgy and feast of the Sacred Heart to the universal Church (after 1856) and dedicated the universal Church to the Sacred Heart (1875). Various religious communities dedicated to the Sacred Heart were also founded in the late eighteenth and early nineteenth centuries.

Nineteenth Century

Catholic spirituality had been negatively affected by the suppression of religious orders, monasteries, and other religious institutions (orphanages, hospitals, libraries) during the French Revolution and by Napoleon's program of secularization, as well as by the eighteenth-century Enlightenment's hostility to the supernatural. After 1830 new orders and congregations were founded, old ones reappeared, monastic life was revived, and various lay movements were initiated. But under pressure from secular states and the restrictive pontificates of Gregory XVI (1831–46) and Pius IX (1846–78), spirituality in the second half of the century tended to become introspective and popular piety turned increasingly to supernaturalism in the form of apparitions of the Blessed Virgin (especially at Lourdes in 1858), miracles, visions, and stigmata. Individualism and even regimented piety (e.g., institutionalized devotions to the Sacred Heart, the Blessed Virgin, the Sacred Wounds, the Eucharist) flourished, and extreme theological ideas were encouraged, and sometimes endorsed, by magisterial interventions of a highly reactionary nature. At the same time, many new ministerial initiatives were undertaken and the number of Catholic institutions multiplied in an accelerated fashion.

The nineteenth century provides a bridge between medieval and modern spirituality, because the forces of renewal were also at work: the renewal of theology, of liturgy, of historical studies, and of social ministry. And so too were the forces of innovation, for example, scientific and technological advances and developments in psychology and sociology. Together these forces of renewal and innovation would have a profound impact on Christian spirituality in the twentieth century. A large number of apostolic congregations of women were also founded at this time, some drawing their main inspiration from Ignatian spirituality.

Although the main currents of spiritual renewal were on the

Continent, this incipient renewal of Christian spirituality was also evident in England and particularly in the Oxford movement, whose driving force was John Henry Newman [August 11]. His spiritual orientation was primarily interior, a life lived in intimate union with God under the guidance of the Holy Spirit. But it was also a Christocentric spirituality, stressing the Incarnation as the basis for an active Christian life in the world. As in Ignatius, therefore, there was a blending of the contemplative and the practical. Newman, however, was not to exert very much influence as a spiritual writer during his lifetime. More influential was Frederick William Faber (d. 1863), who drew his own inspiration from the Italian and French style of spiritual writing, especially that of Alphonsus Liguori and Cardinal Bérulle. Faber too was Christocentric (one of his works was entitled *All for Jesus*), but he was also highly emotional and florid. On the other hand, his emphasis on the psychology of the individual, openness to all people, even non-Catholics and non-Christians, and the frequent reception of the sacraments all anticipated by a century certain developments that would characterize modern Catholic spirituality.

Unfortunately, Catholic spirituality after 1860 and until the Second Vatican Council was hampered by its separation from theology and from the ordinary world of the layperson. The presumption was that spirituality is not for everyone, only for priests and religious.

1900–1950

What the history of Christian and, more specifically, Catholic spirituality makes clear is its decidedly pluralistic character. At the beginning of the twentieth century pluralism was taken for granted. There were spiritualities, not *a* spirituality. And those spiritualities were identified both with charismatic individuals, such as Teresa of Ávila, John of the Cross, Thomas à Kempis, John Vianney (the Curé d'Ars), and with schools, which, in turn, were identified mostly with religious orders. For example, there was Dominican spirituality (Dominic, Aquinas, Catherine of Siena; the priority of truth, or knowledge, which leads to love), Ignatian spirituality (Ignatius of Loyola; finding God in all things), Franciscan spirituality (Francis of Assisi, Clare of Assisi, Bonaventure; a life of poverty, modeled on Jesus', in service of the poor), Benedictine spirituality (Benedict, Joseph Columba Marmion [January 30]; prayer—liturgy and the reading of Scripture—and work), Carmelite spirituality (Teresa of Ávila, John of the Cross, Theresa of the Child Jesus; solitude and contemplative prayer), Carthusian spirituality (Bruno; solitude and prayer), Cistercian spirituality (Bernard of Clairvaux, Thomas Merton [December 10]; solitude and contemplative prayer), and Sulpician spirituality (Olier, Adolfe Tanquerey [d. 1932]; the disciplining of the lower appetites by the higher faculties, especially the intellect). The last has had a profound impact on the formation of future priests, given the Sulpicians' primary commitment to seminary education.

Catholic spiritual writings during the first half of the twentieth century reflected the ambivalent character of Catholic theology itself. On the one hand, traditional neo-Scholastic theology was firmly in place in seminaries, in college religion courses, in catechisms, in sermons, and especially in official magisterial pronouncements. The manuals of spiritual theology were similar—for example, Tanquerey's *The Spiritual Life* and Reginald Garrigou-Lagrange's *The Three Ages of the Interior Life.* On the other hand, the liturgical movement, spurred by the renewal of historical and biblical studies, guided spirituality in a more Christocentric direction through the writings of such Benedictines as Abbot Columba Marmion (e.g., *Christ: the Life of the Soul* and *Christ in His Mysteries*) and, in a very different way, in the life and works of Charles de Foucauld [December 1].

Tanquerey, by his own account, showed "a certain preference for the spirituality of the French School of the seventeenth century."[12] He was himself a member of the Sulpicians, a community of priests founded by Olier, one of the leaders of seventeenth-century French spirituality. Certain elements of Tanquerey's system also remarkably anticipated some of the major theological and pastoral developments of the period of Vatican II: (1) the grounding of spirituality in Sacred Scripture and doctrine; (2) an understanding of human existence as spirituality's starting point; (3) the mystery of the Trinity as its primary theological context; (4) the centrality of Jesus Christ and of our union with Christ in the Church, his Mystical Body; and (5) the call of the whole Church, including the laity, to a life of Christian perfection.

Reginald Garrigou-Lagrange (d. 1964), a Dominican professor at the Angelicum (the Pontifical University of St. Thomas Aquinas) in Rome for many years, also presents an individualistic approach to the spiritual life, but with an emphasis on grace. All are called to sanctity, that is, a life in union with God. Christian life consists of intimate conversation with God in prayer, achieved through a threefold process: passing through the purgative, illuminative, and unitive ways successively. Discipline in life and prayer removes the obstacles and purges the senses, and so the soul moves to a second stage of Christian existence, in which it is progressively illumined by the gifts of the Holy Spirit and finds it increasingly easy to contemplate the mystery of God. And then there is entrance into a state of perfect mystical union with God in which the theological and moral virtues are practiced to a heroic degree.[13]

Although she had died at the end of the nineteenth century (in 1897), Thérèse of Lisieux, a young French Carmelite nun known in religious life as Theresa of the Child Jesus, had a profound impact on twentieth-century, pre–Vatican II Catholic spirituality. At the command of her superiors she wrote her autobiography, which was revised and circulated to all Carmelite houses. Her popular name, the "Little Flower," is taken from the subtitle. Miracles of healing and prophecy were soon reported, and by 1910 proceedings were initiated for her beatification, which occurred in 1923. Two years later she was canonized as "St. Theresa of the Child Jesus and the Holy Face." The popularity of her cult was largely due to the simplicity of her spirituality and its practicality. Sanctity is not achieved through extreme mortification, but through continual renunciation in small matters.

Abbot Columba Marmion (d. 1923), referred to above, marked out an ecclesial, liturgically oriented, Christocentric, and humanistic approach to Christian spirituality. It is the last of these four characteristics that may have been the most significant. Although both Tanquerey and Garrigou-Lagrange assert the importance of the redemptive work of Jesus Christ, they also continue to speak of human existence as if the redemption is, for all practical purposes, a juridical event (i.e., God now "declares" us just) that has not really transformed and renewed the whole human person. The Holy Spirit is given to us in Baptism and Confirmation, filling us with peace and filial confidence in God, Marmion insisted. The Spirit makes us understand that we have everything in Jesus Christ, who is not only holy in himself, but has been given to us to be *our* holiness.[14]

For Marmion, the Lord is not our distant judge, but the source of love, affection, and sympathy, for he is truly human himself. It is above all in the Eucharist that Christ's action in the soul becomes effective and fruitful for us. We are similarly impelled to the love of one another, for we have become one in Christ. This is what *Communion* implies and requires, for "to give oneself to Jesus Christ is to give oneself to others for love of Him, or rather to give oneself to Him in the person of our neighbor. . . . We are neither spirits nor ghosts," he insists, "but human beings."[15] Therefore, we are to love God humanly, that is, with all our heart, soul, strength, and mind, and to love our neighbor in the same way.

A creative move away from the mechanistic spirituality of the neo-Scholastics of the early twentieth century was taken by Charles de Foucauld (d. 1916), founder of the Little Brothers of the Sacred Heart of Jesus. Foucauld was in the tradition of French rather than Benedictine spirituality, and so his focus on Jesus was less liturgical and less ecclesial in orientation than Marmion's. To be a Christian is to follow Jesus in the way of poverty and humility. To take the lowest place among humankind is to be close to Jesus. Foucauld left the Trappist life to establish a small community whose purpose would be to live as nearly as possible the way Jesus lived, following to the letter all the evangelical counsels, possessing nothing, giving to anyone who asks.[16] The great Catholic philosopher Jacques Maritain (d. 1973) spent his own last days living in community with the Little Brothers of Charles de Foucauld.[17]

1950 to Vatican II

Christian spirituality became more oriented to the world in the years leading up to Vatican II, and no Christian spiritual writer contributed more substantially to that new emphasis than Teilhard de Chardin (d. 1955) [April 10]. The more intensely he came to know and experience the world, the closer God seemed to him. The entire universe is one "divine milieu."[18] We attain an experience of God not, as the traditional ascetical manualists argued, exclusively through purgation, contemplation, and mystical union, or a kind of "meditation with closed eyes." Rather, we encounter God by turning toward the things of the earth in love and reverence. The natural delight we take in life and in all that exists is the first dawn of divine illumination.

The great mystery of Christianity is not that God appears *(epiphany)*, but that God shines through the universe *(diaphany)*. Our prayer, therefore, is not that we might see God "as He is in Himself," but that we might see God in all things. Here again we have an echo of the basic Ignatian vision, so characteristically Catholic in its sacramental orientation. It is not merely coincidental that Teilhard himself was a member of Ignatius's company, the Society of Jesus. And yet there is also a trace of Franciscan spirituality in his sense of the presence of God in the physical universe and in his sense of the activating energy of Christ, as the Omega of evolution, across the entire cosmos.

In spite of Teilhard's insistence that spirituality is not for the religiously professed alone, monks continued to exercise profound influence on Catholic spirituality in the years immediately preceding the Second Vatican Council. For Dom Hubert Van Zeller spiritual life is a life in search of truth. But the search for truth is not distinct from the quest for love, for the object of both is God, who is at once Truth and Love. Apart from God there is no end to our search, and Christ is the embodiment of God's truth and love.

For the Christian, therefore, the purpose of life is union with Christ, and the Christian's aim is always to live to the fullest possible extent the life outlined in the gospel. This is no distant ideal proposed only to saints and mystics, but to every baptized person. All are called to a life based on the Christian love ethic, in the individual and the social orders alike. But our search is a prolonged one, involving progressive discovery. We experience frustration and loneliness on the way. "We look for Christ in darkness, and in darkness He reveals Himself. We flounder in unsatisfied longing, and in our floundering we discover love. We think we have lost faith and hope, when in our seeming faithlessness and hopelessness we discover true faith and hope. . . . We discover that the only thing in life which is worth doing is to search. The man in the Gospel who went digging for his buried treasure had already found it."[19]

The change from a negative to a positive attitude toward the world is also apparent in the extraordinarily popular writings by the Trappist monk Thomas Merton (d. 1968). There is a discernible shift from his perception of the world as wicked in his *The Seven Storey Mountain* in 1948 to *Conjectures of a Guilty Bystander* eighteen years later,[20] in which he reports how, on a downtown corner in Louisville, Kentucky, he was suddenly overwhelmed with the realization that he loved all the people he saw coming and going around him and that human beings cannot be alien to one another even though they are total strangers. The whole illusion of a separate holy existence is a dream, he insisted.

In his *Life and Holiness* Merton declares that "a Christianity that despises [the] fundamental needs of man is not truly worthy of the name. . . . There is no genuine holiness without this dimension of human and social concern."[21] Spiritual perfection is available not to those with superhuman powers, but to those who, though weak and defective in themselves, trust perfectly in the love of God, who abandon themselves with confident joy to the apparent madness of the Cross. Perfection means "simple fidelity" to the will of God in every circumstance of our ordinary life. To be a saint means to be oneself, to be what God intended one to be. We are, in fact, called to share with God "the work of *creating* the truth of our identity."[22]

"Finding God," therefore, "means much more than just abandoning all things that are not God, and emptying oneself of images and desires." Rather, "God discovers Himself in us." To find God, one must find oneself. But one cannot find oneself in isolation from the rest of humankind. We must give ourselves to others in the purity of selfless love. "For it is precisely in the recovery of our union with our brothers in Christ that we discover God and know Him, for then His life begins to penetrate our souls and His love possesses our faculties and we are able to find out Who He is from the experience of His mercy, liberating us from the prison of self-concern."[23]

Few preconciliar formulas provide as clear an introduction to post–Vatican II spirituality, however, as the title of Josef Goldbrunner's essay, "Holiness Is Wholeness." God, the All-Holy, he argues, is whole. There is "no blemish of disease . . . , no poison of death. . . . The more we seek the perfection that makes man like God, that makes him holy, the more we should become healthy in body and soul, for holiness is health."[24] This is not to say that the way to God is free of suffering and even death. "Only a slow advance in the spiritual life gives the body time to adapt itself, to expel, as it were, the poison of death which it has come to absorb." But there are also many "illegitimate illnesses" that have come to be associated with the spiritual life: sufferings and risks to health that are embraced for their own sake, assaults upon the laws of nature, and the like. Modern Christians should be ready to tread the way of the Cross that leads to holiness, but they must rebel when "holiness appears in a guise contrary to nature."[25]

Dualism is to be rejected: There is no warring between soul and body as if the two were separate components, the one higher and the other lower and base. The Incarnation teaches us that there is a wholeness to human life that comprehends the bodily as well as the spiritual. But there is more to it even than that. There is as well the universe of the unconscious with which each must get in touch. To live a spiritually healthy life one must find one's own truth; that is, "one must consciously come to terms with the irrational forces within oneself, incorporating them into the total life of the soul, but never allowing them a perfectly free rein."[26] Not every soul is the same. Each has "a certain measure of energy." If the religious life claims a great deal of energy, it must inevitably be subtracted from other spheres of the spirit. It is clear, therefore, that there are limits to our conscious striving for union with God.

It was the French philosopher-poet Charles Péguy (d. 1914) who exposed the self-deception of those who believe that the way to God is the way of repression of all desires for intimacy and interpersonal warmth. "Because they love no one," he wrote, "they imagine they love God." This is not to say, of course, that the spiritual life is without paradox. How is one to be wholly worldly and wholly devoted to God? "Through the cross of Christ, holiness and health become one."[27]

Preconciliar spirituality was also identified with lay movements like the Catholic Worker movement in the United States (and its charismatic leader, Dorothy Day [November 29]), the Young Christian Workers (Jocists) in Belgium and France, the Legion of Mary in Ireland, the Grail movement in Holland, the Cursillo movement in Spain and Latin America, and the Christian Family Movement, also in the United States. These movements also functioned for many as schools of spirituality.

Vatican II

The Second Vatican Council laid to rest, supposedly once and for all, the assumption that spirituality is for priests and nuns alone. The fifth chapter of its keynote Dogmatic Constitution on the Church is entitled "The Call of the Whole Church to Holiness." The Lord addressed all of his disciples when he said: "Be perfect, therefore, as your heavenly Father is perfect" (Matt. 5:48). We are already holy by reason of the Spirit's indwelling within us. Christian spirituality is a matter of living in accordance with who we have become in the Spirit, of manifesting the fruits of the Spirit's presence: mercy, kindness, humility, meekness, patience (Col. 3:12; Gal. 5:22; Rom. 6:22). "Thus it is evident to everyone," the council declares, "that all the faithful of Christ of whatever rank or status are called to the fullness of the Christian life and to the perfection of charity" (n. 40).

The next sentence is almost as significant: "By this holiness a more human way of life is promoted even in this earthly society." Holiness, therefore, is not only for everyone; it also comprehends far more than the individual soul's relationship with God. Furthermore, there is no single mode or style of spirituality for Christians. Each must adapt the call to perfection to his or her own situation. What will always be common to all is love of God and of neighbor. "For charity, as the bond of perfection and the fulfillment of the law (cf. Col. 3:14; Rom. 13:10), rules over all the means of attaining holiness, gives life to them, and makes them work. Hence it is the love of God and of neighbor which points out the true disciple of Christ" (n. 42).

Elsewhere the council reaffirms or elaborates upon these basic principles of Christian spirituality. The call to holiness is a call issued to laity as well as to clergy and religious. The spiritual life of all Christians will be rooted in the mysteries of creation and redemption, in the presence of the Holy Spirit, and in the mission of Christ and the Church (Decree on the Apostolate of the Laity, n. 29; see also n. 4). The Christian enters upon the spiritual life in response to the Word of God (Dogmatic Constitution on Divine Revelation, n. 21), and the Word of God, in turn, is proclaimed and celebrated in the liturgy of the Church, which is the "summit" and the "fountain" of the whole Christian life. "From the liturgy, therefore, and especially from the Eucharist, as from a fountain, grace is channeled into us; and the sanctification of persons in Christ and the glorification of God, to which all other activities of the Church are directed as toward their goal, are most powerfully achieved" (n. 10).

And what the council teaches about Catholic spirituality applies to the whole Body of Christ, for there can be "no ecumenism worthy of the name without a change of heart. . . . Let all Christ's faithful remember that the more purely they strive to live according to the gospel, the more they are fostering and even practicing Christian unity. For they can achieve depth and ease in strengthening mutual solidarity to the degree that they enjoy profound communion with the Father, the Word, and the Spirit" (Decree on Ecumenism, n. 7). The council insists that this is "the soul of the whole ecumenical movement, and can rightly be called 'spiritual ecumenism.'"

Post–Vatican II

The postconciliar period has been marked by a full-scale liturgical renewal (liturgy in the vernacular, diversified worship, active participation), a stronger sense of the ecumenical and global breadth of the Church, a more pronounced concern for social justice and the liberating mission of the Church, a heightened sense of responsibility for the environment, a deepening reverence for Sacred Scripture, an increased striving for a personal experience of the Holy Spirit, and a growing consciousness of the equality of women in the Church and in society at large. All of these developments—many of which are outgrowths of movements already at work in the nineteenth century and actively promoted in the pre–Vatican II period—shape contemporary Christian spirituality. Illustrative of the explosion of interest in spirituality since Vatican II are the charismatic renewal movement, the Cursillo movement, Marriage Encounter, directed retreats according to the original Ignatian mode, weekend youth retreats, the expansion of opportunities for spiritual direction, not only from clergy but also from religious women and laypersons, the resurgence of contemplative prayer, the establishment of many new centers and institutes for the cultivation of the spiritual life, the renewal and reform of religious congregations, and the relatively sudden appearance of new periodicals, monographs, and series in the field of spirituality.[28] Individual spiritual writers, of course, continue to influence the shape and style of Christian life, but there are too many to catalogue and we are still too close to the scene to assess their longer-term influence on Christian spirituality.[29]

The writings of Dom Aelred Graham (d. 1984), especially his *Contemplative Christianity: An Approach to the Realities of Religion*, are worth special mention because they typify the move beyond the traditional ecumenical boundaries between Catholic and Protestant into the wider spiritual dialogue between East and West. What East and West have in common, he writes, is the conviction that there are three paths to God: the path of self-forgetting adoration, expressed in both private worship and in the Church's liturgy; the path of selfless service of others, which finds expression in compassionate activity for the benefit both of the individual and of society as a whole; and the path of truth-realizing experience, through contemplative meditation. Not all three paths have to be traveled. We will be inclined to one or another by temperament. But any one of these paths, selflessly pursued, can lead to union with God.

To be spiritual is to have achieved "God-realization," that is, "to be in a state of awareness such that God is consciously *real*."[30] It means seeing God everywhere and in everything and everyone. Christian spirituality, therefore, is incarnational. It welcomes what is fully human, including the physical, the down-to-earth, the concrete. And yet it is not simply materialistic. There is more to reality than meets the eye. God is present to the world as the power of love, which is to be shared with others.[31]

One of the most significant postconciliar developments has been that of feminist spirituality. Rooted in women's experience of friendship and solidarity and in their search for autonomy and freedom, feminist spirituality not only affirms and recognizes the realities of feminist sisterhood, but also of the broader solidarity of humankind. Because of this sense of universal solidarity, feminist spirituality stands against all forms of human oppression, including racism, classism, sexism, and elitism; it is global in its compassion, and as such stands also against militarism and the exploitation of the environment.

Feminist writers suggest that God should occasionally be imagined and worshiped as mother and sister, and that the Risen Christ be thought of, in a nonandrocentric way, as bearing the feminine qualities of the biblical Wisdom or Sophia as well as the masculine features of the Jesus of history and the *Logos* (Gk., "Word"). The Church, therefore, is a community of equal discipleship, and Mary is the witness to both the strength of autonomy and the compassion of relatedness that human and Christian development implies. Christian virtue, in turn, is both active and passive strength in the solidarity of human community with God that is given in Christ and that is continually energized by the Spirit.[32]

Liberation spirituality represents the spiritual turn in Latin American liberation theology, as represented, for example, in Gustavo Gutiérrez's *We Drink from Our Own Wells: The Spiritual Journey of a People*, *On Job: God-talk and the Suffering of the Innocent,* and *The God of Life.*[33] Leonardo Boff explicitly links liberation and feminist concerns in *The Maternal Face of God: The Feminine and Its Religious Expressions.*[34]

A global (ecumenical, interfaith, and transcultural) spirituality that is at once thoroughly Christian and Catholic has been fashioned by Donald Nicholl (d. 1997), an English philosopher whose book *Holiness*, originally published in 1981, has established itself as a modern classic.[35] Drawing upon an extraordinarily wide range of classical and modern writers, he situates our "place" in creation while reflecting upon the role of solitude and stillness, spiritual companions, suffering, and daily life as an exercise in self-sacrifice and the service of others. He shows why solitude and communion (Gk. *koinonia*) are not incompatible: "because the principle that unites persons in the most intimate *koinonia* is the unique, incommunicable relationship with God which each person shares with every other person."

In the end, spirituality *is* about communion, or *koinonia,* with God, with other human persons, and with the environment, animate and inanimate alike. And it is as richly diverse as the human community in general and as the communion of saints in particular.

PART III

CANONIZATION: PROCESS AND POLITICS

SAINTS DO NOT COME ABOUT THE WAY THE TEN COMMANDMENTS did. No one ascends a high mountain, consults with God, and then returns with a list. It is an essentially human process, which Catholics nonetheless believe is guided by the wisdom and inspiration of the Holy Spirit. During the first Christian millennium saints were popularly acclaimed at the local level, that is, where they lived much of their lives and where they died, often as martyrs. In most instances, it was the prerogative of the local bishop to grant approval for a new cult, usually centered on the tomb. In the second Christian millennium the process shifted from the local church to the papacy. Only those candidates who survived scrutiny by Roman offices (the Congregation of Rites, and later the Congregation for the Causes of Saints) and ultimately by the pope himself could be advanced to canonization in a step-by-step fashion: from "Servant of God" to "Venerable" to "Blessed" to "Saint." To be sure, this process was never completely immune from external and internal pressures, whether from temporal rulers, powerful families, religious orders, or influential bishops and cardinals. In other words, there has been a political as well as a spiritual dimension to the process. This chapter traces the history of canonization through both millennia, and indicates when and how the process has been politicized.

The Process of Canonization

Before 1983

Canonization is the process of adding names of holy people to the list (Gk. *canon*) of saints. Until the year 993, when John XV canonized Ulrich of Augsburg [July 4], the pope was not involved in the process, except in approving the cults of Roman saints under his jurisdiction as Bishop of Rome. Before the end of the first Christian millennium, saints were proclaimed by the local communities among whom they had lived and died. The first saints were the so-called red martyrs (those who had died for the faith). Their tombs and relics were given special honor, and the Eucharist was celebrated over them on the anniversaries of their deaths. Moreover, their names were added to a list of martyrs, called a martyrology, and were read out to the community when it assembled for worship. Various liturgical calendars were later developed, containing the names, dates of death (and hence the feast days), and burial places of the martyrs. Local churches, monasteries, regions, and eventually nations kept their own calendars, which were often exchanged with other local churches. Not until the seventeenth century was a universal calendar established for the Church in the West.

During or soon after the fifth century, veneration was also extended to the so-called white martyrs. They were confessors who had suffered for the faith, but were not put to death. Bishops gradually assumed responsibility for approving the cults of such saints and required written accounts (Lat. *vitae*) of the individual's life and miracles. (The latter were not required in the case of "red martyrs.") These accounts of the holy person's life and miracles were read out in the presence of the bishop. (The common use of the word "legend" with reference to the biographies of saints is derived from the Latin *legenda* ["to be read"], used with reference to this public reading of a proposed saint's life and spiritual achievements.) Some bishops also required eyewitness testimony. Once the bishop or a regional synod approved the cult, the saint's body was exhumed and transferred, or "translated" (the technical term), to an altar. The new saint was assigned a feast day (almost always the day of death, regarded as the day of entrance into eternal glory) and his or her name was added to the local calendar of saints. This whole process was tantamount to canonization.

About the year 1170 Pope Alexander III sent a letter to King Canute of Sweden chastising a local bishop for tolerating the cult of a monk who had been killed in a drunken brawl, notwithstanding claims of local Christians that miracles had been performed through the monk's intercession. The pope insisted that henceforth no cult would be allowed without the approval of the Bishop of Rome. With the publication of his *Decretals* in 1234, Pope Gregory IX formally incorporated his predecessor's new rule into the universal laws of the Western Church. In the next century, when the popes were in Avignon (1309–77), more detailed procedures were put in place. Those petitioning on behalf of a candidate for canonization were now represented by an official procurator, or prosecutor, of the cause. The pope was represented by a new curial official, the Promoter of the Faith, more popularly known as the "Devil's Advocate." Before a cause could be considered, the pope required letters from bishops, temporal rulers, and other important individuals formally requesting that a process be initiated. Because of these new procedures, the number of canonizations declined precipitously, at least for a time.

In spite of the new legislation, local cults were still tolerated and bishops retained the right to approve them. However, the holy persons in question could not be regarded as saints (Lat. *sancti*), only as blessed (Lat. *beati*). Additional procedural reforms were introduced by Pope Sixtus V in 1588 with the creation of the Congregation of Rites, having responsibility for preparing canonizations and authenticating relics. In his constitution of 1634, Pope Urban VIII (1623–44) formally introduced the distinction between beatification and canonization and established detailed procedures for both. Henceforth, no holy person could be venerated publicly or have any of his or her writings published unless the person had been beatified or canonized by the pope. An exception was allowed in the case of saints whose cults could be shown to have existed "from time immemorial" (in some reckonings, for at least a century) or could be justified "on the strength of what the fathers or saints have written, with the ancient and conscious acquiescence of the Apostolic See or the local bishops."[1] Any unauthorized public cult prior to papal beatification or canonization would automatically disqualify the holy person from consideration for canonization. The faithful were only allowed to gather at the person's tomb, to pray for divine favors in the person's name, and to practice private devotions in their homes.

A half century later there was yet another development of the process. Prospero Lorenzo Lambertini, a canonist in the Congregation of Rites and the future Pope Benedict XIV (1740–58), reviewed and clarified the Church's theory and practice of beatification and canonization in a five-volume work entitled *De Servorum Dei beatificatione et Beatorum canonizatione* (Lat., "On the Beatification of the Servants of God and the Canonization of the Blessed"), published between 1734 and 1738. The text quickly acquired the status of a classic. The norms were for the most part incorporated into the 1917 Code of Canon Law (cans. 1276–89).

From this time until the promulgation of Pope John Paul II's apostolic constitution *Divinus perfectionis Magister* (Lat., "The Divine Master of Perfection"), in 1983, these rules and procedures were followed:[2]

1. No cause for beatification and canonization could formally be considered by Rome until fifty years after the candidate's death. (It was later reduced to ten years, and now is five.)

2. Initial petitions had to be submitted to the local bishop in whose territory the prospective saint died. If he decided there was sufficient merit to the case and that there was no public cult, he established a tribunal or court of inquiry. This opened the Ordinary Process. Witnesses were called to testify on one side or the other, and their testimony was notarized, sealed, and placed in the diocesan archives for later transmittal to Rome, should the case merit referral.

3. At the same time, the bishop appointed officials to collect and evaluate for their orthodoxy all of the candidate's published and unpublished writings, including private letters. Since 1940 candidates have had to receive from Rome a *nihil obstat* (Lat., "nothing stands in the way"), indicating that there was nothing objectionable in their files.

4. If, following these procedures, the bishop approved the petition, he submitted the case to the Congregation of Rites. (In 1969 Pope Paul VI divided the Congregation of Rites into the Congregation for Divine Worship and the Congregation for the Causes of Saints, giving the latter a new structure with three offices: judicial, Promoter General of the Faith, and historical-juridical.) A Postulator (representing the petitioners), resident in Rome, was assigned to the case. The Postulator, in turn, selected an advocate, or defense lawyer, to assist him. This lawyer prepared a brief, giving arguments why the case should be introduced.

5. A written "dialectic" followed in which the Promoter of the Faith ("Devil's Advocate") posed objections to the brief, to which the advocate replied. The Promoter, in turn, responded to the reply, and the process continued in that fashion, sometimes for decades. (The new procedures, adopted in 1983, have abolished the entire series of protracted legal dialectics between the advocate and the "Devil's Advocate," who, after nearly six centuries, has been eliminated from the process.)

6. Eventually all of the material developed in the previous steps was printed in a volume known as the *positio* (Lat., "position"), and this was studied by all of the officials of the Congregation. At a formal meeting in the Apostolic Palace, the Congregation decided whether or not to move to a formal process.

7. If the Congregation rendered a positive judgment, the pope issued a Decree of Introduction. Significantly, he did not sign the decree with his papal name, but with his baptismal name, to indicate that the cause had only his administrative approval. The cause was now called an Apostolic Process, one in which the standards of evidence were more exacting.

8. The Promoter of the Faith ("Devil's Advocate") drew up a new set of questions about the virtues or martyrdom of the candidate. These questions were sent back to the diocese, where a new tribunal was established, with judges deputized by the Holy See.

9. Upon completion of the testimony, the documentation was sent to the Congregation in Rome, which translated it into one of the official languages. The documents were examined to be sure that all of the juridical forms and protocols were properly observed. The Holy See then issued a Decree on the Validity of the Process.

10. The Postulator and the advocate prepared another document, called an *informatio* (Lat., "information"), outlining the case for virtue or martyrdom, with citations from the depositions of witnesses. The Promoter of the Faith ("Devil's Advocate") presented his objections, and the advocate replied. This exchange, along with all other relevant documents, was printed and submitted to the officials of the Congregation and their theological consultants.

11. At a formal meeting of the Congregation, the Promoter of the Faith raised new objections and the advocate replied. The process

was repeated at a second meeting of the Congregation, which included its cardinal members. A third meeting included the pope himself. If the judgment was that the candidate had practiced virtue to a heroic degree or was a true martyr for the faith, the candidate was declared "Venerable."

12. Sometime prior to beatification, the body of the candidate was exhumed for identification by the local bishop. If the body was not that of the candidate, the cause could continue, but prayers and devotions at the grave site had to cease. In cases where the body was found to be incorrupt, the cause was often enhanced.

13. Two miracles were required for beatification. It had to be established that the miracles were truly divine in origin and that they occurred because of the candidate's intercession. The initial investigation was done by the local bishop in a manner similar to the Ordinary Process, that is, gathering evidence, taking testimony, notarizing and sealing the data, and transmitting it to Rome.

14. A similar process was followed at the Congregation, but with the traditional dialectical element of objections, replies, more objections, and more replies. This time, however, medical experts were engaged to examine the evidence. If the judgment was positive, theological consultors determined whether the alleged miracle was in fact granted through the intercession of the candidate. The judgments of these parties were circulated through the Congregation and, if the cardinals and the pope certified the miracle, a formal decree to that effect was issued. The same process was followed for each miracle.

15. The candidate was approved for beatification by a general meeting of the cardinals of the Congregation in the presence, and with the acquiescence, of the pope. At the beatification ceremony, an apostolic brief proclaimed the Servant of God as one of the Church's "blesseds." Veneration, however, was limited to a local diocese, region, country, or a religious order. Special prayers and a Mass were also authorized for that purpose.

16. To underscore the considerable chasm between beatification and canonization, the pope did not preside at the Solemn Pontifical Mass that concluded the beatification ceremony. He visited the basilica after the Mass to venerate the new "blessed."

17. After beatification there was no movement in the cause unless and until another miracle was presented in evidence. (Two additional miracles were required for canonization before 1983.) The entire process outlined above was repeated in each instance. When the second required miracle was authenticated, the pope issued a bull of canonization declaring that the candidate was to be venerated as a saint through the universal Church. The pope himself presided at all of the ceremonies of canonization, including the Solemn Pontifical Mass. In his declaration of sanctity, the pope summed up the saint's life and briefly explained the example and message the saint brought to the Church.

In the light of the Second Vatican Council (1962–65), which called for greater participation by the worldwide episcopate in the governance of the universal Church, it became clear that the process of canonization would have to be taken out of the exclusive control of the Vatican and restructured in a manner more consistent with the collegial nature of the Church. That task was left to Pope John Paul II.

Since 1983

On January 25, 1983, Pope John Paul II issued the apostolic constitution *Divinus perfectionis Magister,*[3] which significantly modified the traditional process leading to canonization. The new procedures place the entire responsibility for gathering the evidence in support of a cause in the hands of the local bishop in whose diocese the candidate died. He is expected, however, to consult with the other bishops of his region regarding the wisdom of proceeding with the case, in keeping with the doctrine of episcopal collegiality. There are no longer two canonical processes—Ordinary and Apostolic—but only one, directed by the local bishop. He appoints a Postulator of the cause, who seeks out accurate information about the life of the candidate (known as the Servant of God) and also develops the arguments in favor of moving the cause forward. This process includes the taking of testimony and the examination of historical records. The judgment of orthodoxy is now rendered at the local level rather than in Rome. Thus, if the candidate has written anything for publication, it is the bishop who must see to it that those publications are examined by theological censors. If there is nothing contrary to faith or morals in these publications, the bishop turns his attention to other unpublished writings, such as letters and diaries. If there is nothing objectionable in these documents, the bishop may proceed with the case through the calling of witnesses by the Postulator.

Before the inquiry has been completed, the bishop or his delegate must carefully inspect the tomb of the Servant of God, the room in which he or she lived or died, and any other places where there might be signs of a cult in the Servant of God's honor. The bishop then attests in writing to the fact that there has been no public cult of the candidate, in accordance with the decrees of Urban VIII. When the investigations have been completed, two copies of the record, or transcript, of the proceedings are sent to the Congregation in Rome, along with a copy of the books written by the candidate and of the judgment rendered on them by the theological censors. The bishop or his delegate also must attest in writing to the cardinal prefect of the Congregation for the Causes of Saints that the witnesses were trustworthy and all of the acts of the process were carried out according to law.

Once the cause has been accepted, the Congregation appoints a Relator, drawn from a College of Relators assigned to the Congregation. The Relator is responsible for selecting someone, known as a collaborator, to assist in writing the *positio*. The Relator may select additional collaborators, including specialists in the history of a particular period or country in which the candidate lived. Witnesses are still appropriate, but the chief source of information is now a well-documented biography, written "according to the rules of criticism used in hagiography."[4] The document must contain everything necessary for the consultors (preferably specialists in the field) and prelates of the Congregation to render a judgment about the fitness of the candidate for beatification and canonization, namely, that the candidate was a person of heroic virtue or was truly martyred for the faith. The document is submitted for discussion before the Congregation only after it has been reviewed by theological consultors (appointed by a new official, the Prelate Theologian, who presides over their meetings) and the Promoter of the Faith. Their opinions and conclusions are submitted in writing to the cardinals and bishops of the Congregation.

One Relator is specially assigned to prepare a *positio* on the miracles attributed to the candidate, in consultation with a board of medical doctors and another of theologians. (However, now only two miracles are required: one for beatification and one for canonization. In the case of martyrs, only one miracle is required, and that for canonization. Once evidence of heroic virtue is established at the beatification stage, it need not be investigated further for canonization.) The judgments of the cardinals and bishops of the Congregation are reported to the pope, who alone has the right to declare that a public cult may be accorded to the Servant of God.[5]

At the canonization ceremony itself, the pope proclaims: "We solemnly decide and define that [name] is a saint and inscribe him [or her] in the catalog of saints, stating that his [or her] memory shall be kept with pious devotion by the universal Church."

Infallible?

Ever since the formal definition of papal infallibility at the First Vatican Council in 1870, it has been assumed by many of the Church's theologians that the charism of infallibility, by which the Church is preserved from fundamental error when solemnly defining a matter of faith or morals,[6] applies to the canonization of saints. The principal argument advanced in support of the position is that the pope would be risking the salvation of the faithful if he held up to them as a model of Christian holiness someone who was not, in fact, a saint and the imitation of whom could lead them to eternal damnation.[7]

The arguments against the infallibility of the act of canonization are: (1) The Church has never defined that canonizations are covered by the charism of infallibility. Indeed, the 1983 Code of Canon Law stipulates that "No doctrine is understood to be infallibly defined unless it is clearly established as such" (can. 749.3). (2) The act of canonization does not fulfill one of the essential conditions of an infallible teaching as laid down by the First Vatican Council, namely, that it be clearly a matter of faith or morals, in accordance with the interpretation of infallibility given by the Second Vatican Council.[8] (3) When he teaches infallibly for the whole Church, the pope does not act as an individual bishop, albeit the Bishop of Rome, but as the head of the worldwide College of Bishops. As such, he is morally required to consult the worldwide episcopate before issuing an infallible teaching.[9] Although the canonization process involves the local bishop in a very direct way, especially since the reform of 1983, it does not engage the worldwide episcopate. Indeed, in the case of Pope John Paul II, who canonized more saints during his pontificate than all other popes combined, the bishops could not possibly have kept themselves fully informed of all of his canonizations, much less have given their full and deliberate consent to each and every one of them.[10] (4) Some of the Church's greatest saints were never formally canonized according to the norms of Sixtus V (1585–90), Urban VIII (1623–44), Benedict XIV (1740–58), and John Paul II (1978–); for example, Peter and Paul [June 29], Francis of Assisi [October 4], Mary Magdalene [July 22], and the greatest saint of all, the Blessed Virgin Mary. Conversely, at least a few of the saints canonized according to the precise canonical norms that have been operative since the late sixteenth century are, by today's doctrinal, theological, and spiritual standards, countersigns rather than exemplars of Christian holiness. Their psychologically unhealthy attitudes toward their own bodies and toward the reality of sexual intimacy sanctified by the sacrament of Marriage were contradictions, not affirmations, of the gospel. Thus, on the one hand, the Church has done very well in raising up luminous models of holiness without the aid of papal infallibility and, on the other, has not always prevented the emergence of inappropriate models, notwithstanding the theological appeals to infallibility.[11] (5) It may also be a matter of interest that Pope John Paul II himself makes no claim anywhere in his 1983 apostolic constitution *Divinus perfectionis Magister* that the canonization process is protected by the charism of infallibility.

On balance, therefore, the weightier theological opinion is that papal infallibility is *not* engaged in the act of canonization.

The Politics of Canonization

If the linkage of the words "politics" and "canonization" has a jarring effect on some readers, it may be because "politics" is too often associated in the public mind with *partisan* activity designed to elect or appoint someone to, or keep someone in, office. This type of politics involves the bestowing of favors, usually financial, on one group or another as a reward for its support in a previous election campaign. The word "politics," however, is not being used in that sense here. Rather, it is being used in accordance with its classical meaning, namely, with reference to the use of power and influence to achieve a specific end in the *polis* (Gk., "city"), be it the public or the private sector. Thus understood, politics is a neutral activity. It refers to the process by which people try to get things done by influencing people, directly or through coalitions and alliances, who can help them achieve their goal. Politics is bad only when the goal of the activity is contrary to the common good or to justice and/or the means to the end are unethical. That, of course, is always a matter of interpretation. One side's "good" politics is another side's "bad" politics.

If politics is involved in the election of a pope,[12] a process that determines the successor of Peter and the earthly head of the universal

Church, it does not require a great stretch of logic to conclude that the canonization process may also have a political dimension. If the act of papal succession does not occur through the direct inspiration of the Holy Spirit, neither does the raising of persons to sainthood. Powerful individuals and groups (religious orders, bishops, and temporal rulers) propose candidates for canonization and lobby for their cause, often over many decades, even centuries. A successful outcome is not possible without significant financial resources and a persistence that often exceeds many individual lifetimes.

That is why such a seasoned observer of the canonization process, Lawrence Cunningham, can write: "Every beatification or canonization is, of course, a political statement in the sense that such public gestures of the Church desire to make plain preoccupations, emphases, and iconic representations that are part of the larger church program."[13] Elizabeth Johnson agrees. Once canonization was carefully regulated under the supervision of the pope, she writes, the process became "inevitably . . . political." By means of this honor, the pope was able to reward his allies in battles against heretical groups or recalcitrant monarchs, maintain popular support by naming favored saints, and punish those whose orthodoxy was questionable. Given the length of time and money the process increasingly demanded, it began to favor members of religious orders and royal houses who had resources sufficient for the required research and lobbying.[14]

Examples of overtly political canonizations (in the secular sense of the word "political") abound throughout history.[15] Celestine V [May 19], who is often mistakenly identified as the only pope ever to have resigned the office,[16] was canonized because the king of France, Philip IV (also known as Philip the Fair), pressured a French pope, Clement V (1305–14), to do so. The canonization was a form of posthumous retribution on the part of the king toward his bitter enemy, Boniface VIII (1295–1303), who had coaxed Celestine into resigning the papacy and then placed him under house arrest, lest he become the focal point of a schism. On the other hand, Boniface had canonized Philip IV's grandfather, Louis IX [August 25], as part of the negotiated settlement of a dispute between the pope and the king over the latter's power to tax the French clergy without papal approval. At the time of Rose of Lima's [August 23] canonization, Clement X (1670–76) was engaged in intense struggles with Louis XIV of France over the independence of the Church and was looking to Spain for support. (Rose's home country of Peru was a Spanish colony at the time.) The canonizations of Rose of Lima and of John of the Cross

[December 14], a native Spaniard, were widely applauded in Spain. Finally, Benedict XV (1914–22) canonized Joan of Arc [May 30] in 1920 as part of an effort to restore diplomatic relations between the Holy See and France following World War I.

More often, however, the politics involved in a canonization are internal to the Church. Thus, when many of the bishops at the Second Vatican Council proposed John XXIII (1958–63) [June 3] for immediate canonization, an act that would have appalled the conservative minority at the council, Paul VI (1963–78) finessed the issue by initiating a formal canonical process for both John XXIII and the more conservative Pius XII (1939–58), thus ensuring no action for years. When the controversy over Pius XII's silence during the Holocaust continued to becloud his memory long after the council adjourned in 1965,[17] the ploy was modified. John XXIII's cause for canonization was newly yoked, in John Paul II's pontificate (1978–), with that of an even more conservative pope, Pius IX (1846–78).[18] Both John XXIII and Pius IX were beatified on September 3, 2000.

However, the most blatant example of a politicized process in modern times is that of Josemaría Escrivá de Balaguer (1902–75), founder in 1928 of Opus Dei (Lat., "The Work of God"), a predominantly lay movement that prospered after the political ascendancy of the Spanish Fascist leader General Francisco Franco (1892–1975) and was the first secular institute to be formally recognized by the Church. In 1962 Monsignor Escrivá petitioned the Vatican to declare his movement a personal prelature, which would have removed it from the jurisdiction of local bishops. The Spanish hierarchy strongly objected and permission was not granted during the founder's lifetime. However, soon after his election to the papacy in 1978, John Paul II, who was personally sympathetic with the movement's theological and pastoral agenda, set the procedure in motion and the petition was finally granted in 1982. Opus Dei generated considerable financial resources for the Vatican during John Paul II's pontificate and was particularly generous in support of the pope's efforts on behalf of the Solidarity labor movement in Poland prior to the overthrow of the Communist government there.

Opus Dei has long been controversial because of its historic connections with antidemocratic politics, its opposition to the major reforms of the Second Vatican Council, especially those pertaining to the liturgy, and its secretive character (it does not publish the names of its members or readily identify its secular operations). To judge by its founder's writings alone, Kenneth Woodward has observed, "Escrivá was an unexceptional spirit, derivative and often banal in his thoughts, personally inspiring, perhaps, but devoid of original insights."[19] Nevertheless, his cause for canonization was introduced in Rome less than six years after his death (four years short of a new ten-year minimum, later reduced to five in 1983), thanks to the crucial support of Opus Dei members within the Vatican (Pope John Paul II's press secretary, Dr. Joaquin Navarro-Valls, is a member) and the determined lobbying efforts by other members throughout the world. He was declared "heroically virtuous" in April 1990. Fifteen months later a miraculous healing, authenticated in part by Opus Dei doctors, was attributed to his intercession.

Negative testimony, especially from former members of Opus Dei (dismissed by Cardinal Angelo Felici, then prefect of the Congregation for the Causes of Saints, as "discordant voices"), was ignored and the process was hastily concluded. Monsignor Luigi de Magistris, one of two theological consultants to the Congregation who had voted against proceeding with the beatification, was quoted as saying that the beatification should have been postponed "insofar as it would not be pastorally constructive to offer as a model of virtue a subject not without problems."[20]

At least two cardinals publicly questioned the speed at which the process had moved forward. One of them, Silvio Oddi, a former member of the Roman Curia and regarded generally as an ultraconservative, said that the push to make Escrivá a saint had done Opus Dei "more harm than good," and he reported that many bishops were "very displeased."[21] Many observers were particularly disturbed about Opus Dei's successful efforts to prevent unfavorable witnesses from testifying before the Vatican panel that evaluated the evidence for its founder's sanctity. Some of these witnesses were longtime members of Opus Dei and knew Escrivá personally. His former secretary, Maria del Carmen Tapia, who had been a numerary (celibate lay leader) for eighteen years, claimed that Escrivá had "no respect" for Popes John XXIII and Paul VI, that he was a man of "great ambition," and that he also had "a great ability to manipulate." Another, who had been a member for twenty-two years, charged that the monsignor despised the Second Vatican Council so much that he and his closest associates seriously considered leaving the Catholic Church and joining the Greek Orthodox Church. Escrivá, according to this source, "suffered from deep postconciliar depression at the liturgical changes made by the council. He felt nothing but disgust for them and did not observe them in private."[22]

Still others pointed to Escrivá's lack of humility, his foul temper, his vanity (reflected, for example, in his change of name from the simple Escribá to the more ostentatious Escrivá de Balaguer), and his playing loose with the truth in dealings with parents of young Opus Dei candidates and in business matters. Even his own nephew, Carlos Albas Minguez, had stated that "arrogance was one of my uncle's traits."

So specific and so widespread were these charges that the beatification became the subject of cutting and sarcastic humor in highly placed quarters of the Catholic Church. There was a joke circulating in the Vatican and in the city of Rome that, while it was known that the pope had the power to dispense with the requirement for miracles in a canonization process, it was not known that he could also dispense with the requirement for virtue.

According to Kenneth Woodward, the *positio* (or printed version of the case in support of beatification) was written by the Postulator (the advocate of the cause) with the help of four Opus Dei university professors. When Woodward asked how this was possible in light of the fact that it is the Relator, not the Postulator, who is charged with writing the *positio*, the Relator, Father Ambrose Eszer, O.P., said that he had been "in control" of the writing process, but he admitted that the others did all the work and that he did nothing except cut the "excess" testimony.

Josemaría Escrivá de Balaguer—the name by which he preferred to be known because of its hint of nobility—was beatified on May 11, 1992, more than eight years before the beatification of Pope John XXIII, who had convened the council that Escrivá had so despised. "Escrivá," Woodward pointed out, "may indeed be the great saint that Opus Dei holds him out to be. But the speed and unobstructed ease with which he was passed by the Congregation raises many questions about the process itself: its toughness, impartiality, professionalism, and freedom from ecclesiastical pressure and spiritual politics."[23]

Such have been the exceptions, not the rule. The hundreds of saints who are memorialized and honored in the pages that follow are, in almost all instances, compelling examples of the power of grace to transform the human spirit and of the goodness of God in illuminating our own paths to eternal life. These individuals were recognized as saints because of the transparently heroic virtue of their lives and because of their extraordinary capacity to inspire thousands, even millions, to attempt to follow their example.

Saints, in the end, are not saints for themselves, but for the Church and even for the world, as in the case, for example, of the great Francis of Assisi. They are sacraments, that is, both signs and instruments of grace. This is what the Church proclaims when it raises them, by whatever process, to the heights of sainthood.

PART IV

LIVES OF THE SAINTS

ONE CAN REFLECT THEORETICALLY ON THE NATURE OF sanctity, the various schools of spirituality, and the process and politics of canonization, but in the end saints were, and are, real people with real-life stories. Just as Christianity is not simply an idea, but a way of life, so sanctity is not just a concept, but something that is embodied and lived.

The biographical profiles presented in this section of the book are arranged according to the yearly calendar. The criteria for inclusion, in order of priority, are the following: (1) saints who are on the General Roman Calendar (the official liturgical calendar of the Roman Catholic Church); (2) saints who, although not on the General Roman Calendar, are commemorated by one of the major Christian traditions that have a sanctoral cycle (Orthodox, Anglican, Lutheran), or by one of the Catholic Church's major religious orders, or whose feasts are on the Proper Calendar for the (Roman Catholic) Dioceses of the U.S.A.; (3) saints who are listed in the *Roman Martyrology* (the Catholic Church's official list of saints and their feast days) on a day when no other saint is commemorated on one of the aforementioned liturgical calendars; and (4) historically significant holy persons who have not yet been recognized officially by the Catholic Church as worthy of public veneration. Various feasts of the Blessed Virgin Mary and major feasts on fixed dates, such as Christmas or the Triumph of the Cross, are included, but moveable feasts, such as Easter or Pentecost, are not.

The selections are comprehensive, but not complete. There are many thousands of saints who are not included, including many recently named by Pope John Paul II. As of June 2001, he had already canonized four hundred and fifty-one saints and beatified over a thousand. These figures place his pontificate in a historical class by itself. John Paul II did not simply canonize more saints than any other pope before him—he canonized more saints than all other popes combined.

A point of information: Whenever reference is made to a saint in an entry other than the saint's own feast day, the date of that feast day is given in brackets. Readers may consult that date for the saint's biographical profile. If no date is given in brackets following a proper name, there is no separate entry on that individual.

JANUARY

1 Solemnity of Mary, Mother of God

The *Blessed Virgin Mary* is the greatest of the Church's saints and "Mother of God" (Gk. *Theotokos;* Lat. *Deipara*) is the highest of her titles. It is the basis for every other title and dignity accorded to her. Although she was the Mother of God from the moment she conceived Jesus in her womb by the power of the Holy Spirit (Luke 1:26–38), her motherhood of God was not formally recognized by the Church until the first half of the fifth century, in response to a theological controversy that focused not upon her, but upon her Son.

Nestorius (d. ca. 451), the patriarch of Constantinople (present-day Istanbul, Turkey), argued that there are two whole and distinct natures in Christ, one human and one divine, each having its own "personal" manifestation. For him and for others identified with the school of theology centered in Antioch (present-day Syria), such expressions as "God has suffered" and "God was nursed at his mother's breast" were offensive because they seemed to deny the full meaning of the Incarnation. Nestorius and his supporters wanted to emphasize that the Son of God really took on our humanity. He became one of us in the flesh. It was Jesus, not the Second Person of the Trinity, who nursed at his mother's breast and who later suffered on the cross. According to Nestorius, Mary was the mother of the human person Jesus, and not of the Son of God, "since a true mother should be of the same essence as what is born of her" (*Letter to Pope Celestine,* n. 2).

A crisis erupted when, in his preaching, Nestorius publicly denied to Mary the title "Mother of God" *(Theotokos),* calling her instead the mother of Christ *(Christotokos).* His supporters, led by John, the bishop of Antioch, lined themselves up against those allied with Cyril, the bishop of Alexandria [June 27]. After being condemned by local synods in Rome and in Alexandria in 430, Nestorius appealed to the emperor Theodosius II (d. 450) to convene a general council to address the issue. It met at Ephesus, a wealthy Greek city on the western coast of Asia Minor (in present-day Turkey). Cyril formally opened the council on June 22, 431, even before the arrival of Nestorius and his supporters and that of the delegates from Rome, representing Pope Celestine (d. 432). The council condemned Nestorius's views and deposed him as patriarch of Constantinople. His principal supporter, John of Antioch, was excommunicated, and the Nicene-Constantinopolitan Creed (recited to this day at Sunday Mass and at other great feasts) was established as the only acceptable formula of faith. When the Roman delegation finally arrived at the council, they ratified in the name of the pope what had already been decided and done.

Because of its teaching that in Jesus Christ there are two natures, one human and one divine, and only one divine Person, the council affirmed that Mary was not only the mother of Christ in his human nature, but also of Christ as a divine Person. Therefore, Mary could indeed be proclaimed as the Mother of God. Upon the release of the council's teaching to the general public, crowds began marching through the streets of Ephesus chanting, "*Theotokos! Theotokos!*"

The teaching gave a major impetus to the spread of Marian devotion throughout the Church for centuries to come. Thus, before the Council of Ephesus there had been only one liturgical feast of Mary, the feast of the Purification, and that was celebrated only in certain parts of the Eastern Church. After Ephesus, however, Marian feasts began to multiply and churches were dedicated to her in all major cities. In Rome the major basilica of St. Mary Major (the largest of eighty churches dedicated to her in that city alone) was substantially completed by the middle of the fourth century.

From the beginning of the sixth century various Christian communities celebrated Mary's bodily assumption into heaven. By the middle of the seventh century, four separate Marian feasts were observed in Rome: the Annunciation [March 25], the Purification [February 2], the

Assumption [August 15], and the Nativity of Mary [September 8]. The feast of the Conception of Mary [December 8] began in the East at the end of that century, but remained unknown in the West until the ninth. Popular interest in apocryphal writings about her also increased, especially in the *Protevangelium of James*, and there was a proliferation of Marian icons in both East and West. The iconic tradition, however, gradually disappeared in the West, which eventually adopted a more humanized, sentimentalized form of Marian imagery.

Western piety and theology in the Middle Ages implied that Mary is actually a more reliable source of mercy and compassion toward sinners than is Christ himself. The assumption was that Mary would exercise her maternal influence over her Son and turn away his just anger and wrath. The so-called Theophilus legend, translated into Latin in the eighth century, had a great influence on this devotional development. According to the story, a man bargains his soul away to the devil to gain a lucrative position. Near death, he prays to Mary and beseeches her to retrieve the contract from the devil. She succeeds after a great struggle. Theophilus escapes eternal punishment, and Mary emerges as the great savior of sinners. That mentality continued even into the middle of the twentieth century, when parochial-school children were taught to appeal to Mary, our loving and all-merciful mother, rather than to Christ, who is our stern Judge. Christ locks the front door of heaven to keep out unworthy sinners, while Mary lets them in through a side window.

The growth of Marian piety was accelerated in the nineteenth century with the promulgation of the dogma of the Immaculate Conception by Pope Pius IX in 1854. During the same century, a spate of Marian apparitions were reported: at La Salette and Lourdes (in France) and in many other places. Various devotional customs developed, including the living Rosary, May processions with the crowning of a Marian statue, and the wearing of the Miraculous Medal and the scapular. Marian piety reached a peak during the pontificate of Pope Pius XII (1939–58), with his proclamation of the dogma of the Assumption in 1950, his declaration of a Marian Year in 1954, his establishment in the same year of the feast of the Queenship of Mary (originally celebrated on May 31, later transferred to August 22, the octave of the feast of the Assumption), and his strong personal devotion to Our Lady of Fátima (in Portugal) [May 13].

The Second Vatican Council (1962–65) brought about a major change in Marian devotion by grounding it more firmly in the Bible and the liturgy of the Church and in situating Mary herself in the context of the mystery of the Church, as the first among the redeemed, as the disciple par excellence (for Jesus, his mother's fidelity to the Word of God, not the fact of her motherhood, was the basis of her dignity [Mark 3:33–35; Luke 11:27–28]), and as Mother of the Church, in which she is a "preeminent and altogether singular member" (Dogmatic Constitution on the Church, n. 53). At the same time, the council warned against excesses in Marian devotion. Theologians and preachers, the council declared, must "carefully refrain from whatever might by word or deed lead the separated sisters and brothers or any others whatsoever into error about the true doctrine of the church."

The council continued: "Let the faithful remember moreover that true devotion consists neither in sterile or transitory feeling, nor in an empty credulity, but proceeds from true faith, by which we are led to recognize the excellence of the Mother of God, and we are moved to a filial love towards our mother and to the imitation of her virtues" (n. 67).

Formerly the feast of the Circumcision of Jesus (still celebrated as such by the Greek and Russian Orthodox Churches, which also celebrate the feast of Basil the Great [January 2] on this day), January 1 has been devoted liturgically to Mary, the Mother of God, since 1970, following the revision of the General Roman Calendar in 1969. It has the rank of a Solemnity, which means that it is a feast of the greatest importance. Observance of the Circumcision of Jesus has been incorporated into the new feast of the Presentation of the Lord on February 2. In 1968 Pope Paul VI (d. 1978) instituted an annual observance of a World Day of Peace on this New Year's Day as a means of addressing a message of peace to all of the nations of the world and to their political leaders.

For centuries, however, the Church gave no liturgical notice to this day, because in the so-called pagan world it was an occasion for widespread license. When the Church noted the day at all, it was as a day of fasting and penance. In the seventh century January 1 was made an ecclesiastical holiday in celebration of the octave of Christmas. The appointed church (or "station") for the papal Mass of the day was the Church of St. Mary's in Trastevere, the oldest Roman church dedicated to Mary. Consequently, the day became associated with Mary, and the old Roman calendars refer to it as the feast of Mary. In the Middle Ages, the day also came to be associated with devotion to the Holy Name of Jesus, since the short Gospel reading for the feast (Luke 2:21) includes both the circumcision and the giving of the name of Jesus.

Lutheran and Anglican liturgical calendars retain this medieval connection and celebrate it as the feast of the Name of Jesus and the Holy Name of Our Lord Jesus Christ, respectively. The Church of England, however, also includes the Circumcision with the Naming. The Franciscans celebrate the feast of the Holy Name of Jesus on January 3.

BIBLIOGRAPHY

Brown, Raymond E., et al., eds. *Mary in the New Testament: A Collaborative Assessment by Protestant and Roman Catholic Scholars.* Philadelphia: Fortress Press; New York: Paulist Press, 1978.

Gebara, Ivone, and Maria Clara Bingemer. *Mary: Mother of God, Mother of the Poor.* Maryknoll, NY: Orbis Books, 1989.

Graf, Hilda. *Mary: A History of Doctrine and Devotion.* 2 vols. New York: Sheed & Ward, 1963; reprint, Westminster, MD: Christian Classics, 1985.

Johnson, Elizabeth A. "Blessed Virgin Mary." In *The HarperCollins Encyclopedia of Catholicism.* Ed. Richard P. McBrien. San Francisco: HarperCollins, 1995, pp. 832–38.

2 Basil the Great and Gregory Nazianzen, bishops and Doctors of the Church

Basil, bishop of Caesarea, and Gregory, bishop of Constantinople, were two of the three famous Cappadocian Fathers, a designation taken from the name of the Roman province in east-central Asia Minor. The third of the Cappadocians was Basil's younger brother Gregory of Nyssa [January 10]. Their writings and sermons effectively put an end to Arianism, a fourth-century heresy that denied the divinity of Christ, referring to him instead as the greatest of creatures.

Saint Basil Dictating His Doctrine by Francisco Herrera the Elder, ca. 1639

Basil, also known as "the Great" (ca. 330–79), was born in Caesarea, the capital of the Roman province of Cappadocia. One of nine children, he came from a distinguished and pious family, to say the least. His father and mother, his sister, his two brothers, and his grandmother are all venerated as saints. (His sister Macrina's feast day is

July 19.) His father was a teacher of rhetoric and his mother was a wealthy aristocrat. Basil was educated first at home by his father and grandmother and then in Constantinople and Athens, where he befriended Gregory of Nazianzus, the other saint honored on this day. Upon his return home in 355 Basil taught rhetoric, but he renounced this career after a tour of monastic settlements in Syria, Palestine, and Egypt and following his father's death in 358. He was baptized, along with his friend Gregory, and joined other members of his family in an ascetic community on one of the family estates in Pontus. It was during this five-year period that Basil developed, through dialogues with his monastic disciples, the "long" and "short" Rules that were to influence Benedict of Nursia [July 11] and, through him, all of Western monasticism. They also helped to shape monasticism in the East, including Russia, where he is honored as one of its patron saints. Nearly all of the monks and nuns of the Greek Church to this day follow his longer Rule, which emphasizes community life, liturgical prayer, and manual work. It is sufficiently flexible to allow for almsgiving and work in hospitals and guest houses without sacrificing its strongly contemplative dimension.

With great reluctance on his part, Basil was ordained a priest (presbyter) ca. 362 for the diocese of Caesarea. His bishop later summoned him to the see city to lend support against the persecution waged against the Church by the Arian emperor Valens (364–80) and specifically to rebut the teachings of the Arians. However, the bishop became jealous of Basil's growing reputation and influence, and Basil returned to his life of solitude once more. When illness prevented the bishop from administering his diocese any longer, Gregory persuaded Basil to return to Caesarea to assume this responsibility. Basil led relief efforts during a region-wide famine in 368, distributing his own inheritance to the poor and establishing—and personally serving in—a soup kitchen. Upon the bishop's death in 370, Basil was elected to succeed him.

Basil's episcopal ministry continued to emphasize aid to the poor, but it also drew him inevitably into direct controversy with the Arians and also with the Pneumatomachians, who denied the divinity of the Holy Spirit. His writings provided solid defenses of the teachings of the Council of Nicaea (325) and anticipated the teaching of the Council of Constantinople (381) on the divinity of the Holy Spirit. He also offered carefully crafted critiques of a too allegorical interpretation of the Bible.

Basil preached every morning and evening to large congregations and promoted the construction of a major building complex known as the Basiliad, which included a large hospital. (He is patron saint of hospital administrators.) Ironically, it was on land that the Arian emperor Valens had donated after attending a Mass that Basil celebrated the feast of the Epiphany, 372. In addition to his work on behalf of the sick, Basil was especially concerned about the quality of candidates for the priesthood, the rehabilitation of thieves and prostitutes, the excessive involvement in politics and the accumulation of wealth by clergy; and the severity of rulings by civil officials. Given his own blend of classical and theological education, he was a staunch advocate of a truly catholic approach to secular culture, particularly contemporary philosophy. This openness proved to be crucial not only in his own defense of Catholic orthodoxy against the heretics of the day, but also in the longer-term development of Catholic theology itself.

In 1568 Basil was proclaimed a Doctor of the Church, or outstanding teacher of the faith—one of the four original Doctors of the Church from the East (alongside Athanasius [May 2], John Chrysostom [September 13], and Gregory Nazianzen). In his own lifetime, however, he did not enjoy the unqualified support of the papacy. Pope Damasus (366–84) had refused to recognize Basil's candidate for the bishopric of Antioch, and this led to considerable friction between the two.

Basil died on January 1, 379, at the relatively young age of forty-nine, having been worn out by a lifetime of asceticism, hard work, and a chronic stomach ailment. There was great mourning throughout the East upon news of his death. His feast is celebrated there on January 1 and again on January 30 (with Gregorian Nazianzen and John Chrysostom). It was formerly celebrated on June 14 in the West (the day of his consecration as a bishop). Basil is patron saint of Russia.

Gregory Nazianzen, also known as Gregory of Nazianzus (ca. 329–90) and as Gregory the Theologian, was the son of the bishop of Nazianzus in Cappadocia. Like Basil, Gregory came from a family of saints: his father, mother, sister, and brother. He was broadly educated in Christian writings and in Greek philosophy in Caesarea, Alexandria, and Athens, where he began a deep but sometimes troubled friendship with Basil. The two of them took up the monastic life together at Pontus in 359, where they had frequent discussions on theology and monasticism. After two years Gregory went home to help his aged father manage his diocese and estates. He accepted ordination with great misgivings and even fled back to Basil for ten weeks to avoid his new duties. Later he wrote an *apologia,* or defense, of his flight, which became a classic on the nature and responsibilities of the priesthood.

When the Arian emperor Valens divided the province of Cappadocia in order to diminish Basil's influence, the bishop of the new province of Tyana claimed for it equal ecclesiastical status with Caesarea. Basil resisted the claim on the grounds that the division was only civil, and he pressured Gregory to become bishop of the insignificant and unfriendly border town of Sasima so that he could maintain his influence in the area. (Gregory was functioning at this time as assistant to his father at Nazianzus and did so until his father's death in 374.) Because Sasima was so unpleasant and because he did not wish to be used as a pawn in an ecclesiastical power struggle, Gregory never even visited Sasima. For that, Basil accused him of laxity. Commentators point out that Gregory's sense of personal betrayal was still evident in the eloquent funeral oration he delivered for Basil in 379.

Gregory had continued to administer the diocese of Nazianzus for about a year after his father's death, but poor health forced him to retire to Seleucia in the province of Isauria for five years. Soon after the death of the Arian emperor in 380, bishops of various neighboring dioceses appealed to Gregory to help restore the beleaguered Christian community at Constantinople. It had been under Arian rule for over thirty years, and orthodox Christians (those who had remained faithful to the teaching of the Council of Nicaea on the divinity of Christ) lacked even a church for worship. Gregory, now bent over with age, accepted under protest. He took up residence in a house belonging to relatives and transformed it into a church, which he named the *Anastasis* (Gk., a place where the faith would rise again). Here he preached his famous sermons on the Trinity and, in the process, earned the surname "the Theologian." It was in his theological orations, particularly the *Five Orations on the Divinity of the Word,* that he most clearly displayed his ability to bring together his considerable learning in the classics and his profound understanding of Christian doctrine. As his reputation spread, so too did the size of his congregation.

The new orthodox emperor Theodosius banished the Arian bishop of Constantinople, and Gregory was formally installed as its bishop, to much rejoicing of the people. The emperor then summoned a council at Constantinople in May 381, at which Gregory Nazianzen (and Basil's brother Gregory of Nyssa) were to play a prominent part. The council confirmed the teaching of both Gregorys regarding the divinity of the Holy Spirit: "[We believe] in the Holy Spirit, the Lord and Giver of life, who proceeds from the Father, who together with the Father and Son is adored and glorified, who has spoken through the prophets."

Physically and psychologically drained by the continued opposition of Arian Christians and the conflicts they fomented in the city, Gregory Nazianzen resigned the bishopric of Constantinople before the end of the year and returned home to Nazianzus, which was still without a bishop. He administered that see until a successor was chosen. He subsequently retired to his estates and remained in seclusion for the rest of his life, cultivating his garden and writing poetry and his autobiography. He died in 390 and his remains were taken first to Constantinople and then to Rome, where they are still interred in St. Peter's Basilica.

Gregory and Basil are two of the four original Eastern Doctors of the Church, a title bestowed on Gregory in 1568 because of his teaching on the Trinity. His feast day is celebrated in the East on January 25 and again on January 30 (with Basil and John Chrysostom). In the West it was formerly celebrated on May 9, but since 1969 on January 2, with Basil. The feast of Basil and Gregory Nazianzen is on the General Roman Calendar and is also celebrated on this day by the Church of England. The Russian and Greek Orthodox Churches celebrate the feast of *Pope Sylvester I* [December 31] on this day.

BIBLIOGRAPHY

Meredith, Anthony. *The Cappadocians.* Crestwood, NY: St. Vladimir's Seminary Press, 1995.

Rousseau, Philip. *Basil of Caesarea.* Berkeley and Los Angeles: University of California Press, 1994.

3 Geneviève of Paris, virgin

Geneviève, patron saint of Paris (ca. 422–ca. 500), was born to wealth in Nanterre, on the outskirts of Paris, but moved, after the death of her parents, to the city, where she continued her life of prayer and asceticism as a consecrated virgin. Although her cult is ancient (reference to it can be found in the *Martyrology of Jerome,* in 592), her biography, written many centuries after her death, is not considered reliable. When Paris was besieged by the Franks under Childeric, she is said to have accompanied a group to obtain food and other provisions from neighboring towns and, in the process, to have won the respect of the Frankish leader, who spared the lives of many citizens in response to her pleas. She is also said to have encouraged the Parisians not to flee the city, but to fast and pray in order to avert an attack by Attila and his Huns in 451. The invaders changed the route of their march, and Paris was spared. After her death, Geneviève was buried in the Church of Sts. Peter and Paul [June 29], which the Frankish king Clovis had built at her suggestion. The church became a place of pilgrimage because of the many cures and miracles attributed to her and became known in the mind of the public as St. Geneviève's. A new church was begun in 1746, but was secularized at the time of the French Revolution and is called the Panthéon today, a burial place for distinguished French citizens. The best-known artistic representations of Geneviève are the frescoes in the Panthéon done by Puvis de Chavannes in 1877.

Among the miracles attributed to her, the most famous was in connection with the great epidemic that afflicted France in the early twelfth century. All efforts, both medicinal and spiritual, had failed to halt its progress—until 1129, when the casket containing Genevieve's bones was carried in solemn procession to the cathedral. (She is patron saint of those suffering from fever.) When Pope Innocent II visited Paris the following year (having fled to France during an eight-year schism when an antipope, Anacletus II, held control in Rome), he ordered an annual feast to commemorate the miracle, and it is still celebrated in Paris churches today. Even though Geneviève's shrine and most of her relics were destroyed in the French Revolution, her cult did not die out. Numerous churches in France have been named after her, and she continues to be invoked against drought, flooding, and other natural disasters. Pope John XXIII named her patron saint of French security forces in 1962. Her feast is not on the General Roman Calendar.

4 Elizabeth Ann Seton, widow and foundress; "Seventy Apostles"

Baptized Elizabeth Bayley (1774–1821), *Elizabeth Ann Seton* was the first American-born saint. She was raised in a devout and well-to-do Episcopalian family. Her father was a well-known physician. At age twenty Ann married a wealthy merchant, William Magee Seton. Together they had five children. She became involved in social work and established the Society for the Relief of Poor Widows with Children in 1797, earning the epithet the "Protestant Sister of Charity." By 1803 her husband's shipping business had gone bankrupt and he developed tuberculosis. In search of a sunnier climate, he took Elizabeth and their eldest daughter to Italy, where he died soon after the voyage. Having been inspired by the kindness of an Italian family, Elizabeth became a Catholic in 1805 after her return to the United States. (Her nephew James

Roosevelt Bayley also later became a Catholic, and eventually archbishop of Baltimore.) Rejected by her family and friends and without financial resources, she established a boarding house for schoolboys in New York and performed other assorted jobs to supplement her meager income. The rector of St. Mary's Seminary in Baltimore learned of her plight and invited her to establish a school for girls there. It opened in 1808. With four companions the following year, she founded a religious community, the Sisters of St. Joseph, and also a school for poor children near Emmitsburg, Maryland.

Her community's Rule, based on that of St. Vincent de Paul [September 27], was approved by the bishop of Baltimore (the famous John Carroll) in 1812. She was elected superior and, with eighteen other sisters, took vows the following year. Thereafter, she was known as Mother Seton. Hers was the first American religious society, formally known as the Daughters of Charity of St. Joseph, devoted to the service of the poor and to teaching in parochial schools. Historians often credit her with laying the foundation for the Catholic parochial-school system in the United States.

Mother Seton died in Emmitsburg on January 4, 1821. By then her communities were twenty in number and were spread throughout the United States, the rest of North America, South America, and Italy. Everywhere they went, the sisters opened schools and taught in orphanages. Mother Seton's cause was first taken up by Cardinal James Gibbons of Baltimore (the successor of her nephew, Archbishop Bayley). Three miracles of healing were attributed to her intercession: one from leukemia and the other two from severe meningitis. She was beatified by Pope John XXIII in 1963 and canonized in 1975 by Pope Paul VI. The latter held her up as an example of how one can live an authentically spiritual life in the midst of material prosperity. She is buried under an altar in the chapel of the National Shrine of St. Elizabeth Seton in the provincial house of the Daughters of Charity in Emmitsburg. Her feast is on the Proper Calendar

Mother Elizabeth Seton by Joseph Dawley

for the Dioceses of the U.S.A., but is not on the General Roman Calendar. On this day the Russian and Greek Orthodox Churches honor the *"Seventy Apostles"* whom Jesus sent ahead in pairs to every town and place he intended to visit (Luke 10:1).

BIBLIOGRAPHY

Stone, Elaine Murray. *Elizabeth Bayley Seton: An American Saint.* New York: Paulist Press, 1993.

5 John Nepomucene Neumann, bishop

John Nepomucene Neumann (1811–60), the fourth bishop of Philadelphia, was born in Bohemia of a German father and Czech mother. Named after John Nepomucen [May 16], also Nepomuncene or Nepomuk, the patron saint of Bohemia, he came to the United States with the intention of doing missionary work after the Austrian government forced the local bishop to postpone ordinations. (Another version is that the bishop decided this on his own because of an oversupply of priests in his diocese.) A diminutive man of some five feet, three inches, Neumann arrived in Manhattan in June 1836 and was ordained within three weeks for the diocese of New York. His first assignment was to German-speaking immigrants who were clearing the forests for a settlement around Niagara Falls. After four years of working alone, he yearned for community life and joined the Redemptorists (the Congregation of the Most Holy Redeemer, known by their initials, C.SS.R.), taking his vows in January 1842. Given his facility for languages (he spoke eight), he became a popular preacher among the immigrant communities of Pittsburgh and Baltimore. He was eventually appointed vicar of all the Redemptorists in the United States, with headquarters in Baltimore.

In 1852 he was appointed the fourth bishop of Philadelphia, thanks in large measure to the sponsorship of his friend and penitent, Francis Patrick Kenrick, archbishop of Baltimore and a former bishop of Philadelphia. As the new bishop of Philadelphia, Neumann embarked on a vigorous program of building some one hundred churches and eighty schools. (The diocese at the time covered the eastern half of Pennsylvania and all of Delaware.) He completed the unfinished cathedral and founded a new congregation of women, the Sisters of St. Francis of Philadelphia, to help staff the increasingly crowded schools. He also wrote two German catechisms that were approved by the First

Council of Baltimore in 1852 and were widely used in the United States for the rest of the century.

On January 5, 1860, Bishop Neumann collapsed on Vine Street in Philadelphia and died at age forty-eight. To the surprise of many, half the city's population came to the funeral. The mayor, police and fire brigades, a brass band with muffled drums, and a battalion of military, civic, and Catholic societies were on hand to pay a final tribute. He was buried, as he had requested, in the Redemptorist church of St. Peter, under the altar of the lower church. The burial place quickly became a shrine, attracting pilgrims from all over the region seeking cures. Pope John XXIII had his cause for beatification on his desk when he died in June 1963. Pope Paul VI accepted his predecessor's judgment and formally beatified him the following September, and then canonized him as St. John Nepomucene Neumann on June 17, 1977. His feast is celebrated in the United States according to the Proper Calendar for the Dioceses of the U.S.A., but it does not appear on the General Roman Calendar.

BIBLIOGRAPHY

Murphy, Francis X. "Sainthood and *Politique,*" *The Tablet* 231 (June 18, 1977): 573–75.

Neumann, John. *The Autobiography of Saint John Neumann, C.SS.R., Fourth Bishop of Philadelphia.* Ed. Alfred C. Rush. Boston: St. Paul Editions, 1977.

6 Peter of Canterbury, abbot; Blessed André Bessette, religious

For centuries the feast of the Epiphany was observed in the Roman Catholic Church on January 6. However, the Greek and Russian Orthodox Churches continue to observe the feast of the Theophany of Our Lord, and it is also observed as the Epiphany by the Church of England and the Episcopal Church in the USA. Where this feast is no longer observed in the Roman Catholic Church as a holy day of obligation, it has been assigned to the Sunday between January 2 and January 8. No feast occurs on this day in the General Roman Calendar.

Among the saints commemorated on this day is *Peter of Canterbury* (d. ca. 607), a member of the original group of Benedictine monks who were sent to Briton by Pope Gregory the Great [September 3], under the leadership of Augustine of Canterbury [May 27], to evangelize the Anglo-Saxons. The party landed in Kent in 597, where King Ethelbert [February 24] received them. The king was eventually baptized and gave the monks a house in Canterbury that would become the monastery of Sts. Peter and Paul, later called St. Augustine's. Peter was appointed its first abbot. It was probably Peter whom Augustine sent back to Rome to inform the pope of the first Anglo-Saxon conversions and to seek answers to various questions pertaining to the mission. Peter later drowned in the English Channel while on a missionary journey to Gaul and was buried in Boulogne. His feast is not on the General Roman Calendar.

André Bessette (1845–1937), a Holy Cross brother with a reputation for the power of healing, was born in the village of Saint-Grégoire d'Iberville, in the diocese of Montreal, Canada. Baptized as Alfred, by his twelfth year he had to choose, of necessity, work over education because both of his parents had died. At age twenty-two he moved to the United States, where he labored in various manual occupations, but he returned to Canada three years later and joined the Brothers of Holy Cross, taking final vows in 1874. He was given the religious name André. For some forty years he served as janitor, porter, infirmarian, and in other capacities at the College of Our Lady of the Snows near Montreal and then, at age sixty, was transferred to the city itself, where he founded and helped to build the Oratory of St. Joseph [March 19], the saint to whom he was greatly devoted. The oratory became a place of pilgrimage, and much attention centered on Brother André himself because of the number of cures that were attributed to him, so many, in fact, that he was referred to as the "Miracle Man of Montreal." Upon his death on January 6, 1937, at age ninety-one, over a million mourners paid their respects. He was beatified by Pope John Paul II in 1982. His feast is on the Proper Calendar for the Dioceses of the U.S.A.

7 Raymond of Peñafort, priest

Raymond of Peñafort (ca. 1180–1275) was a distinguished Dominican and canonist. He was born of a family of high station in Catalonia, Spain, and was already teaching philosophy by the age of twenty. He received doctorates in canon and civil law at the University of Bologna and also taught there. It is likely that Raymond was acquainted with Dominic Guzmán [August 8], the founder of the Order of Preachers (Dominicans), who was also in Bologna at the time. The first general chapter of the order was held there in 1220, and Dominic himself died in Bologna the following year. Eight months after Dominic's death, Raymond joined the Dominicans in Barcelona, where he combined the tasks of preaching with those of study and meditation. Pope Gregory IX summoned him to Rome in 1230 and appointed him as his confessor. Over a period of three years Raymond gathered into five books some two thousand decrees issued by popes and councils since the previous collection by Gratian in 1150. These were known as the *Decretals of Gregory IX.* He thereby laid the foundation for a Code of Canon Law that was to last until the 1917 Code (later revised in 1983).

After returning to Barcelona, Raymond was chosen by the pope to become archbishop of Tarragona, but he declined the appointment, preferring to continue his studies, preaching, and confessional ministry. He wrote his *Summa de casibus poenitentiae* (Lat., "A Synthesis of Cases Related to the Sacrament of Penance"), which served as a guide for confessors for many years to come. In 1238 he was elected third master general of the Dominican order—a position he could not refuse, however reluctantly he accepted it. He spent the next two years visiting all of the Dominican houses on foot and revising the new order's constitutions. In 1240, at age sixty-five, he voluntarily resigned his office, in accordance with one of the new constitutional changes that he had promoted. He devoted the rest of his life (another thirty-four years) to preaching and working for the conversion of the Jews and the Moors, the latter especially through dialogue, and was instrumental in establishing the Inquisition in Catalonia. Scholars tend to discount the popular tradition that he also encouraged a young fellow Dominican, Thomas Aquinas [January 28], to write his *Summa contra Gentiles,* a selective synthesis of Catholic theology designed to explain the faith to non-Christians.

Raymond died in Barcelona on January 6, 1275, at the age of ninety-five or thereabouts, and is buried in the chapel of Sts. John and Paul in the Barcelona cathedral. He was canonized in 1601 and is the patron saint of canon lawyers. Formerly celebrated on January 23, his feast was moved to January 6, with the status of an optional memorial, in the 1969 revision of the General Roman Calendar. The Russian and Greek Orthodox Churches celebrate a feast in honor of *John the Baptist* [June 24, August 29] on this day.

8 Apollinaris the Apologist, bishop; Lawrence Giustiniani, bishop

Little is known of the life and writings of *Apollinaris* (d. ca. 179). He is thought to have defended the faith in a letter to the emperor Marcus Aurelius (161–80), pointing out that a recent military victory had been achieved in large part because of the twelfth legion, composed mainly of Christians. Apollinaris argued that it was their prayers as well as their fighting skills that had won the day for the emperor. A supposedly miraculous rain shower first quenched the thirst of the imperial soldiers, and then, when it turned into a thunderstorm, blinded and frightened the enemy. His feast is not on the General Roman Calendar.

This is also the feast day of *Lawrence Giustiniani* (1381–1455), the archbishop of Venice who was renowned for his extraordinary concern for the poor. Born of a noble Venetian family, he entered an Augustinian monastery early in his life, was ordained a priest in 1406, and eventually became general of the congregation of Canons Regular of St. Augustine from 1424 until 1431. During this period he wrote several works of an ascetical and mystical nature—on the love of God, contemplation, and spiritual marriage. He was appointed bishop of Castello, which included a portion of Venice, in 1433. When the region was reorganized, Castello was suppressed and Lawrence became archbishop of Venice (which replaced Grado as the metropolitan see), but not as its patriarch. His episcopal ministry was marked by personal austerity and extraordinary generosity to the poor, more often in the form of food and clothing rather than money, which he felt was subject to abuse. During the course of his final illness, clergy and laity alike flocked to see him, and he insisted that beggars and those most destitute be admitted to his bedside. He died on a bed of straw on January 8, 1455. He was canonized in 1690. His feast is not on the General Roman Calendar.

9 Adrian of Canterbury, abbot

An African by birth, *Adrian of Canterbury* (d. ca. 710) was the abbot of the monastery of Sts. Peter and Paul (later St. Augustine's) in Canterbury. Under his leadership and that of the archbishop, Theodore, the monastery became a major center of learning, producing a number of future bishops and archbishops. Adrian taught at the school for some forty years. He died on January 9, probably in 710, and was buried in the monastery. It is said that when it became necessary to move the remains from several tombs in 1091, during a period of reconstruction, his body was discovered to be "incorrupt and fragrant." His tomb became associated with various miracles, and his feast was added to English liturgical calendars. It does not, however, appear on the General Roman Calendar.

10 Gregory of Nyssa, bishop; William of Bourges, abbot

Gregory of Nyssa (ca. 330–ca. 395) was the third of the three great Cappadocian Fathers (along with his older brother, Basil the Great [January 2], and Gregory Nazianzen [January 2]). He became bishop of Nyssa in 371, a remote outpost near Armenia where Arianism (the heresy that denied the divinity of Christ) was strong. But Gregory was more skilled as a thinker and writer than as an administrator. He played an important role, along with Gregory Nazianzen, in the Council of Constantinople (381), which defined the divinity of the Holy Spirit. The significance of his writings and his own personal stature were not fully appreciated, however, until the second half of the twentieth century, thanks to the work of several leading scholars.

Gregory was born in Caesarea and was educated in Athens, becoming a specialist in rhetoric. Under the influence of Gregory Nazianzen, he abandoned his first academic career for that of a theologian. He was ordained a priest ca. 362, but it is not clear if he remained with his wife (celibacy was not required of priests at the time) or whether she had died or entered a monastic community. Gregory himself spent the first few years of his priesthood in the monastic community founded by Basil. In his spiritual writings, he argued that the purpose of the Christian life is to imitate God in Christ and that the ideal milieu for such a process is the monastic community. His writings had a lasting influence on the development of monasticism in the East.

After accepting the see of Nyssa under pressure from Basil, Gregory encountered fierce opposition from the local Arians. They accused him of embezzling funds and of irregularities in his election. He was arrested by the governor of Pontus, but escaped from captivity. He was not restored to Nyssa until 378. It was only after Basil died the following year that Gregory became an important ecclesiastical figure and theologically productive writer, producing a number of works in defense of Nicene orthodoxy. The emperor Theodosius sent him on missions to counteract Arianism in Palestine and Arabia and invited him to take a leading role at the Council of Constantinople, where Gregory preached the funeral oration for Melitius of Antioch, the first president of the council. Gregory's name does not appear on the General Roman Calendar, but his feast is celebrated in the East on this day and he is commemorated on the Benedictine and Cistercian calendars.

The Cistercians also commemorate *William of Bourges* (d. 1209), a Cistercian abbot who accepted the archbishopric of Bourges under direct obedience to Pope Innocent III and the abbot of Cîteaux. He proved to be a model bishop and was canonized the year after his death.

11 Theodosius the Cenobiarch

Theodosius (423–529) was a leading pioneer of cenobitic, or communal, monasticism. Born in Cappadocia in Asia Minor, he made a pilgrimage early in life to Jerusalem, where he began to attract disciples. Influenced by the writings and example of his fellow Cappadocian Basil the Great [January 2], Theodosius promoted cenobitic monastic life rather than the life of solitude. He built a large monastery at Cathismus near Bethlehem, and it was soon filled. He attached three infirmaries to the monastery: one for the sick, one for the aged, and one for the mentally disturbed. There were also four churches: one for Greeks, one for Armenians, one for Slavs, and one for those doing penance or recovering from mental illness. The Liturgy of the Word was celebrated within each language group, and then all came together for the liturgy of the Eucharist in Greek. The daily agenda consisted of prayer, manual labor, and rest. The monastic complex resembled a small city and became a model of its kind in the East. The patriarch of Jerusalem appointed Theodosius as abbot general of all cenobitic communities in Palestine, which explains his title, "Cenobiarch."

In spite of contrary pressure from the emperor Anastasius, Theodosius became a strong advocate of the Church's teaching against the Monophysites (those who held that in Christ there was only a divine nature, and not a human nature as well, as the Council of Chalcedon had taught in 451). His preaching was so effective that he was banished for a time by imperial edict, but a later emperor revoked it. By this time Theodosius was ninety-five years old! Upon his death, the patriarch of Jerusalem and a great portion of its population attended his funeral. His fame spread as many miracles were attributed to his intercession. His feast is celebrated by the Greek and Russian Orthodox Churches, but it is not on the General Roman Calendar.

12 Benedict Biscop, bishop; Aelred of Rievaulx, monk

The founder and first abbot of Wearmouth and later of Jarrow, both in England, *Benedict Biscop* (628–89) was born Biscop Baducing, of a noble Northumbrian family. He decided at age twenty-five to become a monk, taking the name Benedict, and eventually made six separate visits to Rome (from which he brought back numerous books and artworks) as well to seventeen different monasteries, from which he produced a synthesis of Rules for later use in his own foundations. After serving only two years as abbot of Sts. Peter and Paul (later St. Augustine's) in Canterbury, he founded, with the help of King Egfrith, a new monastery in Wearmouth in 674, for which he later secured the special protection of the Holy See. With the help of the same king, he founded a second monastery in Jarrow in 682, later delegating the abbacy of both to others. Benedict's extensive library holdings made possible the work of the Venerable Bede [May 25], a monk of Jarrow, where he wrote the *Ecclesiastical History of the English People.* Bede's sermon on Benedict's feast was indicative of his early public cult. Benedict Biscop's feast is not on the General Roman Calendar, but he is commemorated by the Church of England on this day. He is the patron saint of English Benedictines.

The Cistercians commemorate *Aelred of Rievaulx* (1110–67) on this day. Although never formally canonized, he is said to have been the Cistercian monk who most resembled the greatest Cistercian saint, Bernard of Clairvaux [August 20]. His feast is also celebrated today by the Church of England and the Episcopal Church in the USA.

13 Hilary of Poitiers, bishop and Doctor of the Church; Remigius, bishop; George Fox, founder

Hilary of Poitiers (ca. 315–ca. 367) was a vigorous and outspoken defender of orthodoxy against Arianism (which held, contrary to the Council of Nicaea in 325, that Jesus Christ was the greatest of creatures, but not the equal of God). Born at Poitiers (in the central southwest of modern-day France) of wealthy pagan parents, Hilary became a Christian in 350 after a long period of study. About three years later he was elected bishop of his hometown, probably while still a married layman. His manner was always courteous and friendly, but his writings were sometimes severe in tone. Some described him as the "Athanasius of the West." Jerome [September 30] referred to him as "the trumpet of the Latins against the Arians," and Augustine [August 28] called him "the most illustrious doctor of the churches." Hilary's reputation was based, first, on his participation in the Synod of Béziers (or Bitterae) in 356, after which he was exiled to Phrygia (in Asia Minor) by the Arian emperor Constantius II for refusing to sign a condemnation of

Athanasius; second, on his role in the Council of Seleucia (just south of Antioch) in 359, which he attended while still in exile in the East; and, third, on his public refutation of Auxentius, the Arian bishop of Milan, in 364. His return from exile was greeted with great enthusiasm in Gaul.

The Arians had regarded him as "the sower of discord and the troublemaker of the Orient" and so were pleased to see him leave. Gaul itself became the center of Nicene orthodoxy in the West, and Hilary its chief proponent. He convened a synod of Gallic bishops in Paris in 361 at which the Nicene Creed was ratified completely and unambiguously. His most famous work was the *De Trinitate* (Lat., "On the Trinity"), written against the Arians and, for the most part, while in exile in the East. He was not yet sixty when he died, exhausted by his travels, his exile, and his constant engagement in controversy. He was named a Doctor of the Church by Pope Pius IX in 1851. His feast is on the General Roman Calendar and is also observed on this day by the Church of England and the Episcopal Church in the USA.

January 13 is also the feast day of *Remigius* (d. 533), bishop of Reims and apostle of the Franks, who baptized their king, Clovis I (481–511), as well as his family and followers, some three thousand in all. He is one of the patron saints of France. The Church of England and the Episcopal Church in the USA celebrate his feast on October 1.

This is also the day of death of *George Fox* (1624–91), founder of the Society of Friends, or Quakers. Fox's life was one of commitment to peace, human equality, and the poor, a commitment for which he paid the price of imprisonment and persecution.

14 Sava of Serbia, bishop; Blessed Odoric of Pordenone, friar

Sava (1174–1237), patron saint of the Serbs, was the youngest of three sons of Prince Stephen I, who secured the independence of the Serbian state from Byzantium. At age seventeen Sava became a monk on Mount Athos in Greece. His father later abdicated and joined his son there, and together they founded a monastery for Serbian monks called Khilandari, which survives as one of the seventeen "ruling monasteries" of Mount Athos. Sava became its abbot for a time, but returned home in 1206 to attempt to settle a dispute between his brothers over their inheritance. He was struck by the sad state of the Church in his homeland. He settled in a monastery at Studenica and from there established a number of smaller monasteries from which his monks engaged in pastoral and missionary work.

The emperor Theodore, who was related to Sava's family, nominated Sava as the first metropolitan of the new Serbian hierarchy and persuaded the reluctant patriarch of Constantinople to ordain him as archbishop of Zica in 1219. On the way back to Serbia, Sava stopped off at Mount Athos to gather some monks and some books for the Church in his homeland. Upon his return to Serbia, he established a number of bishoprics, built churches and monasteries, and generally reformed the religious life of the country. He died on January 14, 1237, on the way home from a pilgrimage to Palestine and the Near East. His feast is not on the General Roman Calendar, but it is observed by both the Serbian Orthodox Church and the Catholic Church in Croatia. He is also commemorated on the Russian Orthodox calendar.

The Franciscans commemorate *Odoric of Pordenone* (ca. 1285–1331) on this day. He was a famous preacher based in Udine, Italy, who in 1317 undertook an extraordinary missionary journey to the Far East, spending three years in Beijing and returning home through Tibet. He died on January 14, 1331. After many miracles were attributed to him, his cult was confirmed in 1755.

15 Paul the Hermit; Ita of Killeedy, abbess; Maur and Placid; Martin Luther King Jr., civil rights leader

Paul the Hermit (ca. 233–ca. 345), also known as Paul of Thebes, is traditionally regarded as the first hermit in Christian history. He fled to the desert during a period of persecution (probably during the reign of the Roman emperor Decius [249–51]) and is reputed to have lived there to well over a one hundred years of age. Life in solitude was regarded not only as a way of following the example of Christ's forty days in the desert, but also of expressing a defiant "no" to the newly comfortable circumstances of the Church under the emperor Constantine (306–37), the persecutions of previous emperors having ended. Paul was visited in the desert by Anthony (also Antony) of Egypt [January 17], who is considered the founder of monasticism, and was also later buried by him, allegedly in a pit dug by lions (thus Paul is depicted in art accompanied by two lions) and in the cloak of Athanasius [May 2]. Jerome's [September 30] Life of Paul is the only source for biographical details, but it is said to be a confusing mixture of fact and fantasy. Paul's feast was suppressed from the General Roman Calendar in 1969, but continues to be celebrated in the East (including the Russian and Greek Orthodox Churches and the Coptic and Armenian rites) on this day.

Ita of Killeedy (d. ca. 570), also known as Ida, is one of the two most famous women saints in Ireland, along with Brigid of Kildare [February 1]. Born near Waterford, allegedly of a royal family, and baptized as Deirdre, she is said to have rejected a prestigious marriage for a life of virginity and asceticism. In any event, she moved early in her life to Killeedy (Limerick), where she founded a small community of nuns and resided for the remainder of her life, in prayer, fasting, and solitude. However, she was also much sought out for spiritual direction. She began a school for boys, some of whose graduates became saints in their own right, the most famous of whom was Brendan of Clonfert [May 16]. She was known as the "foster mother of the saints of Erin." The name "Ita" ("thirst for holiness") was conferred on her because of her saintly qualities.

Ironically, the Celtic Church was more advanced than other churches at the time in recognizing qualities of spiritual leadership in women and in encouraging women in this role. It is thought that Ita may have been abbess of a double monastery of men and women and that she was a confessor to both, giving difficult penances while maintaining a forgiving and compassionate spirit. Auricular confession (direct confession of sins to a priest) had not yet been established as the normal form for the sacrament of Penance (Reconciliation), and ordained priests were not yet regarded as the only members of the Church authorized to hear confessions, forgive sins, and impose penances.

Ita was buried in the monastery she founded, but it was destroyed by Viking invaders in the ninth century. A Romanesque church was later built over its ruins, but that too failed to survive. The site, however, remains a place of pilgrimage today. Although January 15 is the day set aside for her feast, Ita's name is not on the General Roman Calendar. Her feast is celebrated as an optional memorial in Ireland.

On this day Benedictines commemorate the feast of *Maur (Maurus)* and *Placid,* two sixth- or seventh-century figures. Little is known about them that is not laced with legend and fantasy. Maur is said to have succeeded Benedict [July 11] as superior of Subiaco when Benedict retired to Monte Cassino. Placid was the name of a boy whom Maur is said to have rescued from drowning by walking on the water.

Martin Luther King Jr., 1967

Lutherans commemorate the American civil rights leader *Martin Luther King Jr.* (1929–68) on this day as a "renewer of society" and "martyr." The United States Catholic bishops recommended to the Vatican that his name be included on a list of twentieth-century martyrs announced by Pope John Paul II in May 2000. The Episcopal Church in the USA commemorates Dr. King on April 4, the day of his assassination, rather than on January 15, the day of his birth, which is also a national holiday in the United States.

16 Honoratus of Arles, bishop; Berard and companions, martyrs

Honoratus (d. ca. 429), born of an aristocratic pagan Gallo-Roman family, was the founder (ca. 405) of one of the most famous monasteries of the early Church, that of Lérins, off the southern coast of Gaul (France) opposite modern-day Cannes. The island is now called Saint-Honorat in honor of the saint. This monastery produced several of southern Gaul's leading bishops and writers, including Vincent of Lérins [May 24], who gave the Church an enduring criterion of tradition, namely, *quod ubique, quod semper, quod ab omnibus* (Lat., "what [has been believed] everywhere, always, and by all"). Honoratus was named archbishop of Arles against his wishes in 426, and died there about three years later. His remains were transferred from Arles to Lérins in 1391. He is patron saint of bakers and cake makers. His feast is not on the General Roman Calendar.

On this day the Franciscans commemorate *Berard and companions* (d. 1220), five Franciscan friars (Berard, Peter, Odo, Accursio, and Adjutus) who were the order's first martyrs. They were sent by Francis himself [October 4] as missionaries to the Muslims, first in Seville (from which they were banished because of their zeal in preaching) and then in Morocco, where they tried to serve as chaplains to Christian mercenaries, against the warnings of the local sultan. When they continued their preaching, the sultan split their heads open at Marrakesh on January 16, 1220. Martyrdom for Christ became the supreme aspiration of Franciscan missionaries because it was regarded as the "summit of perfection."

17 Anthony of Egypt, abbot

Anthony (also Antony) *of Egypt* (251–356) is generally regarded as the founder of monasticism. Born in Upper Egypt of a prosperous landowning family, at about the age of twenty, following his parents' deaths, he sold all of his possessions and gave the money to the poor in keeping with the Gospel injunction in Matthew 19:21. He took up the life of a hermit, first near his home under the tutelage of an elderly hermit; then for twelve to fifteen years he lived in empty tombs in a cemetery at some distance from his village, and later still in an abandoned fort deep in the desert (286–306). He eventually attracted many disciples and established his first monastery, which was actually a collection of hermits' cells. He later founded a second monastery, Pispir, on the east bank of the Nile, but did not reside there permanently. He returned to a life of solitude with one or several disciples, cultivating a garden and weaving mats. He is the patron saint of basket weavers.

The Temptation of Saint Anthony by Hieronymus Bosch (ca. 1450–16)

The widely read *Life of Antony,* written ca. 357 by Athanasius of Alexandria [May 2], transformed Anthony into a major figure, "the father of monks," and played an important part in the conversion of Augustine [August 28]. Although Anthony was still committed to the solitary life after his lengthy desert experience, his was not an isolated existence. Hermits like him were accessible to each other and to visitors, including pilgrims. Anthony made at least two visits to Alexandria, once in 311 to encourage the local church in a time of persecution (he brought material and spiritual assistance to imprisoned Christians), and a second time in 355 to refute the Arians, who were continuing to deny the divinity of Christ in defiance of the teaching of the Council of Nicaea (325). His words of counsel to hermits and pilgrims alike are preserved in a collection known as the *Sayings of the Fathers,* about forty of which date back to Anthony.

He is revered in the East as the "first master of the desert and the pinnacle of holy monks." He also influenced the Camaldolese monks and the Carthusians, and in the twentieth century Charles de Foucauld (d. 1916 [December 1]), a hermit who inspired the founding of the Little Brothers (and Sisters) of Jesus. Anthony's feast is on the General Roman Calendar and is also celebrated on this day by the Greek and Russian Orthodox Churches under the title "Anthony the Great," and by the Church of England and the Episcopal Church in the USA.

BIBLIOGRAPHY

Athanasius. *The Coptic Life of Antony*. Trans. Tim Vivian. San Francisco: International Scholars Publications, 1995.

Rubenson, Samuel. *The Letters of St. Antony: Monasticism and the Making of a Saint.* Minneapolis, MN: Fortress Press, 1995.

18 Margaret of Hungary, nun

Margaret of Hungary (1242–70), daughter of King Bela IV, was a Dominican nun, having entered the convent at age thirteen. When her father ordered her to withdraw from the convent to marry the king of Bohemia, she adamantly refused, threatening to cut off her nose and lips if forced to leave. Her life in the convent was described as one of self-crucifixion because of her preference for the most menial and even degrading tasks, especially in the care of the sick and dying. She also neglected her own health and personal hygiene, the latter in order to identify more closely with the poor. During Lent she went to excesses in fasting and lack of sleep, the latter probably accounting for some of her alleged visions. She died at age twenty-eight. Although a local cult developed almost immediately, she was not beatified until 1789. She was canonized by Pope Pius XII in 1943, at a time when Hungary was under Nazi domination. The Dominicans commemorate her on this day, but her feast is not on the General Roman Calendar.

The Greek and Russian Orthodox Churches celebrate the feast of *Athanasius* [May 2] and *Cyril of Alexandria* [June 27] on this day.

19 Wulfstan, bishop; Marguerite Bourgeoys, foundress; Macarius the Elder, monk; Henry of Uppsala, bishop

Born of Anglo-Saxon parents and well-educated by the Benedictines as a youth, *Wulfstan* (ca. 1008–95) entered the Benedictine priory at the Worcester cathedral sometime following his ordination as a diocesan priest. He became prior of this small (twelve-member) community and did such an excellent job that, when the local diocese became vacant, he was appointed bishop of Worcester, while retaining his responsibilities at the priory. He visited parishes throughout the diocese, encouraged the building of churches on his own lands and those of other nobles, promoted clerical celibacy, rebuilt the cathedral, and was exceedingly generous to the poor. He also abolished the slave trade between Bristol and Ireland (then under Viking control). After the Battle of Hastings in 1066, he was one of the first bishops to submit to William the Conqueror and, as a result, retained his bishopric.

Wulfstan died at age eighty-seven, and his cult began almost immediately. Many cures were reported at his tomb. He was canonized by Pope Innocent III in 1203. Although he is not on the General Roman Calendar, his feast is celebrated on this day by the Church of England and the Episcopal Church in the USA.

Marguerite Bourgeoys (1620–1700) was the foundress of the Sisters of Notre Dame de Montréal, a community devoted to teaching. Born in Troyes, France, she was recruited by the governor of Montréal in 1652 to become a schoolmistress in that city. Although her work as an educator was successful, her life was also filled with hardships of all kinds, including natural disasters, massacres by local native populations, poverty, and episcopal misunderstanding. She was beatified in 1950 and canonized in 1982. Her feast is not included on the General Roman Calendar, but she is commemorated by Benedictines and Cistercians in Canada on January 12.

The Greek and Russian Orthodox Churches commemorate *Macarius* (also Makarios) *the Elder* (ca. 300–390) on this day. Also known as Macarius the Egyptian or Macarius the Great, he was said to have been a disciple of Anthony [January 17]. He is also commemorated in the Coptic and Armenian rites.

The Lutherans commemorate *Henry of Uppsala* (d. 1156) on this day. English by birth, he accompanied Cardinal Nicholas Breakspear, the future Pope Adrian IV (1154–59), to Scandinavia in 1151 and was ordained a bishop in Uppsala, Sweden, the following year. He was axed to death by a convert whom he had excommunicated for killing a Swedish solider. Miracles were reported at Henry's tomb, and he eventually became recognized as patron saint of Finland.

20 Fabian, pope and martyr; Sebastian, martyr; Euthymius the Great, bishop

Fabian (d. 250) was one of the most respected and accomplished popes of the earliest Christian centuries. Elected as a layman, he reorganized the local clergy, dividing the growing Roman church into seven ecclesiastical districts with a deacon in charge of each, and supervised numerous building projects in the cemeteries, which were also places of worship for the Christian community. Almost all of Fabian's pontificate (236–50) was peaceful, until Decius rose to power in 249 and unleashed a new and vicious persecution against the Church. Fabian was the first to be arrested and put in prison, where he died after suffering brutal treatment. His body was at first buried in the papal crypt in the cemetery of Callistus on the Appian Way, but was later moved to the church of San Sebastiano (where it was discovered in 1915), with whose namesake he shares this feast day. Cyprian of Carthage [September 16], at the time second only to the Bishop of Rome in prestige, praised him as "an incomparable man, the glory of whose death corresponds with the holiness of his life."

Sebastian (d. ca. 300) was martyred under Diocletian and buried on the Appian Way close to the site where a basilica was erected in his honor, possibly by the emperor Constantine [May 21]. He is usually depicted being pierced with arrows (which, according to legend, did not kill him). For that reason, he is regarded as the patron saint of archers. He was also invoked against plagues and is revered as patron saint of physicians, athletes, and local police as well. His feast is celebrated in the East on December 18. Both Fabian and Sebastian are on the General Roman Calendar.

The Greek and Russian Orthodox Churches commemorate *Euthymius the Great* (ca. 378–473) on this day. He spent sixty-eight years in the desert and died at the age of ninety-five, having been ordained a bishop at one point to minister to the growing numbers of Arab converts in Palestine.

21 Agnes, virgin and martyr; Meinrad, hermit

Liturgical sources indicate that *Agnes* (d. ca. 305) was one of the most famous of the early Roman martyrs. There is strong evidence of an early cult. She was killed at a very young age (probably twelve or thirteen) during the persecution of Diocletian in the Stadium of Domitian, now the Piazza Navona. Her head is venerated in a chapel of the church of Sant'Agnese in Agonia on the Piazza Navona, and the rest of her body is entombed in the church of Sant'Agnese on the Via Nomentana. Because of the similarity of her name to the Latin word for lamb *(agnus)*, the lamb has been her emblem since the sixth century, and she is often depicted with the animal. On her feast day in Rome, there is a blessing of the lambs that produce the wool from which the pallia for archbishops are woven by the nuns of St. Agnes's convent. Her feast is on the General Roman Calendar and is also celebrated by the Church of England and the Episcopal Church in the USA. She is patron saint of young girls and the Children of Mary, a pious sodality dedicated to the Blessed Virgin Mary.

The Greek and Russian Orthodox Churches celebrate the feast of *Maximus the Confessor* [August 13] on this day. It is also the feast day of *Meinrad* (d. 861), a hermit at Einsiedeln who, after twenty-five years in ascetical seclusion, was clubbed to death by robbers. Meinrad's hermitage was refounded as a regular Benedictine monastery, which still exists today.

22 Vincent of Saragossa, deacon and martyr; Vincent Pallotti, founder

Vincent of Saragossa (d. 304), a patron saint of Portugal, was a deacon trained by the bishop of Saragossa (or Zaragoza). He was martyred under Dacian, governor of Spain, during the imperial reign of Maximian. The fact of his martyrdom is clear, but not the manner. Some accounts say that he was imprisoned and nearly starved to death, then racked and roasted on a gridiron when he refused to sacrifice to the gods or hand over the sacred books, then returned to prison and placed in stocks. He eventually died from this brutal treatment. In Burgundy and elsewhere he is regarded as patron of vine growers and wine makers because of the protection he offers against frosts, which often occur on or near his feast day. His feast is on the General Roman Calendar.

The Greek and Russian Orthodox Churches commemorate *Timothy the Apostle* [January 26] on this day. This is also the feast day of *Vincent Pallotti* (1795–1850), founder of the Society of the Catholic Apostolate, also known as the Pallottines, and patron saint of missionary priests. He was canonized in 1963.

23 Ildephonsus of Toledo, bishop; Blessed Henry Suso, mystic; Mary Ward, foundress

Ildephonsus of Toledo (ca. 607–77) was a leading figure in the Spanish Church of the seventh century. Born of a noble Spanish family, he became a monk early in his life against the opposition of his parents, was ordained to the priesthood ca. 637, and was appointed abbot of Agalia ca. 650. As an abbot, he participated in the councils of Toledo in 653 and 657 and was appointed archbishop of Toledo in 657, succeeding his uncle. The archdiocese of Toledo dominated the Church in Spain. Neighboring bishops were required to make *ad limina* visits and the archbishop had the right to convene national councils, although the king set the agenda. Church and state were intermingled during this period, a forerunner of even more pronounced developments in medieval Europe. Ildephonsus had great devotion to the Blessed Virgin Mary and wrote a tract on her perpetual virginity that exercised great influence on the development of Marian devotion in Spain. There was a medieval legend that she appeared to him on his episcopal throne and gave him a chasuble. The scene was painted by Velázquez, El Greco, and others. Ildephonsus's feast is not on the General Roman Calendar.

The Dominicans commemorate *Henry Suso* (ca. 1295–1366) on this day. Henry was a German Dominican spiritual writer, preacher, and mystic, who was influenced by Meister Eckhart (ca. 1260–ca. 1328). He had a distinctively Catholic sacramental view of God's presence in nature: "Ah, gentle God, if Thou art so lovely in thy creatures, how exceeding beautiful and ravishing Thou must be in Thyself!" Henry was beatified in 1831.

January 23 is also the day of death of *Mary Ward* (1586–1645), foundress of the Institute of the Blessed Virgin Mary during the period of anti-Catholic persecution in England. She engaged in a clandestine ministry among the Catholics of England and was imprisoned for a time upon exposure. She was permitted to accept exile over death and returned to the Continent to continue her efforts to secure papal approval of her institute, which was based on the apostolate and Rule of the Society of Jesus, namely, nonenclosed, free of episcopal jurisdiction, and committed to service in the world, including the provision of free schools for girls. Her institute was mocked by its critics as a house of "Lady Jesuits." These enemies prevailed, the institute was suppressed in 1631, and she was imprisoned temporarily in a convent. She returned to England, where she died in 1645. The Rule was finally approved by Pope Clement XI in 1703, and the institute had a marked influence on religious life on the Continent. Mary Ward has not been canonized.

24 Francis de Sales, bishop and Doctor of the Church

Francis de Sales (1567–1622) was one of the originators of lay spirituality and author of the classic work *Introduction to the Devout Life.* Several religious congregations have been founded under his patronage, including the Missionaries of St. Francis de Sales, the Oblates of St. Francis de Sales, the Salesians of Don Bosco, and the Sisters of St. Joseph. Born in the duchy of Savoy, he received an excellent education as a young man, becoming a Doctor of Law at the University of Padua. He eschewed a civil career, however, and was ordained in 1593, soon distinguishing himself as a preacher and as a minister to the poor and the sick. After several years of very difficult but eventually successful efforts to reconvert many of the Calvinists of Geneva to Catholicism, he became bishop of Geneva in 1602, an unreformed pre-Tridentine diocese of some 450 parishes (all of which he would visit at great physical cost over a period of four years), where he excelled in administration, preaching, catechesis, clergy education, and spiritual direction. He became a close friend of Jane Frances de Chantal [December 12], a young widow who founded the Order of the Visitation under Francis's guidance in 1610. His voluminous correspondence with her over the years included the line, "With you I speak as I do with my own heart."

Saint Francis de Sales by Giovanni Battista Tiepolo (1696–1770)

Much of his spiritual thought was shaped in reaction to pessimistic Calvinist views on predestination. Francis concluded that one must have a wholly disinterested love of God, without regard for whether one will go to heaven or hell after death. He once wrote, "Whatever happens, Lord, may I at least love you in this life if I cannot love you in eternity since no one may praise you in hell." The central message of his *Introduction to the Devout Life,* written originally as a series of letters containing spiritual advice for the wife of the Duke of Savoy and first published in 1608, was a novel one for the times, namely, that the way of spiritual perfection is not only for the elite few and it does not require great austerities or withdrawal from the everyday life of the world. Some criticized the book for adopting too lax an approach to the spiritual life. By present-day standards, however, it is exceedingly rigorous. In any case, it became an immediate best-seller and was eventually translated into several other languages.

Worn out by his labors and travels, Francis died in Lyons in a Visitation convent on December 28, 1622, was canonized in 1665, and declared a Doctor of the Church in 1877. He was named patron saint of writers in 1923. He is also patron saint of the Catholic press and of the hearing impaired. His feast day is on the General Roman Calendar and is also celebrated by the Church of England.

BIBLIOGRAPHY

Wright, Wendy M. *Francis de Sales: Introduction to the Devout Life and Treatise on the Love of God.* New York: Crossroad, 1993.

25 Conversion of Paul, apostle

Paul (ca. 1/5–ca. 62/67) was the most prominent early Christian missionary, known as the "apostle to the Gentiles." Born in Tarsus in Asia Minor of a Hellenistic-Jewish family and given the name Saul, he received both a Greek and a Jewish education and probably possessed Roman citizenship. A self-described Pharisee (Phil. 3:5), he was zealous in his persecution of the early disciples of Jesus. However, he had a profound conversion experience, liturgically commemorated on this day, while on his way to Damascus around the year 35 (Gal. 1:15–16), an experience he interpreted as a call to preach the Risen Christ to the Gentiles. After remaining in the Damascus area for the next three years, he spent ten years (38–48) on his first great missionary journey, in Syria and Asia Minor. In the early dispute about whether new converts from outside the Jewish community would have to be circumcised before being initiated into the Church, Paul adopted a moderate position, namely, that Gentile converts need not be circumcised or follow Jewish dietary laws. Moreover, he did not demand that Jewish Christians break with their lifelong cultic practices associated with the great Jewish feasts and with the Temple, nor did he insist that Jewish Christians abandon circumcision and the law.

After the resolution of this dispute in a manner satisfactory to Paul (Acts 15:1–35), he spent the next eight years (49–57) establishing Christian communities around the eastern Mediterranean. For his second missionary journey (49–52) he centered his operations in Corinth, Greece. The center for his third journey (53–57) was Ephesus in Asia

Minor. During these journeys (especially the third) he wrote letters to various communities; those that survive form part of the New Testament. In the year 57 he returned to Jerusalem, where he was arrested and imprisoned for two years. Exercising his rights as a Roman citizen, he appealed his case to Caesar and was sent to Rome, where he was held under house arrest for about two more years (59–60). Sometime between 62 and 67 he was executed in Rome by order of the local authorities.

Two of Paul's basic theological convictions, grounded in his own abiding Jewishness, were belief in the oneness of God and in the revelation of God in the Hebrew Scriptures. From his conversion experience on the road to Damascus came his conviction about the centrality of Jesus Christ, and in particular of his death and resurrection. He believed thereafter that "in Christ" there is no distinction between Jew and Gentile (Gal. 3:28; Rom. 3:22). All are saved through faith in Christ rather than through observance of the Mosaic law (Rom. 3:21–30). Christians, no longer under the law, were now to be guided by the presence of the Holy Spirit and by faith working through love, and their lives were to be marked by service to one another (Gal. 5–6).

This feast was originally a commemoration of the moving (or "translation") of Paul's relics from the catacombs to the major basilica of St. Paul Outside the Walls in Rome. The conversion aspect, however, was the feast's dominant motif according to seventh- and eighth-century liturgical calendars, and it has taken on even greater significance by being chosen as the closing day of the annual Week of Prayer for Christian Unity. The feast is on the General Roman Calendar and is also celebrated by the Church of England and the Episcopal Church in the USA.

Paul is the patron saint of Greece and Malta, and also of the Cursillo movement, founded in Spain in 1949, which provides laypeople with an opportunity for shared prayer, spiritual reading, and discussion.

The Greek Orthodox Church celebrates the feast of *Gregory the Theologian* (Gregory Nazianzen) [January 2] on this day.

BIBLIOGRAPHY

Fitzmyer, Joseph. *Paul and His Theology.* 2d ed. Englewood Cliffs, NJ: Prentice Hall, 1989.

———. *According to Paul.* New York: Paulist Press, 1993.

Murphy-O'Connor, Jerome. *Paul: A Critical Life.* New York: Oxford University Press, 1996.

Segal, Alan E. *Paul the Convert: The Apostolate and Apostasy of Saul the Pharisee.* New Haven, CT: Yale University Press, 1990.

26 Timothy, bishop and martyr, and Titus, bishop; Alberic, Robert of Molesmes, and Stephen Harding, monks; Paula, widow

Although the first-century disciples Timothy and Titus are the addressees in three of Paul's New Testament Letters, virtually nothing is known about them. *Timothy* (d. 97) came from Lystra in Asia Minor, the son of a Jewish-Christian mother and a Greek father (Acts 16:1). Paul first met him during his second missionary journey, and Timothy accompanied him on this and the third journey. Paul sent him to strengthen the Thessalonians (1 Thess. 1:1; 3:2,6) and to help solve problems in Corinth (1 Cor. 4:17; 16:10) and Philippi (Phil. 2:19). Timothy's prominence is indicated not only by the fact that Paul gave him such delicate tasks, but also by his being listed by Paul in the opening of 1 Thessalonians, Philippians, and 2 Corinthians. In later Christian tradition Timothy was considered the first bishop of Ephesus (probably based on 1 Tim. 1:3). Paul's Letters to Timothy in the New Testament direct him to correct innovators and teachers of false doctrine and to appoint overseers (bishops) and deacons. His feast, along with that of Titus, is on the General Roman Calendar and is also celebrated on this day by the Church of England, the Episcopal Church in the USA, and the Evangelical Lutheran Church in America. Timothy's feast is celebrated by the Greek and Russian Orthodox Churches on January 22.

Titus was of Greek origin and perhaps a native of Antioch. In the year 48 he accompanied Paul and Barnabas from Antioch to Jerusalem to meet with the leaders of the Jerusalem church about whether Gentile Christians had to be circumcised and observe the Mosaic law. Paul pointed to the example of Titus, a Greek, who was not forced to be circumcised upon his conversion to Christ (Gal. 2:3). Titus served as Paul's co-worker and secretary at least during the latter's stay at Ephesus on the third missionary journey. Just as he had sent Timothy on delicate missions, so Paul sent Titus to Corinth to serve as an intermediary in his bitter dispute with the Corinthian Christians. We know that Titus was successful because, when Paul rejoined him in Macedonia, he was comforted by the news Titus had brought from Corinth (2 Cor. 2:13; 7:6, 13–14). Based on Titus 1:5, it is thought that Titus was the first bishop of Crete, because Paul had left him there to organize its Christian community. He was sent to Dalmatia after that, but returned to Crete, where he died and was venerated. Paul's Letter to Titus in the New Testament instructed him to ordain presbyters and to govern firmly the Cretans, about whom Paul was skeptical. The Russian Orthodox Church celebrates his feast on August 25.

The Benedictines and Cistercians commemorate *Alberic* (d. 1109), *Robert of Molesmes* (1027–1110), and *Stephen Harding* (d. 1134) on this day. They are considered the founders of the Cistercian order, having left the abbey of Molesmes for the abbey of Cîteaux, to provide a stricter and more primitive form of monastic life based on the Rule of St. Benedict [July 11]. This is also the feast of *Paula*, the wealthy Roman widow who accompanied her close friend Jerome [September 30] to Egypt and the Holy Land, where she financed the building of a monastery for men and a convent for women, with a guest house for pilgrims. She remained there with him for the rest of her life, underwriting his studies and assisting him with her knowledge of Greek. She is the patron saint of widows.

27 Angela Merici, virgin

Angela Merici (ca. 1470/74–1540) was the foundress of the Ursuline nuns. Born in Desenzano, in the Republic of Venice, she was orphaned at an early age and moved to Brescia, where she became a Franciscan tertiary (which gave her opportunities for frequent reception of the sacraments) and began to devote her life to the education of poor girls. She and several companions placed themselves under the patronage of Ursula, thought to have been a fourth-century British princess who fled to Cologne to preserve her virginity and was martyred there with some companions. (Formerly celebrated on October 21, her feast was dropped from the General Roman Calendar in 1969.) Ursula's legend had fascinated Angela as a young child. The Company of St. Ursula took no vows and wore lay clothes, but its Rule prescribed virginity, poverty, and obedience. The foundation of the Congregation of the Ursulines is given as November 25, 1535, when Angela and her companions took up formal residence in Brescia, but it was not formally recognized as a congregation until 1544 because church authorities were initially put off by the fact that members did not live a cloistered life. Angela's *Testament* advises those who succeed her in the leadership of the congregation to "be of one heart and mind," because there is "only one sign that is pleasing to the Lord, that of loving and being united to one another." One of her last words of advice was to "do in life what you would have wanted to do in death." The congregation continues to flourish today in various parts of the world.

Angela Merici died on January 27, 1540, and was canonized in 1807. Her feast is on the General Roman Calendar. The translation of the relics of John Chrysostom [September 13] is commemorated on this day in the Greek and Russian Orthodox Churches, and his feast is also observed today by the Episcopal Church in the USA.

28 Thomas Aquinas, priest and Doctor of the Church

Thomas Aquinas (ca. 1225–74), a Dominican friar and a Doctor of the Church, also known as the "Angelic Doctor," is one of the greatest and most influential theologians in the entire history of the Church. Born at the castle of Rocca Secca near the small town of Aquino, Thomas was educated at the Benedictine monastery at Monte Cassino and at the University of Naples, where he first became acquainted with the writings of the Greek philosopher Aristotle (d. 322 B.C.) and the Islamic philosopher Averroës of Córdoba (d. 1198). He entered the Order of Preachers in 1244 over thc strong opposition of his family. His brothers were sent to kidnap him; they held him in a castle for a year, and then tried to seduce him away from his vocation by sending in a courtesan to tempt him. Upon regaining his freedom, he went to Paris the following year for further studies, and then to Cologne, where he studied under Albertus Magnus (also Albert the Great) [November 15] from 1248 until 1252, during which period he was ordained a priest. Albert is said to have predicted that one day "the lowing of this dumb ox" (so called because of Thomas's large size and taciturn manner) "would be heard all over the world."

Saint Thomas Aquinas and a Donor by Ambrosius Benson, 16th C.

Thomas returned to Paris for further studies and some teaching and writing. From 1259 to 1268 he was in Naples and then at Orvieto, Viterbo, and Rome, teaching his fellow Dominicans. It was in Rome that he began writing his most famous work, the *Summa Theologiae* (Lat., "Synthesis of Theology"). He was back in Paris 1268–72, where he continued his Scripture commentaries and completed a large part of the *Summa*. From 1272 to 1274 he was back in Italy, teaching Scripture and theology at the new University of Naples, where he completed the third part of the *Summa*. On the feast of St. Nicholas, December 6, 1273, he suddenly stopped all of his writing. Whether this was due to a recognition of the limitations of his work (captured in the famous statement attributed to Aquinas: "All I have written seems to me like straw compared with what I have seen and what has been revealed to me") or whether it was related to a medical condition from which he died a few months later cannot be known. Invited to the Second Council of Lyons in 1274, he decided to visit his sisters and relatives en route, between Naples and Rome. He became acutely debilitated when he reached them, perhaps as the result of a major stroke, and asked to be taken to the Cistercian monastery at Fossanova, where he died on March 7, 1274.

Thomas's deep immersion in Sacred Scripture fostered his desire as a Dominican to lead a life in complete fidelity to the gospel and to cherish the guidance of the great Fathers of the Church, especially Augustine [August 28] and Gregory the Great [September 3], but also those of the East. His entire ministry as a teacher and preacher was a matter of giving to others what he had himself contemplated, which was for him the highest of all activities when done out of charity (*Summa Theologiae* 2–2.188.6). It was this same openness and generosity of mind and heart that inspired him, against the opposition of those in the Augustinian school, to use extensively the works of any authors—whether Christian, Jewish, or pagan—who might lead him to the truth. Like his mentor Albertus Magnus, Thomas saw no opposition between nature and grace or between reason and revelation. In spite of Thomas's great intellectual acumen, he was universally admired for his modesty and humility and for his prayer life and spiritual insights. He once wrote: "The ultimate human knowledge of God is to know that we do not know God, and that insofar as we know, what God is transcends all that we understand of God."

In spite of Thomas's apparent sanctity and extraordinary breadth and depth of learning, his writings did not escape the critical gaze of ecclesiastical authorities. Stephen Tempier, the bishop of Paris, who was also chancellor of the University of Paris, established a commission to examine his works. On the third anniversary of Thomas's death, the bishop condemned twenty-one theses attributed to Thomas's thought. Even the Dominican archbishop of Canterbury,

Robert Kilwardby, followed suit. These condemnations assured the dominance of the neo-Augustinianism of Bonaventure [July 15] during the next fifty years, although a Thomist school developed among the Dominicans.

Thomas was canonized in 1323, less than fifty years after his death, by John XXII, a pope who evidently understood and appreciated Thomas's theological writings. There were many marginal notes, in the pope's own hand, in his various copies of Thomas's works. He was declared a Doctor of the Church in 1567. Pope Leo XIII, in his encyclical *Aeterni Patris* (1879), commended Thomas's thought to all students of theology, thereby generating a revival of interest in the Angelic Doctor's works. The following year Thomas was named patron saint of Catholic universities. He is also patron saint of students and booksellers, among others. His feast day was originally March 7, the day of his death, but was moved to January 28 in the 1969 revision of the General Roman Calendar. It is also celebrated by the Church of England and the Episcopal Church in the USA.

Ephrem the Syrian [June 9], also Ephraim, is commemorated on this day in the Greek and Russian Orthodox Churches.

BIBLIOGRAPHY

O'Meara, Thomas F. *Thomas Aquinas Theologian.* Notre Dame, IN: University of Notre Dame Press, 1997.

Principe, Walter. "St. Thomas Aquinas." In *The HarperCollins Encyclopedia of Catholicism.* Ed. Richard P. McBrien. San Francisco: HarperCollins, 1995. Pp. 83–89.

Torrell, Jean-Pierre. *Saint Thomas Aquinas: The Person and His Work.* Vol. 1. Trans. Robert Royal. Washington, DC: Catholic University of America Press, 1996.

Weisheiple, James A. *Friar Thomas d'Aquino: His Life, Thought, and Works.* 2d ed. Washington, DC: Catholic University of America Press, 1983.

29 Gildas, abbot

Gildas (ca. 500–ca. 570) was a monastic leader who influenced the development of monasticism in Ireland through his Irish disciples, a visit to Ireland, and subsequent correspondence with Irish monasteries. Born in Scotland, he became a monk probably after being married and widowed. His famous work, *De excidio Britanniae* ("On the Ruin of Britain"), cited by the Venerable Bede [May 25], described the decadence of contemporary British secular rulers and clerics and placed on them the blame for the victory of the Anglo-Saxon invaders. He founded a monastery on an island in Brittany's Morbihan Bay that became the center of his cult. It is still known as the "island of monks." His feast does not appear on the General Roman Calendar. The Russian and Greek Orthodox Churches celebrate the feast of the translation of the relics of Ignatius of Antioch [October 17] on this day.

30 Hyacintha Mariscotti, foundress; Mohandas K. Gandhi, Hindu holy man; Joseph Columba Marmion, abbot

Hyacintha Mariscotti (1585–1640) was the foundress of two confraternities in Viterbo to care for the sick, the aged, and the poor. Born of a noble Italian family, she was christened Clarice and was educated at the local Franciscan convent, where one of her sisters was already a nun. Because of her displays of temper, her parents forced her to enter the same convent, where she took the name Sister Hyacintha. For ten years she lived the life of a nun in name only, while surrounding herself with luxuries. Both illness and the influence of a saintly Franciscan confessor eventually helped her change her ways. As mistress of novices, she exhibited great wisdom and common sense. She mistrusted signs of alleged "divine favor" and was partial to those who showed little evidence of self-love. She died on January 30, 1640, and was canonized in 1807. The bull of canonization indicated that she had won more souls to God through her works of charity than many preachers of her time. Her feast is celebrated today by Franciscans, but it is not on the General Roman Calendar.

The Greek and Russian Orthodox Churches commemorate *Basil the Great* [January 2], *Gregory Nazianzen* [January 2], and *John Chrysostom* [September 13] on this day.

January 30 is also the day of death of one of the twentieth century's spiritual giants, the Hindu holy man and modern pioneer of nonviolent resistance *Mohandas K. Gandhi* (1869–1948), who was assassinated by a young Hindu fanatic, and also of *Joseph Columba Marmion* (1858–1923), the Irish-born abbot of the Benedictine monastery of Maredsous in Belgium from 1901 until his death, who was one of the most influential spiritual writers and directors of the early twentieth century. His spirituality was biblically and liturgically oriented and centered

Mohandas K. Gandhi, ca. 1930

always on the mystery of Christ. His major works included *Christ: the Life of the Soul* and *Christ in His Mysteries.* He was beatified by Pope John Paul II on September 3, 2000.

31 John Bosco, priest

John Bosco (1815–88) was the founder of the Society of St. Francis de Sales [January 24], known as the Salesian order. He is the patron saint of Catholic publishers, editors, and young apprentices. Born in a small town near Turin, he was brought up in severe poverty. He entered the seminary wearing clothes and shoes obtained through charity and was ordained a priest in 1841 (becoming Don Bosco). Soon thereafter he began a lifelong devotion to educating and caring for boys and young men, especially of the working class, for the most part in the newly industrialized city of Turin. He served as a time as chaplain to a refuge for young girls, but soon resigned and invited his mother to join him in his apostolate to poor and homeless boys. He opened workshops to train shoemakers, tailors, printers, bookbinders, and ironworkers, thereby becoming a pioneer in vocational training. As other priests came to help, the nucleus of a religious community emerged. With the encouragement of a professor at the Turin seminary, Joseph Cafasso [June 23], Don Bosco in 1859 organized a religious community to continue his work. The Salesians were formally approved in 1884. In 1872 he collaborated with Mary Mazzarello [May 14] to found a parallel community of women, the Daughters of Mary Help of Christians, or the Salesian Sisters.

Upon his death on January 31, 1888, some forty thousand mourners filed past his body as it lay in church, and virtually the whole population of Turin lined the streets for his funeral. He was canonized on Easter Sunday, 1934, by Pope Pius XI, who, as a young priest, had known Don Bosco. On the next day a national holiday in his honor was observed throughout Italy. His feast day is on the General Roman Calendar and is also commemorated by the Church of England.

FEBRUARY

1 Brigid of Kildare, abbess

Brigid (d. ca. 525), also known as Brigit, Bridget, and Bride (of Ireland), is a patron saint of Ireland along with Patrick [March 17] and

Columba [June 9]. What little is known of her is mixed with myth, Irish pagan folklore, miracle stories, and cultic elements that are difficult to disentangle. The legendary exploits, however, are typically Irish. She distributes butter (a sign of prosperity) to the poor and changes her bathwater into beer to satisfy the thirst of some visiting clerics. Some accounts even have her being consecrated a bishop. Born near Kildare, she is said to have been baptized by Patrick himself. She established a monastery at Kildare, which later became a double monastery (for men and women) that contributed significantly to the spread of Christianity throughout the country. Irish missionaries carried her cult to the Continent and elsewhere. It was second only to that of Patrick. She is patron saint of Kildare and of poets, scholars, and dairy workers. Her feast is not on the General Roman Calendar, but she is commemorated on this day in Ireland and by the Church of England and the Episcopal Church in the USA.

Saint Bridget of Ireland

2 Presentation of the Lord; Cornelius the Centurion; Alfred Delp, priest

On the General Roman Calendar (and on that of the Greek and Russian Orthodox Churches, the Church of England, the Episcopal Church in the USA, and the Evangelical Lutheran Church in America), February 2 is the feast of the *Presentation of the Lord*, when the infant Jesus was brought to the Temple and Mary was purified following childbirth, to fulfill the requirements of Mosaic law (Luke 2:22–40; Exod. 13:2, 12; Lev. 12:6–8). Simeon [February 3] greeted them and pronounced the prayer that came to be known as the *Nunc Dimittis* (Lat., "Now you are dismissing [your servant]"), and the prophetess Anna [February 3] spoke of Jerusalem's redemption.

This is also the feast day of *Cornelius the Centurion* (first century), an officer of the imperial Roman army and the first pagan converted to Christ, according to the Acts (10:45). He is described by the Scriptures as a devout man who feared God, gave alms generously, and prayed constantly to God (10:1–2). Cornelius and the Apostle Peter [June 29] had simultaneous visions that eventually brought them together (10:5; 10:15) at Cornelius's house and in the presence of Cornelius's whole household. Peter assured Cornelius that God shows no partiality and briefly related the history of Jesus' preaching and death. At this, the Holy Spirit was poured out on all who were listening, Jew and Gentile alike. Peter was so astounded that the Spirit was given to the pagans as well as the Jews that he readily acceded to Cornelius's request for baptism for himself and his household. When some of the Jewish Christians back in Jerusalem learned of what had happened, they criticized Peter severely. Later a council had to be convened, headed by James [October 23], to settle the dispute (Acts 15). Peter was vindicated, and a new missionary outreach to the Gentiles was inaugurated. Cornelius's feast is not on the General Roman Calendar, but is observed by the Episcopal Church in the USA on February 4.

This is also the day on which *Alfred Delp* (1907–45), a Jesuit priest, was hanged by the Nazis for his opposition to Hitler. In his final message to friends, he wrote: "If through one man's life there is a little more love and kindness, a little more light and truth in the world, then he will not have lived in vain."

3 Blase, bishop and martyr; Ansgar, bishop; Simeon and Anna

Blase (d. ca. 316), also Blaise, was an early bishop of Sebaste (or Sebastea) in Armenia who was martyred under the emperor Licinius. He is also one of the Fourteen Holy Helpers (see Glossary), a group of saints to whom there was much popular devotion in Germany in the fourteenth and fifteenth centuries. Blase is thought to have been born in Armenia, but little or nothing is reliably known of his life. One legend that has him saving the life of a boy with a fish bone caught in his throat is the origin of the custom of blessing throats on his feast day. The boy's mother is said to have brought Blase food and candles when he was imprisoned. Thus, we have the use of

Saint Blase

two candles (in the form of St. Andrew's cross) in the throat-blessing ceremony, still practiced today. While the candles are held under the chin and against the throat, this prayer is said: "Through the intercession of St. Blase may God deliver you from ills of the throat and other ills." He is also patron saint of veterinarians. There is no evidence of a cult of Blase in either East or West before the eighth century. His feast is still on the General Roman Calendar, although in the 1969 revision it was demoted from a memorial to an optional memorial. The Russian Orthodox Church celebrates his feast on February 11.

Ansgar (801–65), also Anskar or Anschar, was a Benedictine monk who served as a missionary in both Denmark and Sweden and is regarded as the "apostle of Scandinavia." He is also patron saint of Denmark, Germany, and Iceland. Born of a noble family in Amiens in northern France, he became a monk in nearby Corbie in Picardy and then moved to Corvey, Corbie's daughterhouse in Saxony. He became a missionary when King Harold of Denmark, a convert to the faith, brought him back to his country to evangelize his people. After a subsequent missionary journey to Sweden, Ansgar was named abbot of Corvey and a year later bishop, then archbishop, of the new diocese of Hamburg, with responsibilities as papal legate to the peoples of the north. When the city was sacked and burned to the ground by Vikings in 845, he became archbishop of both Hamburg and Bremen (by appointment of the emperor Louis the German), with continuing missionary responsibilities for Denmark and Sweden. The union of the two dioceses, however, was not recognized by the pope until 864. Ansgar was known as a builder of schools, a great preacher, and a servant of the poor. He is commemorated on the General Roman Calendar. His feast is also celebrated by the Church of England, the Episcopal Church in the USA, and the Evangelical Lutheran Church in America.

On this same day the Greek and Russian Orthodox Churches celebrate the feast of *Simeon* and the prophetess *Anna,* who were present when Mary and Joseph brought the child Jesus to the Temple for the first time (Luke 2:22–38). Both spoke of the child as the Messiah who was to come. The Russian Orthodox Church celebrates yet another feast of Simeon alone on April 27.

4 Rabanus Maurus, abbot and bishop

Rabanus Maurus (780–856), also Rhabanus Maurus or Raban Maur, is credited with composing the hymn "*Veni, Creator Spiritus*" (Lat.,

"Come, Creator Spirit"), and for laying the foundation for another hymn, "King of Kings and Lord of Lords," both of which are still sung today. Born in Mainz, where he would eventually become archbishop, he was educated at the monastery of Fulda and then sent to Tours to study under Alcuin, the English biblical scholar and adviser to the emperor Charlemagne. It was Alcuin who conferred on Rabanus the nickname Maurus, after Benedict's favorite disciple [January 15]. Under Alcuin's guidance, Rabanus became a part of the Carolingian renewal of biblical studies and liturgy. He mastered Greek, Hebrew, and some Syriac in order to study Scripture. His scriptural commentaries relied almost literally on the Fathers of the Church and on Origen (ca. 185–ca. 254) in particular. He also developed a spirituality for laity and for clergy, emphasizing in both instances the importance of an organized prayer life. He was ordained a priest in 815 and elected abbot of Fulda in 822, resigning ca. 842. Then in 847, at age seventy-one, he was elected archbishop of Mainz. At first he was rejected by his clergy when he tried to impose rigid standards of obedience to the laws of the Church. He visited every part of his diocese, and during a famine he fed three hundred people at his episcopal residence each day. His own devotion to the Holy See was so intense that he was known as the "pope's slave." He is especially venerated in Germany, where he has sometimes been called a Doctor of the Church, but that title was never conferred upon him. His feast is not observed on the General Roman Calendar.

The Dominicans observe the feast of *Catherine de' Ricci* [February 13] on this day.

5 Agatha, virgin and martyr; Pedro Arrupe, priest

Agatha (d. 251) was a martyr widely venerated in Sicily. Although the dates of her birth and death (both probably in Catania, Sicily) are uncertain and her entire life is shrouded in legend, Agatha's cult developed very early in the history of the Church. Her name is included in the *Martyrology of Jerome* and on the liturgical calendar of Carthage (ca. 530), both of which give February 5 as the day of her death, and she is also mentioned in the Canon of the Roman Mass. Pope Damasus I (366–84) [December 11] composed a hymn in her honor, and two churches were dedicated to her in Rome during the sixth century. Her historically dubious biography indicates that she was born into a wealthy family and made a vow of virginity, which the Roman consul attempted to violate; upon her refusal, she was subjected to torture, including the cutting off of her breasts; subsequently, however, she was healed by a vision of the Apostle Peter [June 29]. She is said to have died in prison as a result of her sufferings, during the Decian persecution (249–51). She is invoked against diseases of the breast as well as against volcanic eruptions and earthquakes. She is said, for example, to have stilled an eruption of Mount Etna the year after her death. Her veil, which had been raised prayerfully on a staff in the latter instance, is still carried in procession on her feast day in Catania. She is also patron saint of nurses and firefighters. In spite of the dearth of reliable information about her, she continues to be one of the most frequently invoked saints in the Church and her feast remains on the General Roman Calendar, even after the revision of 1969. The Russian Orthodox Church also celebrates her feast on this day.

This is also the day of death of *Pedro Arrupe* (1907–91), superior general of the Society of Jesus from 1965 until he resigned in 1983, having suffered a stroke two years earlier. Father Arrupe led his fellow Jesuits, in their Thirty-Second General Congregation (1974–75), in defining their mission as one of living and promoting "a faith that does justice" and of entering into solidarity with the poor and the powerless. He had been affected for most of his adult life by his having been only four miles from the center of Hiroshima when the atomic bomb fell on that city on August 6, 1945.

Father Pedro Arrupe

6 Paul Miki and companions, martyrs; Amand, monk and bishop; Dorothy, martyr

Paul Miki (d. 1597) *and his companions* were the first martyrs of the Far East. The Japanese ruler Hideyoshi initiated a persecution of Christians when he became alarmed by the success of Francis Xavier's [December 3] mission, which had begun in 1549. To strike terror in the hearts of other Christians, the ruler ordered that twenty-six Christians have their left ears cut off, be marched through the streets of various towns with blood streaming down their faces, and then be crucified and pierced with lances on a hill outside of

Nagasaki on February 5, 1597. Those martyred included Paul Miki, a Jesuit priest and popular preacher, two Jesuit lay brothers, and six Franciscans, of whom four were Spanish; the fifth was from Mexico City, namely, *Peter Baptist* (1545–97), Mexico's first saint, who is also patron saint of Japan; and the sixth was from Bombay. The other seventeen included sixteen Japanese laypeople and one Korean. Among them were catechists, interpreters, a soldier, a physician, and three boys. Their bloodied garments were collected as relics and miracles were attributed to the martyrs' intercession. They were canonized in 1862. Missionary work, conversions, and martyrdoms continued in Japan for the next several decades. Christians then went underground, preserving their faith and many of its devotional elements, from the middle of the seventeenth century until 1865, when Japan was reopened to the outside world. Before the martyrs' feast day was included on the revised General Roman Calendar in 1969, it was celebrated principally in Japan and by Franciscans and Jesuits. The martyrs are also commemorated by the Church of England, the Evangelical Lutheran Church in America, and the Episcopal Church in the USA (the last, on February 5). The Franciscans also commemorate them, but the name of the Franciscan Peter Baptist (Blásquez) precedes that of Paul Miki in the title of the feast.

This is also the feast day of *Amand* (ca. 584–ca. 675), abbot and bishop in northern France and Flanders, where he became known as the "apostle of Belgium." He founded several monasteries there and spent his last four years as an abbot. He was considered one of the most spiritually compelling figures of his time. He is patron saint of innkeepers, wine merchants, and brewers.

It is also the feast day of *Dorothy* (d. ca. 304), who was martyred under Diocletian at Caesarea in Cappadocia. According to her legend, a young lawyer jeered at her as she was being led to her execution and challenged her to send him fruits from the garden of paradise. An angel is said to have appeared later with a basket containing three apples and three roses. The lawyer was converted and also martyred. Dorothy is patron saint of gardeners.

BIBLIOGRAPHY

Fujita, Neil S. *Japan's Encounter with Christianity: The Catholic Mission in Pre-Modern Japan*. New York: Paulist Press, 1991.

7 Colette, virgin

Colette (1381–1447) was a Franciscan nun who devoted herself to the reform of Franciscan religious life through the restoration of the Rule of Francis [October 4] and Clare [August 11]. Born in Picardy, France, and baptized Nicolette Boylet, she grew up near Corbie abbey, where her father was a carpenter. After his death, she took up the life of a hermit close to the abbey church and became a Franciscan tertiary. As her reputation for holiness grew, many came to her for spiritual direction. The antipope Benedict XIII (1394–1417), recognized in France as the true successor of Peter during the Great Western Schism (1378–1417), professed her as a Poor Clare and placed her in charge of all convents she would establish or wish to reform. She met with rejection at first, but eventually founded seventeen new convents and reformed several others, mainly in France, Flanders, and Savoy. She was canonized in 1807. Her feast is commemorated on the Franciscan calendar, but it does not appear on the General Roman Calendar.

8 Jerome Emiliani, founder

Jerome Emiliani (1483–1537) was the founder of the Somoscan Fathers, an order that runs schools and orphanages in Italy. Born in Venice, he became an officer of the Venetian army. In 1518, following a conversion experience while a captive of enemy forces, he was ordained a priest and devoted his life to the care of suffering people in a time of widespread famine and plague. After his own recovery from the plague in 1531, he founded orphanages, hospitals, houses for former prostitutes, and a small congregation of priests (named after their place of origin, Somasca, between Bergamo and Milan) to care for them all, but especially the orphans. He died from an infectious disease he had contracted while caring for the sick. He was canonized in 1768 and declared the patron saint of orphans and abandoned children in 1928. His feast is on the General Roman Calendar.

9 Apollonia, virgin and martyr; Miguel Febres Cordero, religious brother

Apollonia (d. ca. 249) was an aged deaconess of Alexandria the form of whose martyrdom has ensured her place in the history of saints. The bishop of Alexandria reported that, during an anti-Christian riot, all of her teeth were broken with blows to the jaw and then she was burned to death. She became known as the patron saint of dentists and of those with toothaches. In Boston there is a dentists' quarterly named after her, *The Apollonian.* Her feast was dropped from the General Roman Calendar in 1969.

Miguel Febres Cordero (1854–1910) was Ecuador's first canonized saint. A Christian Brother, he was born in the city of Cuenca, seven thousand feet up in the Andes, and was baptized as Francisco. He joined the Christian Brothers at age fourteen, taking the name Brother Miguel, and before he was twenty he published a Spanish grammar book that was eventually prescribed for all schools in Ecuador. A number of similar books followed and his reputation grew, not only nationally but internationally. At the same time, he devoted himself to religious education and to the preparation of children for First Communion. He was canonized in 1984. His feast is not on the General Roman Calendar.

10 Scholastica, virgin

Scholastica (ca. 480–ca. 543) was the sister of Benedict of Nursia [July 11] and is the patron saint of Benedictine nuns. Her own nunnery at Plombariola was only five miles from the famous Monte Cassino. She and her brother would meet annually in a house outside Monte Cassino to discuss spiritual matters. (As a woman, she was not allowed to enter the monastery itself.) According to the *Dialogues* of Pope Gregory the Great [September 3], at their last meeting she begged her brother to stay longer in order to continue their discussion. He refused on the ground that his Rule prevented it. She thereupon bowed her head in prayer, and a violent thunderstorm prevented her brother from leaving until the following morning. Benedict accused Scholastica of provoking the storm, to which she replied: "I asked a favor of you and you refused it. I asked it of God, and he has granted it." They spent the night discussing the joys of heaven. Three days later she died. While praying in his cell, Benedict is said to have seen her soul rising to heaven in the form of a dove. She was buried in the tomb Benedict had prepared for himself. Her feast is on the General Roman Calendar and she is also commemorated by the Church of England.

11 Our Lady of Lourdes

Between February 11 and July 16, 1858, the Blessed Virgin Mary is said to have appeared to Marie Bernarde (later Bernadette) Soubirous [April 16], a fourteen-year-old girl, eighteen times at the grotto of Massabielle, near her hometown of Lourdes on the northern slopes of the Pyrenees mountains. Although by March twenty thousand pilgrims had gathered to witness the apparition, only Bernadette could see it. She was instructed by the apparition to bathe and drink from a spring that began to flow the following day. Since then the bath at Lourdes has been associated with miraculous healings. The local bishop eventually authorized the cult of Our Lady of Lourdes in 1862. The site of the apparitions attracts over three million pilgrims a year. Of some five thousand reported cures, at least fifty-eight have been declared miraculous by church officials. In 1907 Pope Pius X made the feast of Our Lady of Lourdes a feast of the universal Church. It remains on the General Roman Calendar.

Benedictines celebrate the feast of *Benedict of Aniane* [February 12] on this day.

BIBLIOGRAPHY

Harris, Ruth. *Lourdes: Body and Spirit in the Secular Age.* New York: Viking, 2000.

12 Benedict of Aniane, abbot

Benedict of Aniane (ca. 750–821) was a major reformer of Benedictine monasteries in France. Born of a noble Visigothic family (his birth name was Witiza) in Languedoc, he became a courtier of Pepin III and Charlemagne and then a monk. After three years in a conventional monastery, he lived as a hermit on his own estate along the river Aniane, but was later joined by others. They devoted themselves to working in the fields, other manual labor, and copying books. When they outgrew their surroundings, they moved to another location where they built a monastery and a church. As Benedict's influence grew, he was appointed to supervise all of the monasteries in the region. He was enlisted by the Frankish emperor Louis the Pious, successor of Charlemagne, to apply the Rule of St. Benedict [July 11] to all monasteries in his domain. Louis had built a small monastery for him along the river Inde, five miles south of the imperial court, so that Benedict would remain close to him in the capital, Aachen. Benedict presided over a council there in 816 at which reform legislation was enacted. It stressed poverty, chastity, and obedience, the importance of the daily conventual Mass and the keeping of the liturgical hours, the standardizing of the intake of food and drink, and an emphasis on teaching, writing, and artistic work over manual labor on the part of monks who were also clerics. The reforms had an extensive effect on monasteries in France and England alike, but with the disintegration of the Holy Roman Empire they were difficult, if not impossible, to enforce universally. Benedict of Aniane's feast is not on the General Roman Calendar, but is a major celebration in Benedictine communities on February 11.

13 Catherine de' Ricci, virgin; Blessed Jordan of Saxony, friar

Catherine de' Ricci (1522–90) was a Dominican nun known for her wisdom, psychological healthiness, and concern for the sick. Born to a wealthy family in Florence and baptized Alexandrina, she is said to have experienced ecstasies each week (from midday on Thursday to about 4:00 P.M. on Friday) over a twelve-year period in which she became physically conformed to the Passion of Christ, including the stigmata. This phenomenon drew much public attention, and Catherine begged the other nuns to pray for the end of the manifestations. Their prayers were heard. In spite of her admiration for Girolamo Savonarola (1452–98), a Dominican priest and religious reformer who preached against papal corruption, Catherine de' Ricci was canonized in 1746. Her feast is not on the General Roman Calendar, but it is observed on the Dominican liturgical calendar on February 4. On this day, February 13, the Dominicans commemorate *Jordan of Saxony* (ca. 1177–1237), who succeeded Dominic [August 8] as master general of the Order of Preachers in 1222.

14 Cyril, monk, and Methodius, bishop; Valentine, martyr

Cyril (826–69) and *Methodius* (ca. 815–85) are known as the "apostles of the Slavs" and were named by Pope John Paul II as the patron saints of Europe, alongside Benedict of Nursia [July 11]. Their principal missions were to territories encompassed by the modern-day Czech Republic, Croatia, Serbia, and Slovenia. Cyril, whose baptismal name was Constantine, was the youngest of seven children born to a senatorial family in Thessalonica. Methodius, his brother, is known only by his religious name. Cyril was educated in Constantinople at the imperial university and acquired such a reputation as a philosopher that he was subsequently appointed as professor of philosophy there. After ordination to the priesthood, he was appointed librarian at the Hagia Sophia, the principal church in Eastern Christendom. He later joined his brother Methodius, who, after a brief government career, entered a monastery in Bithynia.

Both were commissioned by the emperor Michael III ca. 862 to become missionaries in Moravia at the request of the local ruler, Rostislav, who, for political as well as ecclesiastical reasons, was seeking an alternative to the German missionaries who were already ministering there. Rostislav also wanted Cyril and Methodius, who had spoken Slavonic since childhood, to teach in the vernacular. In order to put spoken Slavonic in written form, Cyril invented a Slavonic alphabet (Glagolithic [or Glagolitic], from which Cyrillic was derived), based on the Greek alphabet, and then he and Methodius together translated major portions of the Bible and the liturgy. (Methodius alone translated the rest of the Bible later in his life.)

For mainly political reasons (one might call it, somewhat irreverently, a turf war), the German bishops opposed Cyril and Methodius's missionary efforts, especially their advocacy of the use of the vernacular in the liturgy, and refused to ordain them or their disciples. As a result, they left Moravia and headed back toward Constantinople to seek help. While they were on a stopover in Venice, Pope Nicholas I invited them to Rome, where they were received with great honor by Nicholas's successor, Hadrian II, in 868, largely because they were carrying the supposed relics of St. Clement [November 23]. The pope approved the Slavonic liturgy and ordained Methodius and three of their disciples as priests. The newly ordained celebrated the Slavonic liturgy at St. Peter's Basilica and in other Roman churches. Already afflicted with serious health problems, Cyril became a monk and changed his name from Constantine. He died only fifty days later at age forty-two, on February 14, 869, and was buried in the church of San Clemente, where an ancient fresco depicts his funeral.

Saints Cyril and Methodius

Later that same year Methodius returned to Moravia as papal legate to the Slavs. When the prince of Slovenia petitioned the pope to restore the ancient archbishopric of Sirmium, Methodius was the logical candidate. He returned to Rome in 870, where he was consecrated by the pope. Once again, however, the German bishops and Hungarian clergy opposed him and he was exiled and confined for two to three years in Swabia by order of a synod in Regensberg. The pope (by now John VIII) secured his release and restored him to his see in 873, but on the condition that he cease using the Slavonic liturgy. In 879 Methodius was called to Rome to answer charges of heresy (for not using the "*Filioque*" in the creed) and disobedience (for continuing to use Slavonic in the liturgy). After he was found innocent, he returned to Moravia in 880 with his appointment as archbishop confirmed and with papal permission to use the Slavonic language in the liturgy restored. (Old Slavonic continues as the liturgical language of the Bulgarian, Byelorussian, Hungarian, Romanian, Russian, Ruthenian, Serbian, Slovak, and Ukrainian Churches, both Catholic and Orthodox.) The last four years of his life were not without difficulty, created in large part by continued machinations against him by his ecclesiastical and political enemies. It was during this period that he translated the entire Bible into Slavonic, with the exception of Maccabees. Methodius died on April 6, 885, at Velehrad in what is now the Czech Republic.

The feast of Cyril and Methodius is on the General Roman Calendar and is celebrated on May 11 in the East, where they were venerated long before their feast was made universal in the West (in 1880). Because they are venerated in both East and West, they are also patron saints of ecumenism. Indeed, their feast is also celebrated on this day by the Church of England and the Episcopal Church in the USA and also by the Evangelical Lutheran Church in America.

February 14 is also St. Valentine's Day. *Valentine* was a third-century Roman martyr with a very early cult. His martyrdom most likely took place on the Flaminian Way, two miles outside the city, ca. 250, during the Decian persecution. It is not clear how his cult became linked with lovers. His feast was suppressed in the 1969 revision of the General Roman Calendar.

BIBLIOGRAPHY

Farrugia, Edward G., Robert F. Taft, and Gino K. Piovesana, eds. *Christianity Among the Slavs: The Heritage of Saints Cyril and Methodius.* Rome: Pontificium Institutum Studiorum Orientalium, 1988.

15 Sigfrid, bishop; Claude La Colombière, priest; Onesimus, bishop

Sigfrid (d. ca. 1045) was bishop of Vaxjo and the "apostle of Sweden." English by birth and a monk of Glastonbury, he was sent by King Ethelred to Christianize the Swedes and the Norwegians, baptizing Olaf [July 29], the king of Sweden. During a missionary trip to the more remote areas of the region, Sigfrid's three nephews, who were also his principal helpers, were murdered. On his return Sigfrid persuaded the king not to execute the killers. Their punishment was commuted to a heavy fine, but Sigfrid refused to accept any money, even though he was in desperate need of funds for rebuilding his cathedral. It is uncertain whether he was canonized in 1158 by the only English pope in history, Adrian IV, who had himself been a missionary in Scandinavia, but it is clear that his cult was established in Norway, Sweden, and Denmark by the thirteenth century. He was widely venerated in Sweden until the Reformation. His feast is not on the General Roman Calendar, but he is commemorated on this day by the Church of England.

Claude La Colombière (1641–82), also Claude de la Colombière, was the confessor of Margaret Mary Alacoque [October 16], who was the recipient of private revelations about the Sacred Heart of Jesus. Born into a wealthy French family near Lyons, he entered the Society of Jesus in 1658 and, even before ordination in 1675, displayed a remarkable talent for preaching. Claude often appealed to the new and growing devotion to the Sacred Heart (with its emphasis on the love of God for all) as a spiritual weapon against Jansenism, a largely French movement that incorporated elements of Calvinism and Lutheranism (with an emphasis on predestination and the sinfulness of humanity). During his retreat before making final profession as a Jesuit, he consecrated himself to the Sacred Heart.

Shortly after his arrival at his first priestly assignment in Paray-le-Monial in Burgundy, Claude paid a call at the Visitation convent there. On that occasion Sister Margaret Mary claimed to have heard an inner voice saying, "This is he whom I have sent to you." She told him of her visions and together they worked for the approval of a new feast in honor of the Sacred Heart of Jesus. Eighteen months after arriving in Paray, he was transferred to London. Protestant England at this time still had laws against Catholic priests, and Claude was eventually arrested for traitorous speech. While he was imprisoned in a damp dungeon, his health deteriorated rapidly. At the request of King Louis XIV, he was saved from execution, released from prison, and banished to France. He never regained his health and died in Paray on February 15, 1682. Margaret Mary claimed to have had direct knowledge that Claude's soul went directly to heaven. However, he was not beatified until 1929. He was canonized by Pope John Paul II in 1992. After his death, devotion to the Sacred Heart continued to grow, eventually leading to the inclusion of the feast of the Sacred Heart on the universal liturgical calendar in 1856, celebrated on the Friday after Corpus Christi. Pope Pius XII described the theological foundation of this devotion in his encyclical *Haurietis aquas* (1956). Claude's feast is not on the General Roman Calendar, but is celebrated on this day by the Jesuits.

The Greek and Russian Orthodox Churches celebrate the feast of *Onesimus*, the Phrygian slave about whom Paul [June 29] wrote his Letter to Philemon. According to tradition, Onesimus became bishop of Ephesus in the early second century and was martyred there.

16 Juliana, virgin and martyr; Maruthas, bishop

Juliana (d. ca. 305) was an early-fourth-century martyr who probably died at Naples or at Cumae, which is near Naples, during the persecution of the emperor Maximian. Pope Gregory the Great (590–604) [September 3] requested her relics from the bishop of Naples for an oratory built in her honor. The principal, though legendary, episode associated with her life is the lengthy argument she supposedly had with the Devil, who tried to persuade her to obey her pagan father and to marry a Roman prefect. Condemned to death, she was beheaded after a furnace and boiling oil did no harm to her. There is evidence of her cult in England at least as early as the seventh century, because she appears in the *Martyrology of Bede* [May 25]. Her feast is not on the General Roman Calendar.

This is also the feast day of *Maruthas* (d. ca. 415), the bishop of Maiferkat in Mesopotamia, near the Persian border, who restored the Church in Persia and is considered the father of the Syrian Church. He composed hymns used in the Syriac liturgy and wrote several theological works. He is the patron saint of Persia.

17 Seven Founders of the Order of Servites

Today's feast celebrates the sanctity of seven members of well-to-do thirteenth-century Florentine families who founded a new order of friars called the Servites, or the Order of Friar Servants of Mary (O.S.M.) in 1233. Their names are *Buonfiglio* (also Bonfilius) *Monaldi* (also Monaldo), *Giovanni Bonaiuncta* (also Buonagiunta), *Manettus dell'Antella* (also Benedict dell'Antello, or dell'Antela), *Amadeus degli Amidei* (also Bartholomew), *Ricovero Uguccione* (also Hugh), *Geraldino Sostegni* (also Sosthenes Sostegno), and *Alexis Falconieri.* In reaction to the general moral laxity of the city, they gathered in a house outside Florence where they practiced a life of solitude, prayer, and penance. When they were besieged by visitors, they withdrew to the wilderness, where they built a simple church and hermitage. Visitors found their way there as well, but at first the men refused to accept others into their community. Later, under pressure from the bishop of Florence and in response to an alleged vision of the Blessed Virgin Mary, they did so and adopted a way of life based on the Rule of St. Augustine [August 28], with some additions from the Dominican constitutions. They moderated their extremely austere lifestyle and became friars rather than monks, living in towns rather than in monasteries. The new religious community grew rapidly, but was not recognized until 1259 because of a concern in Rome that there were too many new orders springing up. The community received formal papal approval in 1304.

A principal devotion fostered by the friars is that of the Seven Sorrows of the Blessed Virgin (the prophecy of Simeon [February 3] at the circumcision of Jesus in the Temple, the flight into Egypt, Jesus' being lost in Jerusalem, the encounter with Jesus on the way to Calvary, the crucifixion, the taking of the body down from the cross, and Jesus' burial). Of the seven founders, four became priors general, two founded convents in France and Germany, while the last, Alexis, remained a lay brother all of his life, outliving the other six. They were canonized in 1887, and their feast appears on the General Roman Calendar. It was first made a feast of the universal Church by Pope Pius VII in 1814, in thanksgiving for his return to Rome from captivity under Napoleon. The feast of Our Lady of Sorrows is celebrated on September 15.

18 Colman of Lindisfarne, bishop; Theotonius, abbot; Blessed John of Fiesole (Fra Angelico), painter; Martin Luther, Reformer

Colman of Lindisfarne (d. 676) was a leading figure in the seventh-century Irish Church as bishop-abbot of the great monastery of

Lindisfarne. He played a key role at the Synod of Whitby, an Anglo-Saxon church council held at St. Hilda's Abbey in 664 to resolve differences between the Roman and Celtic practices regarding the dating of Easter and other observances and the relationship of local churches to the see of Rome. After a full-scale debate between Colman, for the Celtic side, and Wilfrid of Ripon [October 12], for the Roman, the king ruled in favor of the latter lest, as he said, he be denied entrance into heaven by St. Peter [June 29], whose successor the pope was. Colman resigned his post at Lindisfarne and returned to Iona (where Colman had originally been a monk) with all of the Irish monks and about thirty English monks from Lindisfarne. Then they migrated to Ireland, where Colman founded a monastery on the isle of Inishbofin, off the coast of Galway, ca. 667.

Because of a dispute between the Irish and English monks (the former had left the monastery during the summer harvest, so the latter had to do all the work), Colman had to settle the English monks on the mainland at Mayo while the Irish remained at Inishbofin. The new monastery at Mayo, known as "Mayo of the Saxons," flourished and was widely praised for its devotion to the Rule, the canonical election of its abbot, and the frugality of its community life. According to the Venerable Bede [May 25], "They had no property except cattle, and whenever they received any money from rich folk, they immediately gave it to the poor." Colman remained abbot of the two communities until his death. His cult was confirmed in 1898, and his feast is observed in some parts of Ireland on this day or on August 8. It is not on the General Roman Calendar, but he is commemorated on this day by the Russian Orthodox Church.

Theotonius (1086–1166) was the abbot of the Monastery of the Holy Cross in Portugal, a country in which he is held in great honor. Born in Spain, he was the nephew of the bishop of Coïmbra in Portugal and was ordained a priest. Soon thereafter he attracted wide attention because of his sanctity, austerity of life, and great skill as a preacher. Every Friday he sang a Solemn High Mass for the souls in purgatory, followed by a vast procession to the town cemetery, where great sums of money were collected for the poor. Although repeatedly urged to accept a bishopric, he refused to do so. After two pilgrimages to the Holy Land, Theotonius decided to enter a monastery, becoming one of the original members of the Canons Regular of St. Augustine [August 28]. He was soon elected prior. Because he was so highly respected by Alphonsus, the king of Portugal, Theotonius was able to persuade him to release his

Mozarabic Christian captives, taken in the reconquest of Portugal from the Moors. Theotonius spent the last thirty years of his life in the Monastery of the Holy Cross and became its abbot before dying at age eighty. His cult was approved by Pope Benedict XIV (1740–58). His feast is not on the General Roman Calendar.

John of Fiesole (ca. 1400–55), better known as *Fra Angelico,* is the patron saint of artists. Born Guido di Pietro in a small village near Fiesole, which is in the hills overlooking Florence, he took up painting early in life, before entering the Dominicans ca. 1420 and taking the name Fra Giovanni. His notable works of art include the *Annunciation, Descent from the Cross,* and the frescoes in the monastic cells at San Marco in Florence. By the fifteenth century he was given the title"Fra Angelico," probably because of the devotional quality of his works and/or the prominence of angels in them. The incomparable Michelangelo once said of him, "One has to believe that this good monk has visited paradise and been allowed to choose his models there." John of Fiesole was beatified by Pope John Paul II in 1982. His feast is celebrated by the Dominicans, but is not on the General Roman Calendar.

The Evangelical Lutheran Church in America and the Episcopal Church in the USA celebrate the feast of *Martin Luther* (1483–1546), the leading figure in the Protestant Reformation, on this day. The Russian Orthodox Church celebrates the feast of *Pope Leo the Great* [November 10] on this day.

19 Conrad of Piacenza, hermit

Conrad of Piacenza (1290–1351) was born of a noble family in Piacenza and eventually married and took up residence there. One day, while he was hunting, a fire that he had lit got out of control and burned a neighboring cornfield. Conrad had to sell all of his possessions to pay for the damages. It was then that he decided to change his life. He gave to the poor his remaining wealth, his wife became a Poor Clare nun, and he became a Franciscan tertiary and a hermit, living a life of great austerity. Because large crowds were attracted by his reputation for sanctity, Conrad moved to Noto in Sicily, where he lived for the next thirty years. His last years were spent in a grotto outside of Noto, where he died and was buried. Numerous miracles were reported at his tomb, and his cult was approved by Pope Paul III (1534–49). His feast is not on the General Roman Calendar, but is celebrated by the Franciscans.

20 Wulfric, priest and hermit

Wulfric (ca. 1080–1154), also Ulric or Ulfrick, of Haselbury was an English hermit. Born in Somerset, he was converted to an austere form of life in the early 1120s, reportedly after a chance conversation with a beggar. He ministered as a parish priest until 1125, when he undertook the life of a hermit (anchorite) in a corner of the parish church at Haselbury Plucknett (near Exeter). His rigorous penitential practices, including fasting and self-scourging, generated a reputation for sanctity. Many made pilgrimages to his cell, including kings Henry I and his successor, Stephen. When Wulfric was not in prayer, he copied and bound books and made other articles for use in church services. His cult began to develop about thirty years after his death on February 20, 1154, when various miracles were reported at his tomb (located in his cell, and later moved to an unknown place). He was never formally canonized and his feast is not on the General Roman Calendar.

21 Peter Damian, bishop and Doctor of the Church

Peter Damian (1007–72) was a major reformer of the papacy, episcopate, clergy, and monasteries. Born in Ravenna of a large poor family, he entered the Camaldolese Benedictine monastery at Fonte Avellana in northern Italy in 1035. This was a community of hermits who lived two to a cell and followed a rigorously austere program of fasting, abstinence, and vigils. Peter also devoted himself to the study of Scripture and the Fathers of the Church and to the transcribing of manuscripts. In 1043 he was elected abbot. Given the unreformed state of the Church at this time, he was outspoken in his criticism of bishops and monks who violated their high calling. He preached against simony and clerical marriage and in favor of a reformed papacy. In 1057 he was appointed bishop of Ostia (one of the ancient dioceses neighboring Rome) and a cardinal. Given his newly elevated status in the Church, he increased his activities on behalf of reform, opposing false claimants to the papacy (various antipopes) and fulfilling diplomatic missions to Milan, Germany, and France. However, Peter remained a monk at heart and successfully persuaded Pope Alexander II to relieve him of his episcopal duties so that he might return to his monastery at Fonte Avellana. He died on February 22, 1072, on the way back from his native town of Ravenna, where he had settled a severe factional dispute that had erupted following the excommunication of its archbishop. Peter was never formally canonized, but in 1828 Pope Leo XII approved his cult for the universal Church and also declared him a Doctor of the Church. His feast is on the General Roman Calendar.

22 Chair of Peter, apostle; Margaret of Cortona, foundress

Today's feast celebrates not only the triumph of Christ's grace in the heart and soul of *Peter* [June 29], but his status as the primary pastor and teacher of the Church. The chair is the symbol of his teaching authority, as it is of every bishop. Peter (d. ca. 64) was Jesus' chief apostle, whom later Catholic tradition regards as the first pope. (Previously the popes were regarded as successors of Peter, who was not himself a pope.) Born in the village of Bethsaida on the Sea of Galilee, his original Hebrew name was rendered in Greek as Simon, but Jesus gave him a new name, the Aramaic word for "rock," rendered in Greek as Kephas. The name Peter is a translation of the Aramaic word. Sometimes he is referred to in the New Testament as Simon Peter. Peter was married and remained so even after becoming a disciple. There is a reference to his mother-in-law (Mark 1:29–31) and to the fact that Peter and the other apostles took their wives on their missionary journeys (1 Cor. 9:5).

Peter enjoyed a unique status within the college of apostles. He was the first disciple whom Jesus called (Matt. 4:18–19); he served as the spokesman for the others (Mark 8:29; Matt. 18:21; Luke 12:41; John 6:67–69); and according to the tradition of Paul [feast day, with Peter: June 29] and Luke [October 18] he was the first to whom the Risen Lord appeared. Peter is the most frequently commissioned of the Twelve following the Resurrection, the most frequently mentioned in all four Gospels, and regularly listed first among the Twelve (Mark 3:16–19; Matt. 10:1–4; Luke 6:12–16). He was prominent in the original Jerusalem community, described by Paul as one of its "pillars" (Gal. 2:9), and well known to many other churches. It was Peter who took the decisive step in ordering the baptism of the Gentile Cornelius without first requiring circumcision (Acts 10). But one must be careful not to exaggerate his role. At the council of Jerusalem (Acts 15), where the circumcision issue was debated and resolved, it was James, not Peter, who presided and issued the final ruling. And although there is increasing agreement among historians and biblical scholars that Peter did go to Rome and was martyred there, there is no evidence that he functioned as Rome's first bishop.

In the Catholic tradition, the biblical basis for associating the primacy with Peter is embodied in three texts: Matthew 16:13–19 (". . . you are Peter, and upon this rock I will build my church. . . . I will give you the keys to the kingdom of heaven"); Luke 22:31–32 (". . . you must strengthen your brothers"); and John 21:15–19 ("Feed my lambs. . . . Tend my sheep. . . . Feed my sheep"). This is not to say that Peter's authority was exclusive and absolute. In the Acts of the Apostles, in fact, Peter is shown consulting with the other apostles and even being sent by them (8:4). He and John [December 27] are portrayed as acting as a team (3:1–11; 4:1–22; 8:14). And Paul confronts Peter for his inconsistency and hypocrisy in drawing back from table fellowship with gentile Christians in Antioch under pressure from some Jewish Christians who arrived later from Jerusalem. Paul "opposed him to his face because he clearly was wrong" (Gal. 2:11; see also vv. 12–14).

Scholars, however, point to a significant trajectory of images relating to Peter and his ministry as an independent basis for the primatial claims. He is spoken of as the fisherman (Luke 5:10; John 21:1–14), an occupation that, in fact, he and his brother Andrew [November 30] had practiced, as the shepherd of Christ's sheep (John 21:15–17), as the Christian martyr (John 13:36; 1 Pet. 5:1), as an elder who addresses other elders (1 Pet. 5:1), as a proclaimer of faith in Jesus as the Son of God (Matt. 16:16–17), as the receiver of a special revelation (Mark 9:2–8; 2 Pet. 1:16–18; Acts 1:9–16; 5:1–11; 10:9–16; 12:7–9), as the guardian of the true faith against false teaching and misunderstanding (2 Pet. 1:20–21; 3:15–16), and, of course, as the rock on which the Church is to be built (Matt. 16:18).

This trajectory of biblical images continued in the life of the early, postbiblical Church, and these images were enriched by others: missionary preacher, great visionary, destroyer of heretics, receiver of the new law, gatekeeper of heaven, helmsman of the ship of the Church, coteacher and comartyr with Paul. This is not to suggest, of course, that Peter was portrayed always and only in a positive fashion. He is also presented as a weak and sinful man. He is reproached by Paul (Gal. 2:11–14), misunderstands Jesus (Mark 9:5–6; John 13:6–11; 18:10–11), weakens in faith after beginning to walk on water (Matt. 14:30–31), is rebuked by Jesus (Mark 8:33; Matt. 16:23), and, in spite of prior boasts to the contrary (Mark 14:29,31; John 13:37), he denied Christ (Mark 14:66–72). But he is always repentant and was eventually rehabilitated. The Risen Lord appears to Peter and he becomes once again a source of strength to the Church (Luke 22:32).

The ministry of pastoral leadership exercised by Peter in the first part of Acts is the model and the norm for the Petrine ministry exercised by every one of his successors. It involves witnessing to the faith, overseeing the way in which local churches preserve and transmit this faith, providing assistance and encouragement to fellow bishops in their own local and universal ministry of proclaiming and defending the faith, speaking in the name of the bishops and their local churches when the need arises, and articulating the faith of the Church in the name of the whole communion of local churches that together constitute the universal Church. In sum, the Petrine ministry is that of a "servant of the servants of God" (Lat. *servus servorum Dei*): a servant of his brother bishops and a servant of the whole People of God. This feast is on the General Roman Calendar.

This is also the feast day of *Margaret of Cortona* (ca. 1247–97), a woman who had lived as a mistress for nine years. Upon her companion's violent death, she returned home with her son and found no one to take them in except for two women. She embarked on a life of rigorous and often excessive penances, but later founded a community to care for the sick poor. She was canonized in 1728 and is patron saint of the homeless and single mothers.

BIBLIOGRAPHY

Brown, Raymond E. *The Churches the Apostles Left Behind.* New York: Paulist Press, 1984.

Brown, Raymond E., Karl Donfried, and John Reumann, eds. *Peter in the New Testament: A Collaborative Assessment by Protestant and Roman Catholic Scholars.* New York: Paulist Press, 1973.

Grant, Michael. *Saint Peter: A Biography.* New York: Scribner, 1994.

McBrien, Richard P. "Peter, Apostle, St." In *Lives of the Popes: The Pontiffs from St. Peter to John Paul II.* San Francisco: HarperSanFrancisco, 1997. Pp. 28–33.

23 Polycarp, bishop and martyr

Polycarp (ca. 69–ca. 155) was a disciple of John the Apostle and Evangelist [December 27]. He became bishop of Smyrna (in present-day Turkey) ca. 107 and one of the most important Christian leaders in all of Roman Asia during the first half of the second century. His letter to the Christians in Philippi, for example, was still being read in churches in Asia at the time of Jerome (d. 420) [September 30]. He defended the faith against the heresies of Marcionism (which rejected the inspired character of the Old Testament) and Gnosticism (which denied the humanity of Christ and held to an understanding of revelation accessible only to an elite few). He also had a great influence over Irenaeus of Lyons (d. ca. 200) [June 28], through whom the faith was transmitted to much of western Europe.

Toward the end of his life, Polycarp journeyed to Rome at the invitation of Pope Anicetus (ca. 155–ca. 166) in the hope of resolving a dispute over the date for the celebration of Easter. Polycarp urged Anicetus to adopt the common liturgical practice in Asia Minor of observing the feast, regarded as the Christian Passover, on the fourteenth day of the Jewish month of Nisan (the day of the Jewish Passover) regardless of the day of the week on which it fell. Until this time, it should be noted, Rome itself observed no special feast of Easter. The Roman church considered every Sunday a celebration of the Resurrection. Anicetus denied Polycarp's request that Rome conform to the practice in Asia Minor, insisting that he felt bound by his predecessors' custom of celebrating the Resurrection every Sunday. The discussion remained friendly and the pope invited Polycarp to preside at the Eucharist. They departed in peace, but Rome and the East continued their separate practices. (Ever since the First Council of Nicaea in 325, Roman Catholics have celebrated Easter on the Sunday following the full moon after the vernal equinox, i.e., between March 22 and April 25. Many Eastern-rite Catholics and Orthodox Christians follow the Julian rather than the Gregorian calendar and celebrate Easter on a different Sunday.)

Soon after Polycarp returned to Smyrna, a young boy was killed at a pagan festival. The crowds called for the death of all "atheists" and focused on the aged Polycarp in particular. He was found calmly waiting at a nearby farm. He invited his captors to have a meal while he prayed alone for an hour. At his subsequent interrogation he refused to deny Christ and readily acknowledged that he was a Christian. When the crowd at the amphitheater learned of his admission, they shouted for his death. He was held for trial, then bound, and killed with a sword thrust to his neck; his body was burned at the stake in the town stadium. The local Christians collected his bones, which they regarded as "more precious than stones of great price, more splendid than gold," and buried them "where it seemed right." They also wrote a careful account of his martyrdom—the first of its kind, and important evidence for the cult of saints and of relics as early as the second century. It was the commemoration of Polycarp's martyrdom that established the custom of celebrating the anniversary of a martyr's death, seen as the *dies natalis* (Lat., "the day of birth" [into heaven]). His feast is on the General Roman Calendar and is also observed on this day by Greek and Russian Orthodox Churches, the Church of England and the Episcopal Church in the USA, and the Evangelical Lutheran Church in America.

24 Ethelbert of Kent, king

Ethelbert of Kent (d. 616), also known as Aethelberht, Aethelberct, Aidilberct, and Edilbertus, was the first Christian Anglo-Saxon king, or *bretwalda* ("overlord"). His wife, Bertha, daughter of the king of Paris, was already a Christian when Ethelbert married her; she had agreed to the marriage on condition that she be allowed to practice her religion and to have a chaplain to minister to her. He offered a friendly welcome to Augustine of Canterbury [May 27] and his monks in 597 when they came, at the behest of Pope Gregory the Great [September 3], to re-Christianize Britain. Although he could not accept Christianity at that time, he did offer them a house in Canterbury and allowed them to preach and to make converts. Ethelbert himself was eventually baptized ca. 601 and received a congratulatory letter and gifts from the pope.

His conversion was decisive for the Christianization of Kent and then of all of England. Augustine restored an old church in Canterbury, dedicated it to Christ, and made it his cathedral. Ethelbert built a monastery for the monks, dedicated to Sts. Peter and Paul (later St. Augustine's), outside the walls of the city. With the king's encouragement and generous support, Augustine also established sees in Rochester (then called Hrofescaestir, after an early chieftain named Hrof) and London, which were at the time the principal towns of the East Saxons. Ethelbert founded the church of St. Paul in London, which later became St. Paul's Cathedral. He also promulgated a code of laws that, among other provisions, protected churches and the clergy from damage or harm. He died on February 24, 616, and was buried alongside his first wife, Bertha, in the side chapel, or *porticus,* of St. Martin in the monastery church of Sts. Peter and Paul. Although there is evidence of a very early, but unofficial, cult in Canterbury (a candle was kept burning at his tomb until the time of the Reformation), his feast is not found in liturgical calendars until the thirteenth century, and generally on February 25 or 26 in England because St. Matthias occupied February 24. (Matthias's feast is still commemorated on this day by the Episcopal Church in the USA and the Evangelical Lutheran Church in America, but in the 1969 revision of the General Roman Calendar, it was moved to May 14, when it is also celebrated by the Church of England.) Ethelbert's feast is not on the General Roman Calendar.

The Greek and Russian Orthodox Churches celebrate on this day the feast of the First and Second Finding of the Head of John the Baptist [August 29].

25 Walburga, abbess

Walburga (d. 779), also Walpurgis, Wilburga, Warpurg, and Vaubourgi, was the abbess of Heidenheim. The sister of Sts. Winnibald [December 18] and Willibald [June 7], she was one of many Anglo-Saxon monks and nuns who assisted her uncle Boniface [June 5] in his missionary work in Germany. She was educated at the monastery of Wimborne (Dorset), then sent to the abbess of Tauberbischofsheim (some twenty miles southwest of Würzburg) for two more years of training, including studies in medicine. She became abbess of the double monastery (one for men, the other for women) of Heidenheim (fifty miles east of Stuttgart), established by her brother Winnibald. When Winnibald died, her other brother Willibald, whom Boniface had appointed the first bishop of Eichstätt, named her superior over both the nuns and the monks. (Given her social status, well above that of the monks and lay brothers, the appointment was not unusual.) Nothing is known about her manner of rule there, although the *Roman Martyrology* refers to it as optimal. Miraculous cures were associated with her tomb in Eichstätt, from which medicinal oils are said to have flowed. The fluid is known as St. Walburga's oil. Indeed, she is usually depicted with a crown and scepter and a vial of oil. When her relics were spread to other countries, so was her cult. She is patron saint of the diocese of Eichstätt. Her feast is not on the General Roman Calendar.

26 Porphyry of Gaza, bishop

Porphyry (353–421), the bishop of Gaza, was renowned for his generosity to the poor. He was born in Thessalonika and came to Macedonia, where, at age twenty-five, he abandoned the world and spent five years as a monk in the desert of Skete. He spent the next five years as a hermit in Palestine, living in a cave near the river Jordan. He became crippled by illness and moved to Jerusalem, where, with the help of a walking stick, he visited the holy places. It was while in Jerusalem that he first met Mark, who would become his deacon and biographer. Porphyry sent Mark back to his family estate in Thessalonika to sell his property for distribution to the poor. When Mark returned to Jerusalem, he found Porphyry restored to full health. Porphyry, now without income, became a shoemaker, while Mark copied books.

In 393, when Porphyry was forty years old, the bishop of Jerusalem ordained him a priest. Three years later he was elected bishop of Gaza without his knowledge. He was ordered to go to Caesarea on the pretext that the local bishop wanted to consult with him about biblical matters. At the instigation of the bishop, Porphyry was effectively kidnapped by some of the townspeople of Gaza and forcibly consecrated as their bishop. After a difficult three-day journey, he arrived in Gaza only to be accused by the local pagans of causing a drought in the area. Both sides—the pagans and the Christians—prayed for rain. When the rains came, the pagans gave credit to the Christians and many conversions followed. Porphyry received permission from the emperor to destroy the remaining pagan temples and personally participated, alongside his clergy and laypeople, in the building of a cruciform church on the site once occupied by the temple of Marnas. He spent the remaining thirteen years of his life in active pastoral service of his see, gaining a wide reputation for his generosity to the poor. His feast is celebrated on this day by the Greek and Russian Orthodox Churches, but it is not on the General Roman Calendar.

27 Gabriel Possenti, religious; George Herbert, priest

Gabriel Possenti (1838–62) was a Passionist who died at a young age and whose sanctity was often compared with that of Thérèse of Lisieux, the Little Flower [October 1]. Also known as Gabriele dell'Addolorata, he was the son of the governor of Assisi (then part of the Papal States), who lived a life of self-indulgence until two serious illnesses made him rethink its direction. After considering the Jesuits, who had educated him, he entered the Passionist novitiate at Morrovalle in 1856, where he was known for his cheerfulness, his commitment to prayer and penance, and his devotion to Our Lady of Sorrows. Indeed, he had taken the religious name Gabriel of Our Lady of Sorrows. He was only twenty-four years old when he died of tuberculosis at Isola del Gran Sasso in the Abruzzi on February 27, 1862. Many noted the similarity between his life and that of the Little Flower, and great numbers of pilgrims visited his shrine. He was beatified in 1908, canonized in 1920, and is considered the patron saint of the Abruzzi region of Italy and of clerics and youth. His feast is not on the General Roman Calendar.

On this day the Church of England and the Episcopal Church in the USA celebrate the feast of *George Herbert* (1593–1633), priest of the Church of England and a renowned poet, who influenced the hymns of Charles Wesley (d. 1788) and the poetry of the Jesuit

Gerard Manley Hopkins [June 8]. The Evangelical Lutheran Church in America commemorates him on March 1.

28 Oswald of Worcester, bishop

Oswald (d. 992) was a Benedictine monk, bishop of Worcester, and archbishop of York. Born into a Danish military family, he was the nephew of the archbishops of Canterbury and York. The latter provided Oswald's early education. He was more formally educated at a famous Cluniac monastery in France, Fleury-sur-Loire, where he became a Benedictine monk; he returned to England as a priest ca. 958 when he learned that his uncle, the archbishop of Canterbury, was dying. The king appointed him bishop of Worcester in 961 on the recommendation of Dunstan [May 19], the saintly archbishop of Canterbury. He founded or supported the foundation of monasteries, especially at Ramsey, and reformed his own cathedral chapter. His biographer referred to Oswald as having a fine physique, a magnificent singing voice, a pleasant and welcoming personality, and a special love for the poor. Other sources, however, underscore his close cooperation with the king in acquiring considerable tracts of land for his diocese and monasteries, and in accepting the archbishopric of York in 972 while retaining the see of Worcester, at the king's request and with the pope's permission—an abuse, nevertheless, known as pluralism.

With the death of his patron, King Edgar, an antimonastic reaction set in. Nevertheless, Oswald continued to administer both of his dioceses, building churches, visiting parishes and monasteries, and administering justice. He also resided for extended periods of time as abbot at Ramsey. He spent his last winter in Worcester, where, at the beginning of Lent, he resumed his usual practice of washing the feet of twelve poor men each day at Mass. He died immediately after doing so on Leap Year Day, February 29, 992. Having been widely recognized for his sanctity in life, it was not surprising that his cult began immediately after his death and remained popular in the region. His feast is not on the General Roman Calendar.

MARCH

1 David of Wales, bishop

David of Wales (ca. 520–ca. 601), also Dewi and Dafydd, is the patron saint of Wales (and of poets) and the only Welsh saint to have been canonized. His nickname was "Aquaticus" (Lat., "water drinker"), because he was the leader of a group of monks who drank neither wine nor beer, but only water. Though he is one of the most famous of British saints, there is no reliable biography of him. He is said to have founded ten or perhaps even twelve monasteries in Wales and England, among them Menevia (now St. David's) and, less likely, Glastonbury, where the monks followed the austere practices of the monks of Egypt, including rigorous manual labor, immersion in cold water, study, and a diet of bread, water, salt, and vegetables. His cult was approved in 1120, and his feast was celebrated in the province of Canterbury from 1398, but his name was already mentioned in Irish martyrologies as early as the eighth century, with the day of his death given as March 1. Devotion to him existed in the south of England and in the Midlands, as well as in his native Wales. More than fifty pre-Reformation churches were dedicated to him in south Wales. His feast is not on the General Roman Calendar, but is celebrated by the Church of England and the Episcopal Church in the USA on this day.

2 Chad of Lichfield, abbot and bishop; John and Charles Wesley, founders

Chad (d. 672), also Ceadda, was the bishop of Lichfield, in service to the Mercians. He is patron saint of the archdiocese of Birmingham, England, whose cathedral is dedicated in his honor. A native of Northumbria and a pupil of Aidan [August 31] at Lindisfarne, he became abbot of Lastingham upon the death of his brother. Soon thereafter he was consecrated under dubious circumstances (by a simoniacal bishop with two coconsecrators of questionable orthodoxy) as bishop of the Northumbrians, with his see at York. King Oswiu had become impatient at the absence of Wilfrid [October 12], who had originally been appointed to the see but had gone to France for his consecration. When Wilfrid returned, Theodore [September 19], the archbishop of Canterbury, refused to recognize Chad's appointment. Chad willingly yielded to Theodore's judgment: "If you consider that I have not been properly ordained, I gladly resign. I never thought myself worthy of the office and agreed to undertake it, though unworthy, only under obedience." Then he retired to Lastingham.

Impressed by Chad's humility, Theodore had him reconsecrated as bishop of the Mercians, with his see in Lichfield. Chad built a small place near his church where he could pray and read with seven or eight other monks and also founded a monastery in his diocese. Chad proved himself such a dedicated pastor to his people that he was venerated as a saint immediately after his death from plague on March 2, 672. He was buried near the church of St. Mary, and his relics were later transferred to the church of St. Peter [June 29], on the site presently occupied by Lichfield Cathedral. Miracles were reported at both sites, including healings from the mixture of water and dust taken from his shrine. His feast is not on the General Roman Calendar, but is celebrated on this day by the Church of England and the Episcopal Church in the USA.

The Lutherans commemorate *John* and *Charles Wesley* (1703–91 and 1707–88, respectively), leading figures in the establishment of the Methodist Church. The Episcopal Church in the USA celebrates their feast on March 3.

3 Katharine Drexel, foundress; Cunegund, empress and nun

Katharine Drexel (1858–1955), also known as Mother Drexel, was the foundress of the Sisters of the Blessed Sacrament for Indians and Colored People (S.B.S.) in 1891. The daughter of a wealthy Philadelphia banker (whose family firm eventually became the Wall Street powerhouse Drexel Burnham Lambert), she was encouraged by Pope Leo XIII himself to follow the example of her generous parents and to devote her fortune (worth more than $80 million today) and her life to the poor. Three days a week her stepmother had opened the doors of their home to distribute food, clothing, and cash to the needy. In 1889, at age thirty, she entered the Sisters of Mercy, but felt a special call to do missionary work among African and Native Americans, her interest in the latter having

Mother Katharine Drexel

been heightened by visits to Indian reservations in the Dakotas. She undertook the humblest work in the convent and faithfully observed the requirements of the vow of poverty.

In 1891 she started her own religious congregation, the Sisters of the Blessed Sacrament, and established her first American Indian school in Sante Fe, New Mexico, three years later. She would create eleven more schools on Indian reservations, nearly a hundred for African Americans in rural areas and the inner cities of the South, and found in 1915 a teachers college that would eventually grow to become the first and only Catholic university for African Americans, Xavier University in New Orleans. In 1922 in Beaumont, Texas, the Ku Klux Klan threatened to tar and feather the local pastor and bomb his church if he did not close down one of Mother Drexel's schools. The sisters prayed, and within days a tornado destroyed the Klan's headquarters. Two Klansmen died, and the Klan never bothered the sisters again.

Mother Katharine suffered a severe heart attack in 1935 and spent the next twenty years in prayerful retirement at her motherhouse in Philadelphia. She continued to fight for, and fund, civil rights causes. Her sisters walked the streets of New Orleans and Harlem during the 1950s and were jeered at and called "Nigger sisters." When they described the name-calling to Mother Katharine, she simply asked, "Did you pray for them?" She died on March 3, 1955, and was beatified by Pope John Paul II in 1988 and canonized on October 1, 2000. Her feast is on the Proper Calendar for the Dioceses of the U.S.A., but is not on the General Roman Calendar. She is the second American-born canonized saint.

This is also the feast day of *Cunegund* (978–1033), the empress of Germany who became a Benedictine nun after the death of her husband, Henry II. She devoted the rest of her life to prayer and care of the sick. She is a patron saint of Lithuania, Poland, and Luxembourg.

4 Casimir, prince

Casimir (1458–84) is the patron saint of Lithuania, Poland, and Russia. Born at Kraków, the third son of the king of Poland, he refused his father's orders to take up arms against other Christian countries and to marry the daughter of the emperor Frederick III, preferring instead a life of celibacy and asceticism. During his father's absence, he is said to have ruled over much of Poland from 1481 to 1483 with justice and prudence. He died at age twenty-six of tuberculosis on March 4, 1484, while on a trip to Lithuania, where he was also Grand Duke, and was buried in the cathedral at Vilna (now Vilnius). Miracles were reported at his tomb. He was canonized in 1521, and his feast was extended to the whole Church in 1621. Devotion to him has been popular among Polish and Lithuanian immigrants in the United States and Canada. His feast is on the General Roman Calendar.

5 John Joseph of the Cross, religious; Martin Niemoeller, pastor

John Joseph of the Cross (1654–1734) was born Carlo Gaetano on the island of Ischia off the west coast of Italy, opposite Naples, of which he is patron saint. At age sixteen he entered the Franciscans of the strict Alcantarine observance (following in the tradition of Peter of Alcántara [October 22]), taking the name John Joseph of the Cross. He was ordained in 1677 and devoted himself particularly to the ministry of the confessional and to spiritual direction. Following a dispute between Italian and Spanish members of the community, the Italians were given papal permission to form their own province and John Joseph was elected minister provincial. At the end of his term, he returned to the house he had originally entered, seeking a life of obscurity. However, he was constantly followed on the street by people seeking his advice or blessing. He died of a major stroke on March 5, 1739. He was beatified fifty years later and canonized in 1839. His relics lie in the friary church of Santa Luca del Monte in Naples. His feast is not on the General Roman Calendar.

This is also the day of death of *Martin Niemoeller* (1892–1984), a German Lutheran pastor whose organized opposition to the Nazis became known as the Confessing Church. A war hero during World War I, he was imprisoned throughout World War II and afterward drafted a confession of guilt acknowledging the churches' responsibility for tolerating anti-Semitism in their country. He became a prominent pacifist, criticizing the nuclear arms race and violations of human rights.

6 Chrodegang of Metz, bishop

Chrodegang of Metz (ca. 712–66) was a reformer of the clergy, the author of a Rule for canons (i.e., priests attached to a cathedral and living in common) that was used in Germany, Italy, the British Isles, and throughout the Frankish kingdom, and the founder of a school of church music at Metz, which became famous for Gregorian chant. Born near Liège in present-day Belgium of noble Frankish parents, he served in a variety of high offices (including chief minister) under Charles Martel and Pepin III, the grandfather and father of the emperor Charlemagne, respectively, and he became bishop of Metz in 742. As Pepin's ambassador to Pope Stephen II (III), he was closely involved in the donation of the exarchate of Ravenna and other territories to the Holy See (the basis of the Papal States), following the defeat of the Lombards, and in the coronation of Pepin as king in 754. Upon the martyrdom of Boniface [June 5], also in 754, he assumed responsibility for church reform in the whole of the Frankish kingdom. He also built and restored churches, monasteries, and charitable institutions and founded the abbey of Gorze, which became a center of monastic reform. His greatest achievement, however, was his reform of the European secular clergy, whose moral conduct had become reflective of society's laxity and general disregard for law.

Chrodegang began his reform at home, with his own clergy in Metz. He obliged them to attend the chanting of the Divine Office in choir and to live a common life according to the Rule he drew up, based on that of St. Benedict [July 11]. The code of canons (rules) he imposed consisted of thirty-four chapters. At each daily meeting of the priests, a chapter had to be read. The meeting itself came to be known as a "chapter," and eventually it was applied to those in attendance. Those who were bound by these canons were themselves called "canons." The communities of clergy governed by their own regulations became known as "regulars." Canons differed from monks in that the former were allowed to hold property and retain their own money. Charlemagne subsequently imposed Chrodegang's Rule on all the secular clergy within his empire. Chrodegang made Metz not only the center of clerical reform, but also of liturgical renewal. He mandated the use of Roman practices and Roman (Gregorian) chant. The choir school at Metz was renowned throughout Europe for centuries to come. In 805 Charlemagne ordered that all choirmasters should be trained in Metz.

Chrodegang died on March 6, 766, and was buried in the abbey of Gorze, which he had founded and for which he always had a special fondness. His feast does not appear on the General Roman Calendar.

7 Perpetua and Felicity, martyrs

Perpetua and her slave *Felicity* (Felicitas) were North African martyrs who were put to death in 203, during the persecution of Septimus Severus. Their feast was widely celebrated throughout the early Christian world and was recorded in the earliest Roman and Syriac liturgical calendars (late fourth century) as well as in the fifth-century *Martyrology of Jerome* [September 30]. Their names were also included in the Canon of the Roman Mass. There is an inscription in their honor in the major basilica at Carthage, where they were buried. They are also depicted in the Ravenna mosaics done in the sixth century.

Perpetua (Vibia Perpetua) was a young married noblewoman of twenty-two who was arrested, along with other North African catechumens, a few months after giving birth to a son. Perpetua's husband and her pregnant slave Felicity were arrested with her. The *Passion of Perpetua and Felicitas,* written in part by Perpetua, in part by Saturus, her catechist, and the rest by an eyewitness, once thought to be Tertullian (d. ca. 225), provides one of the earliest, most valuable, and most revered accounts of Christian martyrdom. Augustine [August 28] frequently quoted from it. In this document Perpetua referred to her prison as "a palace" where she "would rather have been than anywhere else." She refused the constant pleadings of her aged father to renounce her faith, nursed her son, is said to have experienced a number of visions, and was baptized while awaiting the start of the games. Her servant *Felicity* gave birth to a girl. On the day of the games, they left

Saint Perpetua, left, and a detail, right, from *Saint Felicity and her Seven Sons* by Bicci di Lorenzo (1378–1452)

for the amphitheater "joyfully as though they were on their way to heaven." The men were attacked by leopards and bears; the women, by a heifer. Injured but not killed, Perpetua guided the gladiator's knife to her throat. It was March 7, 203. Their feast is on the General Roman Calendar and is also celebrated on this day by the Church of England, the Episcopal Church in the USA, and the Evangelical Lutheran Church in America. Felicity is patron saint of barren women.

BIBLIOGRAPHY

Robeck, Cecil M. *Prophecy in Carthage: Perpetua, Tertullian, and Cyprian*. Cleveland, OH: Pilgrim Press, 1992.

Salisbury, Joyce E. *Perpetua's Passion: The Death and Memory of a Young Roman Woman*. New York: Routledge, 1997.

8 John of God, religious; Stephen of Obazine, abbot

John of God (1495–1550), born John Ciudad, was the founder of the Brothers of the Hospitaller Order of St. John of God (O.H.), also known as the Brothers Hospitallers. Born in Montemor-o-Novo, Portugal, he was taken to Spain by a visiting priest, never to return home again. After the priest abandoned him, he was taken in and raised by another family. He worked for a time as a shepherd and later joined a company of Spanish mercenaries, abandoning his faith and living an immoral life. At about age forty he had a conversion experience and hoped to achieve martyrdom in North Africa, working among Christian slaves. He was dissuaded from doing so by a Franciscan confessor, and returned to Gibraltar to spread the faith by going from town to town, selling religious books and holy pictures. He eventually opened his own shop in Granada.

Spiritually overcome by a sermon preached by John of Ávila [May 10], he pledged himself to a life of sanctity. Initially, however, he went to such great extremes in his devotional and penitential practices that he was committed to an asylum for the mentally disturbed. John of Ávila visited him there and directed his energies to the care of the sick and the poor. His mental health improved almost immediately, but he remained in the hospital for a time, ministering to the other patients and visiting the sick elsewhere. He subsequently rented a house in Granada and filled it with the sick. The townspeople, who had formerly scorned him as a lunatic, came to admire his work on behalf of those in need. The local bishop gave him a religious habit along with a new name, John of God. John continued to attract followers who wished to share in his ministry. His final illness was precipitated by his effort to save a drowning man in a flood, but was undoubtedly the result of the rigors of his labors on behalf of the sick and of his austere lifestyle. He died on March 8, 1550, his fifty-fifth birthday.

After his death, a Rule was drawn up for his followers, who took vows and became a religious order. They claimed him as their founder. He was canonized in 1690 and in 1886 was declared patron saint of all hospitals and sick people, including heart patients and alcoholics. In 1930 he was named patron saint of nurses. He is also regarded by some as patron saint of printers and booksellers. His feast is on the General Roman Calendar.

The Cistercians commemorate *Stephen of Obazine* (d. 1159) on this day. He, as abbot, and his monastic community of Obazine were received into the Cistercian order in 1147.

9 Frances of Rome, religious; Dominic Savio

Frances of Rome (1384–1440) was the foundress of the Oblates of Tor de' Specchi, a community of women without vows with a mandate to serve the poor. She is the patron saint of motorists and widows. Born Francesca dei Roffredeschi in the Trastevere section of Rome of an illustrious and wealthy family, she was married at age thirteen, in spite of her desire to become a nun. She and her husband lived in the same house as her husband's brother and wife. Both women found that they shared the same ideals and, together, devoted themselves to the service of the poor, especially in hospitals.

After the death of two of her six children, Frances founded a society of devout women to carry out this ministry under the Rule of St. Benedict [July 11], but without vows. They were known at first as the Oblates of Mary, but later became the Oblates of Tor de' Specchi ("Tower of the Specchi," where their convent was located). After her husband's death in 1436, she herself entered this community and became its superior for four years, until her own death on March 9, 1440, having subsisted for years on dry bread and occasional vegetables. She was buried in the church of Santa Maria Nuova (now called Santa Francesca Romana), where her relics still rest and where there is a recumbent statue of her by Bernini (d. 1680). During her life, she is said to have had a number of visions, including a continuous vision for several years of her guardian angel. It is conjectured that this may be the reason why she was named patron saint of motorists by Pope

Pius XI (1922–39). She was canonized in 1608, and her feast is on the General Roman Calendar.

This is also the feast day of *Dominic Savio* (1842–57), who had been a student of John Bosco [January 31] in Turin. He was a spiritually precocious young man who died of tuberculosis at age fifteen. John Bosco himself wrote Dominic's Life, which led to his canonization in 1954. He is patron saint of choirboys and of young boys generally.

10 Forty Martyrs of Sebastea; John Ogilvie, martyr

The *Forty Martyrs of Sebastea* (also Sebaste, a city in modern-day Turkey), were a group of soldiers put to death for their faith in 320, during the persecution of the emperor Licinius. The local governor of Sebastea tried to persuade them to renounce their faith and spare their lives. When his entreaties failed, he ordered them to be stripped naked and exposed all night on a frozen lake outside the city. A fire and warm bath were prepared on the bank of the lake to tempt them. Only one of the soldiers weakened, but another, a nonbeliever, immediately took his place and was converted to Christ. All died of exposure. Their cult was widespread in the East and reference to it can be found in the sermons of Basil [January 2], Ephrem [June 9], John Chrysostom [September 13], and Gregory of Nyssa [January 10]. Their relics were sent to Caesarea and to Constantinople, where they were greatly venerated. Their feast is not on the General Roman Calendar, but is celebrated on this day by the Greek and Russian Orthodox Churches. The Episcopal Church in the USA commemorates *Gregory of Nyssa* on this day.

This is also the feast day of *John Ogilvie* (1580–1615), a Jesuit priest who was the only canonized Scottish martyr from the time of the Reformation. Throughout his persecution, he never lost his wit and humor, which even his jailers appreciated. He refused an offer of his freedom and a rich benefice if he adjured his faith and acknowledged the supremacy of King James I's spiritual jurisdiction over that of the pope and was hanged on March 10, 1615. He was beatified in 1929 and canonized in 1976. The Jesuits observe his feast on October 14.

11 Eulogius of Córdoba, martyr

Eulogius of Córdoba (d. 859) was an archbishop of Toledo martyred by the Moors. Born into a wealthy, landowning family in a city under

Muslim occupation, he eventually became a priest and was devoted to the sick. He was imprisoned with the bishop and other clergy of the city for reading the Scriptures to two young women who were about to be martyred. In their honor he wrote his *Documentum Martyrii,* similar to Cyprian of Carthage's [September 16] "Exhortation to Martyrs." Other works followed, including *Memorial of the Saints,* which described the suffering and death of martyrs, and an *Apologia* in praise of them. On the death of the archbishop of Toledo, Eulogius was chosen as his successor, but he did not live long enough to take possession of the see. He was imprisoned and beheaded on March 11, 859, for giving refuge to a convert from Islam and for refusing to abjure his faith. His relics were transferred to the cathedral in Oviedo, where they remain today. His feast is not on the General Roman Calendar.

12 Maximilian, martyr

Maximilian (d. 295), an early example of a Christian conscientious objector, refused to serve in the Roman army. When told he must either serve or die, he replied: "You may cut off my head, but I will not be a soldier of this world because I am a soldier of God." When they pressed him to accept the military seal (or badge), he said: "I will not accept the seal. I already have the seal of Christ. . . . My service is for the Lord; I cannot serve the world." When reminded that there were Christians serving in the army, even as imperial bodyguards, Maximilian answered: "They know what is best for them. I am a Christian and I cannot do what is wrong." "What wrong do those commit who serve in the army?" the proconsul asked. "You know very well what they do," Maximilian replied. Confronted one last time with his choice, he declared: "I shall not perish, and if I do depart from this world, my soul shall live with Christ my Lord." Just before his execution by the sword, he encouraged his companions to persevere and asked his father to give his new clothes to the executioner. He was beheaded in his native town of Theveste (Tebessa) in Numidia (present-day Algeria). His body was buried in Carthage, close to that of Cyprian [September 16]. His feast is not on the General Roman Calendar.

The Episcopal Church in the USA and the Evangelical Lutheran Church in America commemorate *Gregory the Great* [September 3] on this day.

13 Euphrasia of Constantinople, virgin; Ansovinus, bishop; Leander of Seville, bishop

Euphrasia (d. ca. 420), also Eupraxia, was raised in Constantinople by the emperor Theodosius I, who was a relative of her late father. She was betrothed to a senator at age five, but accompanied her mother to Egypt two years later, where she and her mother each received a nun's habit. Her mother died when Euphrasia was only twelve, and she was recalled to Constantinople by the new emperor in order to marry the senator to whom she had been betrothed. Instead, she was allowed to give her inheritance to the poor, free her slaves, and spend the rest of her life as a nun. Her feast is not on the General Roman Calendar.

This is also the feast day of *Ansovinus* (d. 840), who was elected bishop of Camerino, Italy, because of his reputation for sanctity and miracles while living as a hermit. He served as confessor to the emperor Louis the Pious, who approved his election, but only on Ansovinus's condition that he not be required to conscript soldiers for the imperial army. He was a highly effective pastor, exceedingly generous to the poor, and an efficient administrator of scarce resources during times of famine. He is considered the protector of crops.

March 13 is also the feast day of *Leander of Seville* (ca. 550–600), bishop of Seville, who devoted himself to combating Arianism in Spain. He was so successful that Gregory the Great [September 3] rewarded him with the archbishop's pallium. Leander wrote an influential Rule for nuns and introduced into the West the singing of the Nicene Creed at Mass, a practice later adopted in Rome and other Western cities.

14 Matilda, queen

Matilda (ca. 895–968), also known as Mechtildis and Maud, was married to the German king Henry I, with whom she had five children. While her husband was constantly away at war, Matilda lived a pious life and was generous to the poor and to all in need. Upon his death, she removed all of her jewels as a sign of her renunciation of honor and status. Her oldest son, Otto, succeeded to the throne and began to criticize his mother's liberality toward the poor. When her favorite son, Henry, allied himself with his older brother, Matilda gave them both her inheritance and retired to the country residence where she had been born. When her son Henry became ill and the affairs of state lapsed into chaos, many interpreted these developments as a punishment for the sons' ill treatment of their mother.

Matilda returned to court at the urgent invitation of the nobles, the clergy, and Otto's wife, Edith, and resumed her former works of mercy and almsgiving. She built three convents and a monastery and administered the kingdom when her son Otto went to Rome to be crowned by the pope as first sovereign of the Holy Roman Empire in 962. She spent most of her remaining years in one of the convents she had built, at Nordhausen, and died at the monastery of Quedlinburg on March 14, 968. She was buried there beside her husband, Henry. She was venerated locally as a saint from the moment of her death. Her feast is not on the General Roman Calendar. The Russian Orthodox Church celebrates the feast of *Benedict of Nursia* [July 11] on this day.

15 Louise de Marillac, widow and foundress; Clement Mary Hofbauer, religious

Louise de Marillac (1591–1660) was the foundress of the Daughters of Charity of St. Vincent de Paul [September 27]. Born into an aristocratic family, she married and had one son. After her husband's death twelve years later, she met Vincent de Paul, who became her spiritual director. He was at the time encouraging and training devout and wealthy women to care for the sick and the poor. He chose Louise to train girls and widows for this ministry drawn mainly from the lower classes (since the aristocratic women proved unequal to the task). From this small group of women working out of Louise's Paris home, beginning in 1633, there developed the Daughters of Charity of St. Vincent de Paul and all of the other Sisters of Charity communities that were founded and spread all over the world.

Vincent himself had not intended to found a new religious order. For him, the "convents" of his sister associates were to be the homes of the sick and the poor. Their chapel was the parish church; their cloister, the streets. Their original habit was indistinguishable from the usual dress of Breton peasant women of the time. Eventually they took charge of hospitals, orphanages, and even schools. Louise herself nursed those suffering from the plague and reformed a neglected hospital in Angers. She died on March 15, 1642, urging her sisters to be diligent in serving the poor "and to honor them like Christ himself." She was canonized in 1934. In 1960 she was declared patron saint of

Christian social workers. Her remains are in the convent of the Sisters of Charity on the Rue du Bac in Paris. Her feast is not on the General Roman Calendar.

Clement Mary Hofbauer (1751–1820) is regarded as the second founder of the Redemptorists, after Alphonsus Liguori [August 1], because he established the congregation for the first time north of the Alps. Born Johannes Hofbauer at Tasswitz in Moravia, he was the son of a butcher. After work as a baker's apprentice and three pilgrimages to Rome, he joined the Redemptorists in 1784, taking the religious name Clement Mary, and was ordained the following year. Three years later he opened a Redemptorist house in Warsaw and remained in Poland until 1808, serving German-speaking Catholics and promoting charitable and educational ministries. He was arrested and imprisoned when Napoleon suppressed the religious orders, but he was allowed to leave the country. He returned to Vienna, where he became widely known for his preaching and spiritual direction and for his ministry to the sick and the dying. He also established a Catholic college. Suffering from a variety of illnesses, he died on March 15, 1820, six days after braving a snowstorm to sing a requiem Mass for Princess Jablonowska, who had helped him when he was in Warsaw. His funeral in the Vienna cathedral attracted thousands. He was canonized in 1909 and named patron saint of Vienna. His feast is not on the General Roman Calendar.

16 Abraham Kidunaia, hermit

Abraham Kidunaia (sixth century) was a highly venerated Eastern hermit. Born into a wealthy family near Edessa in Mesopotamia, he rejected his parents' plea that he should marry and literally ran off to the desert to live as a hermit. He gave away all of his worldly possessions to the poor, except for a cloak, a goatskin, a bowl, and a mat. That was the sum total of what he owned throughout fifty years of penance. The local bishop ordained him a priest so that he could preach to the local people who had hitherto resisted the faith. Abraham had a church built and destroyed every pagan idol he could find. He was driven out of town, but returned by night to preach once again. They stoned him and left him half dead. This pattern continued for nearly three years. Eventually there was a breakthrough and they began to listen to him and to be converted and baptized. After another year, he returned to his hermitage. He died at the age of seventy, and a popular cult developed immediately. In the Greek and Russian Orthodox calendars, his feast is celebrated, along with that of his niece Mary, on October 29. His feast is not on the General Roman Calendar.

17 Patrick, bishop

Patrick (fifth century, or possibly ca. 389–ca. 461), the "apostle to" and patron saint of Ireland, is one of the Church's most famous and popular saints, even among those who are not Irish. He is also patron saint of Nigeria. Born in Roman Britain, the grandson of a priest and the son of a public official who was also a deacon, Patrick was captured by Irish pirates while in his mid-teens, sold, and kept as a slave herding livestock for six years—a particularly humiliating experience for a person of his family background. He interpreted his situation as a punishment for his lax religious practice and learned to trust more in God and to develop a life of prayer. He either escaped or was freed and somehow made his way home after an arduous journey that included near starvation. By now he was twenty-two years old. A much changed person, he received some rudimentary training for the priesthood, including the study of the Latin Bible. He never had the advantage of a really strong education, however, and he regretted that throughout his life.

His appointment as the successor to the first bishop of Ireland, Palladius, encountered some opposition, probably because of his lack of education, but he made his way to Ireland ca. 435, working principally in the north and establishing his see at Armagh—a choice probably determined by the presence of a powerful king nearby who could offer protection. Armagh, where he also founded a school, became the base of his various missionary journeys. His success in making converts, ordaining clergy, and consecrating virgins astonished him. Indeed, his missionary spirit would mark the Irish Church for centuries to come. His writings reveal a person of sincere simplicity and deep pastoral concern. His *Confession* ends with the words: "I beg of those who believe and fear God, whoever shall deign to look into or receive this writing, which Patrick, the sinner, unlearned indeed, has written in Ireland, that no one may ever say, if I have done or demonstrated anything according to the will of God, however little, that it was my ignorance [that did it]. But judge ye and let it be most truly believed, that it has been the gift of God."

These bare, historically verifiable facts are in stark contrast to the popular legends that have grown up around his name: his driving the snakes out of Ireland, his explaining the Trinity with the use of a shamrock, his single-handed missionary accomplishments, which actually took many missionaries and several generations to achieve. The significance of his connection with several places in Ireland is also dubious, for example, Croagh Patrick, and Saul and Downpatrick. Even the place of his death and burial is uncertain. The cult of Patrick spread from Ireland to the numerous Irish monasteries in Europe during the early Middle Ages, and it flourishes today in the United States and Australia. The most famous church in the United States is dedicated to him, St. Patrick's in New York City. St. Patrick's Day is celebrated by people of all ethnic backgrounds by the wearing of the green and parades. His feast, which is on the General Roman Calendar, has always been given as March 17 in liturgical calendars and martyrologies. The Church of England, the Episcopal Church in the USA, and the Evangelical Lutheran Church in America observe his feast on this day, and he is also commemorated on the Russian Orthodox calendar.

Saint Patrick, Bishop of Ireland by Giovanni Battista Tiepolo (1696–1770)

BIBLIOGRAPHY

Bieler, Ludwig. *Studies on the Life and Legend of St. Patrick.* Ed. Richard Sharpe. London: Variorum reprints, 1986.

De Poar, Déaglán. *Patrick, the Pilgrim Apostle of Ireland: St. Patrick's Confessio and Epistola.* Ed. Máire B. de Paor. Dublin: Veritas, 1998.

Patrick. *The Book of Letters of Saint Patrick the Bishop.* Ed. and trans. D. R. Howlett. Dublin: Four Courts Press, 1994.

18 Cyril of Jerusalem, bishop and Doctor of the Church

Cyril of Jerusalem (ca. 315–ca. 386) was the bishop of Jerusalem from ca. 350 until his death and is a Doctor of the Church, primarily because of his brilliant catechesis, preserved in a series of twenty-three homilies addressed to baptismal candidates and to the newly baptized. Born in or near Jerusalem and well educated there, especially in Scripture, he was ordained a priest in 345 and given the task of instructing catechumens. He became bishop ca. 350 and was soon embroiled in controversy with Acacius, the metropolitan of Caesarea, who had consecrated him, over the relative importance of their two sees (Acacius regarded Jerusalem as one of his suffragan sees) and over doctrinal matters as well. Charged with insubordination, having sold church goods for the sake of the poor, and with supporting the teaching of the Council of Nicaea (325), Cyril refused to appear before a synod of bishops in Caesarea to answer the complaints, either because there would be too many Arians present and he would not get a fair hearing or because he refused to be judged by other than a patriarchal synod. The emperor was drawn into the dispute, and Cyril was exiled in 357. He was recalled two years later after the Council of Seleucia reinstated him and deposed his accuser, Acacius. However, Cyril was banished twice more after that. Indeed, he would spend sixteen of his thirty-five years as a bishop in exile.

The second banishment occurred when he was accused of having sold a gold-brocaded vestment that the emperor Constantine [May 21] had given to Makarios of Jerusalem and that was later seen being worn on stage by a comedian. When the emperor Constantius died in 361, his successor, Julian, recalled all exiled bishops, including Cyril. In 367 yet another emperor, Valens, exiled all the bishops whom Julian had recalled. When the orthodox Theodosius I became emperor, Cyril was restored for the third and last time, only to find Jerusalem in civil and ecclesiastical chaos. Gregory of Nyssa [January 10] wrote a vivid description of the situation in his *Warning Against Pilgrims*.

On doctrinal matters Cyril was attacked by both sides (perhaps because he never used the Council of Nicaea's technical word *homoousios* [Gk., "of the same substance"]): first, by those loyal to the teaching of the Council of Nicaea that Christ is *homoousios* with God the Father, and then by the Arians, who held that Christ was the greatest of creatures but not divine. Nevertheless, he participated fully in the Council of Constantinople (381) and consented readily to its teachings, which included Nicaea's term *homoousios*. Cyril was named a Doctor of the Church in 1882. His feast is on the General Roman Calendar and is also celebrated on this day by the Russian Orthodox Church. He is commemorated today by the Church of England and the Episcopal Church in the USA.

BIBLIOGRAPHY

Walker, Peter W. L. *Holy City, Holy Places?: Christian Attitudes to Jerusalem and the Holy Land in the Fourth Century.* New York: Oxford University Press, 1990.

19 Joseph, husband of Mary

Saint Joseph by Guercino (1591–1666)

Joseph (first century) was the husband of the Blessed Virgin Mary, the mother of Jesus. In the New Testament Joseph is mentioned as the father of Jesus in John 1:45 and 6:42, in Luke 4:22, and in Luke's genealogy of Jesus (Luke 3:23). He appears also in the infancy narratives (Matt. 1–2; Luke 1–2), where he is said to be of Davidic descent (Matt. 1:2–16, 20; Luke 1:27; 3:23–38). According to Luke, Joseph was born in Bethlehem, but lived with Mary in Nazareth, returning to Bethlehem at one point to register for a census (Luke 2:1). Matthew, however, indicates that they lived in Bethlehem and moved to Nazareth after their flight to Egypt (Matt. 2:22–23). Joseph was a carpenter by trade (Matt. 13:55) and trained his son as a carpenter as well (Mark 6:3).

Mary was betrothed to Joseph, but she was already pregnant with Jesus before Joseph took her into his home. The Hebrew Scriptures (Deut. 22:13–21) provided harsh penalties for the infidelity of a betrothed woman if her intended spouse did not choose simply to divorce her. At first, Joseph, being a "righteous" or "just" man, chose the latter option in order to protect Mary from shame. But an angel told Joseph in a dream to take Mary into his home, that the child was conceived through the Holy Spirit, and that his name would be Jesus. In yet another dream, Joseph was also told to take Mary and Jesus to Egypt and to remain there until Herod's slaughter of newborns had come to an end with Herod's own death.

Joseph disappears from the New Testament after the family's pilgrimage to Jerusalem (Luke 2:42–52), which suggests that Joseph died sometime before Jesus' public ministry. There are a number of apocryphal writings that attempt to fill in the blanks of Joseph's personal history. One in particular is of interest, the *Protevangelium of James* (second century), because it represents an effort to explain how the New Testament could refer to Jesus' brothers and sisters (Mark 3:31; 6:3; Matt. 12:46; 13:55; Luke 8:19; John 7:3–5; 1 Cor. 9:5; Gal. 1:19) without undermining the Church's teaching about the virginity of Mary. The *Protevangelium* claims that Joseph was an aged widower with children when he married Mary.

The special veneration of Joseph seems to have originated in the East, where the equally apocryphal *History of Joseph the Carpenter,* a fifth- or sixth-century Greek document, enjoyed widespread popularity. The Copts observed a feast in his honor in the seventh century. The earliest evidence for the cult in the West is in ninth-century Irish martyrologies. Among its earliest promoters in the fourteenth and fifteenth centuries were Vincent Ferrer [April 5], Bridget of Sweden [July 23], and Bernardino of Siena [May 20], partly, it is said, in reaction to medieval mystery plays that made fun of Joseph. Joseph's feast had been celebrated in England before 1100, but was not introduced into the Roman calendar until 1479, thirty-five years after Bernardino's death, and by a pope (Sixtus IV) who, like Bernardino, was a Franciscan. In the sixteenth and early seventeenth centuries devotion to Joseph was popularized by Teresa of Ávila [October 15], who dedicated her reformed Carmelite motherhouse to him, and Francis de Sales [January 24]. Ignatius of Loyola [July 31] also actively promoted the devotion in the sixteenth century. Joseph was declared patron saint of the universal Church by Pope Pius IX at the close of the First Vatican Council in 1870. He is also the patron saint of a happy death, workers, fathers of families, and many countries, including Russia, Canada, Mexico, Peru, Belgium, Korea, Austria, Vietnam, Bohemia, and the mission to China. Many religious congregations, hospitals, and churches are dedicated to him, and his name has been popular for baptisms and confirmations alike. The most impressive monument to Joseph is the basilica dedicated to him in Montreal, Quebec, in Canada, inspired by Brother André Bessette [January 6]. The traditional depiction of Joseph holding a lily is derived from the various apocryphal writings about him.

His feast has the rank of a Solemnity on the General Roman Calendar, and it is also celebrated by the Church of England, the Episcopal Church in the USA, and the Evangelical Lutheran Church in America. In the East his feast is celebrated on the first Sunday after Christmas. A second feast of Joseph the Worker was inaugurated by Pope Pius XII in 1955 to counteract a Communist holiday on May 1. The new feast replaced that of the Patronage of St. Joseph, later called the Solemnity of Joseph, celebrated since 1913 on the third Wednesday after Easter. Joseph's name was added to the list of saints in the Canon of the Mass (now the First Eucharistic Prayer) by Pope John XXIII in 1962.

BIBLIOGRAPHY

Brown, Raymond F. *The Birth of the Messiah.* Garden City, NY: Doubleday, 1977.

Filas, Francis L. *The Man Nearest to Christ: Nature and Historic Development of the Devotion to St. Joseph.* Milwaukee, WI: Bruce, 1944.

20 Cuthbert, bishop

Cuthbert (ca. 634–87) is the most popular saint in northern England. Born of a comfortable Anglo-Saxon family, he became a monk at Melrose in 651, becoming prior about ten years later. After the Synod of Whitby (664), at which Roman liturgical practices were adopted for the whole of England, Cuthbert became prior at Lindisfarne, with the difficult task of persuading many of the monks to accept the new practices, but he later relinquished the office to live a solitary life for some nine years. By 685, however, his saintly qualities, especially his kindness and extraordinary patience and forbearance, were so widely celebrated that he was chosen by the king and the archbishop of Canterbury as bishop of Hexham. Almost immediately he and the bishop of Lindisfarne exchanged sees. He was known for his preaching and teaching, his devotion to visiting parishes throughout his diocese, his ministry to the poor, the sick, and the bereaved, and for his own ascetical lifestyle. Many thought he had gifts of prophecy and healing. He died after only two years of episcopal ministry and following a painful illness on March 20, 687. His cult began immediately thereafter. Eleven years later, when his body was exhumed for reburial in the church of Lindisfarne, the body was found to be uncorrupted. This fact gave great stimulus to the cult.

The Vikings destroyed Lindisfarne in 875. Cuthbert's incorrupt remains and relics were eventually placed in a church built over his shrine in Durham in 999 and later transferred to the new Norman cathedral in 1104. They rest in the Durham cathedral today. More than 135 churches in England and some 17 in Scotland are dedicated to Cuthbert. He is depicted in a famous fifteenth-century stained-glass window in York Minster cathedral. Although his feast is not on the General Roman Calendar, it is celebrated on this day by the Church of England and the Episcopal Church in the USA.

21 Nicholas of Flüe, hermit; Thomas Cranmer, bishop

Nicholas of Flüe (1417–87), a hermit, is the patron saint of Switzerland. Born into a family of Swiss farmers at Flueli near Unterwalden, he belonged from an early age to a group of laity known as the Friends of God, who lived ascetical lives of prayer and service to one's neighbor and who meditated on the Passion of Christ. He served in the army and in 1447 married and eventually had ten children. In 1467, with his wife's consent, he resigned his civil offices as a magistrate and judge and left his wife and children with the intention of taking up the life of a hermit near Strasbourg, the headquarters of the Friends of God. He was advised, however, to turn back because of the hostility of the Alsatians toward the Swiss. On his return, he was struck with a severe gastric disorder. It is said that he subsisted on the Eucharist alone thereafter, spending the next twenty years in a small cottage with an attached chapel at Ranft, not far from his home. Each day he rose at midnight from his bed, consisting of a wooden plank and stone pillow, and prayed into the morning and then prayed again in the early evening.

His reputation as a holy man (known as Brother Klaus) attracted afternoon visitors seeking his advice on spiritual and even worldly matters, including the resolution of a dispute involving the formation of the Swiss Confederation and the prevention of civil war. After a week of intense suffering, he died on March 21, 1487, and was immediately hailed as a patriot and a saint. His cult was approved in 1669, and he was canonized in 1947. In Switzerland his feast is celebrated on September 25. Nicholas is not on the General Roman Calendar.

The Benedictines and Cistercians commemorate the death of *Benedict of Nursia* [July 11] on this day. The Church of England commemorates the Reformation martyr *Thomas Cranmer* (1489–1556), archbishop of Canterbury.

22 Nicholas Owen, martyr; Jonathan Edwards, theologian

Nicholas Owen (ca. 1550–1606) was a Jesuit lay brother and martyr. Born in Oxfordshire of Catholic (recusant) parents, he was trained as a carpenter, a trade that enabled him to construct hiding places for priests—single-handedly and at night—over a period of twenty-six years. Several of them still exist. He was imprisoned three times, the last time giving himself up in order to deter the authorities from pursuing some priests who had escaped. Nicholas was taken to the Tower and tortured on the rack. When he continued to refuse to divulge information regarding the whereabouts of priests, he was racked one last time, on March 22, 1606, during which his inner organs burst out of his body. He died in agony. He was beatified in 1929 and then canonized by Pope Paul VI in 1970 as one of the Forty Martyrs of England and Wales. Their feast is celebrated on October 25. Nicholas's individual feast is not on the General Roman Calendar.

Lutherans commemorate *Jonathan Edwards,* well-known American Protestant theologian, preacher, and missionary to Native Americans, who died on March 22, 1758, while serving as the first president of the College of New Jersey (now Princeton University).

23 Turibius of Mongrovejo, bishop

Turibius of Mongrovejo (1538–1606) was archbishop of Lima and is the patron saint of Peru. Born in Mayorga, Spain (where his father was governor), he was chosen archbishop of Lima while serving as a lay professor of civil and canon law at Salamanca University. He pleaded in vain with King Philip II to be relieved of this appointment. Pope Pius V dispensed Turibius from the usual steps to ordination so that he could receive minor and major orders and then episcopal consecration in a relatively short time. Arriving in Lima in 1581, he found that his new diocese consisted of thousands of square miles, including coastline, mountains, and jungle. It took him seven years to make his first visitation. There were few roads (most routes were better suited to goats and deer, it was said, than to human beings), dangerous conditions, a scandal-ridden clergy (many were rarely in their parishes, while some were engaged in the slave trade), widespread abuses by Spanish conquerors driven by greed and the lust for power, and a poorly educated native Catholic population.

Turibius built churches, hospitals, and religious houses, approved a new catechism in Spanish and two Indian languages, held councils and synods in conformity with the mandate of the Council of Trent (1545–63), and in 1591 established the first seminary in the New World. He also took upon himself the task of learning the Indian dialects, and he championed natives' rights against their oppressive civil rulers, with whom he was often in conflict. He was indefatigable in his service to the poor, Indians and Spaniards alike. He is reported to have personally baptized a half million people, including Rose of Lima [August 23] and Martin de Porres [November 3]. He died on

March 23, 1606, in Santa Clara during one of his lengthy pastoral journeys and was canonized in 1726. His cult has been popular in Latin America for more than three centuries, and his feast is now on the General Roman Calendar.

The Episcopal Church in the USA commemorates *Gregory the Illuminator* (d. ca. 332) [September 30] on this day. He is the "apostle to" and patron saint of Armenia.

24 Catherine of Sweden, abbess; Oscar Romero, bishop and martyr; Walter Hilton, friar

Catherine of Sweden (ca. 1331–81), also known as Catherine of Vadstena, was the daughter of Bridget of Sweden [July 23] and abbess of Vadstena, a monastery founded by her mother. She entered an arranged marriage that was never consummated. She and her husband followed an ascetical way of life that was indistinguishable from that of a religious. Catherine sought always to emulate her saintly mother; she followed her to Rome in 1350, with the blessing of her husband, who died soon thereafter. Bridget had gone to Rome the previous year in hopes of restoring the papacy to the city (the popes resided at this time in Avignon, France) and of securing papal approval for the new monastery in Vadstena. But the years in Rome were very difficult for Catherine. The city was unsafe and, because she and her mother gave away so much to the poor, their living conditions were stark. Catherine was also engaged in a constant struggle with her mother to try to persuade her to return to Sweden. That never happened. Bridget died in Rome soon after returning from a pilgrimage to the Holy Land. It was left to Catherine to return her mother's remains to Sweden.

Upon her return to Sweden, Catherine asked to be received as a novice in Vadstena, but she was immediately acclaimed as abbess. She set about to reorganize the community, but was asked to leave for Rome to promote her mother's cause for canonization. Because of the confusion created by the Great Schism (1378–1417), in which there were two (and later three) claimants to the Chair of Peter, nothing was finally resolved. After five years (1375–80), Catherine returned home. While in Rome, however, she did receive papal approval for the Brigittine order. She arrived at Vadstena in July 1380 and died the following March 24. Catherine's mother, Bridget, was canonized in 1391. The name of Catherine was also added to the *Roman Martyrology* and her cult approved in 1484, but she was never formally canonized. Her feast is not on the General Roman Calendar.

March 24 is also the day on which *Oscar Romero* (1917–80), archbishop of San Salvador, was martyred for his defense of the poor and the powerless. He had been denounced by some of his fellow bishops, hated by the military and many in the wealthiest classes, and even distrusted by the Vatican. His weekly sermons, broadcast throughout El Salvador by radio, contained a list of violations of human rights. "A church that does not unite itself to the poor in order to denounce from the place of the poor the injustice committed against them," he wrote, "is not truly the Church of Jesus Christ." A few weeks before his assassination he sent a letter to U.S. president Jimmy Carter, appealing for an end to further military assistance to the ruling junta.

Archbishop Oscar Arnulfo Romero, 1979

On March 23, the day before his death, Romero appealed directly to members of the military, urging them to disobey illegal and immoral orders: "In the name of God, in the name of our tormented people whose cries rise up to heaven, I beseech you, I beg you, I command you, *stop the repression.*" The next day, as he was celebrating Mass in the chapel of the Carmelite Sisters' hospital for cancer patients, where he lived, a single rifle shot was fired from the rear of the chapel. The archbishop was struck in the heart and died almost instantly. His martyrdom was strikingly similar to that of Thomas Becket [December 29] in Canterbury Cathedral. Two weeks before his murder, the archbishop had acknowledged in an interview that he had received death threats. "If they kill me," he said, "I shall rise again in the Salvadoran people." An individual bishop may die, he declared, "but the church of God—the people—will never die." At an ecumenical prayer service honoring the martyrs and faith witnesses of the twentieth century, held in the Roman Colosseum on May 7, 2000, Archbishop Romero was the only person named in the prayer for the martyrs of the Americas. The prayer honored "zealous pastors like the unforgettable Oscar Romero, killed at the altar while celebrating the eucharistic sacrifice." Although not yet beatified by his own Church, Oscar Romero is commemorated on this day by the Church of England. He was the subject of the 1989 film *Romero.*

The Church of England also commemorates on this same day *Walter Hilton* (ca. 1343–96), an English Augustinian friar, mystic, and spiritual writer known for his concept of the "luminous darkness" of mortification, namely, the transition from disordered self-love to love of God. This concept has been compared to John of the Cross's [December 14] "dark night of the soul."

BIBLIOGRAPHY

Brockman, James R. *Romero: A Life.* Maryknoll, NY: Orbis Books, 1989.
Romero, Oscar. *Voice of the Voiceless.* Maryknoll, NY: Orbis Books, 1985

25 The Annunciation of the Lord; Dismas, the Good Thief; Margaret Clitherow, martyr; Lucy Filippini, foundress

When the feast of the Nativity, or Christmas, was assigned to December 25 before the middle of the fourth century, it was almost inevitable that a feast of the conception of Jesus would be placed nine months beforehand. The basic account of the *Annunciation* appears in Luke 1:26–38. The angel Gabriel appeared in Nazareth to a virgin betrothed to Joseph [March 19], of the house of David. Gabriel proclaimed what has become the first portion of the Hail Mary prayer: "Hail, favored one! The Lord is with you!" (Luke 1:28). Gabriel then predicted the birth of Jesus and his eternal rule over the "house of Jacob." A confused and troubled Mary asked the angel how this was to happen, and Gabriel told her not to be afraid and promised that the Holy Spirit would cause her to conceive (Luke 1:35).

The interchange between Mary and Gabriel provides the opening for the Angelus prayer: "The angel of the Lord declared unto Mary, and she conceived of the Holy Spirit." Mary's response to Gabriel was one of humble submission to God's will: "Behold, I am the handmaid of the Lord. May it be done to me according to your word." It is one of the few direct quotations from Mary in the New Testament, and her "*Fiat*" (Lat., "May it be done") epitomized her role as a servant of God and a disciple par excellence.

The feast of the Annunciation has the highest liturgical rank, that of a Solemnity, on the General Roman Calendar. It is also celebrated in all of the major Christian liturgical traditions. The event of the Annunciation is depicted in a famous mosaic in the Roman basilica of St. Mary Major.

Other saints whose feasts fall on this day include *Dismas, the Good Thief,* who said to Jesus on the Cross, "Jesus, remember me when you come into your kingdom" (Luke 23:42). To which Jesus replied: "Amen, I say to you, today you will be with me in paradise" (v. 43). The *Roman Martyrology* assigns his death to this day because, as Tertullian and Augustine [August 28] both attested, March 25 was traditionally regarded as the day of Christ's death as well. Dismas is the patron saint of prisoners, thieves, and funeral directors.

Margaret Clitherow, martyred on this day in 1586 for hiding priests, is one of the Forty Martyrs of England and Wales, canonized in 1970 and commemorated on October 25. *Lucy Filippini* (1672–1732) was the foundress in 1704 of the Pontifical Institute of Religious Teachers, known simply as the Filippini Sisters, and devoted originally to the education of poor girls. She was beatified in 1926 and canonized in 1930.

26 Ludger of Münster, bishop

Ludger (Liuger) of Münster (ca. 742–809) was bishop of Münster and is its patron saint; he was the founder of a Benedictine monastery on his family estate at Werden. Born of noble and wealthy parents in Frisia, he was educated at Utrecht and York and ordained a priest ca. 777, after which he built several churches, including one at Dokkum, where Boniface [June 5] had died. The churches were destroyed during the Saxon invasions in 784. Two years later Ludger rebuilt the churches, was consecrated bishop of Münster in 804, and built there a monastery for canons under the Rule of Chrodegang of Metz [March 6]. He evangelized Westphalia and Eastphalia and is said to have done more to convert the Saxons by his gentleness than the emperor Charlemagne could accomplish through repressive measures.

On one occasion, Ludger was denounced to the emperor for giving away too much money to the poor to the detriment of the ornamentation of churches, but he never fell out of imperial favor. After saying Mass and preaching in two different places on Passion Sunday, March 26, 809, he died that evening at his monastery in Werden, where his relics were kept until 1984, when they were transferred to Münster. There are many representations of him in that diocese. His feast is recorded in liturgical books as early as the ninth century, but is not included on the General Roman Calendar.

On this day the Greek and Russian Orthodox Churches celebrate the feast of the archangel *Gabriel* [September 29] as a synaxis, or extension, of the feast of the Annunciation.

27 Rupert, bishop

Rupert (d. ca. 710–20) was the bishop of Worms and of Salzburg. He was Frankish and possibly Irish by birth. Having been expelled for whatever reason from his bishopric at Worms, he was invited by the duke of the Bavarians to evangelize his territories, which also comprised parts of present-day Austria. Rupert was a successful missionary bishop in the villages along the Danube River as far as Hungary. Upon his return he was given jurisdiction over Juvavum (Salzburg), a Roman town then in ruins. Using a donation of land from the duke, Rupert built a church and a monastery (with himself as its abbot), both dedicated to St. Peter [June 29], a school, and other necessary buildings. Later he built Nonnberg, a monastery for women, and installed his niece as abbess. He continued his missionary journeys, returning eventually to Salzburg when he felt his life ebbing away, sometime between 710 and 720. Rupert is said to have inaugurated the three-hundred-year-old tradition of the abbot-bishop in this part of Europe. He died on Easter Sunday, and his relics rest today in the new cathedral. His feast is not on the General Roman Calendar.

28 Hesychius of Jerusalem, priest

Hesychius of Jerusalem (d. ca. 450) was a monk in his early life, ordained a priest of Jerusalem in 412, and the author of a now lost history of the Church, cited at the Second Council of Constantinople (553), that endorsed the teachings of Cyril of Alexandria [June 27] against the Nestorians (those who held that in Jesus there were two separate persons, one human, one divine). He was known for his modesty and gentleness. Indeed, his writings display none of the polemical tone one finds in other contemporary works, including those of Jerome [September 30]. Hesychius was a strong supporter of the orthodox Alexandrians in the controversies leading up to the decisive Council of Chalcedon (451), but he may have died before the council actually met. Basil the Great [January 2] informs us that Hesychius wrote commentaries on all of the books of the Bible, but only those on Leviticus and the Psalms still exist. There are also meditations on Job, a few homilies on the Presentation of the Lord in the Temple, some fragments on the prophets, and some homilies on the Blessed Virgin Mary. In his writings, he avoided minutiae and personal digressions and focused instead on the Risen Christ, the light set on the lampstand of the Cross and the guarantor of our own new life. In the Eucharist, he insisted, "our bodies become the body of Christ." He is commemorated on this day by the Russian Orthodox Church, but his feast is not on the General Roman Calendar.

29 Jonas and Barachisius, martyrs

Jonas and *Barachisius* (d. ca. 326/27) were Persian Christians who were cruelly martyred by King Sapor II at the very time when the Roman Empire under Constantine had ended its own persecution of Christians. When Constantine heard of the great numbers (perhaps as many as eighteen thousand) who were put to death in the main cities after excruciating torture, he wrote to the king and asked for clemency, but to no avail. Churches and monasteries were destroyed, and Christians were required to sacrifice to the gods. Those who obeyed were honored; those who did not were tortured mercilessly.

Jonas and Barachisius, two Christian monks, heard of the persecution and set out for Bardiaboc, where some Christians were being held. They found nine awaiting execution and encouraged them to persevere. After the nine were martyred, Jonas and Barachisius were reported to the same judges who had condemned the nine. They refused to offer sacrifice. The two were then separated. Jonas was forced to lie face down with a sharp stake under the middle of his body, while he was heavily flogged. He was then bound and thrown out into the cold winter night. Barachisius was summoned and told that Jonas had renounced his faith. But he knew that was a lie. In fact, Barachisius was so eloquent in defense of his faith that the judges feared he might convert those who heard him, so they postponed his hearing until night. When they realized that they could not prevail over him, they doused him in hot pitch and hung him by one foot all night long in his cell. The next morning Jonas was brought in and told that Barachisius had apostatized. He too knew that to be a lie. When asked if it would not be better to save himself, Jonas replied: "If a person loses his life in this world for the sake of Christ, . . . he will be renewed in light imperishable when the Lord comes again to make all things new." His fingers and toes were cut off, he was thrown into a vessel of burning pitch, and then his body was crushed and his bones broken. Barachisius, in his turn, was impaled on stakes, placed under the same press, and had burning pitch poured down his throat. The vivid details of their martyrdom were supplied by Isaiah, a knight in the service of the king and an eyewitness to the events. The feast of Jonas and Barachisius is not on the General Roman Calendar.

30 John Climacus, abbot; Karl Rahner, theologian; Thea Bowman, religious

John Climacus (ca. 570–ca. 649) was a monk and abbot of Mount Sinai. Born in Palestine, he was married early in life and became a monk upon the death of his wife. After a period of time in community, he took up the solitary life, coming to church for Mass with other hermits on weekends. It was while he was in solitude that John wrote the work that gave him his name, Climacus (Lat., "ladder"), usually called *The Ladder to Paradise*. It was a volume on monastic spirituality, touching upon the virtues and vices of monastic life, both communal and eremetical. It held up as the ideal virtue that of *apatheia* (Gk., "passive disinterestedness"), or complete mastery over one's feelings and emotions. There are thirty steps of the ladder, each with a chapter in the book, corresponding with the age of Christ at his baptism by John [June 24, August 29] in the Jordan. The work has had great influence in the East, having been translated into Syriac, Arabic, Georgian, Armenian, Slavonic, Rumanian, and Russian, and is read today in Orthodox monasteries every Lent. It was translated into Latin by the Franciscans in the fourteenth century.

In his writings, John was careful not to depreciate the body for the sake of exalting the soul. "How can I run away from [my body] when it will be my companion at the resurrection?" he asked. What we strive for is not the soul without the body, but "a body made holy." Although asceticism and obedience are indispensable tools of the spiritual life, he reminded his readers, they are useless without faith, hope, and love, which "bind and secure the unity of the whole."

At age seventy or thereabouts John Climacus was chosen as abbot of Mount Sinai, but after four years he returned to his hermitage. He died at about age eighty. His feast is not on the General Roman Calendar, but it is celebrated in the East on the fourth Sunday of Lent as well as on this day by the Greek and Russian Orthodox Churches.

On this day, *Karl Rahner* (1904–84), a Jesuit and the leading Catholic theologian of the twentieth century, died. Rahner's whole theological approach, like that of his principal mentor Thomas Aquinas [January 28], was sacramental, centered always on grace as the presence of God to the individual person and to the whole created order. For Rahner, religious experience is not to be found in some separate compartment of human experience, but in the ordinary, grace-filled moments of life. At the core of human knowing and loving is the drive toward union with God. His vision of the Church was that of a "world church" and of salvation as available to all people of good will. Toward the end of his life he said that, as a writer and teacher, he "tried in this ordinary everyday way to serve God."

March 30 is also the day of the death of *Thea Bowman* (1937–90), an African American Franciscan sister. Thea Bowman helped to found the Institute of Black Catholic Studies at Xavier University in New Orleans, which became the institutional base for her many lectures and workshops throughout the country. She continued her speaking and her travels even after 1984, when she was diagnosed with breast cancer. At the end, she was bald from chemotherapy treatments and in a wheelchair. Her prayer in her remaining years was: "Lord, let me live until I die," that is, "to live, love, and serve fully until death comes." "I don't make sense of suffering," she once said. "I try to make sense of life."

Thea Bowman

31 Stephen of Mar Saba, monk; John Donne, priest; Anne Frank, martyr

Stephen of Mar Saba (d. 794) was the nephew of John Damascene [December 4], who, upon abandoning his distinguished theological career, took a ten-year-old Stephen with him to Mar Saba, the most famous monastery in Palestine. John mentored Stephen until his own death in 749, when Stephen was twenty-four. Stephen then began an eight-year period of service to the community: as guest master, cantor, and medical dispenser. But he felt a strong call to the eremetical life and asked the abbot to be released for it. The abbot, or *igumen*, suggested a compromise. Stephen could lead a hermit's life (which he did during the week), but he must be available to others for counsel (which he was on Saturdays and Sundays). Stephen thereupon pinned a note on the door of his cell: "Forgive me, fathers, in the name of the Lord, but please do not disturb me except on Saturdays or Sundays." He went through periods of almost total solitude, and then more modified ones. Throughout, he showed great compassion not only for other persons, but also for animals, even worms, and he displayed an extraordinary gift for assisting those in great difficulty. "There is nothing of value in life," he often said, "except the soul's gain, but the soul's gain is to be found only in the love of God."

At the end of his biography of Stephen, his disciple Leontius wrote: "Whatever help, spiritual or material, he was asked to give, he gave. He received and honored all with the same kindness, even unbelievers. He possessed nothing and lacked nothing. In total poverty he possessed all things." He died on March 30, 794. His feast is not on the General Roman Calendar, but he is commemorated on this day by the Russian Orthodox Church.

The Church of England, the Episcopal Church in the USA, and the Evangelical Lutheran Church in America commemorate the English poet *John Donne* (1572–1631) on this day. Born and raised a Catholic, he became a priest of the Church of England and one of its most accomplished preachers.

Sometime toward the end of March 1945, a few weeks before Bergen-Belsen was liberated on April 15, *Anne Frank* (1929–45), a young German Jewish girl, died of typhus there. She was one of humanity's most famous martyrs, having provided a unique witness to the Holocaust in her diary, written while in hiding before her capture.

APRIL

1 Hugh of Grenoble, bishop; Frederick Denison Maurice, priest; Mary the Egyptian, hermit

Hugh of Grenoble (1052–1132) was the bishop of Grenoble for fifty-two years and the virtual cofounder of the Carthusians. Born at Châteauneuf d'Isère, in the Dauphiné region of France, and well educated as a young man, he became a canon in the nearby Valence cathedral (while still a layman), then secretary to the bishop of Die, who was also a papal legate. Hugh accompanied the bishop to the synod of Avignon, which reviewed the severe pastoral problems in the now vacant diocese of Grenoble, including simony, usury, violations of clerical celibacy, religious ignorance, and lay control of church property. Hugh so impressed the delegates to the synod that he was elected as the new bishop of Grenoble and was consecrated in Rome by the pope himself, Gregory VII [May 25].

Hugh took up his episcopal ministry as an avid reformer in the tradition of Gregory VII. He dealt with the abuses in the diocese, restored the cathedral, made civic improvements in the town (building a new bridge, a marketplace, and three hospitals), founded houses of canons regular, and gave a charter to Bruno [October 6] for the mountainous estate of the Grand Chartreuse, where Bruno and six companions formed an eremetical monastic community that developed into the Carthusian order. Hugh's own father died as a Carthusian monk at the age of one hundred, and Hugh himself would spend much time at the monastery for retreats and prayer. He was renowned for his preaching, his skill as a confessor, and his generosity to the poor. He was also such an ardent defender of the papacy against the encroachments of temporal rulers, including kings and emperors, that he was at one time forced into exile, only to return triumphantly to the acclaim of his people. After attempting unsuccessfully on several occasions to resign from his see for a life of solitude and prayer, he died on April 1, 1132, in the company of the monks and was canonized only two years later. His feast is not on the General Roman Calendar.

The Church of England and the Episcopal Church in the USA commemorate *Frederick Denison Maurice* (d. 1872) on this day. He was a priest of the Church of England, a professor of theology at Cambridge University, and a strong advocate of the social mission of the Church. Also on this day the Greek and Russian Orthodox Churches celebrate the feast of *Mary the Egyptian,* a fifth-century hermit.

2 Francis of Paola, hermit

Francis of Paola (1416–1507) was the founder of the Franciscan Minim Friars and is patron saint of Italian seafarers, naval officers, and navigators (because many of his reported miracles were connected with the sea). Born at Paolo in Calabria, in southern Italy, he lived for a year (at age thirteen) as a Franciscan friar, then took up the life of a hermit in a cave overlooking the sea. At age twenty he was joined by two companions. They called themselves the hermits of Brother Francis of Assisi [October 4]. After the neighbors built for them a chapel and three cells, others joined them. Following Franciscan ideals, they led lives marked by charity toward others, poverty, and penance, including a perpetual Lenten fast. They also had a special devotion to the Five Wounds of Christ and to the Blessed Virgin Mary. The community received papal approval in 1474. In 1492 Francis changed the community's name to Friars Minim to indicate that its members were "the least" of all religious. The order reached peak membership in the first half of the sixteenth century, but declined from the end of the eighteenth century. It is confined today to Italy and Spain.

Francis was renowned for his prophecies and miracles even during his lifetime, the last twenty-five years of which were spent in France, where, at the direct request of the pope, he helped prepare King Louis XI for his death in 1483. Francis also helped to restore peace between France and Brittany and between France and Spain. He died at Tours on April 2, 1507, was beatified only six years later, and then was canonized in 1519. His cult is particularly popular in Italy, France, and Mexico. He is depicted in the paintings of a number of celebrated artists, including Murillo, Velázquez, and Goya; is the subject of a sonata by Franz Liszt; and is in Victor Hugo's *Torquemada*. His feast is on the General Roman Calendar.

3 Richard of Chichester, bishop

Richard of Chichester (1197–1253) was the bishop of Chichester in England. Born at Wych (present-day Droitwich), he was educated at Oxford and Paris, and possibly also Bologna. Upon his return to England, he became chancellor of Oxford, then chancellor of the archdiocese of Canterbury, a position in which he earned a reputation for complete moral integrity. After the death of his friend, the archbishop, in 1240, Richard decided to become a priest and studied theology for two years with the Dominicans in Orleans. Ordained in 1242 (or 1243), he served as a parish priest in two places before being reappointed chancellor by the new archbishop of Canterbury. Two years later he was elected bishop of Chichester, but King Henry III and a faction in the cathedral chapter opposed him. A rival was elected and both sides appealed to the pope, who confirmed Richard's election and consecrated him in Lyons in 1245. Richard returned to Chichester, but the diocesan properties, confiscated earlier by the king and now in general disrepair, were not restored to him for two years—and then only under the threat of excommunication. In the meantime, Richard lived in a parish house, visited the diocese on foot, and cultivated figs in his spare time.

He would earn an excellent reputation as a diocesan bishop. He was kindly, accessible, compassionate toward sinners, generous to those stricken by famine, and personally above moral reproach. He also enforced ecclesiastical laws regarding the administration of the sacraments, celibacy, clerical residence, and clerical dress. The laity were obliged to attend Mass on Sundays and holy days and to know the Hail Mary, the Our Father, and the creed by heart. He was also active in promoting the Crusade, not for political reasons but to encourage pilgrimages to the Holy Land. He died at Dover on April 3, 1253, and was canonized in 1262. His shrine in Chichester Cathedral, where many cures were reported, was destroyed by order of King Henry VIII in 1538. However, Richard's cult was to some extent overshadowed by that of Thomas Becket [December 29], and only one medieval church was dedicated to him in England.

He is known for having composed the following prayer, which has been set to popular music: "Thanks be to thee, my Lord Jesus Christ, for all the benefits thou hast given me, for all the pains and insults which thou hast borne for me. O most merciful redeemer, friend and brother, may I know thee more clearly, love thee more dearly, and follow thee more nearly, day by day." Richard of Chichester's feast is not on the General Roman Calendar. He is commemorated on this day by the Episcopal Church in the USA.

4 Isidore of Seville, bishop and Doctor of the Church

A prolific writer, *Isidore of Seville* (ca. 560–636) is often considered the last of the Fathers of the Church. Born in Seville of a noble family, he succeeded his brother Leander as archbishop of Seville ca. 600, where he served for thirty-six years. He converted many Visigoths from Arianism and organized the Church of Spain through synods and councils, especially the Second Council of Seville (619) and the Fourth Council of Toledo (633), over which he presided. The latter council approved a creed based on Isidore's theology of the Trinity and the Incarnation, and fixed a uniform liturgy, the Mozarabic Rite (largely the work of Isidore himself), to be observed throughout Spain. The council also mandated the establishment of a cathedral school in every diocese and of colleges for the education of future priests. Significantly, it stipulated that only gifted students should be advanced to ordination; others were to be directed to the monastic life. As bishop, Isidore also devoted himself to education, the completion of the aforementioned Mozarabic missal and breviary, and an extensive ministry to the poor. He prepared himself for death by giving away all of his possessions, asking forgiveness from everyone he had injured in any way, and dressing in sackcloth and ashes. He died on April 4, 636, but there is no evidence of a cult in his memory until his remains were moved to Léon in 1063. The new shrine was on the route to the famous pilgrimage center at Compostela (traditionally regarded as the burial place of St. James the Apostle [July 25]), and so became popular in its own right as well. Isidore of Seville was canonized in 1598 and declared a Doctor of the Church in 1722.

His reputation in church history, however, is due principally to his many writings on a variety of subjects, including a twenty-volume etymological encyclopedia, a summary of doctrines, and rules for monks and nuns. His writings, although derivative in nature for the most part, were almost as frequently cited in the Middle Ages as were those of Gregory the Great [September 3]. His portrayal of the ideal bishop influenced Pope John XXIII (1958–63): "He who is set in authority for the education and instruction of the people for their good must be holy in all things and reprehensible in nothing. . . . Every bishop should be distinguished as much by his humility as by his authority. . . . He will also preserve that charity which excels all other gifts, and without which all virtue is nothing." His feast is on the General Roman Calendar.

April 4 is also the day on which *Martin Luther King Jr.* (1929–68), a Baptist minister, civil rights leader, and Nobel Prize winner, was assassinated in Memphis, Tennessee. He is commemorated on this day by the Episcopal Church in the USA. The Evangelical Lutheran Church in America commemorates him on January 15, the day of his birth, which is also a national holiday in the United States. The U.S. Catholic bishops recommended to the Vatican that his name be included on a list of twentieth-century martyrs announced by Pope John Paul II in 2000.

5 Vincent Ferrer, priest

Vincent Ferrer (1350–1419) was a renowned Dominican friar and preacher. Born at Valencia, Spain, the son of an English father who had migrated to Spain and a Spanish mother, he became a Dominican in 1367 and quickly distinguished himself as a philosopher and preacher. Ordained ca. 1374 (or perhaps 1379) by Cardinal Peter (Pedro) de

Luna, later the antipope Benedict XIII, he taught at Barcelona, studied theology in Toledo, and in 1379 became prior of the Dominican house in Valencia. As a preacher he was warmly received in various parts of France, Spain, and Italy. In some places he preached in the open air because there were no churches large enough to accommodate the crowds. As a man of his times, he stressed sin and damnation to the extent that he is also known as the "Angel of Judgment." Unfortunately, he was also a man of his times with regard to Jews, whom he viewed as "perfidious" and in need of conversion.

His life and ministry overlapped with the Great Western Schism (1378–1417), during most of which Vincent supported the claims of the Avignon popes over those in Rome. When his friend Cardinal Peter de Luna became the antipope Benedict XIII in 1394, he appointed Vincent his adviser and confessor as well as Master of the Sacred Palace, the pope's personal theologian. Gradually over time, however, Vincent began to see his friend as an obstacle to church unity. He unsuccessfully tried to persuade him to negotiate with Urban VI in Rome. By 1409 there were three, not two, claimants to the papacy, including Benedict XIII. Once again, Vincent urged his friend to resign for the sake of the unity of the Church. When Benedict refused, Vincent persuaded Ferdinand, king of Aragon, to withdraw his support for Benedict. The latter's credibility collapsed and the schism was eventually brought to an end by the Council of Constance in 1417 with the election of Martin V. Worn out by his travels and preaching throughout Europe, as well as his various diplomatic efforts on behalf of church unity, he spent the last three years of his life in Normandy and Brittany and died at Vannes in Brittany, on April 5, 1419. His cult developed immediately and he was canonized in 1455. He is patron saint of builders and plumbers. His feast is on the General Roman Calendar.

6 Peter of Verona, martyr; Michelangelo Buonarroti, artist

Peter of Verona (1205–52) was the first Dominican martyr. He is also known simply as Peter Martyr. Born in Verona of Cathar parents (Catharism denied the goodness and resurrection of the body and the usefulness of the sacraments), he nonetheless became a Dominican at age fifteen while a student at the University of Bologna, receiving the habit from Dominic himself [August 8]. He became prior of various

Dominican houses and was famous as a preacher in Lombardy. He was appointed an inquisitor for Milan and later for most of northern Italy, directing his attention mainly toward Cathars. His work aroused much animosity and he was assassinated, along with a Dominican companion, on his way from Como to Milan on April 6, 1252. One of his assailants later repented of his crime and his heresy and became a saintly Dominican lay brother. He reported that Peter had died with the words of the first martyr, St. Stephen [December 26], on his lips, forgiving his killers. Peter was canonized in 1253, and his tomb in Milan became a popular pilgrimage center. His fellow Dominican Fra Angelico [February 18] depicted him with a wound in his head, a dagger in his shoulder, and his fingers on his lips. His feast is not on the General Roman Calendar. It is celebrated on the Dominican calendar on June 4.

Lutherans commemorate the famous artist *Michelangelo Buonarroti* (d. 1564) on this day.

7 John Baptist de La Salle, priest

John Baptist de La Salle (1651–1719) was the founder of the Brothers of the Christian Schools and is the patron saint of schoolteachers. Born at Reims in northern France of a noble and wealthy family, he was tonsured at age eleven (the custom for young boys who were seriously considering studying for the priesthood) and became a canon of the Reims cathedral at age sixteen (another custom motivated by the need to generate income for one's education). He studied for the priesthood at Saint-Sulpice and was ordained in 1678. He later received a doctorate in theology in 1681.

He would have settled into a life of relative ease as a cathedral canon with an adequate personal fortune had not Adrien Nyel, a layman who had opened four free schools for the poor in Rouen, approached him for help in opening a similar school in Reims. John Baptist helped to open not one but two, and pupils flocked to them. The quality of teachers, however, was low. A priest in Paris urged him to open his own house for the training of teachers. He did so with a great measure of discomfort, since he regarded these teachers as below even his servants in status and living with them as "unbearable." However, he came to see it as God's will, much to the consternation of his own family. The criticism became so intense that he moved out of his own house into rented space. The date was June 24, 1682, the feast of John the Baptist.

By 1684 he had resigned his canonry, sold all of his worldly goods, and donated the proceeds for famine relief while dedicating the remainder of his life to education. In May of that year he and twelve others formed themselves into a community by taking the simple vow of obedience and adopting the name Brothers of the Christian Schools. He opened four more schools and established the first training college for teachers in Reims in 1686, and then others in Paris and Saint-Denis. He also opened a junior novitiate for students who might consider joining the Brothers. In 1694 he and twelve of the Brothers took perpetual vows, committing themselves to providing free education for the poor for the rest of their lives. Among the features of their still unapproved Rule was the forbidding of bodily mortifications beyond the normal fasting required by the Church. John Baptist believed that teaching was sufficiently demanding in itself and, if done properly, would develop the necessary self-discipline in the brothers. The final version of the Rule (following various drafts and revisions) received papal approval in 1726, seven years after his death.

When the exiled king of England, James II, invited John to establish a school for fifty young Irish gentlemen, John's ideas and educational techniques became known in influential social circles. Among his novel approaches were classroom teaching as opposed to one-on-one instruction, the use of the vernacular rather than Latin, insistence on students' silence during instruction, and the combination of religious education and technical training for future artisans. He also provided special instruction for troubled boys. There was much opposition to his efforts to educate the poor. Many believed that the poor should only be taught to perform manual labor. He and his work were also affected by the tensions created by the Jansenists (a group that was pessimistic about human nature and free will), then powerful in France and for whom he had no sympathy. There were also sharp conflicts within his religious community and at one point there were efforts to depose him as superior. Nevertheless, he remained in charge until his resignation in 1717. He died on Good Friday, April 7, 1719, having devoted most of his adult life to an apostolate for which he felt no natural attraction. He was canonized in 1900 and declared patron saint of all schoolteachers in 1950. His feast is on the General Roman Calendar.

8 Julie Billiart, foundress; Walter of Pontoise, abbot

Julie Billiart (1751–1816) was the foundress of the Sisters of Notre Dame de Namur. She was born at Cuvilly in Picardy, France, of a relatively prosperous family, but she had to take up manual labor after her family lost its money. At the same time, she became engaged in various parish ministries as a catechist and a visitor of the sick. When she was in her early twenties, her life was changed when an attempt was made on her father's life. A shot was fired through one of the windows in their home. Julie became so frightened that she developed a nervous paralysis that eventually prevented her from walking. She was completely disabled by the time she was thirty. She had to be smuggled out of Cuvilly during the French Revolution because of accusations that she was harboring priests and supporting the Church. When the worst of the Reign of Terror was over, she was moved to Amiens, where she met an aristocratic woman, Françoise Blin de Bourdon, who looked after her and eventually became the cofoundress of Julie's new institute. With the renewal of the persecution, both women moved to Bettencourt, where they met Father Joseph Varin. He assisted them in laying the foundations of the Institute of Notre Dame in 1803, with a dedication to Christian education, the instruction of the poor, and the training of teachers. The institute would combine the contemplative and the active lives, each depending upon the other. Father Varin provided them with a provisional Rule and the first sisters made their vows as religious in 1804. Julie also recovered from her paralysis that same year.

From 1804 until her death in 1816 she was constantly on the road, expanding her institute and opening schools in France and Belgium. However, when Father Varin was replaced as chaplain, problems developed for the two cofoundresses. The new chaplain was less sympathetic and turned the bishop against them. Julie and Françoise left Amiens and moved their motherhouse to Namur. Julie kept her community together by her constant visits from convent to convent and by her abiding cheerfulness and optimism. By the end of the nineteenth century the community had spread to the United States, Great Britain, and parts of Latin America and Africa, and in the twentieth, to other parts of Latin America and Africa, and to Japan and China as well. Julie Billiart died on April 8, 1816. She was beatified in 1906 and canonized in 1969. Her feast is not on the General Roman Calendar.

This is also the feast day of *Walter of Pontoise* (ca. 1030–95), the first abbot of the monastery at Pontoise, a position he did not covet and one he tried unsuccessfully to abandon more than once. He was an outspoken critic of corruption among the clergy, for which criticisms he sometimes endured much abuse. Although he had spent most of his life trying to find solitude, he proved to be an able administrator and committed reformer. Fittingly, he is the patron saint of those suffering stress. His feast is not on the General Roman Calendar.

9 Waldetrude, anchoress; Dietrich Bonhoeffer, martyr

Waldetrude (d. ca. 688), also known in France as Waltrude or Waudru, was a married woman whose husband, Vincent Madelgarius, and four children have all been venerated as saints: Landericus, who became bishop of Paris; Dentilin, who died at a very young age; Aldetrude, who became abbess of Mauberge; and Madelberta, who also became abbess of the same monastery. Waldetrude's own parents were venerated as saints, as was her sister. After the birth of their fourth child, Waldetrude's husband withdrew to an abbey he had founded at Haumont and took the name Vincent. Two years later Waldetrude took a similar path, moving into a small house in semisolitude. When her sister invited her to join the community at Mauberge, Waldetrude insisted that she could live a life of greater austerity outside the abbey. As in so many other instances, her reputation for sanctity began to attract visitors seeking spiritual direction. Consequently, she founded her own convent at Chateaulieu in the center of what is today the Belgian town of Mons, of which she is patron saint. She was known for her works of mercy, and miracles were attributed to her intercession. She died ca. 688 and her cult dates from at least the ninth century. Her feast is not on the General Roman Calendar.

On this day the Evangelical Lutheran Church in America, the Church of England, and the Episcopal Church in the USA commemorate the Lutheran pastor, theologian, and martyr *Dietrich Bonhoeffer* (1906–45), whose writings warned Christians against a soft understanding of Christian discipleship and who gave personal witness to Christ in the face of the enormous evil of Nazism. He was hanged on April 9 for his alleged involvement in a plot to assassinate Adolf Hitler. Bonhoeffer influenced Christian spirituality not only through his heroic witness to the gospel in the face of one of the greatest evils of human history, but also through such writings as *The Cost of Discipleship* and his *Letters and Papers from Prison.*

10 Magdalen of Canossa, foundress; William Law, spiritual writer; William of Ockham, friar; Pierre Teilhard de Chardin, scientist and theologian

Magdalen of Canossa (1774–1835) was the foundress of the congregation of the Daughters of Charity, also known as the Canossian Sisters of Charity. Born Maddalena Gabriella di Canossa into a wealthy family, she was only five years old when her father died and her mother abandoned the family to marry again. Magdalen was raised by a French governess and, after surviving a serious illness at age fifteen, she declared her intention to become a nun. She joined the Carmelites for a short time, but did not take to the strict rules of enclosure. She wished to be able to assist people in need, especially the poor. Indeed, she felt her vocation was captured in the words "to serve Christ in the poor." As her apostolate developed, she worked with the sick in hospitals and in their homes, organized retreats, gave money and food to the poor, and assisted delinquent and abandoned girls.

In 1799 she lodged two girls in her own house and by 1802 she had established a permanent refuge and school in the poorest and most notorious part of the city. She recruited teachers and outlined a form of religious life for them, but few were willing to stay for long. In 1808 she received permission to take over the buildings of a suppressed Augustinian monastery and use them for a school. The school flourished. She opened a second house in Venice and in 1812 drew up a definitive version of the Rule of her new congregation. She received papal approval in 1824. Additional houses were opened in various Italian cities. She also founded the Institute of the Sons of Charity, a congregation of priests and lay brothers to share in her work. For her, "Religious life is only the gospel translated into practice." She died in Verona on April 10, 1835. She was beatified in 1941 and canonized in 1988. Magdalen of Canossa's feast in not on the General Roman Calendar.

The Church of England and the Episcopal Church in the USA celebrate the feast of *William Law* (1686–1761) on this day. A prolific spiritual writer, he laid the foundation for the evangelical movement in England and the Great Awakening in America. The Church of England also commemorates today *William of Ockham* (ca. 1285–1347), a Franciscan friar who had great influence on medieval philosophy and theology. April 10 is also the day of death of *Pierre Teilhard de Chardin* (1881–1955), a Jesuit paleontologist and theologian, who viewed Christianity from an evolutionary perspective in which the movement of history is always toward greater complexity and higher consciousness, culminating in the Risen Christ. Forbidden to publish in his lifetime, his writings—rooted in science, but spiritual in character—became highly influential after his death, especially *The Divine Milieu* and *The Phenomenon of Man.*

11 Stanislaus, bishop and martyr; George Augustus Selwyn, bishop

Stanislaus (ca. 1030–79), or Stanislaw, was the bishop of Kraków and is the patron saint of Poland and the city of Kraków. Born in Szczepanow, Poland, he was ordained a priest and became a canon at the Kraków cathedral. He was appointed bishop of Kraków in 1072 and went on to establish a record as a great preacher, a reformer of his clergy, and a generous benefactor of the poor. At first he was supposedly on good terms with King Boleslaus (or Boleslaw) II, but some conflict developed that led to Stanislaus's death. Some Polish historians have questioned whether Stanislaus was a martyr in the strict sense of the word. They have viewed the bishop's death in political terms, that is, as retribution for his having sided with the king's brother, Ladislaus (Wladyslaw), against the king. But the more widely accepted explanation is that the king resented the bishop's attacks on him for his personal behavior and his treatment of his subjects.

When Stanislaus excommunicated the king, the king ordered the bishop killed. The king and his guards entered the cathedral and services were suspended. Other accounts have it that the bishop fled directly to the chapel of St. Michael upon hearing of the king's edict condemning him to death and that there was no incident at the cathedral itself. In any case, the king and his soldiers did pursue Stanislaus to the chapel of St. Michael just outside of the city. When the king ordered his guards to enter the chapel and kill Stanislaus, they refused, so the king himself stepped in and killed the bishop, on April 11, 1709. Stanislaus's martyrdom has been likened to those of Thomas Becket [December 29] and John Nepomucen [May 16], patron saint of the Czechs, both slain at the order of their kings. Because of Stanislaus's murder, Pope Gregory VII [May 25] placed the whole country under interdict until the king fell from power. Boleslaus escaped and sought refuge with his royal relatives in Hungary, where he eventually adopted the life of a penitent at the Benedictine monastery at Osiak.

Stanislaus's relics were moved in 1088 to the Kraków cathedral, and he was canonized in 1253. Many churches in Poland and the United States are dedicated to him. His cult is also strong in Lithuania, Byelorussia, and Ukraine. When Karol Wojtyla, archbishop of Kraków, was elected pope in 1978, he thought seriously of taking the name Stanislaus, but decided finally on John Paul II. Stanislaus's feast is on the General Roman Calendar. The Church of England, the Episcopal Church in the USA, and other churches in the Anglican Communion, particularly in New Zealand, commemorate *George Augustus Selwyn* (d. 1878), the first Anglican bishop of New Zealand, on this day.

12 Teresa of Los Andes, virgin

Teresa of Los Andes (1900–20) was a Carmelite nun who fashioned her spiritual life after those of St. Thérèse of Lisieux, also known as Theresa of the Child Jesus [October 1] and the Little Flower, and St. Teresa (or Theresa) of Ávila [October 15], whose name she took in religion, Teresa of Jesus. Born Juana Enriquita Josefina de los Sagrados Corozones Fernández Slar in Santiago, Chile, of pious and well-to-do parents (sufficiently well-to-do, in fact, to have had a family oratory where Teresa attended daily Mass), she made a private vow of virginity at age fifteen and began thinking about joining the Carmelites after reading Thérèse of Lisieux's *Story of a Soul.* In the meantime, she joined the Children of Mary and helped in the teaching of catechism in her parish. Her desire to become a Carmelite, "to learn how to love and to suffer," intensified with her reading of the biographies of Teresa of Ávila and Blessed Elizabeth of the Trinity.

At age nineteen she entered the Carmelite convent in the town of Los Andes, a run-down house without electricity and adequate sanitary facilities, but whose nuns impressed her as happy in their devotion to a strict observance of the Rule and a simple lifestyle. She took the name Teresa of Jesus and offered her new life of prayer and sacrifice for the sanctification of priests and the repentance of sinners. She began an apostolate of letter writing on the spiritual life to a large number of people, but she contracted typhus and died a few days later, on April 12, 1920, having made her final vows on her deathbed. She was beatified in 1987 and canonized in 1993. Her cult is popular, with some one hundred thousand pilgrims visiting her shrine every year. She is sometimes referred to as the "little saint" of America in imitation of the Little Flower. Her feast is not on the General Roman Calendar.

13 Martin I, pope and martyr

Martin I (d. 655, pope 649–54) was the last pope to be recognized as a martyr. Born at Todi in Umbria, he became a deacon in Rome, where his reputation for intelligence and charity won him appointment as nuncio to Constantinople, the center of the Byzantine Empire. He was elected pope in 649 and was the first pope in decades to be consecrated as Bishop of Rome without waiting for imperial approval, an act that infuriated the emperor, Constans II, who refused to recognize him as pope. Three months after his election, Martin held a synod at the Lateran Basilica, attended by 105 Western bishops and a number of exiled Greek clergy, which affirmed the doctrine of the two wills in Christ (human and divine) and condemned both Monothelitism (the heresy that held to only one divine will) and the imperial decree that forbade further discussion of it. The pope sent a copy of the synodal decision to the emperor, urging him to renounce the heresy. The emperor, in his turn, sent a newly appointed exarch of Italy to arrest the pope and bring him to Constantinople. However, when the exarch saw how much support the pope enjoyed in Rome, he decided to join forces with him against the emperor.

In the summer of 653 a new exarch seized the pope, now bedridden from gout, in the Lateran Basilica, where he had taken sanctuary. After declaring the pope deposed, the exarch smuggled Martin out of Rome and forced him onto a ship to Constantinople. Weakened by the long voyage (some say it was a year and three months; others, three months) and ridden with dysentery, Martin was placed upon arrival in three months of solitary confinement, in which he was served wretched food and was not allowed to wash. Then he was put on trial for treason. During the trial he was treated not as pope, but as a rebellious deacon and former papal nuncio. He was publicly stripped of his episcopal robes, his tunic was torn from top to bottom, and he was put in chains. He was found guilty, condemned to death, and publicly flogged. However, the dying patriarch of Constantinople pleaded for the pope's life and the sentence was commuted to exile. After three more months in prison under miserable conditions, Martin was taken by ship to Chersonesus in the Crimea, where he died on September 16, 655, from the effects of starvation and harsh treatment.

Martin's suffering was intensified by feelings that his local community in Rome had forgotten him. Indeed, they had elected a new pope, Eugenius, in August 654, probably because they knew Martin would never return and for fear that the emperor would impose a candidate favorable to Monothelitism. (It is interesting that the Vatican's official listing of popes in the *Annuario Pontificio* begins Eugenius's pontificate on August 10, 654, and lists the end of Martin's as September 16, 655, thereby suggesting that the Church had two legitimate popes serving simultaneously.) Martin was buried in Chersonesus in a church dedicated to the Blessed Virgin Mary. His feast is on the General Roman Calendar. It is also celebrated by the Russian Orthodox Church, but on April 14.

14 Blessed Peter González, friar

Peter (Pedro) González (d. 1246) was a Dominican friar who excelled at preaching, especially to Spanish and Portuguese seamen. He is still invoked as patron saint of seamen, but under the name St. Elmo, because he is confused with St. Erasmus, an Italian bishop martyred during the Diocletian persecution who is also patron saint of sailors. Born in Castile of a noble family, Peter was educated by his uncle, the bishop of Astorga, and appointed as canon of the cathedral even though he was under age. As Peter pompously rode into the city, his horse stumbled and he fell off and into the mud, much to the delight of jeering spectators. This incident is said to have convinced Peter that he should embark upon a more spiritually serious course for his life. He decided to enter the Dominicans. He became a popular preacher and served as royal chaplain to the court of Ferdinand III, king of Castile and Léon. Peter tried to elevate the morals of the courtiers and also to mitigate the severity of the king's treatment of the defeated Moors. After being allowed to retire from court, he devoted the rest of his life to preaching in the rural areas of northwestern Spain and along the coast, where he developed a special mission to seamen. He died on April 14, 1246. A large church was built over his tomb in the sixteenth century, and his cult was approved in 1741. He has not been canonized, however, nor is his feast on the General Roman Calendar. It is observed on the Dominican calendar on this day.

15 Blessed Damien de Veuster, priest

Damien de Veuster (1840–89) is better known as Damien of Molokai, "apostle to lepers." Born Joseph de Veuster in a small village near Malines, Belgium, he joined the Fathers of the Sacred Hearts of Jesus and Mary, also known as the Picpus Fathers, in 1859, taking the religious name Damien. When his brother, who was also a member of the congregation, was taken ill and unable to embark on his assignment in the Hawaiian Islands, Damien went in his place, arriving in Honolulu five months later. He was ordained a priest there in 1864. For nine years he served at two of the mission stations. In 1873 he responded to the local bishop's call for volunteers to work on Molokai, an island used in part as a leper colony. At the time there was no cure for leprosy, and those who contracted the disease were shunned not only because of the effects it had on its victims' physical appearance, but also because of the belief that the disease was the result of immoral behavior. Indeed, when Damien himself later contracted it, he was accused of having violated his vow of celibacy and was subjected to demeaning physical examinations.

There were about eight hundred lepers on the island when Damien arrived, and the number continued to grow. Living conditions were so terrible that Damien referred to the place as a "living cemetery" and a "human jungle." But he was not deterred from his mission. He visited the lepers in their huts and brought them the sacraments as often as possible. He also made efforts to improve the roads, harbor, and water supply and to expand the hospital. He also founded two orphanages at the colony. His multiple responsibilities were said to have included those of a pastor, physician, counselor, builder, sheriff, and undertaker. In one of his letters home, he wrote: "I make myself a leper with the lepers, to gain all to Jesus Christ."

In order to better the living conditions of the lepers, he returned to Honolulu to beg for money, clothing, and medicine. As news of his work spread, donations began to pour in from all over the world. But criticisms of him also increased. Some perceived him to be autocratic and quarrelsome; others found him coarse and boorish and were put off by his standards of personal hygiene. He himself was diagnosed with leprosy in January 1885. At first he was distraught, wondering about the future of his work, and confused about why he had not been immunized by his prayers to Jesus, Mary, and Joseph. He was forbidden to leave the island, and visitors, including priests who might have heard his confession, stopped coming. Later that year, however, he became resigned to his condition, accepting it as God's will and describing himself as the "happiest missionary in the world."

Suddenly, things improved dramatically. He spent a week in a Honolulu hospital, where he was visited by the king, the prime minister, and the bishop. Money and offers of prayers began once again to pour in from Europe and the United States. In May 1886 an American layman, Joseph Dutton, joined him as an assistant (and would remain on Molokai for over forty years), and in 1888 another priest arrived, followed later in the year by three Franciscan nuns who came to look after the orphans. Having sensed that his own end was near and newly confident that his work would continue through these recent arrivals, Damien died on April 15, 1889. His remains were transferred from Molokai to Louvain, Belgium, in 1936. He was beatified in 1995. His feast is not on the General Roman Calendar.

16 Bernadette Soubirous, nun

Bernadette Soubirous (1844–79) was the young French girl to whom the Blessed Virgin Mary is believed to have appeared in Lourdes, France, and is the first saint to have been photographed. Born Marie Bernarde Soubirous to a poverty-stricken family, at age fourteen she experienced a series of eighteen visions in six months (February 11–July 16, 1858) at the rock of Massabielle, Lourdes. The Virgin called herself the Immaculate Conception [December 8], a dogma that had just been solemnly defined four years earlier by Pope Pius IX. According to the dogma, Mary was conceived without original sin. Her message was simple: do penance for the conversion of sinners and urge people to come to pray at the place of the apparitions. The Blessed Mother also ordered that the church be built over the site and that Bernadette should drink from, and bathe in, a hidden spring, which, since then, has produced some 27,000 gallons of water per week. Many cures were later attributed to the water. As news of the apparitions and the healing power of the water spread, Lourdes became, following the Franco-Prussian War of 1870, the most popular pilgrimage site in all of Europe.

Bernadette Soubirous, 1858

Bernadette had to overcome a great measure of skepticism, ridicule, and harassment from local townspeople as well as civic and religious leaders. She was a simple, uneducated child, and many assumed that she had manufactured the account of her visions. A series of intense interrogations, however, could not shake her story. In 1866 she joined the Sisters of Notre Dame of Nevers, where she spent the rest of her life as Sister Maria Bernarda. She did not even leave the convent to take part in the celebrations that marked the opening of the new basilica in Lourdes in 1876. She died on April 16, 1879, at age thirty-five, after a prolonged and painful illness involving tuberculosis of the bones, which she bore valiantly. As the distinguished hagiographer David H. Farmer pointed out: "The only 'extraordinary' months in her life were those of the apparitions; before and after, her life was humdrum in the extreme." Her story was told in a novel by Franz Werfel, *The Song of Bernadette* (1942), which was made into an Oscar-winning film of the same name. She was canonized as Maria Bernarda in 1933, not for her visions but for her life of prayer, simple devotion, and faithful obedience to the will of God. Her feast is not on the General Roman Calendar, but a feast in honor of Our Lady of Lourdes, instituted in 1907 and celebrated on February 11, is.

17 Blessed Clare of Pisa, nun; Benedict Joseph Labre, pilgrim

Clare of Pisa (1362–1419) was a Dominican nun who has been compared to Bernardino of Siena [May 20] and Teresa of Ávila [October 15] as one of the great reformers of religious life. Born Theodora, or Thora, in either Venice or Florence, of the highly respected Gambacorti family, she was betrothed at an early age and eventually went to live with her future husband's parents. She developed a deep interest in assisting the poor and the sick. Her husband died during an epidemic when she was only fifteen, and she refused the opportunity for a second marriage, deciding instead to become a religious, inspired by a letter to her from Catherine of Siena [April 29]. Theodora gave away all of her most expensive clothes to the poor and joined the Poor Clares, taking the name Clare. Her relatives, however, forced her to leave the convent, but her father eventually gave in and allowed her to enter a Dominican convent. It was a lax house, and most of the nuns refused to cooperate with Clare's efforts to reform it. Her father built a new convent for her, and several of the nuns who supported her efforts joined her there. She became prioress of the convent, which became a training center and model of religious life according to a strict observance of the Rule. The nuns led an enclosed life of prayer, manual work, and study. Regarding the last item, Clare's spiritual director had urged her never to "forget that in our order very few have become saints who have not likewise been scholars." Despite financial problems suffered by her own convent, she used a large inheritance to found an orphan hospital rather than spend it on the convent. She died in 1419, and a cult developed soon thereafter. She was beatified in 1830. Her feast is not on the General Roman Calendar, but she is commemorated on the Dominican calendar on this day as Blessed Clara Gambacorti.

The Franciscans celebrate today the feast of *Benedict Joseph Labre* (1748–83). After being rejected by three different religious orders, he became a lifelong pilgrim in imitation of Christ, who had "nowhere to lay his head." He visited all the major shrines of western Europe and spent his last years in Rome. He was canonized in 1883 and is the patron saint of wandering people and the homeless.

18 Blessed Mary of the Incarnation, nun

Mary of the Incarnation (Barbe Acarie, 1566–1618) was responsible for the introduction of the Discalced Carmelite nuns into France, for which she has been known as the "mother and foundress of Carmel in France." Born Barbe Avrillot, the daughter of a high government official in Paris, she married Pierre Acarie, an aristocrat, at age seventeen. They had six children, three of whom became Carmelite nuns and one a priest. Barbe became known throughout Paris for her charitable work: feeding the poor, visiting the sick, ministering to the dying, instructing converts from Protestantism, and assisting several religious houses. She persuaded the king to allow Carmelite nuns to open a convent in Paris. Several other convents were opened subsequently. She helped to prepare young women for entrance into these convents, gaining the unofficial title "married novice-mistress."

Among her own spiritual advisers were Francis de Sales [January 24] and her cousin, Cardinal Pierre de Bérulle (1575–1629), perhaps the leading spiritual director of the time in France. When Barbe's husband died in 1613, Barbe entered the Carmelite convent in Amiens as a lay sister, taking the name Mary of the Incarnation. Disagreements with Cardinal Bérulle, however, led to her transfer to Pontoise in 1616, where she wished to become "the last and poorest of all." She died on April 18, 1618. Miracles were reported at her tomb, and she was beatified in 1791. Her feast is not on the General Roman Calendar.

19 Leo IX, pope; Alphege of Canterbury, bishop and martyr

Leo IX (1002–54; pope 1049–54) was a leading reformist pope who laid the foundation for the Gregorian reform of the latter half of the eleventh century. Born in Alsace and baptized as Bruno, the son of Count Hugh of Egisheim, who was a close relative of the imperial family, he was educated at Toul, a center of monastic reform, and became canon of the cathedral there. He was a member for a time of the German emperor's court and was appointed bishop of Toul in 1027, where he served for twenty years as an energetic reformer of clerical and monastic life. When Pope Damasus II, a Bavarian, died after less than a month in office in August 1049, Bruno accepted the emperor's nomination to the papacy only on condition that it would subsequently be approved by the clergy and laity of Rome. When he reached Rome, dressed in the simple garb of a pilgrim, he was greeted with acclaim and crowned on February 12, 1049, taking the name Leo to recall the ancient, still uncorrupted church.

Two months later he convened a synod in Rome that denounced simony and violations of clerical celibacy. Several simoniacal bishops were deposed. Leo gathered a "kitchen cabinet" of distinguished persons to assist him in the reorganization of the Curia. These included Hildebrand (later Pope Gregory VII [May 25]), Frederick of Lorraine (the future Pope Stephen IX), and Humbert of Moyenmoutier (later cardinal-bishop of Silva Candida). He also sought counsel from Hugh [May 11], the abbot of the reformist monastery of Cluny, and from Peter Damian [February 21]. Leo traveled so extensively throughout Europe to promote the reforms that he was called the "Apostolic Pilgrim." He also held a dozen synods in Italy and Germany and insisted that bishops must be elected by the local clergy and laity and abbots, by their monks.

Unfortunately, Leo's final years in office were marred by his own personal involvement in the military campaign against the Norman invaders in southern Italy (he was held captive for several months) and by the beginning of the schism between East and West. His last days were marked by illness and deep regret. He placed his bed next to his coffin in St. Peter's Basilica and died there on April 19, 1054. It is said that within forty years seventy cures were attributed to his intercession. He was acclaimed a saint and in 1087 his relics were enshrined. His feast is not on the General Roman Calendar.

Alphege of Canterbury (ca. 953–1012), also Aelfheah, was the archbishop of Canterbury who was captured and killed by Danish invaders. He began his adult life as a monk at Deerhurst. After a period of solitude in Somerset, he was appointed abbot of Bath and then as bishop of Winchester in 984, where he gained a reputation for personal austerity and great generosity to the poor. In 1006 Alphege became archbishop of Canterbury. At the time England was being subjected to continual raids and invasions by the Danes. By 1011 they had overrun much of southern England and eventually captured Canterbury. Alphege was imprisoned and an enormous ransom was demanded. Alphege refused to pay it and also forbade his people to do so. The Danes were so infuriated that, following a drunken feast at Greenwich, they axed him to death. Alphege was buried in St. Paul's Cathedral, London, and became a national hero in death. The Danish king Canute (or Cnut) [July 10] had the body transferred to Canterbury Cathedral eleven years later, where it was venerated by the monks at the beginning and end of each day. The discovery of the body as incorrupt in 1105 led to an increase in his cult, although it was always overshadowed by that of Thomas Becket [December 29] who, just before his own death, commended himself to God and to St. Alphege. Alphege's feast is not on the General Roman Calendar, but it is celebrated by the Church of England and by the Episcopal Church in the USA on this day. He is also commemorated by the Russian Orthodox Church.

20 Agnes of Montepulciano, nun

Agnes of Montepulciano (ca. 1270–1317) was a Dominican nun known for her simplicity of life and piety. Born of well-to-do parents in a small Tuscan village a few miles from Montepulciano, she entered a local convent of the Sisters of the Sack (so called because of their rough clothes) and adopted an austere lifestyle, including a diet of bread and water, the ground for a bed, and a stone for a pillow. When the convent moved to another location near Viterbo, Agnes moved with it. As her reputation for sanctity spread, the people of Montepulciano demanded her return. She did so and opened a new convent under the care of the Dominicans, because she was convinced it needed to be affiliated with a major order to achieve stability. She became prioress in 1306. She died after a long and painful illness on April 20, 1317, and her tomb, with her incorrupt body, became a popular place of pilgrimage, visited even by the emperor Charles IV and by Catherine of Siena [April 29], with whom she is often associated in Italian art. Agnes of Montepulciano was canonized in 1726. Her feast is not on the General Roman Calendar, but it is celebrated by the Dominicans on this day.

21 Anselm of Canterbury, bishop and Doctor of the Church

Anselm (1033–1109), a major theologian and archbishop of Canterbury, gave the Church the most enduring definition of theology, "faith seeking understanding." Born at Aosta in Lombardy, he spent his early childhood in Burgundy, France with his mother's family. Because of the reputation of Lanfranc, abbot of Bec in Normandy, Anselm moved to Normandy and, after much hesitation, became a monk at Bec ca. 1060. He studied in depth the writings of Augustine [August 28] and wrote several major works, including the *Proslogion* (Gk., "Allocution"), in which he presented his famous argument for the existence of God (as an idea greater than which no other idea can be conceived). In 1078 he was elected abbot, keeping all the while in close contact with his mentor Lanfranc [May 28], who had become archbishop of Canterbury. Upon Lanfranc's death in 1089, Anselm was the clear choice of the clergy to succeed to the office. But King William II resisted and kept the see open for four years (and kept its revenues for himself as well). Only when the king seemed sick unto death did he relent and approve the appointment. But the king survived, and the two men found themselves constantly at loggerheads over papal jurisdiction, lay investiture, and the primacy of the spiritual over the temporal.

When Anselm steadfastly refused to support the antipope against Urban II, William exiled him in 1097. Anselm spent some time at first at Cluny and then at Lyons. He offered his resignation to the pope, but the pope instead threatened the king with excommunication—a threat that became moot upon the king's sudden death in 1100. It was in exile that Anselm wrote his famous work on the Incarnation, *Cur Deus Homo?* (Lat., "Why God Became Man"), which described Christ's death on the cross as an act of satisfaction, returning to God the honor stolen by human sin. He also took a leading role at the Council of Bari (1098) in defense of the double procession of the Holy Spirit ("from the Father and the Son"; Lat. *Filioque*) against the Greeks ("from the Father through the Son"). At a council in Rome soon thereafter, Anselm spoke strongly against the interference of temporal rulers in the investiture of bishops and abbots.

Anselm returned to England in 1100 with the accession of Henry I, but he was exiled again in 1103 over the very same investiture issue. A compromise was reached in 1106, and Anselm was allowed to return to England yet again. He remained there for the rest of his life, enjoying such an excellent relationship with the king that the king appointed him guardian of his son and viceroy of the whole kingdom while he, the king, was away in Normandy. As bishop, Anselm insisted on a strict enforcement of clerical celibacy, and he strengthened the primatial claims of the see of Canterbury, especially with relation to York. Anselm died on April 21, 1109, but his cult was slow to develop and, in any case, was destined to be overshadowed by Thomas Becket's [December 29]. There is no formal record of his canonization, but a late twelfth-century Canterbury calendar lists two feast days, one for his death and one for the transfer of his remains. In 1734 he was named a Doctor of the Church. His feast is on the General Roman Calendar and is also celebrated by the Church of England, the Episcopal Church in the USA, and the Evangelical Lutheran Church in America. The Russian Orthodox Church celebrates the feast of *Januarius* [September 19] on this day.

BIBLIOGRAPHY

Shannon, William Henry. *Anselm: the Joy of Faith.* New York: Crossroad, 1999.

Southern, Robert W. *Saint Anselm: A Portrait in a Landscape.* Cambridge: Cambridge University Press, 1990.

22 Theodore of Sykeon, bishop

Theodore of Sykeon (d. 613) was a hermit, a miracle worker, and a bishop in Asia Minor. Born in the Galatian town of Sykeon, he was taken under the wing of the elderly and devout cook at an inn operated by his mother and aunt. The cook taught Theodore how to pray and fast. Theodore became a hermit at Arkea, about eight miles from his home, and lived there in a cave underneath a chapel. His reputation as a exorciser of evil spirits rapidly spread, and many visitors came to him for spiritual advice and physical help. He retreated to the mountains, but had to be rescued because of his deteriorating health. Although only eighteen, he was ordained a priest and went on a pilgrimage to Jerusalem, where he received the monastic habit. Upon his return, he took up once again the austere life of a hermit, living in cages suspended from the rock over his cave, and he began once again to attract visitors and disciples. He eventually established a monastery, a guest house, and a church to accommodate them all. Then he was chosen, against his will but with the support of the local clergy and landowners, to become bishop of Anastasiopolis, where he served for ten years before his resignation was finally accepted so that he could return to his life of contemplation.

Little record of his episcopal ministry survives, but there is some indication that Theodore was in conflict with some of the landowners who mistreated their people. After his resignation, he settled near Heliopolis, but was invited to Constantinople by the emperor and the patriarch. While he was there, he cured the emperor's son. He spent the rest of his life in his own monastery, giving both spiritual and medical advice and help to the many who visited him. He died in 613 and his remains were later transferred to Constantinople. His feast is not on the General Roman Calendar, but it is celebrated on this day by the Russian Orthodox Church.

23 George, martyr; Adalbert of Prague, bishop and martyr; Cesar Chavez, union leader

George (d. ca. 303) is the patron saint of England and is best known as the legendary slayer of the dragon and savior of the maiden. It is likely but not certain that he was a soldier. The story about the dragon gained immense popularity through the translation and printing of the thirteenth-century *Golden Legend*, a collection of saints' lives and short treatises on Christian feasts. According to that source, there was a dragon who terrorized a whole country, poisoning with its breath all who approached it. It had to be appeased on a daily basis with the offering of two sheep, but when these grew scarce, a human victim, chosen by lot, was substituted. The victim, however, was the king's daughter, dressed as a bride. George saved her by attacking the dragon with his lance and taking it captive with the princess's girdle, as if it were perfectly tame. George assured the people that he would rid them of the monster if they would believe in Jesus Christ and be baptized. The king and the people agreed,

Saint George and the Dragon by Andres Marzal de Sas, 15th C.

and George slew the dragon. Fifteen thousand men were baptized. The legend concluded with an account of George's death in Lydda (present-day Lod in Israel), during the persecution of Diocletian and Maximian.

George's cult was ancient and widespread. In the East he was referred to as the *megalo martyros* (Gk., "magnificant martyr"), and in the West he was mentioned in the fifth-century *Martyrology of Jerome* [September 30] and the seventh-century *Gregorian Sacramentary.* There was a monastery dedicated to him in Jerusalem in the fifth century, and churches dedicated to him in both Jerusalem and Antioch date from the sixth century. He was known in England and Ireland from the seventh or eighth centuries, gaining mention in the eighth-century *Martyrology of Bede* [May 25] and the ninth-century Irish *Martyrology of Oengus.* During the Crusades King Richard put himself and his armies under the protection of St. George. The chapel at Windsor Castle is dedicated to him.

In 1415, after the battle of Agincourt, when Henry V invoked St. George as England's patron saint, his feast was raised in rank to become one of the principal feasts of the year. By the late Middle Ages, he had become such a personification of the ideals of Christian chivalry that he was taken as the patron saint of Venice, Genoa, Portugal, and Catalonia as well. He was also venerated in Germany, Russia, and Ethiopia. With the invention of gunpowder, his popularity began to recede, except in England. For a time in the seventeenth and eighteenth centuries his feast day was a holy day of obligation for English Catholics, and Pope Benedict XIV (1740–58) declared him Protector of England. His feast is still on the General Roman Calendar and is celebrated by the Church of England and by the Greek and Russian Orthodox Churches as well. He is also patron saint of soldiers and the Boy Scouts.

Adalbert of Prague (956–97) was a missionary bishop in Hungary, Bohemia, and Prussia who contributed greatly to the Christianizing of eastern and central Europe. Born Wojciech, of the princely Slavnik family in Bohemia, he was educated by Adalbert, archbishop of Magdeburg (who gave him the Confirmation name Adalbert), returning to Prague after the latter's death. In 982, although less than thirty years old, he was chosen as bishop of Prague, entering the city barefoot and to an enthusiastic welcome. As bishop, he worked tirelessly to bring the gospel to Hungary and Bohemia, but his clergy resisted his reforms and he was exiled for nationalist reasons in 990. He went to Rome, where he became a monk. By order of the pope, he was recalled to

Bohemia, where he founded a Benedictine monastery. But an incident involving a penitent adulteress to whom he had given sanctuary forced him into exile once again in Rome in 995. (The woman had been dragged out of the nunnery in violation of the law of sanctuary, but when Adalbert excommunicated the perpetrators, the people thought the penalty extreme.) Some of his relatives were massacred, and the people of Prague refused to accept him back. The pope ordered him to return a second time, but with the concession that Adalbert could also function as a missionary bishop.

His last years were spent, from a base in Poland, on a mission to the Prussians in Pomerania along the Baltic coast. He was executed on April 23, 997, as a suspected Polish spy, perhaps near Gdansk (reports vary), and was buried at Gniezno. In 1039 his relics were moved to Prague. Because of early medieval Europe's fascination with martyrdom and monasticism, Adalbert's cult developed rapidly in Bohemia, Hungary, Germany, Poland, and Kiev and was actively promoted by the emperor Otto III and Boleslaw (Boleslaus) the Great in the interests of Polish unity. Adalbert's missionary efforts were said to have inspired similar efforts to evangelize the eastern and central Europeans, and he is patron saint of Poland and Bohemia. His feast is on the General Roman Calendar.

April 23 is also the day of death of *Cesar Chavez* (1927–93), organizer and leader of the United Farm Workers. In 1968 he undertook a twenty-five-day fast to strengthen discipline and morale in the movement. His nonviolent marches and boycotts always had a religious cast to them, and he was frequently supported by Catholic bishops, priests, and sisters as well as clergy of other religious traditions. "To be a man," he once said, "is to suffer for others."

24 Fidelis of Sigmaringen, priest and martyr

Fidelis of Sigmaringen (1578–1622) was a Capuchin Franciscan friar who was martyred while preaching to the Zwinglians in Switzerland (Ulrich Zwingli [d. 1531] was a Protestant Reformer who denied that sacraments confer grace and that Christ is truly present in the Eucharist). Fidelis is also one of the patron saints of lawyers. Born Mark Roy at Sigmaringen (Hohenzollern), he was educated at the university of Freiburg-im-Breisgau, where he received doctorates in philosophy and civil and canon law. He was ordained a priest sometime after 1610 and entered the Capuchin branch of the Franciscan order in

1612, taking the name Fidelis (Lat., "faithful"). He served as superior of three different houses and fashioned a reputation as a preacher, confessor, minister to the sick, and ascetic. He also wrote a book of spiritual exercises that was translated into several languages. Fidelis was killed on April 24, 1622, during a mission to Zwinglians in Seewis, Switzerland, in an attempt to reconcile them to the Catholic Church. He had been asked to do so by the bishop of Chur and with the direct mandate of a new Roman Congregation in charge of missionary work, *De Propaganda Fide* (Lat., "Propagation of the Faith"). The Zwinglians had not only abandoned Catholicism, but were in revolt against the Austrian Hapsburgs. They regarded Fidelis as a Hapsburg agent. Fidelis of Sigmaringen was canonized in 1746. When he was honored by *Propaganda* in 1771 as its protomartyr (first martyr), his cult was extended to the universal Church. His feast is on the General Roman Calendar.

25 Mark, Evangelist

Mark (d. ca. 74), who is also identified with the John Mark of the New Testament, was, according to Christian tradition, the author of the Second Gospel. (He is not the same person as the man who fled naked when Jesus was arrested [Mark 14:51–52].) According to the Acts, his mother, Mary, owned a house in Jerusalem in which the earliest Christian community gathered (12:12). After visiting Jerusalem, Paul [January 25; June 29] and Barnabas [June 11] took Mark back with them to Antioch (12:25). Mark assisted them in the proclamation of the gospel in Cyprus (13:1–12), but upon their arrival by ship in Perga, he left them and returned to Jerusalem (13:13). Later, after returning to Antioch, Paul and Barnabas had an argument over Mark. Barnabas wanted to take Mark on their next journey, but Paul objected on the grounds that Mark had not persevered on the previous journey. Accordingly, Barnabas took Mark back to Cyprus, and Paul set out for Syria and Cilicia with Silas (15:36–41).

In the Letter to Philemon, Mark is mentioned among Paul's fellow workers (v. 24). When Paul was held captive in Rome, Mark was with him, giving him "comfort" (Col. 4:10). In the same verse, Mark is mentioned as the cousin of Barnabas, and the Christians at Colossae are urged to receive Mark hospitably, if he should come there. Elsewhere Timothy [January 26] is asked to bring Mark to Paul, since he is useful for the apostle's ministry (2 Tim. 4:11). The first letter attributed to

Peter [June 29], written in all likelihood from Rome, mentions Mark as the "son" of Peter, a term either of simple affection or an indication that Peter was Mark's father in the faith. Mark's presence in Rome with Peter would be consistent with the tradition that Mark took notes that recorded Peter's memories of Jesus' teachings and deeds. This tradition was written down by Papias of Hierapolis, according to the historian Eusebius, who also said that Mark was Peter's "interpreter." Mark probably wrote his Gospel there in Rome, but another tradition suggests that it was written in Alexandria.

Eusebius also recorded the tradition that Mark was the first to bring the Christian faith to Egypt, that he had made known there the Gospel that he had written, and that he had established churches in Alexandria. Eusebius also indicates that Mark was the first bishop of Alexandria. He is said to have been martyred there in the eighth year of Nero's reign. Mark was venerated as a martyr in both East and West since the fourth century.

Early in the ninth century his body was brought by merchants to Venice to save it from desecration by the Arabs. The original church of St. Mark was destroyed by fire in 976, but the rebuilt cathedral contains both the relics from Alexandria and the twelfth-to-thirteenth-century mosaics of his life and death and of the transfer of his remains to Venice. Depicted as a winged lion, Mark is patron saint of Venice, Egypt, notaries, basket weavers, glass workers, opticians, and cattle breeders. His feast is on the General Roman Calendar and is also celebrated on this day by all the major Christian liturgical traditions.

26 Stephen of Perm, bishop

Stephen of Perm (ca. 1340–96), venerated by Catholics and Orthodox alike, is considered by the Russian Orthodox Church to be its outstanding missionary. Born in the town of Velikij Ustyug, about five hundred miles northeast of Moscow, he became a monk in the monastery of St. Gregory Nazianzen [January 2] in Rostov, where he had received his education. Stephen was unusual among Russian monks in that he knew Greek well and was an expert in Byzantine theology. To prepare himself for missionary work among the Zyrani, which he began ca. 1379, he learned their language, created an alphabet, and then translated the Scriptures and liturgy into the vernacular. (Unfortunately, this work was not destined to survive.) The Zyrani were readily attracted by the beauty of the liturgy and by the icons, which Stephen himself painted. In 1383 he was appointed the first bishop of Perm and proceeded to establish churches and schools, including a seminary for future priests. He also organized the distribution of food during times of shortage and served as an advocate of the people with politicians. He made several trips to Moscow, where he died on April 26, 1396. He was canonized by the Russian Orthodox Church in 1549, but the canonization was later recognized by the Catholic Church as well. His feast is not on the General Roman Calendar, but he is commemorated on this day by the Russian Orthodox Church.

27 Zita, virgin

Zita (ca. 1218–78), also known as Sitha, Citha, and other variations, is the patron saint of domestic servants or maids. Born at Monsagrati, a few miles from Lucca in Italy, she served as a maid in the Fatinelli household from age twelve until her death. Her fellow servants and the Fatinelli family resented her devotional life, but she eventually won them over by her goodness and constancy. She was generous to the poor and kind to the sick and to prisoners. After her death on April 27, 1278, her cult became popular among those in low stations of life. She became one of the most popular minor saints in medieval England, especially among servants, under the name of Sitha, probably because of the influence of a colony of Lucchese merchants in London. Her remains are in the church of San Frediano in Lucca, where she worshiped most of her life. Her cult was approved in 1696, and her name was included in the *Roman Martyrology* in 1748. She became patron saint of Lucca, and the poet Dante used her name in his *Inferno* as synonymous with the city. In 1935 Pope Pius XI declared her the principal patron saint of domestic servants. Her feast is not on the General Roman Calendar.

Peter Canisius [December 21] is commemorated by his fellow Jesuits on this day.

28 Peter Chanel, priest and martyr; Louis Grignion de Montfort, founder

Peter Chanel (1803–41) is regarded as the protomartyr of Oceania (of which he is patron saint) and the Marists. Born into a peasant family in a small village in eastern France, about fifty miles northeast of Lyons, he impressed his parish priest for his intelligence and piety and was encouraged to study for the priesthood himself. He successfully completed his studies and was ordained a priest for the diocese of Belley in 1827. After one year as a curate and three years as a pastor, he joined the recently founded Society of Mary (Marists), a congregation of missionary priests, in 1831. He had hoped for an immediate assignment to the foreign missions, but instead was sent to teach in the local seminary, where he also became vice rector. He accompanied the founder of the congregation, Jean Colin, to Rome in 1833 to try to win papal approval for the Rule. It was granted in 1836 and the congregation was assigned a vast area in the southern Pacific as its mission territory.

Peter finally got his wish and was sent to preach the gospel in the islands of the South Pacific, although the founder actually had little knowledge of the vast area. Peter and a companion landed by chance on the island of Fatuna, between Fiji and French Samoa. They received a friendly welcome, probably because the natives had been told that they were simply travelers seeking to learn the local language and customs. They earned a great measure of respect and appreciation because of their care of the sick, but when the chief's son asked for baptism, the chief was so enraged that he sent a group of warriors to kill Peter. On April 28, 1841, he was clubbed and then killed with an ax, and his body was cut up with knives. Less than a year later, however, the entire island became Christian, perhaps because the islanders feared reprisal from the French, who landed the following year and began to make inquiries about the priest's death. The French took his remains with them, but they were returned to the island in 1977. Peter was canonized in 1954. His feast was formerly celebrated only in Australia and New Zealand, but it is now on the General Roman Calendar. He is also commemorated by the Church of England.

Louis Grignion de Montfort (1673–1716) was the founder of the Company of Mary (Montfort Fathers) and the Daughters of Wisdom. Born at Montfort in Brittany and educated by the Jesuits at Rennes, he began his studies for the priesthood in Paris in 1693. He could not afford to reside at the seminary, but living conditions in the student hostel were so poor that his health was seriously affected and he had to be hospitalized. Upon his release, he was granted permission to live at the seminary, but he displayed a difficult personality and little interest in theology. Ordained in 1700, Louis was so affected by the great gap between rich and poor that he decided to devote his entire priestly life to the spiritual care of the poor and the sick. He taught catechism in the worst sections of Paris and founded an institute of sisters to care for the sick in hospitals. The sisters were themselves patients. However, opposition developed against him, whether because of Louis's personality and methods or because of envy at his success. As a consequence, he was forbidden to preach in the diocese of Poitiers. But after a period of uncertainty and aimlessness, he went to Rome in 1706, impressed the pope with his zeal and sincerity, and secured a papal appointment as a "missionary apostolic." He was granted permission to preach missions once again in Brittany.

His style of preaching tended toward the emotional, almost revivalist in character, and his piety was centered strongly, as always, on Mary and the Rosary. Although he publicly burned books he regarded to be irreligious and at times played the dramatic part of a sinner at the point of death, about to be claimed by either his guardian angel or the devil, he also opened or refurbished a number of schools for poor boys. Indeed, service to the poor was so central to his entire priestly ministry that it set him apart among the French clergy of his day.

In 1712 Louis founded the Missionaries of the Company of Mary, an association of missionary priests who shared his pastoral and devotional ideals, but by the time of his death he had attracted only two priests and a small number of lay brothers. He had been more successful with the female branch, the Daughters of Wisdom. In addition to a large number of hymns, letters, and other writings, he is best known for his *True Devotion to the Blessed Virgin,* which has been criticized for its exaggerated language (the reader is asked to become a "slave" of Mary) and excessive emphasis on Mary's role in the redemption. Because of Mary's sinlessness, he wrote, she has from God "the same rights and privileges that Christ possesses naturally." Nonetheless, it is a book that had enormous influence for more than two centuries, and interest in it increased even more when he was canonized in 1947. However, its influence waned considerably after the Second Vatican Council (1962–65) introduced a more biblically based and Christ-centered approach to Marian devotion. Louis died on April 28, 1716, in Saint-Laurent-sur-Sèvre, and is buried there in a basilica dedicated to him. The feast of Louis Grignion de Montfort is on the General Roman Calendar.

29 Catherine of Siena, virgin and Doctor of the Church

Catherine of Siena (1347–80), a reformer of popes, was the first layperson and one of the first two women named a Doctor of the Church (with

Teresa of Ávila [October 15]). She is also one of the two primary patron saints of Italy (along with Francis of Assisi [October 4]). In 1999 Pope John Paul II named her co–patron saint of all of Europe, along with Bridget of Sweden [July 23] and Teresa Benedicta of the Cross (Edith Stein) [August 9]. Born Caterina di Giacomo di Benincasa in Siena, the twenty-fourth of twenty-five children, she decided early in life not to marry and joined the third order of Dominicans. After several years of prayer and fasting in virtual solitude, during which she is said to have become mystically espoused to Christ, she felt a call to a more apostolic life and became involved in the nursing of the sick in a local hospital. (She is also patron saint of nursing.) She was especially active in assisting people during the famine of 1370 and the plague of 1374.

Saint Catherine of Siena by Fra Bartolomeo (1472–1517)

Later, she gathered a disparate group of disciples (known as her "family") who accompanied her on her frequent journeys to call people to reform and repentance in the spirit of Christ crucified. She evoked opposition, however, from those who resented her presumption to preach as a laywoman. Nevertheless, she had such extraordinary success that additional confessors had to accompany her on her preaching missions. During a preaching mission to Pisa in 1375, while kneeling before the crucifix in the church of Santa Cristina, she claimed to have received the stigmata (bleeding wounds similar to those suffered by Christ on the cross), visible only to herself. (In 1471 Pope Sixtus IV forbade pictures of her showing the stigmata because of a dispute between the Dominicans and the Franciscans about the veracity of her claim. The ban was lifted by Pope Urban VIII in 1630, but on condition that the stigmata not be shown bleeding.)

Her general attitude toward church authority was mixed. On the one hand, she believed the Church to be "the sweet bride of Christ" and "the body of the living Lord" and the pope, the bishops, and the clergy to be his representatives on earth. On the other hand, she was fully aware of the weaknesses and ambitions of the hierarchy and lower clergy and of the many abuses committed by and under them. "They ought to be mirrors of freely chosen poverty, humble lambs, giving away the Church's possessions to the poor," she declared. "Yet here they are, living in worldly luxury and ambition and pretentious vanity a thousand times worse than if they belonged to the world! In fact, many laypersons put them to shame by their good and holy lives." She excoriated bishops for ordaining unqualified candidates for the priesthood, "little boys instead of mature men," "idiots who scarcely know how to read and could never pray the Divine Office" because of their ignorance of Latin.

But Catherine knew that there could be no lasting reform of the Church without papal leadership. Throughout the summer of 1376 she met with Gregory XI in Avignon, where the papacy had been lodged in "Babylonian captivity" since 1309, and urged him to return to Rome. (She also urged him to combat abuses in the Church and to mount a Crusade against the Turks.) In a letter sent before her visit to Avignon, she insisted that he must be "courageous" and "not a coward." Gregory had already decided to return to Rome, but Catherine's appeal solidified his resolve. The two left Avignon on the same September day: the pope by boat for Rome, and Catherine on foot for Siena. The pope arrived in Rome on January 17, 1377. After Gregory's death the next year and the election of the unstable Urban VI, the Great Schism began, in which, for the next thirty-nine years, there would be at least two, and sometimes three, concurrent claimants to the Chair of Peter. Catherine sent frequent letters to Urban (most of which she dictated, because she did not learn how to write until late in life) in the hope of moderating his severity toward his opponents, and also to various Catholic rulers and cardinals, urging them to recognize Urban as the legitimate pope.

The anti-Urban party was so enraged by her stance that they tried to kill her at one point. She regretted that she had not been granted martyrdom and began to blame herself for the rupture of church unity. If only she had prayed more or fasted more, she said to her spiritual director. However, during this same period (1377–78), she dictated her major work, *The Dialogue,* on the spiritual life. Some commentators insist that it stands alongside the great spiritual classics produced by Teresa of Ávila and John of the Cross [December 14], both of whom were also declared Doctors of the Church for their mystical theology.

Urban had invited Catherine to Rome to support his cause, but she became exhausted by the journey, by her subsequent efforts to convene a "council" of holy men and women to promote church unity, and by her severe program of fasting, in which she refused to take even water. By the end of January 1380 she suffered a complete physical collapse, leading to convulsions and a coma. She recovered slightly, but only temporarily. Meanwhile, her critics continued their barrage of ridicule, charging that she had been following her own will, not God's, all along. She suffered a stroke and died eight days later, on April 29, 1380. Her body lies in the basilica of Santa Maria sopra Minerva in Rome, but her head was later removed and taken to the church of San Domenico in Siena. (The dismemberment and distribution of a saint's remains as relics was a common occurrence in the Middle Ages.) Her biography, written by her friend and spiritual director, Raymond of Capua [October 5], later master general of the Dominican order, brought great attention to her person and her cause, and she was eventually canonized by Pope Pius II, also a native of Siena, in 1461. She was declared a Doctor of the Church in 1970. Her feast is on the General Roman Calendar and is also celebrated by the Church of England, the Episcopal Church in the USA, and the Evangelical Lutheran Church in America.

BIBLIOGRAPHY

Cavallini, Giuliana. *Catherine of Siena.* London: Geoffrey Chapman, 1998.

Meade, Catherine M. *My Nature Is Fire: Saint Catherine of Siena.* New York: Alba House, 1991.

Noffke, Suzanne. *Catherine of Siena: Vision Through a Distant Eye.* Collegeville, MN: Liturgical Press, 1996.

30 Pius V, pope; Adjutor, monk

Pius V (1504–72; pope 1566–72) enforced the decrees of the Council of Trent (1545–63), published the *Roman Catechism,* reformed the Roman Missal and the Roman Breviary, and excommunicated Queen Elizabeth I of England. Born Antonio (Michele) Ghislieri of poor parents in Bosco, near Alessandria in northern Italy, he was a shepherd until he became a Dominican at age fourteen, taking as his religious name Michele. After ordination to the priesthood in 1528, he taught philosophy and theology for sixteen years and then served as inquisitor for Como and Bergamo. So zealous was he that he came to the notice of Cardinal Gian Pietro Carafa (later Pope Paul IV), who recommended him to Pope Julius III for appointment to the Roman Inquisition in 1551. When Carafa became pope, he named his protégé as bishop of Nepi and Sutri in 1556, then as a cardinal of the titular church of Santa Maria sopra Minerva, headquarters of the Dominican order, in 1557, and as grand inquisitor of the Roman Inquisition in 1558. He was known as Cardinal Alessandrino, after his native city.

He was elected pope on January 7, 1566, after a nineteen-day conclave, with the strong support of Cardinal Charles Borromeo [November 4], who looked upon him as a reformer. When he was crowned on January 19, Pius V did away with the traditional pomp and feasting, insisting that they were anachronistic and offensive to the poor. He directed that the money traditionally thrown indiscriminately to the crowds be distributed among the poor and hospitals and that money saved on the banquets be given to needy religious houses.

His agenda as pope was to implement the decrees of the Council of Trent. He imposed strict standards of lifestyle on himself, the Curia, and the city of Rome. He followed a monastic regimen, including simple, solitary meals, whose solitary character remained a papal custom through the pontificate of Pius XII (1939–58). He continued to wear his white Dominican habit, which became the standard dress of all subsequent popes. He opposed nepotism (although he appointed his grandnephew and fellow Dominican a cardinal and secretary of state to keep watch on an unfriendly faction within the College of Cardinals), insisted that clerics reside in their pastoral assignments, and maintained close supervision over religious orders. He published the *Roman Catechism* in 1566, a revised Roman Breviary in 1568, and a revised Roman Missal in 1570. The use of the Missal was made obligatory for the whole Church, except where local rites were already in place for at least two hundred years; it remained in force until the Second Vatican Council (1962–65). He restricted the use of indulgences (whose sale had been a major factor in the disruption of church unity at the time of the Reformation) and dispensations (relaxations of, or outright exemptions from, church laws). He also saw to the distribution of the decrees of the Council of Trent outside of Italy and Europe.

The pope's background as a grand inquisitor, however, led him to an inordinate reliance upon the Inquisition and its often inhuman methods. He built a new palace for the Inquisition, toughened its rules and practices, and often attended its sessions. Even though many distinguished individuals were tried and sentenced during his pontificate, Pius thought himself too lenient! He was unusually severe on the Jews. He allowed some to remain in Rome's ghettos and in Ancona for commercial reasons, but otherwise his policy was to expel Jews from the Papal States. In 1571 he established the Congregation of the Index to oversee and censor the publication of books.

His excommunication of Queen Elizabeth I of England in 1570 and concomitant declaration that her subjects were absolved from allegiance to her exposed English Catholics to persecution, imprisonment, torture, and execution, and also antagonized France, Spain, and the empire. His one significant achievement on the political-military front was the victory of the Holy League (with Spain and Venice) over the Turkish fleet at Lepanto in the Gulf of Corinth on October 7, 1571, thereby breaking their power in the Mediterranean. Lepanto made the pope a hero throughout Catholic Europe. Because the pope attributed the victory to the Blessed Virgin Mary, he declared October 7 as the feast of Our Lady of Victory (changed by his successor, Gregory XIII, to the feast of the Most Holy Rosary). It is called today the feast of Our Lady of the Rosary.

It was Pius V who, in 1567, declared his fellow Dominican, St. Thomas Aquinas [January 28], a Doctor of the Church. He died on May 1, 1572, and was buried first in St. Peter's Basilica, but his remains were later transferred to the basilica of St. Mary Major. He was beatified in 1672 and canonized in 1712. His feast is on the General Roman Calendar. The Greek and Russian Orthodox Churches celebrate the feast of *James the Apostle* [July 25] on this day.

It is also the feast day of *Adjutor* (d. 1131), an obscure Norman knight who went on the First Crusade in 1095, was captured by the Muslims, escaped, returned to France and became a monk at the abbey of Tiron. He is the patron saint of swimmers and yachtsmen.

MAY

1 Joseph the Worker

The principal feast of Joseph, husband of Mary, is celebrated on March 19. (See the March 19 entry on Joseph for biblical references to his life and for the history of his cult within the Church.) This second feast of *Joseph the Worker* was inaugurated by Pope Pius XII in 1955 to counteract a Communist holiday on May 1. The new feast replaced that of the Patronage of St. Joseph, later called the Solemnity of Joseph, which was celebrated since 1913 on the third Wednesday after Easter. The appropriateness of this new feast is grounded in that fact that Joseph was a carpenter by trade (Matt. 13:55) and trained his son Jesus as a carpenter as well (Mark 6:3).

The *Roman Martyrology* refers to today's feast as the "Memory of St. Joseph the worker, who as a carpenter at Nazareth provided for the needs of Jesus and Mary by his labor, and initiated the Son of God into human work. Therefore, on the day when a holiday in honor of workers is celebrated in many countries, Christian workers venerate him as their exemplar and protector." Joseph is the patron saint of carpenters and other manual laborers. His feast is on the General Roman Calendar.

The Church of England, the Episcopal Church in the USA, and the Evangelical Lutheran Church in America celebrate the feast of the apostles *Philip and James* [May 3] on this day, while the Greek and Russian Orthodox Churches commemorate the prophet *Jeremiah*.

2 Athanasius, bishop and Doctor of the Church

Athanasius (ca. 295–373) was the outstanding defender of the teaching of the First Council of Nicaea (325) on the divinity of Jesus Christ against the Arians, who held that Jesus was not divine, but only the greatest of creatures. Born of Christian parents in Alexandria and educated at its famed catechetical school, Athanasius became deacon and secretary to his bishop, Alexander, whom he accompanied to the Council of Nicaea. In 328, while still in his early thirties, Athanasius became the bishop (or metropolitan patriarch) of Alexandria, a see comparable in prestige to Jerusalem and Antioch. He took his new responsibilities seriously, making extensive pastoral visits throughout the region. However, he came under heavy personal attack by those opposed to the teaching of the council, who questioned even the validity of his election. (His election had been the result of popular acclaim, given his growing reputation as a theologian and defender of the faith. Moreover, his predecessor, Alexander, had indicated his preference for Athanasius as his successor.) Given reports about violence allegedly perpetrated by some of his supporters and charges of personal misconduct against him as well, Athanasius was summoned to a regional council in Tyre, composed

The Prophet Athanasius

almost entirely of his enemies, and was exiled to Trèves (Trier) in northern Gaul by order of the emperor Constantine [May 21] in 335.

Upon the emperor's death two years later, Athanasius was allowed to return to his diocese, but his opponents continued to deny the legitimacy of his election as part of their ongoing campaign against the Council of Nicaea's teaching. He was deposed once again, this time at a synod of Antioch (337 or 338), and a rival bishop was installed in his place. Athanasius appealed his case to Rome, where Pope Julius I convened a synod attended by some fifty bishops in the fall of 340 or the spring of 341. Athanasius was cleared of the charges that had been brought against him at the council of Tyre, but his opponents in the East refused to accept the verdict. Athanasius remained in the West, where he promoted monastic ideals in his travels through Italy and Gaul. The two emperors of East and West, Constantius II and Constans, summoned a general council in Sardica in 343, but the Eastern bishops refused to attend because Athanasius would be sitting among the Western bishops. The council met instead as a regional council and exonerated Athanasius once again.

Upon the death of the rival bishop of Alexandria, Constantius II allowed Athanasius to return to his see in October 346, where he remained for ten years. During this period, the Arians kept up their campaign against Athanasius, condemning him at the councils of Arles in 353 and Milan in 355. In February 356 a military detachment surrounded the church where Athanasius was holding a vigil service. With the help of monks, he managed to escape and went into hiding in the Libyan desert, while an Arian bishop was installed in his place in Alexandria. Athanasius moved from one hiding place to another over the next six years, protected by his clergy and the monks. He continued to govern his flock from afar and even made a few secret visits to Alexandria. During this period he produced some of his major writings, including his *Life of Antony* [January 17].

After the death of Constantius II in November 361, the rival bishop of Alexandria was murdered and the new emperor, Julian, allowed the exiled bishops to return to their sees. Athanasius returned in triumph to Alexandria, where he held a synod that condemned Arianism, but dealt leniently with bishops who had signed Arian formulas under duress. Julian, however, wanted to promote a revival of paganism and, jealous of the revitalization of Christianity, exiled Athanasius for a short time, from October 362 to June 363, when Julian died. Jovian served only briefly as Julian's successor. Upon Jovian's death the following February, the next emperor, Valentinian, made his brother Valens coemperor, with responsibility for the Eastern empire. Valens favored the Arians and resumed the persecution of those faithful to Nicaea, including Athanasius. Thus, for the fifth time Athanasius was forced into exile, but under pressure from the Alexandrians Valens was forced to rescind the exile after four months. On balance, much of Athanasius's life as bishop was spent in exile, but through it all he received the unwavering support of successive popes and of subsequent ecumenical councils.

From 366 until his death in 373 he functioned once again, and without harassment, as bishop of Alexandria. His liturgies and sermons were well attended, and candidates for monastic life multiplied. Indeed, several of his writings were addressed to monks, and, as mentioned above, he wrote a celebrated biography of Anthony of Egypt that was enthusiastically received in both East and West. He was an extraordinarily prolific author during his periods of exile. His *On the Incarnation* and the *Discourses Against the Arians* clarified the notion of the Trinity and the central Christian belief in the enfleshment of the Son of God in Jesus of Nazareth. He also emphasized the divinity of the Holy Spirit, equal to that of the Son, several decades before that doctrine was formally approved by the First Council of Constantinople in 381. He died in Alexandria during the night, between May 2 and May 3, 373, and was immediately venerated as one of the Church's first confessors, that is, as one who suffered for the faith without actually being put to death. A commemorative sermon preached by Gregory Nazianzen [January 2] in 379 linked Athanasius with the prophets, apostles, and martyrs and etched his reputation in the West as a champion of orthodoxy who suffered persecution and exile for his defense of the faith. He is viewed in the East as an ascetical teacher and mystical theologian.

Athanasius was proclaimed in 1568 one of the four great Doctors of the Church in the East, alongside Basil the Great [January 2], Gregory Nazianzen, and John Chrysostom [September 13]. His feast is on the General Roman Calendar and is celebrated by all of the major Christian liturgical traditions on this day. His feast is also celebrated in the East on January 18.

BIBLIOGRAPHY

Arnold, Duane W. H. *The Early Episcopal Career of Athanasius of Alexandria.* Notre Dame, IN: University of Notre Dame Press, 1991.

Pettersen, Alvyn. *Athanasius.* London: Geoffrey Chapman, 1995.

3 Philip and James (the Less), apostles

Philip (first century) was one of the original twelve apostles and, with James, is the patron saint of Uruguay. He came from Bethsaida in Galilee (John 1:43–51) and was one of Jesus' first disciples (John 1:43–44), along with Peter [June 29] and Andrew [November 30]. At the feeding of the five thousand, it is Philip who points out to Jesus that they have only two hundred denarii worth of bread and that this would not be enough to feed the crowd (6:5–7). Because he has a Greek name, it is not surprising that "the Greeks" came to him looking for Jesus (12:21–22). At the Last Supper, Philip asked Jesus to show the Father to the Twelve, eliciting Jesus' response that the one who has seen Jesus has seen the Father (14:8–9). He is listed among those who were in the upper room awaiting the Spirit at Pentecost (Acts 1:12–14).

There are various traditions about the life and death of Philip. One says that he preached the gospel in Phrygia and died in Hierapolis. His supposed remains were taken to Rome and placed in the basilica of the Twelve Apostles. An ancient inscription there indicates that the church was originally dedicated to Philip and James. This explains why the two share the same feast day. At least two apocryphal works attributed to Philip circulated in the early Church, both called the *Gospel of Philip*.

James the Less (first century), to be distinguished from James the Great [July 25], was also one of the original twelve apostles. He was the son of Alphaeus (Matt. 10:3; Mark 3:18; Luke 6:15), and his mother Mary was present at the Cross on Good Friday (Mark 15:40). Almost nothing else is known about him. He has been identified with James of Jerusalem [October 23], who was described as the "brother" of the Lord (Matt. 10:3; 13:5) and who presided over the council of Jerusalem (Acts 15). However, the New Testament clearly distinguishes the Twelve from the brothers of the Lord (Acts 1:13–14). James the Less is believed to have been clubbed to death upon sentence of the Sanhedrin ca. 62. According to biblical scholars, it is extremely unlikely that he was the author of the Letter (Epistle) of James in the New Testament. He is a patron saint of the dying.

The traditional feast day of Philip and James, May 1, was changed to May 11 in 1955 to make room for the new feast of St. Joseph the Worker. In the revision of the General Roman Calendar in 1969, the feast was changed once again, from May 11 to May 3. Anglicans, Lutherans, and others continue to celebrate the feast on May 1. The

Greek and Russian Orthodox Churches celebrate Philip's feast on November 14 and that of James the Less on October 9.

4 Florian, martyr; English saints and martyrs of the Reformation era

Florian (d. 304), one of the patron saints of Poland and of Austria, was martyred in the last and most violent of the imperial persecutions, that of Diocletian, in Lorch (Lauriacum). An army officer and civil administrator at Noricum in present-day Austria, he gave himself up as a Christian to the local governor. He was scourged and his skin was stripped off before he was thrown with a stone tied around his neck into the Emms River, which flows into the Danube. He was buried by a pious woman, but his remains were later moved to St. Florian's Abbey near Linz. Some of his relics were brought to Rome, and Pope Lucius III (1181–85) gave them to King Casimir of Poland and to the bishop of Kraków. Many cures were attributed to his intercession, and he was especially invoked against dangers from fire and water, and is patron saint of firefighters. His feast is not on the General Roman Calendar.

The Episcopal Church in the USA and the Evangelical Lutheran Church in America celebrate the feast of *Monica* [August 27], mother of Augustine [August 28], on this day, while the Church of England commemorates the *English saints and martyrs of the Reformation era.*

5 Gotthard of Hildesheim, abbot and bishop; Irene of Thessalonica, martyr

Gotthard (or *Godehard*) *of Hildesheim* (ca. 960–1038) was a monastic and episcopal reformer. Born at Reichersdorf in Bavaria, he was educated by canons at the abbey of Nieder-Altaich and later participated in its reform by restoring the Rule of St. Benedict [July 11] there. He was ordained a priest and became a monk at Nieder-Altaich in 990 and was eventually elected its abbot. During his twenty years in that post, he also guided the reform of three other monasteries and provided nine abbots for several houses. His efforts so impressed Emperor Henry II [July 13] that, upon the death of the bishop of Hildesheim, Henry nominated Gotthard to succeed to the see in 1022. Although already sixty years old, he embraced his new pastoral responsibilities with extraordinary energy. He built and restored churches, established schools, reformed the cathedral chapter, and built a hospice for the sick and the poor. He was canonized in 1131. The famous pass of St. Gotthard over the Alps derives its name from a chapel built on the summit and dedicated to him. His feast is not on the General Roman Calendar.

The Russian Orthodox Church celebrates the feast of the "great martyr" *Irene of Thessalonica* (d. 304) on this day. She was convicted and executed during the Diocletian persecution for possessing copies of the Scriptures and then for refusing to sacrifice to the gods. Irene was sent to a house of prostitution where she was stripped naked and chained, but left untouched. She was put to death either by fire or by an arrow in the throat.

6 Marian and James, martyrs

Marian and *James* (d. 259) were North African martyrs, born in Numidia. Marian was a lector, or reader, and James, a deacon. Both were martyred in 259, during the reign of Valerian, at Cirta Julia (later Constantina), the chief city of Numidia. Before their martyrdom, they were inspired by the example of two bishops, Agapius and Secundinus, both of Numidia, who stopped at their house to offer encouragement. The bishops were themselves martyred soon thereafter. Marian and James confessed their faith and were tortured on the rack and imprisoned. They were said to have experienced visions there, including one of Cyprian of Carthage [September 16], who had just been martyred during the same persecution, and another of Bishop Agapius. They were executed by beheading in a river valley with high banks on each side, and their bodies were thrown into the water. Augustine [August 28] referred to their martyrdom in his *Sermon 284*. Their relics are in the Gubbio cathedral. Their feast is not on the General Roman Calendar.

The Russian Orthodox Church commemorates *Job*, "the long-suffering," on this day.

7 John of Beverley, bishop

John of Beverley (d. 721) was the English saint whom King Henry V invoked on John's feast day during the battle at Agincourt (1415). Born at Harpham in Yorkshire, John studied at Canterbury and upon his return became a monk at St. Hilda's [November 19] double monastery at Whitby, where he was renowned for his concern for the poor and for learning. He was consecrated bishop of Hexham in 687. As bishop he ordained the Venerable Bede [May 25] as a deacon and then as a priest. In his *Ecclesiastical History* Bede attested to various miracles that occurred during the bishop's ministry. In 705 John was appointed bishop of York, but little is known of his ministry there. He did found a monastery at Beverley and eventually retired to it in 717; he died there on May 7, 721. His shrine was for centuries one of the most popular pilgrimage sites in England. He was canonized in 1037.

The famous anchoress and mystic popularly known as "Blessed" Julian of Norwich [May 8] referred to John of Beverley in her *Revelations* as "a dear worthy servant to God, greatly God-loving and dreading. . . . God sheweth in earth with plenteous miracles doing about his body continually." At the request of King Henry V, a synod in 1416 ordered that John of Beverley's feast be kept throughout England. It may be a matter of interest that his feast is not, in fact, kept by the Church of England today, but that Julian of Norwich's is, on the following day. John of Beverley's feast is also not on the General Roman Calendar.

8 Peter of Tarentaise, bishop; Julian of Norwich, anchoress

Peter of Tarentaise (ca. 1102–74), not to be confused with Pope Innocent V (1276) who was also Peter of Tarentaise, was the archbishop of Tarentaise in Savoy with a special ministry to the sick and the poor. Born near Vienne, France, he became a Cistercian monk at nearby Bonnevaux ca. 1122. About ten years later he was elected abbot of Taimé, where he built a guest house and hospital for travelers between Geneva and Savoy. He was elected archbishop of Tarentaise in 1142, an appointment he accepted because of the insistence of his fellow Cistercian Bernard of Clairvaux [August 20]. The previous bishop had been deposed from office because of corruption.

Peter appointed men of high quality as cathedral canons and parish clergy. He visited his largely mountainous diocese regularly, established educational, charitable, and medical institutions, recovered property that his predecessor had alienated from the Church, and improved the quality of worship. He was so personally involved in the ministry to the poor and the sick that he developed a reputation for miraculous healings and multiplication of food. Distressed by the general acclaim for his spiritual feats, Peter suddenly disappeared from his diocese in 1155 and was not discovered until a year later in a Swiss Cistercian abbey, living as a lay brother. Persuaded to return to his diocese, Peter resumed his ministry on behalf of the poor, instituting the practice of distributing soup and bread from the month of May until harvest time. The custom lasted until the French Revolution.

Peter supported Pope Alexander III against the antipope Victor, who, in turn, had the support of the emperor Frederick Barbarossa. Peter spoke on behalf of Alexander III in Alsace, Burgundy, and Italy, and even at councils in the emperor's presence. Toward the end of his life, Peter was sent by Pope Alexander to make peace between Henry II of England and Louis VII of France. One eyewitness at the English court described Peter as joyful, modest, and humble, with an obvious love for the poor. This eyewitness's testimony was all the more significant because of his cynicism about Cistercians. Peter died on September 14, 1174, at Bellevaux Abbey, near Besançon, while on his way back to his diocese. He was canonized in 1191. Most of his relics are at Cîteaux, the Cistercian motherhouse. His feast is not on the General Roman Calendar, but it is observed on the Cistercian calendar on September 12.

The Church of England and the Episcopal Church in the USA celebrate the feast of *Julian of Norwich* (ca. 1342–ca. 1420) on this day. She lived a life of solitude as an anchoress in a cell attached to the church of St. Edmund and St. Julian in Norwich, East Anglia. She is said to have received sixteen mystical visions on the Passion of Christ and the Trinity, described in her *Book of Showings,* also known as the *Revelations of Divine Love,* and on other mysteries of faith. She looked upon Christ also as a mother, who allows people to get hurt, but protects them from ultimate harm. By the time of her death, her reputation for sanctity was widespread. Pilgrims came to her cell from all over England. Although she is popularly called "Blessed," there is no record of any formal ecclesiastical process of beatification.

Julian of Norwich by Lu Bro

In the Greek and Russian Orthodox Churches this is the feast of *John the Theologian,* the same individual as the apostle and Evangelist [December 27].

9 Pachomius, abbot; Catherine of Bologna, prioress

Pachomius (d. 346) was the founder of cenobitic, or communal, monasticism. Born in Upper Egypt of pagan parents, he was drafted into the army and became a Christian upon discharge in 313. He lived as a hermit for a few years, but then organized others in a monastic community. He founded his first monastery at Tabennisi, near the Nile, in 320, and ruled over nine monastic communities for men and two (possibly three) for women by the time of his death. Pachomius's military background and organizational skills led him to divide the monks into occupational groups, for example, farmers, bakers, weavers, and pottery makers. Functioning as a kind of general, he assumed the authority to transfer monks from one monastery to another, although each had its own local superior and assistant. All superiors met for liturgical celebrations and to share semiannual reports at Easter and in August. Complete obedience was expected of all the monks, and an ascetical lifestyle was followed regarding food, drink, and sleep. Pachomius himself was engaged in a continual fast, and often spent the whole night in work and prayer. Meditation consisted of reflecting upon memorized passages from Scripture. His Rule, translated by Jerome [September 30], influenced those of Basil [January 2] and Benedict [July 11]. In the East his teaching was known largely through the writings of Theodore the Studite [November 11]. Pachomius's feast is not on the General Roman Calendar, but is celebrated in the Coptic Church on this day and in the Greek and Russian Orthodox Churches on May 15.

The Greek Orthodox Church commemorates the prophet *Isaiah* on this day; the Episcopal Church in the USA commemorates *Gregory Nazianzen* [January 2].

The Franciscans celebrate the feast of *Catherine of Bologna* (1413–63), also known as Catherine de' Vigri, who was part of a semimonastic community that eventually affiliated with the Poor Clares. She became prioress of the Poor Clares' Corpus Christi convent in Bologna, which became famous because of her sanctity and spiritual gifts. She died there on March 9, 1463, and was canonized in 1712. She is patron saint of artists.

10 John of Ávila, priest

John of Ávila (1500–69) was the spiritual counselor of Teresa of Ávila [October 15] and facilitated the conversions of Francis Borgia [October 3] and John of God [March 8]. Born at Almodóvar del

Campo in Spain of wealthy Jewish parents, he first studied law, then undertook a life of prayer and penance for three years, followed by studies in philosophy and theology. He was ordained as a diocesan priest in 1525, gave away most of his inheritance to the poor, and accepted a mandate from the archbishop of Seville to reevangelize Andalusia, the southernmost province of Spain, which had been ruled by the Moors. In spite of his success as a preacher over the course of nine years there, he was brought before the Inquisition because of some of his teachings, including the charge that he unduly favored the poor and excluded the rich from heaven. The accusations were not proved, and John was released from confinement. He produced many letters and sermons and a treatise on Christian perfection. He also established more than a dozen schools for the laity and two for the clergy. His last fifteen years of life, however, were marked by much illness. He was canonized in 1970 and is a patron saint of Spain and of the diocesan clergy. His feast is not on the General Roman Calendar. In the Greek and Russian Orthodox Churches May 10 is the feast of the Apostle *Simon the Zealot* [October 28].

11 Ignatius of Laconi, religious; Odo, Maiolus, Odilo, Hugh, and Peter the Venerable, abbots; Mamertus of Vienne, bishop; Matteo Ricci, missionary

Ignatius of Laconi (1701–81) was a Capuchin lay brother whose sanctity was expressed, like that of Thérèse of Lisieux [October 1], also known as Theresa of the Child Jesus and as the Little Flower, in fulfilling the ordinary obligations of life in an extraordinary way. Born at Laconi (Sardinia) of a poor family, one of nine children, he decided during a serious illness to join the Franciscans as a lay brother, a decision his mother supported but his father did not. He finally joined the order in 1721 following an incident when his horse bolted out of control, but then resumed its normal pace, leaving him unharmed. For the first fifteen years he worked as a weaver at Cagliari. In 1741 he was appointed *questor,* one who begs for alms, a task he fulfilled on foot in all types of weather and for the rest of his life. He was especially devoted to the sick and to children. Many cures were attributed to him during his lifetime as well as after his death. He was canonized in 1951. His feast is not on the General Roman Calendar.

The Benedictines and Cistercians celebrate on this day the feast of *Odo, Maiolus, Odilo, Hugh,* and *Peter the Venerable,* abbots of Cluny.

Odo (879–942) was the second abbot of Cluny, known as a reformer and widely respected throughout Europe. *Maiolus* (904–94), or Maieul, was abbot for thirty years and declined an opportunity to become pope in 974. *Odilo* (ca. 962–1049) was abbot for fifty-five years. Under him Cluny became the most important abbey in western Europe. It was he who instituted the feast of All Souls [November 2], first for deceased monks and then for all the deceased faithful. He sold or melted down much of Cluny's treasure to relieve the poor in time of famine and was known for his saying that he would rather be damned for being too merciful than for being too severe. *Hugh* (1024–1109) served as abbot for sixty years, a period of great Cluniac expansion. He was an adviser to popes and one of the most influential figures in the second half of the eleventh century. *Peter the Venerable* (ca. 1092–1156) was the eighth abbot of Cluny. He added studies to the traditional monastic elements of prayer and manual labor. Although never formally canonized, he has always been honored as a saint.

On this day the Russian Orthodox Church celebrates the feast of *Methodius and Cyril,* "Holy Equals to the Apostles" [February 14].

As a matter of minor interest, this is also the feast day of *Mamertus of Vienne* (d. ca. 475), a bishop who in a time of crisis instituted the penitential processions, known as the Rogations, on the three days preceding the feast of the Ascension. The Rogation Days were dropped from the General Roman Calendar in the reform of 1969.

Finally, this is the day of death of *Matteo Ricci* (1552–1610), Jesuit missionary to China and a scientist in his own right. He adapted Christianity to Chinese culture, promoted the use of Chinese rites, and assumed the status and dress of a mandarin. Because of their rivalry with the Jesuits, the Dominicans secured papal prohibition of Chinese rites in 1742, effectively closing China to Catholicism for centuries.

12 Nereus and Achilleus, martyrs; Pancras, martyr

Nereus and *Achilleus* (early second century) were Roman martyrs whose ancient and well-established cult was centered on their relics in the cemetery of Domitilla. Former Praetorian soldiers who left military life after their conversion, according to their legendary "Acts" they were beheaded during the reign of Trajan (98–117) for refusing to sacrifice to idols. The most ancient and reliable historical source is an inscription written in their honor by Pope Damasus I [December 11] during the fourth century.

Pancras (ca. 304) was a Roman martyr whose cult was centered on his body in a church on the Via Aurelia in Rome. He is said to have been beheaded at age fourteen during the reign of Diocletian (284–305) and buried on the Via Aurelia in the cemetery of Calepodius, later renamed in his honor. Otherwise, almost nothing is known of him. Pope Gregory the Great [September 3] dedicated a monastery to him in Rome, and Augustine of Canterbury [May 27] dedicated a church to him in Canterbury. His relics were sent by Pope Vitalian to King Oswiu of Northumbria ca. 664, which may explain why his name appears in the *Martyrology of Bede* [May 25] and in most medieval English liturgical calendars. Six ancient churches were dedicated to him in England, including one in north London, from which the cemetery, railway station, and hotel take their name. The feasts of Nereus and Achilleus, and Pancras, are on the General Roman Calendar.

13 Andrew Fournet, founder; Our Lady of Fátima

Andrew Fournet (1752–1834) was the founder of the Daughters of the Cross, also known as the Sisters of St. Andrew [November 30]. Born at Maillé, near Poitiers, of a comparatively wealthy family, he dissipated his early years in idleness and amusements. His attitude changed when in 1774 he was sent to live with an uncle who was a parish priest in a remote rural area. Under the influence of his uncle, he took up the study of theology and in 1776 was ordained a priest. He served first as his uncle's curate and then took an appointment in a nearby town. In 1781 he was appointed parish priest in his hometown of Maillé. He adopted a life of simplicity and of generosity to the poor. However, when he refused to take an oath of loyalty to the new revolutionary government, he became by that fact an outlaw. His bishop sent him to Spain in 1792 for safety's sake, but he returned in 1797 in secret, keeping one step ahead of his pursuers.

When Napoleon came to power in 1799 and made peace with the Church soon thereafter, Andrew was restored to his parish. He became spiritual director of Elizabeth Bichier des Ages [August 26], whose group of women who cared for the sick and the poor became the nucleus of his new congregation. It was Elizabeth who preferred to call them the Sisters of St. Andrew rather than the Daughters of the Cross. Andrew resigned from his parish at age sixty-eight because of illness and fatigue and devoted himself to his new congregation of sisters. One miracle attributed to him involved the multiplication of grain and other food, which his nuns needed for themselves and the children in their care. He was beatified in 1926 and canonized in 1933. His feast is not on the General Roman Calendar.

This is also the feast of *Our Lady of Fátima,* commemorating the reported apparitions of the Blessed Virgin Mary in Fátima, a small town in Portugal, to three illiterate peasant children on May 13, 1917, and on five later occasions. She identified herself as Our Lady of the Rosary and urged the practice of penance, the daily recitation of the Rosary, and devotion to the Immaculate Heart of Mary. Two of the three children—Francisco and Jacinta Marto–died in 1919 and were later beatified by Pope John Paul II in Fátima itself on May 13, 2000. They were the first children to be beatified who were not martyrs. As of that date, the surviving child, Lucia de Santos, a Carmelite nun, was still alive at age ninety-three. An attempt had been made on Pope John Paul II's life in St. Peter's Square on May 13, 1981. The pope attributed his survival to the intercession of Our Lady of Fátima. Speculation about the nature of the three secrets alleged to have been revealed to the children by the Blessed Virgin focused on the third (the first two were accepted as the forecasting of the end of the First World War and the start of the Second, and the rise of Communism). Cardinal Angelo Sodano, Vatican secretary of state, disclosed on the occasion of the beatification of the two children that the third secret concerned the attempted assassination of John Paul II in 1981. The feast is not on the General Roman Calendar.

14 Matthias, apostle; Mary Mazzarello, foundress

Matthias (first century) was the apostle chosen to replace Judas (Acts 1:15–26). The bases of his election by lot (against Joseph, called Barsabbas, also known as Justus) was that he was a disciple of Christ from the time of Jesus' baptism in the Jordan and a witness of the Resurrection. Nothing certain is known of Matthias's apostolic activity, although he is said to have preached first in Judea and later in Cappadocia near the Caspian Sea. The historian Eusebius (d. ca. 339) reports that he was one of the seventy disciples (Luke 10:1), but this is based on inference alone. The apocryphal *Acts of Andrew and Matthias* tells of Matthias's mission to a nation of cannibals, where he is taken prisoner and rescued by Andrew. The story was preserved in Latin by Gregory of Tours (d. 594) [November 17] as a preface to his version of the *Acts of Andrew* and also in the Anglo-Saxon poem "Andreas," attributed to Cynewulf (d. early ninth century). A spurious *Gospel According to Matthias* is mentioned by Origen (d. ca. 254) and Eusebius. According to Hippolytus (d. ca. 236) [August 13], some Gnostics appealed to secret traditions handed down from Matthias to support their own heretical doctrines.

Matthias is said to have suffered martyrdom either at Colchis or in Jerusalem. According to some traditions he was crucified and hacked to pieces with an ax or a halberd. He is often represented holding a cross or a halberd, and is a patron saint of carpenters. His relics were claimed by Jerusalem, then taken, at least in part, to Rome by the empress Helen [August 18], and some were removed to St. Matthias's Abbey in Trier. His feast is on the General Roman Calendar and is also celebrated by the Church of England on this day. The feast is celebrated on August 9 in the Greek and Russian Orthodox Churches.

This is also the feast day of *Mary Mazzarello* (1837–81), collaborator of John Bosco [January 31] and foundress of the Salesian Sisters, who educate young girls, while the Salesian Fathers educate young boys. She is buried alongside side him in Turin and was canonized in 1951.

15 Isidore the Farmer

Isidore the Farmer (ca. 1080–1130) is patron saint of Madrid, farmers, and laborers. Born in or near Madrid, he worked as a farm laborer all of his life. He married a peasant like himself and had a son who died at a young age. Thereafter, he and his wife lived as brother and sister. Although his life was lived in obscurity, marked by many devotional practices and generosity to the poor, he achieved great fame after his death. In 1170 his remains were transferred to a beautiful shrine via a process that was equivalent in those days of canonization. Miracles were attributed to his intercession, including the cure of King Philip III ca. 1615. The king then petitioned for Isidore's formal canonization, which was achieved in 1622, in the same ceremony that elevated Ignatius of Loyola [July 31], Francis Xavier [December 3], Teresa of Ávila [October 15], and Philip Neri [May 26]. Isidore's incorrupt remains lie in the church of St. Andrew, Madrid. His feast is not on the General Roman Calendar.

The Cistercians and the Greek and Russian Orthodox Churches celebrate the feast of *Pachomius the Great* [May 9], founder of cenobitic (communal) monasticism, on this day.

16 Andrew Bobola, martyr; Margaret of Cortona, penitent; Simon Stock, friar; Brendan of Clonfert, abbot; John Nepomucen, martyr; Peregrine of Auxerre, bishop

Andrew Bobola (1591–1657) was a Polish Jesuit martyr who is venerated as "apostle of Lithuania" and a patron saint of Poland. Born in the Palatinate of Sandomierz, he studied under the Jesuits in Vilna, Poland (now Vilnius, Lithuania), and entered the Jesuit novitiate there in 1611. Ordained a priest in 1622, he served as pastor of the church at Nieswiez, then of St. Casimir's [March 4] in Vilna, where he was known for his outstanding preaching and for his ministry to prisoners and the poor. In 1630 he was transferred to Bobruisk as pastor and superior of the Jesuit house there. He ministered heroically to the sick and dying during a subsequent plague.

Andrew became caught up in the midst of the bitter conflict between Catholics and Russian Orthodox at the time. He inspired opposition because of his successful efforts in bringing large numbers of Orthodox back into communion with Rome. By 1655 the Cossacks had forced many Catholics out of the territory, and Andrew was in Vilna when it was sacked by Russian troops at war with Poland. The Jesuits were driven from their churches and colleges and given refuge by Prince Radziwill in Pinsk. The Cossacks captured Pinsk in 1657, and Andrew himself was taken prisoner at nearby Peredil. He was whipped, then tied to horses and dragged for miles back to Janov, where he was stretched out on a butcher's table and the skin torn off his body. Holes were cut into the palms of his hands, he was stabbed in the chest, and then he was beheaded. His body was later placed in a local church and then buried at Pinsk. In 1808 it was transferred to Polotsk (Byelorussia), and in 1922 taken to a Moscow museum by the Bolsheviks. In 1923 two American Jesuits requested Andrew's remains in the name of Pope Pius XI, and they were taken to Rome. They were later returned to Poland and placed in the Jesuit church in Warsaw. Andrew Bobola was beatified in 1853 and canonized in 1938. His feast is not on the General Roman Calendar.

On this day the Franciscans celebrate the feast of *Margaret of Cortona* (ca. 1247–97), a member of the third order of St. Francis who lived a life of extreme austerity in reparation for her having served, under force, as a mistress to a knight for nine years, bearing him a son.

The Carmelites celebrate the feast of *Simon Stock* (d. 1265), a

Carmelite friar who led his order in its development from a hermit order into a mendicant one, similar to the Franciscans and Dominicans. In response to an alleged vision of the Blessed Virgin Mary, he is said to have commended the wearing of the brown scapular as an assurance of salvation. Simon Stock was never formally canonized, but his feast was approved for the Carmelite order in 1564.

This is also the feast day of *Brendan of Clonfert* (ca. 486–575), also Brandon, founder of several Irish abbeys, including one at Clonfert ca. 559. Mount Brandon, the westernmost point of Europe, on the Dingle peninsula, is named after him. The legendary story in *The Navigation of St. Brendan* contributed greatly to his popularity and to his reputation as patron saint of sailors and whales.

May 16 is also the feast day of *John Nepomucen* (1350–93), or Nepomuk, martyr and patron saint of the Czechs. He is also patron saint of Bohemia, confessors, and those who have been slandered.

Finally, this is also the feast day of *Peregrine of Auxerre* (d. ca. 261), regarded as the first bishop of Auxerre, who was martyred for opposing the dedication of a local temple to Jupiter. He is patron saint of cancer patients.

17 Paschal Baylon, religious

Paschal Baylon (1540–92) was a Franciscan lay brother who is patron saint of eucharistic devotions, congresses, and confraternities. Born at Torre Hermosa on the borders of Castile and Aragon of a poor shepherd family, he tended flocks as a youth (he is also patron saint of shepherds) and in his early twenties joined the reformed Friars Minor of Peter of Alcántara [October 22]. He devoted himself to the care of the sick and the poor and was known for his devotion to the Mass and the Blessed Sacrament; he remained for long periods of prayer before the tabernacle day after day and night after night and served one Mass after another each morning. While carrying letters to the minister general of the Observant Franciscans in France, he suffered injuries inflicted by Protestant Huguenots from which he never fully recovered. He died at age fifty-two. Many cures and miracles, as well as curious knocking sounds that were said to have continued for two hundred years, were reported at his tomb. He was beatified in 1618 and canonized in 1690. During the Spanish Civil War (1936–39) his grave was desecrated and his relics burned. His feast is not on the General Roman Calendar.

18 John I, pope and martyr; Felix of Cantalice, religious; Eric of Sweden, king

John I (d. 526; pope 523–26) was a Tuscan by birth who became archdeacon of Rome and was elected pope in 523, when aged and infirm. Italy was ruled at the time by an Arian, Theodoric the Goth, who was infuriated by the persecution of Arians, many of whom were Goths, in the Eastern empire. He summoned John to Ravenna and sent him as head of a delegation to Constantinople to persuade the emperor Justin I to end the persecutions. If John failed, Theodoric threatened to exact reprisals from Catholics in the West. The first pope to travel to the East, John was welcomed with great honors when he arrived in Constantinople in late 525. The emperor even prostrated himself before the pope "as if he were Peter in person." A few months later, in the Hagia Sophia church, he was given a throne higher than the patriarch's, sang the Mass in the Latin rite, and placed the traditional Easter crown on the emperor's head, a custom usually reserved to the patriarch. Justin agreed to all of Theodoric's demands, except that of allowing Arians who had conformed under pressure to return to Arian belief and practice.

When John returned to Ravenna with the agreement in hand, Theodoric was furious and accused the pope of having sold out to the emperor in return for all the adulation John had received from him. Theodoric forced the pope to remain in Ravenna until he decided what to do with him. Already exhausted by his long journey and terrified by the prospect of severe punishment at the hands of the king, the elderly pope collapsed and died, some said because of maltreatment and starvation. His body was taken back to Rome, where it was venerated as that of a martyr's and as possessing miraculous powers. He was buried in the nave of St. Peter's Basilica, with the epitaph "a victim for Christ." His feast is on the General Roman Calendar.

On this day the Franciscans celebrate the feast of *Felix of Cantalice* (1515–87), a Capuchin lay brother who devoted his life to collecting food and alms for the poor and the sick. The Lutherans commemorate *Eric of Sweden* (d. 1160), king of Sweden, who consolidated Christianity in his native land and saw to its spread to Finland. He is a patron saint of Sweden.

19 Dunstan of Canterbury, abbot and bishop; Celestine V, pope; Ivo Hélory of Kermartin, priest

Dunstan (909–88) was abbot of Glastonbury and archbishop of Canterbury, the restorer of Benedictine life in England, and is the patron saint of goldsmiths, jewelers, silversmiths, locksmiths, and musicians. Born at Baltonsborough, near Glastonbury, of a noble family with royal connections, he was educated at the local monastery and joined the household of his uncle Athelm, archbishop of Canterbury, and then the court of the king. He was expelled from the court for studying "vain poems" and pagan stories and for being a "magician." After considering marriage, he made private monastic vows and was ordained a priest by the bishop of Winchester. He returned to Glastonbury, where he lived as a hermit, practicing the crafts of painting, embroidery, and metalwork. The new king recalled Dunstan to court and then appointed him abbot of Glastonbury, where he restored the Rule of St. Benedict [July 11], beginning in 940. With another change at court, his enemies maneuvered his exile to France. Yet another king recalled him and appointed him bishop of Worcester in 957, then bishop of London in 959, and finally archbishop of Canterbury in 960.

As archbishop he preached and taught frequently, enforced the Church's marriage and fasting-and-abstinence laws, built and repaired churches, and served as a judge. Toward the end of his life, Dunstan spent most of his time in Canterbury with the monks of his household, teaching, correcting manuscripts, and administering justice. Visions, prophecies, and miracles were attributed to him even in his lifetime. He preached three times on the feast of the Ascension, 988, and died two days later, on May 19, just short of his eightieth birthday. After his death his cult spread widely and quickly. By 999 he was recognized as "the chief of all saints who rest at Christchurch" (the Canterbury cathedral). His feast is not on the General Roman Calendar, but it is celebrated by the Church of England, the Episcopal Church in the USA, and the Evangelical Lutheran Church in America.

On this day Benedictines and Cistercians celebrate the feast of *Celestine V* (1210–96; pope 1294), born Pietro del Murrone, one of the few popes in history to have resigned his office, only a few months after his election at about age eighty-five. He returned to his life as a Benedictine hermit, but under house arrest imposed by his successor, Boniface VIII, who feared that some of Celestine's supporters would try to make him a rival pope and create a schism in the Church. He is patron saint of bookbinders.

This is also the feast day of *Ivo Hélory of Kermartin* (1253–1303), a civil and canon lawyer in France who defended the poor without fee, served as a parish priest, and established a hospital. He is a patron saint of lawyers, judges, and abandoned children.

20 Bernardino of Siena, priest; Alcuin of York, abbot

Bernardino of Siena (1380–1444) was a Franciscan friar best known for his fostering of devotion to the Holy Name of Jesus and for the popularizing of the "IHS" emblem (a compression of the Greek word for Jesus) surrounded by rays, as if from the sun. Born in a small town near Siena, where his father was governor, he was left an orphan at age six and was raised by an aunt. After a broad education, including a degree in canon law, he became a Franciscan in 1402. He quickly established a reputation as a great preacher. He would travel by foot all across Italy, sometimes preaching for three or four hours at a time. The crowds were often so large that he spoke in the open air rather than in a church. His sermons focused on the need for penance and voluntary poverty. He denounced gambling, superstition, and political intrigue. Pope Pius II (1458–64) said that people listened to Bernardino as they might have listened to St. Paul himself [June 29].

He also wrote works of theology in both Latin and Italian, and, as vicar general of the Observant Franciscans, established schools of theology for his fellow friars in Perugia and Monteripido, insisting that ignorance in a friar was as dangerous as riches. He is thought to have written the statutes for the Observants in 1440. During his lifetime, he turned down three episcopal appointments: Siena, Ferrara, and Urbino. In 1442 he resigned his position as vicar general of his order and resumed his preaching, traveling now by donkey rather than on foot. By this time he was regarded as the most influential religious in Italy. Two years later he preached a course of fifty sermons on consecutive days in his hometown, Massa Marittima, then set out for Naples, preaching as he traveled. He died on May 20, 1444, at Aquila, where he was buried and where miracles were soon thereafter attributed to his intercession. He was canonized only six years later in 1450. Foremost among the many portraits of him is El Greco's in the Museo del Greco in Toledo. It depicts him with three baroque miters at his feet, representing the three bishoprics he refused. He is patron saint of many groups and causes, including advertisers, communications personnel, public relations, weavers, fire prevention, and those suffering from hoarseness. His feast is on the General Roman Calendar.

The Episcopal Church in the USA and the Church of England commemorate *Alcuin of York* (ca. 730–804), abbot of Tours and a leading educator, prolific writer, and theological adviser to the emperor Charlemagne. Alcuin has never been canonized or recognized as a saint in the Catholic Church, however.

21 Godric of Finchale, hermit; Constantine, emperor

Godric of Finchale (ca. 1069–1170), an English hermit, was the author of the earliest surviving Middle English verse, which he himself set to music, similar in style to Gregorian chant. Born of Anglo-Saxon parents in Walpole (Norfolk), he became by turns a peddler, a pilgrim (to Rome and Jerusalem), a sailor, a sea captain, a bailiff, a writer of music and verse, and then a hermit for fifty years or more. He settled finally at Finchale on land owned by the bishop of Durham. There he followed a regime of austerity and penance in reparation for the sins he committed as a sailor and a merchant. The prior of Durham gave him a Rule and offered him an association with the Durham monks. His holiness and other gifts attracted visitors, including his future biographer, Reginald of Durham. Godric received messengers from Thomas of Canterbury [December 29] and even the pope, Alexander III, wrote to him, commending his way of life and asking for prayers for himself and the whole Church. Godric died on May 21, 1170, after a long illness during which he was nursed by Durham monks. He was never formally canonized, and his cult seems to have been confined to Durham and Finchale. His fame eventually spread, however, through his biography and hymns. His feast is not on the General Roman Calendar.

On this day the Greek and Russian Orthodox Churches celebrate the feast of the emperor *Constantine* (ca. 288–337), patron saint of the Church and its liberator from persecution, and his mother, *Helen* [August 18], or Helena, protector of the holy places and founder of the True Cross. She is also commemorated on this day in the Church of England.

22 Rita of Cascia, widow and nun; Joachima of Vedruna, foundress

Rita of Cascia (1377–1457) is patron saint of desperate cases, much like St. Jude [October 28]. Born at Roccaporena in Umbria, she wished to become a nun from her earliest years, but married at the age of twelve in deference to her parents' wishes. The marriage was an unhappy one, but it produced two sons. After eighteen years of inflicting abuse and infidelity, Rita's husband was murdered in a vendetta. The two sons vowed to avenge their father's death, but both died before they could do so. Rita became an Augustinian nun ca. 1407 at Santa Maria Maddalena at Cascia, but she was refused the habit three times because she was not a virgin. The Augustinian authorities did not relent until 1413.

It is said that she meditated so intensely on the Passion of Christ that a wound appeared on her forehead, as if she had been pierced by a crown of thorns. Her reputation as a mystic grew. In the meantime, she also devoted herself to the care of sick nuns and to counseling laypersons who visited the convent. She died of tuberculosis on May 22, 1447, and only ten years later the local bishop approved of her cult. Because of miraculous cures attributed to her intercession, she was beatified in 1626 and canonized in 1900. Her cult remains popular in Spain, South America, the Philippines, Ireland, and parts of the United States, but especially in Italy. In 1946 a new basilica was built at Cascia with a hospital, school, and orphanage. Given the miserable marriage she patiently endured, she became a role model and inspiration for others in desperate marital situations. Her symbol is roses, which are blessed in Augustinian churches on her feast day. It is not on the General Roman Calendar, however.

On this day the Carmelites celebrate the feast of *Joachima of Vedruna* (1783–1854), also known as Joaquina de Mas de Vedruna, who, after the death of her husband and the raising of her children, founded a new religious community in Spain, the Carmelites of Charity. She was canonized by Pope John XXIII in 1959.

23 John Baptist Rossi, priest

John Baptist Rossi (1698–1764) was a Roman priest who devoted his life to those on the most distant margins of society. Born at Voltaggio near Genoa, he studied at the Roman College and was ordained a priest in 1721. In spite of his vulnerability to epileptic seizures, he worked tirelessly among the poor, the sick, the homeless, beggars, and prostitutes. He was also a gifted confessor to people of all social classes and a compelling preacher, particularly to religious communities. He lived a life of extreme poverty, giving away what little he had to others. Pope Benedict XIV entrusted him with courses of instruction for prison officials and other civil servants, including even the public hangman. His cause was begun in

1781 and he was canonized in 1881. On his feast day in 1965 his relics were transferred to a new parish church in Rome dedicated to him. His feast is not on the General Roman Calendar.

24 Simeon Stylites the Younger, hermit; Nicholas Copernicus, astronomer; Vincent of Lérins, monk

Simeon Stylites the Younger (ca. 517–92) was one of the so-called Stylite saints who lived on top of stone pillars in the desert, the most famous of whom is Simeon Stylites the Elder [September 1]. Born at Antioch, Simeon the Younger lived atop pillars near his birthplace for some fifty years. By age twenty he had already acquired a reputation for holiness and was attracting large crowds of visitors. He retired to a more inaccessible location on a mountain, which came to be known as Mons Admirabilis (Lat., "Wonderful Mountain"). He was ordained a priest at age twenty-three (another source says he was thirty-three). The bishop had to climb a ladder to lay hands on him. A steady stream of visitors came to seek his advice or to be cured. His diet was one of fruit and vegetables. Although many contemporaries questioned the way of life adopted by the Stylites, they enjoyed popular support because of their apparent sanctity (especially in an age of licentiousness and luxury), the spiritual assistance they rendered to those who sought it, their success in converting pagans to Christianity, their occasional interventions to achieve reconciliation in the political world, and various cures attributed to them. The cult of the Stylites has been popular in the East, but not in the West. The feast of Simeon the Younger is celebrated on this day in the Russian and Greek Orthodox Churches, but it is not on the General Roman Calendar.

Saint Simeon Sitting on a Column

The Church of England celebrates the feast of the Methodist evangelists and hymn writers *John* and *Charles Wesley* [March 2]. The Evangelical Lutheran Church in America commemorates *Nicholas Copernicus* (1473–1543), the famous astronomer who concluded that the earth revolves around the sun, not vice versa. This is also the feast day of *Vincent of Lérins* (d. ca.

450), a monk of the island monastery of Lérins, near Cannes, and the author of one of the most widely cited criteria for orthodoxy, namely, that a belief has been held "everywhere, always, and by all."

25 Venerable Bede, priest and Doctor of the Church; Gregory VII, pope; Mary Magdalene de Pazzi, virgin; Madeleine Sophia Barat, foundress; Blessed Mary MacKillop, foundress

The *Venerable Bede* (673–735), as he is best known, was the most important historian of the Church in England and a key agent in the preservation of classical and Christian culture. It is fitting that he is the patron saint of scholars. Born near Sunderland, he was educated from age seven, first by Benedict Biscop [January 12], abbot of Wearmouth, and then by Ceolfrith [September 25], abbot of Jarrow in Northumbria, both of whose biographies Bede would subsequently write. He entered the monastery at Jarrow and remained there until his death.

The Venerable Bede

Ordained a deacon at the young age of nineteen and a priest at age thirty, he devoted himself (thanks to the extraordinary library assembled by the abbey's founder and abbot, Benedict Biscop) to the study of Scripture, to the writing of biblical commentaries based on the commentaries of the great Latin Fathers of the Church, to lives of the saints, chronologies, and computational works, to translations of the writings of others, and to the teaching of Scripture and of Latin to the many Anglo-Saxons who, like himself, had come to the monastery with no knowledge of the language. He popularized the use of "A.D." (*Anno Domini,* Lat., "year of the Lord") for the years of the Christian era. His most significant achievement, however, was his *Ecclesiastical History of the English People,* which he completed in 731. It was widely read on the Continent as well as in England and became a classic that is still reprinted and studied. In spite of these considerable scholarly achievements, Bede's daily life was uneventful.

He rarely traveled, but attended faithfully to his monastic duties and to his scholarship. His last days were devoted to teaching, meditation, the chanting of psalms, translating the Gospel of John into Old English (his mother tongue) as well as some extracts from Isidore of Seville [April 4], and dictating the results to the boy who served as his scribe. He is said to have died singing the doxology "Glory be to the Father and to the Son and to the Holy Spirit." When Boniface [June 5], the "apostle to Germany" and a fellow Anglo-Saxon, received the news of Bede's death, he wrote this epitaph: "The candle of the Church, lit by the Holy Spirit, is extinguished." Bede's cult was established within fifty years of his death, with its main centers in Durham and York. Less than a century after his death, he was given the title "Venerable," and in the eleventh century his remains were transferred to the Durham cathedral, where a conspicuous tomb honors him. Pope Leo XIII named him a Doctor of the Church in 1899, the only English saint to achieve this honor. His feast is on the General Roman Calendar and is also celebrated by the Church of England and the Episcopal Church in the USA.

Gregory VII (ca. 1020–85; pope 1073–85), one of the greatest reformer popes in the history of the Church, inspired the so-called Gregorian reform. Born Hildebrand at Rovaco in Tuscany, he was educated in Rome under John Gratian, who became Pope Gregory VI (1045–46). He served under several popes as chaplain, treasurer of the Roman Church, archdeacon, chancellor, and counselor. Upon the death of Alexander II he was elected pope by acclamation and took the name Gregory, after his patron, Gregory VI, and Gregory the Great [September 3]. He made reform the centerpiece of his pontificate, targeting in particular abuses associated with simony, nepotism, clerical marriage, and lay interference in the appointment and investiture of bishops and abbots. In order to achieve his goals, however, he inflated traditional papal claims over the spiritual and temporal spheres.

His famous *Dictatus papae* (Lat., "Pronouncements of the Pope") contained twenty-seven propositions, including, for example, that the pope alone can wear imperial insignia, that his feet alone can be kissed by all princes, that he has the power to depose emperors, and that he can be judged by no one else. Because of his efforts against temporal rulers, he was twice "deposed" from the papacy by bishops under the control of the emperor Henry IV, who had been himself excommunicated by the pope. The Norman forces who invaded Rome to rescue Gregory VII from his imperial enemies behaved so violently that the Roman people turned on the pope who had invited them in. Gregory fled Rome for Monte Cassino and then to Salerno, where he died on

May 25, 1085. His last words were: "I have loved justice and hated iniquity. That is why I die in exile." He was buried in the Salerno cathedral.

It was Gregory VII who decreed that all bishops should visit Rome on a regular basis (the so-called *ad limina* visits "to the thresholds" of the apostles) to report on the state of their dioceses, and that archbishops should come to Rome to receive the pallium (their insignia of office). He also restricted the title of "pope" to the Bishop of Rome, created the position of papal legate (today called nuncios and apostolic delegates) to represent the pope in foreign countries, and fixed the Ember Days (four series of penitential days of fast and abstinence throughout the year, which are no longer observed). So strong and divisive was his personality that subsequent papal elections were often marked by bitter conflict between Gregorian and anti-Gregorian cardinals. The late Cardinal Yves Congar (d. 1995) referred to Gregory VII's pontificate as "the great turning point in ecclesiology," because it transformed the papacy of the first Christian millennium into a highly legalistic, juridical, and even monarchical institution. Gregory VII was beatified in 1584 and canonized in 1606. His feast is on the General Roman Calendar, but he is commemorated on May 26 on the Cistercian and Benedictine liturgical calendars, along with Philip Neri.

Mary Magdalene de Pazzi (1566–1607) was a Carmelite nun and mystic. Born Caterina di Geri de' Pazzi in Florence of a very wealthy family closely associated with the Medicis, she entered the Carmelites against her family's opposition and was professed in 1584, later becoming novice mistress and subprioress. From 1604 on, however, she was bedridden and in much pain, given even to temptations of suicide. She endured frequent and extended periods of spiritual desolation, feeling herself abandoned by God and unable to lift her mind and heart in prayer. Nevertheless, one of her sayings stressed that "God does not germinate in sad souls; [God] wants a heart that is free and happy."

She is said to have had numerous ecstatic visions, particularly of the Passion, and to have conversed with Christ and the saints. At the insistence of her confessor, her words uttered during these mystical experiences were written down by sister secretaries and incorporated in seven large volumes. Indeed, these detailed records make her one of the best-documented saints of her type and time. Some also attributed to her the power to foretell future events and to read the secrets of hearts. She died on May 25, 1607, and her cult began almost immediately, centered on her still incorrupt body at St. Maria degl'Angeli in Florence. She was beatified in 1626 and canonized in 1669. Her feast is on the

General Roman Calendar and is, of course, celebrated by the Carmelites on this day. She is commemorated on May 26 on the Cistercian and Benedictine liturgical calendars, along with Philip Neri.

May 25 is also the feast day of two foundresses who are not on the General Roman Calendar. *Madeleine Sophia Barat* (1779–1865) was a post-Revolutionary French nun who founded the Society of the Sacred Heart (R.S.C.J.) in 1800, also formerly known as the Madams of the Sacred Heart, who were renowned in the United States for educating the daughters of the wealthy. The community is engaged today in religious and secular education in parishes and schools and in social and health-care ministries.

Mary MacKillop (1842–1909), the cofoundress (with Father Julian Tenison Woods) of the Sisters of St. Joseph of the Sacred Heart (Josephites), is Australia's first native-born "blessed." Her original intention was to join one of the established religious orders, but, with the encouragement of her spiritual director, Father Woods, she founded her own community of sisters to provide schools for poor children, to establish orphanages, and to engage in other works of charity. Father Woods, however, was also at least partially responsible for the many difficulties Mary MacKillop would later have with the local hierarchy. He had indiscreetly encouraged some of her nuns who had allegedly experienced visions, insisted on an excessive standard of poverty, and refused all state aid for their schools and social welfare institutions. Mary's repeated clashes with the local bishops included even at one point her excommunication for her alleged disobedience. A year later the bishop absolved her and apologized for having been misled by bad clerical advisers. Hostility and suspicion toward her and her work continued sporadically within the Australian hierarchy, but each time the Vatican eventually supported her. Protestants in Australia were especially appreciative of the work of her sisters because of its ecumenical character and the stark simplicity of their lives. Mary MacKillop suffered a fatal stroke on May 25, 1909. She was beatified in 1995.

BIBLIOGRAPHY

Bede. *Bede: A Biblical Miscellany.* Trans. W. Trent Foley and Arthur G. Holder. Liverpool: Liverpool University Press, 1999.

Blair, Peter Hunter. *The World of Bede.* Cambridge: Cambridge University Press, 1990.

Ward, Benedicta. *The Venerable Bede.* Harrisburg, PA: Morehouse, 1990.

26 Philip Neri, priest; John Calvin, Reformer

Philip Neri (1515–95) was the founder of the Congregation of the Oratory, also known as the Oratorians. The Oratorians are best known in England through their most distinguished member, Cardinal John Henry Newman [August 11], who founded the Birmingham and London Oratories. Born in Florence, Philip left the city when the Medicis returned to power in 1532, disavowed a budding career as a merchant at San Germano near Naples, and went to Rome after a possible conversion experience in 1533. There he lived in an attic in extreme poverty, eking out an existence by giving lessons to his landlord's two sons. He spent some time studying philosophy and theology from the works of Thomas Aquinas [January 28], but then turned to apostolic work among young Florentines employed in banks and shops, whom he encouraged to serve the sick in hospitals and to visit the churches of Rome with him. In 1544, while on one of his frequent visits to the catacombs, he is said to have experienced a vision in which a ball of fire entered his mouth and dilated his heart—a physical condition that allegedly affected him for the remainder of his life. (An autopsy disclosed some broken ribs that had enabled his heart to expand and contract beyond a normal range.) In 1548 he founded the Confraternity of the Most Holy Trinity to look after pilgrims to Rome and to care for convalescents.

With the encouragement of his spiritual director, he was ordained a priest in 1551, lived with a community of diocesan priests at San Girolamo della Carità, and spent long hours in the confessional and in spiritual direction. He is said to have had extraordinary insights into people's hearts. It was also a time of vigorous reform and pastoral renewal in the Church. The Council of Trent met in three different convocations during his lifetime: 1545–48, 1551–52, and 1562–63. Ignatius of Loyola [July 31] and Francis Xavier [December 3], pioneers of the new Society of Jesus, were among his friends. So too were Camillus de Lellis [July 14], John Leonardi [October 9], Charles Borromeo [November 4], and Francis de Sales [January 24]. But he also had enemies—people who accused him of pride and ambition, of introducing novelties into spiritual and pastoral practice, and of using his small groups to plot against the pope. The first wave of suspicion was alleviated with the election of a new, more moderate pope, Pius IV, in 1559. The second wave began under Pope Pius V in 1567. Philip was accused of having laymen preach and of using vernacular hymns. The intervention of his friend Cardinal Charles Borromeo saved him from further scrutiny.

He and five priest-disciples began using an oratory built over the nave of San Girolamo, to which they would summon the faithful by ringing a small bell. They shared a common life under Philip's direction, but without vows. "If you want to be obeyed," he once said, "don't make commandments." The group developed into the Congregation of the Oratory, which was approved by his friend Pope Gregory XIII in 1575. Because of his reputation as a confessor and spiritual adviser, Philip received many visitors, including cardinals, foreigners, the poor, and the troubled. Many were attracted by his warm personality, easy sense of humor, and cheerfulness. He once said that it was "easier to guide cheerful persons in the spiritual life than the melancholy." He is reported to have experienced ecstasy in prayer during the celebration of Mass, to the point where his server would occasionally have to absent himself for two hours at a time, returning when the saint returned to normal consciousness and was able to continue with Mass. In 1575, the same year he approved the group, Gregory XIII gave the community the small and dilapidated church of Santa Maria in Vallicella. Philip decided to pull it down and build a larger church, known as the Chiesa Nuova (Ital., "new church"). It was occupied by the Oratorians in 1577, but Philip himself did not move there until 1584. In 1593 he resigned as superior in favor of Baronius, who would later become a cardinal.

Philip and his Oratorians had introduced a whole new style of personal spirituality integrated with the pastoral life and ministries of the Church. They also encouraged sermons by laypeople, the presentation of plays with biblical themes, and the composition of cantatas and songs on religious themes.

After spending a normal day of celebrating Mass, hearing confessions, and seeing visitors, Philip suffered a stroke at midnight on May 25, 1595, and died early the next morning. His body rests in the Chiesa Nuova. Regarded as a saint even in his lifetime and known as the "apostle of Rome" for reviving Christian life in a city that had absorbed the worst elements of the Renaissance, Philip Neri was beatified in 1615 and canonized in 1622. He is the patron saint of the city of Rome. His feast is on the General Roman Calendar.

The Church of England and the Episcopal Church in the USA celebrate the feast of *Augustine of Canterbury* [May 27] on this day, the day of his death, with a commemoration of Philip Neri and also of the Protestant Reformer *John Calvin* (d. 1564).

BIBLIOGRAPHY

Türks, Paul. *Philip Neri: The Fire of Joy.* Trans. Daniel Utrecht. New York: Alba House, 1995.

27 Augustine of Canterbury, bishop

Augustine of Canterbury (d. ca. 604) was the "apostle of the English" and the first archbishop of Canterbury. He is one of the patron saints of England. An Italian by birth, Augustine became a monk and later prior of the monastery of St. Andrew [November 30] on the Celian Hill in Rome. In 596 he was chosen by his friend Gregory the Great [September 3] to lead a mission of monks to evangelize the Anglo-Saxons in Britain, Welsh missionaries having previously failed in the task. When they reached Gaul, many of them wished to turn back because of the uncertainty, the difficulty, and the dangers involved in their journey. But Gregory encouraged them and appointed Augustine as their abbot. (He was later consecrated a bishop by the bishops in the Reims area.) With the addition of perhaps ten Frankish priests to act as interpreters, the group numbered forty in all.

Having traveled by way of Lérins, Marseilles, Aix-en-Provence, Arles, Vienne, Lyons, Autun, and Tours, they crossed the English Channel at Boulogne or Quentavic and landed at Ebbsfleet, Kent, in 597. They were received cautiously by Ethelbert [February 24], king of Kent, the most important of the seven Anglo-Saxon kingdoms, who asked them to remain on the isle of Thanet until he decided what to do about them. He eventually met with them in the open air (for fear of spells), gave them a house at Canterbury, and granted them permission to preach. He himself was converted to Christianity sometime within the following four years. Augustine established a small, Roman-style church at Canterbury dedicated to St. Martin [November 11], a Frankish saint. He received additional missionary recruits from Rome, together with books, relics, and altar vessels. The relics were probably of Roman martyrs to whom the earliest Kentish churches were then dedicated.

He built the first cathedral and school at Canterbury, dedicating the cathedral as Christ Church, and founded the monastery of Sts. Peter and Paul (called St. Augustine's after his death), just outside the walls of the city but very near the cathedral. It is likely that the monks joined the local diocesan clergy for Mass and for the chanting of the morning and evening Divine Office. He also established the suburban see of Rochester and later the see of London.

It seems that Augustine was not a confident administrator, because he constantly sought guidance from Pope Gregory on the smallest pastoral details. Through regular correspondence, Pope Gregory carefully instructed Augustine in his missionary endeavors. He urged him not to destroy pagan temples but only the idols contained in them. Otherwise, he insisted, Augustine should proceed slowly and deliberately in eliminating erroneous religious practices. He also recommended, for example, that revenues should be divided four ways: one part for the bishop and his household, one for the clergy, one for the poor, and one for the repair of churches. The pope subsequently conferred the archbishop's pallium on Augustine as a sign of his pastoral authority over the whole of the southern province, which Augustine centered not in London (as the pope had expected) but at Canterbury, the main town of England's most powerful ruler. The pope also proposed the establishment of a northern province centered at York, with each province having twelve suffragan bishops. The plan was never fully realized. The conferring of the pallium also established Canterbury's independence of the Church in Gaul. Neither church would have authority over the other.

Relations with Welsh Christians and the Christian Britons in the west country, however, were difficult. They resisted Augustine's overtures of cooperation in the evangelization of the Anglo-Saxons, whom they detested, as well as other pagan groups in eastern England, and they were put off by his Roman ways. Contrary to the Roman approach of centering the local church in a major city or town, the Celtic Christian unit was the rural monastery. They also had a different system for calculating the date of Easter, an issue that would eventually be resolved in favor of the Roman standard at the Synod of Whitby in 664.

Augustine consecrated Laurence as his successor before his own death on May 26, sometime between 604 and 609. He was buried in his monastery, and his relics were transferred with great solemnity in 1091 to the place of greatest honor in the east end of the new cathedral. His feast day is on the General Roman Calendar, although it is celebrated on May 26, as noted above, within the Anglican Communion.

The Evangelical Lutheran Church in America celebrates the feast of *John Calvin* [May 26], major Protestant Reformer, on this day.

BIBLIOGRAPHY

Brooks, Nicholas. *The Early History of the Church of Canterbury: Christ Church from 597 to 1066.* London/New York: Leicester University Press, 1996 (orig. ed., 1984).

Deansley, Margaret. *Augustine of Canterbury.* Southampton: Saint Austin Press, 1997.

Farmer, David Hugh, ed. *Benedict's Disciples.* Leominster: Fowler Wright, 1980.

Green, Michael A. *St. Augustine of Canterbury.* London: Janus, 1997.

28 Germanus of Paris, bishop; Mariana of Jesus de Paredes, mystic; Blessed Lanfranc of Bec, bishop; Bernard of Montjoux, priest

Germanus of Paris (ca. 500–576) is, alongside Geneviève [January 3], patron saint of Paris. Born at Autun in Burgundy, he lived a semimonastic life for fifteen years, was ordained a priest in 530, and then was appointed abbot of the monastic church of St. Symphorien (d. ca. 200) in Autun, where the patronal saint had been martyred for refusing to pay honor to the pagan gods. Germanus proved to be an efficient administrator both of the monastery and the lands it owned as well as a generous benefactor of the poor. When the bishop of Paris was removed from office for some unspecified malfeasance (probably an act of disloyalty to the king), Germanus was appointed to succeed him by the other Gallic bishops and the Frankish king, Childebert, who built a cathedral and monastic basilica for the new bishop. The latter building was originally the basilica of St. Vincent and Holy Cross, but was subsequently named in Germanus's honor as Saint-Germain-des-Prés.

Germanus played important parts in at least three church councils, two in Paris (562 and 573) and a third in Tours (567). Childebert's successor, Charibert, was at once oppressive and corrupt. When the king married two sisters at the same time, Germanus excommunicated him. (It was Charibert's daughter Bertha who married Ethelbert [February 24], king of Kent, the one who received the missionaries from Rome under the leadership of Augustine of Canterbury [May 27].)

Germanus was devoted to the cult of saints and was renowned for his healing powers. He was especially devoted to the pastoral care of prisoners and slaves of all races. He died in Paris on May 28, 576, and was buried close to his patron Childebert in his abbey church. His cult began very early. By 600 his name had been added to martyrologies. His relics were placed behind the altar of Holy Cross in 756, removed for a time because of the Viking invasions, then transferred to a splendid reliquary in 1408 and above the high altar in 1704. The reliquary was destroyed during the French Revolution in 1793. His abbey had become a great center of historical scholarship during the seventeenth century, but it too suffered severe damage in the Revolution. Germanus's feast is not on the General Roman Calendar.

On this day, the Franciscans celebrate the feast of *Mariana of Jesus de Paredes* (1614–45), a Franciscan tertiary who is one of the few canonized saints of South America (1950). She died at age thirty-one after a life of penance, solitude, and ecstatic and prophetic experiences. Following an earthquake and epidemic in her native Quito, Ecuador, in 1645, Mariana offered her own life of prayer and sacrifice in reparation for the sins of its people. She died soon thereafter, worn out by an illness that had been aggravated by her self-imposed austerities.

The Church of England commemorates *Lanfranc of Bec* (ca. 1010–89), an Italian by birth, who was appointed archbishop of Canterbury by William the Conqueror in 1070. A distinguished theologian and canon lawyer and a highly effective bishop, Lanfranc was beatified by the Catholic Church, but never canonized. His feast is not on the General Roman Calendar.

Finally, May 28 is the feast day of *Bernard of Montjoux* (d. 1081), also known as Bernard of Aosta and of Menthon, a priest of the diocese of Aosta who took special care of Alpine travelers, always at risk from snowdrifts and robbers. He founded some houses for them, and a specially trained breed of dogs, Saint Bernards, were named after him. He was declared patron saint of mountain climbers by Pope Pius XI, who had himself engaged in the sport.

29 Maximinus of Trier, bishop; Theodosia of Constantinople, nun; Bona of Pisa, pilgrim and mystic

Maximinus of Trier (d. ca. 347) was regarded by both Jerome [September 30] and Athanasius [May 2] as one of the most courageous bishops of his time. A native of Poitiers, he went to Trier, the imperial capital of the Western empire, for his education, attracted by the reputation of its bishop, Agritius. He eventually succeeded Agritius as bishop in 333 and became celebrated for his staunch opposition to Arianism and for the hospitality and assistance he gave to its victims, including Athanasius, the bishop of Alexandria, who was the leading figure at the First Council of Nicaea in 325 and the strongest opponent of Arianism throughout much of the fourth century. Athanasius was Maximinus's guest for two years (336–38). Paul of Constantinople, exiled from his patriarchate by the emperor Constantius, also enjoyed his protection and hospitality. Maximinus vigorously opposed Arianism in councils (including the Synod of Cologne, which he himself convened) and also personally warned the emperor Constans, a frequent visitor to Trier, against the heresy. Although he is known to have written several treatises, none of his writings survive. His feast is not on the General Roman Calendar.

On this day the Russian and Greek Orthodox Churches celebrate the feast of *Theodosia of Constantinople* (d. 745), a nun at the monastery of St. Anastasia [December 22] in Constantinople who led a group of nuns in resisting a band of soldiers sent to enforce the iconoclastic decrees of the emperor Leo III. The emperor had ordered the destruction of the image of Christ over the monastery's main entrance. Theodosia was imprisoned and tortured to death, along with twelve other women.

This is also the feast day of *Bona of Pisa* (1156–1207), a mystic and pilgrim who traveled several times to the Holy Land, Rome, and Compostela in Spain. Probably for that reason she is the patron saint of flight attendants.

30 Joan of Arc, virgin; Josephine Butler, social reformer; Ferdinand of Castile, king; Isaac of Constantinople, abbot; Dymphna

Joan of Arc (1412–31) is one of the patron saints of France. Born at Domrémy in Champagne, the daughter of a peasant farmer, she was a young girl during the Hundred Years' War between France and England and the civil war within France between the houses of Orléans and Burgundy. As the English armies regained the ascendancy, Joan claimed to have heard the voices of saints urging her to save France. (Two of those "saints" were Margaret of Antioch [July 20] and Catherine of Alexandria [November 25], who almost certainly never existed.) At first, no one paid any attention to Joan, but she was taken more seriously when some of her predictions of further defeats were fulfilled. She was sent to the Dauphin (the future Charles VII), who was impressed that Joan recognized him through his disguise. She also passed review by a group of theologians at Poitiers. Her credentials established, she asked for troops to relieve Orléans in 1429 and was accorded the honor of leading them into battle in full white armor and accompanied by a special banner bearing a symbol of the Trinity and the words, "Jesus, Maria." Orléans was saved and

Joan of Arc at the Coronation of Charles VII in Reims Cathedral by Jean Auguste Dominique Ingres, 1851–54

English forts in the vicinity were captured. (Thus, her title, the "Maid of Orléans.")

Joan also took part in another successful campaign at Patay, and stood at the side of the new king when he was crowned at Reims. The predominantly male court, Church, and army, however, resented her newly elevated stature. Military reversals (including a failed attack on Paris) and her own capture by the duke of Burgundy changed the situation drastically in 1430. The king made no attempt to save her. The Burgundians sold her to their English allies, who attributed her military successes to witchcraft and spells. She was imprisoned at Rouen and tried for witchcraft and heresy in the court of the bishop of Beauvais. She defended herself vigorously, but her lack of theological sophistication led her into damaging mistakes. Indeed, she could neither read nor write. With the support of the University of Paris, her judges declared that her visions were false and even diabolical and demanded that she recant. At first, she made some form of recantation and was returned to prison. But when she appeared once more in male clothes (which she had promised not to wear again) and repeated her conviction that God had sent her and that the voices were from God, she was declared a lapsed heretic, handed over to the secular authorities, and burned at the stake in the marketplace at Rouen on May 30, 1431. Her gaze fixed on the cross, she died calling on the name of Jesus.

A member of the English royal court made the comment: "We are lost. We have burned a saint." Some twenty years later her family asked that the case be reopened. Pope Callistus III appointed a commission, which in 1456 set aside the verdict and declared her innocent. She was beatified by Pope Pius X [August 21] in 1910 and canonized in 1920 by Pope Benedict XV, a gesture that helped in the restoration of diplomatic relations between the Holy See and France. Her feast is not on the General Roman Calendar.

Although the Church of England also commemorates Joan of Arc on this day, it accords the principal festal celebration to *Josephine Butler* (1828–1906), an English social reformer who combated prostitution and the slave trade, taking as her model of holiness Catherine of Siena [April 29].

On this day the Franciscans commemorate *Ferdinand of Castile* (1199–1252), the king of both Castile and of Léon, who recaptured much of southern Spain from the Moors. He was buried not in royal robes, but in the habit of a Franciscan tertiary. He was canonized in 1671 and is the patron saint of engineers, governors, the poor, and prisoners.

The Russian Orthodox Church celebrates the feast of *Isaac of Constantinople* (d. ca. 410), the founder of the first monastery in Constantinople. It was named the Dalmatian monastery, after Isaac's successor, Dalmatus.

Finally, this is also the feast day of *Dymphna,* a seventh-century Irish woman, whose life is almost wholly fictional. She is said to have been murdered by her own father after she fled to Belgium to escape his advances. She is the patron saint of the mentally ill and of sleepwalkers.

BIBLIOGRAPHY

Gordon, Mary. *Joan of Arc.* New York: Lipper/Viking, 2000.

Pernoud, Régine. *Joan of Arc: Her Story.* Trans. Jeremy du Quesnay Adams. New York: St. Martin's Press, 1998.

Tavard, George H. *The Spiritual Way of St. Jeanne d'Arc.* Collegeville, MN: Liturgical Press, 1998.

Warner, Marina. *Joan of Arc: The Image of Female Heroism.* New York: Knopf, 1981.

31 The Visitation of the Blessed Virgin Mary

This feast commemorates the visit of the *Blessed Virgin Mary* to her cousin Elizabeth [November 5]. According to Luke 1:39–56, Mary, having learned that both she and her aged cousin had conceived, visited Elizabeth and remained with her for three months. Upon her arrival, Mary uttered the song of praise known as the Magnificat. The Latin title derives from the opening word of the hymn in the Vulgate. The Magnificat praises God's salvific power manifested in the overthrow of the mighty, the vindication of the lowly, and the divine mercy perpetually shown to Israel. The event is also commemorated as one of the Joyful Mysteries of the Rosary [see October 7].

The feast itself is Franciscan in origin. The general chapter of 1263 introduced it at the request of Bonaventure [July 15], who was minister general of the order. Urban VI (1378–89), the pope whose election precipitated the Great Schism (1378–1417), decided to place this feast on the liturgical calendar for the universal Church with the hope that it might help to end the schism, and Boniface IX (1389–1404) actually prescribed that it be done in 1389. Because of the deep divisions in the Church, however, Boniface's decree was accepted only in those parts of the Church that acknowledged his primacy. The Council of Basel again ordered its celebration in 1441, but it was not until the pontificate of Pius V (1566–72) [April 30] that the feast in fact attained universal status, to be celebrated on July 2.

In 1969, with the revision of the General Roman Calendar, the date of the feast was changed to May 31 in order to stress its spiritual connection with the feasts of the Annunciation [March 25] and the Birth of John the Baptist [June 24]. It was the announcement of the angel Gabriel [September 29] that gave rise to Mary's visit to Elizabeth. And it was John the Baptist whom Elizabeth had conceived in her womb. Because the Magnificat prayer is recited daily at Vespers, in a real sense the Visitation is commemorated by the Church every day of the year. The feast of the Visitation is also celebrated by the Church of England and the Episcopal Church in the USA and by the Evangelical Lutheran Church in America.

JUNE

1 Justin, martyr

Justin (ca. 100–ca.165) was one of the first great apologists, or defenders of the faith, and is regarded as the first significant Christian philosopher. (He is the patron saint of philosophers.) Indeed, he may have been the greatest Christian figure between the apostles and Irenaeus (d. ca. 200) [June 28]. Born Flavia Neapolis at Shechem (modern Nablus) in Samaria, of Greek parents, he was well educated in rhetoric, poetry, and history, and then studied philosophy in Ephesus and Alexandria in search, as he put it, of "the vision of God." After studying with Stoics, Pythagoreans, Peripatetics, and Platonists, he became a Christian ca. 130, having been impressed with the connection between Christ and the Old Testament prophecies as well as with those who suffered martyrdom for their faith. He had found deficiencies in the first three philosophies, but was attracted to the fourth as a second stream of divine truth alongside its fulfillment in Christian revelation, the criterion of all truth. Nevertheless, it was the teachings of Christ that became for him "the only sure and useful philosophy."

For Justin, the Son of God is the generative or germinative Word (Gk. *Logos spermatikos*) who had sown the seed of truth in all people and who had become incarnate in Jesus of Nazareth, in whom the prophecies of the Old Testament were fulfilled. Christ is also the new Adam, and his mother, the new Eve. The Incarnation, Justin insisted, was not a break in history, but its fulfillment.

After his conversion, he continued his role as a philosopher, complete with the traditional garb of a philosopher, but now as a Christian, teaching first at Ephesus and eventually in Rome. He publicly debated Jews, Gnostics, and those who worshiped Roman gods. He went to Rome ca. 150, where he founded a school of philosophy, taught Christian apologetics, and wrote his major works. His writings disclose important information about the contemporary rites of Baptism and the Eucharist (he wanted to show that they were not magical, as the pagans charged) as well as the distribution of alms. They also contain refutations of charges of immorality (incest and cannibalism) and atheism (the refusal to participate in public worship) commonly leveled against Christians, demonstrating that loyalty to the emperor was consistent with the teachings of Christ. It is important to remember that Justin taught from a living and lived tradition of the Church and not from the New Testament, since that portion of the Scriptures had not yet taken its current form.

Justin was arrested during the reign of Marcus Aurelius. At his trial he openly confessed his Christian faith, refused to sacrifice to the gods, and accepted suffering and death as a means to salvation. He was scourged and then beheaded with six other Christians ca. 165. His feast is on the General Roman Calendar. It is also celebrated by the Russian Orthodox Church (along with those martyred with him in Rome), the Church of England, the Episcopal Church in the USA, and the Evangelical Lutheran Church in America.

2 Marcellinus and Peter, martyrs; Nicephorus, bishop; Martyrs of Lyons; Erasmus (Elmo), bishop and martyr

Marcellinus and *Peter* (d. 304) were Roman martyrs whose names were included in the Roman Canon of the Mass. Marcellinus was a prominent priest of Rome, and Peter was an exorcist. They were arrested, imprisoned, and later beheaded, probably during the persecutions of the emperor Diocletian. They were buried in the catacomb of Tiburtius on the Via Laviana. Constantine [May 21] built a church over their tomb and his mother, Helen [August 18], was buried there ca. 330. Part of the tomb forms a portion of the church named for the two martyrs. In 828 Pope Gregory IV sent some of their relics to Einhard, the former secretary and biographer of the emperor Charlemagne, to enrich his monastery at Seligenstadt. Miracles were later associated with the relics. The feast of Marcellinus and Peter is on the General Roman Calendar.

On this day the Russian Orthodox Church commemorates *Nicephorus* (758–828), patriarch of Constantinople, who was a vigorous opponent of iconoclasm. The Episcopal Church in the USA commemorates the *Martyrs of Lyons* (d. 177), who were tortured and killed during the reign of Marcus Aurelius. This is also the feast day of *Erasmus* (d. ca. 300), also known as Elmo, the bishop-martyr of Formiae in Italy, who became invoked as one of the Fourteen Holy Helpers (see Glossary), a group of saints who enjoyed a special cult in the Rhineland from the fourteenth century. Because so little is known of his life, there is much confusion about him, which may account for the fact that he is patron saint of sailors, stomach ailments, childbirth, and women in labor.

3 Charles Lwanga and companions, martyrs; Blessed John XXIII, pope; Kevin, abbot

Charles Lwanga (ca. 1860–86) *and his companions* are regarded as the protomartyrs (first martyrs) of black Africa. He was one of twenty-two African Catholics who were executed for their faith, including Joseph Mkasa, Denis Sebuggwawo, Matthias Murumba, and Andrew Kagwa. Twenty-four Protestants were also martyred. In 1920 Pope Benedict XV declared Charles Lwanga patron saint of youth and Catholic Action for most of tropical Africa. Born in Buddu County, Uganda, Charles became a catechumen after learning of Christianity from two members of the chief's court. He served as an assistant to Joseph Mkasa, who was in charge of the king's pages. On the night of Mkasa's martyrdom by beheading upon the orders of the new chief, or *kabaka*, Charles requested and received Baptism (November 15, 1885). He became head of the pages and spent much of his energy protecting them from the chief's sexual designs upon them. He instructed the pages in the Christian faith and then, when their lives were threatened, he baptized them. Charles and the pages were forced to confess their faith, arrested, and then taken on a brutal sixteen-mile march to Namugongo on Lake Victoria. Three of the youths were killed on the way. Charles and six others were wrapped in mats of reed and slowly burned alive on the feast of the Ascension, June 3, 1886. It is said that their courage and cheerfulness in the face of death were reminiscent of the spirit of the early Christian martyrs.

The martyrs of Uganda were beatified in 1920 and canonized by Pope Paul VI in 1964, and their feast was placed on the General Roman Calendar in 1969. That same year Paul VI made a pilgrimage to Namugongo as part of the first papal visit to the African continent. The Church of England and the Episcopal Church in the USA also commemorate the Martyrs of Uganda on this day. However, the Anglicans also include the Anglican and Protestant martyrs, as well as those martyred by the Muslim military dictatorship in the 1970s.

This is also the feast day of *Pope John XXIII* (1881–1963; pope 1958–63), who convened the historic Second Vatican Council (1962–65) and is widely regarded as the most beloved pope in history. Born Angelo Giuseppe Roncalli, the third of thirteen children in a family of peasant farmers, at Sotto il Monte near Bergamo, he was ordained a priest in 1904 and served as secretary to the bishop of Bergamo and as a lecturer in church history at the diocesan seminary. He was a conscripted hospital orderly during World War I and then a military chaplain. In 1921 Pope Benedict XV appointed him national director of the Congregation for the Propagation of the Faith. Because of his deep interest in history, and especially in Charles Borromeo [November 4], whose life he researched at the Ambrosian Library in Milan, Father Roncalli came to the attention of its librarian, Achille Ratti, the future Pope Pius XI (1922–39). It was Ratti, after his election as pope, who launched Roncalli's diplomatic career in Bulgaria, Turkey, Greece, and then France during World War II.

Pope John XXIII, 1958

Archbishop Roncalli established friendly relations with the Orthodox churches and did what he could to prevent the deportation of Jews after the German occupation of Greece. In France he dealt tactfully with the new worker-priest movement and with bishops who had collaborated with the Nazis. He also served as the Vatican's first permanent observer at the United Nations Educational, Scientific, and Cultural Organization (UNESCO). In 1953 he was appointed cardinal-patriarch of Venice. He was elected pope on October 28, 1958, just shy of his seventy-seventh birthday. Many regarded him as a "transitional pope." The new pope was to prove them wrong.

He was crowned on November 4, the feast day of his hero Charles Borromeo, and, contrary to custom, preached at his own coronation Mass, insisting that he wanted to be, above all, a good shepherd. When he took possession of his cathedral church as Bishop of Rome, the Basilica of St. John Lateran, he reiterated that he was not a prince, but "a priest, a father, a shepherd." That Christmas he revived a custom of visiting prisoners at Regina Coeli, where he recalled the jailing of one of his own relatives, and of visiting patients at one of the local hospitals. He also made frequent appearances at local parishes, other hospitals, convalescent homes, and educational and charitable institutions. He announced a new ecumenical council on January 25, 1959, referring to it as a "new Pentecost." His opening address to the council on October 11, 1962, was the most important speech given in the council's four years of existence. He insisted that the council had not been called to refute errors, but to update the Church and to "let some fresh air in." Separating himself from many of his close advisers, whom he described as "prophets of gloom," his talk was full of hope for the future of the Church.

His encyclicals emphasized the unity of the Church, world peace, social justice, and human rights. Indeed, no pope in history was so committed to Christian unity as he was. He established the Secretariat for Promoting Christian Unity (now the Pontifical Council for Promoting Christian Unity) and opened channels of communication with other major Christian leaders and with the World Council of Churches. Out of concern for the Jews, he removed the word "perfidious" from the prayer for Jews in the Good Friday liturgy, and on one occasion greeted a group of Jewish visitors with the words, "I am Joseph, your brother."

Diagnosed with stomach cancer in September 1962, his last public appearance from the window of his apartment was on Ascension Thursday, May 23, 1963. Over the next several days, he was filled with pain, but he remained conscious and communicative. His statements were relayed around the world, drawing the global community into an unprecedented solidarity. He prayed for the council and for church unity, for workers, for the sick and the suffering, and for so many others. When he died on the evening of June 3, virtually the whole world mourned his loss. Even the Union Jack was lowered to half-staff in the bitterly divided city of Belfast. In the early Church he would have been proclaimed a saint by popular demand. He was beatified on September 3, 2000. The Evangelical Lutheran Church in America also commemorates him on this day.

This is also the feast day of *Kevin* (d. ca. 618), or Coemgen ("the fair-begotten" in Gaelic), founder and abbot of Glendalough (County Wicklow) and a patron saint of Dublin. His feast is celebrated throughout Ireland. Little is known of his life apart from legendary accounts, but he is reputed to have lived to the age of 120.

BIBLIOGRAPHY

Hastings, Adrian. *The Church in Africa: 1450–1950.* Oxford: Oxford University Press, 1994.
Hebblethwaite, Peter. *Pope John XXIII: Shepherd of the Modern World.* Garden City, NY: Doubleday, 1985.

4 Metrophanes, bishop; Optatus of Milevis, apologist; Francis Caracciolo, founder

Metrophanes (d. ca. 325) was the first patriarch of Constantinople and one of the major reasons the emperor Constantine [May 21] chose Byzantium as the new capital of his empire. Dometius, the father of Metrophanes, after converting to Christianity took his family to live in Byzantium, which was then a small town. Dometius was a close friend of the bishop of Heracles, who ordained him and whom he succeeded as bishop. He, in turn, was succeeded by his older son, and then in 313 by his younger son, Metrophanes. It is not clear whether the see was moved from Heracles to Byzantium, or whether it was divided when Constantine transformed Byzantium into his new capital. In any case, it is clear that Metrophanes was the first bishop of Byzantium (later Constantinople). Illness and old age prevented his attending the Council of Nicaea (325), but the emperor paid a visit to him a week before his death. Metrophanes had a great reputation for sanctity throughout the East, and a church was built in his honor soon after Constantine's own death. His feast is not on the General Roman

Calendar, but is celebrated by the Greek and Russian Orthodox Churches on this day. The Dominicans commemorate *Peter of Verona* [April 6].

June 4 is also the feast day of *Optatus of Milevis* (d. ca. 387), one of the outstanding apologists, or defenders of the faith, in the Church of North Africa during the fourth century. Augustine [August 28] referred to him as ranking with Cyprian of Carthage [September 16] and Hilary of Poitiers [January 13], and Fulgentius of Ruspe, less than one hundred years later, regarded Optatus to be a saint and ranked him with Ambrose of Milan [December 7] and Augustine himself. Optatus was bishop of Milevis in Numidia and a leading opponent of Donatism, a schismatic movement that deeply divided the Church of North Africa. The Donatists took their name from Donatus, who was an unsuccessful candidate for the bishopric of Carthage in 311. When Donatus and his followers established a church of their own in opposition to Rome, Optatus rebutted their claims, but in a conciliatory manner. He asked them how they could consider themselves to be the one, true Church when they represented only a tiny corner of North Africa and one small Roman colony. He also refuted their argument that Donatus had a stronger claim to the bishopric because he was holier than the victorious candidate. Optatus articulated a theological principle that holds to this day, namely, that the validity or efficacy of the sacraments does not depend upon the holiness of the minister. His feast is not on the General Roman Calendar.

Francis Caracciolo (1563–1608) is a patron saint of Naples and was the cofounder of the Order of the Minor Clerks Regular in 1588. Baptized Ascanio, he took the name Francis at his solemn profession out of devotion to Francis of Assisi [October 4]. He was a relative of Thomas Aquinas [January 28] through his mother and to Neapolitan princes through his father. As superior of his order, he refused to take precedence over his brothers, insisting on taking his own turn at the most menial tasks. He heard confessions every morning, begged in the streets on behalf of the poor, and gave away what little he owned to those in greater need. He was canonized in 1807. His feast is not on the General Roman Calendar.

5 Boniface, bishop and martyr

Boniface (ca. 675–754) was the "apostle of Germany" and is a patron saint of the country. Born probably at Crediton in Devon, England, of land-owning Anglo-Saxon peasants, he was baptized as Wynfrith, or Winfrid, and was educated in Benedictine monasteries at Exeter and then Nursling, between Winchester and Southampton. As a young monk and schoolmaster, he compiled the first Latin grammar in England. He was ordained a priest at age thirty and, because of his deep knowledge of Scripture, was an effective preacher and teacher. Rather than follow a promising career path in England, he chose to leave his monastery to become a missionary in present-day Germany. He went first to Frisia (the northern part of the Netherlands today) in 716, where Wilfrid [October 12] and Willibrord [November 7] had been pioneers. Resistance from the pagan tribes, however, was so strong that he returned to Nursling.

The following year he was elected abbot, but remained in office only a short time. He relinquished the office and traveled to Rome, where in 719, with a supporting letter in hand from the bishop of Winchester, he received a mission directly from Pope Gregory II to preach the gospel in Bavaria and Hesse. On his way there, he learned that conditions had changed for the better in Frisia following the death of its anti-Christian leader, Radbod, so he went to assist the aged Willibrord, who was bishop of Utrecht, for three years. Thereafter, he went to Hesse and later to Rome, where the pope consecrated him a regional bishop (i.e., without a specific diocese) in 722 with jurisdiction over Germany. It may have been during this visit to Rome that Wynfrith (Winfrid), or perhaps even the pope himself, changed his name to Boniface, in honor of the martyr whose feast had been celebrated the day before.

With the aid of a papal letter, he received the support of the Frankish king, Charles Martel, to evangelize Hesse. There was a famous incident at Geismar, near the abbey of Fritzlar, where Boniface cut down an oak tree sacred to the pagans (called the Oak of Thor) and feared for its magical powers. When no evil befell Boniface, there were widespread conversions to Christianity. He moved on to establish monasteries in various places, including Fritzlar, Amöneburg, Ohrdruf, Erfurt, Würzburg, Eichstätt, and Fulda. The monasteries gave stability and permanence to his missionary work, especially in rural areas. In 732 the new pope, Gregory III, sent Boniface the pallium, making him an archbishop (again, without any specific see) with the authority to consecrate missionary bishops in Germany beyond the Rhine. It should be noted that Rome at the time was also concerned about the abiding influence of the Celtic missionaries who had preceded Boniface and who had introduced various forms of Celtic monastic Christianity, with wandering missionary bishops. Boniface was a willing instrument of Romanization.

Wherever he went, many were converted to the faith. Given the continuing shortage of missionaries, he sent a famous letter to the English people in which he appealed for their prayers and help in the mission to "those who are of one blood and bone with you." English monasteries sent money, books, vestments, and relics, and many monks and nuns crossed the sea to join him. Some of these volunteers were later recognized as saints themselves, including Lull of Malmesbury, who would succeed Boniface as archbishop of Mainz, Willibald [June 7], later bishop of Eichstätt, Winnibald [December 18], later abbot of Heidenheim, and their sister Walburga [February 25], later abbess of the double monastery of Heidenheim, the only one of its kind in Germany.

In 738–39 Boniface made another visit to Rome and was appointed papal legate to Germany. Upon his return, he convened a synod for all the areas of Germany and established a hierarchy for Bavaria. In 741, when the results of his work in Germany were secure, he was asked to help reorganize the Frankish Church. Bishoprics were bought and sold, even to laymen, or left vacant for long periods, and the clergy were poorly educated and worldly. Boniface presided over five synods (there had not been one for eighty-four years) between 741 and 747. Many abuses were corrected and the Rule of St. Benedict [July 11] was established for all monasteries. In 744 Boniface was appointed bishop of Mainz, succeeding one who had been deposed for killing his father's murderer. Boniface is said to have crowned Pepin as king of the Franks in 751 (other sources question whether he even attended the ceremony). By now Boniface was nearly eighty years old.

In 752 he relinquished the leadership of the Frankish Church to Chrodegang of Metz [March 6] and the diocese of Mainz to Lull of Malmesbury. (Mainz did not become an archdiocese until ca. 781.) Boniface then returned to what has been described as his first love, the evangelization of the Frisians, many of whom had lapsed in the meantime. Boniface led a new and more vigorous missionary effort, pressing even into territory occupied by hostile tribes. While reading in his tent at Dokkum, awaiting the arrival of some candidates for Confirmation, Boniface's camp were attacked by a band of tribesmen. Boniface forbade any resistance; he and fifty-three companions were massacred. His body was taken to Fulda, where it still rests along with a copy of the book he was reading, dented with sword cuts and stained with his blood.

Boniface left behind a large corpus of letters written to popes, bishops, abbots, abbesses, and former pupils who sought his advice. He was, before all else, a pastor—loving, kind, simple, and devoted to the gospel. Boniface never became a principal saint in England, particularly after the Norman Conquest of 1066 when he and other Anglo-Saxons saints suffered an eclipse. The center of his cult was at Fulda, and he is still widely venerated in Germany and the Netherlands. His feast was extended to the universal Church in 1874 and is on the General Roman Calendar. It is also celebrated by the Church of England, the Episcopal Church in the USA, and the Evangelical Lutheran Church in America, and he is commemorated by the Russian Orthodox Church on this day.

BIBLIOGRAPHY

Farmer, David Hugh, ed. *Benedict's Disciples.* Leominster: Fowler Wright, 1980 (reprinted 1995). Especially chap. 1, pp. 21–40.

6 Norbert, bishop

Norbert (ca. 1080–1134) was the founder of the Premonstratensians, also known as the Canons Regular of Prémontré or simply the Norbertines, and is patron saint of Magdeburg (where he was archbishop) and Bohemia. Born of a noble family at Xanten in the duchy of Cleves, in the Rhineland, Norbert, like other sons of noblemen, became a subdeacon and canon while still living a worldly life. A narrow escape from death—he was thrown from his horse during a violent thunderstorm in 1115—is said to have brought about a conversion similar to the Apostle Paul's [January 25]. After a period of prayer and fasting and then a retreat at the abbey of Siegberg near Cologne, he was ordained a priest the same year; after that he made yet another retreat, this time for forty days. His zeal was now such that he elicited charges of hypocrisy from other canons, who also challenged his right to preach without a commission. To establish his sincerity, Norbert resigned his canonry, sold his estates, and gave away the proceeds to the poor. Then he traveled barefoot in wintry weather to Saint-Gilles in the Languedoc to meet with Pope Gelasius II, who was in exile from Rome, to confess his sins and to ask for a penance. In response, the pope authorized him to preach the gospel wherever he chose.

Norbert became a celebrated itinerant preacher in northern France, Germany, and present-day Belgium. His efforts to reform the canons at Xanten and later at St. Martin's in Laon, where he had been assigned by the new pope, Callistus II, were rebuffed. Indeed, Norbert met with such resistance that, with the blessing of the local bishop in

1121, he made a fresh start with thirteen disciples (some of whom were at St. Martin's) in the valley of Prémontré. Their number soon increased to forty, and all made their solemn profession according to the Rule of St. Augustine [August 28] on Christmas Day, 1121. They were not regarded as a new order but as a reform movement within the canons regular of Laon. They wore a simple white habit (for which they were known as the white canons) and were set apart from traditional monks by their preaching and other pastoral work. At the same time, however, they adopted an austere form of life marked by strict poverty, in the spirit of the Cistercians and of Bernard of Clairvaux [August 20] in particular. The movement spread to other countries, attracting both men and women.

When the order had eight abbeys and one or two convents, Norbert sought papal approval, which Honorius II granted in 1126. The canons of Laon, who had previously resisted his Rule, now joined with him. In the same year, Norbert was appointed archbishop of Magdeburg, giving him even greater influence in the reform of the Church at this time. Significantly, he arrived at Magdeburg barefoot and so poorly dressed that the porter at the episcopal palace at first refused him entrance, ordering him to join the other beggars. As bishop, he was especially opposed to the alienation of church property by certain laymen, whom he described as robbers, and he vigorously pursued a course of clerical reform, enforcing celibacy and striking against corruption and absenteeism. Because of his zeal on such issues, his life was threatened and he was forced to leave Magdeburg for a time. Under pressure from the emperor and the threat of ecclesiastical censure, the people asked Norbert to return.

Upon the death of Pope Honorius II in 1130, two cardinals were separately elected to the papacy. Innocent II represented the new reformers, and Anacletus represented the old Gregorians (followers of Pope Gregory VII, who had died in 1085). An eight-year schism followed, ending only upon Anacletus's death. Norbert had worked hard in Germany for the recognition of Innocent II as the legitimate pope, especially while Innocent was in exile from Rome. Innocent extended Norbert's metropolitan jurisdiction to the whole of Poland. In 1132–33 Norbert accompanied the emperor Lothair II to Rome in the hope of persuading the antipope Anacletus to resign. He failed, and so too did Bernard of Clairvaux. Norbert returned to Magdeburg in 1134, but as a sick man. He died on June 6 and was buried in Magdeburg, in the church of his canons. He was canonized in 1582 and his relics were transferred to Strahov, near Prague, in 1627. His feast was extended to the universal Church in 1672 and is on the General Roman Calendar.

7 Willibald, bishop; Colman of Dromore, abbot; Blessed Anne of St. Bartholomew, nun; Noah Seattle, chief

Willibald (d. ca. 786), the bishop of Eichstätt, was the brother of Winnibald [December 18], abbot of Heidenheim, and Walburga [February 25], abbess of Heidenheim, and the nephew of Boniface [June 5]. Born in Wessex, he became a monk early in life following an illness that almost killed him. After his education was completed, he became one of the most traveled Anglo-Saxons of his time. In 720 he and other members of his family embarked on a pilgrimage to Rome, Sicily, Cyprus, modern-day Turkey, Syria, and Palestine. He spent a long period in Constantinople and returned to Italy in 730, residing for ten years in the monastery of Monte Cassino, where he contributed to the restoration of the primitive Benedictine Rule.

Around the year 740 Pope Gregory III, a Syrian, who was fascinated with Willibald's accounts of his pilgrimage, sent him to Germany to participate in the mission of his uncle Boniface, at Boniface's request. Willibald joined Boniface in Thuringia and was ordained a priest there ca. 741. He then evangelized in Franconia, in the southern part of the Rhine valley, and in 742 was consecrated bishop of Eichstätt. One of his first acts, sometime before 750, was the establishment of the double monastery at Heidenheim, with the same Rule as that at Monte Cassino. His brother and sister, Winnibald and Walburga, came to join him as abbot and abbess, consecutively. Willibald conducted the pastoral affairs of his diocese from the monastery and outlived both his brother and his sister, serving as bishop for forty-five years. His remains were placed in Eichstätt's cathedral and still lie there today. His feast is not on the General Roman Calendar.

This is also the feast day of *Colman of Dromore*, a sixth-century Irish bishop who founded the monastery of Dromore, the seat of his own diocese, ca. 514. He was venerated in Ireland and Scotland soon after his death and is mentioned in the ancient liturgical calendars of both countries.

The feast of *Anne of St. Bartholomew* (d. 1626) is celebrated by the Carmelites on this day. She was the companion and secretary of Teresa of Ávila [October 15], who died in her arms. She is venerated as the protectress of Antwerp for having prayed through the night to save the city on two occasions from a siege mounted by the prince of Orange.

The Evangelical Lutheran Church in America commemorates *Noah Seattle* (ca. 1790–1866), chief of the Suquamish tribe and then of the Duwamish Confederacy and a convert to Catholicism who constantly pursued the path of peace. The city of Seattle, Washington, is named in his honor.

8 William of York, bishop; Thomas Ken, bishop; Gerard Manley Hopkins, poet and religious

William of York (d. 1154) was a highly controversial archbishop of York. Born into a noble family with royal connections, William FitzHerbert became canon and treasurer of York Minster at a young age (ca. 1130) and chaplain to King Stephen, who selected him to be the new archbishop of York in 1140. The canons of the cathedral, however, were divided over the appointment, and Theobald, the archbishop of Canterbury, refused to consecrate him. His election was also opposed by Bernard of Clairvaux [August 20] and the Yorkshire Cistercians, who accused William of simony and unchastity. Both sides appealed to Pope Lucius II, who decided that William could be consecrated if the dean of York could clear him of the charges and if William would purge himself of them by an oath. That is what happened, and so William was consecrated by his uncle, the bishop of Winchester, who was also the king's brother. Pope Lucius II died before William could be granted jurisdiction (Cardinal Imar had failed to give William the pallium sent from Rome), and Lucius was replaced by a Cistercian, Eugenius III, who accepted Bernard's complaint and suspended and deposed William. He appointed Henry Murdac, the Cistercian abbot of Fountains, in his place, but it was five years before Murdac was able to enter England, and even then the people of York refused to accept him. (The abbey of Fountains, it should be noted, had been violently attacked by William's relatives.)

In the meantime, William retired to Winchester and lived humbly and devoutly as a monk until 1153, when the pope, Bernard, and the Cistercian archbishop of York all died. William was restored to his see and given the pallium in Rome by the new pope, Anastasius IV. Soon after his triumphant return to York in 1154, during which a bridge collapsed under the weight of the jubilant crowds, he died suddenly after Mass on June 8. It was charged at the time that his chalice had been poisoned by

Osbert, the archdeacon of York, but the case was later dropped for lack of proof. William was buried in the cathedral and miracles were subsequently reported at his tomb. He was regarded as the victim of injustice and as a saint. Pope Honorius III appointed the Cistercian abbots of Fountains and Rievaulx to investigate William's life and miracles, and then he canonized him in 1227. A great window in the north choir transept of the York Minster cathedral celebrates the events of his life and miracles in a hundred and ten separate panels. The altar in the chapel of St. William in the crypt was a gift from the Catholic diocese of Leeds. William of York's feast is not on the General Roman Calendar.

The Church of England celebrates the feast of *Thomas Ken* (1637–1711) on this day. Ken was bishop of Bath and Wells, a nonjuror who declined to take the oath of allegiance to the Protestant William III, son of the prince of Orange, because he had previously taken an oath to James II, a Catholic, whom William had defeated at the Battle of the Boyne in Ireland. Thomas Ken was deposed from his see and went into retirement. He is best known for his evening hymn "All Praise to Thee, My God, This Night," which concludes with the doxology "Praise God from whom all blessings flow." His feast is celebrated on March 21 by the Episcopal Church in the USA.

June 8 is also the day of death of the Jesuit poet *Gerard Manley Hopkins* (1844–89), whose poetry embodied the distinctively Catholic understanding of all created reality as sacramental, that is, as embodying and mediating the presence of God. Like other saintly figures, he went through periods of spiritual desolation and doubt, broken only by bursts of poetic brilliance.

9 Ephrem, deacon and Doctor of the Church; Columba of Iona, abbot

Ephrem (ca. 306–73), also Ephraem of Syria, was the author of numerous hymns and works of biblical exegesis for which he was named a Doctor of the Church in 1920, the only Syrian to be so honored. Born in Nisibis (Mesopotamia), he was baptized ca. 324 and joined the cathedral school there, eventually becoming its head. After the Persians captured Nisibis in 363, Ephrem took up the life of a monk in a cave near Edessa. It was during this period that he produced his many hymns (over five hundred survive) and exegetical writings on nearly the whole of the Old Testament and much of the New Testament. His hymns were sung during the liturgy, and his exegetical writings were translated into several languages and often read immediately after the reading of the Scriptures. He was also renowned for his preaching and is referred to by Catholic and Orthodox Syrians alike as "the harp of the Holy Spirit." He was ordained a deacon, perhaps late in his life. In 372 he organized a relief effort on behalf of famine victims in and around Edessa and died a month later in his cave. Ephrem's feast is on the General Roman Calendar and he is commemorated by the Church of England on this day. His feast is celebrated by the Russian and Greek Orthodox Churches on January 28, and he is commemorated by the Episcopal Church in the USA on June 10.

Columba of Iona (ca. 521–97), also Columcille and Columbkille, although Irish by birth, is the most celebrated of the Scottish saints. Born at Gartan in Donegal of a royal clan, he was educated by monks and then founded the monasteries of Derry (546), called Londonderry by its English conquerors, Durrow (ca. 556), and Kells. For reasons unknown or at least not agreed upon by historians, he left Ireland with twelve companions in 565, setting out for the island of Iona off the southwest coast of Scotland. He established the famous monastery of Iona and devoted himself to the training of its monks, spiritual direction, peacemaking between civil rulers, and copying sacred texts. It is said that he transcribed three hundred copies of the Gospels. He remained in Scotland for the rest of his life, with only occasional visits back to Ireland. He died before the monastery's altar, just as his monks gathered for Matins.

Columba's influence increased after his death, in Scotland, Ireland, and Northumbria. Celtic Christians in these lands upheld Columban traditions in matters of ritual and discipline against the Roman traditions brought by Augustine of Canterbury [May 27], who arrived the year Columba died. The differences remained even after the Synod of Whitby (664) decided in favor of Roman practice, especially on the dating of Easter. The Venerable Bede [May 25] noted that the Iona monks "held on to their own manner of keeping Easter for another 150 years." Columba's monastic Rule was followed by many monasteries in western Europe until it was superseded by the less rigorous Rule of St. Benedict [July 11]. Columba's feast is not on the General Roman Calendar, but it is celebrated in the Anglican Communion by the Church of England and the Episcopal Church in the USA, and also by the Evangelical Lutheran Church in America. He is the patron saint of Ireland, Scotland, and poets.

The Russian and Greek Orthodox Churches celebrate the feast of *Cyril of Alexandria* [June 27] on this day.

10 Landericus of Paris, bishop; Ithamar of Rochester, bishop; Bogumilus, bishop; Blessed John Dominici, bishop

Landericus (d. ca. 660), or Landry, was the bishop of Paris who founded Paris's first hospital, an institution that still exists today under the name Hôtel-Dieu. He became bishop of Paris in 650 and is remembered for his care of the poor and the sick. During a great famine in 651, he sold his own possessions and those of the Church in order to relieve the sufferings of the people. He also founded at this time the city's first real hospital near Notre Dame and dedicated it to St. Christopher [July 25]. His feast is not on the General Roman Calendar.

This is also the feast day of *Ithamar of Rochester* (d. ca. 656), the first Anglo-Saxon to become a bishop in the English Church, and of *Bogumilus* (d. 1182), archbishop of Gnesen (Gniezo), Poland, who resigned after five years because his clergy rebelled at his strict discipline. He retired to a Camaldolese monastery for the remainder of his life. His cult was approved in 1925. Neither feast is on the General Roman Calendar.

The Dominicans celebrate the feast of *John Dominici* (1376–1419) on this day. One of the leading theologians and preachers of his time, he spearheaded the reform of his order in northern Italy, introducing or restoring the strict Rule of St. Dominic [August 8]. He was the confessor and spiritual adviser of Pope Gregory XII, whom he persuaded to resign the papacy in 1415 in order to bring a definitive end to the Great Western Schism (1378–1417). By then a cardinal-archbishop, it was he who conveyed the pope's resignation to the Council of Constance. His cult was confirmed in 1832.

11 Barnabas, apostle; Rembert, bishop; Paola Frassinetti, foundress

Barnabas (first century) was not one of the original twelve apostles, but was regarded as an apostle by Luke [October 18] and the early Fathers of the Church because of his missionary work beyond Jerusalem. He was a Levite from Cyprus (Acts 4:36) whose original name was Joseph. The apostles gave him the name Barnabas, which means "son of consolation (or encouragement)," perhaps because of his pleasant disposition. When he became a follower of Jesus, he sold some property and donated the proceeds to the apostles (Acts

4:36–37). He introduced Paul [June 29] to the leaders of the Church in Jerusalem (Acts 9:27), and then collaborated with Paul in Antioch (Acts 11:22–30), where the disciples were first called Christians, and then in missionary work (Acts 13–14; 1 Cor. 9:6). He and Paul attended the assembly in Jerusalem that settled the question of circumcision for Gentile converts (Acts 15; Gal. 2:1–10). Barnabas supported the gentile Christians who did not see why they should have to be circumcised and observe Jewish dietary laws. The council decided in their favor. Barnabas and Paul parted ways, however, over a disagreement about the presence of his cousin John Mark, who had irritated Paul by his desertion from the first missionary journey (Acts 15:39), and about the appropriate form of table fellowship to be observed between Jewish and gentile Christians.

Like Peter [June 29], Barnabas did not always practice the principle agreed upon at the council of Jerusalem that there should be freedom from Jewish law on the matter (Gal. 2:11–14). Paul nevertheless continued to use Barnabas as an example of apostolic behavior (1 Cor. 9:6). Barnabas and Mark later sailed to Cyprus together (Acts 15:39), where according to tradition Barnabas was stoned to death in the Greco-Roman city of Salamis before the year 60 or 61 and after his founding of the Cypriote church. His remains were taken to Constantinople, where a church was built in his honor. The fifth-century *Acts of Barnabas* is an elaboration upon the account in Acts. No certain writings of Barnabas survive. The *Letter of Barnabas* is not his, since it was written ca. 130. He is the patron saint of Cyprus, and his feast is on the General Roman Calendar; it is also celebrated in the Anglican Communion by the Church of England and the Episcopal Church in the USA, as well as the Evangelical Lutheran Church in America. The Greek and Russian Orthodox Churches celebrate his feast on this day as well, but in conjunction with the Apostle *Bartholomew* [August 24].

This is also the feast day of *Rembert* (d. 888), archbishop of Hamburg and Bremen and missionary to Scandinavia and northern Germany. His predecessor Anskar once said of him: "Rembert is more worthy to be archbishop than I am to be his deacon."

Finally, June 11 is the feast of *Paola Frassinetti* (1809–82), foundress of the Sisters of St. Dorothy [February 6]. She was canonized in 1984.

12 Onouphrios, hermit; Peter of Mount Athos, hermit; Alice, nun

Onouphrios (d. ca. 400) was an Egyptian hermit in whose honor a church (San Onofrio) was erected on the Janiculum Hill in Rome in the fifteenth century. The author of his Life presents himself as Paphnoutios, a monk who allegedly wandered in the desert trying to discern whether he had a vocation to the eremetical life. He came across Onouphrios, a naked and hairy man with a long white beard, who told him the story of his life and deeds. He had been a monk in a large monastery in the Thebaïd, but felt called to a solitary life. For more than sixty years since then, Onouphrios had lived as a hermit. Paphnoutios stayed with Onouphrios for the night, during which food (an "immaculate communion") is said to have appeared miraculously at the hands of an angel. Paphnoutios shared with Onouphrios a message from the Lord to the effect that Onouphrios was to die and he was to bury him. Onouphrios did die, and Paphnoutios did bury him—in a hole in the mountainside. The site allegedly disappeared immediately, which Paphnoutios took as a sign that he should not remain there. The story became popular in the sixth century. Paphnoutios himself had suffered much hardship and cruelty during the persecution by Maximin Daza (305–13) and his mutilated body was the object of great wonder and veneration at the Council of Nicaea (325), during which he dissuaded the council from ordering all priests to put away their wives. The feast of Onouphrios is not on the General Roman Calendar, but it is celebrated on this day by the Greek and Russian Orthodox Churches, along with that of *Peter of Mount Athos* (eighth century), the first Christian hermit on Mount Athos.

The Cistercians commemorate *Alice* (d. 1250), also known as Aleydis, a Belgian Cistercian nun who spent almost her entire life, from age seven, at the convent of La Cambre. She contracted leprosy, lost her sight, and suffered paralysis. She was renowned for her humility and devotion to the Eucharist. Her cult was approved in 1907.

13 Anthony of Padua, priest and Doctor of the Church

Anthony of Padua (1195–1231), a Franciscan friar and a Doctor of the Church, is considered one of the greatest preachers in the history of the Church. He is best known, however, as the saint to whom one prays to find a lost article. He is also the patron saint of Brazil, Portugal, travelers, the poor, barren women, and harvests. Born in Lisbon of a noble Portuguese family and baptized Fernando (Bulhon, Bouillon, or de Buglione), he joined the Augustinian Canons Regular, a group of friars, at the age of fifteen or sixteen and studied (especially the Bible) under prominent European scholars at Coïmbra. He became a Franciscan in 1220 after meeting a group of friars who were on their way to Morocco to refute the Moors and other heretics and who were subsequently martyred there. He later viewed their relics.

Anthony felt a call to missionary work, but that would have been impossible had he remained a canon regular. After receiving permission to join the Franciscans, he sailed to Morocco hoping to continue the mission of the slain friars, but ill health forced his return. The ship that was to return him to Portugal was blown far off course, and he landed in Sicily. From there he made his way north to attend a general chapter of Franciscans to be held at Assisi in 1221. Francis himself [October 4] was still alive and attended the chapter, still a deacon and sitting at the feet of Brother Elias, the vicar general. At the close of the chapter Anthony was assigned to a small hermitage near Forli. He lived there in relative obscurity until his considerable theological, spiritual, and homiletical gifts were manifested in a sermon he gave on short notice at an ordination ceremony attended by the bishop, Anthony's fellow friars, and a number of Dominicans. As a result, he was sent to preach in different parts of Lombardy, where he attracted people by the thousands. Francis himself confirmed his appointment to teach theology to the friars at Bologna and Padua, and he became one of Francis's favorite disciples and closest friends.

A few years later, Anthony preached against the Albigensians (adherents of a movement that rejected both civil and ecclesiastical authority and denied the goodness of the flesh) in various cities in southern France, where he was called "the hammer of the heretics." After the death of Francis in 1226, Anthony was called back to Italy and was elected provincial of northern Italy. He traveled widely to visit the friaries under his supervision. During these three years he wrote his "Sermons for Sundays" and later was called to Rome to discuss the Rule and legacy of Francis. Deep divisions had developed between those who favored a

Saint Anthony of Padua by Alvise Vivarini (c. 1445–1505)

more pragmatic approach to the vow of poverty and those who insisted on a strict observance. At the papal court his preaching was described as a "jewel case of the Bible," and he was commissioned to write "Sermons for Feast Days."

He returned to Padua for the last months of his life, which were taken up with preaching, hearing confessions, and assisting those in debt. He was instrumental in getting a law passed so that debtors who were willing to sell their possessions to pay their creditors would not be imprisoned—a forerunner of bankruptcy laws. Anthony was so popular a preacher that he often had to speak in public squares and marketplaces rather than churches. He died at Arcella, near Padua, on June 13, 1231, and his body was taken to the Franciscan church of Our Lady in Padua, where a basilica was built in his honor. He was canonized less than a year after his death. His feast is on the General Roman Calendar.

Since the seventeenth century Anthony has been frequently invoked as the finder of lost articles. When a novice took his Psalter without permission, Anthony prayed for its return. After a frightening apparition, the novice rushed to restore the book to its rightful owner. Anthony's devotion to the poor also inspired the institution of St. Anthony's Bread, a movement devoted to the relief of the starving and others in dire need; it is still operative today, especially in the Third World. In Sicily huge loaves of bread in the shape of a crown are baked on his feast day. Pope Pius XII named him a Doctor of the Church in 1946, with the title *Doctor evangelicus* (Lat., "Evangelical Doctor"), a gesture that drew greater attention to the biblical and liturgical character of Anthony's preaching. He is often depicted with an open book (symbol of the Bible) and a lily (symbol of purity), together with the Infant Jesus seated on the book. His tomb was reopened in 1981, and a scientific examination of his remains disclosed that he had a long, thin face with deep-set eyes, and long, delicate hands. The condition of his bones indicated that he ate poorly (he undertook long and frequent fasts) and suffered from fatigue (caused by frequent journeys on foot). His cult is especially strong today in Italy, France, Portugal, Brazil, Ireland, and the United States.

BIBLIOGRAPHY

Clasen, Sophronius. *St. Anthony, Doctor of the Church.* Trans. Ignatius Brady. Chicago: Franciscan Herald Press, 1987.

Hardick, Lothar. *He Came to You So That You Might Come to Him: The Life and Teaching of St. Anthony of Padua.* Trans. Zachary Hayes. Chicago: Franciscan Herald Press, 1989.

14 Methodius of Constantinople, patriarch

Methodius of Constantinople (d. 847) is the object of great veneration in the East because of the role he played in the final defeat of iconoclasm (a movement, with imperial support, that rejected the use of icons and other sacred imagery as well as the veneration of the saints) and his suffering in prison. He is often called "the Confessor" and "the Great." Born and educated in Syracuse in Sicily in the second half of the eighth century, he went to Constantinople with the hope of securing a position at court but, under the influence of a monk, he instead entered the monastery of Chenolakkos in Bythynia, eventually becoming its *hegoumenos* (Gk., "superior"). Later he built a monastery on the island of Khios (Chios) and was called back to Constantinople from there by the patriarch Nicephorus. Iconoclasm had been revived by the emperor Leo V the Armenian, partially in response to pressure from the growing population of Muslims, who forbade any representation of images or sacred objects.

After Nicephorus was deposed and exiled, Methodius was sent to Rome by the bishops (after 815) to inform the pope of the situation. He remained there until after the emperor's death. The pope sent a letter to the new emperor, requesting the reinstatement of the patriarch. Upon Methodius's return in 821, he was accused by the civil authorities of instigating the papal letter and was thrown into prison for at least seven years. Those years of imprisonment were wretched. He was confined for a time with two thieves. When one of them died, his body was allowed to rot in the cell. Upon Methodius's release from prison in 829, he was scarcely recognizable. He was skeletal and bald, and his skin was blanched from years of living in darkness.

When another emperor resumed the attack on veneration of images, Methodius asked him: "If an image is so worthless in your eyes, how is it that when you condemn the images of Christ, you do not also condemn the veneration paid to representations of yourself?" The emperor had Methodius flogged and thrown back into prison, his jaw broken. Friends rescued him that same night and the emperor died soon thereafter. His widow, Theodora, succeeded to the throne and immediately reversed the work of the iconoclasts. The persecutions stopped, the exiled clergy were called home, and the sacred images were restored to the churches. The iconoclast patriarch was deposed and Methodius was installed in his place, still wearing the bandages on his broken jaw.

Methodius was patriarch for four years, during which time he called a synod to reaffirm the use of images. He had the relics of his predecessor Nicephorus brought back from his place of exile and paid honor to them. He instituted the annual Festival of Orthodoxy, still observed in Orthodox churches on the first Sunday of Lent, and wrote a statement of faith (the *Synodicon*) to be read on that occasion. Methodius's feast is not on the General Roman Calendar, but is celebrated by the Russian Orthodox Church, along with that of the Old Testament prophet *Elisha,* who is also commemorated by the Greek Orthodox Church. The Evangelical Lutheran Church in America commemorates the Cappadocians on this day: *Basil the Great* [January 2], *Gregory Nazianzen* [January 2], and *Gregory of Nyssa* [January 10]. The Episcopal Church in the USA commemorates only Basil the Great on this day.

15 Vitus and companions, martyrs; Evelyn Underhill, spiritual writer

Vitus (d. ca. 300), martyred during the Diocletian persecution, is the patron saint of those suffering from various diseases associated, correctly or not, with neurological disorders. Thus, the term "St. Vitus's dance" to refer to a variety of conditions causing convulsive and involuntary movements. By extension, he is also considered the patron saint of dancers and comedians. According to tradition, Vitus was the son of a Sicilian senator and was raised as a Christian by his tutor and nurse. After his father and the civil ruler of Sicily tried unsuccessfully to dissuade him from his faith, Vitus and his two companions, *Modestus* and *Crescentia,* escaped by boat to Lucania in southern Italy and subsequently to Rome. Vitus was thought to have cured the emperor Diocletian's son of devil possession, but the emperor attributed it to sorcery and had the three arrested, tortured, and condemned to death. Nothing is known of their martyrdom. What is clear is that his cult is ancient and is mentioned in the *Martyrology of Jerome* [September 30] as well as that of Bede [May 25].

His cult spread among the Slavs and the Germans, as well as in Rome, Sicily (of which he is a patron saint), and Sardinia. His alleged relics were placed in Saint-Denis [October 9] in Paris in 775 and then moved to Corvey in Saxony in 836. So great was the devotion to him in Germany that he is named as one of the Fourteen Holy Helpers (see Glossary), who were venerated in the Rhineland from the fourteenth century. His feast is not on the General Roman Calendar.

On this day the Church of England and the Episcopal Church in the USA commemorate the spiritual writer *Evelyn Underhill* (1875–1941), who had been drawn to Catholicism but turned away from it with the condemnation of Modernism by Pope Pius X (1903–14). Her major works were *Mysticism* (1911) and *Worship* (1936). She was a much sought after retreat director and was active in the pacifist movement.

16 Lutgardis, nun; Joseph Butler, bishop

Lutgardis (1182–1246), or Lutgard, was a Cistercian nun and one of the leading mystics of the thirteenth century. Born at Tongeren, between Brussels and Maastricht, she was placed in a Benedictine monastery at the age of twelve because her father no longer could pay her dowry. Since she had no apparent vocation to religious life, the nuns regarded her as a boarder rather than a future nun. However, after an alleged apparition of Christ in which he is said to have shown her his five wounds, she renounced all worldly interests. The nuns remained skeptical, but she persevered in her new life of prayer and meditation on the Passion of Christ. Her transformation was such that the other nuns wanted to make her their abbess, but she declined. She remained at the convent for twelve years, having become a nun herself at age twenty, but then moved to a stricter Cistercian house at Aywières, south of Liège, on the advice of her confessor. She would remain there for thirty years, until her death.

Since her native language was a form of Low German, she could not converse fluently in the French that was spoken in her new home. The difficulty in communication became a form of mortification for her. In spite of her broken French, however, she became a sought after spiritual director and healer. In 1235, eleven years before her death, she lost her sight, which she accepted as yet another opportunity for mortification and self-denial. She died on June 16, 1246, just as the nuns were about to begin Matins for Sunday. Her Cistercian abbey was destroyed during the French Revolution and her relics were carried from place to place by the wandering nuns, until they were finally secured in the parish church of Ittré in 1804. Her feast is on the Cistercian liturgical calendar, but not the General Roman Calendar.

The Church of England celebrates the feast of *Richard of Chichester* [April 3] on this day. It also commemorates (along with the Episcopal Church in the USA) *Joseph Butler* (1692–1752), bishop of Bristol and then of Durham, whose fame rests, however, on his philosophical works in defense of Christian faith and morality.

17 Rainerius of Pisa, hermit; Botulf, abbot

Rainerius of Pisa (1117–61), also Rainier or Ranieri, is the patron saint of Pisa. Born in Pisa, Rainerius Scaccieri was the son of a prosperous merchant. In 1140, under the influence of a local monk, he repented of his worldly ways and went on a pilgrimage (initially a business trip) to the Holy Land, remaining there as a hermit (or barefoot beggar) and visiting the holy places until 1153. When he returned to Pisa, he was welcomed by the archbishop and people. He took up residence with monks, but without actually becoming one himself. His knowledge of Latin gave him access to the Bible and enabled him to preach on occasion. He enjoyed a reputation for austerity of life, facilitating conversions, and healing. He was sometimes called Rainerius "De Aqua" (Ital., "of water") because of his use of holy water in his healings. Upon his death, he was buried with great honor in the Pisa cathedral, where his body remains to this day in his chapel at the end of the south transept. One of the bells in the famous leaning tower is named after him. He was probably canonized by Pope Alexander III (1159–81) and then was named patron saint of Pisa sometime during the thirteenth century. His name was entered in the *Roman Martyrology* in the seventeenth century, but it is not on the General Roman Calendar.

This is also the feast day of *Botulf* (d. 680), also Botolph, Botulph, or Botwulf, the founding abbot of Icanhoh, also Icanho or Ikanhoe, a site that is usually identified as Botulf's town (later corrupted to "Boston") in Lincolnshire, although it is more probably Iken in Suffolk. He began building his abbey in 654 and soon had a group of disciples. Other monks came to visit the monastery from time to time because of Botulf's reputation for sanctity and learning. He remained in his monastery until his death. Because he was an Anglo-Saxon, his cult suffered an eclipse after the Norman Conquest in 1066. However, some sixty-four English churches were dedicated to him and three of those, known as St. Botolph's, were rebuilt by the great architect Christopher Wren (d. 1723) in the city of London. There is a St. Botolph's Street in Boston as well as a St. Botolph Club, founded in 1880, that is devoted to the arts, literature, music, architecture, business, and public affairs. Botulf's feast day is not on the General Roman Calendar.

18 Gregory Barbarigo, bishop; Bernard Mizeki, catechist

Gregory Barbarigo (1625–97) was an active seventeenth-century church leader. Born into a noble and wealthy Venetian family, he took part, as an assistant to the Venetian ambassador, in the Congress of Münster in 1648 that ended the Thirty Years' War through the Treaty of Westphalia. He was ordained a priest in 1655 and ministered heroically to the sick during the plague of 1657. He was appointed bishop of Bergamo the same year, created a cardinal in 1660, and transferred to Padua in 1664. He founded a seminary and a college, to which he donated a printing press, collected a superb patristic library, and was active in efforts to secure reunion with the separated churches of the East. His pastoral activities, marked by extraordinary generosity to the poor, have been compared to those of Charles Borromeo [November 4]. He died on June 15, 1697, and was buried in the Padua cathedral. He was beatified in 1761 and canonized in 1960. His feast is not on the General Roman Calendar.

On this day the Anglican Communion commemorates an African martyr, *Bernard Mizeki* (ca. 1861–96), a catechist known as the "apostle of the MaShona" (in present-day Zimbabwe) and who is revered by Anglicans in central and southern Africa.

19 Romuald, abbot; Juliana Falconieri, foundress; Gervase and Protase, martyrs

Romuald (ca. 950–1027) was the founder of the Camaldolese order. Born of a noble Ravenna family, Romuald Onesti fled to a local Cluniac monastery after his father had killed a relative in a duel over property. His austere lifestyle and devotional practices irritated some of the other monks, and after about three years he left the monastery and placed himself under the spiritual direction of a hermit near Venice. He lived a solitary life for some ten years and only returned to his home area to assist his father, who had also become a monk after his duel and was having doubts about his vocation. In 998 the emperor Otto III appointed Romuald abbot of San Apollinare in Classe (the very monastery he had originally entered some years earlier), but he resigned after only a year or two to live once again as a hermit, this time at Pereum, which became an important center for the training of clergy for the Slavonic missions. He later wandered through northern Italy, setting up hermitages, and obtained a mandate from the pope to carry out a mission to the Magyars in Hungary, desiring a martyr's death. Illness upset his hopes, and he returned to Italy.

After prolonged study of the Desert Fathers, he concluded that the way of salvation was along the path of solitude. He founded a monastery at Fonte Avellana, later refounded by his disciple Peter Damian [February 21], and another at Camaldoli, in an isolated valley in Tuscany. (Its name is derived from Campus Maldoli, a combination of *campus* [Lat., "field, plain"]and the name of the lord of the district, Maldolo.) The years of its founding are given by various sources as covering a fifteen-year span, from 1012 until as late as 1027. After Romuald's death, this latter community developed into a separate congregation, known as the Camaldolese order (Monk Hermits of Camaldoli). Romuald did not leave a written Rule.

His distinctive contribution to Benedictine monasticism was to provide a place for the eremetical life within the framework of the Rule of St. Benedict [July 11]. The hermits would come together for liturgical worship and certain meals, but otherwise lived in isolation. Although Benedict had high regard for the solitary life, he had rejected it for his own community. The Camaldolese observance influenced Bruno [October 6] and the Carthusian order, which Bruno founded in 1084. After some years at Camaldoli, Romuald began to travel again. He died alone in his cell at the monastery of Val-di-Castro on June 19, 1027, and his incorrupt body was transferred to nearby Fabriano on February 7, 1481, which was originally kept as his feast day. His feast is now observed today, June 19, on the General Roman Calendar. In art he is shown in the white robe of his order with his finger to his lips, requesting silence.

This is also the feast day of *Juliana Falconieri* (1270–1341), regarded as the foundress of the Servite nuns, the women members of the Order of Friar Servants of Mary, which was originally founded by a group of young Florentine merchants, including Alexis Falconieri, Juliana's uncle. They are known as the Seven Founders of the Order of Servites [February 17], or the Seven Holy Founders of the Servants of Mary.

The Greek and Russian Orthodox Churches celebrate the feast of *Jude the Apostle* [October 28] on this day.

Finally, it is the feast day of the protomartyrs of Milan, *Gervase* and *Protase* (unknown dates, possibly the second century), whose bodies were discovered by Ambrose [December 7], the local bishop, in 386 on the eve of the dedication of the basilica. Ambrose's secretary Paulinus and Augustine of Hippo [August 28], whom Ambrose baptized, were both present and testified to the miracles associated with the relics, especially the cure of a sightless butcher. Ambrose chose to be buried beside the two martyrs.

20 Alban, martyr

Alban (third century) is the protomartyr of Britain. His death is the earliest recorded execution in that country on the charge of being a Christian. Alban must have been a prominent citizen of Verulamium, perhaps of Romano-British extraction. He had a house large enough to conceal a fugitive for some time and was a Roman citizen, with the right to a trial. His martyrdom by beheading, rather than by being thrown to wild beasts, was also an indication of his civil status. According to the eighth-century church historian the Venerable Bede [May 25], Alban was martyred during the persecution of Diocletian in 301. More recent historical scholarship, based on excavations, places his death in the middle of the third century. Alban was allegedly a pagan who gave shelter to a Christian priest who was being hunted by imperial forces. It is fitting, therefore, that he is regarded as the patron saint of refugees.

Alban is said to have been so impressed with the priest's demeanor that he was converted and took instruction in the faith from him. When the soldiers heard of the fugitive's location, they came to Alban's house and found Alban dressed in the fugitive's clerical garments. He surrendered himself in place of his guest and teacher. When the deception was discovered, the magistrate demanded to know Alban's name. He gave it, along with a confession of faith and a refusal to sacrifice to the Roman gods. The magistrate had Alban flogged, with the hope that he would recant. When he did not recant, Alban was sentenced to death by beheading.

As the story goes, he was led out to a nearby river, which suddenly dried up so that he could cross it. His assigned executioner was so moved by this miracle that he too was converted and refused to carry out the execution. Both were beheaded. The second executioner's eyes were said to have dropped out of their sockets just as Alban's head fell. The judge was so astonished by these miracles that he called a halt to the persecution. Bede was precise about the month and the place: "St. Alban suffered on the twenty-second day of June near the city of Verulamium, which the English now call Verlamcestir or Vaeclingacaestir."

The abbey and town of St. Alban's developed on the site of Alban's execution. His tomb is thought to have been on the hill where the abbey now stands. It was a Roman cemetery until the fourth century. In 1257 the monks discovered a mausoleum under the eastern end of the abbey church and concluded that it was the tomb of Alban. The abbey was dissolved and destroyed in 1549, and then rebuilt in 1872. Alban's feast is not on the General Roman Calendar, but it is liturgically celebrated in the Church of England and the Episcopal Church in the USA on June 22.

21 Aloysius Gonzaga, religious

Aloysius Gonzaga (1568–91) was a member of the Society of Jesus who died in his early twenties and is the patron saint of young people and of students in Jesuit colleges and universities. Born into a high-ranking family in Castiglione, near Mantua, in Lombardy and destined by his father for a military career, Aloysius decided to become a Jesuit during a family trip to Spain in the company of the empress of Austria in 1581–83. His family's return to Italy in 1584 did nothing to change his mind in spite of heavy-handed pressures, especially from his father, to the contrary. Aloysius renounced his inheritance and entered the novitiate in Rome in November of 1585. The vow of obedience and poor health combined to curb his penchant for excessive austerities. He studied philosophy at the Roman College, pronounced his first vows in November 1587, and then began his study of theology. Four years later, after nursing the sick in a Jesuit hospital during an outbreak of plague, he contracted the disease himself, partially recovered, and then died on June 21, 1591.

His spiritual director during his last years was Robert Bellarmine [September 17], the theologian and future cardinal. Bellarmine once commented that Aloysius's example of piety was so extreme that others should not be encouraged to follow it. Indeed, he was exceedingly scrupulous in prayer, almost masochistic in the exercise of self-mortification, often uncommunicative, frightened of women, refusing even to gaze at his mother, and obsessed with the idea and hope of an early death. Some commentators attribute these odd personality traits to a determined reaction against his privileged upbringing. Aloysius was beatified in 1621, canonized in 1726, and declared patron saint of youth in 1729, a title confirmed in 1926. His feast is on the General Roman Calendar.

22 Paulinus of Nola, bishop; John Fisher, bishop and martyr; Thomas More, martyr; Eusebius of Samosata, bishop

Paulinus of Nola (ca. 355–431) was a wealthy noble who retired from public office, gave his fortune to the poor, became the bishop of Nola (in Campania, Italy) and, along with his wife, founded an ascetic community. Born Pontius Meropius Anicius Paulinus at Bordeaux of a wealthy, patrician, and politically powerful non-Christian family, he practiced law, held public office, probably in Campania, traveled widely, and married a Spanish woman, Therasia. He became a Christian ca. 389 (his wife may already have been a Christian at the time of their marriage). Following the death of an infant son, they gave away most of their immense fortune to the poor and to the Church. The bishop of Barcelona persuaded Paulinus to accept ordination to the priesthood, and so he was ordained on Christmas Day, ca. 393.

Paulinus and his wife did not remain in Barcelona, however. They moved to Italy to settle on his estates there in Nola, a small town near Naples. He built a church at Fondi, an aqueduct for Nola, and a guest house for pilgrims, debtors, and others who were down on their luck. These occupied the ground floor of his house, while he, his wife, and a few friends followed a semimonastic regime on the upper floor, praying the Divine Office together daily. Paulinus had his own cell near the tomb of St. Felix of Nola (a third-century Christian who suffered for the faith, but was also known for making many converts and for his miracles), while his wife, Therasia, had a separate cell. He had a special devotion to the saints, and particularly to Felix of Nola, who was buried in the church close to Paulinus's house and cell. From that house, Paulinus wrote poems and letters to some of the most important Christians of the day, including Ambrose [December 7], Jerome [September 30], Augustine [August 28], and Martin of Tours [November 11].

Many felt that he was wasting his considerable talents for public and ecclesiastical affairs by living the life of a recluse. Thus, when the bishop of Nola died in 409, Paulinus was chosen to succeed him. Little, however, survives of his episcopal tenure. Some have speculated that it was in response to the pastoral needs of his people that he wrote to the prominent saints mentioned above, seeking their insights and advice. He went to Rome once a year on the feast of Sts. Peter and Paul [June 29], but otherwise never left Nola. He died on June 22, 431, having just celebrated the Eucharist with two visiting bishops and given his last present of fifty silver pieces to the poor. He was buried in the church he had built in honor of St. Felix. His remains were later transferred to Rome, but then returned again to Nola by order of Pope Pius X [August 21] in 1909. His feast is on the General Roman Calendar.

John Fisher (1469–1535) was chancellor of Cambridge University, bishop of Rochester, a cardinal, and a vigorous defender of the Catholic faith in England at the time of the Reformation. Born at Beverley in Yorkshire, he was educated at Cambridge from the age of fourteen, elected a Fellow of Michaelhouse (now Trinity College), and ordained a priest in 1491. In 1502 he became chaplain to the king's mother, Lady Margaret Beaufort, who richly endowed both Cambridge and Oxford universities, and was himself appointed the first Lady Margaret Professor of Divinity at Cambridge. In 1504, at age thirty-five, he became both chancellor of the university and bishop of Rochester, England's smallest diocese, while declining appointments to other, wealthier sees. He had reluctantly accepted the episcopal appointment, but once in office he executed his pastoral responsibilities with great energy and care.

He was such a famous preacher that he was chosen to preach at the funerals of King Henry VII and Lady Margaret herself in 1509. But he was always the scholar. He began the study of Greek at age forty-eight and Hebrew at fifty-one. He also built up one of the finest libraries in all of Europe. Fisher wrote four volumes against Martin Luther, which constituted the first serious refutation of Lutheran teachings in England, and upheld the doctrines of the Real Presence and the sacrificial nature of the Mass against Protestants in various English universities. His theological works were influential at the Council of Trent (1545–63). At the same time, he too was committed to church reform. At a synod called by Cardinal Wolsey in 1518, Fisher had spoken out strongly against the worldliness and laxity of the higher clergy. However, he also believed that, for the sake of unity, reforms should be initiated within the Church rather than against it. Among his idiosyncracies was his habit of keeping a skull on his desk and on his table at meals to remind him of death.

When King Henry VIII began contemplating divorce and remarriage, it was John Fisher who argued for the validity and indissolubility of his first marriage. He later protested Henry's new title as "Supreme Head of the Church of England," suggesting that it be qualified with the words "so far as the law of Christ allows." The king rejected his proposal, and from that point on (perhaps even earlier) John Fisher lost the royal favor and was a marked man. He was arrested as a traitor and imprisoned in the Tower of London in 1534 for refusing to take the oath required by the Act of Succession because it was tantamount to an oath attesting royal supremacy and repudiating papal authority. The king deposed him from office and declared his see vacant. Pope Paul III named John Fisher a cardinal, but Henry VIII retorted that, even if the pope sent Fisher a red hat, he would have no head to wear it on. After ten months in the Tower, Fisher was condemned to death on June 17, 1535, and was beheaded five days later. Although he was sixty-six at the time of his execution, Fisher is said to have looked more like eighty-six, given his poor health and the strain of his imprisonment. He had to be carried to Tower Hill on a chair. On the scaffold, however, he retained his dignity, pardoning his executioner and declaring in a clear voice that he was dying for the faith of Christ's Church. He asked for the spectators' prayers and then recited the Te Deum and a psalm.

The king's contempt for John Fisher continued even after Fisher's death. His naked body was left on the scaffold all day and then buried without rites or shroud in a local churchyard near the Tower. His head was displayed on London Bridge for two weeks and then thrown into the Thames. John Fisher was beatified in 1886 and canonized in 1935. His feast, along with that of Thomas More, is on the General Roman Calendar. It is celebrated by the Church of England on July 6.

Thomas More (1478–1535) was the most famous victim of King Henry VIII's persecution of Catholics who refused to accept royal supremacy over the Church in England. He is the patron saint of Catholic lawyers. The son of a lawyer and judge, More joined the household of the archbishop of Canterbury at age thirteen. He studied for two years at Oxford, but was called home by his father to study law. He was a member of Parliament for four years (1504–8), during which time he also contemplated entering religious life or becoming a diocesan priest. He did neither, deciding instead to pursue his legal career and marriage. He began at this time a lifelong habit of wearing a hair shirt and reciting the Little Office of the Blessed Virgin Mary daily. He slept on the floor with a log for a pillow and spent all day Friday in prayer.

Sir Thomas More by Hans Holbein the Younger, 1527

Thomas More's reputation for intelligence, wit, integrity, and loyalty to family, friends, and king brought him to the attention of the new king, Henry VIII, who promoted him to a series of public offices, including Speaker of the House of Commons in 1523. His reputation as a man of learning and of letters was definitively established with the publication of his Latin classic, *Utopia,* in 1516 and later translated into several European languages. (He had written it originally in Latin so that the unlearned should not come to any harm by reading it without understanding.) In 1523 he wrote a defense, against Martin Luther, of Henry VIII's own book on the seven sacraments, for which the pope gave the king the title "Defender of the Faith."

Thomas More's first wife died in 1511, and he married again a few weeks later. His second wife helped him raise his three daughters and one son. Their home life was remarkable for its time. There was Scripture reading at table and family prayers each night; visitors were in and out constantly, including the king himself on occasion. More himself maintained a deep curiosity about nature and science. In the late 1520s, when the issue was still under papal review, the king asked Thomas for his opinion of the marriage question. More at first declined for lack of expert knowledge, but when the king persisted, More acknowledged that he did not share the king's opinion. Nevertheless, Henry chose Thomas More as his lord chancellor in 1529—a post in which More excelled because of his fairness and integrity. After some hesitation, he accepted the king's new title, "Protector and Supreme Head of the Church of England," but with John Fisher's qualification, "so far as the law of Christ allows." As he became increasingly concerned, however, about the king's real intentions regarding the Church of England, he resigned the chancellorship on May 16, 1532.

When Henry married Anne Boleyn while the validity of his first marriage to Catherine of Aragon was still being reviewed in Rome, Thomas More refused to attend Anne's coronation as queen. Then in March 1534 the Act of Succession required all of the king's subjects to recognize the offspring of the second marriage as successors to the throne, the nullity of his first marriage, and the validity of his second. Like John Fisher, Thomas More could have assented to the first proposition, but not to the second and third, especially since the pope had just decided in favor of the validity of the first marriage. Opposing the Act of Succession was considered tantamount to treason. Upon his second refusal to take the oath, More, along with John Fisher, was arrested and consigned to the Tower of London on April 13, 1534. He remained there for the final fifteen months of his life. More forfeited all of his lands and his family shared his poverty. While in the Tower, he wrote such works as *Dialogue of Comfort Against Tribulation* and the *Treatise on the Passion of Christ.* Once the Act of Supremacy came into force in late 1534, the executions for treason began. Thomas More watched the Carthusian monks of London go to their deaths on May 4, 1535. The beheading of his friend and adviser John Fisher followed on June 22.

More's trial was held on July 1. In his own defense he argued that his indictment was based on an act of Parliament that was against the laws of God and the Church, that no temporal prince can declare himself superior to the pope in spiritual matters, and that the king's new title was contrary to his coronation oath. He insisted that he had the Fathers, councils, and saints of the Church on his side on the issue. Nevertheless he was condemned to death, on perjured evidence, at which point he expressed the hope that he and his judges would "hereafter in heaven all meet merrily together, to our everlasting salvation." He was beheaded on Tower Hill on July 6. His last words were that he was dying for the faith of the Holy Catholic Church and was "the king's good servant, but God's first."

His body was buried in the church of St. Peter in Chains inside the Tower, but his head was first exhibited on Tower Bridge (replacing John Fisher's) and then buried in the Roper vault at St. Dunstan's [May 19], Canterbury. His death and that of Fisher sent shock waves throughout Europe. Both were beatified in 1886 and canonized in 1935. They are among the few English saints whose cult is worldwide. Along with John Fisher's, Thomas More's feast is on the General Roman Calendar, and, as in the case of John Fisher, it is celebrated by the Church of England on July 6. Portraits of Thomas More, painted by Hans Holbein (d. 1543) and others, hang in the Royal Collection at Windsor, the National Portrait Gallery in London, the Frick Collection in New York, and elsewhere. He was also the subject of a major play by Robert Bolt and of a subsequent motion picture, *A Man for All Seasons* (1966). On November 5, 2000, Pope John Paul II named Thomas More patron saint of politicians and those in public life.

The Anglican Communion celebrates the feast of *Alban* [June 20] on this day.

The Russian Orthodox Church commemorates *Eusebius of Samosata* (d. 379), a staunch defender of the teaching of the Council of Nicaea (325) on the divinity of Christ. He made several trips at great risk to himself into Syria and Palestine to strengthen Catholics in their faith, ordain priests, and assist bishops in electing other orthodox bishops. The Arian emperor Valens banished him from Samosata in 374. After Valens's death in 378, Eusebius returned to his see, where he continued to work for unity. On his way to install a bishop in Dolikha, he was struck on the head by a tile thrown by an Arian woman. He died several days later, but only after making the local people promise that they would take no revenge on the woman. His feast is not on the General Roman Calendar.

BIBLIOGRAPHY

Ackroyd, Peter. *The Life of Thomas More.* New York: Nan A. Talese, 1998.

Bradshaw, Brendan, and Eamon Duffy, eds. *Humanism, Reform, and the Reformation: The Career of Bishop John Fisher.* Cambridge: Cambridge University Press, 1989.

Marius, Richard. *Thomas More.* New York: Knopf, 1984.

Martz, Louis Lohr. *Thomas More: The Search for the Inner Man.* New Haven, CT: Yale University Press, 1990.

23 Etheldreda, abbess; Joseph Cafasso, priest; Blessed Innocent V, pope

Eltheldreda (d. 679), also Aethelthryth or Audrey, the foundress and abbess of Ely, was one of the best known Saxon women saints. (The word "tawdry" is derived from a corruption of "Audrey" and was applied to the cheap necklaces and other items that were offered for sale at her annual monastery fair.) Born probably at Exning in Suffolk, she was the daughter of the king of East Anglia and the sister of three saints. She was married twice, but according to her biography she remained a virgin in both marriages. After her first husband died, she retired to the Isle of Ely for a life of prayer. After five years she returned at the request of her family to enter a second marriage to a young man of fifteen. He agreed to her remaining a virgin, but changed his mind twelve years later. When the matter could not be resolved, both parties appealed to Bishop Wilfrid of York [October 12]. The husband attempted to bribe the bishop, but Wilfrid decided that Etheldreda should be allowed to enter a convent if she wished.

She left her husband and became a nun at Coldingham, where her aunt was abbess, in 672, and then founded a double monastery (i.e., one for men and one for women) at Ely a year later. She restored an old church and built her monastery on the site of the present Ely

Cathedral. For seven years she served as abbess, living a life of austerity, praying for long hours, wearing woolen rather than linen clothes (the latter were common even in monasteries and convents), and eating only one meal a day. She died of the plague in 679. Seventeen years later her body was found incorrupt, and her burial place became a popular center for pilgrims. Although her shrine was destroyed in 1541, some relics were salvaged and can be found today at St. Etheldreda's Church, Ely Place, London, and at St. Etheldreda's Church in Ely. Her feast is celebrated by the Church of England on this day, but it is not on the General Roman Calendar.

Joseph Cafasso (1811–60), spiritual adviser to John Bosco [January 31], is regarded as the second founder (after John Bosco) of the Sale-sian congregation. Born into a wealthy peasant family at Caselnuovo d'Asti in the Piedmont region of Italy, he was ordained a priest of the Turin diocese in 1833. He taught moral theology for a time, but his good reputation—notwithstanding his small stature and twisted spine—was based on his preaching and spiritual direction. In 1848 he was appointed superior of the Institute of St. Francis [October 4] at Turin, where he himself had studied theology after ordination. The institute's enrollment consisted of sixty young priests from various dioceses and of differing political views. Joseph Cafasso constantly reminded them that the great enemy of the priesthood was worldliness. He also directed a retreat house for clergy and laity at Lanzo and worked pastorally with prisoners, including those awaiting public execution. It was Joseph Cafasso who directed John Bosco into his apostolate for boys (Bosco had studied with Cafasso at the Institute of St. Francis), helped him to settle in Turin, and introduced him to wealthy patrons. Cafasso also inspired others to establish charitable institutions, a college, and religious communities. He died of pneumonia on June 23, 1860, not yet fifty years of age. John Bosco preached at his funeral. Joseph Cafasso was canonized in 1947 and is considered the patron saint of prisoners and of prisons. His feast is not on the General Roman Calendar.

On this day the Dominicans celebrate the feast of *Innocent V* (1224–76; pope 1276), the first pope who was a member of the Dominican order. His pontificate lasted only five months. He had been a friend of Bonaventure [July 15], the eminent Franciscan theologian, and preached at his funeral. He was also twice elected Dominican provincial of France and served as archbishop of Lyons. He was beatified in 1898, but has never been canonized.

24 Birth of John the Baptist

John the Baptist (first century) was the prophet who prepared the way for Jesus Christ and who baptized him in the Jordan River. He is the patron saint of Jordan, the city of Florence, monks, and highways. This celebration of his birth is primarily concerned with the events recorded in the first chapter of the Gospel of Luke (1:5–80). John was a cousin of Jesus, of priestly descent, and the son of Zechariah and Elizabeth [November 5]. Zechariah had a vision while exercising his priestly duties in the temple. The angel Gabriel [September 29] appeared to him in the sanctuary and told him that his wife, Elizabeth, would bear him a son and that he was to be called John. When Zechariah expressed doubts because of his and his wife's age, the angel struck him speechless and said he would not speak again until the child was born. In the sixth month of her pregnancy Elizabeth received a visit from her kinswoman Mary. When Elizabeth heard Mary's greeting, her child "leapt in her womb." This event is liturgically celebrated on the General Roman Calendar as the feast of the Visitation [May 31]. After John was born, his father was still unable to speak until the eighth day, when an argument arose about his name. Relatives wanted him to be named after his father, but Elizabeth insisted that his name be John. Zechariah asked for a writing tablet and wrote, "His name is John." At that moment he recovered his power of speech.

Nothing more is known of John's life until the fifteenth year of Tiberius (A.D. 28) when, as Luke reports (3:1), he began his public ministry of preaching repentance and of baptizing in the Jordan. Matthew 3:7–10 and Luke 3:7–9 record John's diatribes against sinners, and all of the Gospels report John's proclamation of a stronger one to come after him (Matt. 3:11–12; Mark 1:7–8; Luke 3:15–18; John 1:24–28). His basic message about Jesus was that "He must increase, while I must decrease" (John 1:30). The Synoptics also report that John baptized Jesus.

Head of John the Baptist by Aleksandr Andreevic Ivanov, 1840s

One finds in the Gospels a contrast between the ministries of John and Jesus. John insisted on ascetical practices (Matt. 3:4; Mark 1:6), while Jesus was more lenient (Mark 2:18; Matt. 11:16–19). Jesus, however, respected John (Matt. 11:11; Luke

7:28), applied Malachi 3:1 to him (Matt. 11:10; Luke 7:27), and identified him as Elijah (Matt. 11:14; Mark 9:11–13). John was executed by Herod Antipas, ruler of Galilee, who resented John's denunciation of his immoral behavior (Matt. 14:3–12; Mark 6:17–29; Luke 3:19–20). His disciples constituted a community after his death, in some areas rivaling those of the early Christians (Acts 18:25; 19:1–7).

This feast, which is on the General Roman Calendar, is one of the oldest feasts of the Church, and the date is verified by a sermon delivered by Augustine [August 28] on this day. It is also observed by the Greek and Russian Orthodox Churches, the Anglican Communion, and the Evangelical Lutheran Church in America. This is, however, only one of two feasts dedicated to John the Baptist on the General Roman Calendar. The other, on August 29, commemorates his beheading. The Lateran Basilica in Rome, originally built in the fourth century, was rededicated to John the Baptist in 905.

25 Prosper of Aquitaine, theologian

Prosper of Aquitaine (ca. 390–ca. 460) was an influential fifth-century theologian. Little is known of his life, however. Prosper Tiro was probably a layman from Provence in southwestern France, where he spent most of his adult life. He was an intellectual disciple of Augustine [August 28] and was in correspondence with him. The extracts he drew from Augustine's writings were used at the Council of Orange (529). Like Augustine, Prosper was thoroughly involved in the controversy provoked by Pelagianism, a heresy that held that salvation can be obtained by human effort alone, without the grace of God. Although heavily indebted to Augustine, Prosper softened Augustine's views on grace, free will, and predestination, insisting that grace was a free gift of God that is available to all people because of divine mercy. (In Augustine's view, most of the human race is damned. Only a minority is given the unmerited grace of salvation.)

Following Augustine's death in 430, Prosper went to Rome with a priest friend, Hilary, to secure papal support for Augustine's teachings, and he returned with a strong anti-Pelagian letter from Pope Celestine I (422–32) addressed to the bishops of Gaul. Prosper eventually returned to Rome, where he is said to have served as secretary to Pope Leo the Great (440–61) [November 10], collaborating with him on some of his doctrinal pronouncements. Prosper's writings also exercised considerable influence on the Carolingian theologians of the late eighth and early ninth centuries. He died in Rome sometime between 460 and 463. His feast is not on the General Roman Calendar.

26 John and Paul, martyrs

John and *Paul* (d. before 410) were Roman martyrs of the fourth century. Although their cult is both early and well established, little is known of their lives. Their feast, however, is recorded both in the *Martyrology of Bede* [May 25] and in the Sarum liturgical calendar in wide use throughout England. In 1222 the Council of Oxford decreed that the faithful should attend Mass on their feast before going off to work. The popularity of their biography, or Acts, however unreliable it may be, contributed to the spread of their cult. According to these Acts, John and Paul were brothers and soldiers of the emperor Constantine [May 21] who continued to serve him after their military service and until the time of his death. Constantine's successor, his nephew Julian the Apostate, was unsympathetic to their Christian ways. He is said to have summoned them both to his court and commanded them to renounce their faith. When they refused even after a ten-day grace period, they were executed in their house on the Celian Hill, owned by the wealthy Roman Pammachius, a close friend of Jerome [September 30], and their bodies were buried in the garden. (Pammachius died in 410; therefore, the deaths of John and Paul probably occurred before then.)

The house was later converted into a church, and in the fifth century a basilica was erected on the old foundation. This may have been dedicated originally to Sts. Peter and Paul, but it came to be associated in the popular mind with John and Paul, who were thought to be brothers and martyrs. Excavations of the present basilica of SS. Giovanni e Paolo in 1887 uncovered rooms of an ancient house beneath the church dating back to the second century. The great church dedicated to Sts. John and Paul in Venice was built by Dominican friars who were from the convent of SS. Giovanni e Paulo in Rome. The feast of John and Paul is not on the General Roman Calendar.

In the Russian and Greek Orthodox Churches this is the feast day of *David of Thessalonike* (ca. 450–ca. 540), a hermit who lived in a cell outside the walls of Thessalonike (also Thessalonica) and who was sent by the local archbishop to Constantinople to request the transfer of the eparch's residence from Sirmium (then endangered by invasions) to Thessalonike. David, who was already nearly ninety years of age and whose hair was down to his loins, impressed the emperor and empress, in whose presence he is said to have worked a "miracle": holding hot charcoal embers without burning his hands. He died after his successful mission. The church of Hosios David in Thessalonike is dedicated to him.

27 Cyril of Alexandria, bishop and Doctor of the Church; Sampson the Hospitable of Constantinople, priest and physician

Cyril of Alexandria (ca. 376–444) was one of the leading theologians of the fifth century, the patriarch of Alexandria, and a Doctor of the Church. Born in Alexandria, he was the nephew of the patriarch of Alexandria, Theophilus, whom he succeeded in 412. The early years of his ministry were marred by violent attacks on Jews and pagans and a fatal attack on a philosopher, Hypatia, who had been critical of Cyril. Although Cyril himself was not directly involved in these attacks, he perhaps created an atmosphere of intolerance by his excessively sharp condemnations of non-Christians and schismatics. Cyril's principal theological adversary was Nestorius, the patriarch of Constantinople, who held that there were two persons in Christ, one divine and one human, which were bound together by a merely moral union. For that reason, the Blessed Virgin Mary should not be called the Mother of God, but only the mother of Christ.

When Nestorius refused to retract his teaching, even after condemnation and deposition from the patriarchate by Pope Celestine I, the Council of Ephesus was convened in 431, in which two hundred bishops took part and over which Cyril presided. He chose not to wait for the papal legates or the oriental bishops, who were largely in support of Nestorius. Nestorianism was condemned, and Mary was proclaimed as the Mother of God (Gk. *Theotokos*) since she is the mother of one divine Person. Six days later the archbishop of Antioch and forty-one bishops of his jurisdiction arrived, accused Cyril himself of heresy, and deposed him. The emperor had both Nestorius and Cyril arrested for three months, but the pope ruled in favor of Cyril. The result was a schism that involved the creation of a Nestorian Church, which did missionary work in China and India before being overwhelmed by the Mongol invasions of the fourteenth century.

The Council of Chalcedon appealed to Cyril's authority in its own teaching on the humanity and divinity of Christ in 451. Perhaps too little attention has been paid to the rich spiritual dimension of Cyril's theology and too much to the more systematic and controversial aspects. The focal point of his spirituality was his doctrine of the image of God in the human person, wherein lies human dignity and happiness. The image of God had been corrupted by sin, but restored by Christ in his Incarnation, Crucifixion, Resurrection, and Ascension. Cyril of Alexandria was declared a Doctor of the Church in 1882, and his feast is on the General Roman Calendar.

The feast of *Sampson the Hospitable of Constantinople,* a fifth-century philanthropic priest and physician, is observed on this day in the Greek and Russian Orthodox Churches. With his own funds he established a great hospital for the poor in Constantinople and was popularly known as Sampson the Hospitable even in his lifetime.

BIBLIOGRAPHY

McGuckin, John Anthony. *St. Cyril of Alexandria: The Christological Controversy: Its History, Theology, and Texts.* Leiden: E. J. Brill, 1994.

28 Irenaeus, bishop and martyr

Irenaeus of Lyons (ca. 130–200) was one of the greatest bishops and theologians of the second century. Born in the East, perhaps in Smyrna, whose bishop, Polycarp [February 23], he had known as a boy, Irenaeus studied at Rome and then was ordained a priest of Lyons (in east-central France). The city was a flourishing trade center and the principal diocese in all of Gaul. During a persecution of Christians, Irenaeus was sent to Rome with a letter for the pope, Eleutherius, urging leniency toward a heretical sect of Christians in Phrygia (in Asia Minor) for the sake of peace and unity. (The links with the Church of the Middle East were very strong in Lyons, given the fact that its first bishop and Irenaeus himself were both from Asia Minor.) On his return ca. 178, he was chosen to succeed the bishop who had been killed during the persecution.

Irenaeus acted as a peacemaker again in 190 when he successfully urged Pope Victor I to take a more moderate stance toward the Quartodecimans of Asia Minor, those who observed Easter on a different day than Rome did. Irenaeus was also a significant theologian, whose work was not fully appreciated until the early twentieth century, when one of his principal works was discovered. He was a strong and effective opponent of Gnosticism, the first major Christian heresy, which denied the goodness of the flesh and held that revelation (or saving knowledge [Gk. *gnosis*]) was available only to an elite few. He appealed to the principle of apostolic succession to show that saving revelation is available to everyone and that its authenticity is guaranteed by a body of public ministers, the bishops, whose pastoral authority is traceable back to the apostles themselves. He also argued that the Incarnation and the Resurrection gave ultimate value to human flesh because Christ "recapitulated" God's loving intentions in creating the world, revealing its destiny, and providing the "firstfruits" of that destiny. He saw all of human history and Jewish history as an educational process by which the human race was schooled in divine revelation and formed in grace. Jesus Christ was the climax and personification of this whole process.

Irenaeus died in Lyons in 200 and was buried in the crypt of the church of St. John (now Saint-Irénée), where his shrine remained until it was destroyed by Calvinists in 1562. He is usually venerated as a martyr, but there is no reliable evidence to support that belief. His feast is on the General Roman Calendar. It is also celebrated by the Church of England and the Episcopal Church in the USA and by the Evangelical Lutheran Church in America. His feast is observed in some portions of the Eastern Church on August 23, when he is commemorated by the Russian Orthodox Church.

BIBLIOGRAPHY

Donovan, Mary Ann. *One Right Reading?: A Guide to Irenaeus.* Collegeville, MN: Liturgical Press, 1997.

Grant, Robert M. *Irenaeus of Lyons.* London: Routledge, 1997.

Minns, Denis. *Irenaeus.* Washington, DC: Georgetown University Press, 1994.

29 Peter and Paul, apostles

Peter (d. ca. 64) was the first disciple chosen by Jesus and was the leader of the twelve apostles. A native of Bethsaida, near the Sea of Galilee, his original name was Simon. He was the son of Jonah (Matt. 16:17) and the brother of Andrew [November 30], who introduced him to Jesus. Peter and his brother were fishermen, like their father, working their father's trade possibly in a consortium with Zebedee and his sons. Peter was the first disciple whom Jesus chose, on which occasion he gave him a new name, Cephas, or Peter, which means "rock" (Matt. 16:18), and designated him a "fisher of men" (Mark 1:17; also Luke 5:10). Peter was married (Mark 1:30) and apparently traveled

Byzantine mosaic of Saint Peter, 11th C.

with his wife (1 Cor. 9:5). He was regarded as an "uneducated common man" (Acts 4:13).

Peter enjoyed a special status and role within the company of Jesus' disciples, especially in Matthew's Gospel. He is portrayed as walking on water (14:28–29), receiving special revelations (16:17), and performing miracles (17:27). He is the one who asks Jesus key questions and is the conduit of information from Jesus about an important range of topics (15:15; 17:25–26). He is also, of course, designated by Jesus as the rock upon which his Church will be built (16:18–19). On the other hand, Peter was not without human flaws and weaknesses. He rebuked Jesus when Jesus first began to speak of his own impending death in Jerusalem, and Jesus called him a "Satan" (Mark 8:33). Peter's faith failed as he was walking on the water (Matt. 14:30–31). And he made various boasts about his loyalty to Jesus (Mark 14:29, 31), but then denied him three times (Mark 14:66–72). Just as Paul is remembered as the one who persecuted the Church before his own conversion on the road to Damascus, Peter is remembered for all time as the apostle who denied the Lord. John [December 27], "the beloved disciple," noted that Peter's insights were inferior to his own (John 20:6–9; 21:7). Jesus prayed for Peter that his faith might be strengthened (Luke 22:31–32).

Peter was both the chief apostle and one of the three who were closest in Jesus (along with James [July 25] and John). The three of them were with Jesus when he raised Jairus's daughter (Mark 5:37), at the Transfiguration [August 9] (Mark 9:2), on the Mount of Olives for a special farewell discourse (Mark 13:3), and in the Garden of Gethsemane (Mark 14:33). Paul acknowledges that Peter was the first to whom the risen Lord appeared (1 Cor. 15:5) and that he functioned not only as the "pillar" of the church in Jerusalem, but also as the leader of the mission to the Gentiles (Gal. 2:27). Luke also describes Jesus at the Last Supper commissioning Peter as the head of the disciples (22:32) and notes that Jesus appeared first to him after the Resurrection (24:34). The angel of the Lord instructs the women to convey the word of Jesus' Resurrection to "the disciples and Peter" (Mark 16:7). In this and other Resurrection appearances, Peter is the most commissioned of the Twelve.

Peter's role in the early Church is described in Acts. He functioned as the chief witness of Jesus (2:14–36). He defended the gospel before legal courts (4:7–12), and he himself functioned as a judge within the Christian community (5:1–10) and an arbiter of conflict (15:7–11). He was also the one who received the vision of foods descending from heaven that led to the opening of the mission to the Gentiles (10:13–15), at the beginning of which he baptized the pagan centurion Cornelius [February 2] and his household (10:44–48), without requiring circumcision or the imposition of Jewish dietary laws. Peter was later imprisoned and then escaped from Jerusalem (12:17).

He is credited with writing two Letters that are part of the New Testament. The case for his authorship of the first is strong, but not for the second, even though there is much information about Peter therein. It is a synthesis of traditions about Peter. The New Testament indicates that Peter traveled to Lydda, Joppa, and Caesarea (Acts 9–10), and also visited Antioch (Gal. 2:11) and probably Corinth (1 Cor. 9:5). There is increasingly reliable evidence that he did travel to Rome and was martyred there. It is difficult, if not impossible, to say how Peter functioned in Rome. Paul's Letter to the Romans never mentions Peter. However, Ignatius of Antioch [October 17] and Irenaeus [June 28] assumed that Peter and Paul exercised special authority over the church of Rome and even that they jointly founded it and inaugurated its succession of bishops, or popes. But not until the late second or early third century did the tradition identify Peter as the first Bishop of Rome—a tradition that continues, of course, to this day.

Clement of Rome [November 23] describes Peter's trial in Rome (*1 Clement* 5:4), and the historian Eusebius reports an ancient story about his crucifixion, upside down, just as he had requested (*Ecclesiastical History* 2.25.5, 8). Tertullian also says that Peter was crucified. According to a very old tradition Peter was confined in the Mamertine prison, where the church of St. Peter in Chains now stands. His place of execution is thought to have been the gardens of Nero, where many executions took place during his reign. Eusebius quotes Gaius, a priest of Rome during the pontificate of Zephyrnus (198/9–217), as stating that Peter's body was interred in the Tropaion, a memorial shrine in a cemetery on the Vatican Hill. The relics were subsequently transferred to the catacombs for safety during later persecutions. When they were returned to Vatican Hill, they were placed in the new basilica built by the emperor Constantine [May 21] in the early fourth century. Recent archeological evidence supports the traditional belief that Peter was indeed buried under the present site of St. Peter's Basilica. In fact, no other city or town has ever claimed to possess the remains of St. Peter, and no historian through the centuries has contradicted Rome's claim.

The best early representation of Peter and Paul is on a bronze medal dating from the first half of the second century. It was found in the catacombs of Domitilla and is now in the Vatican Museum. Peter is shown, just as he has always been portrayed in art, as a sturdy and thickset man, with a bald or tonsured head and a curly beard, while Paul appears as thin and bald, with a long head, a scantier beard, and deep-set eyes. Peter was invoked as a saint of the universal Church from very early times and is considered the patron saint of the Church and the papacy. His feast, along with that of Paul, is on the General Roman Calendar, and is celebrated also on this day throughout the East, in the Anglican Communion, and by the Evangelical Lutheran Church in America. This is one of two major feasts of Peter on the General Roman Calendar. The other is the feast of the Chair of Peter on February 22.

Paul (ca. 1/5–ca. 62/67) was the most prominent early Christian missionary, known as the "apostle to the Gentiles." He is patron saint of Greece and Malta, as well as the lay apostolate and the Cursillo movement. Born in Tarsus and raised as a Pharisee, he was originally named Saul. He was at first a persecutor of Christians, having been present at the stoning to death of Stephen [December 26]. He had a conversion experience while on the way to Damascus (commemorated in the feast of the Conversion of Paul on January 25), was baptized and given the name Paul, and then became a Christian missionary to the Gentiles. (The main events of his life and missionary journeys are summarized in the entry for January 25.)

Saint Paul Preaching to the Jews in the Synagogue of Damascus

Paul was first introduced to Peter by Barnabas [June 11] in Jerusalem (Acts 9:25–29; Gal. 1:18–19). He came into contact with Peter again at Antioch, where they had an intense argument (Gal. 2:11–21). Peter had preached the gospel to the Gentiles and at first enjoyed meals with his Gentile converts in accordance with the decision reached by the council of Jerusalem (Acts 15:19). But after a group of conservative Jewish Christians came to Antioch from Jerusalem, Peter "began to draw back and separated himself, because he was afraid of the circumcised" (Gal. 2:12). Peter's example affected others as well. So Paul "opposed him to his face because he clearly was wrong" (2:11). "If you, though a Jew, are living like a Gentile and not like a Jew," Paul said, "how can you compel the Gentiles to live like Jews?" (2:14).

Paul's movements following his three missionary journeys are uncertain, but he did end up in Rome, where he was detained and kept under house arrest for two years. Though he was eventually released, he was evidently arrested again because he was executed in Rome at Tre Fontane sometime in the 60s. As a Roman citizen, Paul would have been beheaded instead of suffering one of the crueller deaths reserved for others. He was buried on the present site of the basilica of St. Paul's Outside the Walls. The building has been ascribed to the emperor Constantine, but was principally the work of the emperor Theodosius I (d. 395) and Pope Leo the Great (440–61) [November 10]. It was destroyed by fire in 1823 and later rebuilt and consecrated in 1854.

Peter and Paul, the two greatest missionaries of the early Church, are forever linked because of the tradition that they "founded" the church in Rome through their martyrdom there. The earliest witnesses to this tradition are Ignatius of Antioch and Irenaeus. The joint commemoration of the two saints in Rome is attested from the year 258. Indeed, it is one of the rare liturgical commemorations the West has given to the East. Until 1969, however, there was a separate feast of Paul on June 30. The two were liturgically rejoined in the reform of the General Roman Calendar approved by Pope Paul VI in 1969.

BIBLIOGRAPHY

Farmer, William Reuben. *Peter and Paul in the Church of Rome: The Ecumenical Potential of a Forgotten Perspective.* New York: Paulist Press, 1990.

(Separate bibliographies for Peter and for Paul are available at the end of the entries on February 22 and January 25, respectively.)

30 First Martyrs of the Church of Rome; Blessed Raymond Lull, missionary; Theobald of Provins, hermit

This feast commemorates those who were martyred during the persecution of Nero, who reigned from the years 54 to 68. Peter and Paul also died during this persecution, and this feast follows immediately upon theirs on June 29. It was introduced in 1969 with the reform of the General Roman Calendar partly in compensation for the several Roman martyrs whose feasts are no longer on the universal calendar.

The Roman historian Tacitus reports that on July 19, 64, a great fire broke out in the city, beginning near the Circus Maximus (Lat., "the great circus") in a district full of shops and booths filled with inflammable goods and spread rapidly in the summer heat in all directions. The fire raged for seven days and nights and destroyed palaces, temples, and other public monuments. It was contained for a time, and then it reignited for three more days. By the time it was completely over, two-thirds of the city was in ruins. Given Nero's odd behavior, bordering on delight, during the fire, there was widespread suspicion that he himself had ordered the fire set, or at least ordered it not to be extinguished. Nevertheless, he announced that Christians had been responsible and ordered their arrest and execution. Some were crucified; some were covered with wax and set afire; and some were sewn into animal skins to be devoured by animals. These barbarous acts were perpetrated as public entertainment in Nero's palace gardens. The cruelty and horror of the spectacle appalled even those who had been hardened by previous imperial spectacles. Tacitus noted that "it was felt that [the Christians] were being sacrificed to one man's brutality rather than to the national interest." A wave of uprisings followed, Nero lost public support, and he committed suicide four years later. By the time a later historian, Suetonius, wrote his account, it was taken for granted that Nero had "brazenly set fire to the City."

The Franciscans commemorate *Raymond Lull* (1232–1316), also Ramon Llull, on this day. He was a Franciscan tertiary and lay missionary to the Muslims, and, through his mystical writings, is considered a forerunner of Teresa of Ávila [October 15] and John of the Cross [December 14]. Beatified in 1847, he is the patron saint of Majorca, his birthplace.

This is also the feast day of *Theobald of Provins* (d. 1066), a hermit who, along with a companion, hired himself out by day, doing unskilled work. He later became a priest and a Camaldolese monk. He was canonized in 1073 and is patron saint of janitors.

JULY

1 Blessed Junipero Serra, priest; Antonio Rosmini-Serbati, priest

Junipero Serra (1713–84) was a Spanish Franciscan priest who established the first mission in present-day California in 1769. Born in Majorca, Spain, he entered the Franciscans in 1730 and was ordained a priest in 1737. After teaching for a time, he went to the New Spain (present-day Mexico and Texas) in 1749, where he did missionary work for the next twenty years. He expanded his ministry into Upper California in 1769 and established nine of the twenty-one Franciscan missions along the Pacific coast, serving as their president until his death. He is credited with having baptized some six thousand converts.

His statue, representing the state of California, has been in the National Statuary Hall in the U.S. Capitol since 1931. Nevertheless, his cause for canonization became the source of controversy between the Catholic Church and leaders of the Native American community, who objected to the Franciscan missionaries' treatment of those whom they sought to convert. Serra himself, however, defended the local people against abuse and exploitation and stressed their equality before God. He died at Monterey on August 28, 1784, and was beatified in 1988 by Pope John Paul II, who called him "an exemplary model of the selfless evangelizer." His feast is on the Proper Calendar for the Dioceses of the U.S.A., but is not on the General Roman Calendar, nor even on the Franciscan liturgical calendar. Serra Clubs, which encourage vocations to the priesthood, operate under his patronage. On this day, the Greek and Russian Orthodox Churches celebrate the feast of *Cosmas* and *Damian* [September 26], early fourth-century martyrs.

July 1 is also the day of death of *Antonio Rosmini-Serbati* (1797–1855), an Italian priest-philosopher who founded the Institute of Charity, also known as Rosminians, a congregation of priests committed to the pursuit of holiness in and through their service to the Church. His best known and most controversial work was *Five Wounds of the Church,* which named five major areas in need of reform: the division between clergy and laity at worship, a poorly educated clergy, a divided hierarchy, the nomination of bishops by secular powers, and the riches of the Church. Although the book anticipated some of the reforms of the twentieth century, it was placed on the Index of Forbidden Books and Rosmini lived under a cloud thereafter.

2 Bernardino Realino, Francis Regis, and Francis Jerome, priests

Bernardino Realino (1530–1616) was an Italian Jesuit who served as a parish priest in Lecce in Apulia for forty-two years. His work was that of an ordinary pastor: celebrating the Eucharist, preaching, hearing confessions, ministering to the sick, educating children in the faith, providing spiritual direction, and visiting prisoners. He also gave conferences and retreats to religious. He was so highly respected and deeply beloved by the townspeople that the mayor came to him on his deathbed and made him promise that he would be Lecce's patron saint in heaven. Bernardino Realino was beatified in 1895 and canonized in 1947.

Francis Regis (1597–1640), also John Francis Regis, was a French Jesuit who spent most of his priestly life as a missionary among those who had lapsed from the faith during the Wars of Religion between Calvinists (Huguenots) and Catholics. In addition to his normal pastoral duties of saying Mass, preaching, and hearing confessions, he visited prisons, collected food and clothing for the poor, and established homes for the rehabilitation of prostitutes. People came flocking to him for confession even when he was on his deathbed. He was beatified in 1716 and canonized in 1737. He is patron saint of social workers and of marriage.

Francis Jerome (1642–1716) was an Italian Jesuit who spent forty years of his priesthood in parish work in Naples, where he was an indefatigable preacher. He also had a special ministry to slaves and criminals, as well as to the sick. He was beatified in 1806 and canonized in 1839.

The feast of all three is celebrated on this day by the Jesuits, but is not on the General Roman Calendar.

3 Thomas, apostle

Thomas (first century), called Didymus, "the twin" (John 11:16 20:24; 21:2), was one of the twelve apostles, best known for his doubts about the reports of Jesus' Resurrection (John 20:24–29). Thus, he is also known by the epithet "doubting Thomas." He was the first apostle to insist that he was ready to die with Jesus (11:16). At the Last Supper he admits that he does not know where Jesus is going, to which Jesus replies that he is the Way, the Truth, and the Life (14:4–6). Thomas's confession of faith, upon seeing the Risen Lord, is the only instance in the New Testament where Jesus is explicitly addressed as God: "My Lord and my God" (20:24–29). Thomas is also mentioned as being among the disciples on the shore of the Sea of Galilee after the Resurrection who witnessed the miraculous catch of fish (21:1–14).

There is much uncertainty about Thomas's missionary activities after Pentecost. One tradition, supported by the historian Eusebius (d. ca. 339), indicates that he preached to the Parthians in what is now Iran. The strongest tradition links him with southern India and indicates that he founded the Church there after preaching in Syria and Persia. The Syrian Christians of Malabar, known as Thomas Christians, claim that they were evangelized by him and that he was killed by a spear and buried at Mylapore, near Madras. An ancient stone cross marks the spot where he was buried, until his remains were transferred to Edessa, Syria, in 394, and eventually to Ortona in Italy. Indian Christians, however, insist that he is still buried in India at what they call San Tome, the place of his martyrdom, on which site was built the Cathedral of St. Thomas. The Indian government is satisfied that this is the case. It issued postage stamps in his honor in 1964 and again in 1972 to mark the nineteenth centenary of Thomas's death.

Various writings are associated with Thomas, but they are all apocryphal: the *Acts of Thomas*, the *Apocalypse of Thomas*, the *Gospel of Thomas*, and the *Infancy Gospel of Thomas*. Legend has it that he built a palace for an Indian king, and so he is considered a patron saint of architects. Because of his earlier spiritual blindness in refusing to accept the Resurrection until the Lord himself appeared to him, he is also invoked by those who suffer from physical sightlessness. His name became one of the most popular Christian names in the West.

In the Syrian churches and in Malabar, July 3 was believed to be the date of his death, in the year 72. The Episcopal Church in the USA and the Evangelical Lutheran Church in America still commemorate him on December 21, which was the former date of his feast in the Catholic Church. With the reform of the General Roman Calendar in 1969, the Catholic Church, along with the Church of England, celebrates his feast today, while the Greek and Russian Orthodox Churches celebrate it on October 6. He is patron saint of India, the East Indies, Pakistan, surveyors, construction workers, carpenters, and, as mentioned above, architects.

4 Elizabeth of Portugal, queen; Ulrich of Augsburg, bishop; Andrew of Crete, bishop

Elizabeth of Portugal (1271–1336) was queen of Portugal by marriage to King Denis, or Diniz. Born in Zaragoza, Spain, the daughter of the king of Aragon, she was always known in her own country as Isabella. She married the king of Portugal at age twelve, and eight years later had a daughter and then a son a year after that. The marriage, however, was not a happy one, given the king's many dalliances and his fathering of various illegitimate children. She diverted her energies to prayer and the care of the sick, orphans, the poor, pilgrims, and prostitutes. After her husband's death in 1325, she became a Franciscan tertiary and lived in great simplicity. Toward the end of her life she prevented a war between Portugal and Castile, but the effort exhausted her and she died at Estramoz on July 4, 1336. She was buried in the convent of the Poor Clares in Coïmbra, after which many miracles were said to have occurred. She was canonized in 1625. Elizabeth is the patron saint of Coïmbra and one of the patron saints of Portugal. Her feast is on the General Roman Calendar.

This is also the feast day of *Ulrich of Augsburg* (890–973), a bishop whose principal "claim to fame" in church history is that his canonization in 993 was the first one performed by a pope. It is said that Ulrich visited the local hospital in Augsburg every day to wash the feet of twelve poor people and to distribute alms. His feast is not on the General Roman Calendar.

The Greek and Russian Orthodox Churches celebrate the feast of *Andrew of Crete* (ca. 660–740) on this day. Born in Damascus, he became a monk at Jerusalem and represented the patriarch of Constantinople at the Third Council of Constantinople (680–81). He was appointed archbishop of Gortyna (Crete) ca. 700 and was considered one of the greatest preachers and hymn writers in the Byzantine Church. Some of his homilies are still read in the Divine Office, and his hymns continue to be sung in the Liturgy.

5 Anthony Mary Zaccaria, priest

Anthony Mary Zaccaria (1502–39) was the founder of the Barnabite order. Born at Cremona in northern Italy, he studied medicine at the University of Padua and served as a doctor in his hometown until he decided to change from physical to spiritual healing. He was ordained a priest in 1528. Two years later, together with two Milanese noblemen, he founded an order of priests to regenerate the love of the liturgy and a Christian way of life by frequent preaching, with emphasis on the writings of St. Paul [June 29] and the faithful administration of the sacraments. His small community ministered to victims of the plague and won widespread acclaim for their work. One of the noblemen with whom he cofounded the order was the brother of a papal secretary. The brother brought the new order to the attention of Pope Clement VII, who granted it formal approval in 1533. The order adopted the name Clerks Regular of St. Paul and later added "the Beheaded" to the title.

At first the order encountered opposition from the local clergy because of the reforms it tried to introduce, but Rome stood behind it. Anthony himself organized conferences for the clergy, established associations for married people, preached in the open air, and ministered to the sick. His spirituality was based on devotion to the Eucharist and to the Passion of Christ. He and the other members of his order lived a life of strict poverty. He also helped Countess Ludovica Torelli to found the Angelicals of St. Paul for religious women, which received papal approval in 1535. In the last year of his life, he began negotiations to make the church of St. Barnabas [June 11] in Milan the headquarters of his order. This is why its members became known in the popular mind as Barnabites. The Barnabites were credited with preparing the way for the reforms of Charles Borromeo [November 4] in Milan.

Anthony fell gravely ill while giving a parish mission and was taken to his mother's house in Cremona, where he died on July 5, 1539, at age thirty-seven. In 1893 his remains were moved from the church of St. Paul in Milan to the crypt of the Barnabite church, where they are still venerated. Anthony Mary Zaccaria was canonized in 1897. His feast is on the General Roman Calendar.

6 Maria Goretti, virgin and martyr

Maria Teresa Goretti (1890–1902) was killed by a rapist at the age of twelve. Born of a peasant family in Corinaldo, near Ancona, in Italy, she was left to take care of the house while her mother worked in the fields following her father's death. A young man in the neighborhood made sexual advances and, when she resisted an attempted rape, he stabbed her repeatedly. Maria died the next day, July 6, 1902, in the hospital at Nettuno, but not before voicing a word of forgiveness for her attacker, "for the love of Jesus." Her killer was sentenced to thirty

Saint Maria Goretti

years in prison. He later repented, expressed remorse for what he had done, and lived to see his victim beatified in 1947 and canonized in 1950 as a martyr for chastity. Maria's mother and other members of her immediate family were also present for the ceremony held in St. Peter's Square and attended by some 250,000 people. Her remains are in the church of Our Lady of Grace in Nettuno. Her cult was popular in Italy, but she was also held up as a model of chastity for parochial-school children in the United States in the 1950s. She became the patron saint of the Children of Mary and of teenage girls. Her feast is on the General Roman Calendar. On this day the Church of England commemorates *Thomas More* and *John Fisher* [June 22].

7 Blessed Benedict XI, pope

Benedict XI (1240–1304; pope 1303–4) was born Niccolò Boccasini in Treviso of an ordinary working-class family. He studied in Venice and joined the Dominicans at age seventeen. In 1268 he was appointed lecturer in theology and preacher in Venice and Bologna. In 1286 he became provincial in Lombardy and ten years later master general of the order. He was a strong supporter of Pope Boniface VIII (1295–1303) against the Colonna cardinals and the Spiritual Franciscans (a dissident group within the Franciscan order that insisted on an absolute standard of poverty), and in 1298 the pope made him a cardinal and then bishop of Ostia. Upon the death of Boniface VIII at Anagni, his place of exile (where Niccolò had stood with him in support against his enemies), the cardinals unanimously elected Niccolò as pope, and he took the name Benedict because it was the baptismal name of his patron, Boniface VIII.

Benedict's pontificate was marked by a weak acquiescence to the demands of the king of France, Philip IV (Philip the Fair). A quiet, scholarly man, Benedict seemed to feel at ease only among his fellow Dominicans. Indeed, it is said that, even as pope, he remained a friar at heart, following an austere spiritual regime and abating none of his humility and moderation. He revoked his predecessor's bull restricting the rights of Dominicans and Franciscans to preach and to hear confessions, and also lifted his predecessor's excommunications of the two Colonna cardinals, but without restoring them to their previous rank. Although his conciliatory gesture did not completely satisfy the Colonnas, it did manage to exasperate the supporters of Boniface VIII. The factional conflict that erupted afterward forced Benedict XI to leave Rome for Perugia in April 1304. While in Perugia, he made one concession after another to appease the anger of the king of France, who was demanding that the pope call a council to denounce the memory of Boniface VIII. The king was temporarily satisfied by Benedict's gestures, and his call for a council subsided. However, the pope became ill with acute dysentery and died in Perugia on July 7, 1304. He was buried there, in accordance with his wishes, in the church of San Domenico, and there were reports of miraculous cures at the tomb. Benedict XI was beatified in 1736. His feast is not on the General Roman Calendar, but it is celebrated on this day by the Dominicans.

8 Aquila and Prisca, martyrs; Procopius, martyr; Blessed Eugenius III, pope; Kilian, bishop

Aquila and *Prisca* (first century), also known as Priscilla, were husband and wife and disciples of Paul [June 29]. They had to leave Italy for a short time because of an imperial edict, rendered in the year 49 or 50, prohibiting Jews from living in Rome. Paul visited them in Corinth and discovered that Aquila was a tentmaker like himself, so he lodged with them and they worked together (Acts 18:1–3). It is not clear whether they were already Christians at the time, or whether they were converted by Paul during his stay with them. When Paul left Corinth, Aquila and Prisca went with him, but stopped at Ephesus while he went on to Syria. In Ephesus they instructed Apollos, a Jew from Alexandria (18:18–19, 24–26). They returned to Rome eventually, and Paul sent them greetings there, referring to them affectionately as "co-workers in Christ Jesus, who risked their necks for my life, to whom not only I am grateful, but also all the churches of the Gentiles" (Rom. 16:3–4). He also greeted "the church at their house," a reminder that Christians at this time gathered for the Eucharist in private homes, not in churches. At some point, the couple left Rome again and moved to Ephesus. When Paul wrote from there to the church in Corinth in 57, he included "many greetings" from Aquila and Prisca "together with the church at their house" (1 Cor. 16:19). And when he wrote to Timothy from prison, he sent them his greetings (2 Tim. 4:19).

The *Roman Martyrology* states that they died in Asia Minor, but there is also a tradition that indicates that they were martyred in Rome, perhaps because of the existence of the church of St. Prisca on the Aventine Hill, known as *titulus Aquilae et Priscae* (Lat., "in the title of Aquila and Prisca"). Their feast is not on the General Roman Calendar.

On this day the Russian and Greek Orthodox Churches celebrate the feast of *Procopius* (d. 303), the protomartyr (first martyr) of the Diocletian persecution in Palestine. A lector and exorcist, he refused to sacrifice to the gods and was beheaded in Caesarea on July 7, 303.

The Cistercians celebrate the feast of *Eugenius III* (pope 1145–53). He had been a Cistercian monk at Clairvaux and then abbot of Sts. Vincent and Anastasius just outside of Rome before his election. At the urging of his fellow Cistercian, Bernard of Clairvaux [August 20], Eugenius III promoted clerical and monastic reform. The pope himself retained the habit and lifestyle of a monk while in office. Because of his austere simplicity of life, he was beatified in 1872. He is patron saint of the Czech Republic.

July 8 is also the feast day of *Kilian* (d. 689), an Irish monk who went to the Continent, became bishop of Würzburg, and was murdered after a dispute with the king over the propriety of his marriage to his widowed sister-in-law. Kilian is the principal patron saint of the city and of Bavaria as a whole, and his feast day is celebrated each year with a *Kilianfest,* during which a modern mystery play about the saint's life is performed. His feast, however, is not on any liturgical calendar.

9 Martyrs of Gorkum; Pancratius, martyr; Rose Hawthorne, nun

This feast commemorates a group of nineteen martyrs put to death by Dutch Calvinists in a deserted monastery at Ruggen, in the Netherlands, in 1572. The group included eleven Franciscans, including their guardian *Nicholas Pieck,* two Norbertines, a Dominican, an Augustinian, and four diocesan priests. They had been arrested and imprisoned at Gorkum from June 26 to July 6, then taken by ship to Briel. When they refused an offer of freedom in return for denying Catholic teaching on the Eucharist and the papacy, they were hanged at Ruggen, near Briel. Their bodies were mutilated before and after death, buried in a ditch, and left there until they were transferred to the Franciscan church in Brussels in 1616. The political context for their martyrdom was a long struggle for Dutch independence from Spain that pitted Calvinists against Catholics. Nevertheless, the Prince of Orange, who was the leader of the anti-Spanish forces, had tried unsuccessfully to obtain their release. The martyrs were beatified in 1675 and canonized in 1867. Their feast is not on the General Roman Calendar, but is celebrated on this day by the Franciscans (as "John Pieck and Companions") and by the Dominicans (as "John of Cologne and Companions").

The Greek and Russian Orthodox Churches celebrate the feast of *Pancratius* who, according to legend, was a disciple of Peter [June 29] and had accompanied the apostle on his journeys, converted the governor of Sicily, and became the first bishop of Taormina. He was said to have been killed by pagan bandits.

This is also the day of death of *Rose Hawthorne* (1851–1926), who became a Dominican nun after the death of her husband, George Lathrop. She was the daughter of the American writer Nathaniel Hawthorne (1804–64) and the foundress of the Servants of Relief for Incurable Cancer. She was inspired by the example of Vincent de Paul [September 27], and, in turn, her biography inspired Dorothy Day [November 29] to launch the Catholic Worker movement.

10 Veronica Giuliani, abbess; Canute, king

Veronica Giuliani (1660–1727) was a Franciscan nun who has been described as the most representative figure of Baroque mysticism. Born Orsola Giuliani at Mercatello, in Urbino, of a well-to-do, middle-class family, she became a Capuchin nun at Città di Castello in Umbria in 1677, against her father's wishes. She took the name Veronica and had a difficult novitiate because of the severity of her superiors. After her profession she is said to have had numerous mystical experiences in which she received the stigmata, including those of a crown of thorns on her head. These phenomena were subjected to much scrutiny and investigation during her lifetime. She was mistress of novices for thirty-four years and then was elected abbess in 1717. As abbess, she made a number of physical improvements of the convent, including its enlargement and the introduction of running water. She was reelected every three years until her death on July 9, 1727. She is said to have combined a high degree of contemplation with common sense and administrative skill.

She was an avid reader and her own writings were influenced by those of Catherine of Siena [April 29], Teresa of Ávila [October 15], John of the Cross [December 14], and Francis de Sales [January 24]. Upon orders from her confessor, she left a ten-volume spiritual diary in which she described various aspects of her visions of the suffering Christ and claimed that instruments of Christ's Passion were imprinted on her heart. These documents were carefully reviewed in connection with her canonization process. She was beatified in 1804 and canonized in 1839. Her feast is not on the General Roman Calendar, but it is celebrated by the Franciscans on this day. This is also the feast day of *Canute* (d. 1086), also Cnut, the king of Denmark who lavished benefits on the Church, but made two unsuccessful attempts to invade England, whose throne he also claimed. He was killed when his own subjects rebelled against the heavy taxes he imposed. Canute is a patron saint of Denmark.

11 Benedict of Nursia, abbot; Olga, grand duchess

Benedict of Nursia (ca. 480–ca. 550) was the founder of Western monasticism, the author of the famous Rule that bears his name, and a patron saint of Europe (declared as such by Pope Paul VI in 1964). He is also the patron saint of monks, speleologists, farmworkers, and victims of poisoning. Little is known about his life, apart from Gregory the Great's [September 3] *Dialogues*. Born at Nursia in central Italy, he studied for a time in Rome, but was so distressed by the immorality of society that he left the city ca. 500 to become a hermit at Subiaco. Disciples later joined him, and he organized them into twelve deaneries of ten monks each. He stayed at Subiaco for about twenty-five years, but left there, it is thought, because of some local disturbances, perhaps created by a jealous local cleric. It is even said that an attempt was made on his life. Whatever the reason for the change, he took a small group of his monks to Monte Cassino, near Naples. It was there that he wrote the final version of his Rule, which borrowed from previous monastic writers such as Basil [January 2], John Cassian [July 23], Augustine [August 28], various Desert Fathers, and the anonymous author of the *Regula Magistri* (Lat., "Rule of the Master").

Detail from *Life of Saint Benedict* by Consolo, 13th C.

Benedict's Rule emphasized authority and obedience, and stability and community life. The monks' primary occupation was the praying of the Divine Office in common, complemented by the reading of sacred texts and manual work of various kinds. Benedict insisted that an abbot should be elected by all of the monks and that he should be wise, discreet, flexible, learned in the law of God, and a spiritual father to his community—just as he was. The flexibility of his Rule allowed it to be adapted readily to the needs of society, so that monasteries shaped by it became centers of scholarship, agriculture, medicine, and hospitality.

Benedict remained in Monte Cassino for the rest of his life. It is interesting to note that he never became a priest, nor did he intend to found a new religious order. Nevertheless, he influenced the growth not only of Western monasticism, but of Western civilization itself. After his death on March 21, ca. 550, he was buried in the Oratory of St. John the Baptist [June 24; August 29] at Cassino alongside his sister, Scholastica [February 10], whom he used to meet once a year outside his monastery for the exchange of spiritual insights.

At first his cult was limited. Indeed, there is no indication of it before the destruction of his monastery by the Lombards ca. 577. After its restoration ca. 720 there is the first sign of a cult connected with his tomb. The martyrologies and liturgical calendars of Cassino, the earliest of which go back to the eighth century, mention a solemnity on March 21, his day of death, celebrated in concurrence with a feast on July 11, the day his remains were transferred to another site within the monastery.

His Rule was followed in France, England, and Germany by the seventh and eighth centuries, but there was still no federation of monasteries constituting the Benedictine order. When the emperor Charlemagne (d. 814) initiated a reform of monasticism, he chose the Rule of St. Benedict as the most suitable instrument, and his son and successor Louis the Pious imposed it on all monasteries within the empire. For a time there was considerable tension between the claims of autonomy on the part of individual monasteries and the reformers' conviction that common action was required. With the Cluniac reform of the tenth century, establishing networks of monasteries attached to a center in Cluny, this situation began gradually to change. The first liturgical evidence of Benedict's cult in England is from that same century.

His feast is on the General Roman Calendar, having been moved in the liturgical reform of 1969 to this day for two reasons: July 11 is the day of the transfer of his remains, and the former feast day, March 21, the day of death, often occurred during Lent. The moving of the feast to July ensured that it would always be observed outside of Lent. The feast is also celebrated on July 11 by the Church of England, the Episcopal Church in the USA, and the Evangelical Lutheran Church in

America. The Benedictines themselves continue to celebrate his main feast on March 21, but observe this day as well.

On this day the Russian Orthodox Church celebrates the feast of *Olga* (ca. 879–969), one of the first Russian converts to Christianity. As a grand duchess, she tried unsuccessfully to introduce Christianity to her people, even asking the Holy Roman emperor Otto I to send missionaries. Her grandson Vladimir of Kiev [July 15] brought her aspirations to some measure of fulfillment. Her cult was confirmed in Russia in 1574. Her feast is not on the General Roman Calendar.

BIBLIOGRAPHY

Kardong, Terrence. *Benedict's Rule: A Translation and Commentary.* Collegeville, MN: Liturgical Press, 1996.

———. *The Benedictines.* Wilmington, DE: Michael Glazier, 1988.

Vogüé, Adalbert de, ed. *The Life of St. Benedict–[by] Gregory the Great.* Trans. Hilary Costello and Eoin de Bhaldraithe. Petersham, MA: St. Bede's Publications, 1993.

12 John Gualbert, abbot; John Jones and John Wall, martyrs; Nathan Söderblom, bishop; Veronica

John Gualbert (ca. 995–1073) was the founder of the Vallombrosian monks. Born Giovanni Gualberto in Florence of a noble family, he spared the life of his brother's murderer and soon after entered the Benedictine monastery of San Miniato in Florence. He left four years later, after a disputed election for abbot, to seek a more austere way of life that was untouched by contemporary abuses in the Church, namely, clerical concubinage, nepotism, and simony, the last practiced in a notorious manner by the archbishop of Florence. After visiting the hermitage of Romuald [June 19] at Camaldoli, Gaulbert decided to establish his own monastery and chose Vallombrosa, a site about twenty miles east of Florence.

As his community grew, he adopted a modified form of the primitive Rule of St. Benedict [July 11], laying greater stress on silence, poverty, and strict enclosure. He regarded manual labor as a distraction from a monk's need for prayer and contemplation, and so he developed the use of lay brothers to take care of the monastery's physical needs. He established a number of other monasteries on the model of Vallombrosa, some with hospices for the sick and the poor. Out of humility, John refused to accept ordination to the priesthood. He died on July 12, 1073, and was canonized in 1193. His order expanded during the Middle Ages, mostly in Italy, and was reformed by John Leonardi [October 9] in the sixteenth century. Since 1966 it has been part of the Benedictine federation, but it is now much smaller in numbers. His feast is not on the General Roman Calendar, but it is celebrated on this day by Benedictines and Cistercians.

Also on this day, Franciscans commemorate *John Jones* (d. 1598), a Franciscan priest who was hanged, drawn, and quartered outside the church of St. Thomas Waterings in London on July 12, 1598, and was canonized in 1970; and *John Wall* (d. 1679), also a Franciscan priest who suffered exactly the same fate, but almost a century later and at Redhill, Worcester, on August 22, 1679. He too was canonized in 1970 as one of the Martyrs of England and Wales.

This is also the day of death of *Desiderius Erasmus* (1466–1536), one of the greatest Christian humanists in all of history and a courageous critic of abuses in the Church and of social injustices. A friend of Thomas More [June 22], he dedicated his masterpiece, *In Praise of Folly,* to him.

On this day the Evangelical Lutheran Church in America commemorates *Nathan Söderblom* (1866–1931), archbishop of Uppsala and primate of the Church of Sweden, a leading ecumenist and winner of the Nobel Peace Prize in 1930 in recognition of his advocacy of peace through church unity and his work on behalf of war prisoners and displaced persons in the World War I.

July 12 was also the traditional feast day of *Veronica,* a legendary woman who is said to have greeted Jesus along the Way of the Cross and wiped his face with a cloth on which was left his facial imprint. The cloth was widely venerated during the later Middle Ages when devotion to the Passion of Christ was particularly strong, and it has been preserved in St. Peter's Basilica in Rome since the eighth century. However, she was not included in any of the early martyrologies, including the *Roman Martyrology,* and Charles Borromeo [November 4] suppressed her feast and Office in sixteenth-century Milan. Veronica is in all probability a fictional person created to explain the relic. Needless to say, her feast is not on the General Roman Calendar.

BIBLIOGRAPHY

Belting, Hans. *Likeness and Presence: A History of the Image Before the Era of Art.* Chicago: University of Chicago Press, 1994.

Kuryluk, Ema. *Veronica and Her Cloth.* Cambridge, MA, and Oxford: Blackwell, 1991.

13 Henry II, king; Mildred, abbess

Henry II (973–1024) was a Holy Roman emperor and benefactor of the Church. The son of the duke of Bavaria, whom he succeeded in 995, he was educated by Wolfgang, the saintly bishop of Regensberg, and in 1002 succeeded his cousin, Otto III, as emperor of the Holy Roman Empire. He repaired and endowed the dioceses of Hildesheim, Magdeburg, Strassburg, and Merseburg, and in 1006 founded the diocese of Bamberg, building a cathedral and monastery there. He was also a supporter of the Cluniac reform of monasticism, centered at the abbey of Gorze, and of the papacy's claim over the Papal States in Italy. However, he had his critics within the Church, including German bishops who were unhappy when portions of their own dioceses were taken away to form Henry's newly created sees and Catholic missionaries who objected to his tolerance of pagan practices in mission lands. He died on July 13, 1024, and was canonized in 1146 (others put the date at 1152). Pope Pius X [August 21] named him patron saint of Benedictine oblates. His feast (formerly celebrated on July 15) is on the General Roman Calendar. His wife, *Cunegund* [March 3], was canonized in 1200.

This is also the feast day of *Mildred* (d. ca. 700), or Mildrith, who succeeded her mother as abbess at Minster-in-Thanet. Her biographer wrote: "She was merciful to widows and orphans, and a comforter to all the poor and afflicted, and in all respects of easy temper and tranquil." Her tomb was a popular place of pilgrimage. Her remains were removed in 1035 to St. Augustine's abbey in Canterbury, where they were venerated above all the relics there. Her feast is not on the General Roman Calendar.

14 Camillus de Lellis, priest; Blessed Kateri Tekakwitha, virgin

Camillus de Lellis (1550–1614) was the founder of the Order of Camillians and is co–patron saint (with John of God [March 8]) of hospitals, nurses, nurses associations, and the sick. Born at Bucchioanico in the Abruzzi region of Italy, at age seventeen he fought with the Venetian army against the Turks. A very large man, six feet, six inches tall, he contracted an incurable disease of the leg, and sometime between 1574 and 1575 lost all of his money through gambling. He had a religious conversion and tried to enter the Franciscans after a brief period as a lay brother, but was denied profession because of his health. Instead, he became a member of the staff of the hospital of San Giacomo in Rome, where he himself had previously been a patient. He began by caring for the incurably sick, but his skill as an administrator eventually won him a promotion to the position of bursar. He was so appalled by the state of medical care at San Giacomo, that, with the support of his spiritual director, Philip Neri [May 26], he left that hospital and established his own, with the help of a wealthy patron. Meanwhile, he also studied at the Roman College and was ordained a priest in 1584. The following year he rented a larger house where he drew up a simple Rule for his helpers, committing himself and them to the service of plague victims, the sick in hospitals and homes, and prisoners.

Camillus obtained provisional approval of the Rule in 1586 and two years later opened a new house in Naples, where they ministered to those suffering from the plague. Two of his associates, now calling themselves Ministers of the Sick, died from it themselves. Pope Gregory XIV gave formal approval to their Rule in 1591 and allowed the members to call themselves clerks regular. In that same year, Camillus and twenty-five others made their solemn profession, adding to the vows of poverty, chastity, and obedience a fourth vow of "perpetual physical and spiritual assistance to the sick, especially those with the plague." Their habit was black, with a large red cross on the breast and on their capes. The cross was to remind them that the only reason for their existence was to spend themselves in the service of the sick, in the spirit of the crucified Christ. In 1595 and again in 1601 some members of the congregation served the wounded on battlefields in Hungary and Croatia—the first recorded examples of medical field units. Among the first in the field of medical care to insist on fresh air, suitable diets, and the isolation of infectious patients, Camillus was personally involved in the physical and spiritual care of the sick until the end of his life, having resigned from the generalship of his order in 1607. He died at his motherhouse in Rome (the Maddelena) on July 14, 1614, and was canonized in 1746. His remains are in the church of Santa Maria Maddelena [July 22] in Rome. His feast is on the General Roman Calendar.

Kateri Tekakwitha (1656–80) is the first Native American to have been beatified. She is also known as the "Lily of the Mohawks." Born Tekakwitha (Kateria, or Catherine, was her Christian name), the daughter of a Christian Algonquin and a pagan Mohawk chief, in present-day Auriesville, New York, she was orphaned at age four. A bout of smallpox left her disfigured and partially blind. She made a vow early in life not to marry, which ran counter to the culture of her people and created great personal difficulty for her. In 1667 she met Christian missionaries for the first time, but did not seek baptism. Eight years later she met another missionary, Father Jacques de Lamberville, a Jesuit, who baptized her on Easter Sunday, 1676. Finding life in her village stressful, she walked two hundred miles to settle in a Christian mission in Sault St. Louis, near Montreal, where she made her First Holy Communion in October 1677. For the next three years she led a devout Catholic life, attending Mass twice a day, fasting on Wednesdays and Saturdays, teaching children, and caring for the sick and the aged. One of the missionaries who knew her later wrote: "Her soul was well disposed toward perfection." She died on April 17, 1680. A number of miracles and appearances were reported after her death and were attested to by the Jesuit missionaries. The Council of Baltimore in 1884 petitioned the Holy See to begin Kateri's beatification process. She was beatified in 1980. Her feast is on the Proper Calendar for the Dioceses of the U.S.A., but not on the General Roman Calendar.

15 Bonaventure, bishop and Doctor of the Church; Vladimir of Kiev, prince

Bonaventure (1221–74), known as the Seraphic Doctor, was one of the greatest theologians in the history of the Church. A Franciscan, he is sometimes referred to as the second founder of the order. Born Giovanni di Fidanza of a noble family at Bagnoreggio, near Orvieto, he became a Franciscan in 1243 and took the name Bonaventure. His intellectual gifts were quickly recognized and he was sent to Paris to study under another celebrated Franciscan theologian, Alexander of Hales. In 1253 Bonaventure became master of the Franciscan school in Paris. As a theologian he was more Augustinian than Aristotelian, unlike his contemporary Thomas Aquinas [January 28]. He also emphasized an affective over a rational approach to the study of the divine mysteries. For Bonaventure, the purpose of human knowledge, including theology, is not to speculate, but to love. His main theoogical work was his commentary on Peter the Lombard's *Sentences*, but he also wrote works of mystical theology, particularly the *Breviloquium* (Lat.,

Saint Bonaventure by Fra Angelico (1387–1455)

"Abbreviated Statement") and the *Itinerarium mentis ad Deum* (Lat., "The Journey of the Mind Toward God").

Those seeking God, he wrote, pass through three stages: purification from sin that brings the "calm of peace"; illumination, based on the imitation of Christ, leading to the "splendor of the truth"; and union with God, leading to the "sweetness of love." In 1257, at age thirty-six, he was elected minister general of the Franciscan order. There were already deep divisions within the community, only thirty years after the death of Francis [October 4] in 1226. Although Bonaventure strongly defended Franciscan ideals, he differed with Francis himself on the need for study and, therefore, on the need for possessing books and buildings. He confirmed the existing practice of Franciscans teaching in universities and also their work of preaching and spiritual direction, by way of complementing the ministry of a poorly educated diocesan clergy. He rejected the extreme position of the Spiritual Franciscans, who held that Franciscans can own no property of any kind and who exalted poverty above everything else, including learning and pastoral ministry. Nevertheless, Bonaventure himself lived a life of austere simplicity. Indeed, he was detached not only from riches, but from the rich as well. He also wrote an official biography of Francis.

In 1265 he was nominated by Pope Clement IV as archbishop of York, but Bonaventure declined the appointment. In 1273 he was nominated again, this time by Pope Gregory X as cardinal-bishop of Albano, with a command not to refuse. When the papal messengers reached him, he was washing the dishes in a friary near Florence. He told them to wait until he had finished his task. He was consecrated in November of that year.

Bonaventure took a leading part in the Second Council of Lyons (1274), convened to seek ways of healing the division between the Churches of East and West. (Thomas Aquinas died on the way to that same council.) He supported the council's efforts toward reunion and preached at the Mass of Reconciliation to mark the agreement between the two Churches (an agreement that would be repudiated in the East a few years later). Bonaventure died in Lyons on July 15,1274, while the council was still in session, and was buried there in the local Franciscan church in the presence of the pope. There seems to have been no evidence of an early cult, perhaps because of continued internal strife in the order and the serious disruptions in the life of the Church created by the Great Western Schism (1378–1417), but he was eventually canonized in 1482 by Pope Sixtus IV, a Franciscan, and declared a Doctor of the Church in 1588 by Sixtus V, another

Franciscan. Bonaventure's feast is on the General Roman Calendar, and he is commemorated on the liturgical calendar of the Church of England. He is patron saint of workers.

The Russian Orthodox Church celebrates the feast of *Vladimir of Kiev* (ca. 955–1015) on this day. The grandson of Olga [July 11], he is regarded as the "apostle of the Russians and the Ukrainians" because, as prince of Kievan Rus', he Christianized so many of his subjects—those from whom present-day East Slavic peoples are derived (e.g., Ukrainians, Russians, Belorussians). He himself became a Christian ca. 988 when the opportunity of marrying the sister of the Byzantine emperor presented itself. With that marriage also came military aid. After his conversion, he was reluctant to impose capital punishment on murderers and robbers, and he was notable for his generous almsgiving. He also vigorously promoted the evangelization of Rus', sometimes by force, and the organization of the Church in his realm. He was recognized as a saint in Russia sometime in the thirteenth century. His feast is not on the General Roman Calendar, but he is also commemorated on this day by the Evangelical Lutheran Church in America. He is patron saint of converts.

BIBLIOGRAPHY

Hayes, Zachary. *The Hidden Center: Spirituality and Speculative Christology in St. Bonaventure.* New York: Paulist Press, 1981.

16 Our Lady of Mount Carmel; Mary-Magdalen Postel, foundress

July 16 is one of several feast days on the General Roman Calendar in honor of the *Blessed Virgin Mary*. Mount Carmel, about three miles south of Haifa in present-day Israel, is the place traditionally associated with the beginnings of the Carmelite order ca. 1200, when a group of lay hermits formed a community on its western slope. Between 1206 and 1214 they received a "formula of life" from the patriarch of Jerusalem, commending daily Eucharist, continual prayer (especially the psalms) with silence otherwise, manual labor, and other traditional forms of eremetical asceticism. It was to be a life of both solitude and community, with a structure of individual cells surrounding an oratory. The order received formal papal approval in 1298. From the very beginning the Carmelites identified themselves with the Blessed Virgin Mary. The oratory on Mount Carmel was dedicated to her, and the

Carmelites became known as the Brothers of Our Lady of Mount Carmel, whom they saw as their patroness. In time, the feast of Our Lady of Mount Carmel, celebrated on this day, became the patronal feast of the order.

Mary-Magdalen Postel (1756–1846) was the foundress of the Sisters of St. Mary-Magdalen Postel, formerly known as the Sisters of the Christian Schools of Mercy. Born Julie Françoise Catherine Postel in a small French port near Cherbourg, she secretly took Communion to the sick during the French Revolution. When she was beatified by Pius X [August 21], the pope called her a "maiden-priest." After the Concordat of 1801 she engaged in various parochial ministries, especially the preparation of children and adults for the sacraments, and in works of mercy. She moved to Cherbourg and established a house, dedicated to Our Lady, Mother of Mercy, with three other teachers. When she made her religious vows in 1807, she took the name Mary-Magdalen. Their work flourished during the first three years, but in 1811 the Sisters of Providence returned to Cherbourg and Mary-Magdalen's little community left to make room for them. They actually came close to disbanding because they could find no other place to continue their teaching. After enduring extreme poverty for several years, they finally settled in Tamerville and opened a school. Once again the community began to grow and in 1832 took over an old abbey.

In 1837 Mary-Magdalen was required to give up the Rule that she had been using for twenty-eight years because authorities in Rome insisted that she adopt the Rule approved for the Brothers of the Christian Schools. Her community's name was changed to the Sisters of the Christian Schools of Mercy, and then changed again after the Second Vatican Council (1962–65). Their work as teachers expanded to include the nursing of the poor and elderly at home. Mary-Magdalen died on July 16, 1846. The congregation's constitution received full approval in 1925, the year of Mary-Magdalen's canonization. Her feast is not on the General Roman Calendar.

17 Hedwig of Poland, queen

Hedwig (1374–99), or Jadwiga, was queen of Poland. Born in 1374, the daughter of Louis Angevin, the king of Hungary and Poland, she was only ten when crowned queen of Poland. At age twelve she married Jagiello, the grand duke of Lithuania and Ruthenia, in spite of rumors that she had consummated a marriage already with Wilhelm, the Hapsburg heir to the grand duchy of Austria. Jagiello kept his marriage promise to assist in the evangelization of Lithuania. A diocese was established in the capital, Vilnius, and both Jagiello and Hedwig sent chalices, holy pictures, and vestments for the new cathedral and other churches. She endowed a college in Prague for the education of Lithuanian priests and worked for the reunion of Latin and Orthodox Christians, importing monks from Prague, who used the Slavonic rite to help build bridges between the two churches. Early in 1399 she retired from public life because of a pregnancy. A daughter was born prematurely in June, but died three weeks later. Hedwig herself died four days after that, on July 17. She was buried in Wawel Cathedral in Kraków. In her will she asked that all of her possessions be sold and the proceeds given for the restoration of Kraków University. Her cult spread rapidly and in later years, as Poland was partitioned, she became a symbol of Polish nationalism. Although her cause was first opened in 1426, she was not beatified until 1986 and then canonized in Kraków in 1997 by John Paul II, the first Polish pope in history. Her feast is not on the General Roman Calendar.

18 Pambo, hermit

Pambo (ca. 303–ca. 390), or Pamo, was an Egyptian hermit who was a disciple of Anthony [January 17] and who was held in high regard by Athanasius [May 2], not only because of the quality of his life, but also for his vigorous defense of the teachings of the Council of Nicaea (325), at which Athanasius was the major figure. Pambo was ordained ca. 340. He led a life typical of contemporary desert monks: hard manual labor, long fasts, physical penance, and sustained periods of prayer. He looked upon the capacity for silence as a basic first step toward a deeper spirituality and is said to have meditated for six months on the opening words of Psalm 39: "I will watch my ways, so as not to sin with my tongue; I will set a curb on my mouth" (v. 2). At the same time, he did not hold the view, common among monks, that the monastic life was more spiritually elevated than life in the world. "There are other roads to perfection besides being a monk," he said. The constant theme in his teaching was: "Guard your conscience toward your neighbor, and you will be saved." As he lay dying, he said to one of his disciples that, in spite of all of the rigors of his life and his constant effort to be faithful to God's will, "I am going to God as one who has not yet begun to serve him." His feast is not on the General Roman Calendar, but he is one of the saints commemorated on this day by the Russian Orthodox Church.

19 Macrina the Younger, virgin

Macrina the Younger (ca. 327–79) was the older sister of Basil [January 2] and Gregory of Nyssa [January 10]. She is to be distinguished from her grandmother, Macrina the Elder (d. 340). Born in Caesarea in Cappadocia, the oldest of ten children, she was betrothed to be married at age twelve, but after her intended spouse died, she vowed never to marry and remained at home to assist in the education of her brothers and sisters. When Basil returned from his studies in Athens, he had a high estimation of himself as an orator. Macrina took him aside and persuaded him eventually to renounce his property and prospects for a civil career and to become a monk. Basil later provided an estate (Annesi) for his mother and sister in Pontus, along the river Iris, where they lived a communal life with other women who came to join them. The mother died ca. 373 and Macrina gave away all of their possessions, living thereafter on the fruits of her own labor. When she herself died nine months after Basil in 379, she had so little left that there was nothing but a coarse veil to cover her body. As she lay dying on two planks of wood on the floor of her cell, she and her brother Gregory of Nyssa conversed about spiritual matters. From that conversation came Gregory's treatise *De anima et resurrectione* (Lat., "On the Soul and Resurrection"). Her final prayer included the words: "You have freed us from the fear of death. You have made the end of this life the beginning of true life." Macrina is said to have performed miracles during her lifetime, including the healing of a young girl's eye. She was buried in the church of the Forty Martyrs of Sebastea [March 10]. Her feast is not on the General Roman Calendar, but she is one of the saints commemorated on this day by the Russian Orthodox Church.

20 Frumentius, bishop; Elijah, prophet; Bartolomé de Las Casas, missionary; Margaret of Antioch, martyr

Frumentius (ca. 300–ca. 380) is regarded as the "apostle of the Ethiopians" (sometimes "the Abyssinians"). He was called "Abuna" ("Our Father"), a title still given to the primate of Ethiopia. Born in Tyre, Palestine, Frumentius and another young man, Aedesius, accompanied a merchant named Meropius on a voyage to Arabia. On their way home, their ship set into port on the Ethiopian coast, where an altercation broke out between some local inhabitants and the ship's crew. The latter, along with most of the passengers, including Meropius, were killed. Frumentius and Aedesius survived and were taken to the king's court at Aksum, where they were given minor roles of service. One account says that Frumentius became a cupbearer. When the king died, they were given their freedom, but they decided to remain at the request of the queen regent. Frumentius seems to have risen in the ranks and began using his influence to promote the growth of Christianity in the country. He persuaded several Christian merchants to settle there and obtained special trading privileges for them as well as the right to practice their faith.

When the new king came of age, Aedesius returned to Tyre and Frumentius went to Alexandria. He wanted to persuade its bishop, Athanasius [May 2], to send missionaries to Ethiopia to build on the work he had already begun there. Athanasius was so impressed with Frumentius that, sometime between 340 and 356, he made Frumentius bishop of Axum, the capital of a kingdom in northern Ethiopia, and sent him back to continue his work of preaching the gospel. Frumentius had great success at first, even converting two of the royal princes, and he came to be known in Ethiopia as Bishop Salama ("Bishop of Peace"). However, the emperor at the time was Constantius (d. 361), who was an Arian so strongly opposed to Athanasius that he exiled him from his diocese. Because the emperor knew that Frumentius was a protégé of Athanasius, he tried to turn the Ethiopian king against him. The emperor failed, and Frumentius continued his missionary work in the country, ratified, it is said, by several miracles. Frumentius's feast day in the most recent edition of the *Roman Martyrology* was changed from October 27. The feast is not on the General Roman Calendar. He is commemorated in the East on November 30.

On this day the Greek and Russian Orthodox Churches and the Carmelite order celebrate the feast of *Elijah* (Elias), the ninth-century B.C. prophet who upheld the true worship of God against the pagan worship of Baal (1 Kings 16:29–19:18) and condemned a royal murder (1 Kings 21; 2 Kings 9). Some thought Jesus to be Elijah (Matt. 16:14), but Jesus identified John the Baptist [June 24; August 29] as Elijah (Matt. 17:9–13; Mark 9:9–13). An unsubstantiated tradition developed in the fourteenth century that Elijah was the founder of the Carmelite order, and consequently that it is the most ancient religious order in the Church. Elijah's shrine survives on Mount Carmel.

The Church of England commemorates two figures on this day, one of whom, *Bartolomé de Las Casas* (1474–1566), a Dominican missionary to the Americas known as "apostle to the Indies," has never been beatified by the Catholic Church, much less canonized (although his cause was introduced by the Dominicans in 1976). He was the son of a landowner in present-day Dominican Republic, became critical of the Spaniards' treatment of the indigenous people, joined the Dominicans, and became one of the most vigorous advocates on behalf of those abused by Spain. The other, *Margaret of Antioch* (supposedly fourth century), almost certainly never existed. Nevertheless, her cult was popular in medieval England and over two hundred ancient English churches were dedicated to her. Joan of Arc [May 30] believed that she had heard Margaret of Antioch encouraging her in her mission to the French king, which, of course, raises questions about the authenticity of those claimed visions and voices. (The Evangelical Lutheran Church in America commemorates Bartolomé de Las Casas on July 17.)

21 Lawrence of Brindisi, priest and Doctor of the Church

Lawrence of Brindisi (1559–1619) was an Italian Franciscan and is a Doctor of the Church. Born Giulio Cesare Russo in Brindisi, in the kingdom of Naples, of a well-to-do family, he was orphaned early in life and became a Capuchin friar in Verona at age sixteen, taking the name Lawrence. He developed a reputation as a scholar at the University of Padua and was particularly adept at learning languages, ancient and modern alike, which he put to effective use in the study of the Bible. After ordination in 1582 he became a highly respected preacher in Padua, Verona, and other northern Italian towns. He was elected provincial of Tuscany and then of Venice. In 1596 he was called to Rome to serve as definitor general of the Franciscan order and was appointed by Pope Clement VIII to take special responsibility for the conversion of the Jews. After his term in Rome he established, along with other friars, Capuchin houses in Vienna, Prague, and Graz, partially as a way of combating Protestantism in those regions, and spent considerable time and energy caring for plague victims. In 1601 he actually led a German imperial army into battle against the Turks, armed only with a crucifix.

The following year he was elected minister general of the order, now some nine thousand strong in Italy, France, Belgium, Switzerland, and

Spain. He visited most of these areas on foot, preaching to large crowds en route. Three years later he refused election to a second term, although he accepted other, lower-level positions in the order after that. He retired to the friary in Caserta in 1618, but was required to go to Spain and then to Portugal on a diplomatic mission. He died shortly thereafter in Lisbon, on July 22, 1619, and was buried in the cemetery of the Poor Clares at Villafranca del Bierzo in northern Spain. He was beatified in 1783, canonized in 1881, and declared a Doctor of the Church in 1959. His writings consist mainly of sermons, but also include a commentary on Genesis and a number of controversial works against Lutheranism. Among his popular relics were the handkerchiefs he is said to have used to wipe away his tears during Mass. He is reported to have taken three hours or more to celebrate the Eucharist! Because of his devotion to the Blessed Virgin Mary, he received papal permission to say the votive Mass of Our Lady every day. His feast is on the General Roman Calendar.

22 Mary Magdalene, disciple

Mary Magdalene (first century) was a witness of the Resurrection and is patron saint of repentant sinners, hairdressers, and the contemplative life. Known also as Mary of Magdala, she was, according to Luke 8:2, healed of seven demons by Jesus. She was also among the women who accompanied and supported Jesus and the twelve apostles and was present at the Crucifixion and burial (Matt. 27:56; Mark 15:40; John 19:25). Mary Magdalene is mentioned in five of the six Resurrection narratives in the Gospel tradition: Mark 16:1–8; Matthew 28:1–20; Luke 23:56b–24:53; John 20:1–29; and Mark 16:9–20 (she is not mentioned in John 21:1–23). Peter [June 29] is mentioned in four of the six narratives and is linked with Mary Magdalene in three. He is not mentioned in Matthew 28, the chapter that announces both the Resurrection and the post-Resurrection command to evangelize the world. In Matthew, John, and the appendix to Mark's Gospel, she, not Peter, is the primary witness to the Resurrection. Peter is

The Repentant Magdalen by El Greco, ca. 1577

the primary witness in the tradition of Paul and Luke (1 Cor. 15:5; Luke 24:34). These facts do not undermine the authority of Peter in any way, but they do underscore the complementary roles of women, Peter, and the other disciples as witnesses to the Risen Christ. Among the women, Mary Magdalene is clearly portrayed in Scripture as having the primary role. Later traditions erroneously equated Mary with both the sinful woman of Luke 7:36–50, who anointed Jesus, and with Mary of Bethany, who also anointed Jesus (John 11:1–12:8; Luke 10:38–42).

Her feast, which has been observed in the West since the eighth century, is on the General Roman Calendar and is celebrated on this day across the ecumenical spectrum: by the Greek and Russian Orthodox Churches, the Church of England, the Episcopal Church in the USA, and the Evangelical Lutheran Church in America. Both Oxford and Cambridge Universities have colleges named after her, and there are many famous representations of her in art, for example, Giotto's *Crucifixion* and Titian's *Noli Me Tangere* (Lat., "Do not touch me"), which depicts her meeting with the Risen Christ in the garden (similarly depicted by Rembrandt). Her reputed burial place was at Saint-Maximin in modern-day France. The Benedictine church was destroyed by Saracens in the eighth century and later rebuilt by Dominicans in 1295. Her alleged relics are contained in a splendid bronze casket in the crypt. Her feast is also on the Dominican and Cistercian liturgical calendars for this day.

BIBLIOGRAPHY

Haskins, Susan. *Mary Magdalene: Myth and Metaphor.* New York: Harcourt Brace, 1993.

Maisch, Ingrid. *Mary Magdalene: The Image of a Woman Through the Centuries.* Trans. Linda M. Maloney. Collegeville, MN: Liturgical Press, 1998.

Ricci, Carla. *Mary Magdalene and Many Others: Women Who Followed Jesus.* Trans. Paul Burns. Minneapolis, MN: Fortress Press, 1994.

Thompson, Mary R. *Mary of Magdala: Apostle and Leader.* New York: Paulist Press, 1995.

23 Bridget of Sweden, religious; John Cassian, monk

Bridget of Sweden (1303–73), or Birgitta, was the founder of the Brigittine order (Order of the Most Holy Savior) and is the patron saint of Sweden and of nuns. In 1999 Pope John Paul II named her a co–patron saint of all of Europe along with Catherine of Siena [April 29] and Teresa Benedicta of the Cross (Edith Stein) [August 9]. The daughter of a wealthy governor of Uppland, Bridget married at age fourteen and bore eight children, one of whom was Catherine of Sweden (also known as Catherine of Vadstena) [March 24]. After gaining a reputation for nursing the sick in her neighborhood, in 1335 she was appointed lady-in-waiting to the queen and began having what she took to be revelatory experiences. She tried unsuccessfully to change the behavior of the royal couple. After her youngest son died, she made pilgrimages to shrines in Norway and Spain and then entered the Cistercian monastery at Alvastra after her husband's death in 1343. Three years later she founded a double monastery at Vadstena on Lake Vättern for sixty nuns and twenty-five men (thirteen priests, four deacons, and eight laymen), who lived in separate enclosures but shared the same church for worship. Bridget was abbess, in charge of temporal matters, while the superior of the monks directed both sides in spiritual matters. Luxuries were forbidden, but there was no limit on the number of books one could have for study. Indeed, the monastery became the literary center of Sweden during the fifteenth century.

Saint Bridget of Sweden

In 1349 Bridget went to Rome to obtain approval for her new order and to receive the Jubilee indulgence of 1350. Her daughter Catherine followed her to Rome the next year. The years in Rome proved to be very difficult for Catherine. The city was unsafe and, because mother and daughter gave so much away to the poor, their living conditions were stark. Catherine unsuccessfully implored her mother to return to Sweden. Instead, Bridget spent the rest of her life in Italy or on various pilgrimages, including one to the Holy Land. She served the poor, the sick, and pilgrims to Rome and also continued to have visions, one of which prompted her to warn Pope Clement VI to return to Rome from Avignon and to make peace between England and France (she had seen the devastation wrought by the war while on pilgrimage in France). Bridget was canonized in 1391—for her heroic virtue, not for her alleged revelations. She died in Rome on July 23, 1373, in a house on the corner of the Piazza Farnese, which is still a Brigittine convent. Her remains were eventually brought in triumph through central Europe to the abbey at Vadstena in Sweden. Her daughter Catherine obtained formal papal approval for the Brigittine order in 1376. Bridget's feast is on the General Roman Calendar. She is also commemorated on this day by the Church of England and the Evangelical Lutheran Church in America.

This is also the feast day of *John Cassian* (ca. 365–ca. 435), one of the most important early monastic figures in the West. His *Institutes* and *Conferences,* which were expositions of Egyptian monasticism (he had been a monk in Egypt for many years before establishing two monasteries near Marseilles), influenced the Rule of St. Benedict [July 11]. His feast day is not on the General Roman Calendar. He is the patron saint of stenographers.

24 Declan, bishop; Thomas à Kempis, priest

Declan (early fifth century), an Irish bishop in the Waterford area, was one of four bishops ministering in Ireland before the arrival of Patrick [March 17]. According to his biography, Declan was born of noble blood near Lismore. He studied first at home, then abroad, probably in Gaul. He was consecrated bishop and founded the church of Ardmore, where there are remains of a monastery and a hermitage as well as a holy well (restored in 1951), where cures have been reported, and an ancient St. Declan's stone (actually a boulder in size) on the beach. His choice of Ardmore in County Waterford is said to have been the result of a miraculous boulder that followed him from Wales. In any case, there is a boulder on the beach, and numerous pilgrims visit it during the week nearest to his feast, known at Ardmore as "Pattern week." In his old age, Declan retired to a hermit's cell, but returned to the main settlement at Ardmore to die. The *Martyrology of Oengus* (early ninth century) commemorates him thus: "If you have a right, O Erin, to a champion of battle to aid you, you have the head of a hundred thousand, Declan of Ardmore." His feast is not on the General Roman Calendar.

The Episcopal Church in the USA commemorates *Thomas à Kempis* (ca. 1380–1471), a priest who authored the classic *The Imitation of Christ,* which has been translated into more languages than any other book apart from the Bible. It stresses personal piety over learning and the inner life over active service in the world. He has been neither beatified nor canonized.

25 James (the Great), apostle; Christopher, martyr

James the Great (or the Greater; first century), the son of Zebedee and the older brother of John [December 27], was one of the twelve apostles and one of the three closest disciples of Jesus, along with Peter [June 29] and John. He may also have been the cousin of Jesus through his mother, who, in turn, may have been the sister of the Blessed Virgin Mary (cf. Matt. 27:56; Mark 15:40; John 19:25). He is called "the Great" (or "Greater") to distinguish him from a younger apostle of the same name [May 3]. He is the patron saint of Spain, Chile, Guatemala, and Nicaragua as well as of pilgrims, pharmacists, laborers, and those suffering from arthritis. Born in Galilee, James was, like his father and brother, a fisherman whom Jesus called among his first disciples (Matt. 4:21; Mark 1:19; Luke 5:10). The list of apostles in Mark 3:17 indicates that Jesus gave James and John the nicknames "sons of thunder," perhaps because of their zeal and perhaps because of their temperament. On one occasion, when a Samaritan village refused to welcome Jesus, they urged Jesus to call down fire from heaven to destroy it (Luke 9:51–56).

Saint James Major by Antonio Veneziano, 14th C.

According to the synoptic Gospels, James, along with his brother and Peter, were among Jesus' closest followers. Jesus brought these three with him into the home of Jairus, whose daughter he raised (Mark 5:37; Luke 8:51), and the same three accompanied Jesus at his Transfiguration [August 6] (Matt. 17:1; Mark 9:2; Luke 9:28). They also asked Jesus about the end of the world (Mark 13:3), and together they failed him in the Garden of Gethsemane (Matt. 26:37; Mark 14:33). Both James and John requested seats of honor on Jesus' right hand when he sits in royal glory (Mark 10:35–37; but Matt. 20:20–21 attributes the request to their mother). Jesus asked them if they were also ready to drink the cup that he was going to drink. They answered confidently that they could, and Jesus promised that they would do so. We do not know if James left Jerusalem after Pentecost to preach the gospel elsewhere, but there is an early tradition that says that none of the apostles left the city until after James's death.

James was beheaded during the persecution of Herod Agrippa I between the years 42 and 44 (Acts 12:1–3) and was buried in Jerusalem. He was the first of the Twelve to be martyred. An expanded version of James's miracles and martyrdom appears in the sixth-century *Apostolic History of Abdias.* Later traditions report that James preached in Spain or that his body was transferred from Jerusalem to Compostela in Spain, which, in any case, became a major pilgrimage site in the Middle Ages. James was invoked there as a powerful defender of Christianity against the Moors (Muslims who had conquered and ruled over large portions of Spain). Although the tradition may be difficult to support, the shrine of Compostela does rest on the site of an early Christian cemetery, where a martyrology testifies to the cult of a saint of early Christian times. James's feast is on the General Roman Calendar and is also observed by the Church of England, the Episcopal Church in the USA, and the Evangelical Lutheran Church in America. The Greek and Russian Orthodox Churches celebrate his feast on April 30.

July 25 is also the feast day of *Christopher,* a third-century martyr who is best known as the patron saint of motorists. His name, which means "Christ-bearer" (from the Greek), has been given to many Christian children. He was put to death in Lycia during the persecution of Decius (249–51). A church in Bithynia was dedicated to him in 452. There were many legends about him, and he became one of the most popular saints in the Middle Ages, especially in Germany. He was included among the Fourteen Holy Helpers (see Glossary), a group of saints known for their assistance to people in need. Christopher's specialty was the care of travelers and protection against sudden death. It was believed that anyone who looked upon his statue or painting would not die that day. In one of the legends a child asked Christopher to carry him across a river on his shoulders. When Christopher admitted that he was too heavy to carry, the child revealed that he was Jesus and that he had carried the weight of the whole world. He told Christopher to plant his staff in the ground and the next day it would sprout flowers and dates as a sign of the truth of the child's words. His feast was removed from the universal calendar of the Catholic Church in 1969, but it may still be observed locally. In other words, the Church is not saying that Christopher never existed, but only that he (along with many other saints) no longer merits a place on the General Roman Calendar. In addition to motorists, he is also the patron saint of bus and truck drivers, porters, and sailors.

26 Joachim and Anne, parents of Mary

Neither *Joachim* nor *Anne* (first century) is even mentioned in the New Testament. The belief that they were the father and mother of the Blessed Virgin Mary is based on the *Gospel of James* (also known as the *Protevangelium of James*), an unreliable, second-century apocryphal document that became popular in the Middle Ages when devotion to Our Lady became more widespread. Joachim and Anne are portrayed as old and childless, a situation that serves as a source of embarrassment especially for Joachim, a rich and respected figure in Israel. He retired to the desert to fast and pray. Still at home, Anne also bewailed her fate. Suddenly she was visited by an angel who told that she would conceive and bear a child and that the child would become famous throughout the world. Joachim also received the same message in the desert. He rushed home to find his wife at the city gate to meet him. The account of Mary's birth is followed by her presentation in the Temple [November 21]. In the remainder of the apocryphal Gospel, the parents no longer appear.

The emperor Justinian built a church in honor of Anne in Constantinople in the sixth century, and another was built in Jerusalem at the traditional site of her birthplace. Relics and pictures of her in Rome date from the eighth century. The feast of Anne and Joachim was first observed in the East toward the end of the sixth century, probably at her church in Constantinople or the one in Jerusalem, but it was not until the mid-fourteenth century that it was generally kept in the West. In 1584, however, her feast, on July 26, was extended to the universal Church, and Gregory XV (1621–23) even made it a holy day of obligation. It was later briefly suppressed and then restored in 1621, and was eventually raised to an even higher rank by Pope Leo XIII toward the end of the nineteenth century. Anne's cult is especially strong in Canada. She is the country's patron saint, along with Joseph [March 19]), and her liturgical feast is of major importance there. She is also the patron saint of childless women, expectant mothers, women in labor, homemakers, and even cemeteries. The feast of Joachim and Anne is on the General Roman Calendar and is also observed in the Anglican Communion by the Church of England and the Episcopal Church in the USA.

27 Pantaleon, martyr

Pantaleon (d. ca. 305), or Panteleimon, a name that means "the all-compassionate," was venerated in the West as one of the Fourteen Holy

Helpers (see Glossary) and in the East as the "Great Martyr and Wonder-worker." He is a patron saint of physicians, second only to Luke [October 18]. Born in Nicomedia of a pagan father and Christian mother, he studied medicine and, because of his subsequent success and favorable reputation, was appointed physician to the emperor Galerius, in whose court he abandoned his faith. He was later reconverted by another Christian. Unfortunately, his life is clouded by legends of miraculous cures, the raising of a dead child to life, and various feats of strength. After his reconversion he was condemned to death during the persecution of Diocletian and, after many tortures, was beheaded.

There is ample evidence for his early cult. Sanctuaries in his honor existed already in the reign of Justinian (527–65). He was venerated for many reasons, including his reputation for rendering medical service without requiring any payment. Thus, he was considered one of the "Holy Moneyless Ones." Alleged relics of his blood exist in Constantinople, Madrid, and Ravello. Those at Ravello are said to liquefy on his feast day in a manner similar to the blood of Januarius [September 19] in Naples. He is depicted in an eighth-century fresco in Santa Maria Antiqua in Rome, in a tenth-century cycle of pictures in the crypt of San Chrysogono in Rome, and in a window in the cathedral at Chartres. There are also paintings of him by Veronese and Fumiani in the church of San Pantaleone in Venice. His feast is not on the General Roman Calendar, but it is celebrated on this day by the Russian and Greek Orthodox Churches.

28 Prochorus, Nicanor, Timon, and Parmenas, deacons

This feast, which is observed by the Greek and Russian Orthodox Churches, honors four of the seven men listed in Acts (6:5) as the Church's first deacons. The full text reads: "At that time, as the number of disciples continued to grow, the Hellenists complained against the Hebrews because their widows were being neglected in the daily distribution. So the Twelve called together the community of the disciples and said, 'It is not right for us to neglect the word of God to serve at table. Brothers, select from among you seven reputable men, filled with the Spirit and wisdom, whom we shall appoint to this task, whereas we shall devote ourselves to prayer and to the ministry of the word.' The proposal was acceptable to the whole community, so they chose Stephen, a man filled with faith and the holy Spirit, also Philip, Prochorus, Nicanor, Timon, Parmenas, and Nicholas of Antioch, a convert to Judaism. They presented these men to the apostles who prayed and laid hands on them. The word of God continued to spread, and the number of the disciples in Jerusalem increased greatly; even a large group of priests were becoming obedient to the faith" (6:1–7).

The work of two of the Seven, namely, Stephen (6:8–8:2) [December 26] and Philip (8:5–40; 21:8), makes it clear that the Seven did not limit themselves to serving at table, but functioned for the Hellenist Christians in the way that the Twelve did for the Jewish Christians. They are thought to have been among the seventy appointed by Jesus (Luke 10:1). Tradition also says that *Nicanor* later went to Cyprus, where he suffered martyrdom during the reign of Vespasian (69–79). *Parmenas* is said to have preached for years in Asia Minor, becoming bishop of Soli on Cyprus (Acts 11:19, 20) before being martyred at Philippi in Macedonia ca. 98, during the persecution of Trajan. *Timon* is thought to have become bishop of Bostra in Arabia and eventually been martyred by fire in Basrah at the instigation of heathen Greeks. *Prochorus* is said to have been the scribe to whom John [December 27] dictated the Fourth Gospel and who later became bishop of Nicomedia and was martyred at Antioch. Their feast is not on the General Roman Calendar.

29 Martha, disciple; Olaf, king; James E. Walsh, bishop

Martha (first century) is the sister of Lazarus [December 17], who was raised from the dead by Jesus, and of Mary, with whom Jesus compared her. Martha is mentioned in three biblical situations. In the first, Jesus visits her home in Bethany. Martha busies herself with household chores, while Mary sits at Jesus' feet listening to his words. When Martha asks Jesus to encourage Mary to help her in the kitchen, he replies that Mary "has chosen the better part" (Luke 10:38–42).

The second occasion is the raising of her brother Lazarus from the dead (John 11:1–44). Again, it is Martha who takes the active role, going out to meet Jesus while Mary remains at home. When Jesus assures Martha that her brother will rise again, Martha utters a confession of faith that has echoed down through all of the Christian centuries: "I know he will rise, in the resurrection on the last day." And then Jesus said to her: "I am the resurrection and the life; whoever believes in me, even if he dies, will live, and everyone who lives and believes in me will never die." When he asked Martha if she believed this, she replied: "Yes, Lord. I have come to believe that you are the Messiah, the Son of God, the one who is coming into the world" (11:24–27). When Jesus ordered the stone removed from the tomb, again it was the practically minded Martha who said: "Lord, by now there will be a stench; he has been dead for four days" (11:39).

The third situation is just before the Passion, when Martha, Mary, and Lazarus entertain Jesus at dinner in Bethany (John 12:1–8). Martha "served," while Mary anointed his feet. Martha, however, is not mentioned after the Resurrection and there is no indication of when or where she died. There are legends that she accompanied her sister and brother to the south of France, where she was thought to have saved the people of Tarascon from a dragon. The town's principal church has been dedicated to her since the early ninth century. In 1187 claims were made that her relics were discovered there when the church was being rebuilt.

She is invoked as the patron saint of homemakers, cooks, hospital dieticians, innkeepers, domestic workers, restaurants, and waiters and waitresses. Her feast is on the General Roman Calendar, but it was formerly celebrated (before the reform of the liturgical calendar in 1969) in tandem with Mary and Lazarus. On this day the Benedictines and Cistercians continue to commemorate all three, and so too does the Church of England and the Evangelical Lutheran Church in America. The Episcopal Church in the USA commemorates two of three: Martha and Mary.

The Evangelical Lutheran Church also commemorates *Olaf* (ca. 990–1030), king of Norway and its patron saint. He used force as well as persuasion to Christianize his country, but his methods were so harsh that he was overthrown and exiled and then killed in battle while trying to regain his crown.

This is also the day of death of *James E. Walsh* (1891–1981), second superior general of the Catholic Foreign Mission Society, better known as Maryknoll. Ordained a bishop in 1927, he spent twelve years in prison under the Communist government in China, where he served as a missionary for forty years. He is to be distinguished from Bishop James A. Walsh (1867–1936), the cofounder and first superior general of Maryknoll and a great visionary leader in his own right.

BIBLIOGRAPHY

Carter, Nancy Corson. *Martha, Mary, and Jesus: Weaving Action and Contemplation in Daily Life.* Collegeville, MN: Liturgical Press, 1992.

30 Peter Chrysologus, bishop and Doctor of the Church; William Wilberforce, philanthropist and politician

Peter Chrysologus (ca. 380–ca. 450) was archbishop of Ravenna and a Doctor of the Church. Born in Imola in northeastern Italy, he was a deacon there before the emperor Valentinian III appointed him archbishop of Ravenna, the capital of the Western empire, sometime between 425 and 430. The title "Chrysologus" (Gk., "Golden-worded") may have been given him in the ninth century or later, so that the Western Church would have a preacher of equal status to the East's John Chrysostom (Gk., "Golden-tongued") [September 13], although he is not generally regarded as having been as eloquent as Augustine [August 28] or Ambrose [December 7], or for that matter as Chrysostom himself. Peter's first sermon as bishop was preached before the empress, who became a generous patroness. A large number of his sermons survive, but almost none of his writings.

The sermons are suggestive of careful preparation, warmth, and zeal. Most are homilies on the Gospels and other parts of the Bible or exhortations to conversion and penance. Unlike many of his contemporary bishops, his message was positive. He eschewed polemical tirades against pagans and Jews. The sermons are also valuable for the picture they give of Christian life in fifth-century Ravenna. He died at Imola on December 3 (others say July 31), ca. 450, and was declared a Doctor of the Church in 1729. His feast is on the General Roman Calendar.

William Wilberforce

The Church of England and the Episcopal Church in the USA commemorate *William Wilberforce* (1759–1833), a member of Parliament who was an eloquent and forceful opponent of slavery and the slave trade. He also supported Catholic emancipation.

31 Ignatius of Loyola, priest

Ignatius of Loyola (1491–1556) was the founder of the Society of Jesus, better known as the Jesuits. (His original Christian name was Iñigo, a common name among Basques, but when he moved to Paris and Rome, he changed it to Ignacio, or Ignatius, as more recognizable to non-Basques.) Born Iñigo López de Loyola, the youngest of eleven children, in the ancestral castle of the Loyola family in the Basque province of Guipúzcoa, he left home in 1506 to become a page in the household of a distinguished noble. He received his early education there and traveled with the family. His early life was marked by gambling, womanizing, and fighting, but it changed suddenly in 1516 when his patron lost his position at court and had to retire. Ignatius went to Pamplona, the capital of Navarre, and obtained a position in the army of the local duke. During a siege of the city in 1521, he was struck by a cannonball, which broke one leg and injured the other. He was taken prisoner and was cared for by the French. His leg had to be reset a few weeks later and he fell dangerously ill. He went to Confession and promised that, if he lived, he would devote his life as a knight to the Apostle Peter [June 29]. His leg had to be reset a second time, which required an extended period of recuperation and also an opportunity for reading. (He would suffer a limp for the remainder of his life.)

Saint Ignatius of Loyola, 19th C.

During this period of recuperation, he was strongly influenced by the life of Christ and the lives of the saints, especially Francis [October 4], Dominic [August 8], and Onouphrios [June 12], even though Ignatius himself did not approve of their specific forms of asceticism. He still harbored thoughts of marriage to a woman of high standing, but then began to think also about the need to do penance for his sins. One night it is said that he had a vision of Our Lady that filled him with an intense joy for several hours, but also a feeling of shame over his former ways. He was determined to change. As soon as he was well enough, he set out for Barcelona to board a ship to Jerusalem as a humble pilgrim. He stopped on the way at the monastery of Montserrat, where he exchanged his knight's dress for that of a pilgrim. But something happened while he was at the monastery, and he decided to defer his trip and instead to live as a hermit at nearby Manresa. One of the monks at Montserrat had given him a copy of a book by a monastic reformer, Garcia Jiménez de Cisneros, entitled

Exercitatorio de la Vida Espiritual (Sp., "Manual of the Spiritual Life"), which would influence the writing of his own *Spiritual Exercises.*

Ignatius stayed at Manresa for ten months, living in meager circumstances, begging food on the streets, and praying and studying about the spiritual life. He focused not only on Cisneros's work, but also on Thomas à Kempis's *Imitation of Christ,* which came to be regarded as second only to the Bible in popularity and which was the product of the so-called Devotio Moderna (Lat., "Modern Devotion"), a northern European movement popular in the fourteenth and fifteenth centuries. He eventually made friends and found support among a group of well-to-do women. At the same time, he passed through periods of inner darkness marked by remorse and scrupulosity over his many past sins and also by sickness, both of which were compounded by his austere program of fasting and physical penance. Gradually, however, he came to experience an inner peace that he claimed to have enjoyed for the rest of his life—a peace, he often said to others, that comes from knowing that one is doing the will of God. He would later refer to his mystical life at Manresa as his "primitive church."

It was also here at Manresa that he developed his *Spiritual Exercises,* one of the classics of Western spirituality, based on his own experiences and noted for its practical orientation. The *Exercises* lay out a program (usually for thirty days, in solitude) of examination of conscience, contemplation, meditation based on vivid representations of biblical events, and discernment (a key term) of God's will in one's life. Three years later in Paris, the Inquisition examined the *Spiritual Exercises* for heresy, and revisions were made.

Ignatius felt drawn to the monastic life, but decided that his vocation was to the active apostolate, one built on the foundation of personal conversion and individual sanctification. He left Manresa in 1523, resuming his long delayed pilgrimage to Jerusalem. He stayed there for three weeks—long enough to realize that his implicit agenda for the trip, the conversion of Muslims, was too daunting a task. The Franciscan guardians of the holy places ordered him to leave the city to avoid capture and even death at the hands of the Turks. He returned to Spain, where, now in his early thirties, he began to study Latin, theology, and the humanities for the first time, at the university in Alcalá. At the same time, he continued to provide spiritual direction to others. It was at this point in his life that he began to show the moderation that had been absent from his own previous spiritual life and that would become the hallmark of Jesuit confessional practices and approaches in moral theology.

He was joined at the university by a mixed group of disciples, men and women alike, and he began to wear clerical dress, having already received the tonsure as a young man. This brought him to the attention of the local Inquisition. He was summoned before it and released only on condition that he and his friends not dress as members of a religious order. Other, more rigorous examinations followed, including questions about his recommendations that people receive Holy Communion as often as every two weeks! There were no charges of heresy, but he was ordered once again to dress as an ordinary student and not to hold meetings. Because he could not accept the latter condition, he moved to Salamanca to continue his studies there, but encountered similar trouble. He was actually imprisoned for three weeks while his *Spiritual Exercises* was examined. The verdict was the same, but Ignatius concluded that he had to leave Spain entirely. He moved to Paris in 1528, where he studied philosophy for three years, earning a Master of Arts degree in 1534.

In Paris he was joined by other followers who were to become the core of his group, or company, including the great missionary-to-be Francis Xavier [December 3]. They took vows of poverty and chastity and also one to go to Jerusalem to convert the Muslims or, failing that, to place themselves at the service of the pope. All the while, Ignatius continued to refine his *Exercises*. However, a setback in his health forced him to return to Spain in 1535. After three months' recuperation, he went to Venice, where he studied more theology and discussed ecclesiastical matters with leading church reformers. His companions, now nine in number, joined him there from Paris. They worked among the sick and dying in the city. Their plans to travel to Jerusalem were postponed because of the outbreak of war between the Turkish empire and Venice, and they took advantage of the delay to get ordained and make a long retreat together (which Ignatius called his "second Manresa"). Then they split into twos and threes to work in different cities on the Italian peninsula. Before leaving Venice, they decided to call themselves the Company of Divine Love.

Ignatius set out with two companions for Rome toward the end of 1537. About twelve miles from the city, in La Storta, Ignatius is said to have had a profound spiritual experience assuring him of divine approval for his work with his companions. (Ironically, Ignatius himself was always suspicious of reports of mystical phenomena, and he strongly discouraged members of his society from aiming for the higher reaches of contemplative prayer, because it distracted people from action and exposed them to illusions, some of which, he insisted, have their origin in the devil.) In Rome the three heard confessions, preached, and taught catechism to children. Again their orthodoxy came under scrutiny, and again they were cleared of all charges. The rest of the company joined them in the winter of 1538/39. Together they cared for the victims of a terrible famine that had gripped the city.

Ignatius drew up an initial constitution, or "formula," for his company in 1539. The apostolate was to focus on preaching, hearing confessions, teaching, and caring for the sick, but it involved none of the traditional elements of a religious order, such as praying the Divine Office in common or other prescribed prayers and penances. The element of direct obedience to the pope was also a novel feature. There were criticisms, but Ignatius refused to compromise, especially on the matter of Office in common. He insisted that his company must have sufficient flexibility to engage in the apostolate, wherever and whenever they were needed. Papal approval was granted a year later (1540) and the company was given the name "Society of Jesus." Ignatius was elected superior in 1541.

Ignatius spent the rest of his life in Rome, administering the Society and caring for the poor, the sick, orphans, and prostitutes. He kept in touch with his members through voluminous correspondence and the exchange of reports. He also wrote to people in high places to provide spiritual direction and to win financial support for his charities. His governing style was collegial rather than authoritarian. He preferred to leave decisions to the judgment of those closest to the situation. He guided rather than controlled. All the members had done the *Exercises*, and that was sufficient for him. Nevertheless, he regarded obedience as the best means of self-denial and the surest sign of its achievement. The model was always Jesus, who was "obedient to death, even death on a cross" (Phil. 2:8). Because Ignatius placed such a high premium on obedience, however, he also stressed the importance of selecting the right people for positions of leadership in the Society.

In accordance with his constitutions, which were completed between 1544 and 1550, the amount of study required of Jesuits would be far more extensive than in other orders, and solemn vows were to be postponed until an aptitude for such study had been tested. He was convinced of the need for an educated clergy and of the importance of an educated laity as well. The first of many colleges and universities founded by the

Jesuits were opened in Padua in 1542, in Bologna in 1546, and in Messina in 1548. Above all, Ignatius wanted colleges in Rome, and the first of these was opened in 1551. Courses in philosophy and theology, leading to ordination, were added in 1553. Thus was born the famous Gregorian University. He also established a German College to train missionaries to Lutheran Germany in 1552. Within a decade of his death there were colleges in Spain, Portugal, France, Germany, India, Brazil, and Japan.

Ignatius died suddenly on July 31, 1556, and was buried next to the high altar in Santa Maria della Strada. The church was later pulled down and replaced by the Gesù, where his remains are enshrined today. He was beatified in 1609 and canonized in 1622, along with Teresa of Ávila [October 15], Philip Neri [May 26], Francis Xavier, and Isidore the Farmer [May 15]. He is patron saint of many schools, churches, and colleges and was declared patron saint of spiritual exercises and retreats by Pope Pius XI in 1922. His feast is on the General Roman Calendar, and he is also commemorated on this day by the Church of England and, since 1997, by the Episcopal Church in the USA.

BIBLIOGRAPHY

Boyle, Marjorie O'Rourke. *Loyola's Acts: The Rhetoric of Self.* Berkeley: University of California Press, 1997.

Caraman, Philip. *Ignatius Loyola: A Biography of the Founder of the Jesuits.* San Francisco: Harper & Row, 1990.

Meissner, William W. *Ignatius of Loyola: The Psychology of a Saint.* New Haven, CT: Yale University Press, 1992.

Munitiz, Joseph. A., and Philip Endean, eds. and trans. *St. Ignatius Loyola: Personal Writings.* New York: Penguin Books, 1996.

O'Malley, John W. *The First Jesuits.* Cambridge, MA: Harvard University Press, 1993.

Tellechea Idígoras, José Ignacio. *Ignatius of Loyola: The Pilgrim Saint.* Trans. Cornelius M. Buckley. Chicago: Loyola University Press, 1994.

AUGUST

1 Alphonsus Liguori, bishop and Doctor of the Church

Alphonsus Liguori (1696–1787) was the founder of the Redemptorists (Congregation of the Most Holy Redeemer) and one of the greatest moral theologians in the history of the Church. Born Alfonso Maria de'Liguori, the son of a Neapolitan noble, he studied and practiced law successfully until, after losing an important case through his own fault and seeing it as a sign of God's will, he decided to enter the priesthood.

He studied theology privately and was ordained in 1726. Soon thereafter he established a reputation as an effective preacher and understanding confessor in and near Naples—but all the while continuing to live at home with his father. In 1729 he left his father's house to become a chaplain to a college training missionaries for China. At the college he met an older priest, Thomas Falcoia, who became a close friend and spiritual associate. Father Falcoia had spent years trying to establish a new religious institute but succeeded only in founding a convent of nuns at Scala, near Amalfi. One of the nuns, Sister Maria Celeste Crostarosa, claimed to have had a vision that disclosed that the original Rule Father Falcoia had devised from a previous vision of his own should be adopted in the convent. After Falcoia was appointed bishop of Castellamare, he asked Alphonsus to give a retreat to the nuns at Scala. At the same time, Alphonsus investigated Sister Celeste's claim. He decided that her vision was authentic and that the convent should be reorganized according to the Rule specified in her vision. The local bishop agreed and the nuns adopted the new Rule. This was the beginning of the Redemptoristines.

At his friend Bishop Falcoia's urging, Alphonsus founded in 1732 the Congregation of the Most Holy Redeemer for priests dedicated to preaching the gospel, especially to the rural poor in the kingdom of Naples. Because of internal divisions about authority, however, the new order did not flourish until after his death. Alphonsus continued to preach and hear confessions with great success throughout the kingdom, especially in villages and hamlets, until 1752 when his health failed. He was especially gentle with the scrupulous (i.e., those with an unhealthy sense of anxiety and guilt), because he himself suffered from scrupulosity.

In 1745 he published the first of his thirty-six theological and devotional works, the most important of which was his *Moral Theology* (first edition, 1748; revised and reprinted nine times during his life). In this work he created a new moral principle known as equiprobabilism, which held that one can follow in conscience the milder of two equally probable opinions about the morality of some human action, the one opinion favoring the law and the other favoring liberty. In this way, Alphonsus marked a path between Jansenistic rigorism (which insisted that the stricter moral opinion is always to be followed) and laxism (which allowed an individual to follow any moral opinion so long as there was at least some theological support for it). His approach was always one of simplicity and kindness. His devotional writings, especially about the Blessed Virgin Mary, were given to flights of rhetorical exuberance. His

Glories of Mary (1750) influenced Marian piety well into the nineteenth century. His followers used similar techniques in their preaching, which stressed the fear of God and the Day of Judgment. In 1749 he was elected superior general of his order for life.

After at first refusing the appointment, in 1762 Alphonsus was consecrated bishop of Sant'Agatha dei Goti (between Benevento and Capua), a diocese of some thirty thousand people, seventeen religious houses, and four hundred diocesan priests, some of whom did no pastoral work at all. He organized parish missions and urged his priests to be simple in the pulpit and compassionate in the confessional. He was especially critical of priests who celebrated Mass too quickly. When a famine broke out in the winter of 1763, he sold everything he had, including his carriage and mules and his uncle's episcopal ring, to buy food for the starving. The Holy See also gave him permission to dip into the assets of the diocese for relief work. In 1767 he suffered an attack of rheumatic fever that almost killed him and left him with an incurably bent neck. He eventually resigned his see in 1775 because of poor health. He lived another twelve years in Pagani, but they were marked by personal sadness generated by serious divisions in his order and constant attacks upon it by secular forces who resented its stress on morality and concern for the poor.

Because of his age and deteriorated eyesight, Alphonsus signed a doctored version of the Rule to secure royal approval for the order. When other members of the order in the Papal States discovered what had happened, they strongly protested and placed themselves directly under the protection of the pope. Alphonsus found himself between the rock and the hard place. The Holy See had already approved the correct version of the Rule, but if he repudiated the version he had just signed, the Redemptorists would be banned throughout the kingdom of Naples. Pope Pius VI forbade the Redemptorists in the Papal States to accept the Rule and removed them from Alphonsus's jurisdiction. He provisionally recognized those members in the Papal States as the only true Redemptorists and made the decision final in 1781. Alphonsus was thus excluded from the order he had founded.

During 1784–85 Alphonsus suffered temptations against virtually every article of faith and morality and then bouts of depression and scrupulosity. There were also reports of ecstasies, prophecies, and even miracles, but these are impossible to evaluate, especially given his advanced age and medical condition. He died during the night of July 31/ August 1, 1787, within two months of his ninety-first birthday. In 1793 the Neapolitan government recognized the original Rule, and the two branches of the Redemptorists were reunited.

In 1796, the same pope, Pius VI, who had condemned Alphonsus because of the confusion surrounding his signing of the doctored version of the Rule now authorized the introduction of his cause for canonization. Alphonsus Liguori was beatified in 1816, canonized in 1839, declared a Doctor of the Church in 1871, and made patron saint of confessors and moral theologians in 1950. His feast is on the General Roman Calendar.

BIBLIOGRAPHY

Jones, Frederick M., ed. *Alphonsus de Liguori: Selected Writings.* New York: Paulist Press, 1999.

———. *Alphonsus de Liguori: The Saint of Bourbon Naples, 1696–1787.* Westminster, MD: Christian Classics, 1992.

2 Eusebius of Vercelli, bishop; Peter Julian Eymard, priest; Blessed Joan of Aza

Eusebius of Vercelli (d. 371) was a fourth-century bishop who was noted for his strong opposition to Arianism. He is thought to have contributed to the formulation of the Athanasian Creed. Born on the island of Sardinia, where his father was said to have died in chains as a Christian martyr, he was taken to Rome as an infant by his mother. He was ordained a lector and served in that capacity at Vercelli, in Piedmont, where he so impressed the local clergy and laity that he was chosen their bishop ca. 344. Indeed, he is the first bishop of Vercelli whose name is recorded. Ambrose [December 7] indicated that Eusebius was also the first bishop in the West to unite monastic and clerical disciplines and that he lived in community with several of his priests, some of whom were later recruited to be bishops of other dioceses. He was also known as an effective teacher and preacher. Eusebius is specially venerated by the canons regular, or Augustinian Canons, as their virtual cofounder with Augustine [August 28].

In 354 Pope Liberius asked Eusebius to try to persuade the Arian emperor Constantius to convene a council to bring an end to the division between Arians and Catholics faithful to the teaching of the Council of Nicaea (325). The council, or synod, was held the next year in Milan. Although the latter were in the majority, the power at the assembly lay with the Arian bishops. When the bishops were asked to sign a condemnation of Athanasius [May 2], the foremost exponent of Nicene orthodoxy, Eusebius refused, placed the Nicene Creed on the table, and insisted that all the bishops sign that before even considering the case against Athanasius. The emperor sent for Eusebius and two other bishops and ordered them to condemn Athanasius. He threatened them with death but, upon their refusal, sent them into exile instead.

Eusebius was sent first to a diocese in Palestine, where an Arian bishop was placed in charge of him. At first he lived with an orthodox count who protected him, but after his death, Eusebius was dragged half naked through the streets and confined to a small room to make him conform. The Arians would not allow any of his deacons from Vercelli to see him. Eusebius wrote to the local bishop, addressing him as his jailer, and asked him to allow the deacons to visit. Then he went on a four-day hunger strike, after which he was returned to his former lodgings. Three weeks later his house was broken into, his possessions were taken, and his attendants were ejected. He was dragged away and was eventually moved from Scythopolis to Cappadocia and then to Egypt. When Constantius died in 361, the new emperor, Julian, allowed the exiled bishops to return to their sees. Eusebius continued his efforts throughout the East to heal the Arian conflict, to assure the wavering, and to reconvert those who had gone over to the Arian side. He also stood with Hilary of Poitiers [January 13] against the Arianizing bishop of Milan. Little is known of his final years, except that he died, probably at Vercelli, on August 1, 371. His feast is on the General Roman Calendar.

Peter Julian Eymard (1811–68) was the founder of the Blessed Sacrament Fathers, dedicated to the perpetual adoration of the Blessed Sacrament. Born at La Mure d'Isère, a small town in the diocese of Grenoble, France, he entered the seminary in 1831 and was ordained a diocesan priest in 1834. After five years of parish work, he received permission from his bishop to become a Marist. By 1845 he had risen to the rank of provincial at Lyons. One Corpus Christi Sunday, while carrying the Blessed Sacrament in procession, he had an overwhelming experience of faith and love for Jesus in the Eucharist. Eventually he received permission to leave the Marists and, in 1856, he took the first steps toward the establishment of a new order of priests dedicated to the adoration of the Blessed Sacrament. They were called the Congregation of Priests of the Most Blessed Sacrament, or simply the Blessed Sacrament Fathers. He served as their superior general for the rest of his life, obtaining papal approval for his new order in 1863. The priests prayed the Divine Office in common and fulfilled other pastoral duties as well, but their principal duty was the perpetual adoration of the exposed Sacrament.

In 1858 he founded a community of sisters known as the Servants of the Blessed Sacrament and later the Priests' Eucharistic League, which was approved in 1905. He also organized the Archconfraternity of the Blessed Sacrament, which the 1917 Code of Canon Law recommended for every parish. Peter Julian Eymard, however, did not look upon adoration of the Blessed Sacrament as an end in itself or as purely an act of individual devotion. He expected an overflow from it into works of charity and apostolic service. Nevertheless, his concept of the Eucharist, so typical of nineteenth-century France, was in large measure transcended by theological developments before, during, and after the Second Vatican Council (1962–65). The Eucharist is now understood as a communal, sacrificial meal, an act of worship involving the whole congregation. Ironically perhaps, Peter Julian Eymard was canonized during the council itself, on December 9, 1962. His feast is on the General Roman Calendar.

On this day the Dominicans commemorate *Joan of Aza* (d. ca. 1190), mother of Dominic [August 8].

3 Lydia, disciple

Lydia (first century) was a devout Jew from Thyatira (in present-day western Turkey) who was converted by Paul [June 29] in the city of Philippi and the first one he baptized there (Acts 16:11–15). She was also his first "European" convert. She was the founding member of the Christian community that met in her house (16:40), having previously invited Paul and his companions, although complete strangers, to come and stay there (16:15). This fact underscores the important point that women, especially those who owned their own homes, exercised a leadership role in the early Church.

Lydia's hometown was an industrial center where purple dye was made. She herself sold cloth colored with this royal purple dye (16:14), which was a luxury item. It is thought, therefore, that she was a woman of independent means whose house would have been large enough to accommodate a community at worship. Others believe that she may have been of the working class, even a freed slave. It is likely that she met Paul in Philippi after having traveled there to sell her goods to some of the wealthy residents of that city. Cardinal Baronius

(1538–1607) added her name to the *Roman Martyrology,* but she was not formally canonized by the Eastern Church in Constantinople until 1982. Her feast is not on the General Roman Calendar.

4 John Vianney, priest

John Vianney (1786–1859), better known as the Curé d'Ars, is the patron saint of parish priests. Born Jean-Baptiste Marie Vianney at Dardilly, near Lyons, he spent his early years as a shepherd boy on his father's farm. It was during the French Revolution that he began to study for the priesthood, at age twenty, but this was interrupted by a call to military service. (His name had mistakenly been left off the list of exempted ecclesiastical students.) He never actually joined a company. His first attempt was thwarted by an illness that required hospitalization; the second, when he missed a troop train. He met a deserter and stayed in his town for fourteen months, teaching children, working on a farm, and continuing his studies for the priesthood in secret. When a general amnesty was declared in 1810, he returned to Lyons a free man. He entered a minor seminary the following year and the major seminary in Lyons in 1813. Just as his popular image portrays, he was not a good student and had particular difficulty with Latin, in which all courses were taught. He was dismissed from the seminary and had to be privately tutored by Abbé Balley, the parish priest at Écully, who arranged for two special exams with seminary officials. They were so impressed with John Vianney's evident piety and goodness that they approved him for ordination in 1815.

Saint John Vianney

He served as a curate under his old friend and tutor at Écully for two years and then, in 1817, was appointed as parish priest of Ars-en-Dombes, a remote village with a population of less than 250. He restored the church, visited every parishioner, and taught catechism. He would remain there for the rest of his life, living mainly on potatoes for the first six years. His sermons were often about hell and the Last Judgment, and he railed publicly against dancing and other forms of human amusement. Nevertheless, he was perceived as a compassionate priest and came to be revered as a confessor and spiritual counselor.

He also became an attraction for visitors—about 300 a day between 1830 and 1845—as his reputation for miracle working spread, including the report that he had multiplied loaves of bread to supply food for an orphanage he had founded. A special booking office for Ars had to be established at the train station in Lyons. John Vianney preached every day at eleven o'clock and spent long hours—sometimes as many as twelve—in the confessional. He is said to have spent as much as sixteen hours there in the years just before his death, when visitors numbered 20,000 annually.

On three different occasions he left Ars with the intention of becoming a monk, but each time he returned to his simple rectory. He refused all offers of ecclesiastical promotion except for the canonry, which he received under protest. Nevertheless, he sold the robes and gave the money to the poor. He also refused to be invested as a knight of the Imperial Order of the Legion of Honor and never wore its decoration, the imperial cross. He died on August 4, 1859, at age seventy-three, worn out by years of hearing confessions and offering spiritual counsel to the thousands of visitors who came to see him. He was canonized in 1925 and named patron saint of parish priests. His feast is on the General Roman Calendar, and he is commemorated by the Church of England on this day. Pope John XXIII wrote an encyclical letter on him as an example to priests in 1959, *Sacerdotii Nostri primordia* (Lat., "The Foundation of Our Priesthood").

5 Dedication of St. Mary Major; Oswald, king

Today's feast on the General Roman Calendar celebrates the dedication of the basilica of *St. Mary Major,* known in Italian as Santa Maria Maggiore, one of Rome's four major basilicas (along with St. Peter's, St. John Lateran, and St. Paul's Outside the Walls). Founded in the fourth century by Pope Liberius on the Esquiline Hill, the present church was built by Pope Sixtus III in the fifth century. Relics of the manger in Bethlehem are reputed to be held there. The basilica was formerly called Our Lady of the Snows because, according to legend, the pope built it on a site where the Blessed Virgin Mary left her footprints in an August snowfall. This legend was formerly commemorated as the feast of Our Lady of the Snows on this day, now renamed the feast of the Dedication of St. Mary Major.

The Church of England celebrates the feast of *Oswald* (d. 642) on this day. He became king of Northumbria after defeating and killing the tyrant Cadwalla at the battle of Heavenfield, even though Oswald's forces were badly outnumbered. After the battle many of his subjects became Christian, thanks in large part to the missionary efforts of Aidan (d. 651) [August 31], Irish monk of Iona, who became the first bishop and abbot of Lindisfarne, an island near the royal residence of Bamburgh, which the king had donated to the Church. It is said that Oswald himself served as Aidan's interpreter until the latter learned the English language. Oswald united both parts of Northumbria (Bernicia and Deira) under his rule, which was marked by concern for the sick and the poor, but his reign ended after eight years when he was killed in battle by the pagan king Penda of Mercia on August 5, 642. As he lay dying, Oswald prayed for the soul of his bodyguard who lay next to him. Oswald's body was sacrificially mutilated to the god Woden, and the fragments were placed on stakes. His feast has been observed in England since the late seventh century, and his cult spread later to many other European countries. He was remembered as one of England's national heroes. His feast is not on the General Roman Calendar.

6 Transfiguration; Justus and Pastor, martyrs

The *Transfiguration* refers to the appearance of Jesus to his disciples in glorified form. The three synoptic Gospels record the episode: Matthew 17:1–9; Mark 9:2–10; Luke 9:28–36. Jesus took Peter [June 29], James [July 25], and John [December 27] with him onto a mountain. (Tradition locates it on Mount Tabor, but many scholars prefer Mount Hermon.) He appeared there before them in a luminous form with Moses and Elijah at his side. Peter proposed that they build three tabernacles, or tents. A heavenly voice declared Jesus to be the "beloved son" and enjoined the disciples to heed him. Jesus then appeared in his usual form and commanded his disciples to keep silence.

There are various interpretations of the episode. Some view it as a misplaced account of a resurrection appearance. Others view it as a mystical experience that Jesus' disciples had in his presence. Others as a symbolic account devised by Matthew or the tradition on which his Gospel relied. Whatever its origin, the episode of the Transfiguration serves at the very least as a literary device to place Jesus on the same level as the Law (represented by Moses) and the Prophets (represented by Elijah) and as a foreshadowing of his future glory. He is the authentic source of divine truth for those who would listen to him.

The feast of the Transfiguration originated in the East and became widely celebrated there before the end of the first Christian millennium.

The feast was not celebrated in the West until a much later date. Pope Callistus III ordered its celebration in 1457 in thanksgiving for the victory over the Turks at Belgrade on July 22, 1456, news of which reached Rome on August 6. The feast is on the General Roman Calendar and is also celebrated by the Russian and Greek Orthodox Churches, the Church of England, and the Episcopal Church in the USA.

This is also the feast day of *Justus* and *Pastor* (d. 304), two young brothers (one thirteen, the other nine) who are said to have been beheaded by Dacian, the governor of Spain, under the Roman emperors Diocletian and Maximian. Their Acts, or account of their martyrdom, report that, during an official search for Christians, they willingly showed themselves to be Christians, infuriating the judge, who then had them whipped. To the astonishment of onlookers, the two boys continued in their defiance. Dacian ordered them to be beheaded. Their relics are enshrined at Alcalá (formerly Complutum), and they are the patron saints of that city and of Madrid. Paulinus of Nola [June 22] had his little son buried next to them at Alcalá, and Prudentius (d. ca. 410), himself a Spaniard and the only lay Latin Father of the Church, numbers them among the most glorious martyrs of Spain. Their feast is not on the General Roman Calendar.

7 Sixtus II, pope, and companions, martyrs; Cajetan, priest; Albert of Sicily, hermit; Afra, martyr

Sixtus II (d. 258; pope 257–258) is one of the Church's most highly venerated martyrs. Today's feast also commemorates his companions in martyrdom, seven Roman deacons: *Agapitus, Felicissimus, Januarius, Vincent, Magnus, Stephen, and Lawrence* [August 10]. More correctly known as Xystus, Sixtus was elected Bishop of Rome just as the emperor Valerian abandoned his policy of toleration toward Christians, ordering them to participate in state-sponsored religious ceremonies and forbidding them from gathering in cemeteries. Sixtus II managed to avoid personal troubles with the authorities until Valerian issued a second, more severe edict ordering the execution of bishops, priests, and deacons and imposing assorted penalties on laypersons. On August 6, 258, while the pope was seated in his episcopal chair addressing the congregation at a liturgical service in the private (and presumably safe) cemetery of Praetextatus, imperial forces rushed in and seized and beheaded the pope and four deacons. It is said that the pope refused to flee lest there be a massacre of the entire congregation. Two other deacons were executed later the same day, and the seventh, Lawrence, was put to death four days after that.

Before his death, however, Sixtus had successfully devoted his energies to healing the breach between Rome and the churches of North Africa and Asia Minor created by the issue of the rebaptism of heretics and schismatics who wished to enter or be reconciled to the Church and, in particular, by the intransigent approach taken by his predecessor, Stephen I. Although Sixtus too upheld the Roman policy of accepting the validity of baptisms administered by heretics and schismatics, he restored friendly relations with Cyprian [September 16], bishop of Carthage, and the estranged churches of Asia Minor, probably by tolerating the coexistence of the two practices. Much credit for the reconciliation has been given to Dionysius (d. 264/5), bishop of Alexandria, who had tried in vain to persuade Stephen I to adopt a less confrontational approach. Cyprian's biographer, however, also gives credit to Sixtus himself, describing him as "a good and peace-loving priest."

After Sixtus II's martyrdom, his body was transferred to the papal crypt in the cemetery of Callistus on the Appian Way. The bloodstained chair on which he had been sitting when killed was placed behind the altar in the chapel of the crypt. A century later Pope Damasus I [December 11] composed an epitaph, describing the execution, that was placed over the tomb. The name of Sixtus II was included in the Eucharistic Prayer, or Canon of the Mass, situated between those of Popes Clement [November 23] and Cornelius [September 16]. He is portrayed with Lawrence in a well-known sixth-century mosaic in the church of San Apollinare Nuovo in Ravenna, and he also appears in one of the most famous and most often copied and reproduced paintings in the world, the "Sistine Madonna," or "Our Lady and Child with Sts. Sixtus II and Barbara," by Raphael (1483–1520), now in the Dresden Art Gallery in Germany. Because the painting was commissioned by the warrior-pope Julius II to commemorate his victory over the French in 1512, Raphael gave Sixtus the features of his aging patron. Since there is strong evidence that Sixtus II was martyred on August 6, his feast was originally celebrated on that day. It was moved to August 7 in the 1969 revision of the General Roman Calendar.

Cajetan (1480–1547) was the leading founder of the Theatine order (Theatine Clerks Regular). Born Tommaso de Vio Cajetan (Gaetano) of a noble family at Vicenza, he was educated in theology and law at Padua University, became senator from Vicenza, and served for a time in the Roman Curia. Upon the death of Pope Julius II in 1513, he resigned his curial post and spent the next three years studying for the priesthood. He was ordained in 1516. While in Rome he refounded a confraternity of priests known as the Oratory of Divine Love. He returned to Vicenza in 1518 and joined the Oratory of St. Jerome [September 30], which included only men on the lowest rungs of the economic and social ladders and whose apostolate included service to the sick and the poor. He said that he tried to serve God by worship, but "in our hospital we can say that we actually find him." He subsequently founded another Oratory in Verona and in 1520 began a three-year period of service in a hospital in Venice.

In 1523 he founded, in conjunction with Giovanni Pietro Carafa (the future Pope Paul IV, but at this time bishop of Theate, or Chieti), a congregation of diocesan clergy bound by vows and the Rule of St. Augustine [August 28]. Their move was inspired by the need to address the widespread corruption common among the clergy of the day. The new order, which derived its name Theatines from Bishop Carafa's diocese, emphasized traditional priestly responsibilities: preaching and sacramental ministry, biblical and theological study, and care for the sick and the poor. The order would own no property and would rely on divine providence, not begging, for its income. Cajetan succeeded Carafa as its provost general for a term of three years, spent in Venice, where the members fled after the sack of Rome and the demolition of their house. When Carafa returned as superior, Cajetan went to Verona and then to Naples to establish the order there. He founded *montes pietatis* (Lat., loosely translated as "benevolent pawnshops"), which had been sanctioned by the Fifth Lateran Council (1512–17) and became the Bank of Naples. Overall, however, the order was somewhat eclipsed by the larger and better organized Society of Jesus, and may have suffered from the unpopularity of its intransigent cofounder Giovanni Pietro Carafa. Worn out by the civil strife in Naples, Cajetan took sick in the summer of 1547, refusing a mattress for his bed so that he could emulate Christ on the cross. He was beatified in 1629 and canonized in 1671. His feast is on the General Roman Calendar.

On this day the Carmelites commemorate *Albert of Sicily* (d. ca. 1307), a Carmelite famous for his preaching and healing in Messina. He spent his last years living as a hermit there. His cult was approved in 1476.

This is also the feast day of *Afra* (d. 304), one of the patron saints of the diocese of Augsburg. After she was martyred during the Diocletian persecution, her burial place in the Roman cemetery in Augsburg became a place of pilgrimage and the site where almost all bishops of Augsburg, including Ulrich [July 4], were buried until the year 1000. Her memory was a powerful force in the evangelization of the Franconian tribes. The basilica of St. Ulrich and St. Afra stands on their burial site.

8 Dominic, priest

Dominic (ca. 1170–1221) was the founder of the Order of Preachers, or Black Friars, better known as the Dominicans. Born Dominic de Guzmán at Calaroga (now Caleruega) in Old Castile, Spain, not far from the Benedictine abbey of St. Dominic of Silos [December 20] and after whom he may have been named, he was at first educated by a priest-uncle, then studied theology at the cathedral school of Palencia (which became shortly afterward the first university in Spain). During a famine there, he sold his books and furniture to raise money for the poor. This gesture attracted the attention of Diego de Azevedo, the prior of the reformed cathedral chapter of Osma, who persuaded Dominic to join his group, which lived a common life under the Rule of St. Augustine [August 28]. Dominic became a canon of Osma ca. 1196 and later succeeded Diego when he was appointed bishop of Osma. On their way together to Denmark in 1203 and again in 1205 to help negotiate a marriage for the son of the king of Castile, Dominic met for the first time Albigensian heretics at Toulouse, in southern France.

Saint Dominic by Giovanni Bellini, ca. 1515

The Albigensians, also known as Cathari, or the "perfect ones," regarded matter as evil and believed that perfection required a restrained diet and abstinence from sexual intimacy. Their conduct, however extreme, was appealing to the people because of its striking contrast to the corrupt lifestyle of the clergy. Diego and Dominic remained among them, adopting an austere lifestyle and traveling barefoot as they preached from place to place. When Diego returned to Spain in early 1207, he left Dominic in charge of a center for training preachers, educating girls, and promoting prayer. Diego returned for a time later in the year to conduct another one of his public debates with the Cathari and suggested the use of a band of full-time preachers to deal with the Albigensian problem. Diego died on December 30, leaving Dominic now completely in charge of preaching and of a community Diego had established at Prouille for women who had been converted from heresy. (The community would evolve into a convent of Dominican nuns.)

In 1208 the murder of the papal legate unleashed a brutal reaction in the form of a crusade. Dominic took no part in the violence, but relied only on instruction and prayer in his campaign against the Cathari. He helped found Toulouse University, modeled on that of Paris, and three times declined appointment to the hierarchy because he felt called to preaching. Dominic followed his friend Diego's example and preached tactfully and lived modestly so that the Cathari would be more disposed to hear his message. His familiarity with the Cathar way of life may have even influenced his conception of the religious order he would found. In late 1214 or early 1215 the new papal legate appointed him head of the preaching mission centered at Toulouse, where the local bishop wished to establish a permanent institute of preachers for his diocese. Peter Selhan, a rich burgher who had donated the house, and another man named Thomas attached themselves to Dominic by religious profession.

In 1215 Dominic's embryonic order was given an episcopal charter, with the charge not only to combat heresy but also to assist the bishop in various facets of his doctrinal ministry. A few months later Dominic accompanied the bishop to the Fourth Lateran Council in Rome. Agreeing that something more was needed than a diocesan institute, particularly in light of Pope Innocent III's decree that emphasized the obligations of bishops and priests to preach, Dominic and the bishop petitioned the pope for approval of a wider apostolate. Even though the council had forbade the multiplication of new religious orders, the pope gave tentative approval and asked Dominic to decide on an appropriate Rule. He and his brothers met at Prouille in 1216 and chose the Rule of St. Augustine along with the strict observances borrowed from the Cistercian-oriented Premonstratensians (Norbertines). The first Dominican community began its common life under vows at Toulouse. Bertrand de Garrigues [September 6] was chosen as superior, and Dominic remained in charge of preaching.

Innocent III died in July 1216. Dominic left for Rome in October and the new pope, Honorius III, confirmed the order's papal protection in December. The following year the Cathari regained ground at

Toulouse, and the friars scattered in many different directions, establishing an important foundation in Paris. Dominic eventually left Rome and crossed the Alps, as usual on foot, at the end of the summer, 1219. When he arrived in Bologna, he met many of the friars for the first time. The city became his ordinary residence for the remainder of his life, except for most winters, which he spent in Rome. Houses were established from there in Milan, Bergamo, Verona, Piacenza, Brescia, and possibly Florence. In December 1219 Honorius III issued a papal bull that characterized the new order as "necessary" and called upon bishops to cooperate with it. The following year the pope confirmed Dominic as master general. At the first general chapter the same year, he asked to be relieved of the post but the chapter refused.

The order's commitment to begging (thus it is called a "mendicant" order) was confirmed. It was to own only its churches and monasteries. Superiors, who were to be elected and not appointed, were allowed to dispense friars from observances that might impede their pastoral work. There was to be an emphasis upon study and presence in universities, especially Paris and Bologna, which became pivotal centers of Dominican pastoral activity. Indeed, one of the early laws of the order was that no house was to be founded without a lecturer in theology. The work of Albert the Great [November 15] and Thomas Aquinas [January 28] represented the fruition of this ideal. After the chapter Dominic went to Milan, a center of heresy, where he fell ill. Upon his return to Bologna in 1220 he found that the friars' convent was being built in too opulent a fashion, inconsistent with the corporate vow of poverty. The work stopped until after his death.

In 1221 he accepted a gift from the pope—a monastery on the Aventine, along with the church of Santa Sabina. He also received various papal bulls approving of the order's spread into other countries, within and beyond Christendom. Indeed, expansion was the main topic at the order's second chapter in Bologna in June 1221. After the chapter Dominic traveled to Trevisa and Venice and then returned to Bologna. He was exhausted from the heat, but continued working and praying through the night. The next day he was very ill. He was taken to the country to the church of St. Mary in the Hills to escape the heat, but he knew he was dying. "My dear sons," he said, "these are my bequests: practice charity in common; remain humble; stay poor willingly." After a final sermon to the friars on the evening of August 6, 1221, he was taken to the monastery, where he died. (August 6 was his original feast day.) His friend Pope Gregory IX authorized the solemn transferal of

Dominic's body to the new Dominican church in Bologna in 1233 as his cult began to increase. In 1234 the pope signed a decree of canonization, calling him a "man of the gospel in the footsteps of his Redeemer." Popular devotion to him spread, as did legends about his childhood and miracles. He is patron saint of the Dominican Republic and of astronomers.

Contrary to conventional wisdom, Dominic did not invent the Rosary. Its origins are largely unknown. However, it became associated with the Dominicans with the establishment of many confraternities of Our Lady and St. Dominic in which the recitation of the Rosary was a condition of membership. Dominic's feast is on the General Roman Calendar. It is also celebrated in the Church of England and the Episcopal Church in the USA.

BIBLIOGRAPHY

Koudelka, Vladimir J., and Simon Tugwell, eds. *Dominic.* London: Darton, Longman and Todd, 1997.

Tugwell, Simon. *Saint Dominic.* Strasbourg: Éditions du Signe, 1995.

Vicaire, Marie-Humbert. *Saint Dominic and His Times.* (English trans.) New York: McGraw-Hill, 1964.

9 Teresa Benedicta of the Cross, martyr; Franz Jägerstätter, martyr

Teresa Benedicta of the Cross (1891–1942), whose original name was Edith Stein, was a convert from Judaism who was gassed to death by the Nazis at Auschwitz during World War II. In 1999 Pope John Paul II named her a co–patron saint of all of Europe, along with Bridget of Sweden [July 23] and Catherine of Siena [April 29]. Born at Breslau (then in Germany, now Wroclaw, Poland) of Jewish parents, she was a self-proclaimed atheist as a young woman. She studied at the universities of Göttingen and Freiburg, with special emphasis on philosophy. The great influence in her life was Edmund Husserl (1859–1938), a philosopher with whom she did her doctorate and for whom she worked. Through another philosopher, Max Scheler (1874–1928), she was drawn to contemporary Catholic thought. The autobiography of Teresa of Ávila [October 15] had a profound effect on her. When she closed that book, she told herself, "This is the truth." She was baptized a Catholic on January 1, 1922.

For years after the completion of her doctorate Edith Stein was unable to secure a university position, because women were not at that time eligible for such in Germany. She taught in the Dominican sisters' high school in Speyer and then in a pedagogical institute in Münster. She was among the first to attempt, in her writings on and translations of Thomas Aquinas [January 28], a dialogue between phenomenology and medieval thought.

Just over a decade after her baptism and with Hitler now in power in Germany, she joined the Carmelites at Cologne on October 12, 1933, taking the name Teresa Benedicta of the Cross, and made her final profession in 1938. With the escalation of anti-Semitism in Germany, she became convinced that her people's destiny was intertwined with her own. To escape persecution, however, she left Cologne for the Netherlands, where she wrote her major work, *The Knowledge of the Cross.* The Nazi government later ordered that Christians of Jewish descent and converts from Judaism resident in the Netherlands be rounded up and sent to Poland for "resettlement." Edith and her sister Rosa, also a convert from Judaism, were arrested on August 2, 1942. As they left the convent, she took Rosa's hand and said, "Come, Rosa, we are going for our people." Edith Stein was executed at Auschwitz (Oswiecim) on August 9. She was beatified in Cologne in 1987, during a papal visit to Germany, and canonized in Rome on October 12, 1998.

Both acts were the subject of controversy between some Jewish leaders and the Vatican because, in the eyes of the former, she was technically a "public apostate" from Judaism. Indeed, in her spiritual last will and testament, required of Carmelite nuns, she offered her life for "the sins of the unbelieving people so the Lord will be accepted by his own." Some of her defenders pointed out that she wrote those words at a time when the Church itself continued to pray for unbelieving or "perfidious" Jews at the Good Friday liturgy. The reference was later dropped during the pontificate of John XXIII (1958–63). Continued ill feeling among Jews because of the silence of Pope Pius XII (1939–58) during the Holocaust also contributed to the negative reaction to the canonization, as well as to the beatification earlier in the same month of *Alojzije Stepinac* (d. 1962), a Croatian cardinal accused of collaboration with a Nazi-backed government during the war. The feast of Teresa Benedicta of the Cross is not on the General Roman Calendar. The Russian and Greek Orthodox Churches celebrate the feast of the Apostle *Matthias* [May 14] on this day.

August 9 is also the day of death of *Franz Jägerstätter* (1907–43), an Austrian peasant who was beheaded by the Nazis in 1943, for refusing to serve in Hitler's army. His story was later told in a book by Gordon Zahn, *In Solitary Witness* (1964, 1991).

10 Lawrence, deacon and martyr

Lawrence (d. 258) was one of the deacons to Pope Sixtus II (257–58) [August 7] and whose name appears in the First Eucharistic Prayer, or Canon, of the Mass. He was Rome's most famous postapostolic martyr. There is no doubt of Lawrence's existence and martyrdom, mentioned in an ancient martyrology, but few details of his life are historical. He was martyred, like the pope, during the persecution of Valerian. He was also prominent in almsgiving to the poor. According to a tradition repeated by the Latin poet Prudentius (d. ca. 410), Ambrose [December 7], and Augustine [August 28], when Lawrence was commanded by the Roman prefect to surrender the Church's riches, he assembled the poor, to whom he had distributed the Church's possessions, and said that they (the poor) were the Church's real treasure. For this he was roasted alive on a gridiron, during which he asked his executors to turn him over so that he could be done on the other side as well. Most scholars, however, believe that he was beheaded four days after Sixtus II's own beheading and was buried in the cemetery of Cyriaca on the Via Tiburtina, where the emperor Constantine [May 21] built the first chapel on the site of the present basilica of St.-Lawrence-Outside-the-Walls. The basilica itself was built at the order of Pope Pelagius II (579–90). There are four other ancient basilicas dedicated to Lawrence in Rome. It is said that his martyrdom had such an impact in the city that some senators became converts to Christianity and various idolatrous activities were brought to an end. Lawrence is patron saint of Sri Lanka, cooks, the poor, and firefighters.

The most complete cycle of his life was painted by Fra Angelico [February 18] for the chapel of Pope Nicholas V (1447–55) in the Vatican, and there are notable stained-glass windows of his life in the cathedrals of Bourges and Poitiers in France. Titian's famous *Martyrdom of St. Lawrence* (1564–67) was sent to King Philip II of Spain for the high altar of the old church in the Escorial, the monastery of St. Lawrence, where it remains today.

As with so many other saints, the vitality of his cult in the universal Church has not been based so much on the few scraps of information we have of his life, but on the way in which his saintly example has inspired the imagination and behavior of countless Christians throughout history. In other words, like official church teachings on faith and morals, Lawrence's "authority" as a saint rests not only on the Church's official inclusion of him in its martyrologies and liturgies, but also on the general acceptance (the technical theological term is "reception") of those inclusions by the rank-and-file membership of the Church at large. His feast is on the General Roman Calendar and is also celebrated by the Greek and Russian Orthodox Churches, the Church of England and the Episcopal Church in the USA, and by the Evangelical Lutheran Church in America.

11 Clare of Assisi, virgin; John Henry Newman, theologian and cardinal

Clare of Assisi (ca. 1193–1253) was the close friend and spiritual associate of Francis of Assisi [October 4] and the foundress of the Poor Clares, or Minoresses. Born in Assisi, at age eighteen she was so moved by the Lenten sermons of Francis in the church of San Giorgio in Assisi that she renounced all of her possessions and took the habit of a nun, much to the dissatisfaction of her family and friends, who tried very hard to dissuade her and to bring her home. She was formed in the religious life at Benedictine convents near Bastia and at Sant'Angelo di Panzo and then accepted Francis's offer of a small house for herself and her companions adjacent to the church of San Damiano, which Francis had restored, in Assisi. He appointed Clare abbess ca. 1215, much against her will. She would govern her convent for the next forty years without ever leaving it. The community, which eventually included her mother and two sisters, followed a rudimentary Rule that Francis drew up for them. Later she became the first woman to write a Rule for other women. It was approved in 1253.

The way of life of those in the new order was marked by poverty and austerity and sustained itself entirely by alms (something they would not have been allowed to do without explicit papal permission, which they received in 1228). They wore no stockings, shoes, or sandals, slept on the ground, never ate meat, and remained silent unless spoken to or in order to perform a work of charity. Clare herself was first up in the morning to ring the choir bell and light the candles. She wore a rough hair shirt close to her skin, and on vigils and throughout Lent she subsisted on bread and water. Eventually Francis and the local bishop ordered her to use a mattress for sleep and to eat some bread every day. In later years, Clare herself urged her nuns to moderate their own austerities, offering Christ "reasonable service and a sacrifice seasoned with the salt of prudence." Clare's nuns soon spread to other countries in Europe, including Spain, Italy, Germany, France, England, and Bohemia. By the late twentieth century they were established in the Middle East, Asia, Africa, Oceania, and the Americas. Clare, however, never left her own convent in Assisi.

From the time Francis died in 1226 until her own death twenty-seven years later, Clare suffered various illnesses, probably as the result of a lifetime of penances, and she was often bedridden. All the while, she lived a simple, but dedicated, religious life, doing such menial tasks as sewing altar clothes. Twice when the town of Assisi was under attack, Clare was transported on her bed to the wall, while another carried a pyx containing the Blessed Sacrament. The armies were said to have ended their siege and fled. This is why she is often depicted in art with a pyx or monstrance.

Clare was canonized in 1255, only two years after her death. This was not surprising, given her reputation for sanctity during her lifetime. She had been visited by the pope, cardinals, and bishops in the course of her final illness. She was buried at first in the church of San Giorgio, but her remains were later transferred to Santa Chiara in Assisi. Divisions persisted among her nuns, as among the Franciscan friars, over the issue of poverty, until Colette [February 7] reformed the Poor Clares in the fifteenth century. Already patron saint of embroiderers, good weather, those in childbirth, and those suffering diseases of the eye, Clare was named patron saint of television in 1958. Pope Pius XII chose her for this because, he said, one Christmas Eve when she lay sick in her bed, she saw the crib and heard singing just as if she had been present in the church. Her feast is on the General Roman Calendar and is also celebrated by the Church of England and the Episcopal Church in the USA. The Franciscans and Poor Clares celebrate the feast of the finding of her body on September 23.

This is also the day of death of *John Henry Newman* (1801–90), leader of the Oxford movement in nineteenth-century England and a convert to Catholicism. Although a loyal Catholic, he opposed the First Vatican Council's dogma of papal infallibility (1870) as inopportune and emphasized the primacy of conscience over all else. Nevertheless, he was named a cardinal in 1879 by Pope Leo XIII. Newman's thought, especially regarding the development of doctrine, had such influence on the Second Vatican Council that Pope Paul VI once referred to it as "Newman's Council." He was declared "Venerable" (the first step to canonization) in 1991.

BIBLIOGRAPHY

Francis Teresa, Sister. *This Living Mirror: Reflections on Clare of Assisi.* Maryknoll, NY: Orbis Books, 1995.

Peterson, Ingrid, ed. *Clare of Assisi: A Medieval and Modern Woman.* St. Bonaventure, NY: Franciscan Institute, 1996.

12 Euplus, martyr

Euplus (d. 304), or Euplius, was martyred in Catania, Sicily, during the persecution of the emperor Diocletian. He is said to have stood outside the governor's court and taunted the authorities to arrest him. "I am a Christian and willing to die for it," he is reported to have shouted. When brought inside, he was carrying a forbidden book of the Gospels, which he admitted belonged to him. He was imprisoned for three months and then interrogated again. Asked if he still had the forbidden writings, he replied that he did, but now they were in his heart. The exasperated governor ordered him to be tortured until he agreed to offer sacrifice to the gods. When Euplus continued to refuse, he was beheaded. His feast is not on the General Roman Calendar, but it is celebrated by the Russian and Greek Orthodox Churches on the preceding day, August 11. The Russian calendar refers to him not only as a "holy martyr," but also as an "archdeacon."

13 Pontian, pope and martyr; Hippolytus, priest and martyr; Maximus the Confessor, monk; Florence Nightingale, nurse

Pontian (d. 235; pope 230–35) was the first pope to have abdicated, or resigned, his office, and *Hippolytus* (ca. 170–ca. 236) was not only the first of thirty-nine antipopes, but also the only antipope to be recognized as a saint, with a feast on the General Roman Calendar. Both were martyred together on Sardinia, the so-called island of death.

Pontian, or Pontianus, was a Roman by birth, the son of Calpurnius. All except the last few months of his pontificate had been peaceful because the tolerant emperor Severus was still reigning. The only matter for which Pontian's pontificate was known was the Roman church's formal approval of the condemnation of Origen (d. ca. 254), one of the first great theologians of the early Church, by Demetrius, bishop of Alexandria, in 230 or 231. It is assumed that, as Bishop of Rome, Pontian must have presided over the Roman synod that endorsed the expulsion of Origen from Egypt, from his teaching post, and from the priesthood itself.

A fourth-century martyrology lists Pontian as the first Roman bishop-martyr (after Peter [June 29]). After succeeding Severus as emperor in March 235, Maximinus Thrax abandoned his predecessor's policy of toleration and launched a violent campaign against Christian leaders. He arrested Pontian and the antipope Hippolytus, who had been a strong critic of popes Zephrynus (198/9–217) and Callistus (217–22) [October 14] and was the leader of a schism in the Roman church, beginning with the election of Callistus. The schism continued through the pontificates of Urban I (222–30) and Pontian. Both Pontian and Hippolytus were imprisoned in Rome and then exiled to Sardinia to work in the mines. Since deportation was normally for life and few survived it, Pontian abdicated to allow a successor to assume the leadership of the Roman community as soon as possible. According to the fourth-century *Liberian Catalogue,* Pontian abdicated on September 28, 235, the first precisely recorded date in papal history.

In fact, neither Pontian nor Hippolytus survived the harsh treatment and conditions on Sardinia. Pontian died less than a month after his resignation. It has been suggested that Pontian and Hippolytus were reconciled while in prison or in exile and that when Pontian abdicated, Hippolytus also renounced his claim to be Bishop of Rome and urged his followers to end their schism. Unity was thereby restored to the Roman church.

Their bodies were brought back to Rome by Pope Fabian [January 20] in 236 or 237. Pontian was solemnly buried in the newly completed papal crypt in the catacombs of Callistus on the Appian Way on August 13. Fragments of Pontian's tomb slab were discovered there in 1909, with his name and episcopal title inscribed in Greek. On the same day the remains of Hippolytus were interred on the Via Tiburtina in a cemetery that thereafter bore his name. In 1551 a third-century marble statue of him, in the conventional dress of a philosopher or teacher and inscribed with an incomplete list of his writings, was discovered near the Via Tiburtina. It was installed in the Vatican Library in 1959 by Pope John XXIII.

Hippolytus had been born in the Greek-speaking East and was a man of Greek philosophical culture. He came to Rome and was ordained during the pontificate of Victor I (189–98). He was the author of a number of theological and exegetical works, most notably the *Apostolic Tradition,* which contains invaluable descriptions of contemporary baptismal and eucharistic rites in use in Rome. His differences with the newly elected Callistus were both personal and theological. Hippolytus accused Callistus of laxity toward sinners and, like his patron Zephrynus, of failing effectively to combat modalism, a Christological heresy that denied the divinity of Christ because it refused to accept the doctrine of the Trinity, which posits three distinct divine Persons in the one God. Thus, the Father, Son, and Holy Spirit are merely modes, aspects, or energies of the one divine Person, who exercises three distinct functions on behalf of humanity. Hippolytus himself was accused of ditheism for appearing to hold that the Father and the Son are divine, but that the Spirit is not a distinct divine Person. Hippolytus was also a rigorist in other matters, insisting, for example, that the validity of the sacraments depends upon the sanctity of those who administer them. He is the patron saint of prison guards and horses.

The feast of Pontian and Hippolytus is on the General Roman Calendar. The feast of Hippolytus alone is celebrated in the East on January 30. In the Russian Orthodox calendar he is identified as "pope of Rome."

On this day the Greek and Russian Orthodox Churches celebrate the feast of *Maximus the Confessor* (ca. 580–662). He was a famous Byzantine theologian and monk who vigorously defended the teaching of the Council of Chalcedon (451) on the humanity and divinity of Christ against the subsequent heresies of Monenergism and Monothelitism, both of which, in effect, denied the full humanity of Christ. Thus, his title, "the Confessor." These heresies enjoyed imperial favor, however, because they were seen as useful compromises with the still powerful Monophysite community in the East. Monophysitism held that Christ had a divine nature but not a human nature. The Council of Chalcedon taught that there are two natures in Christ, one divine and one human, united "hypostatically" in one divine Person.

Maximus has always enjoyed particular favor in the East, especially in Eastern monastic communities, because of his mystical approach to theology. Christians, he said, already participate in the mystical union of the human and the divine in Christ. Eastern monks also identified with his literary device known as the "century": one hundred terse paragraphs written as much to invite the reader's contemplation as to develop a sustained argument. On order of the emperor Constans, who had already arrested and exiled the pope, Martin I [April 13], Maximus was taken into custody in Rome at age seventy-five because of his criticism of the imperially favored Monothelitist heresy. In order to encourage him to recant, a bishop was sent to him in his prison cell to offer him ecclesiastical honors. When he refused, he was sent into exile in various Eastern locales. Maximus spent six hard years in Perberis and then, in 661, was taken again to Constantinople, where he was tortured and then had his tongue and right hand amputated. He died soon thereafter. His feast is not on the General Roman Calendar.

On this day the Church of England and the Evangelical Lutheran Church in America commemorate the famous nurse and reformer of hospital care, *Florence Nightingale* (1820–1910).

BIBLIOGRAPHY

Brent, Allen. *Hippolytus and the Roman Church in the Third Century: Communities in Tension Before the Emergence of a Monarch-Bishop.* Leiden: Brill, 1995.

14 Maximilian Maria Kolbe, priest and martyr

Maximilian Kolbe (1894–1941) was put to death in a Nazi concentration camp when he volunteered to take the place of another prisoner who had been designated for execution. Born Raimund Kolbe in Russian Poland near Lodz, he entered the Franciscans in 1910, taking the name Maximilian Maria. After studies in Rome, he was ordained a priest in 1918, but returned to Poland when he contracted tuberculosis. A year before ordination he organized the Militia of Mary, dedicated to advancing devotion to the Blessed Virgin. He taught church history in Kraków and, following a near fatal relapse, founded in 1922 a monthly bulletin, *Knight(s) of the Immaculata,* which was apologetical in content and tone and which also reflected his deeply personal Marian piety—a piety, however, that was divorced from Christ and from its biblical roots. Although the publication and Militia grew rapidly in several countries, his colleagues found it difficult to work with him, and he was transferred to a half ruined friary at Grodno, near Warsaw, where he continued his pastoral work, writing, editing, and printing. He founded a Franciscan community there, which thrived for a time until he had yet another relapse of tuberculosis.

After eighteen months of recuperation he relocated once more, this time in Niepokalanów, or "town of the Immaculata." One day he met some Japanese students and decided he would like to go to Japan, where many Christians had died for their faith. Early in 1930 he set off with four brothers for Nagasaki, where he tried to spread the message of the Knights of Mary via the printing press. He founded a second Niepokalanów, but illness forced his return to Poland after five years. Soon after that he was off to India to found a third Niepokalanów, then back to Nagasaki to build a church. He was recalled to Kraków in 1936 and made superior of more than 760 friars at the original Niepokalanów. He also started more magazines and papers and conducted regular radio broadcasts.

It is a sad indication of the anti-Semitic atmosphere in Catholic Poland at the time—an atmosphere that affected Maximilian's papers and magazines as well—that the primate of Poland, Cardinal August Hlond, could have written such words as these in a pastoral letter: "There will be the Jewish problem as long as the Jews remain. It is a fact that the Jews are fighting against the Catholic Church, persisting in free thinking, and are the vanguard of godlessness, Bolshevism, and subversion. . . . It is a fact that the Jews deceive, levy interest, and are pimps. It is a fact that the religious and ethical influence of the Jewish people on Polish young people is a negative one."

When the Germans invaded Poland in 1939, Maximilian sent all the friars home to help with the Polish Red Cross, but with a warning not to become involved in the underground resistance. He and others who had remained in the monastery were arrested by the Gestapo, but released after two and a half months. Their monastery became a refugee camp for some three thousand Polish refugees from Poznan (now called Posen, a purely German city) and fifteen hundred Jews. He continued publishing his papers, which took an independent, anti-Nazi, patriotic line. He refused an opportunity to become a legal German national, given his origins, which were more likely Germanic than Slavic. On February 17, 1941, he was arrested again and imprisoned in Warsaw, where he was subjected to physical and psychological brutality. On May 28, without trial or sentence, he was transferred to Auschwitz. In spite of the hard labor and physical abuse, Maximilian continued his priestly ministry, hearing confessions and saying Mass with smuggled bread and wine.

Near the end of July, there was an escape attempt from his unit of the camp. The penalty was always the same. Men from the block were selected for death by starvation, by way of reprisal. When Francis Gajowniczek was picked, he cried out in despair. Kolbe stepped forward. "I am a Catholic priest," he said. "I wish to die for that man. I am old; he has a wife and children." The officer agreed and Maximilian went to the death chamber, helping the others prepare to die with dignity. Two weeks later only four were still alive. Maximilian alone was still fully conscious. He was injected with phenol and died on August 14, 1941, at age forty-seven. The next day his body was thrown into an oven. He was beatified in 1971 and canonized in 1982 in the presence of the man he had saved. His canonization was the source of some controversy within the Jewish community because of the indications of anti-Semitism in some of his writings and publications. His feast is on the General Roman Calendar, and he is commemorated by the Anglican Communion in England and Canada on this day. He is the patron saint of those suffering from drug addiction.

BIBLIOGRAPHY

Stone, Elaine Murray. *Maximilian Kolbe: Saint of Auschwitz.* New York: Paulist Press, 1997.

15 Assumption of Mary; Tarcisius, martyr

Great portions of the universal Church, both East and West, annually celebrate the feast of the *Assumption of Mary* into heaven on this day. Although the feast is relatively ancient in origin, the dogma was not formally proclaimed by the Catholic Church until Pope Pius XII did so in 1950. The definition holds that, "when the course of her earthly life was finished," the Blessed Virgin Mary "was taken up body and soul into the glory of heaven." The definition does not take a position on the long-disputed question of whether Mary actually died.

There are a number of ancient texts from the late fourth century onward that purport to record the death of Mary in Jerusalem amid various miraculous circumstances. *When* the death occurred is another matter. Some sources indicate that it was as early as three years after the death and Resurrection of Christ; others place it as late as fifty years after that. Likewise, some sources claim that Mary's body was assumed into heaven while on its way to burial. Others assert that her body was raised after three days, just like her Son's. Still others believe that she did not die at all, that she was assumed directly into heaven during her natural life. Catholic teaching leaves the question open.

However, feasts celebrating the death of Mary were observed in Palestine during the fifth century and possibly as early as the fourth century in Antioch. In Rome, there was no separate feast day for the Assumption until the late seventh century. Previously, there had been one general feast in honor of Mary, celebrated on January 1. That ancient tradition was restored in 1970 when Pope Paul VI decreed that the Solemnity of Mary, Mother of God, should be celebrated on the first day of the year, replacing the feast of the Circumcision of Jesus. By the end of the eighth century the feast of the Assumption was universally observed in the West on August 15, and in 863 Pope Nicholas I raised it to the liturgical level of Easter, Christmas, and Pentecost. In various parts of the East, a separate feast of the Assumption was celebrated either on January 18 (in association with the Epiphany) or August 15 (probably in connection with the dedication of a church in Mary's honor).

Popular belief in the Assumption had been developing in the early centuries mainly through preaching and various devotional practices. Preachers insisted that, given Mary's sublime dignity as the Mother of God, her body could not have undergone the corruption of the tomb after death. Others made the same argument against her having died at all. The medieval writers were characteristically graphic. It was inconceivable, they declared, that the very same flesh that gave birth to the Savior should be "consumed by worms." In the Scholastic theology of the period, this argument was known as the argument from convenience, or fittingness: God *could* preserve Mary from corruption; it was *fitting* that God should have done so; therefore, God *did* so.

In proclaiming the dogma of the Assumption, Pope Pius XII intended to send a message to a world newly emerging from the horrors of World War II. His pronouncement deplored the destruction of life, the desecration of the human body, and the prevalence of moral corruption. He pointed to Mary's Assumption as "the exalted destiny of both our soul and body." It proclaims the ultimate victory of God's grace over sin and underscores the impact of that grace on the material world as well as the spiritual realm. Her victory gives strength to our own faith and hope in the resurrection of the body.

The Second Vatican Council made the same point more than a decade later in its Dogmatic Constitution on the Church: "The Mother of Jesus in the glory which she possesses in body and soul in heaven is the image and beginning of the church as it is to be perfected in the world to come. Likewise, she shines forth on earth, until the day of the Lord shall come, a sign of certain hope and comfort to the pilgrim people of God" (n. 68).

The feast of the Assumption is on the General Roman Calendar and is one of the four Solemnities (the highest liturgical rank for a feast) devoted to Mary; the others are Mary, Mother of God [January 1], Annunciation [March 25], and Immaculate Conception [December 8]. In the Orthodox East the feast is that of the Dormition (or "falling asleep") of Mary. In the Church of England, the Episcopal Church in the USA, and the Evangelical Lutheran Church in America it is simply a feast of the Blessed Virgin Mary, or of the Mother of Our Lord.

This is also the feast day of *Tarcisius*, a Roman martyr of the third or fourth century, who is said to have been attacked by a pagan mob while carrying the Eucharist. Rather than surrender the Sacrament, he suffered death by stoning and clubbing. He is patron saint of First Communicants.

16 Stephen of Hungary, king

Stephen of Hungary (ca. 975–1038) united and Christianized the Magyars, who had settled in Hungary at the end of the ninth century. Born Vajk, the son of the third Magyar duke of Hungary, he was baptized István, or Stephen, at about age ten, when his father became a Christian. Stephen married at age twenty and succeeded his father as leader of the Magyar people two years later, in 997. He consolidated his political power over rival leaders and established Christianity as the religion of his country. Pope Sylvester II gave him the title of king and a crown in 1000, when Hungary became a nation. The coronation took place in 1001. By then he had already founded various dioceses and monasteries, the most famous of which was the primatial see of Esztergom and the monastery of Pannonhalma. He reduced the power of nobles, abolished tribal divisions, and reorganized political structures, thereby forming the Hungarians into a single kingdom. He imposed a narrow and strict form of Christianity on the nation as well. Blasphemy and adultery were criminalized, pagan practices were ruthlessly suppressed and punished, everyone was commanded to marry, except clergy and religious, and marriages between Christians and pagans were forbidden. At the same time, he was devoted to the poor and often distributed alms to them in disguise. After his death at Szekesfehervar on August 15, 1038, miracles were attributed to him at his tomb. Forty-five years later his remains were enshrined in a chapel dedicated to

Our Lady at Buda, and he was canonized in 1083. In August 2000, the ecumenical patriarch, Bartholomew I of Constantinople, "recognized" Stephen as a saint for the Orthodox Church as well. Stephen was always considered a national hero and the most important of Hungary's Christian kings. His feast is on the General Roman Calendar.

17 Joan of the Cross, foundress; Hyacinth of Poland, friar; Roch, hermit; Myron of Cyzicus, martyr

Joan of the Cross (1666–1736) was the foundress of the Sisters of St. Anne of Providence. Born Jeanne Delanoue, the youngest of twelve children, at Saumur in Anjou, France, she managed her family's religious goods shop after her parents had died. Her attitude, however, was dominated by greed and insensitivity to the beggars who came looking for food. On the eve of the Epiphany 1693, an elderly, unkempt woman who was on pilgrimage from shrine to shrine showed up at her door, claiming to be on intimate terms with God. For some inexplicable reason, Joan allowed her to stay in the back of the house for little or no rent. During Lent Joan began listening to sermons as she made her own tour of shrines, and then, after consulting with the local hospital chaplain, she began closing her shop on Sundays and started fasting three days a week. Otherwise, her unpleasant temperament remained unchanged. On Pentecost the elderly women reappeared with more alleged instructions from God. Joan took out her best dress and gave it to the woman. It is said that Joan subsequently went into a trance for three days, after which she announced her conversion to a life dedicated to the poor. At the suggestion of the old woman, Joan began to care for six poor children in a stable and later for others as well. Many poor people began coming to her on their own. In 1698 she closed her shop and began to practice various acts of mortification, like sleeping in a hard chair, for her past sins. In 1700 she took a poor child into her own home, then some sick, elderly, and destitute people, as well as orphans. Her residence became known as Providence House. In 1702 the cliff behind the house collapsed in an earthquake, destroying the house and killing one of the children. She moved into another house, but it was too small to accommodate all the needy.

In 1704 she found two other young women to help her, and these became the nucleus of a new religious congregation to be known eventually as the Congregation of St. Anne of Providence. On the feast of St. Anne [July 26] they were clothed with the religious habit as Sisters of St. Anne. The bishop of Angers approved their Rule in 1709, and Joan took the religious name of Joan of the Cross. She founded the first local hospice and, with the aid of benefactors, her house expanded to become Great Providence House, with forty helpers. Her hard work and various mortifications eventually caught up with her, and she died on August 17, 1736, after a violent fever. By the time of her death she had founded twelve communities, hospices, and schools, and was already recognized as a saint. Joan of the Cross was beatified in 1947 and canonized in 1982. Her feast is not on the General Roman Calendar.

On this day the Dominicans celebrate the feast of *Hyacinth of Poland* (1185–1257), a first-generation Dominican friar and "apostle of Poland." He was personally converted by Dominic [August 8] and received the habit from him at Santa Sabina in Rome. Hyacinth (also Iazech) preached throughout Poland, where he founded five Dominican houses. He is buried in the Dominican church in Kraków and was canonized in 1594. The Franciscans celebrate the feast of *Roch* (ca. 1350–ca. 1380), also known as Rocco and Rock, a hermit around whom many legends developed, including one in which, while suffering from the plague, he was fed in the woods by a dog. Afterward, he is reputed to have cured many people as well as their sick cattle. And so he is patron saint of the plague-stricken. His cult subsided during the sixteenth century, but was revived in the nineteenth during a cholera epidemic. His feast is not on the General Roman Calendar. The Russian Orthodox Church commemorates *Myron of Cyzicus,* a third-century priest who was martyred during the persecution of Diocletian. He is said to have used his great inherited wealth for the building of churches, hospitals, and orphanages and for the relief of the poor.

18 Helen, empress

Helen (ca. 250–330), also known as Helena and Ellen, was the mother of the first Christian emperor, Constantine [May 21]. Born at Drepanum (later Helenopolis) in Bithynia, she married the Roman general Constantius Chlorus, who divorced her in 292 to marry the stepdaughter of the emperor and eventually become an emperor himself. However, their son Constantine, who also later became emperor in his own right, greatly honored and respected her. She became a Christian ca. 312 when she was already over the age of sixty. She dressed simply, was generous to the poor and to churches, reached out to those in prison, and made a pilgrimage to the Holy Land, where she devoted herself to the building of basilicas (on the Mount of Olives and at Bethlehem) and shrines, the endowing of convents, the collecting of relics, and the care of the poor, orphans, and prisoners. She is also believed to have found the True Cross there ca. 320, but there is no evidence to support that claim.

She died in Palestine, but her body was later transferred to Rome and placed in a tomb attached the church of Sts. Peter and Marcellinus. From the ninth century, however, the abbey of Hautvillers, near Reims, has claimed to have her body. Her feast is not on the General Roman Calendar, but it is celebrated in the East (along with that of her son Constantine) on May 21. The island of St. Helena, where Napoleon died in exile, was discovered by Spaniards on her feast day. She is patron saints of converts and the divorced. The feast of *Jane Francis de Chantal* [December 12] is on the Proper Calendar for the Dioceses of the U.S.A. on this day, while the Cistercians celebrate the feast of *John Eudes* [August 19].

19 John Eudes, priest; Bernard Tolomei, abbot; Louis of Anjou, bishop

John Eudes (1601–80) was the founder of the Congregation of Jesus and Mary (Eudists). Born of a farming family at Ri in Normandy, he was educated by Jesuits and in 1623 joined the newly established French Oratorians in Paris, was ordained in 1625, and remained in that community for twenty years, earning a reputation as one of the great preachers of France. By 1676 he had preached over one hundred parish missions, some lasting several weeks or even several months. He fell seriously ill on more than one occasion (requiring in one instance two years of recuperation) and devoted himself frequently to the physical and spiritual care of plague victims. In 1637 he published *The Life and Kingdom of Jesus in Christian Souls,* which contained the essence of his devotional thought. It went into sixteen editions during his lifetime.

For him, Jesus is the source of all sanctity and Mary is the model of the Christian life. He also promoted devotion to the Sacred Heart and urged the establishment of a feast day (which was not approved until

1765). It was a time of weak religious practice among Catholics and of a poorly educated and weakly motivated diocesan clergy. In 1641 he began giving conferences for priests directed toward improving the performance of their pastoral duties. He realized that something more fundamental was needed, and he tried to establish a seminary in Caen, where he was superior of the local Oratory. In spite of his winning the approval of the bishop, his plan encountered opposition from the new superior general of the Oratorians. In 1643, therefore, he left the Oratory and founded a society of diocesan priests, without vows, calling it the Congregation of Jesus and Mary.

The new group was dedicated to the education and spiritual formation of future diocesan priests in seminaries. Seminaries were established at Caen and in five other French cities by 1670. He also founded a religious society of women, the Congregation of Our Lady of Charity of the Refuge, under the Rule of St. Augustine [August 28] and dedicated to the Sacred Heart of Mary. It was intended to provide a refuge for former prostitutes who wished to be rehabilitated and to do penance. John Eudes died at Caen on August 19, 1680. He was beatified in 1909 and canonized in 1925. His feast is on the General Roman Calendar.

The Greek Orthodox Church and the Cistercians celebrate on this day the feast of *Bernard Tolomei* (1272–1348), founder (in 1319) and abbot of the Benedictine Congregation of Our Lady of Monte Oliveto (the Olivetans), a community that followed a primitive observance. Although the Olivetans venerate him as a saint, he has only been beatified (in 1644). His feast is not on the General Roman Calendar.

The Franciscans celebrate the feast of *Louis of Anjou* (1274–97), a person of royal blood, who was commanded by Pope Boniface VIII to be ordained a priest and a bishop (of Toulouse) at age twenty-three. Beforehand, however, he fulfilled an earlier vow by going to Rome and making his profession as a Franciscan on Christmas Eve, 1296. He was consecrated a bishop there five days later. He lived simply as a bishop and was devoted to his pastoral duties, but they soon exhausted him and he asked to resign. He was denied permission, but died on August 19, 1297, following a voyage to visit his sister in Catalonia. He was buried in the Franciscan convent in Marseilles (although his remains were later transferred to Valencia) and was canonized in 1317. His feast is not on the General Roman Calendar.

20 Bernard of Clairvaux, abbot and Doctor of the Church; Gerard Groote, founder

Bernard of Clairvaux (1090–1153) was one of the greatest monastic leaders and theologians in the history of the Church. He has sometimes been referred to as the last of the Western Fathers of the Church. Born to an aristocratic family at Fontaines, near Dijon, he became a monk at age twenty-two at a poverty-stricken, reformed monastery at Cîteaux, located a few miles south of his family's estate. It had the strictest monastic Rule of the time. He persuaded about thirty of his relatives and friends to join him. Three years later he was made abbot of a new foundation at Clairvaux, a post he would hold for the next thirty-eight years. At first, and by his own admission, he was too strict on the monks, but later relented. The monastery prospered, establishing other foundations in France, Britain, and Ireland. By the time of his death there were some seven hundred monks at Clairvaux itself.

Detail from *The Lactation of Saint Bernard of Clairvaux* by Jan Van Eeckele

In spite of his commitment to a life of solitude and seclusion from the world, Bernard was extremely active in the affairs of the Church. He secured approval for the new order of Knights Templar, whose Rule he had written, dedicated to supporting the Crusades and to the care of the sick and of pilgrims. After a disputed papal election in 1130, he strongly supported the claims of Innocent II against the antipope Anacletus and, between 1130 and 1138, rallied the whole Church to his side. With the lavish support of a grateful Innocent II, his own Cistercian order continued to increase rapidly, and especially after his former pupil Pope Eugenius III was elected in 1145. Bernard was quick to condemn unjustly scholars like Peter Abelard and Gilbert de La Porrée, bishop of Poitiers, for their theological opinions, criticized other monastic foundations, in particular Cluny, for their luxuriant ways, and intervened in various episcopal elections in various parts of Europe. He preached an exhausting campaign against the Cathari (Albigensians) in southern France and concluded, mistakenly, that he had restored the region to orthodoxy. At the request of Eugenius III, he vigorously preached the Second Crusade throughout northern Europe, and many rallied to his call, but the Crusade itself ended in disaster in 1149 and some actually blamed Bernard for it. Bernard, in turn, blamed the Crusaders for their lack of faith. He was an exception to most of his contemporaries, however, in his opposition to the persecution of Jews.

Some of his theological and devotional writings have become classics, particularly his treatise *On Loving God*. Perhaps the best known of all his works were his eighty-six sermons on the Canticle of Canticles, which ranged from reflections on the practical life of a monk to the mystical union between Christ the bridegroom and the Church (and sometimes even himself) as the bride. He was also influential in promoting devotion to the humanity of Christ and to the Blessed Mother. He made a profound impact on the development of Western monasticism, especially through his emphasis on mystical prayer within the ordinary framework of monastic observance. His final years were taken up with the writing of his long work *On Consideration,* also requested by Eugenius III, who wanted a comprehensive treatise on papal spirituality. After acting successfully as a mediator in an armed conflict between the duke of Lorraine's forces and the inhabitants of Metz, Bernard returned from Lorraine to Clairvaux a sick man and died there on August 20, 1153. At the time of his death there were some four hundred Cistercian houses in Europe. Because of Bernard's reputation for healing, his cult began even during his lifetime, but he was formally canonized in 1174 and declared a Doctor of the Church in 1830. Because of his eloquence, he has been called *Doctor mellifluus* (Lat., "Mellifluous Doctor"). Indeed, that was the title of an encyclical letter in his honor written by Pope Pius XII in 1953. His feast is on the General Roman Calendar. It is also observed by the Church of England, the Episcopal Church in the USA, and the Evangelical Lutheran Church in America. He is patron saint of Gibraltar and of candle makers.

August 20 is also the day of death of *Gerard Groote* (1340–84), also Geert Groote, the founder of the Devotio Moderna (Lat., "Modern Devotion") movement, sometimes known as the Brethren of the Common Life, which swept across the Netherlands and Germany in the fourteenth century. Groote had renounced all of his wealth, preached as a deacon in the diocese of Utrecht for four years, and then directed communities of followers who neither took vows nor followed any Rule, who supported themselves by common labor, and who made no distinction within their ranks between lay and clerical members. Groote's condemnation of the worldliness of the clergy won him many enemies, and his license to preach was revoked the year before his death from the plague. The movement's most famous text was *The Imitation of Christ* by Thomas à Kempis [July 24].

BIBLIOGRAPHY

Bredero, Adriaan Hendrik. *Bernard of Clairvaux: Between Cult and History.* Grand Rapids, MI: Eerdmans, 1996.

21 Pius X, pope

Pius X (1835–1914; pope 1903–14) was the pope best known, unfortunately, for the war he waged against Modernism, an ill-defined grab bag of liberal but not necessarily unorthodox opinions, in the course of which campaign he set back Catholic theological, biblical, and historical scholarship at least fifty years. On the other hand, he was also the pope who encouraged frequent Communion and determined that First Communion should be received at the "age of discretion," usually interpreted to mean seven. Born Giuseppe Melchior Sarto of a poor family at Riese in upper Venetia, the second of ten children, he studied for the priesthood at the seminary in Padua and was ordained in 1858. After service as a country curate and then as a pastor, he was appointed in 1875 as the bishop's chancellor and as spiritual director of the Treviso diocesan seminary. In 1884 he was consecrated bishop of Mantua, a run-down diocese that he successfully revived. In 1893 he was appointed patriarch of Venice and named a cardinal. In Venice he earned a reputation not only for his simplicity of life and humility, but also for his strong-willed opinions. In his first pastoral letter he wrote that, with regard to the pope, "there should be no questions, no subtleties, no opposing of personal rights to his rights, but only obedience." He characterized liberal Catholics as "wolves in sheepskin."

Cardinal Sarto was elected pope on August 4, 1903, even though the clear favorite going into the conclave was Pope Leo XIII's secretary of state, Cardinal Mariano Rampolla del Tindaro. When it had appeared that no one could stop Rampolla's election, Cardinal Puzyna de Kozielsko, archbishop of Kraków, solemnly proclaimed the veto of Rampolla's candidacy by Franz Joseph, emperor of Austria and king of

Hungary. Many of the cardinals, especially the French, protested this act of interference and one even proposed that Rampolla be elected by acclamation as a repudiation of the emperor. However, the third ballot had already begun and the cardinals were obliged to count the votes. This time Sarto had twenty-one votes, more than double his support on the previous ballot. It began to appear that the cardinals wanted a different kind of pope from Leo XIII, with whom Rampolla was so closely identified. The next morning Rampolla's vote dropped to ten and Sarto's rose to fifty, sufficient for election. He took the name Pius X out of respect for recent popes of that name who had courageously resisted persecution and fought against error. The following January he decreed that vetoes of papal candidates by Catholic temporal rulers were henceforth prohibited.

In adopting as his papal motto "To restore all things in Christ," a text from Ephesians 1:10, he made it clear that he intended to be a pastoral rather than political pope. However, he found himself immersed in politics almost immediately. He appointed as his own secretary of state Cardinal Merry del Val, an ultraconservative Spaniard who began reversing Pope Leo XIII's more accommodating approach to secular governments. This led the following year to a diplomatic break between the Holy See and France. The pope also raised hackles when he adopted the same stance toward Portugal and voiced his support for Catholic minorities in Ireland and Poland. Pius X's popularity in the United States plummeted when, in 1910, he refused to receive ex-president Theodore Roosevelt because Mr. Roosevelt was scheduled to speak at the Methodist church in Rome. He condemned *Le Sillon,* a French social movement, ecumenical in composition, that tried to reconcile Catholicism with more liberal political views. He also opposed trade unions that were not exclusively Catholic. At the same time, he supported the right-wing, monarchist *Action Française.*

Pius X devoted much of his energy, however, toward the repression of dissent in the Church. In the decree *Lamentabili sane exitu* (Lat., "A lamentable departure indeed"), issued in his name by the Holy Office in July 1907, sixty-five propositions concerning the nature of the Church, the sacraments, and other doctrinal matters were condemned. The following September he issued an encyclical, *Pascendi Dominici gregis* (Lat., "Feeding the Lord's flock"), that characterized Modernism as the "synthesis of all heresies." Three years later he imposed an Oath against Modernism on all clerics. He also explicitly encouraged a network of informants known as the *Sodalitium Pianum* (League of St. Pius V), whose members reported perceived deviations from orthodoxy to Rome. Many seminary professors were dismissed from their teaching positions without a hearing, and some were even defrocked and excommunicated. The oath had a chilling effect on Catholic scholarship and at the same time encouraged reactionary Catholics to wage a kind of war on theologians and biblical scholars who did not toe the line. Pius X's successor, Benedict XV (1914–22), declared an end to this internecine conflict in his first encyclical, published within three months of his election, and the oath itself was finally rescinded in July 1967, during the pontificate of Paul VI (1963–78).

Pius X's pontificate had another, brighter side as well. The Roman Curia was reorganized, a new Code of Canon Law was created (but not promulgated until the next pontificate), seminaries were reformed, the Pontifical Biblical Institute was established, laity were encouraged to cooperate with their bishops in the apostolate, Gregorian chant was restored in the liturgy, the Breviary recited by priests was revised and shortened, and frequent Communion was encouraged. After suffering a heart attack in 1913, the pope lived in the shadow of death. He lapsed into melancholia as the events leading up to World War I began to transpire.

Less than two months after the assassination of the archduke Francis Ferdinand, heir apparent to the Austro-Hungarian throne, Pius X died, on August 20, 1914. He was buried in a simple, unadorned tomb in the crypt of St. Peter's, in accordance with his wishes and in keeping with the reputation for self-effacement that he had gained among the faithful. Indeed, he had a clear distaste for all the pomp and ceremony with which he was surrounded. In his last will and testament, he wrote: "I was born poor, I have lived poor, and I wish to die poor." Venerated as a saint by some even during his lifetime, he was beatified in 1951 and canonized in 1954 by another Pius, Pius XII. He was the first pope to be canonized since yet another Pius, Pius V (1566–72) [April 30]. Because Pius X had left instructions that his body not be embalmed, no subsequent popes have been embalmed after death. His feast is on the General Roman Calendar.

22 Queenship of Mary; Philip Benizi, founder

The feast of the *Queenship of Mary* was first instituted by Pope Pius XII in 1954 and was formerly celebrated on May 31. It is now observed as a memorial rather than a major feast on this day, August 22, which is the octave of the Solemnity of the Assumption [August 15]. The two feasts are connected by the traditional belief that, after her Assumption into heaven, Mary was crowned Queen of Heaven. Christian poetry has referred to Mary as "queen" since the fourth century (by Ephrem [June 9]), and shortly after that Christian art has portrayed her in royal attire, enthroned with her child Jesus, who was himself given "the throne of David . . . [to] rule over the house of Jacob forever, and of his kingdom there will be no end" (Luke 1:33).

This is also the feast day of *Philip Benizi* (1233–85), founder of the Servite nuns. Born of noble Florentine parents, he studied and practiced medicine, but joined the Servites as a lay brother, doing ordinary chores of gardening, manual labor, and begging for alms for nearly three years. However, his educational background surfaced in a theological discussion in Siena (he had a doctorate not only in medicine but also in philosophy) and he was ordained to the priesthood and eventually became prior general of the order. He took an active part in the Second Council of Lyons in 1274 and, at the request of the pope, successfully mediated a conflict between the Guelfs and the Ghibellines in 1279. He was considered a serious candidate for the papacy at one time, but hid in a cave for three months to escape the possibility of election. In 1285, when he felt that his life was drawing to an end, he summoned a general chapter and announced his departure with the words, "Love one another." He went to the smallest and poorest house of the order, at Todi, and went immediately to Our Lady's altar, where he prostrated himself saying, "This is my place of rest for ever." He entered his final illness that afternoon and died seven days later. He was canonized in 1671. His feast is not on the General Roman Calendar.

23 Rose of Lima, virgin

Rose of Lima (1586–1617) is the first canonized saint of the Americas. Born in Lima, the capital of Peru, she was baptized Isabel de Flores. An Indian maid was struck by the infant's beauty and declared in a phrase, still common in Spanish, that she was "*como una rosa*" (Sp., "like a rose"), and her mother agreed that this is how she was to be known. As an adolescent she took Catherine of Siena [April 29] as her model, not only for her mystical experiences, but also for her acts of severe penance, including vomiting after meals (a sickness known today as bulimia) and self-flagellation. She was determined to avoid marriage at all costs, having vowed herself to God. At age twenty she became a Dominican tertiary and slept on a bed of broken tiles in a tiny hermitage that she built behind her house. On her head she wore a crown of thorns, or spikes, but with a garland of roses on the outside to please her mother.

Saint Rose of Lima by Carlo Dolci, 17th C.

Her spirituality, however, was not centered entirely on herself. She set up a small infirmary in one of the rooms of the family home to care for destitute children and sick elderly people. This ministry, rather than her acts of mortification, probably accounted for her extraordinary popularity in Lima by the time of her death. She spent the last years of her life in the home of a government official and his wife. She died there on August 24, 1617, at age thirty-one. The crowds at her funeral were enormous, and the service itself had to be delayed for several days. She was buried, in accordance with her request, in the cloister of the church of St. Dominic [August 8], but her body was later moved to the church itself and then to a place under the altar of the crypt. She was beatified in 1668 and canonized in 1671 in the same ceremony in which John of the Cross [December 14] was elevated. She was the first canonized saint of the New World and was proclaimed patron saint of Peru and all of South and Central America, the West Indies, and the Philippines.

As noted in Part III, canonizations are not without political dimension. At the time of Rose's, the pope, Clement X, was engaged in struggles with Louis XIV of France and looked to Spain for support. The canonizations of Rose of Lima and of John of the Cross, a native Spaniard, were widely applauded in that country. Her feast is on the General Roman Calendar.

24 Bartholomew, apostle

Bartholomew (first century) was one of Jesus' original twelve apostles, according to four lists in the New Testament (Matt. 10:3; Mark 3:18; Luke 6:14; Acts 1:13). His name in Hebrew, *Bar-Talmai,* means "son of

Tholami," or "son of Tholomaeus." Nothing certain is known of him, however. Some scholars identify him with Nathanael of John 1:45–51, because both are closely associated with Philip [May 3]. If the identification with Nathanael is correct, Philip brought Bartholomew (Nathanael), a native of Cana of Galilee (John 21:2), to acknowledge Jesus as the Messiah (John 1:45–46), and Jesus referred to him, in turn, as an Israelite "in whom there is no guile" (1:47). If the identification is not correct, we know nothing of Bartholomew from the New Testament other than that he was one of the Twelve. The earliest church tradition about Bartholomew is a report from the second-century Alexandrian teacher Pantaenus, preserved in Eusebius's *Ecclesiastical History* (5.10.3). Pantaenus had visited India sometime between 150 and 200, probably the Malabar Coast, which had trading relations with the Roman Empire. He discovered a Christian community there that revered Bartholomew as its founder and possessed a Hebrew "Gospel of Matthew" that Bartholomew had left them. Bartholomew is also thought to have preached the gospel in Phrygia, Lycaonia, Mesopotamia, and Persia, and to have been martyred by being skinned alive and beheaded at Albanopolis, on the west coast of the Caspian Sea, in Greater Armenia. (He is patron saint of Armenia.) The *Martyrdom of Bartholomew* states that he was placed in a sack and cast into the sea. His legendary loss of skin (by flaying) made him patron saint of tanners. He appears in Michelangelo's *Last Judgment* in the Sistine Chapel holding his own flayed skin over one arm.

There are several apocryphal works that have circulated under his name: a *Gospel of Bartholomew;* the *Questions of Bartholomew,* a fifth-century document containing a post-Resurrection dialogue between Jesus and his disciples about hell and the virgin birth; and the Coptic *Book of Bartholomew on the Resurrection,* also from the fifth or sixth century, containing loosely connected stories about the death, Resurrection, and descent into hell of Jesus, along with several hymns.

His feast is on the General Roman Calendar, but is celebrated in the East on June 11. It is also observed today by the Church of England, the Episcopal Church in the USA, and the Evangelical Lutheran Church in America. Sadly, it is also the day on which a mass slaughter of French Huguenots occurred in Paris and elsewhere in France, known as the St. Bartholomew's Day Massacre.

25 Louis IX, king; Joseph Calasanz, priest; Genesius, martyr

Louis IX (1214–70) was king of France and a model Christian ruler. Born at Poissy, the son of Louis VIII, he became king upon his father's death in 1226, but his mother served as queen-regent until 1235. Louis married Margaret of Provence in 1234 (he was fourteen and she, thirteen) and thereby became the brother-in-law of Henry III, king of England. He ruled France at a time of great cultural achievement, symbolized in the building of great Gothic cathedrals and the development of universities. He himself was generous to the poor, often distributing food to them in person, founded a hospital for the destitute and the sight-impaired, established three monasteries, and was impartial but often merciful in the execution of justice. He built the Sainte-Chapelle in Paris (1245–48) to house what was believed to be the relic of Christ's Crown of Thorns, a gift of the Latin emperor in Constantinople. It also served as a private chapel for himself and his family. At the same time, he had many of the faults of his contemporaries, particularly in his attitude toward Jews, Muslims, heretics, homosexuals, and even lepers. He regarded Judaism as a perfidious religion, and he countenanced the public burning of the Talmud. In 1269, he decreed that all Jews should wear a distinctive red badge on their chest and back, a precursor of the yellow star they were forced to wear during the Nazi era.

In 1248 Louis sailed to Cyprus with his army on a crusade to the Holy Land. After a victory at Damietta in the Nile Delta the following year, the tide turned against him. His army was afflicted with disease and then was defeated at Marsuna (Mansourah) in 1250, where Louis himself was taken prisoner. He is said to have prayed the Divine Office daily with two chaplains. He obtained his own release and that of other prisoners in return for the surrender of Damietta and a large sum of money. He then sailed to Palestine, visited the few holy places that were still accessible in Caesarea, fortified the Christians in Syria, and returned to France in 1254 after learning of his mother's death. Another Crusade got underway in 1270, but Louis caught typhoid fever soon after landing near Tunis, and died on August 25. His body was chopped up and boiled in wine to separate the flesh from the bones. His remains were taken back to France and buried at the abbey-church of Saint-Denis [October 9] in Paris the next year. Miracles were reported en route and at his tomb. He was canonized in 1297. The next year his bones were exhumed and distributed by Philip the Fair to important people and churches. Those still enshrined in Saint-Denis were scattered at the time of the French Revolution. Louis's entrails were eventually relocated in the cathedral in Carthage, not far from where he had died. In France he was regarded as the country's patron saint and an example of royal sanctity. His feast is on the General Roman Calendar

Joseph Calasanz (1556–1648), also Calasanctius, was the founder of the Clerks Regular of Religious Schools, known today as the Order of the Pious Schools, or Piarists, or Scolopi. Born at Peralta de la Sal of a noble Aragonese family, he was ordained a priest in 1583 and was appointed vicar general of the diocese of Lerida a few years later. In 1592 he resigned his post and distributed his wealth in order to promote the education of the urban poor in Rome. He nursed the sick and dying during the plague of 1595 with his friend Camillus de Lellis [July 14], but thereafter returned to the task of educating poor children and founded a free school with three other priests in 1597. A few years later there were more than twelve hundred pupils. Other schools were opened, and his group of teachers obtained recognition as a religious congregation, with Calasanz as superior general. His commitment to the education of the poor already made him a controversial figure in some circles because of the belief that, if the poor are educated, there will be no one left to do their jobs in society. However, he suffered far more from dissension within his own congregation. One of his priests denounced him to the Holy Office, probably on the grounds of senility, and Calasanz was led through the streets like a criminal. He was spared imprisonment through the intervention of a cardinal, but was suspended from office. His accuser went unpunished until his own death in 1643, but he was succeeded by another who harbored the same ill feeling against Calasanz. In 1645 a commission of cardinals recommended Calasanz's reinstatement as general, but the dissension continued, and in 1646 Pope Innocent X in effect dissolved the congregation by making it a society of diocesan priests subject to their local bishops. Calasanz died in Rome on August 25, 1648, just short of his ninety-second birthday. His society was reconstituted as a religious congregation in 1656 and made into a religious order in 1669. He was beatified in 1748 and canonized in 1767. In 1948 he was declared patron saint of Christian schools. His feast is on the General Roman Calendar.

This is also the feast of *Genesius* (d. ca. 300), a Roman actor who was martyred and who is patron saint of actors. He is often confused with Genesius of Arles (d. ca. 303), a French martyr.

26 Elizabeth Bichier des Ages, foundress; Teresa of Jesus, foundress

Elizabeth Bichier des Ages (1773–1838) was the foundress of the Daughters of the Cross. Born Jeanne Elisabeth Marie Lucie Bichier des Ages at Le Blanc, between Poitiers and Bourges in France, she led a life of prayer and care of the poor. Father Andrew Fournet [May 13] devised a rule of life for her and suggested that she found a community of nuns to continue her work among the poor. By 1811 there were twenty-five nuns, and five years later the local bishop approved their Rule. They took the name Daughters of the Cross. Thirteen new convents were opened between 1819 and 1820, and between 1821 and 1825 fifteen houses were founded in at least a dozen dioceses. By 1830 there were sixty convents. Elizabeth's community was part of the first phase of the extraordinary expansion of French religious orders in the nineteenth century dedicated to social service. In 1836 her health began to fail, and she died on August 26. She was canonized in 1947. Her feast is not on the General Roman Calendar.

This is also the feast day of *Teresa of Jesus* (1843–97), also known as Teresa de Jesús Jornet e Ibars, foundress of the Little Sisters of the Abandoned Aged. She was canonized in 1974 and is patron saint of senior citizens.

27 Monica, widow; Poemen, abbot; Helder Câmara, bishop

Monica (332–87) was the mother of Augustine [August 28]. Most of the information about her comes from her son's *Confessions* (Book IX). Born probably at Tagaste in North Africa, she married Patricius, who lived a dissolute life marked by a violent temper, heavy drinking, and infidelity. Monica's mother-in-law lived in the same house and compounded her difficulties. But Monica's patience eventually won them over. Her husband was baptized a year before his death. Monica had three sons, including Augustine. She exercised the same patience with him as she had with her husband and mother-in-law. When she realized that he was not ready for conversion, she turned to prayer, fasting, and vigils. Augustine went to Italy in 383 with his female companion of many years and their son, stopping first in Rome and then continuing on to Milan, but without informing his mother of his time of departure.

Monica followed him to Milan, where he had settled, and she was befriended and influenced by its bishop, Ambrose [December 7]. Ambrose helped Augustine toward not only his conversion to Christianity, but to a deep moral conversion as well. Consequently, Augustine renounced his mother's plans for a suitable marriage to an heiress and decided instead to remain celibate, having also separated from his companion. After a period of preparation with Monica and a few chosen friends, Augustine was baptized in 387. The party then set off for Africa, but Monica died on the way, at Ostia. She was fifty-five. She is reported to have said to her son before her final illness that she had fulfilled her life's purpose in seeing him converted and baptized. Monica was buried at Ostia, and there seems to have been no early cult of her. Her relics were later taken to Arrouaise, where the Augustinian Canons kept her feast on May 4, the day before Augustine's conversion. From this house her cult spread to others in the same order. In 1430 other relics were transferred from Ostia to Rome, where they rest in the church dedicated to her son. Various associations of Christian mothers have taken Monica as their patron saint. She is also patron saint of alcoholics. Her feast is on the General Roman Calendar and is also celebrated by the Church of England.

The Greek and Russian Orthodox Churches celebrate the feast of *Poemen,* a fifth-century Egyptian abbot, on this day. On the one hand, he was often excessive in his fasting and in his craving for solitude, refusing even on one occasion to see his mother. On the other hand, he was known for his pithy sayings, such as: "Silence is no virtue when charity demands speech." He also encouraged frequent Communion. Byzantine liturgical books refer to him as the "lamp of the universe and pattern of monks." His feast is not on the General Roman Calendar.

This is also the day of death of *Helder Câmara* (1909–99), archbishop of Olinda and Recife, Brazil. He was one of the earliest proponents of liberation theology and the Church's "preferential option for the poor" and was an outspoken critic of Brazil's military dictatorship, for which he received death threats. A leading figure within the Latin American hierarchy, he insisted that private charity toward the poor, while important in itself, fails to address the systemic causes of poverty. Câmara advocated such fundamental social changes as land redistribution and wider access to education. For that he was denounced as "the Red bishop" and "Fidel Castro in a cassock." The archbishop's famous response was: "When I fed the poor, they called me a saint. When I asked, 'Why are they poor?' they called me a Communist."

28 Augustine of Hippo, bishop and Doctor of the Church

Saint Augustine in His Study by Sandro Botticelli (1444–1510)

Augustine of Hippo (354–430) was one of the most distinguished theologians in the history of the Church and may have exercised more influence on the shape and character of Western theology, both Catholic and Protestant, than any other, including even Thomas Aquinas [January 28]. Patron saint of theologians, he was born Aurelius Augustinus at Tagaste (also Thagaste) in Numidia (present-day Algeria), North Africa, to Monica [August 27], a Christian, and Patricius, who was a pagan until just before his death in 371 or 372. One of three sons, Augustine was raised a Christian and was registered as a catechumen, but, in accordance with contemporary custom, baptism was delayed until adulthood. He took a concubine at age seventeen or eighteen, following his formal education as a rhetorician and lawyer in Carthage, and had a son of his own, Adeodatus (Lat., "given by God"), ca. 373.

At age eighteen or nineteen Augustine experienced a kind of conversion through reading Cicero's *Hortensius.* He became enthralled with wisdom, or "philosophy," particularly Plato's as interpreted by Plotinus. When he turned to Scripture, he found it insufficiently philosophical and stylistically unsatisfactory. He then joined the Manichees, a religious sect that not only rejected the Old Testament, but also renounced most of the ordinary pleasures of life associated with eating, drinking, and sexual expression. Augustine taught rhetoric for a brief period in his home town of Tagaste, but moved back to Carthage ca. 376, where he conducted his own school of rhetoric and grammar. In 383 he, his companion, and their son sailed for Rome in order to seek professional advancement. After teaching rhetoric there for a year, and with the help of Manichaean friends and the pagan prefect of Rome, he was appointed professor of rhetoric in Milan, the seat of the imperial court. His mother, Monica, had followed him to Rome (arriving there after he had already left for Milan) and then to Milan. She attempted to arrange a socially advantageous marriage for him, but Augustine refused. His companion returned to Africa, after having lived fifteen years in all with him, and Augustine took another concubine.

As he became progressively disenchanted with Manichaeism (he had had, for example, a disappointing encounter with a Manichaean bishop who was unable to answer his most fundamental questions), he came under the influence of a circle of Christian Neoplatonists in Milan, the most prominent of whom was the local bishop, Ambrose [December 7]. Ambrose's eloquent sermons captivated Augustine, first for their style and then for their theological content. Ambrose demonstrated for him that it is possible to interpret the Bible allegorically in such a way that it was consistent with the Platonic ideas of which Augustine had become so enamored. After a long interior conflict that is vividly described in his *Confessions,* he abandoned Manichaeism, changed his mind about the nature of evil (viewing it no longer, as the Manichaeans insisted, as an eternal substance coexistent with God, but as the privation or corruption of the good), and turned his attention to stories of monks and nuns in Italy and Egypt.

He was particularly affected by the *Life of Antony* by Athanasius [May 2]. He wrote a letter on the ascetical life to a woman who would become the first "abbess" of a community of women he would later found and two sermons on the subject, which included elements that would form the basis of a famous Rule. These writings would influence Western monasticism and religious life for centuries to come, even down to the present day. In 386 he retired from teaching, largely because of continued asthmatic attacks, and withdrew to a country villa at Cassiciacum, near Milan, with his mother, brother, fifteen-year-old son (d. 389), friends, and former students to take up what he expected to be a permanent communal life centered on leisurely philosophical discussion. He wrote four works of dialogues during this period as well as rebuttals of Manichaeism. One of his enduring sayings from this corpus of writings was his comment: "Do not try to understand in order to believe, but believe in order to understand" (*On the Teacher* 11.37). He was also especially influenced by the writings of St. Paul [June 29] and drew particularly upon the Letters to the Galatians and to the Romans in his own *Confessions.*

It was while walking in a garden that he claimed to have heard the words "*Tolle, lege*" (Lat., "Pick up [and] read"). He began reading Romans 13:12–14 ("Let us then throw off the works of darkness [and] put on the armor of light; let us conduct ourselves properly as in the day, not in orgies and drunkenness, not in promiscuity and licentiousness, not in rivalry and jealousy. But put on the Lord Jesus Christ, and make no provision for the desires of the flesh"), and he was filled "with a light of certainty, and all shadow of doubt disappeared" (*Confessions* 8.12.29). He returned to Milan in 387, took a catechetical course offered by Ambrose, and at age thirty-three was baptized at the Easter Vigil. The party then set off for Africa, but his mother, Monica, died en route, in Ostia. He spent a year in Rome before returning to Africa, first to Carthage and then to Tagaste, where he established on his family's estates a quasi-monastic community of educated laymen.

During a visit to the port city of Hippo (also Hippo Regius) in 391, he attended a sermon given by the aged bishop Valerius in which the bishop spoke of the need for a priest for service in the city. Augustine was recognized and acclaimed by the local Christian community and practically compelled to accept ordination. The bishop, however, allowed Augustine to continue his monastic way of life and provided him with a house and garden near the church. In 395 he became their bishop, serving at first as coadjutor with the current bishop, and then succeeding him upon his death soon thereafter. Augustine's consecration had not been without controversy, given his known Manichaean past.

He remained bishop of Hippo for the rest of his life, preaching, writing, administering the sacraments, engaging in a broad range of other pastoral activities (he was especially devoted to the care and relief of the poor), presiding over synods and councils, and adjudicating civil as well as ecclesiastical cases—all while living ascetically in community with his clergy. Much time, however, was also devoted to travel, including twenty to thirty trips to Carthage, which required nine days each way. Nevertheless, he produced a number of major works during the course of his busy episcopate. They include not only the *Confessions*, but also his sermons on the Gospels, Epistles, and Psalms, the *De Trinitate* (Lat., "On the Trinity"), and the *De Civitate Dei* (Lat., "On the City of God"), completed toward the end of his life. His writings were especially influential in the development of the doctrines of creation (written against the Manichees), grace (written against the Pelagians), and the sacraments and the Church (written against the Donatists). In his sermon on Baptism, he insisted (in paraphrase) that: "Many whom

God has, the Church does not have; and many whom the Church has, God does not have."

Only on the matters of predestination, sexual intercourse in marriage, and the relationship of Church and state was his thinking inconsistent with the subsequent teaching of the Church. (The first two were influenced by his Manichaean background.) For Augustine, the human race as a whole was a *massa damnata* (Lat., "damned mass"), from whom only a few are to be saved to manifest the mercy and glory of God. He consigned unbaptized infants to hell. The Church teaches today that God offers everyone the gift of salvation and that it is theirs to lose by the exercise of their own free will, not because of some preordainment by God. Unbaptized infants, once thought to be in limbo, a place of natural happiness outside of heaven, are now regarded as capable of enjoying the eternal presence of God in heaven. Regarding sexual intercourse, Augustine held that original sin is transmitted through it and that it is sinful in any case except for purposes of procreation. Today, however, the Church teaches that everyone is born with original sin (except for the Blessed Virgin Mary), that it has nothing to do with sexual intercourse, and that sexual intimacy is good and holy even when the possibility of procreation is not present, as in the case of infertile periods or in the case of those beyond the age of conceiving a child. Regarding Church and state, Augustine held that the state could function as an arm of the Church, imposing civil punishments on heretics and other sinners. For Augustine, it was better to suffer coercion in this life than damnation in the next. The Church has since taught that the Church and the state are two independent and autonomous entities, albeit cooperative on matters affecting the common good.

Augustine died on August 29, 430, during the fourteen-month-long siege of Hippo by the Vandals. His cult was early and widespread, and he is one of the four original Western Doctors of the Church, proclaimed in 1298, along with Ambrose, Jerome [September 30], and Gregory the Great [September 3]. The earliest surviving painting of him—a sixth-century fresco—is in the Lateran Library. There are many depictions of him by Renaissance painters, among the most famous of which are Sandro Botticelli's fresco of 1480 in the church of All Saints in Florence and van Dyck's in Antwerp (1628), showing Augustine contemplating the Trinity. His feast is on the General Roman Calendar and is also observed by the Church of England, the Episcopal Church in the USA, and the Evangelical Lutheran Church in America.

BIBLIOGRAPHY

Brown, Peter. *Augustine of Hippo: A Biography.* Berkeley: University of California Press, 1967.

Cavadini, John. "St. Augustine of Hippo." In *The HarperCollins Encyclopedia of Catholicism,* ed. Richard P. McBrien. San Francisco: HarperCollins, 1994. Pp. 113–18.

Chadwick, Henry. *Augustine.* Oxford: Oxford University Press, 1986.

Van der Meer, Frederik. *Augustine the Bishop.* London and New York: Sheed & Ward, 1961.

Wills, Garry. *Saint Augustine.* New York: Viking, 1999.

29 Beheading of John the Baptist, martyr; Blessed Mary of the Cross, foundress

John the Baptist (first century) was the prophet who prepared the way for Jesus Christ and who baptized him in the Jordan River. He is the patron saint of monks and of the city of Florence. This feast commemorates his death by beheading. There is another feast, on June 24, that celebrates his birth. This latter feast, which dates from the late fourth century, was long considered to be more solemn than the feast commemorating his death, which dates from about the fifth century.

John had condemned the Jewish ruler Herod Antipas for his marriage to Herodias, which was technically both adulterous and incestuous. She was not only his niece, but also the wife of his brother, who was still alive. At Herodias's insistence, Herod imprisoned John (Matt. 4:12; Mark 1:14; Luke 3:19–20). While John was in jail, Herod sent his own disciples to ask Jesus directly whether he was the Messiah (Matt. 11:2–6; Luke 7:18–23) or were they to look for another. It was in response to these inquiries that Jesus pointed to his own messianic activities, restoring sight to the blind, hearing to the deaf, and so forth. During a banquet, Herodias's daughter Salome danced provocatively in front of Herod, and he rashly promised to grant her any wish (Matt. 14:1–12; Mark 6:14–28; Luke 9:7–9). Herodias took revenge on John the Baptist by telling her daughter to ask for his head on a dish. Herod reluctantly acceded. John was beheaded.

The mention of John in the Canon, or Eucharistic Prayer, of the Mass is evidence of a very early cult. This feast is on the General Roman Calendar and is also celebrated by the Greek and Russian Orthodox Churches and by the Church of England. John the Baptist is one of the most often represented saints in Christian art, especially during the Renaissance and above all in Florence. A medieval mosaic in St. Mark's Cathedral, Venice, is an early version of the presentation of John's head on a dish. Benozzo Gozzoli's (1420–97) *Beheading*, in the National Gallery of Art in Washington, D.C., shows Salome as a young Florentine maiden in a flowing robe (although she almost certainly danced naked). More recent depictions include Puvis de Chavannes's (1824–98) *The Beheading of St. John the Baptist*, in the National Gallery in London, and Gustave Moreau's series of paintings: *Salome Dancing Before Herod* (1876), in the Los Angeles County Museum of Art; *Salome in the Garden* (1878), in a private collection in Paris, and especially *The Apparition* (1876), in the Fogg Art Museum, Cambridge, Massachusetts, in which John's head rises up from the platter to confront Salome.

This is also the feast day of *Mary of the Cross* (1792–1879), born Jeanne Jugan at Cancale, France, the foundress of the Little Sisters of the Poor (1839). The order is devoted to the care of the aged poor. She died on August 29, 1879, and was beatified in 1982.

30 Margaret Ward, martyr; Guérin and Amadeus, bishops; Blessed Ildefonsus Schuster, abbot; Fiacre, hermit

Margaret Ward (1558–88) is one of the few women among the known Catholic martyrs of the British Isles to have been canonized. Born in Congleton, Cheshire, she lived in London as a housekeeper. She was herself imprisoned for aiding a priest's escape from prison. For eight days she was suspended by her hands while beaten, before being brought before the court. She was offered her release if she would disclose the priest's hiding place, begged Queen Elizabeth I's pardon, and agreed to attend services at the established Church. When she refused, she was hanged at Tyburn on August 30, 1588, together with a priest and four laymen. She was beatified in 1929 and canonized in 1970 as one of the Forty Martyrs of England and Wales [October 25]. Her individual feast is not on the General Roman Calendar.

On this day the Cistercians celebrate the feast of *Guérin* (d. 1150), also known as Guarinus, and *Amadeus* (1110–59). *Guérin* was a monk of Molesmes who became bishop of Sion in Switzerland and was highly esteemed by Bernard of Clairvaux [August 20]. *Amadeus* was a Cistercian monk at Clairvaux who later became abbot of Hautecomb in Savoy and then bishop of Lausanne.

This is also the feast day of *Ildefonsus Schuster* (1880–1954), born Ludovico Alfredo Luigi Schuster. Ildefonsus was his name in religion.

He was a Benedictine monk and abbot of St. Paul's Outside the Walls in Rome before being appointed archbishop of Milan in 1929 with the rank of a cardinal. He was devoted to pastoral visitations to every parish in this, the largest diocese in Italy, with three million inhabitants and two thousand priests. He had opposed Italy's entrance into the war on the side of Germany and urged Mussolini to surrender and seek peace. He was strongly opposed to Communism, but was equally committed to social justice for the poor. He died at the archdiocesan seminary on August 30, 1954, and his last words to the seminarians were: "You want something to remember me by? All I can leave you is an invitation to holiness." He was beatified in 1996.

Finally, August 30 is the feast day of *Fiacre* (d. ca. 670), an Irish hermit who moved to France to live a solitary life there. He built a hospice for travelers and established a reputation for charity and spiritual wisdom. He is the patron saint of gardeners and of the cab drivers of Paris, whose vehicles are called "fiacres" because the first cab for hire was located near the Hotel Saint-Fiacre. His feast is celebrated on September 1 in Ireland and France.

31 Joseph of Arimathea and Nicodemus; Aidan, bishop; Raymond Nonnatus, friar

Joseph of Arimathea (first century) was a righteous, respected, and wealthy member of the Sanhedrin (or at least a member of the local council) who had become a clandestine disciple of Jesus and took responsibility for his burial, out of respect for Jewish law that burial was a duty to be performed even for enemies. Fittingly, he is the patron saint of funeral directors and pallbearers. In all four Gospels (Matt. 27:57, 59; Mark 15:43, 45; Luke 23:50–51; John 19:38), Joseph asks Pilate for Jesus' body, which he places in a new rock tomb. The tomb was in a garden near the place of crucifixion (John 19:41). Matthew [September 21] and John [December 27] refer to Joseph as a disciple. Mark [April 25] and Luke [October 18] simply say that he awaited the Kingdom of God. In any case, it took courage for Joseph to go to Pilate and ask for the body, given Jesus' status as an executed criminal (Mark 15:43). With the help of others (though no family members), Joseph prepared and laid the body of Jesus in the tomb and rolled a stone across its opening. Joseph is associated with the Holy Grail legend as the one who collected the blood of the crucified Jesus in a cup.

Nicodemus (first century) was a Pharisaic leader, presumably a prominent member of the Sanhedrin, who was at least partially sympathetic to Jesus. In the Fourth Gospel, Nicodemus is instructed by Jesus about entry into the Kingdom, through "being born of water and Spirit" (John 3:1–21), protests to the chief priests and Pharisees that Jesus must have an opportunity to respond to the accusations against him (John 7:50–51), and participates in Jesus' burial, "bringing a mixture of myrrh and aloes weighing about one hundred pounds" (John 19:39). The fourth-century *Gospel of Nicodemus* (originally called the *Acts of Pilate*) recounts Jesus' descent into hell, following his Resurrection and before his Ascension. The feasts of Joseph of Arimathea and Nicodemus are not on the General Roman Calendar. Joseph of Arimathea is commemorated by the Episcopal Church in the USA on August 1.

On this day the Church of England and the Episcopal Church in the USA celebrate the feast of *Aidan* (d. 651), Irish monk of Iona, who became the first bishop and abbot of Lindisfarne, an island near the royal residence of Bamburgh that King Oswald [August 5] had donated to the Church. After the battle of Heavenfield, many of Oswald's subjects became Christian, thanks in large part to the missionary efforts of Aidan. It is said that Oswald himself served as Aidan's interpreter until Aidan learned the English language. Aidan was known for his learning, his eloquent preaching, his kindness to the poor, and his distaste for pomp. His feast is not on the General Roman Calendar.

This is also the feast day of *Raymond Nonnatus* (1204–40), who, as a member of Peter Nolasco's [December 25] Mercedarians, ransomed Christian slaves in Algeria and then offered himself as a ransom when he ran out of money. Because of his sometimes successful efforts to convert local Muslims, he was subjected to the cruelest of tortures until Peter Nolasco himself ransomed him and insisted upon his return to Spain. Raymond was made a cardinal, but continued to live a humble life. He died on the way to Rome and was declared a saint in 1657. He became the patron saint of midwives and expectant mothers because he had been taken from his mother's womb just after her death.

SEPTEMBER

1 Giles, abbot; Simeon Stylites the Elder, hermit; Teresa Margaret Redi, nun

Giles (d. ca. 710), also Aegidius, was a popular saint in the Middle Ages whose monastery, Saint-Gilles, near Arles in Provence, became an important pilgrimage center on the route to both Compostela in Spain and the Holy Land. Little else is known about him. From Provence his cult spread rapidly to other regions of Europe, partly through the Crusaders. He is patron saint of the disabled, lepers, and nursing mothers, based in part on the tenth-century legend that he gave shelter to a female deer that had once nursed him and that had later been wounded and crippled by the king during a hunt. It is said that when the king searched for the hind, he found only Giles with the arrow in him, not the deer. The king continued to visit him and eventually gave him land for a monastery, provided that Giles was its first abbot. At least some of Giles's popularity was rooted in the medieval belief that he could obtain pardon for sins without the need to confess them directly to a priest.

In England 162 ancient churches were dedicated to him and at least 24 hospitals. His churches were often found at road junctions so that travelers could visit while their horses were being shod by blacksmiths, of whom he is also a patron saint. In the late Middles Ages Giles was included in Germany as one of the Fourteen Holy Helpers (see Glossary)—the only nonmartyr in the group. At least fifteen locations in France are named after him, as is one of the quarters in the city of Brussels, Belgium. His feast was widely celebrated in England and throughout Europe and is still celebrated today by the Church of England, but it is not on the General Roman Calendar. He is also patron saint of the poor and the disabled.

September 1 is the beginning of the liturgical year for the Greek and Russian Orthodox Churches. Both celebrate on this day the feast of *Simeon Stylites the Elder* (390–459) and of his mother, *Martha*. Simeon, the son of a shepherd on the Syrian border of Cilicia, was the first and most famous of the hermits who lived in the desert atop stone pillars. In his lifetime he was the object of veneration and pilgrimage to his pillar. His early years as a monk were marked by such rigorous penances that he was actually dismissed from one monastery for his excesses. At his next monastery, he refused all food and drink during Lent and lay unconscious by Easter. He is said to have been revived by the Eucharist and a few lettuce leaves. He then moved to the top of a mountain, where he chained himself to a rock. He took off the chain when challenged by a representative of the patriarch of Antioch, who said that he should be able to remain in place without artificial support.

Because his solitude and meditation were continually interrupted by visitors, Simeon set himself on a series of pillars, where he spent the rest of his life. He lived on the first pillar, which was 9 feet high and 6 feet wide, for four years. He lived on the second, which was 18 feet high, for three years. He lived on the third, which was 33 feet high, for ten years. His fourth and final pillar, built by the people, was 60 feet high. He lived on it for the last twenty years of his life. During Lent his penances were particularly austere. His visitors included pagans and Christians alike, and even emperors, and many corresponded with him. Simeon's preaching, given twice daily, was practical, unlike his own peculiar lifestyle, and was marked by a concern for justice, charity, and prayer. He was also a strong defender of the teachings of the Council of Chalcedon (451) on the humanity and divinity of Christ. Simeon's life and witness were in striking contrast to the age of excessive licentiousness and luxury. After thirty-seven years living atop pillars, he died on September 1, 459, and his body was taken for burial to Antioch, accompanied by the bishops of the province and many of the faithful. The stylite tradition was continued by Simeon the Younger (ca. 517–92) [May 24]. Simeon the Elder's feast is not on the General Roman Calendar.

On this day the Carmelites commemorate *Teresa Margaret Redi* (1747–70), an Italian Discalced Carmelite who joined the order in Florence in 1765 and died at age twenty-three after a life of prayer and rigorous penance. She was canonized in 1934.

2 Mamas, martyr; John the Faster, patriarch; Martyrs of Papua New Guinea

The Greek and Russian Orthodox Churches celebrate the feast of *Mamas* (d. ca. 275) and *John the Faster* (d. 595) on this day. *Mamas* was a shepherd at Caesarea in Cappadocia noted for the depth of his faith, for which he was executed. The *Roman Martyrology* indicates that he was martyred in old age, during the reign of the emperor Aurelian, but an Eastern tradition says that he was stoned to death while still a boy. Both Basil [January 2] and Gregory Nazianzen [January 2] mention him in their writings.

John the Faster was the patriarch of Constantinople (John IV) from 582. He was renowned for his ascetical lifestyle and for his lack of personal ambition. Nevertheless, he had great influence at court and was jealous of the claims of the patriarchate of Constantinople, insisting that it was second in honor after Rome. At a synod in 588, however, he assumed the title "Ecumenical Patriarch," which had been applied to his predecessors by the emperor Justinian. Pope Pelagius II refused to endorse the acts of the synod because of his conviction that the title infringed upon papal primacy. His successor, Gregory the Great [September 3], insisted that there is no universal patriarch in the Church, including even the pope, and that his own primatial claim as Bishop of Rome required humility. He referred to himself, in fact, as the "servant of the servants of God." However, John the Faster ignored the protests and passed on the title to his successors. Neither his feast nor that of Mamas is on the General Roman Calendar.

The Church of England and the Episcopal Church in the USA commemorate the *Martyrs of Papua New Guinea* (d. 1942) on this day. During World War II eight missionaries and two Papuans were betrayed by non-Christians to the Japanese invaders and were executed. This feast, which is also celebrated in many dioceses of the (Anglican) Church of Australia, honors those of various Christian traditions who risked their lives in the care of the wounded and in the service of the native population.

3 Gregory the Great, pope and Doctor of the Church

Gregory the Great (ca. 540–604; pope 590–604), only the second pope in all of church history to be called "the Great" (Leo I [440–61] was the first), was the first pope to have been a monk and was one of the papacy's most influential writers. His *Pastoral Care,* which defined the episcopal ministry as one of shepherding souls, became the textbook for medieval bishops. The son of a Roman senator, he entered the service of the state as a young man and became prefect of Rome, but in 573 sold his extensive properties, founded six monasteries in Sicily and a seventh in Rome, and distributed much of

Detail from *Pope Gregory I*

his wealth to the poor. The next year he entered his own monastery on the Celian Hill as a monk and was distinguished for his austere lifestyle. Although only a junior deacon at the time of Pope Pelagius II's death in 590, he was unanimously elected to the papacy. However, Gregory immediately wrote to the emperor, asking him to withhold his consent from the election, which he had neither sought nor wanted. In the meantime, Gregory engaged in intense pastoral work among the plague-stricken inhabitants of Rome. After the imperial mandate arrived, however, he accepted consecration as Bishop of Rome under protest.

His early letters disclose his unhappiness over having been forced to leave the contemplative life to assume the burdensome responsibilities of the papacy. Indeed, those responsibilities were far heavier than usual because of the general breakdown of civil order at the time. Gregory found himself drawn as deeply into temporal and political affairs as into spiritual and ecclesiastical concerns. He immediately organized the distribution of food to the starving, and, in order to expand the reservoir of resources, he also reorganized the papal territories in Italy, Sicily, Dalmatia, Gaul, and North Africa. He admonished each rector of the papal estates "to care for the poor" and "to promote not so much the worldly interests of the Church, but the relief of the needy in their distress." He insisted that he was not dispensing his own property, but property that belonged by right to the poor, given originally by St. Peter [June 29], who continued to care for his flock through Gregory.

When the imperial exarch (viceroy) in Ravenna proved incapable of doing anything about the Lombard threat, the pope took the lead and fashioned a truce with the duke of Spoleto. When the exarch broke the truce and the Lombards moved against Rome, Gregory saved the city by bribing the Lombard king and promising yearly tributes. As a result of all these efforts, Gregory became virtually the civil as well as the spiritual ruler of Rome. He negotiated treaties, paid the troops, and appointed generals and governors. At the same time, he carefully attended to the need for reform in the government of the Church. He imposed a detailed code, for example, for the election and conduct of bishops in Italy and enforced clerical celibacy. He also secured better relationships with the churches of Spain and Gaul (modern-day France). When he discovered that the Anglo-Saxon invaders had not been evangelized by the native clergy of Britain, he dispatched Augustine (later "of Canterbury") [May 27], with forty other monks, to England in 596, and later conferred the pallium (the woolen vestment worn around the neck as a symbol of pastoral authority) on Augustine as archbishop of the English.

His relations with the East were complicated by the presence of the emperor, to whom the pope himself was subject. Gregory frequently had to defer to the emperor even in matters of ecclesiastical governance. But the pope continued to insist on papal primacy and on the Roman see's role as a court of appeals even for the East. The conflict with the patriarch's use of the title "ecumenical patriarch" continued throughout Gregory's pontificate. Gregory insisted that there is no universal patriarch in the Church (including the pope!) and that his own primatial claim required humility. Indeed, he referred to himself constantly as the "servant of the servants of God."

Given his own monastic background, Gregory was a vigorous promoter of monasticism and of the liturgy, particularly of liturgical music. Indeed, his name was so closely identified with plainsong that it came to be known as Gregorian chant. Many of the prayers recited in the Eucharist are said to be attributable to Gregory, for example, the Christmas Preface and the Prefaces of Easter and the Ascension. He is also credited with the placement of the Our Father in the Mass. His support of monasticism and of monks, however, created divisions within the ranks of the Roman clergy that were to last for many years and affect several subsequent papal elections, with the electors divided between pro-Gregorian and anti-Gregorian forces, that is, between promonastic clergy and prodiocesan clergy.

His writings were more practical than theoretical and more derivative than original. But he was such an effective synthesizer, especially of the work of Augustine of Hippo [August 28], that he came to be included, in 1298, with Ambrose [December 7], Augustine, and Jerome [September 30] among the four original Western Doctors of the Church. Even in his own lifetime his *Pastoral Care* was translated into Greek and Anglo-Saxon. He set out therein a vision of pastoral care that is adapted to the needs of the people and rooted in personal example and preaching, with a fine balance between the contemplative and active aspects of all ministry. In four books he treated the type of person and motives necessary for pastoral ministry, the virtues required in a pastor, the manner of preaching to many different types of people, and the need for pastors to examine their own consciences. The *Dialogues* describe the miracles and deeds of Italian saints, especially Benedict of Nursia [July 11]. One of his goals was to encourage people to bear the trials of earthly life as preparation for the eternal life to come. His *Forty Homilies on the Gospels* are examples of his popular preaching, blending storytelling with doctrine and biblical texts, and the *Homilies on Ezekiel* are examples of more learned discourse addressed to clerics and monks. His *Moralia,* a mystical and allegorical exposition of the book of Job, was an influential spiritual text centuries later. Thomas Aquinas [January 28], for example, cited him 374 times in the second part of the *Summa Theologiae.*

Gregory's own spirituality was marked by a vivid sense of the imminent end of the world, intensified perhaps by the ill health that hindered him throughout his pontificate. He was so racked with gout that, by the time of his death, he could no longer walk. Unfortunately, Rome, under yet another siege, was once again in the grip of famine. In their desperation, the Romans turned against the pope who had done so much for them. He died on March 12, 604, and was buried in St. Peter's Basilica with the epitaph "consul of God." His feast is on the General Roman Calendar and is also observed by the Church of England. He is a patron saint of England, musicians, singers, popes, teachers, and victims of plague.

BIBLIOGRAPHY

Cavadini, John C., ed. *Gregory the Great: A Symposium.* Notre Dame, IN: University of Notre Dame Press, 1995.

Markus, Robert A. *Gregory the Great and His World.* Cambridge: Cambridge University Press, 1997.

4 Rose of Viterbo, virgin; Bablyas, bishop; Albert Schweitzer, humanitarian

Rose of Viterbo (1234–52) had a short and spiritually undistinguished life when viewed in the light of current theological and ascetical criteria. Born of poor parents in Viterbo, Italy, she is said to have had a vision of the Blessed Virgin Mary at the age of eight and thereafter began preaching in the streets in support of the pope and on the side of the Guelfs against the occupying Ghibellines. She constantly denounced the emperor Frederick II, whose allies sought her death. She fled to Soriano and in 1250 predicted the emperor's death, which occurred a few days later. She was refused admittance to the convent of St. Mary of the Roses in Viterbo because she lacked a dowry, and when she moved to a house nearby, the nuns had the house closed down. Rose returned to her parents' home in Viterbo and died there on

March 6, 1252, at age seventeen. She was canonized in 1457. Her feast is not on the General Roman Calendar, but is celebrated on this day by the Franciscans.

The Greek and Russian Orthodox Churches celebrate the feast of *Bablyas* (d. ca. 250), the bishop of Antioch and a martyr (whether by execution or through ill-treatment in prison) under the emperor Decius. He is the first martyr whose remains are recorded as having been transferred from their original place of burial to another, in this case from Antioch to its suburb Daphne, probably to counteract the influence of the local pagan shrine to Apollo. The Greek and Russian calendars also commemorate the prophet *Moses* on this day.

The Evangelical Lutheran Church in America commemorates *Albert Schweitzer* (1875–1965), renowned theologian, biblical scholar, physician, and missionary to Africa. He won the Nobel Peace Prize in 1952 for his work on behalf of the "brotherhood of nations." Many regard him as the twentieth century's greatest humanitarian; others propose Mother Teresa of Calcutta [September 5].

Albert Schweitzer, medical missionary

5 Bertinus, abbot; Blessed Mother Teresa of Calcutta, foundress

Bertinus (d. ca. 698) was a monk of the abbey of Luxeuil, founded by the Irish missionary Columban [November 23]. Bertinus was sent to assist the new bishop of Thérouanne, where a people known as the Morini lived, who posed great obstacles to the mission. The Morini had been evangelized a century earlier, but had since lost their faith and become exceedingly belligerent toward the Church. In spite of the difficulties, Bertinus and his companions persevered in their work of evangelization and began to make progress. A new monastery was built along the river and it soon proved inadequate for the number of those who sought entrance. A second monastery was built on a donated plot of swamp land, and Bertinus became its abbot after the first abbot was appointed a bishop. The monastery was initially dedicated to St. Peter [June 29], but was later renamed in honor of Bertinus himself, as Saint-Bertin. He and his monks spent much of their time and energy draining the swamp and passed on their techniques to the Morini. In 663 he collaborated in the building of a church dedicated to Our Lady, which eventually became the cathedral of the diocese of Saint-Omer. Bertinus is known to have lived to a great age, and by 745, not long after his death, he was already regarded by many as a saint. His feast is not on the General Roman Calendar.

On this day the Greek and Russian Orthodox Churches celebrate the feast of *Zechariah* and *Elizabeth* [November 5], parents of John the Baptist [June 24; August 29].

Mother Teresa

This is also the day of death of *Mother Teresa of Calcutta* (1910–97), one of the twentieth century's most highly respected and venerated figures. In the early Church, she would have been popularly proclaimed a saint upon her death. Born in Albania, she was the foundress of the Missionaries of Charity, a congregation that ministers to the poorest of the poor and to those nearest to death. She once said: "The biggest disease today is not leprosy or tuberculosis, but rather the feeling of being unwanted, uncared for and deserted by everybody. The greatest evil is the lack of love and charity, the terrible indifference toward one's neighbor who lives at the roadside, assaulted by exploitation, corruption, poverty and disease." She won the Nobel Peace Prize in 1979 as well as prestigious awards from the governments of India and the United States for her extraordinary humanitarian work around the world. She was beatified on October 19, 2003.

6 Blessed Bertrand de Garrigues, friar

Bertrand de Garrigues (d. ca. 1230) was one of the original members of the Order of Preachers and a close associate of its founder, Dominic [August 8]. Born in Garrigues sometime in the second half of the twelfth century, he joined the Cistercian mission against the heretical Cathari, or Albigensians, whose influence continued to spread, especially throughout southern France. In 1208 Pope Innocent III gave approval for a Crusade against the heretics, but unfortunately it spawned more violence and bloodshed than conversions. Through prayer and preaching, Dominic tried to limit the damage being done by the Crusade and to bring about a reconciliation with the Albigensians. Bertrand was impressed with Dominic's approach and began working with him. By 1215 they were joined by five other preachers, and by the following year their number had increased to sixteen. The group met at Prouille, where Dominic had already founded a community of nuns, to lay the foundations for the Order of Preachers. They lived for a year in community in Toulouse, and then Dominic dispersed the friars into different parts of France.

Bertrand and six others were sent to Paris, where they founded a house near the university. Soon thereafter, Dominic called Bertrand to join him in Rome, and from there he founded a house in Bologna. He also accompanied Dominic on the founder's only visit to Paris. At the second general chapter of the order in 1221, the year of Dominic's death, Bertrand was appointed prior provincial in Provence, and for the remaining nine years of his life he preached throughout the south of France, founding the priory of Marseilles and generally expanding the work of the order. He died ca. 1230 at the abbey of Bouchet, near Orange. His cult began there, but declined along with the abbey itself during the Avignon papacy (1309–77). His cult was approved by the bishop of Valence in 1870 and he was beatified in 1881. His feast is not on the General Roman Calendar, but it is celebrated by the Dominicans on this day.

7 Sozon, martyr; Regina, martyr; Mark Körösi, Stephen Pongrácz, and Melchior Grodecz, martyrs

Sozon (date unknown) was a shepherd, perhaps in Cilicia, who was executed for destroying a golden idol with his staff and for refusing to worship the pagan god of the place. His birth name was Pharisius, or Tarasius, but he took the name Sozon at baptism. According to legend, Sozon had a vision of Christ while asleep under a tree in which he was told to leave his sheep and follow the Lord to death. He went to the nearby town of Pompeiopolis during a pagan festival, walked into the temple, and shattered the golden idol with his shepherd's crook. He gave the golden fragments to the poor. Sozon later gave himself up when he learned that other Christians were being punished for his deed. After refusing to worship a false god and to play a tune on his pipe for the magistrate (Sozon said he would only make music for the one, true God), he was sentenced to be burned. His feast is on the Greek and Russian Orthodox calendars on this day.

This is also the feast day of *Regina* (date unknown), whose life is similarly shrouded in legend. Her cult began in the early seventh century and by about the year 750 a cathedral had been built in her honor and to house her relics in Alise-Sainte-Reine in Burgundy. The *Roman Martyrology* indicates only that she died for the faith in the region of Autun (France). She is said to have been imprisoned, tortured, and beheaded for having refused marriage to the local prefect. Her legend says that many spectators were converted by the sight of a shining dove hovering over her as she died.

Finally, the Jesuit liturgical calendar commemorates three priests martyred in Košice (then in northern Hungary) in 1619: *Mark Körösi, Stephen Pongrácz,* and *Melchior Grodecz* (d. 1619), the first a diocesan priest and the other two, Jesuits. The three priests were invited by the Catholic king's deputy in Košice to minister to the beleaguered Catholics in the city, then a stronghold of Hungarian Calvinists. A Calvinist prince in Transylvania, in an attempt to expand his territories at the expense of the king, sent a force to occupy Košice in September 1619. The three priests were arrested, imprisoned, and subjected to the most brutal forms of torture. Mark and Melchior were eventually beheaded on September 7, but Stephen lived another twenty-four hours in agony, lying in a foul-smelling ditch along with the bodies of his two companions. The Calvinist leaders refused to allow their bodies to be buried for six months, at which time a devout countess was given permission to do so. They were beatified in 1905 and canonized in 1995.

8 Birth of Mary; Blessed Antoine Frédéric Ozanam, founder

Nothing is known of the circumstances of the birth of the *Blessed Virgin Mary*. Her parents, traditionally known as Joachim and Anne [July 26], are not mentioned in the Bible. The belief that they were Mary's father and mother is based on the *Gospel of James* (also known as the *Protevangelium of James*), an unreliable, second-century apocryphal document that was popular in the Middle Ages when devotion to Our Lady became more widespread. The account of Mary's birth is followed by that of her presentation in the Temple. In the remainder of the apocryphal Gospel, the parents no longer appear. An ancient tradition in the West identifies Nazareth as her birthplace, but another favors Jerusalem, even specifying the neighborhood of the pool of Bethsaida, where a crypt under the church of St. Anne is venerated as the actual location. Indeed, a small oratory existed there from the early third century and perhaps even from the end of the second. A basilica dedicated to Mary was built over this oratory in the fifth century, possibly by the empress Eudoxia (d. 460). The basilica was destroyed by the Persians in the seventh century, but was quickly rebuilt. In its present form, the church dates from the time of the Crusades, when the name was changed from St. Mary's to St. Anne's.

This feast originated in the East and was probably modeled on that of the Birth of John the Baptist [June 24], which was known at least from the beginning of the sixth century. In some parts of the West, the feast of the Birth of Mary was observed before the middle of the seventh century, and it finally reached Rome during the pontificate of Sergius I (687–701), who ordered that four feasts of Our Lady—her Birth, the Annunciation [March 25], the Purification, or Presentation, in the Temple [November 21], and the Assumption [August 15]—should be celebrated in Rome and marked by processions. September 8 may have been chosen for this particular feast because it is exactly nine months after the feast of Mary's Immaculate Conception [December 8]. The feast of the Birth of Mary is on the General Roman Calendar and is also celebrated by the Greek and Russian Orthodox Churches and the Church of England.

This is also the feast day of *Antoine Frédéric Ozanam* (1813–53), founder of the Society of St. Vincent de Paul [September 27]. A French intellectual leader who distinguished himself as a literary scholar, a professor of rhetoric, and a defender of doctrine, he founded the Society of St. Vincent de Paul in 1833 as a religious association of laymen dedicated to the service of the poor. Originally created in reaction to the poverty that gripped Paris in the early stages of the industrial revolution, the organization spread to more than a hundred other countries, where it is continues to operate used clothing and furniture stores throughout the United States. When he beatified Ozanam in 1997 in Notre-Dame Cathedral in Paris, Pope John Paul II proposed him as a model for all laypeople in the Church. Today the Society has nearly a million members in more than 130 countries. Ozanam's feast is not on the General Roman Calendar.

9 Peter Claver, priest; Constance and companions, martyrs

Peter Claver (1580–1654) was a Spanish Jesuit priest whose ministry to African slaves brought forcibly to the New World (modern-day Colombia in South America) earned him the title "the saint of the slaves." He is the patron saint of Colombia and of missionary endeavors among people of color. Born into a working-class family at Verdú in Catalonia, Spain, he was educated at the university in Barcelona and became a Jesuit in 1602. Under the influence of Alphonsus Rodríguez [October 31], a porter at the Jesuit college on Majorca, Peter was inspired to serve as a missionary in the New World. He was sent to Cartagena, Colombia, in 1610 and was ordained a priest six years later. At the time, Cartagena was major center for the African slave trade. Alongside another Jesuit missionary, Alfonso de Sandoval, who had been involved in the apostolate to the slaves for forty years and had written two important books on the subject, Peter devoted his energies to the spiritual and physical care of the slaves, bringing them food, medicine, and other necessities. He also used interpreters and pictures to educate the slaves about Christianity and to prepare them for baptism. It is said that he baptized more than three hundred thousand by 1615.

When he was not engaged directly in his ministry to the slaves, Peter Claver counseled and brought the sacraments to prisoners, prepared criminals for death, regularly visited the city's hospitals, and conducted annual missions for traders and seamen. At seventy years of age, he took ill while preaching to Africans along the coast and returned to Cartagena, where he succumbed to a virulent plague that almost killed him. For the last four years of his life he was in constant pain and suffered such a severe tremor that he could no longer celebrate Mass. Although he had devoted most of his life to the care of others, his own care was largely in the hands of a surly young man who generally neglected him. Soon after welcoming a newly arrived missionary from Spain who had a royal commission to work among the slaves, Peter lapsed into a coma and died two days later, on September 8, 1654. People flocked to his cell before his death to kiss his hand and take whatever they could as a relic. He was given a large civic funeral, and another by Africans and Indians. His reputation spread after his death, and he was canonized along with his friend Alphonsus Rodríguez in 1888. At the same time, Pope Leo XIII named him patron saint of all missionary activities among Negroes. His cult has been particularly strong in the United States and Latin America. His feast is not on the General Roman Calendar, but is on the Proper Calendar for the Dioceses of the U.S.A.

The Greek and Russian Orthodox Churches celebrate the feast of *Joachim* and *Anne* [July 26] on this day, and the Episcopal Church in the USA commemorates the Episcopal nun *Constance and her companions,* the so-called Martyrs of Memphis, who gave their lives in the service of the sick during a virulent epidemic in the city of Memphis, Tennessee, in 1878.

10 Nicholas of Tolentino, friar

Nicholas of Tolentino (1245–1305) was an Augustinian friar who is the patron saint of mariners. Born in the March of Ancona, Italy, he joined the Augustinian friars just before his eighteenth birthday. Even prior to his ordination to the priesthood in 1269, he had earned a reputation as a healer. After serving in various friaries, he finally settled at Tolentino, a town sharply divided between the propapal Guelfs and the proimperial Ghibellines. Nicholas was soon recognized as an eloquent preacher, gentle confessor, and devoted minister to the sick, the dying, the poor, and prostitutes. Among the many miracle stories associated with him, one is related to the custom of blessing and distributing bread on Augustine's feast day [August 28]. In his later years, weakened by chronic illness, he is said to have had a vision of the Blessed Virgin, who told him that he would recover if he asked for a small piece of bread, dipped it in water, and ate it. After that, he followed the same prescription for the sick he visited.

His final illness lasted for nearly a year. Almost immediately after his death on September 10, 1305, a commission was established to gather evidence to support his canonization. The tribunal investigating his cause accepted as authentic thirty of his reported miracles, all of which were performed to relieve some manifestation of human distress. His canonization was delayed, however, until 1446 because of the transfer of the papacy from Rome to Avignon in 1309 (and until 1377) and then the onset of the Great Western Schism (1378–1417), in which there were two, and sometimes three, simultaneous claimants to the Chair of Peter. From the sixteenth century Nicholas of Tolentino's cult spread through Europe, and there are five paintings of him from that period in the National Gallery in London alone. He is also the patron saint of babies, mothers, animals, and the souls in purgatory. His feast is not on the General Roman Calendar.

11 Protus and Hyacinth, martyrs

Protus and *Hyacinth* were Roman martyrs of unknown date, who are mentioned in the fourth-century list of martyrs, the *Depositio*

Martyrum, in the early sacramentaries, including the *Gelasian Sacramentary*, and in the Naples calendar of stone. Pope Damasus I (366–84) [December 11] thought they were brothers, perhaps because they were buried close to one another. The *Martyrology of Jerome* [September 30] refers to them as "teachers of the Christian Law." One tradition identifies them as eunuchs who were slaves of Eugenia, Christian daughter of the prefect of Egypt. They were said to have accompanied her when she fled from her father and were beheaded for their faith along with Basilla, a Roman woman whom they had converted. Another tradition has them as servants of Basilla herself. In any case, Hyacinth's tomb was discovered in 1845 in the cemetery of Basilla on the Old Salarian Way, with his name and date of burial (September 11). Inside the tomb there were charred bones, which indicated death by fire. Nearby was another inscription bearing the name of Protus M(artyr), but this tomb was empty, probably because the relics had been removed to another location in Rome by Pope Leo IV (847–55). Protus's remains are now in the church of San Giovanni dei Fiorentini, while those of Hyacinth are also in Rome, at the Pontifical Urban University (It. *Pontificia Università Urbaniana*), known as the Urbanianum, after its founder, Pope Urban VIII (1623–44). The cult of Protus and Hyacinth was early and widespread. Their feast is mentioned in the oldest English martyrologies and liturgical calendars. However, it is not on the General Roman Calendar. They appear full length in the mosaics in the basilica of Sant'Apollinare Nuovo in Ravenna and their martyrdoms are depicted in the menology (a liturgical book containing the lives of saints, arranged by months) of St. Basil [January 2] in the Vatican Library.

12 Ailbe, bishop; Stephen Biko, freedom fighter

Ailbe (d. ca. 526), or Ailbhe, is the patron saint of the diocese of Imlech (Emly) in County Tipperary, Ireland. Unfortunately, much of the material about his life is unreliable. What does seem certain is that he preached, mainly in southern Ireland, with such power and authority that many were not only converted to Christianity, but inspired by his example of Christian living as well. He is also thought to have written a monastic Rule and founded the diocese of Imlech. According to his legend, he persuaded Oengus (Angus), king of Munster, to hand over the Aran Islands (County Galway) to the king's brother-in-law, Enda (d. ca. 530), who built the monastery of Killeaney there, from which ten other monastic foundations on the islands developed. Indeed, Enda is considered the founder of monasticism in Ireland along with Finian of Clonard. There seems little or no basis to the belief that Ailbe preached in Ireland before Patrick [March 17] did. His feast is not on the General Roman Calendar.

This is also the day of death of *Stephen Biko* (1946–77), a leader in the fight against apartheid in South Africa, who was imprisoned and later died of injuries from beatings and maltreatment.

13 John Chrysostom, bishop and Doctor of the Church

John Chrysostom (347–407) was the most prolific of the Fathers of the Church and is the patron saint of preachers. His surname "Chrysostom" (Gk., "golden mouth") was given him in the sixth century and has largely supplanted his baptismal name. He is one of the four great Greek Doctors of Church, named in 1568: Athanasius [May 2], Basil the Great [January 2], and Gregory Nazianzen [January 2] are the other three. Born in Antioch, he was raised by his widowed mother (his father had been an army officer), who saw to it that he was well educated in oratory and law as well as Christian doctrine and Scripture. He was baptized at age eighteen and, when his mother no longer needed him, he became a monk ca. 373 in a mountain community not far from Antioch. The experience nearly ruined his health because of his austerities and the damp conditions of the cave hermitage. He returned to Antioch in 381 and was ordained a deacon for service in the local church. In 386 he was ordained a priest and became a special assistant to the bishop in the ministry to the numerous Christian poor in the city. He acquired a reputation as a compelling preacher and as a commentator on the Letters of Paul and the Gospels of Matthew and John, emphasizing always their literal meaning and practical application. He used his gifts most famously in a series of twenty-one sermons that helped to bring peace to a troubled situation brought about by the destruction of statues of the emperor and members of his family in retaliation for the imposition of new imperial taxes.

In 397 he was appointed patriarch of Constantinople, but had to be taken secretly out of Antioch lest the people protest his departure. (One source says that he was lured out of the city on a ruse.) He was consecrated on February 26 of the following year by Theophilus, patriarch of Alexandria, who had wanted the appointment to go to his own candidate. John immediately initiated a program of reform—of the court, the clergy, and the people generally. Clergy were no longer allowed to have virgins or deaconesses living in their homes, monks were required to reside in their monasteries, and worldly widows were ordered to remarry or show the decorum proper to their state. The reforms alienated many of the clergy, but met with broad support among the laity. The upper classes, however, were not pleased by his blunt denunciations of their extravagances and luxurious living. At the same time, however, he reduced his own household expenses, gave the surplus to the poor, and provided hospitals for the sick.

The empress Eudoxia regarded his denunciations of the court as directed at herself, and Theophilus made common cause with her. When the emperor summoned Theophilus to a synod to discuss the status of some monks he had excommunicated and who had appealed to the emperor, Chrysostom objected on the grounds that Theophilus should first be heard by a synod in Chrysostom's own province. On Theophilus's arrival in Constantinople in 403, he convened and presided over his own synod, known as the Synod of the Oak (named after a suburb), consisting of thirty-six bishops, of whom twenty-nine were his suffragans. Twenty-nine charges were leveled against Chrysostom, including the charge of treason for calling the empress "Jezebel." The bishops called for his banishment. The emperor agreed, and Chrysostom was exiled to Bithynia. However, a subsequent earthquake and popular riots at Constantinople terrified the empress, and he was recalled. But his relations with the empress did not improve, especially after he denounced from the pulpit a celebration she had organized just outside the cathedral. He was again banished in 404, by order of an Arian council at Antioch, arranged by Theophilus, for resuming the pastoral duties of a see from which he had been "lawfully deposed." The emperor acceded to the council's wish because of mounting tensions in Constantinople.

Chrysostom went first to Cucusus, a remote outpost in Armenia, then to a fortress at Arabissos, from which he carried on a correspondence with many, including the pope, to win support for his cause. He was moved next to Pityus, a remote village six hundred marine miles from Constantinople across the Black Sea. But the trip had to be made overland, by foot, across six mountain ranges and numerous streams. Chrysostom was forced to walk bare-headed in sun and rain. Exhausted by hardship and fever, he died at Comana in Pontus on September 14, 407, uttering as his last words, "Glory to God for all things." In 414 he was rehabilitated by Pope Innocent I, who had refused to recognize his deposition in the first place, and his feast was celebrated from 438 on. In 448, thirty-one years after his death, his body was taken back to Constantinople and reburied in the Church of the Apostles. In 1204 the Venetians plundered the city and sent his relics to Rome. They are now in the choir chapel of St. Peter's Basilica.

John Chrysostom was recognized as a Father of the Church at the Council of Chalcedon in 451 and was proclaimed a Doctor of the Church in 1568. In the East he is considered one of the Three Holy Hierarchs, along with Basil the Great and Gregory Nazianzen. His commentaries on the Bible and his treatise on the priesthood are among his most enduring writings. His feast is on the General Roman Calendar and is also celebrated by the Church of England. The Russian and Greek Orthodox Churches celebrate his feast on November 13.

BIBLIOGRAPHY

Kelly, J. N. D. *Golden Mouth: The Story of John Chrysostom—Ascetic, Preacher, Bishop.* Ithaca, NY: Cornell University Press, 1997.

14 Triumph of the Cross

This feast, formerly known in the West as the Exaltation of the Cross (and still known by that name in the East), celebrates the finding of the True Cross of Christ under a Roman landfill by the emperor Constantine's mother, Helen [August 18], ca. 320, and the subsequent dedication of a basilica built by Constantine [May 21] on the site of the Holy Sepulcher and Calvary on September 14, 335. It is also known as "Holy Cross Day." Constantine's shrine included two principal buildings: a large basilica used for the Liturgy of the Word and a circular church, known as the "Resurrection" (its altar was placed on the site of the tomb), used for the Liturgy of the Eucharist and for the singing of the Divine Office.

The feast may have originally celebrated the recovery of the True Cross from the Persians by the emperor Heraclius in 629. The first clear record of this feast is by Pope Sergius I (687–701). In the East the feast is marked by veneration of the cross through elevation and blessings in the directions of the four compass points. In Rome a procession from the basilica of St. Mary Major to the Lateran preceded a veneration of the cross before Mass. The exalted cross, prefigured in Moses' lifting up the serpent's staff in the desert (e.g., Exod. 14:15–16; 17:8–13), is glorified on this feast as the instrument of Christ's victory over death. This feast is on the General Roman Calendar and is also celebrated by the Greek and Russian Orthodox Churches, and by the Church of England, the Episcopal Church in the USA, and the Evangelical Lutheran Church in America, for whom it is known as Holy Cross Day.

15 Our Lady of Sorrows; Catherine of Genoa, mystic

This feast celebrates the spiritual martyrdom of the *Blessed Virgin Mary*, particularly in the Passion and death of her son Jesus Christ. By the fourteenth century her sorrows were fixed at seven: the presentation of Jesus in the Temple [February 2], the flight into Egypt, Jesus' being lost in Jerusalem, the encounter with Jesus on the way to Calvary, the Crucifixion, the taking of the body down from the cross, and Jesus' burial. This feast is on the General Roman Calendar, but is not observed by any other churches.

This is also the feast day of *Catherine of Genoa* (1447–1510), an Italian mystic who underwent a spiritual conversion as a married woman in 1473. Thereafter, her difficult and unfaithful husband agreed to live sexually apart, and together they devoted their lives to serving the poor and the sick in a Genovese hospital. Catherine became matron of the hospital and proved herself an able administrator. Her husband died in 1497, after having become a Franciscan tertiary. Her spiritual life became even more intense, and she is said to have undergone various mystical and visionary experiences. Her spiritual teachings concerned the purification of the soul.

She died after a long, painful, and undiagnosed illness on September 15, 1510, and was beatified in 1737. A few years later Pope Benedict XIV added her name to the *Roman Martyrology* with the title of saint. She is patron saint of Genoa and of Italian hospitals. Her feast is not on the General Roman Calendar.

16 Cornelius, pope, and Cyprian of Carthage, bishop, martyrs; Ninian, bishop

Cornelius (d. 253; pope 251–53) was the pope who insisted that those baptized by heretics or schismatics need not be rebaptized upon entering or returning to the Catholic Church. Little is known of his early life except that he was a Roman and perhaps belonged to a patrician family. He was a member of the Roman clergy and was elected pope more than a year after the death of his predecessor Fabian [January 20]. The Roman clergy had postponed the election because of the violent persecution under the emperor Decius and because several members of the clergy, including a leading candidate for the papacy, were in prison. During the interregnum of fourteen months the Roman church was governed as it had been during the first century of its existence, that is, collegially, with the presbyter Novatian acting as spokesman.

The following spring the emperor left Rome to fight the Goths. During his absence, the persecution subsided and the election of a new Bishop of Rome was held. By this time, however, the leading candidate, a presbyter by the name of Moses [November 25], had died in prison. Novatian fully expected that he would be elected, but the clergy voted instead for Cornelius, whom Cyprian, bishop of Carthage (who shares this feast day with Cornelius), had described as an unambitious priest who had come up through the ranks. Novatian reacted bitterly to the result and had himself ordained a bishop, setting himself up as a rival (antipope) to Cornelius. What was clearly at the basis of Novatian's opposition was Cornelius's readiness to readmit to communion, albeit after suitable penance, those Christians who had lapsed during the persecution. Novatian flatly opposed reconciliation, under any conditions. Indeed, this may also have been the central issue in the papal election itself.

Novatian tried to persuade the bishops of other Christian centers to accept his own title to the Roman see, and in Rome itself a faction of rigorist clergy and laity refused to recognize Cornelius's authority. However, Cornelius's election was upheld by Cyprian, who had some influence over the African clergy in Rome, and by Dionysius (d. 264/5), bishop of Alexandria. Cyprian also supported Cornelius when, in October 251, he excommunicated Novatian and his followers at a synod in Rome attended by sixty bishops and many presbyters and deacons. The synod affirmed the pope's policy (and that of a Carthaginian synod) of readmitting, after appropriate contrition and "the medicines of repentance," those Christians who had lapsed during the Decian persecution. Cornelius sent copies of the decisions of the Roman synod and of Cyprian's letter of support to Fabius, the rigorist, pro-Novatian bishop of Antioch. The pope wanted Fabius to suspend his support for Novatian and to accept the moderate course adopted by the majority of churches.

In spite of Cyprian's support of the pope, some bad blood had developed between these two leading bishops of the early Church.

When Cornelius had sought backing for his election to the papacy against the challenge from Novatian, Cyprian took some time before finally giving that support. Over a year later, the pope received representatives of Fortunatus, who, like Novatian, was a schismatic bishop in opposition to Cyprian. Even though Cornelius rejected their advocacy on behalf of Fortunatus, Cyprian was upset that the pope had received these envoys in the first place, and he sent Cornelius a sharp rebuke. A flurry of correspondence followed between the pope and Cyprian, and also between the pope and other bishops. Cornelius made known his position on the schism and also strongly defended his moderate stance toward the lapsed.

Although it has been noted that Cornelius wrote far too harshly, even falsely, about Novatian, the letters (particularly the one to Fabius, bishop of Antioch) provide historians with detailed statistics for the Roman church at the time. It included forty-six priests, seven deacons, seven subdeacons, forty-two acolytes, fifty-two exorcists, readers, and porters, and more than fifteen hundred widows (who were also considered officers of the church). On the basis of these figures, it has been estimated that the membership of the Roman church in the mid-third century may have reached fifty thousand members.

When the new emperor, Gallus, resumed the persecutions in June 252, Cornelius was arrested and deported to Centumcellae (present-day Civitavecchia, the port of Rome). Before dying there the following June (more likely as the result of the hardships of his imprisonment than by beheading), Cornelius received a warm letter of support from Cyprian. His body was later taken back to Rome and was buried in the crypt of Lucina in the cemetery of Callistus on the Appian Way. The inscription on his tomb is the first papal epitaph written in Latin (all others had been in Greek). Both his name and that of Cyprian are included in the Eucharistic Prayer (Canon of the Mass), immediately after the names of Popes Linus, Cletus (Anacletus), Clement [November 23], and Sixtus [August 7].

Cyprian (ca. 200–58) was one of the most prominent and influential bishops of the early Church. Born Thascius Caecilianus Cyprianus in Carthage, he became an orator, rhetorician, and lawyer before his conversion to Christianity ca. 245. A few years later he was ordained a priest and in 248 was elected bishop of Carthage by the laity, clergy, and neighboring bishops. He accepted only because of the widespread support. Almost immediately he was confronted with the persecution conducted by the emperor Decius, and he fled to safety, ruling and encouraging his flock by letter. A number of Christians apostatized by sacrificing to idols or they lapsed by buying certificates that falsely stated that they had sacrificed. Cyprian reconciled those who lapsed, but only after a period of penance. The antipope Novatian held out for a more severe approach, insisting that the Church could not absolve apostates. Cyprian's more moderate position was approved by the Council of Carthage in 251.

Cyprian tangled with Cornelius's successor plus one, namely, Stephen I (254–57), over the issue of the rebaptism of heretics and schismatics. Along with most of the churches of North Africa, Syria, and Asia Minor, Cyprian held that they had to be rebaptized; Stephen insisted, along with the churches of Alexandria and Palestine, that they did not. Cyprian convened another synod in Carthage in 255, which upheld his view, but some of the North African bishops objected and sided with Rome. Cyprian thereupon convened yet another synod, consisting of seventy-one bishops, the following year. The second synod came to the same conclusion as the first. When Cyprian sent envoys to inform the pope of these decisions, the pope refused to receive them. On September 1, 256, a third council of some eighty-seven North African bishops again supported Cyprian. As tensions mounted, Dionysius, bishop of Alexandria, who agreed with Cyprian's position, nonetheless urged him to adopt a more conciliatory approach for the sake of church unity.

The situation might have deteriorated even further if Pope Stephen had not died in the midst of the controversy and had Cyprian himself not been martyred a year later under the emperor Valerian. Because he refused to sacrifice to the gods, he was exiled to a small town on the sea, sixty miles from Carthage, in 257. He was brought back to the city and put on trial twice, the second time receiving a death sentence. He was executed by the sword on September 14, 258. Although his cult was most active in North Africa, where his relics were distributed, there is evidence of it in Rome from the beginning of the fourth century. At some point, however, his name and his cult, especially in the East, became confused for a time with that of an imaginary magician known as Cyprian of Antioch. He is the patron saint of North Africa and Algeria.

Cyprian's greatest legacy are his writings, which were translated into Greek—a rarity for a Latin writer. His concerns were focused on the unity of the Church, the office of bishop, the primacy of the Bishop of Rome (his views on that topic have been the object of much dispute over the years), and the sacraments, especially Baptism, Penance, and the Eucharist. He is cited several times by the Second Vatican Council in its Dogmatic Constitution on the Church (1964).

The feast of Cornelius and Cyprian is on the General Roman Calendar. Cyprian's feast alone is celebrated by the Church of England on September 15, and by the Episcopal Church in the USA on September 13.

On this day, September 16, both churches celebrate the feast of *Ninian* (d. ca. 430), a British missionary bishop of Galloway, England, who is also regarded as the "apostle to the Picts" of northern Scotland.

17 Robert Bellarmine, bishop and Doctor of the Church; Hildegard of Bingen, abbess; Albert of Jerusalem, bishop

Robert Bellarmine (1542–1621) was the most influential ecclesiologist (a theologian who specializes in the doctrine of the Church) between the time of the Council of Trent (1545–63) and the Second Vatican Council (1962–65). Born Roberto Francesco Romolo Bellarmino at Montepulciano in Tuscany, the son of the town's chief magistrate, he entered the Society of Jesus in 1560, taught classics for several years, and was ordained a priest in 1570. Having lectured for seven years at Louvain in modern-day Belgium, where he had completed his own studies for the priesthood, he was appointed in 1576 as professor of "controversial theology" in a recently established chair at the Roman College (now the Pontifical Gregorian University), which had been founded by Ignatius of Loyola [July 31] in 1551. His lectures provided the basis for his celebrated three-volume work, *Disputations on the Controversies of the Christian Faith Against the Heretics of This Age,* which was so comprehensive that it was thought mistakenly to have been the product of a team of scholars rather than of one author. It has been pointed out that his writings and lectures were never marked by personal animosity or severity, that he seemed able always to separate an opinion from the person holding it, and that he prayed daily for his opponents. Others have noted, on the other hand, that he was involved in the trial and execution of the dissident Giordano Bruno in 1600.

Bellarmine became rector of the Roman College in 1592, provincial of Naples in 1594, and then was recalled to Rome in 1597 to serve as the pope's theologian. The following year he was appointed a cardinal, a position that carried with it certain privileges of rank, including servants and a carriage. His private life, however, remained one of simplicity and even austerity. Extremely small of stature, he lived on bread and garlic and even used the curtains of his apartment to clothe the poor. He had a special devotion to Francis of Assisi [October 4].

In 1602 he was appointed archbishop of Capua and immediately plunged into the pastoral work of the diocese. He resigned his see in 1605 after narrowly escaping election to the papacy and upon being asked by the new pope, Paul V (1605–21), to become Prefect of the Vatican Library and a member of various Roman Congregations. His moderate views on the temporal power of the papacy alienated Pope Sixtus V (1585–90) and are generally regarded as the cause for the delay in his canonization, which did not occur until 1930, although he had been declared Venerable in 1627. Bellarmine had held that the pope has only indirect power in temporal matters. He may act regarding temporal matters only when they affect the spiritual order. But not even his moderate views are accepted today. Contrary to Bellarmine's belief at the time, the state is not an arm of the Church, but is autonomous in its own sphere. Church and state are two perfect (i.e., self-sufficient) societies that should be cooperative with one another, but that cannot co-opt each other's rightful responsibilities.

In his old age Bellarmine withdrew from controversy, and his writings turned instead to devotional topics. In August 1621 he persuaded Pope Gregory XV (1621–23) to allow him to retire to the Jesuit novitiate on the Quirinal Hill. He arrived there on August 25, but was taken ill three days later. For the next three weeks a stream of visitors came to see him for one last time. He died at age seventy-nine on September 17, 1621, and was buried in the Lady Chapel of the Gesù Church. The year he was beatified (1923), his remains were transferred to the church of St. Ignatius. He was named a Doctor of the Church in 1931, a year after his canonization by Pope Pius XI. He is the patron saint of catechists. His feast is on the General Roman Calendar.

On this day the Benedictines, the Church of England, and the Episcopal Church in the USA celebrate the feast of *Hildegard of Bingen* (1098–1179), a Benedictine abbess and visionary. Born in present-day Germany, she was educated from age eight by a recluse, Blessed Jutta von Spanheim, an anchoress who lived in a small cottage attached to the abbey church founded by St. Disibo. As others joined Jutta there, a monastic community took form under the Rule of St. Benedict [July 11], with Jutta as abbess. Hildegard joined this community at age fifteen and led an uneventful life until she began to experience visions and revelations seventeen years later. Jutta died in 1136 and Hildegard succeeded her as abbess. With the approval of the archbishop of Mainz and later of Pope Eugenius III, the latter having been encouraged by Bernard of Clairvaux [August 20], she began a long process of dictating the content of her visions to establish a written record. They eventually comprised three volumes and were entitled *Scivias* (which was an abbreviation of the Latin *sci vias Domini*, "know the ways of the Lord"), with illustrations drawn by Hildegard herself.

When her community grew too large for the convent, she moved it to Rupertsberg, near Bingen, sometime between 1147 and 1152. From that base, she engaged in correspondence with rulers and other prominent people, including the pope and the emperor, sometimes reproaching them for their behavior. She also wrote poems, plays, and hymns, as well as works of medicine and natural history. In addition, she composed commentaries on the Gospels, the Athanasian Creed, the Rule of St. Benedict, and the lives of various saints. She was also a musician and an artist. She founded a daughterhouse at Eibingen, near Rüdensheim. Toward the end of her life she found herself in trouble with church authorities for having buried an excommunicated person in the convent cemetery. When the archbishop of Mainz ordered her to have the body exhumed and removed, she challenged him to come and dig it up himself. Before the bishop arrived with his retinue, Hildegard had seen to it that all traces of the burial had been erased. They left empty-handed, but the bishop subsequently placed her church under interdict, only to lift it later. Hildegard of Bingen was over eighty when she died on September 17, 1179. Attempts to have her declared a saint failed during the thirteenth and fourteenth centuries, but her name was added to the *Roman Martyrology* in the fifteenth and her cult was approved for German dioceses. She has never been formally canonized, and her feast is not on the General Roman

Saint Hildegard of Bingen

Calendar. She became a popular spiritual figure, especially for women, in the 1990s.

The Carmelites celebrate the feast of *Albert of Jerusalem* (ca. 1150–1214) on this day. He was patriarch of Jerusalem, but his see was at Akka, because Jerusalem was under Muslim control. He was invited by the prior of the hermits of Mount Carmel to codify their observances into a Rule, for which Albert is regarded as the first legislator of the Carmelite order. He met a violent death at Akka on September 14, 1214, at the hands of a Hospitaller, a member of a military order of crusading monks whom he had deposed from the office of master. Albert has been formally venerated by the Carmelites at least since 1411.

BIBLIOGRAPHY

Brodrick, James. *Robert Bellarmine, Saint and Scholar.* London: Burns and Oates, 1961.

Flanagan, Sabina. *Hildegard of Bingen 1098–1179: A Visionary Life.* New York: Routledge, 1989.

Schipperge, Heinrich. *The World of Hildegard of Bingen: Her Life, Times, and Visions.* Trans. J. Cumming. Toronto: Novalis, 1998.

18 Joseph of Cupertino, priest; John Massias, religious; Dag Hammarskjöld, statesman

Joseph of Cupertino (1603–63), a Franciscan, is known as the "flying friar" because of his reported levitations. It is not surprising that he is the patron saint of aviators. Born Giuseppe Desa of a poverty-stricken family in Cupertino near Brindisi, he was considered an intellectually dull child, acquiring the nickname "*Boccaperta*" (It., "open-mouthed," or "gaper"). He was dismissed from the Capuchin Franciscans after eight months as a lay brother for his almost complete incompetence, having neglected his assignments, dropped dishes on the floor, and failed to tend the kitchen fire. He then became a stable boy and tertiary with the Conventual Franciscans at Grotella, where his conduct was so improved that he was admitted as a novice in 1625. Although a poor student, he managed to pass his examinations for the diaconate when asked about one of the few biblical texts with which he was familiar and was approved for ordination to the priesthood in 1628 when the examination was waived.

He was reputed to have the power of healing and of flying through the air by no apparent physical force. In one instance, he is said to have lifted a 36-foot-tall altar cross into place after ten workmen had failed to do so. There were seventy instances of levitation recorded during his seventeen years at Grotella alone. He was also thought to have had ecstatic experiences during which he could not be awakened by any means. His superiors were so disturbed by his behavior that they forbade him to celebrate a public Mass, attend choir, walk in processions, or eat in the refectory for thirty-five years.

He was sent to Assisi in 1639, where he remained for thirteen years in a state that has been characterized as complete spiritual aridity. In July 1653 the Inquisition of Perugia looked into his case because of all the public attention he drew and decided, for reasons unknown, to remove him from the Conventual Franciscans and place him under the Capuchin Franciscans. For the next four years he lived almost incommunicado in two remote friaries, until he was "discovered" by some pilgrims. Finally, in 1657 he was sent back to the Conventual friary in Osimo, at the request of his own friars in Assisi. He died in Osimo on September 18, 1663, and was buried there. His cult began immediately and miracles were reported at his tomb. His cause for canonization was subjected to careful scrutiny by the "Devil's Advocate," Prosper Lambertini, who was satisfied that the eyewitness reports were reliable. When Lambertini himself became Pope Benedict XIV (1740–58), he beatified Joseph of Cupertino in 1753. His canonization followed in 1767, not for his levitations, it was insisted, but for his patience, gentleness, and humility. His feast is not on the General Roman Calendar, but is celebrated by the Franciscans.

The Dominicans celebrate the feast of *John Massias* (1585–1645), a Spaniard who became a Dominican lay brother in Peru, where he ministered to the poor and the sick. He also had a reputation for ecstatic experiences, visions, and miracles. He was canonized in 1975.

Dag Hammarskjöld, Secretary General of the United Nations, 1960

Also on this day the Evangelical Lutheran Church in America commemorates *Dag Hammarskjöld* (1905–61), who was an indefatigable peacemaker during his ten years as Secretary General of the United Nations. His book *Markings*, published after his death in a plane crash while on yet another peacekeeping mission, disclosed him to be a man with a deeply spiritual life.

19 Januarius, bishop and martyr; Theodore of Tarsus, bishop

Januarius (d. ca. 305) is best known for the annual liquefaction of his blood in Naples on three of his feast days. He is not only the patron saint of Naples, but also of blood banks. Born Gennaro in either Naples or Benevento, he was bishop of Benevento when the persecution of the emperor Diocletian was unleashed in 303. When he went to visit four imprisoned Christians in Nola, he himself was arrested. He was tortured, heavily manacled, made to walk with other prisoners in front of the governor's chariot from there to Pozzuoli, and then thrown to the wild beasts. When the animals ignored them, the prisoners were beheaded and buried near the town. Sometime in the fifth century Januarius's relics were brought to Naples, moved elsewhere for a time, and then returned to the cathedral in Naples in 1497. Since then, his blood is reported to liquefy each year on three feast days associated with him: today, December 16 (the day on which he supposedly averted a threatened eruption of Mount Vesuvius in 1631), and the Saturday before the first Sunday of May (commemorating the transfer of his relics).

The blood is kept in a special cathedral chapel. There, in a metal reliquary is a vial that is half filled with a dark, solid, opaque mass. Six times on each of the three feast days the vial is brought out and held up in front of a silver reliquary that is said to contain the martyr's head. A special group of women known as the *zie di San Gennaro* (It., "aunts of St. Januarius"), in unison with the rest of the congregation, say prayers, while the solid mass begins to liquefy, turn reddish in color, and increase in volume. Sometimes it also bubbles up. The priest announces: "The miracle has happened." Then a Te Deum is sung in thanksgiving and the relic is venerated by the people. Although the phenomenon cannot easily be dismissed, its authenticity has not been scientifically established and there are other blood relics in the Naples area (of John the Baptist [June 24, August 29], Stephen [December 26], and others) that behave in the same way but are unquestionably fakes. Januarius's feast is on the General Roman Calendar. It is celebrated by the Russian Orthodox Church on April 21.

On this day, the Church of England and the Episcopal Church in the USA celebrate the feast of *Theodore of Tarsus* (ca. 602–90), one of the greatest archbishops of Canterbury (668–90), who was appointed to the see while living in a Greek monastery in Rome and when he was already over sixty-five years old. He unified the English Church, which had been divided along Roman, Celtic, and Gallic lines, reorganized its diocesan structures, established the metropolitan authority of Canterbury, and founded an outstanding school there, famous for the breadth of its scholarship and curriculum and for educating many future English bishops. His feast is not on the General Roman Calendar.

20 Paul Chõng Hasang, Andrew Kim Taegõn, and companions, martyrs; Francis Mary of Camparosso, religious

Andrew Kim Taegõn (d. 1846) and *Paul Chõng Hasang* (d. 1839), one, the first native-born Korean priest and the other, a layman, are among 103 Korean martyrs who were canonized by Pope John Paul II in the Catholic cathedral in Seoul on May 6, 1984. (The more accurate rendition of their names is Chõng Hasang Paul and Kim Taegõn Andrew; Ha-sang and Tae-gõn may also be hyphenated.) Other lay leaders who originally established the Church in Korea after 1784 and who died for their faith before the persecutions between 1839 and 1867 are not included in the list of those who were canonized in 1984—much to the disappointment of many Korean Catholics who are proud of the lay origins of their Church.

Paul Chõng Hasang was a nobleman, whose father and brother had died for the faith at the beginning of the nineteenth century and whose mother and sisters were martyred shortly after his own martyrdom in 1839. From age twenty he devoted himself to the revitalization of the Church in Korea and made no fewer than nine trips to Beijing, China, to recruit priests. He also welcomed French missionaries into the country and then into his home, where they celebrated Mass and the sacraments or simply hid. Between May 20, 1839, and April 29, 1841, 67 of the 92 lay Catholics among the 103 martyrs died for their faith after being held for weeks and months in wretched conditions of overcrowding, filth, and torture. The usual method of martyrdom was to be tied to a cross, taken on an oxcart to the place of execution, stripped naked, and then beheaded. Their heads and bodies would be publicly exposed for three days to terrify other Christians. Then they would be buried at the site.

In January 1845 *Andrew Kim Taegõn* was sent to Macao with two other Korean youths for seminary training. He returned to Korea in 1845, reentering the country only with great difficulty by way of

Manchuria, and made contact with a few catechists. He then left again to escort two priests and a bishop into the country. The bishop ordained Andrew on August 17 in Shanghai, making him the first native-born Korean priest. He returned to Korea at the end of the month and began making arrangements for another group of French missionaries and two newly ordained Korean priests to enter the country. But Andrew was arrested the following June and was condemned to death. He spent three months in prison, during which time he wrote a letter of encouragement to his people. He was only twenty-six when he was beheaded at Saenamt'o, at the River Han near Seoul, on September 16, 1846. He was beatified in 1925, along with his father Ignatius, and was named patron saint of the Korean clergy. Not until a treaty was signed between Korea and France in 1886 did the century of persecution come to an official end. Paul's and Andrew's feast, along with that of more than one hundred other Korean martyrs, is on the General Roman Calendar.

On this day the Franciscans celebrate the feast of *Francis Mary of Camparosso* (1804–66), a Capuchin lay brother who gained a reputation in Genoa for healings and supernatural knowledge of persons and events. He died on September 17, 1866, during a cholera epidemic and was canonized in 1962 by Pope John XXIII.

21 Matthew, apostle and Evangelist

Matthew (first century) is one of the twelve apostles and the Evangelist traditionally regarded as the author of the First Gospel, whose message is that in Jesus Christ the Reign, or Kingdom, of God has drawn near and will remain with the Church until the end of time. Matthew's name occurs in all lists of the Twelve: Matthew 10:3; Mark 3:18; Luke 6:15; and Acts 1:13. Matthew and Levi (Mark 2:14; Luke 5:27–28) may be two names for the same person, in which case Matthew is the son of Alphaeus and the brother of James [May 3] (not James, the son of Zebedee [July 25]), or else two different persons confused in the traditions. In any case, both Matthew and Levi are referred to as "tax collectors." Nothing is known for certain about what Matthew did after the Resurrection. According to one tradition he preached the gospel in Judea and then went farther to the East. Some have suggested Ethiopia, Persia, Syria, Macedonia, and even Ireland as possibilities. He is venerated as a martyr, but nothing is known of his martyrdom. A Gnostic writer reported that he died a natural death, and this seems to have been taken for granted by Clement of Rome [November 23]. Earlier versions of the *Roman Martyrology* have him dying in Ethiopia, while the *Marytrology of Jerome* [September 30] says it was in Persia. Some of his relics were claimed to have been in Brittany and then Salerno, and four different churches in France have claimed to have his head. Matthew is the patron saint of the diocese and city of Salerno, as well as of tax collectors, accountants, customs officials, and money changers. For some reason, he is also patron saint of alcoholics, hospitals, and ships. He has been frequently represented in art and sculpture and is often depicted sitting at a desk writing his Gospel with an angel to guide the pen or hold the inkwell. He is also depicted with a spear or similar weapon in his hand as an allusion to his martyrdom, and his symbol as an Evangelist is that of a winged man. Matthew's feast is on the General Roman Calendar and is also celebrated on this day by the Church of England, the Episcopal Church in the USA, and the Evangelical Lutheran Church in America. In the East it is celebrated on November 16.

22 Thomas of Villanova, bishop; Phocas of Sinope, hermit; Maurice, soldier

Thomas of Villanova (1486–1555) was archbishop of Valencia and an Augustinian friar before that. Born in Fuentellana, he took his surname from the town of Villaneuva de los Infantes, where his parents were from and where Thomas himself was raised. He studied at the famous Complutensian University at Alcalá, which was founded as an instrument of intellectual renewal in the Church. He was made professor of philosophy at age twenty-six, but after four years he left the university and joined the Augustinian friars in Salamanca. He was ordained a priest in 1518, taught theology in his own convent, and served as prior in a number of houses after 1519 and for a period of some twenty-five years. He also held several regional positions, including that of vicar general. Sometime before 1534 he was appointed provincial of Castile and then was nominated to become archbishop of Granada, an appointment he successfully declined. In 1544, however, the emperor Charles V nominated him for the archbishopric of Valencia, and this time he did not refuse.

He traveled to the diocese on foot, wearing his old monastic habit and a battered hat that he had worn for years. Seeing his poverty, the cathedral canons gave him a large monetary gift to furnish his episcopal residence, but Thomas gave it away to the local hospital. He immediately undertook a visitation of all the churches in the diocese. His subsequent episcopal ministry was marked by personal austerity, devotion to the care of orphans, the sick, captives, and the poor (he was called the "Almsgiver" because of the many people who came to his door every day for a meal and a little money). He also worked energetically to reform the diocese and especially the clergy in accordance with pastoral principles of the sort that were later adopted by the Council of Trent (1545–63). For some reason, he did not attend the council itself, although he was represented by another bishop and consulted with the Castilian bishops before they left for Trent. He died of heart disease on September 8, 1555, and was buried in the Augustinian church in Valencia. His relics are now in the cathedral. Thomas of Villanova was beatified in 1618 and canonized in 1658. Universities have been named after him in the United States, Australia, and Cuba. His feast is not on the General Roman Calendar.

The Greek and Russian Orthodox Churches celebrate the feast of *Phocas of Sinope* (ca. fourth century) on this day. (Sinope was on the Black Sea.) He was a gardener and a hermit who used his produce to feed visitors, pilgrims, and the poor. According to legend, when he was accused of being a Christian, soldiers were sent to apprehend and kill him. Unaware of his true identity, they stayed the night at his guest house. When they inquired of his whereabouts, Phocas assured the soldiers that he would help them in their search in the morning. During the night, he dug his own grave and prepared for death. The soldiers carried out their mission after he persuaded them that he welcomed martyrdom as the greatest spiritual gain. He is the patron saint of gardeners and of sailors on the Black Sea and in the Eastern Mediterranean.

September 22 is also the feast day of *Maurice* (d. ca. 287), a military officer in the imperial army who, with his soldiers, refused to sacrifice to the gods or to execute innocent Christians. He may or may not have been martyred. He is patron saint of Austria, Sardinia, infantrymen, and the papal Swiss Guard.

23 Thecla of Iconium, virgin; Adomonán of Iona, abbot

Thecla of Iconium (first century), also Thekla, was, according to ancient tradition, a convert and companion of Paul [June 29], whom Paul commissioned to teach and to baptize. According to the apocryphal *Acts of Paul,* a portion of which circulated separately and widely as the *Acts of Paul and Thecla,* she established a ministry in Seleucia of

Isauria, where she taught, cared for the poor, and healed the sick. Gregory Nazianzen [January 2] called Seleucia "the city of the holy and illustrious virgin Thecla," and archaeologists found there a huge, richly decorated basilica as well as other shrines in honor of "St. Thecla." A fifth-century resident of Seleucia wrote a two-volume work entitled *The Life and Miracles of Saint Thecla.* The first half merely paraphrases the *Acts of Paul and Thecla,* but the second half contains forty-six miracles attributed to her by the local faithful, indicating the widespread veneration of her throughout Asia Minor. The fact that there is no burial tradition suggests that she may not have ever existed. Be that as it may, her name was often taken by vowed virgins in the fourth century, including Macrina [July 19], the older sister of Basil the Great [January 2] and Gregory of Nyssa [January 10]. Her name was removed from the calendar of saints in 1969. Her feast is still celebrated, but on September 24, in the Greek and Russian Orthodox Churches.

This is also the feast day of *Adomnán of Iona* (ca. 627–704), abbot of Iona from 679 and the author of a Life of Columba [June 9]. He was responsible for the Law of Innocents, known as Adomnán's Law, which ruled that women should not go into battle and that they and their children should be treated as noncombatants, that is, not subject to physical harm or capture. The same was to apply to boys and clerics. His feast is not on the General Roman Calendar.

Likewise, this is the feast day of *Padre Pio* (1887–1968), an Italian Capuchin friar known for his bearing of the wounds of Christ (the stigmata) on his body from 1918 until the day after his death on September 23, 1968. Born Francesco Forgione in a village near Naples (Pio, or Pius, was his religious name), he was a renowned confessor, said to have heard as many as twenty-five thousand confessions a year. In 1956 he established a hospital and an international research center in the field of biomedicine. He was beatified in 1999 in the presence of some 250,000 people, and was canonized in June 2002.

24 Gerard Sagredo, martyr

Gerard Sagredo (d. 1046) is venerated as Venice's first martyr. He is also regarded as the "apostle of Hungary," where he is known as Collert. He had been a Benedictine monk and later prior at San Giorgio Maggiore in Venice before setting out on a pilgrimage to Jerusalem. He took a circuitous route, traveling through Hungary. King Stephen [August 16] invited him to become his son's tutor. Not long afterward, the diocese of Csanad was established (one of many founded by the king), and Gerard was named its first bishop in 1035. He devoted himself to the combating of paganism and to the reclaiming of imperfectly converted Christians, in much the same fashion as Boniface [June 5] and Willibrord [November 7] had done in Frisia. When Stephen died in 1038, a fierce conflict broke out among competing claimants to the throne and there was also a revolt against Christianity. At Buda Gerard was attacked by one of the factions, stoned, and driven through with a lance. His body was thrown off the Blocksburg cliff into the Danube. In 1083 his relics were enshrined with Stephen's, but in 1333 Venice obtained a share of them and placed them on the island of Murano. His feast is not on the General Roman Calendar.

25 Sergius of Radonezh, abbot; Finnbarr, abbot; Ceolfrith, abbot

Sergius of Radonezh (ca. 1315–92) is regarded as the greatest of the Russian saints and the first Russian mystic, venerated by Orthodox and Catholics alike. Considered the patron saint of Russia, he has been called "the Russian Orthodox Francis of Assisi" [October 4]. He was also the founder of some forty monasteries, and a mediator and peacemaker in political disputes, preventing four civil wars between princes. Born of noble parents at Rostov and baptized as Bartholomew, as a teenager he fled with his family to Radonezh, a small village about fifty miles northeast of Moscow. After his parents' death, he withdrew in 1335 with his widowed brother Istvan (Stephen), who was already a monk, to the forests of Radonezh and took up a life of monastic solitude. In 1336 he built a chapel in honor of the Trinity and soon attracted disciples who lived a "lavriot," or semi-eremetical, monastic life. He became their abbot and was ordained a priest. His name was changed to Sergius.

In 1354 he and his disciples adopted a cenobitic (communal) Rule, that of Theodore the Studite [November 11], and the great monastery that developed, now known as the Trinity–St. Sergius Lavra, became a center of pilgrimage and the spiritual heart of Russian Orthodoxy. It reestablished monastic community life, which had disappeared from Russia through the Tartar invasions of the thirteenth century. Sergius slipped away from the monastery for four years when his brother Istvan's return divided the community. As the monastery declined, the metropolitan of Moscow sent a message to Sergius urging him to return. He did so, to the great joy of the monks. In 1378 he refused election to the patriarchate of Moscow. He became a national hero when he gave his blessing to Prince Dimitri to defeat the Tartars at the Battle of Kulikov Polye in 1380.

Sergius died peacefully on September 25, 1392, and was buried in the principal church of the monastery. It became a popular place of pilgrimage and has remained so to this day. His feast is celebrated in the Russian and Greek Orthodox Churches and by the Church of England and the Episcopal Church in the USA. Because he was canonized before the Orthodox rejection of the Union of Florence (1439), his feast is also found in the Eastern Catholic sanctoral cycle, and it is commemorated on this day by the Evangelical Lutheran Church in America. However, it is not on the General Roman Calendar.

Other feasts on this day that are not on the General Roman Calendar are those of the abbot *Finnbarr* (ca. 560–ca. 610), founder and patron saint of Cork in Ireland, and *Ceolfrith* (d. 716), mentor to the Venerable Bede [May 25] and abbot of Wearmouth and Jarrow.

26 Cosmas and Damian, martyrs; Teresa Couderc, foundress

Cosmas and *Damian* (d. ca. 287) are the patron saints of physicians, along with Luke [October 18] and Pantaleon [July 27]. They are also patron saints of nurses, surgeons, pharmacists, dentists, barbers, the sightless, and even confectioners. Unfortunately, there is little reliable information about them. Their legend says that they were twin brothers born in Arabia and doctors who practiced medicine without taking any fees for service. Thus, in the East they are known as the *anargyroi* (Gk., "moneyless ones"). Many cures were attributed to them. They made no secret of their Christian faith and were arrested during the Diocletian persecution. They were brought before the governor of Cilicia, then tortured and beheaded in Cyrrhus, north of Antioch, in Syria, where a great basilica was built in their honor and from which their cult spread throughout the Christian world. Another church was built in their honor in Constantinople in the fifth century, and still another in Rome in the sixth century, when Pope Felix IV (526–30) brought their relics there and erected a basilica by joining two pagan temples in the Forum. Probably at the same time their names were included in the Canon of the Roman Mass (First Eucharistic Prayer). Six other Roman churches were dedicated to them. Their cult continued to spread from Rome, and many other churches were dedicated to them in Greece and eastern Europe especially. One of the most famous paintings of them was done by Fra Angelico [February 18]. Their cult was encouraged and promoted by the Medici family of Florence, a number of whom were named Cosimo. Their feast is on the General Roman Calendar and is celebrated in the Russian and Greek Orthodox Churches on both July 1 and November 1.

This is also the feast day of *Teresa Couderc* (1805–85), the foundress of the Congregation of Our Lady of the Retreat in the Cenacle in 1826. She was beatified in 1951 and canonized in 1970.

27 Vincent de Paul, priest

Vincent de Paul (1581–1660) was the founder of the Vincentians and the Sisters of Charity and is the patron saint of all charitable societies and works. Vincent himself always signed himself "Depaul," not "de Paul." The latter would ordinarily convey a noble parentage. Born of a peasant family at Pouy (now Saint-Vincent-de-Paul) in southwestern France, he studied for the priesthood at a local Franciscan college and then at Toulouse University and was ordained at the early age of nineteen. He became a court chaplain, but then his biography becomes clouded. According to one version, he was falsely accused of theft and underwent some sort of religious conversion, perhaps while in prison. He is also reported to have been captured by pirates during a boat trip from Marseilles to Narbonne in 1605 and to have spent two years as a slave in Tunisia. He finally managed to escape with his third and last master, whom he had converted to Christianity, and the two of them crossed the Mediterranean by rowboat, arriving in Provence in April 1607. From there they went to Rome, where Vincent remained for a year. Some scholars tend to dismiss this account as legendary.

Saint Vincent de Paul and the Sisters of Charity by Antoine Ansiaux (1764–1840)

What does seem certain is that Vincent did spend a year in Rome, possibly studying, before returning to France. In Paris he joined a group of priests headed by his friend and mentor Pierre de Bérulle (later a cardinal), who established the Congregation of the Oratory in

France. On Bérulle's advice, Vincent became the parish priest of Clichy, on the northern outskirts of Paris, in 1612, and the following year became tutor in the powerful Gondi family.

Again the details of his life become cloudy. For some unknown reason there was a cooling of the relationship with Bérulle ca. 1618, and Vincent chose another director. It was also about this time that he came to know Francis de Sales [January 24], whose writings, especially the *Introduction to the Devout Life,* had a strong influence on him. While he remained with the Gondi family for twelve years, Vincent also spent some time as a parish priest at Châtillon-les-Dombes, where he discovered the needs of sick and poor families. He decided to form a confraternity of caring individuals who would help these families by turns. The first group—all women—came into being in August 1617 and were known as the Servants of the Poor. Three months later Vincent produced a Rule, which had the approval of the archbishop of Lyons. After returning to Paris, he began to establish similar groups of *Charités* in the many villages on the Gondi estates.

Vincent wanted to have male groups as well, but these would not develop until after his death. In 1833 Frédéric Ozanam [September 8] would found the Society of St. Vincent de Paul. Vincent did establish in 1618 a society of priests known variously as the Priests of the Mission, Vincentians, and Lazarists. With the financial support of Madame Gondi, who wanted priests to preach regularly to the peasants on the Gondi estates, Vincent and his new band of priests went from village to village conducting missions. The project was so successful that, with the continued financial support of the Gondis and with the approval of the archbishop of Paris, the group established a base in the city, provided by the archbishop, where they lived a common life without vows, and from which they carried on their village missions, doing other pastoral work as needed. As their work and community grew, the archbishop gave them an even larger accommodation in the priory of Saint-Lazare (thus, the name Lazarists), which became one of the great centers of spiritual and pastoral renewal in France. At the request of the archbishop, Vincent began training diocesan seminarians at Saint-Lazare.

Meanwhile, the women's groups, or *Charités,* began to multiply as many other parishes recognized the needs of their sick and poor. The women came to Paris in 1629 and became known as the *Dames de Charité* (Fr., "Ladies of Charity"). However, because many of the middle-class women in these groups could not personally do the work to which the association was committed, Vincent founded yet another, the *Filles de Charité* (Fr., "Daughters of Charity"), consisting of young women from the country whose life experiences were closer to those of the poor and the sick to whom they would minister.

In 1633 he decided, in collaboration with an aristocratic widow, Louise de Marillac [March 15], to provide training for this new group. She took four women into her home in November, and by the following July there were twelve. At this point they both began to think in terms of a new order, but one without vows or enclosure. His point was: "When you leave your prayer to care for a sick person, you leave God for God. To care for a sick person *is* to pray." He would tell his sisters: "For a cell, your rented room; for your chapel, the parish church; for a cloister, the streets of the city; for enclosure, obedience. . . . Fear of God is your grill, and modesty your veil." The new order grew rapidly, ministering in hospitals, orphanages, prisons, old-age homes, and elsewhere. It was formally approved by the Holy See in 1668. In the meantime, Vincent became directly involved in the struggle against Jansenism, then raging in France. He found its teaching elitist and pessimistic about the possibility of salvation. His approach, by contrast, was simple, practical, and confident in God's love and mercy.

The last three or four years of his life were marked by serious illness and physical incapacity. His legs became ulcerated to the point where he could no longer walk. He died on September 27, 1660. At his funeral the bishop said that Vincent had "changed the face of the Church" in his lifetime. Vincent's cult developed almost immediately. He was beatified in 1729 and canonized in 1737. In 1885 Pope Leo XIII named him universal patron saint of all works of charity. His feast is on the General Roman Calendar and is also celebrated by the Church of England. There have been more than four hundred biographies of Vincent de Paul as well as a motion picture, *Monsieur Vincent* (1947).

28 Wenceslaus, martyr; Lawrence Ruiz and companions, martyrs; martyrs of China

Wenceslaus (907–29) is best known as the subject of the Christmas carol "Good King Wenceslaus," although its contents are not based on any known incident in his life. He is the patron saint of the Czech Republic, Slovakia, Bohemia, and Moravia. The son of a duke, Wenceslaus, or Václav, was educated mainly by his grandmother (St. Ludmilla), the wife of the first Christian duke of Bohemia. Ludmilla was murdered in 921 at the instigation of Wenceslaus's mother, who resented her influence in government. The following year Wenceslaus himself seized the reins of power, becoming duke of Bohemia, in order to bring an end to the struggle between Christian and anti-Christian factions and also to block (as he successfully did) the invasion of Bohemia by the Bavarians. In 929, facing superior military force, he recognized the German king Henry I as the rightful successor of Charlemagne (d. 814) and as overlord of Bohemia. When a son was born to Wenceslaus, his brother Boleslav saw that he had lost his chance to succeed. He invited his brother to his residence and murdered Wenceslaus as he was on his way to chapel for the singing of Matins. Nevertheless, it may have been Boleslav who had his brother's relics taken to the church of St. Vitus [June 15] in Prague, where they became the center of a cult and a strong attraction for pilgrims. Wenceslaus's feast was celebrated from 985 and, early in the next century, he became Bohemia's patron saint. His picture was engraved on its coins and his crown was regarded as a symbol of Czech nationalism and independence. There is a large statue of him as an armed knight on a horse in Wenceslaus Square in Prague. His feast is on the General Roman Calendar.

Lawrence Ruiz (d. 1637) is the first Filipino saint. Lawrence, or Lorenzo, was born to Christian parents in Manila, but fled to Japan to escape some false charge in July 1636. At this time, however, Japan was under severe anti-Christian rule. Christians were required to trample on images of the Blessed Virgin and Child. Refusal was punished by torture (slow burning and "the pit") and death by beheading if the victims were still alive after some days. Lawrence died in this manner on September 28, 1637. He was one of fifteen martyrs cruelly put to death in Japan between 1633 and 1637. They were canonized in 1987 and their feast is on the General Roman Calendar.

The *martyrs of China,* consisting of eighty-seven native converts and thirty-three foreign missionaries, were put to death between 1648 and 1930. Most had been killed during the anti-Western and anti-Christian Boxer Rebellion (1898–1900). Included among them were four young girls who had been raised in a Catholic orphanage: Wang Cheng, Fan Kun, Ji Yu, and Zheng Xu. When they were pressured to renounce their faith, they replied: "We are daughters of God. We will not betray Him." Canonized by Pope John Paul II on October 1, 2000, they were the first Chinese Catholics to be raised to sainthood. The canonization, however, provoked anger and resentment on the part of the Chinese government. Its leaders denounced plans to hold the ceremony on

National Day, the anniversary of the founding of the People's Republic of China in 1949. (The Vatican had chosen October 1 because it is the feast of Theresa of Lisieux, patron saint of the missions.) Although the list of martyrs included none killed under Communist rule, the government excoriated them as "evildoing sinners." In response John Paul II insisted that the Church intended only to "recognize that these martyrs are an example of courage and consistency for all of us and an honor to the noble Chinese people."

29 Michael, Gabriel, and Raphael, archangels

September 29 is known as Michaelmas Day because it is the feast of *Michael the Archangel,* the leader of the ranks of angels and the guardian and protector of the people of Israel (Dan. 10; 12). According to Jude 9 Michael (Heb., "Who is like God?") conducted warfare with the devil over the body of Moses, and in Revelation 12:7–9 he and his angels fight the dragon and hurl him and his followers from heaven. He is venerated as the head of the heavenly armies and as patron saint of soldiers. He is also believed to protect Christians against the devil, especially at the hour of death, and to lead their souls to God. His cult began in Phrygia and soon spread to the West, given impetus by an alleged apparition of him on Monte Gargano in southeastern Italy in the fifth century. He was the only individual angel with a liturgical feast prior to the ninth century, and churches were dedicated to him from as early as the fourth century. His most famous shrine in western Europe is Mont-Saint-Michel in Normandy, where a Benedictine abbey was founded in the tenth century. His original sole feast day on September 29 was celebrated since the sixth century to commemorate the dedication of a basilica in his honor on the Salerian Way in Rome. In the revision of the General Roman Calendar in 1969, his feast was joined with those of Gabriel and Raphael and is celebrated on this day. He is also patron saint of Germany, England, Papua New Guinea, Gibraltar, the Solomon Islands, the sick, radiologists, grocers, mariners, police officers, paratroopers, and cemeteries.

Archangel Michael

The archangel *Gabriel* (Heb., "man of God") is portrayed in the Old Testament as an instrument of revelation (e.g., Dan. 8:15–26; 9:20–27) and in the noncanonical *1 Enoch* (9:1) as a heavenly intercessor. He is one of those who stand in the presence of God (Rev. 8:2), and he is sent to announce the birth of John the Baptist [June 24; August 29] to Zechariah [November 5] (Luke 1:11–20) and the conception of Jesus to Mary [March 25] (Luke 1:26–38), having addressed the Blessed Virgin in the memorable words, "Hail, full of grace. The Lord is with you." This scene is depicted in a fifth-century mosaic in the basilica of St. Mary Major in Rome. It is the oldest known representation of an angel with feet and two wings. In 1951 Pope Pius XII declared Gabriel to be patron saint of those engaged in telecommunications (telephone, radio, television). He is also patron saint of Argentina, messengers, diplomats, postal employees, and stamp collectors.

Raphael (Heb., "God heals"), one of the seven archangels "who stand before the Lord" (Tob. 12:12, 15), healed Tobit's blindness and provided Sarah with a husband (Tob. 3:16–17). He is God's messenger, who hears people's prayers and brings these before God (Tob. 12:12, 15). He is identified as the angel who healed the earth when it was defiled by the sins of the fallen angels (*1 Enoch* 10:7). Raphael's cult, unlike those of other two archangels, developed late and then only infrequently. A Venetian church was dedicated to him in the seventh century, but only in the seventeenth century did Masses in his honor become more numerous. A universal feast was instituted for him in 1921, but it has been merged now with that of Michael and Gabriel. He has been widely depicted as the patron saint of travelers, but he is also patron saint of physicians, nurses, lovers, health inspectors, and the sightless. This feast is celebrated by the Church of England, the Episcopal Church in the USA, and the Evangelical Lutheran Church in America as the feast of Michael and All Angels. The feast is celebrated by the Russian and Greek Orthodox Churches on November 8.

30 Jerome, priest and Doctor of the Church; Gregory the Illuminator, bishop

Jerome (ca. 345–420) is the most famous biblical scholar in the history of the Church, also known for his cantankerous temperament and sarcastic wit. He is patron saint of scholars and librarians. Born Eusebius Hieronymus Sophronius at Stridon, near Aquileia, in Dalmatia, he was well educated, especially in grammar, rhetoric, and the classics, and was baptized sometime before 366. (It was the custom then to defer baptism until later in life.) After a period of travel in Gaul, Dalmatia, and Italy, he decided to become a monk, along with a number of friends, ca. 370 in Aquileia, which was a major Christian center at the time. After a quarrel of some kind, the group broke up. Because of a chance meeting with a priest from Antioch, Jerome and three of his friends left for the East, arriving in Antioch in 374. Two of his friends died there, and Jerome himself became seriously ill. While sick, he had a dream in which he appeared before the judgment seat of God and was condemned for being a Ciceronian rather than a Christian. He became a hermit at Chalcis in the Syrian desert for four or five years, gave up the study of the classics, and learned Hebrew in order to study the Scriptures in the original languages (he already knew Greek). He was ordained a priest in Antioch, even though he had no real desire to be a priest and, in fact, never celebrated Mass. Then he studied the Scriptures in Constantinople under Gregory Nazianzen [January 2]. While there, he translated some of the works of Eusebius and Origen from Greek into Latin and did his first biblical commentary, on the vision of Isaiah (6:1–13).

Detail from *Saint Jerome in His Study* by Joos van Cleve

When Gregory left Constantinople in 382 to retire to his family estates, Jerome returned to Rome to act as interpreter for Paulinus, one of the claimants to the see of Antioch, at a council called by Pope Damasus I (366–84) [December 11] to discuss the schism in Antioch. Once the council was over, he was enlisted by the aged pope to serve as his secretary. While in Rome, Jerome did some biblical translations and began the enormous task of producing a Latin text of the entire Bible that would be faithful to the original languages. This would later be called the Vulgate version, which became the official Latin translation of the Bible. He also wrote a number of commentaries on various books of the Bible. The one on Matthew's Gospel became a standard work. He also became the spiritual guide of a group of wealthy widows who were living a semimonastic life. However, his relationship with them, especially Paula [January 26], gave rise to gossip, exacerbated, no doubt, by the various enmities he had fashioned because of his acidic temperament and his harsh criticisms of certain members of the Roman clergy and some of the laity. Therefore, when he left Rome with his brother Paulinian and some monks in August 385, following the death of his protector Pope Damasus the previous December, it was under something of a cloud.

He returned to Antioch and eventually settled in Bethlehem, where he was joined by Paula, her daughter Eustochium, and some of the other Roman women who decided to join Jerome in his exile. (Jerome had met them earlier and toured the deserts of Egypt and Palestine with them, talking with hermits and taking copious notes about the geography and the local saints.) With Paula's generous financial support, he established a monastery for monks, and she, convents for three communities of nuns. Jerome would spend the remainder of his life in Bethlehem—living in a cell hewn from a rock near the traditional birthplace of Jesus—teaching, studying, writing, and advocating an asceticism that clearly preferred virginity over marriage. On one occasion, he wrote: "Marriage, I praise it because it produces virgins; from the thorns I pluck the rose." Nevertheless, he himself had close relationships with women, especially Paula, and upon her death in 404 he was described as inconsolable.

One of the most unfortunate episodes during the period was his bitter controversy with his old friend Rufinus, now living in a monastery in Jerusalem, over the teachings of Origen (ca. 185–ca. 254), one of the most prominent theologians of the early Church. Rufinus had translated some of Origen's works (just as Jerome had some years earlier), but Jerome believed secondhand reports that Rufinus also agreed with Origen's views. He sharply attacked his friend in harshly personal terms, destroying their friendship in the process and in spite of the efforts of Augustine [August 28] to calm the situation. When Rufinus died in Sicily in 410, Jerome wrote: "Now that the scorpion lies buried in Tinacria . . . ." Nevertheless, it has to be said that Jerome's great learning was unmatched during this period of church history except for that of Augustine himself.

After having endured the sacking and burning of his monastery by thugs in 416 and with his health and eyesight failing, Jerome died in Bethlehem on September 30, 420, and was buried under the church of the Nativity, close to the graves of Paula and her daughter. Later his body was removed to the basilica of St. Mary Major in Rome. He was proclaimed one of the four original Latin Doctors of the Church in 1298, along with Ambrose [December 7], Augustine, and Gregory the Great [September 3]. In 1920 Pope Benedict XV named him patron saint of those who study Sacred Scripture. His feast is on the General Roman Calendar and is also observed by the Church of England, the Episcopal Church in the USA, and the Evangelical Lutheran Church in America.

On this day the Greek and Russian Orthodox Churches celebrate the feast of *Gregory the Illuminator* (ca. 240–ca. 330), also known as the "Enlightener." He was the "apostle" and patron saint of Armenia and served as bishop of Ashtishat.

OCTOBER

1 Theresa of the Child Jesus, virgin and Doctor of the Church

Theresa of the Child Jesus (1873–97), or Theresa (or Thérèse) of Lisieux, is better known as the "Little Flower," a name drawn from the subtitle of her famous autobiography. She was a highly influential model of sanctity for Catholics in the first half of the twentieth century because of the simplicity and practicality of her approach to the spiritual life. Born Marie Françoise Thérèse Martin at Alençon, France, of pious Catholic parents, she moved with her family to Lisieux after the death of her mother in 1877. Following the example of two of her sisters, she became a Carmelite nun at Lisieux, but with the special permission of the bishop because she was only fifteen. Her name in religion was Theresa of the Infant Jesus; later she was allowed to add the words "and of the Holy Face" as a reminder of Jesus' suffering.

Saint Thérèse of Lisieux or de l'Enfant Jesus, 1895

Her life in the convent was uneventful, even though the community was divided into two factions, largely because of the mercurial temperament and behavior of its superior. Theresa eschewed the traditional medieval and Baroque path of excessive self-mortification and ecstatic and visionary experiences, as well as the rigidity, complexity, and formalism of much nineteenth-century spirituality, and instead followed a simple and straightforward path to holiness. In addition to the Carmelite Rule and the liturgical life of the convent, her spiritual life was nurtured by the Scriptures, the *Imitation of Christ* (a highly popular and influential fifteenth-century work attributed to Thomas à Kempis [July 24]), and the writings of John of the Cross [December 14], Teresa of Ávila [October 15], and Francis de Sales [January 24]. Although she saw Christian perfection to be within the grasp of every person, not just clergy and religious, she devoted her prayers in a particular way for the benefit of priests.

In 1895 she had a hemorrhage, the first sign of the tuberculosis that would eventually bring about her death. Although she had hoped to volunteer for missionary service in Hanoi, in French Indochina (modern-day North Vietnam), her state of health kept her at Lisieux, where she is said to have suffered in silence. However, she took two foreign missionaries under her spiritual care and some of her most moving letters in the last two years of her life were written to encourage them in their work. In June 1897 she was moved to the convent infirmary and, after a period of spiritual as well as intense physical suffering, she died on September 30, at age twenty-four. It is likely that she would have remained unknown if she had not written under obedience a short spiritual autobiography, *The Story of a Soul,* edited in a sanitized fashion by one of the sisters and first published in 1899, two years after her death. After being circulated at first to all Carmelite houses, the work was translated into several languages and became widely popular. Many people attributed cures and simple favors to her intercession, and her cult spread at an extraordinary rate, helped in part by her well-known promise to spend her life in heaven continuing to do good on earth, "as long as there are souls to be saved." She said that she would let fall a "shower of roses" from heaven.

At the time of her death, there was a fifty-year waiting period required by canon law before a cause for canonization could be initiated, but this was waived in her case and she was beatified in 1923 and canonized in 1925, less than twenty-eight years after her death. In his bull of canonization, Pope Pius XI noted that she had achieved sanctity "without going beyond the common order of things." She was declared the patron saint of the missions (along with Francis Xavier [December 3]) in 1927, a secondary patron saint of France (along with Joan of Arc [May 30] in 1947, and then a Doctor of the Church by Pope John Paul II on

Mission Sunday, October 19, 1997. She is also patron saint of Russia, aviators, and florists. Because of the large number of pilgrims visiting her place of burial, a basilica was erected in Lisieux in 1926.

On this day the Church of England and the Episcopal Church in the USA celebrate the feast of *Remigius* [January 13], bishop of Reims and "apostle of the Franks."

BIBLIOGRAPHY

O'Donnell, Christopher. *Love in the Heart of the Church: The Mission of Thérèse of Lisieux.* Dublin: Veritas, 1997.

Six, Jean-François. *Light of the Night: The Last Eighteen Months in the Life of Thérèse of Lisieux.* Notre Dame, IN: University of Notre Dame Press, 1998.

2 Guardian angels

According to the belief of many Catholics (and of some pagans and Jews before the time of Christ), guardian angels are spiritual beings who protect individual persons from spiritual and physical harm. The belief has some basis in the New Testament (e.g., Matt. 18:10; Acts 12:15), and the *Catechism of the Catholic Church* assumes their existence and traditional function (n. 336). However, the Church has never defined anything about them. The Matthean text in particular ("See that you do not despise one of these little ones, for I say to you that their angels in heaven always look upon the face of my heavenly Father") has led to a close connection in prayer and art between guardian angels and the protection of children. The guardian angels were originally commemorated with Michael the Archangel on September 29, but an independent feast, first found in Portugal in 1513, was later extended to the whole Church by Pope Clement X in 1670 and assigned to this day. It remains on the General Roman Calendar.

3 Francis Borgia, priest; Thomas of Hereford, bishop

Francis Borgia (1510–72) was the third superior general of the Society of Jesus and is sometimes referred to as the second founder of the Jesuits. Patron saint of Portugal, he was born Francisco de Borja y Aragón in the family palace in Valencia, Spain. His great grandfather on his father's side was the infamous Pope Alexander VI (1492–1503) and his mother's grandfather was Ferdinand V, king of Aragon. His uncle was the archbishop of Saragossa, with whom he went to live after his mother died in 1520. He served for a time as page to his cousin Catherine, the sister of the emperor Charles V. Upon Catherine's marriage to the king of Portugal in 1525, Francis returned to Saragossa to study philosophy. He returned to court at the emperor's invitation in 1528 and married the empress Isabella's lady-in-waiting, Eleanor de Castro of Portugal, in 1529. For the next ten years the Borgias and their eight children lived happily with the emperor and empress until May 1, 1539, when the empress died unexpectedly. Francis was profoundly affected by her death because it made him think about the transitoriness of life and of material possessions and honors. He would always regard that date as the day of his conversion, thereafter dedicating himself to a life of prayer and to striving for perfect holiness.

Upon his father's death in 1542, he returned home to assume his responsibilities as the fourth duke of Gandía. His attempts at political reforms, however, provoked much opposition and he retired to his family estates to lead a more secluded life. In 1545 he founded a Jesuit university and a hospital in Gandía. When his wife died in 1546, he vowed to become a Jesuit as soon as he could arrange his temporal affairs. On February 1, 1548, while still living in a manner befitting his noble rank, he secretly pronounced his first vows as a Jesuit and in August 1550 earned a doctorate in theology from the university he himself had founded. Although 1550 was a Holy Year and he wished to visit Rome anyway, his primary purpose in going was to see Ignatius of Loyola [July 31], the founder of the Society of Jesus, to arrange his official entrance into the order. He set out from Gandía in late August with one of his sons, several Jesuits, and servants and arrived in Rome at the end of October. He declined Pope Julius III's offer to use the Borgia apartments and chose instead to live at the Jesuit residence with Ignatius. While in Rome he visited shrines and monuments like any pilgrim and tourist, but lived as a Jesuit while in the community. He also assisted Ignatius in the founding and financing of the Roman College (later the Pontifical Gregorian University).

In February 1551 he left for Spain, resigned his title in favor of his eldest son, and, upon the emperor's acceptance of the resignation, put on the Jesuit habit for the first time. He was ordained a priest on May 26 and celebrated his first Mass in a tiny oratory in Ignatius's ancestral home at Loyola. Francis spent the next three years fulfilling the role of a parish priest, but in 1554 Ignatius appointed him commissary general of the order for Spain, a position that placed him over the Spanish and Portuguese provincials. While in this post, he founded some twenty colleges and Spain's first Jesuit novitiate. However, his great influence in high places also won him many enemies, and the new king, Philip II, placed some credence in the complaints. To avoid further trouble, Francis went to Portugal in 1559, but less than two years later Pope Pius IV called him to Rome.

He served there as vicar general of the order while the general, Father James Laynez, was at the Council of Trent (where he made a decisive contribution to its formulation of the doctrine of justification against the Protestants). When Laynez died in 1565, Francis Borgia was elected to succeed him. He would remain in the position for seven years, during which he revised the Society's Constitutions, supervised the order's expansion into Poland, France, and elsewhere, promoted its missions in India and North and South America, and began the famous Gesù Church in Rome. During the great plague of 1566, he raised large sums of money for the sick and sent his priests out to serve in hospitals and the poorest sections of the city. His spiritual writings during this period stressed self-knowledge and humility, the humanity of Jesus and his sufferings, the Eucharist, prayer, and the importance of sanctifying all of our daily actions. Ironically, some of his earlier writings had been placed on the Index of Forbidden Books in 1559 because it was thought dangerous to make works of spirituality available to the less educated laity by publishing them in the vernacular. Although the problem was largely resolved with his return to Rome, it was not until some years after Francis's death that the inquisitor general formally withdrew the condemnation.

In 1571, at the pope's request, he traveled to Spain with Cardinal Bonelli to secure Spain's military help against the Turks. He was overwhelmed by his reception in his homeland, as crowds gathered everywhere to see "the saintly duke." He also had an opportunity while there to see and to bless his many children and grandchildren. That mission was no sooner ended when the pope asked them to go to France on another assignment. Because of the unusually severe weather conditions that winter of 1571–72, the traveling had a devastating effect on Borgia's already frail health. The trip was aborted in mid-course, however, when they received word that the pope was dying. Francis had to be carried by litter over the Alps, stopping for periods of rest in Turin and then in Ferrara. He arrived finally in Rome at the end of September and was immediately put to bed. Three days later, on September 30, after receiving many distinguished visitors, he died at age sixty-one. He was beatified in 1624 and canonized in 1671. His feast is celebrated by the Jesuits on this day, but it is not on the General Roman Calendar.

Also on this day the Church of England and the Episcopal Church in the USA celebrate the feast of *Thomas of Hereford* (ca. 1218–82), also known as Thomas de Cantilupe, the bishop of Hereford who fought against simony, nepotism, and the interference of lay rulers in the affairs of his diocese. Toward the end of his life he was engaged in jurisdictional disputes with John Pecham, the archbishop of Canterbury, for which he was excommunicated in 1282. He appealed the sentence to the papal court, but died before a judgment could be rendered. Nevertheless, his reputation for sanctity and miracles led to his canonization in 1320. His feast is not on the General Roman Calendar.

4 Francis of Assisi, friar

Francis of Assisi (1181/82–1226) was the founder of the Franciscans and is one of the most popular saints in the history of the Church. Born Francesco Bernardone in a makeshift manger on the ground floor of the family house in Assisi in Umbria, in deliberate imitation of the birth of Jesus, he was baptized Giovanni in honor of John the Baptist [June 24; August 29], but his father, upon his return from a business trip to France (he was a wealthy cloth merchant), added the name Francesco to mark his own love for that country. Francis's early life was marked by high living and a concern for social status. He was taken prisoner in 1202 during a war between Assisi and neighboring Perugia. Upon his release and return home a year later, he became seriously ill. During his convalescence, he experienced a profound change in his values. He thought first of serving in the papal army in southern Italy, but in Spoleto he is said to have had a dream that urged him to "follow the Master rather than the man." He returned to Assisi, where he was drawn increasingly to a life of prayer, penance, pilgrimages, and almsgiving.

Saint Francis Preaching to the Birds by Giotto, 1297–1300

After a chance encounter with a leper, to whom Francis gave money and whose hand he kissed, he "left the world" and began to spend more time working among social outcasts and the poor. His father was not happy with the new direction his son's life had taken, and there were increasingly tense conflicts between the two. Everything came to a climax in 1206 when Francis sold some valuable cloth from the family store to raise money for the rebuilding of the ruined chapel of San Damiano. He claimed to have heard a call while praying in the church: "Go and repair my house, which you see is falling down." When his father brought charges against him in the local ecclesiastical court, Francis returned the money, renounced his patrimony, and gave back his fine clothes in a dramatic scene before the bishop of Assisi. He spent the next several years living as a penitent hermit, caring for lepers and helping to repair three ruined churches in the town.

In the spring of 1208 his life took yet another turn. In response to what he took to be a personal call (reflected in Matt. 10:7–19) during Mass in the Portiuncula (the church of St. Mary of the Angels), he gave away his shoes, tunic, and staff and donned the simple tunic and hood of a shepherd, with a cord tied around the waist. He began to preach publicly and to attract followers. By the next year there were twelve in his company, which became known as Penitentiaries of Assisi, although Francis preferred the name *fratres minores* (Lat., "lesser brothers"), which eventually became their official ecclesiastical name, Friars Minor. Francis wrote a brief statement on their way of life, based on a few texts from the Gospels, and took this primitive Rule to Rome to secure the approval of Pope Innocent III in 1210. Francis also became a deacon around this time, but, out of humility and a high regard for the priesthood, did not proceed to the next step of ordination.

When Francis returned to Assisi, his friars took up residence together at the rural chapel of the Portiuncula. This became the base from which they spread out in small groups through central Italy, doing manual labor and preaching. Wherever the Franciscans settled, they lived in simple wood huts without tables or chairs, their churches were modest and small, they slept on the ground, and they had very few books. (Only later did the order encourage its members to pursue a life of scholarship in university settings, producing such major theologians as Bonaventure [July 15].) In 1212 Clare [August 11], a young aristocratic woman in Assisi, joined the movement and founded her own community of women, known as the "Poor Ladies of San Damiano" (later the Poor Clares). At about the same time, Francis began to form groups of devout lay people that became the basis of the third order of St. Francis. They were known initially as the Brothers and Sisters of Penance.

At the first general chapter of 1217 Francis sent his friars beyond the Alps and even to the Near East, where the Crusaders had established their rule. After a couple of failed attempts to visit the East in hopes of converting the Muslims, Francis went to Egypt with a dozen friars in 1219, where the Crusaders were mounting an attack on the local sultan. Appalled by the behavior of the Crusaders themselves, he somehow managed to pass through the lines and met the sultan, who was deeply impressed with Francis as a person, but who remained unconverted. After a brief visit to the Holy Land, Francis returned to Italy upon receiving word of growing tensions among his friars, now about three thousand in number, and growing criticisms from some bishops. Concluding that he was not up to the task of dealing with these pressing crises, he resigned as minister general of the order at the chapter of 1220 and obtained a cardinal-protector, Hugolino da Segni (later Pope Gregory IX) for the movement. Still considered the spiritual driving force of the order, however, Francis revised his Rule and secured papal approval for it in 1223. He spent Christmas that same year in Grecchio, where he invented the Christmas crib.

By now his health had begun to fail, and he had to withdraw from normal activities for long periods of rest and prayer. While on one of these retreats on Mount La Verna in the fall of 1224, he is said to have had a profound mystical experience that left the wounds of Christ's Passion on his hands, feet, and side—the first recorded case of the stigmata. He became ill and then blind. He paid a final visit to Clare at San Damiano and, while there, composed his famous "Canticle of the Sun." The popular "Prayer of St. Francis" ("Lord, make me an instrument of your peace") is a modern compilation with no direct connection to Francis himself.

Francis died at age forty-five at the Portiuncula on October 3, 1226, and was canonized two years later by his friend Pope Gregory IX (1227–41), who also canonized Dominic [August 8], the founder of the Dominicans, in 1234. (Unlike the older orders of monks and canons whose primary concern was the spiritual advancement of the members through the liturgy, prayer, and monastic observance, these new orders—the Franciscans and Dominicans, in particular—were directly involved in the life of the world and the Church and dedicated to their renewal and reform.) His remains are now in the crypt of St. Francis in the lower church of the basilica of St. Francis in Assisi (although he had asked to be buried in the criminals' cemetery). The structure was partially destroyed in the earthquake of 1997, but Francis's tomb was not damaged.

Although Francis's cult was widespread from the earliest years, it experienced an even more remarkable revival in the twentieth century, among nonbelievers as well as Christians. His simple lifestyle and piety, his devotion to the poor, and his love for the whole of God's created order, including animals, have made him one of the Church's most beloved saints. He is the patron saint of Italy, of Catholic Action, and also of the environment. In 1926 Pope Pius XI described him as the *alter Christus* (Lat., "another Christ"). His feast is on the General Roman Calendar and is also observed on this day by the Church of England, the Episcopal Church in the USA, and the Evangelical Lutheran Church in America.

BIBLIOGRAPHY

Frugoni, Chiara. *Francis of Assisi: A Life.* London: SCM Press, 1998.

Green, Julien. *God's Fool: The Life and Times of Francis of Assisi.* Trans. Peter Heinegg. San Francisco: Harper & Row, 1985.

Robson, Michael. *St. Francis of Assisi: The Legend and the Life.* London: Geoffrey Chapman, 1997.

5 Blessed Raymond of Capua, priest; Maria Faustina Kowalska, nun

Raymond of Capua (1330–99) was the spiritual director of Catherine of Siena [April 29] and master general of the Dominican order. Born Raymond delle Vigne of a noble family in Capua, a town north of Naples, he studied at the University of Bologna and, while there, joined the Dominicans. He held various positions within the order in Rome and Florence before moving to Siena in 1374. It was there that he met Catherine of Siena, who, while attending one of his Masses, heard a voice saying: "This is my beloved servant; this is he to whom I shall entrust you." For the last six years of her life, he offered her spiritual guidance and encouragement. They also collaborated on apostolic works, beginning with the people of Siena who were suffering from an outbreak of plague. Raymond took ill and seemed to be at the point of death, until Catherine prayed for an hour and a half at his bedside. The next day he was completely recovered. This episode convinced him of

Catherine's spiritual powers and inspired him to dedicate himself to the support of her mission. Thus, when she wanted to launch a new crusade against the Turks in the Holy Land, Raymond preached about it at Pisa and personally delivered a letter of hers to John Hawkwood, a famous English pirate, soliciting his help. This enterprise was interrupted, however, when some Italian city-states revolted against the pope, then residing in Avignon, France. Catherine and Raymond tried unsuccessfully to act as peacemakers and to persuade the pope to return to Rome.

In 1378 the Great Western Schism began with the election of the temperamentally unstable Urban VI and of an antipope, Clement VII. Catholic rulers lined up on either side of the conflict. When Raymond was sent by Urban to preach against Clement in France, he was stopped at the border and threatened with execution by soldiers loyal to Clement. When Raymond returned to Italy, Catherine rebuked him for his faint-heartedness. He stayed in Genoa preaching against the antipope and studying theology. Catherine died soon thereafter, in 1380, but not before promising to be with him in every danger. (He later wrote a Life of Catherine of Siena that has been criticized by some scholars for exaggerating her influence in the Church.) Raymond tried to pick up where Catherine had left off. He assumed the direction of her companion-disciples and devoted the remainder of his life to achieving what had been her greatest wish, the end of the schism. (It did not come to an end until 1417.)

Around the time of Catherine's death Raymond was elected master general of that part of the Dominican order that supported Urban VI's claim to the papacy. His first concern was to revitalize the order in the aftermath of the Black Death and in the teeth of the Great Schism. He placed renewed emphasis on the monastic side of Dominican life and established a number of houses of strict observance in several provinces. Some criticized him for reducing the importance of studies in university settings and for limiting the kinds of apostolic activities in which Dominicans might engage in the world. Those who supported his efforts referred to him as the second founder of the order. He was also committed to the spreading of the third order of St. Dominic [August 8] throughout the world, given the fact that his famous associate Catherine of Siena was herself a Dominican tertiary. After nineteen years as master general, Raymond of Capua died on October 5, 1399, at Nuremberg, where he was involved in efforts to reform the German Dominicans. He was beatified in 1899. His feast is not on the General Roman Calendar, but it is celebrated on this day by the Dominicans.

This is also the feast day of *Maria Faustina Kowalska* (1905–38), the first female Polish saint, canonized on April 30, 2000, by a fellow Pole, John Paul II. Her baptismal name was Helena (or Elena). When she entered the Sisters of the Virgin Mary of Mercy in Warsaw, however, she took the name Faustina (or Faustyna). Serving as her cloistered community's cook, gardener, and housekeeper, she claimed to have had visions of Jesus. Her spiritual diary was translated into ten languages.

6 Bruno, priest; Blessed Mary-Rose Durocher, foundress

Bruno (ca. 1032–1101) was the founder of the Carthusian order. Born in Cologne and educated at Reims, Tours, and Cologne, he became a canon at the Cologne cathedral before being ordained a priest in 1055. He was appointed a lecturer in grammar and theology at the prestigious cathedral school in Reims, where he himself had been a student. He held the post for more than eighteen years. One of his students was the future Pope Urban II (1088–99). Bruno was appointed chancellor of the diocese of Reims, whose simoniacal bishop was a notorious figure who was eventually deposed for corruption (but later reinstated). Because Bruno had denounced the bishop in council, he and some other priests left the diocese. When he eventually returned, there was some talk about electing him the next bishop. Instead, he resigned his various offices, gave away his money, and retired with a few companions to the abbey of Molesmes, where he placed himself under the direction of its abbot, Robert [January 26], the founder of the Cistercians. He and his six companions lived in a hermitage away from the monastery, but Bruno felt that their solitude was not severe enough. They applied to a former pupil of Bruno's, Hugh [April 1], the bishop of Grenoble, for permission to settle in his diocese. When they arrived in 1084, Hugh gave them a remote, forested, mountainous piece of land called Cartusia or La Chartreuse, and in 1085 they built an oratory with some small cells around it. This was the beginning of the Carthusian order and its motherhouse, La Grande Chartreuse.

Their eremetical way of life, which emphasized poverty, solitude, and austerity, was inspired by the Desert Fathers of Egypt and Palestine rather than the Rule of St. Benedict [July 11]. The monks prayed Matins and Vespers together in church during the night, but the rest of the Divine Office in private. They also gathered in church for the

Eucharist and for more of the Divine Office on Sundays and great feast days and took their main meals in common (the other meals were brought to their cells). Their daily life otherwise consisted of prayer, reading, and manual work, the last also performed by Carthusian brothers.

Six years later Bruno's former student, Pope Urban II, summoned him to Rome to consult on the state of the Church. Bruno took up residence in a makeshift cell among the ruins of the baths of Diocletian. When the pope had to flee Rome because of an antipope's hostility, Bruno went with him to Calabria. The pope offered him the bishopric of Reggio, but he declined. Instead, he founded a second hermitage at La Torre, also in Calabria, and brought with him some recent disciples from Rome. From Calabria he wrote to his community back at Chartreuse in the diocese of Grenoble and helped to organize their way of life with greater specificity. However, he never left a written Rule for his community. Bruno died at La Torre on October 6, 1101. His body was found incorrupt in 1513. Although he was never formally canonized (he was simply declared a saint by Pope Leo X in 1514), his cult developed quickly in Calabria itself and was approved for the Carthusians in 1514. It was extended to the universal Church in 1623. His feast is on the General Roman Calendar. He is the patron saint of Ruthenia and of the possessed.

On this day the Catholic Church in the United States also celebrates the feast of *Mary-Rose Durocher* (1811–49), foundress of the Congregation of the Sisters of the Most Holy Names of Jesus and Mary. She was born Eulalie Mélanie Durocher in the village of Saint-Antoine-sur-Richelieu in Quebec, Canada, the youngest of ten children. Because of poor health, she was unable to fulfill her desire to join a religious order. Instead, she assisted one of her priest-brothers for twelve years in various parochial tasks, including the distribution of aid to the needy. During this period she established the first Confraternity of Mary in Canada and bound herself privately to the observance of the three religious vows of poverty, chastity, and obedience. When her local bishop's effort to bring a community of teaching sisters to his diocese fell through, he gave her his approval in 1843 to found a congregation of her own that would be dedicated to the work of teaching the children of the poor. The Congregation of the Sisters of the Most Holy Names of Jesus and Mary was given canonical approval the following year. She made her own religious profession and took the name Mary-Rose. Her spirituality was focused on devotion to Jesus in the Blessed Sacrament and on imitation of Our Lady. The bishop appointed her superior, and she governed the congregation until her death. She was beatified in 1942.

7 Our Lady of the Rosary

The Rosary, also known as the "Psalter of Mary" because its 150 Hail Marys correspond to the number of psalms in the Bible, is a form of prayer originating sometime in the twelfth or thirteenth century, in which fifteen decades of Hail Marys are recited, using beads as counters, while meditating on a sequence of Mysteries associated with the life of the Blessed Virgin. The Mysteries themselves (see below) did not become linked with these repetitive prayers until the fifteenth century. Each decade is preceded by an Our Father and ends with a "Glory be to the Father, and to the Son, and to the Holy Spirit, as it was in the beginning, is now, and ever shall be, world without end. Amen." The usual devotional practice, however, is to recite only five, not the full fifteen, decades of the Rosary at one time. The five decades are called a "chaplet," from a French word meaning "crown" or "wreath." The whole sequence of Hail Marys, Our Fathers, and "Glory be to the Fathers" is introduced by the sign of the cross, the Apostles' Creed, an Our Father, three Hail Marys, and a "Glory be to the Father." The Mysteries of the Rosary are divided into Joyful, Sorrowful, Glorious, and Luminous. The Joyful Mysteries are the Annunciation [March 25], the Visitation (of Mary to her cousin Elizabeth) [May 31], the Nativity [December 25], the Presentation (of Jesus in the Temple) [February 2], and the Finding of Jesus in the Temple. The Sorrowful Mysteries are the Agony in the Garden, the Scourging at the Pillar, the Crowning with Thorns, the Carrying of the Cross, and the Crucifixion. The Glorious Mysteries are the Resurrection, the Ascension, the Descent of the Holy Spirit upon the Apostles (Pentecost), the Assumption [August 15], and the Coronation of Mary (as Queen of Heaven) [August 22]. The Mysteries of Light, added by Pope John Paul II on this feast day in 2002, are the baptism of Jesus in the Jordan, the Wedding at Cana, the proclamation of the Kingdom of God, the Transfiguration [August 6], and the institution of the Eucharist at the Last Supper. It is customary to meditate on the Joyful Mysteries on Mondays and Thursdays, the Sorrowful Mysteries on Tuesdays and Fridays, the Glorious Mysteries on Wednesdays, Saturdays, and Sundays, and the Luminous Mysteries, or Mysteries of Light, on Thursdays.

The development of the cycle of meditations owes much to the Carthusians in Trier in the early fifteenth century. They, in turn, influenced the Dominican Alain de la Roche (ca. 1428–75), who used this devotion to revive the Dominican Confraternity of the Blessed Virgin Mary. The tradition that the Blessed Virgin gave the Rosary to Dominic [August 8] as a weapon to combat the heresy of Albigensianism has no basis in history and is probably derived from Alain's claims to have received a revelation. The Rosary gained popularity through the establishment of Rosary confraternities in the fifteenth century, which were increasingly under Dominican supervision. In 1559 Pope Pius V [April 30], himself a Dominican, gave the Dominican master general exclusive control over these confraternities.

This feast of Our Lady of the Rosary had its origins in the devotional life of these lay confraternities, for whom it became customary to celebrate a feast of the same name, usually on the first Sunday in October. When Christian forces won a decisive sea battle against the Turks at Lepanto, in the Gulf of Corinth, on October 7, 1571, which happened to be the first Sunday of the month that year, the victory was attributed to the intercession of Our Lady of the Rosary. The Roman confraternities had, in fact, been saying the Rosary in the basilica of Santa Maria sopra Minerva and in street processions as the battle was being fought. In thanksgiving Pius V declared October 7 the feast of Our Lady of Victory. In 1573, his successor, Gregory XIII, changed the name of the feast to Our Lady of the Most Holy Rosary. (The new edition of *Butler's Lives of the Saints* indicates that Pius V only granted a Spanish confraternity the right to celebrate the feast in honor of Our Lady of Victory, and on the first Sunday in October, not October 7.) In 1716 the feast was extended to the whole Church in thanksgiving for yet another Christian victory over the Turks. Finally, in 1913 the date of the feast was fixed at October 7.

There was an upsurge in devotion to the Rosary in the nineteenth century, especially because of the Marian apparitions to Bernadette Soubirous [April 16] at Lourdes [February 11] in 1858, in which the Blessed Virgin was reported to have been carrying a rosary. Pope Leo XIII (1878–1903) also promoted the devotion through no less than nine encyclical letters on the subject. He was known in some circles as "the pope of the Rosary." The Rosary remained a highly popular Catholic devotion through most of the twentieth century. Many Catholics prayed it daily, either individually or as a family. There were also liturgically incorrect uses of the Rosary, however. Sometimes it would be recited aloud by a parish congregation during the celebration of weekday Masses in May or October (both months traditionally set aside for Marian devotions), but more often it would be recited quietly by individuals during the celebration of Mass as a substitute for the missal (a book containing in the vernacular all the prayers and readings of the Latin Mass). With the Second Vatican Council came a reorientation of Catholic devotional life, centered on the Eucharist, which was now entirely in the vernacular with full congregational participation. The Mass was no longer to be simply a backdrop for private devotion. Whereas Marian and other devotions once satisfied the need for popular participation in religious rites, the reformed Mass provided the same, but far richer, opportunity, and private devotions receded in importance. In his apostolic exhortation *Marialis cultus* (1974), Pope Paul VI made it clear that the Rosary is not to be recited during Mass (n. 48). The feast of Our Lady of the Rosary is on the General Roman Calendar.

8 Pelagia, virgin

The Greek and Russian Orthodox Churches celebrate the feast of *Pelagia* (d. ca. 311) on this day. Unfortunately, her life is shrouded in legend. The genuine St. Pelagia was a young virgin martyr of Antioch, who was venerated there on October 8, at least since the fourth century. She is mentioned by both John Chrysostom [September 13] and Ambrose [December 7], both of whom lived through the second half of the fourth century. Indeed, her name is included in the canon of the Ambrosian Mass of Milan. She is also commemorated on this day in the Syriac Breviary of the early fifth century. As a young girl of fifteen, she was arrested during a persecution. She asked the soldiers to allow her to go upstairs to change her clothes, whereupon she jumped off the roof to her death in the river below in order to escape dishonor.

The story of this Pelagia became enmeshed in one told by Chrysostom in his sixty-seventh homily on Matthew's Gospel. It concerned a morally notorious, but nameless, actress from Antioch who had a sudden conversion and pursued thereafter a life of extreme austerity and solitude. A later writer attached the name of Pelagia to the story and called her Pelagia the Penitent, the name by which she has been known ever since. According to the story, Pelagia put on men's clothes after her baptism and went to Jerusalem to live as a solitary in the grotto of the Mount of Olives. She was revered by the local people as "Pelagius" and was referred to as the "beardless monk." Only upon her death was her true identity revealed. This legendary Pelagia is the one commemorated on this day on the Greek and Russian Orthodox calendars. Her feast, however, is not on the General Roman Calendar.

9 Denis, bishop, and companions, martyrs; John Leonardi, priest; Louis Bertrán, friar

Denis (d. ca. 258), also known as Denys and Dionysius, is the patron saint of France. Italian by birth, he was one of six (or seven) missionary bishops sent by the pope ca. 250 to evangelize Gaul. He preached in Paris with great success and established a Christian presence on an island in the River Seine, aided by the priest Rusticus and the deacon Eleutherius. They were so effective that they were arrested, imprisoned, and then beheaded during the Valerian persecution. Their bodies were thrown into the river, but later recovered and buried. A chapel, built over their graves, served as the foundation in the seventh century of the great abbey of Saint-Denis, later the burial place of French kings. According to a ninth-century legend propagated by Hilduin, abbot of Saint-Denis, Denis walked two miles to Montmartre, carrying his head in his own hands and led by a choir of angels. The future abbey of St. Denis was an offspring of this walk, although not located where the walk ended. Hilduin's account advanced the tradition that Denis, the evangelizer of the Parisians, was also two other persons: a Dionysius, known also as Pseudo-Dionysius, who wrote influential works of Christian Neoplatonist theology around the end of the fifth century in Syria, and the even earlier Dionysius (the Areopagite), an Athenian official mentioned in the Acts of the Apostles (17:34) who was converted on the Areopagus by St. Paul's [June 29] address. The historian Eusebius reported the belief that the latter Dionysius became the first bishop of Athens. This conflation of three different individuals into one led to a revision of the legend of Denis, according to which Clement of Rome [November 23] was responsible for sending him to France and for Denis's establishment of Christianity there even earlier than supposed.

Denis has been recognized as the first bishop of Paris (so identified by Gregory of Tours [November 17]) and is the principal patron saint of France. (He is also patron saint of the possessed and those suffering from headaches.) His cult was especially popular in the Middle Ages. His feast is on the General Roman Calendar and he is commemorated by the Church of England as well.

John Leonardi (ca. 1542–1609) was the founder of the Clerks Regular of the Mother of God. Born Diecimo Leonardi near Lucca, he served as an apprentice to a pharmacist before studying for the priesthood. Ordained ca. 1572, he founded a confraternity for teaching Christian doctrine and for ministering to those in hospitals and prisons. Two years later he established a congregation of diocesan priests living under vows and committed to the reform of clerical life. The same year he published a compendium of Christian doctrine that remained in use until the nineteenth century, and in 1579 he formed the Confraternity of Christian Doctrine. In 1583 his congregation of priests was officially recognized by the bishop of Lucca, with the approval of Pope Gregory XIII. Leonardi was also encouraged and assisted by Philip Neri [May 26], who made available the premises of San Girolamo della Carità, where Philip had lived with a community of diocesan priests after his own ordination. In 1595 Pope Clement VIII formally recognized Leonardi's community as a religious congregation. At the same time, the pope commissioned him to reform the monks of Vallombrosa and Monte Vergine and to help in the planning of a special Roman seminary for the foreign missions, later known as the College for the Propagation of the Faith (Prop-aganda, for short) and now as the Pontifical Urban University, or Urbanianum, after its founder, Pope Urban VIII (1623–44). On October 9, 1609, he died from influenza, contracted while visiting and nursing the victims of an epidemic. His relics were enshrined at Santa Maria in Campitelli, Rome. In 1621 members of his congregation were allowed to take solemn religious vows and adopted their present name of Clerks Regular of the Mother of God. John Leonardi was beatified in 1861 and canonized in 1938. His feast is on the General Roman Calendar, having been added to the universal calendar in 1941.

The Greek and Russian Orthodox Churches celebrate on this day the feast of the Apostle James, the son of Alphaeus, also known as *James the Less* [May 3].

The Church of England and the Episcopal Church in the USA commemorate *Robert Grosseteste* (ca. 1170–1253), bishop of Lincoln from 1235 and, before that, professor of theology at Oxford. Even though he is regarded as one of the greatest bishops of thirteenth-century England, he has been neither beatified nor canonized.

On this day the Dominicans celebrate the feast of *Louis Bertrán* (1526–81), a Spanish Dominican friar who is the patron saint of Colombia, where he served as a missionary.

10 Paulinus of York, bishop

Paulinus of York (d. 644), one of the second group of monks sent to England by Pope Gregory the Great [September 3] in 601, was the first "apostle of Northumbria" in England and the first bishop of York. The saintly historian-monk Venerable Bede [May 25] described Paulinus as "a tall man, stooping a little, with black hair, thin face, and narrow aquiline nose, venerable and awe-inspiring in appearance." After being consecrated a bishop in 625, Paulinus traveled north as chaplain to Ethelburga, Christian daughter of the king of Kent, with the hope that he would convert her pagan husband-to-be Edwin and his subjects in Northumbria. Paulinus eventually did so and baptized Edwin and his infant daughter at Easter 627 in a wooden church at York. He also baptized a number of nobles and others in various parts of the kingdom. Paulinus built a stone church in Lincoln and later consecrated Honorius as archbishop of Canterbury in the church. He began building a cathedral in York, but his northern apostolate was cut short in 633 by the death of Edwin in battle against pagan forces. Queen Ethelburga fled back to Kent, and Paulinus went with her, thinking there was no future for Christianity in Northumbria. (It was the common assumption of Roman missionaries at the time that the work of conversion was impossible without the support of local kings and princes.) His saintly assistant James the Deacon (who is commemorated by the Church of England on October 12) remained behind, doing what he could to preserve Christianity in the midst of political turmoil. Paulinus served as bishop of Rochester for the remainder of his life. He died on October 10, 644. His cult developed both at Canterbury and Rochester and in a number of English monasteries. His feast is not on the General Roman Calendar.

11 Mary Soledad, virgin

Mary Soledad (1826–87) was for thirty-five years the head of the Handmaids of Mary, a Spanish congregation of sisters whose mission was the service of the sick and the needy. Born Manuela Torres-Acosta in Madrid, she thought at first of becoming a Dominican nun, but was persuaded by the local parish priest, Michael Martinez y Sanz, to become part of his new community founded to minister to the sick. Manuela took the religious name Mary Soledad (Maria Desolata) in honor of Our Lady of Sorrows [September 15], to whom she had a special devotion. Five years later, whether or not because of internal disagreements, the priest took half of the community to establish a new foundation in an African colony. Mary Soledad was left in charge of those who remained in Madrid. Although the local bishop was inclined to suspend his approval for the now smaller group as a religious congregation, the queen and local civil authorities offered their own powerful support because of the community's work on behalf of the poor and the sick in Madrid. In 1861 their Rule received diocesan approval, and the community took the name Handmaids of Mary Serving the Sick. The community's pastoral outreach expanded greatly, and it won special praise for its care of the sick in the cholera epidemic of 1865. In 1875 the first overseas foundation was established in Cuba. Mary Soledad remained in charge of the congregation until her death on October 11, 1887. She was beatified in 1950 and canonized in 1970. In the canonization homily, Pope Paul VI said that her life could be summed up in two words: humility and charity. Her feast is not on the General Roman Calendar.

12 Wilfrid of York, bishop; Seraphin of Montegranaro, religious

Wilfrid (634–709) was bishop of York from 664 and a supporter of the Roman position on the dating of Easter. Born in Northumbria of a noble family, he studied first at Lindisfarne, then at Canterbury and Rome (in 653). Upon his return home, he became abbot of Ripon, where he introduced the Rule of St. Benedict [July 11] and, with the king's approval, adopted the Roman method for the dating of Easter. At the Synod of Whitby (664) Wilfrid was the leading advocate of the Roman system, which prevailed. He was then chosen bishop of Northumbria (centered in York) by King Alcfrith, but had to cross the English Channel to France to be consecrated, so few validly consecrated bishops were there in England at the time. The ceremony was conducted with excessive splendor. Wilfrid was accompanied by a large retinue to demonstrate his wealth and importance, and it was said that twelve bishops carried him into the sanctuary on a golden throne. Unfortunately, Wilfrid remained in France too long. Upon his return to England in 666, he found that Alcfrith had died or was in exile and that his own place as bishop of York had been taken by Chad [March 2], nominated by King Oswiu and dubiously consecrated. Wilfrid retired to Ripon but was later reinstated by Theodore [September 19], the archbishop of Canterbury, in 669.

With the support of King Egfrith and his wife, Etheldreda [June 23], Wilfrid obtained large tracts of land for the building of monasteries and churches. The monastery church of Hexham was said to have been the largest church north of the Alps. He himself adopted the lifestyle of the Frankish bishops he had come to know while in France. He had a large household and presided over a diocese, centered at York, that was coextensive with the whole of Northumbria. His power and wealth had already become subjects of gossip and criticism when he encouraged Etheldreda to separate from her husband, the king, and become a nun in 672. With the collaboration of King Egfrith and without Wilfrid's consent, Archbishop Theodore divided Northumbria into three, and then five, smaller dioceses. Theodore's action was based on a theology of the episcopate that differed from Wilfrid's and from those in Gaul whom he emulated. While the Franks looked upon their bishops as quasi-princes legitimately engaged in matters of court, Theodore's episcopal ideal, consistent with that of Italy and the Mediterranean, was that of an active pastor of a small area centered on a town rather than a kingdom or a tribe. In any event, Wilfrid decided to appeal Theodore's action to Rome.

On his way to Rome, his ship was blown off course and landed in Friesland. He stayed there for the winter and spring, preaching and converting many, and even helping in the development of more efficient methods of fishing. He thereby became the forerunner of the Anglo-Saxon Christian mission on the Continent. The pope did rule in favor of Wilfrid in the matter of his restoration to his see, but he upheld Theodore's division of the diocese, with the stipulation that Wilfrid be allowed to select his own suffragan bishops. The king rejected the decision, accused Wilfrid of having bribed the pope, and placed him in prison for nine months before releasing him on condition that he leave the kingdom. Wilfrid went to Sussex, which was the last stronghold of paganism in Anglo-Saxon England, preaching there and on the Isle of Wight and founding a monastery at Selsey (which later developed into Chichester). With the approval of the new king, Aldfrith, Theodore reinstated Wilfrid in Northumbria in 686, but with reduced jurisdiction, and he remained there until 691. Because of subsequent disputes with King Aldfrith, Wilfrid retired this time to Mercia, where he functioned as bishop of Lichfield and founded several more monasteries. In 703 a new archbishop of Canterbury, Bertwald, decreed that Wilfrid should resign from York and hand over his monasteries. Once again he appealed to the pope, and once again he was vindicated.

Wilfrid's exile came to an end in 705 when he agreed to yield his claim to York in return for which he resumed full episcopal authority over the see of Hexham and the monasteries of Hexham and Ripon. He died in 709 at the monastery of Oundle in Mercia, one of several monasteries he had founded outside of his own diocese, and was buried at Ripon, where a cult developed, as it had also in Hexham. In his will, he divided his considerable wealth among the poor, his churches and monasteries, and those who had shared exiles with him. With the diffusion of his relics in the tenth century to Canterbury and Worcester, his cult became nationwide. His feast is celebrated on this day by the Church of England, but it is not on the General Roman Calendar.

The Franciscans commemorate on this day *Seraphin of Montegranaro* (1540–1604), an Italian Capuchin lay brother who was noted for his devotion to the Blessed Sacrament and to the poor and revered for his spiritual wisdom and holiness. He was canonized in 1767.

13 Edward the Confessor, king

Edward the Confessor (1003–66) was the king of England from 1042 to 1066—the last king of the Anglo-Saxon line—and virtual founder of Westminster Abbey. The son of King Ethelred II, known as the "Unready," and his second (Norman) wife, Emma, Edward was educated at Ely and then in Normandy, during the time when two Scandinavians, Sweyn and Cnut, ruled in succession as kings of England. Edward was proclaimed king in 1042. His political record is a matter of some debate within the historical community, but he was accessible to his subjects, generous to the poor, and had a reputation for visions and healings. He also had a close working relationship with the papacy. He appointed diocesan priests, sometimes from abroad, to bishoprics, thereby diminishing the near monopoly of monastic bishops. Nevertheless, he was the virtual founder of Westminster Abbey, which he richly endowed. His decision to do so was the result of a vow he had once made to visit Rome as a pilgrim, if his family fortunes were restored. Later the pope released him from the vow when he could not fulfill it, but on condition that he should endow a monastery dedicated to St. Peter [June 29]. Edward chose an existing monastic house at Thorney, to the west of London, and that became Westminster Abbey. He also built a huge Romanesque church alongside it, 300 feet long, with a nave of twelve bays. It was completed and consecrated just before Edward's death on January 5, 1066, and has since been used for the coronations and burials of English kings and queens. Edward himself is buried there, and his relics remain undisturbed to this day. His body was found to be incorrupt in 1102.

Edward was canonized at the request of King Henry II in 1161, but only after Henry gave his support to Alexander III against an antipope. Edward's relics were solemnly transferred to a new shrine in the abbey on October 13, 1163, which became his principal feast (replacing January 5, his day of death). In the Middle Ages Edward was widely regarded as the patron saint of England, but by ca. 1450 St. George [April 23] was accorded that distinction. Edward's depiction in art is consistent with the details of his biography, namely, that he was a tall man with a long face, blond hair and beard, ruddy complexion, and long, thin fingers. His feast is celebrated on this day by the Church of England, but it is not on the General Roman Calendar. It was on the universal Roman calendar from 1689 until its revision in 1969.

14 Callistus I, pope and martyr

Callistus I (d. 222; pope 217–22), also known as Calixtus, was the first pope, after Peter [June 29], whose name is commemorated as a martyr in the oldest martyrology of the Roman church, the *Depositio Martyrum* (ca. 354). Much of the information that survives about Callistus comes filtered through the highly derogatory writings of Hippolytus [August 13], a leading and learned Roman presbyter who also had been a persistent critic of Callistus's predecessor Zephrynus (199–217). Callistus was a Roman by birth and in his youth had been a slave of a Christian who set him up in banking. When, to the dismay of its many Christian customers, the business failed (perhaps through some unsavory activity of his), Callistus fled. After his return, he was charged with fighting in a synagogue on the Sabbath and sentenced to hard labor in the mines of Sardinia. He was released at the same time a number of other Christian slaves were liberated, through the good offices of the emperor's Christian mistress, Marcia, and Pope Victor I (189–98). Victor had deliberately excluded Callistus from the list he had submitted to Marcia, but Callistus prevailed upon the governor to free him as well. Upon Callistus's return to Rome, the pope sent him to live in Anzio on a monthly pension, but Victor's successor, Zephrynus, recalled him and appointed him his deacon, with supervisory authority over the clergy of Rome and over the church's official cemetery on the Appian Way (now known as the catacombs of San Callisto). Because of Zephrynus's own intellectual and administrative limitations, Callistus exerted enormous influence as the pope's deacon and was elected to succeed him. Hippolytus, however, refused to accept the election and seems to have sought and received election as bishop by a schismatic group, thereby becoming the first of the Catholic Church's thirty-nine antipopes (the last was Felix V [1439–49]).

Callistus's five-year pontificate was defined in large part by his constant battles with Hippolytus and his faction, who accused the pope of doctrinal deviations (Modalism, in particular) and laxity in discipline (e.g., ordaining men who had been married more than once, recognizing marriages between partners of different social classes, and readmitting heretics and schismatics to the Church without adequate prior penances). Both charges were unfair. Callistus was clearly not a Modalist, but neither did he support Hippolytus's teaching that the Word (Gk. *Logos*) is a distinct Person, a view the pope regarded as ditheistic (positing two Gods). And Callistus's approach to sinners was actually closer to that of Jesus than to that of the new rigorists in the Church. The Church, he believed, is a place where the wheat and tares grow together. As Jesus reminded his disciples, the sorting out of saints from sinners must be left to the merciful God. The Church, the pope insisted, must offer reconciliation to anyone seeking forgiveness for sins committed after baptism.

Callistus is said to have laid the foundation for Ember Days (days of fast and abstinence, occurring in sets of three, four times a year), which are no longer observed in the Catholic Church. Although his name appears in the oldest Roman martyrology, it is questionable whether he was, in fact, a martyr. Historians point out that there was no persecution during his pontificate. His tomb in the cemetery of Calepodius on the Via Aurelia (and not in the cemetery named after him on the Appian Way) was discovered in 1960 in the remains of an oratory erected by Pope Julius I (337–52) in the fourth century. The crypt is decorated with frescoes depicting his martyrdom. His feast is on the General Roman Calendar.

The Jesuits commemorate Scottish martyr *John Ogilvie* [March 10] on this day.

15 Teresa of Ávila, virgin and Doctor of the Church

Teresa of Ávila (1515–82), also Theresa, was the foundress of the Discalced Carmelites and one of the first two women to be named a Doctor of the Church (with Catherine of Siena [April 29]). She is also the patron saint of Spain. Born Teresa de Ahumada y Cepeda near Ávila, Spain, of a large, aristocratic Castilian family with Jewish ancestry, she

Saint Teresa of Ávila by Gregorio Fernandez, 1625

entered the Carmelite monastery of the Incarnation at Ávila in 1535 after reading the letters of St. Jerome [September 30] during a period of convalescence from an illness that may have been psychosomatic. A year after her solemn profession, she fell seriously ill again and had to leave the community for a three-year period of treatment and recovery. Whatever the source of this second illness, however, the cure was extreme and painful: purges and bloodlettings that left her paralyzed for almost a year. Except for that interruption, her first twenty years as a religious were marked by devotion and fidelity to the way of life, but she felt that something was missing and found it very difficult to pray. The atmosphere in the convent was relatively relaxed, and there was much contact between the nuns and the ladies and gentlemen of the town.

In 1554, while praying before a statue of the wounded Christ, she underwent a profound spiritual conversion. She later wrote: "When I fell to prayer again and looked at Christ hanging poor and naked upon the Cross, I felt I could not bear to be rich. So I besought him with tears to bring it to pass that I might be as poor as he." Identifying herself spiritually with Mary Magdalene [July 22] and Augustine [August 28], whose *Confessions* deeply influenced her, she received encouragement from Francis Borgia [October 3] and Peter of Alcántara [October 22] to accept her mystical and visionary experiences as having their origin in God. Between then and 1560, these experiences became the subject of gossip, and she was exposed to misunderstanding, ridicule, and even persecution. Then, after twenty-five years or more of unreformed Carmelite life, she felt the need to found a house of her own where the primitive Carmelite Rule would be strictly observed.

In 1562, with thirteen other nuns, she established such a convent in Ávila, under the patronage of St. Joseph [March 19], and in the same year composed the first draft of her *Life,* which included a treatise on mystical prayer using the imagery of water. Thereafter, she always signed herself Teresa de Jesus. This first reformed convent would become the prototype for sixteen others she would found in her lifetime. Their mode of life would be marked by personal poverty, signified by the coarse brown wool habit, leather sandals, and beds of straw, manual work, abstinence from meat, and solitude. Teresa herself wore a hair shirt under her habit and nettles for bracelets and carried a scourge, which she used on herself whenever spiritually required. On one occasion she donned a halter and saddle weighted with stones and was led by another nun into the refectory on all fours. But there were also experiences of levitation, and their frequent occurrence led to great envy and resentment on the part of others. Through all this, Teresa was an extraordinarily gifted administrator, so gifted, in fact, that her most recent biographer has observed: "It was a wonder, given the complexities of her personal and business transactions, that Teresa had any spiritual life at all." She was especially attentive to the task of weeding out unacceptable candidates for convent life. "God preserve us from stupid nuns!" she once declared.

Her many writings were done under obedience, but also with the encouragement of the Dominican Domingo Báñez, one of the most prominent theologians of the time, who became her spiritual director and confessor and who defended her before civil and ecclesiastical tribunals. In 1566 she wrote *The Way of Perfection* and her *Meditations on the Song of Songs.* In 1567 she met for the first time a newly ordained priest, John of St. Matthias (later known as John of the Cross [December 14]), whom Teresa convinced to remain a Carmelite (rather than become a Carthusian) and to collaborate with her in the reform of the order. Not surprisingly, this effort would evoke as much opposition from the unreformed friars as her earlier reforms of Carmelite nuns had done. In 1568 she saw to the inauguration of the first of the reform houses of friars at Duruelo. Between 1562 and 1582 she would found seventeen Discalced convents and this one friary, while traveling across the rugged Castilian countryside by mule. After 1576, however, her reform program also came to an end. So virulent was the resistance that John of the Cross was kidnapped and imprisoned, and her closest friend and superior of the Discalced friars, Father Jerome Gracián, was placed under house arrest, while the papal nuncio to Spain derided her as "an unstable, restless, disobedient and contumacious female." Teresa appealed to the king, Philip II, for support. As a result of it, peace was made in 1580 when the Discalced Carmelites were given their own province separate from the Calced. This proved to be the first step toward complete independence as a distinct order in 1594.

In 1577 she began the composition of her masterpiece, *The Interior Castle,* a disguised autobiography written in the third person, while her

Life was in the hands of the Inquisition. The book describes the mystical life through the symbolism of seven mansions, with the first three mansions as the premystical journey to God and the next four mansions as growth in the mystical life. With the imagery of the Song of Songs in the background, Teresa saw spiritual betrothal occurring in the sixth mansion and spiritual marriage in the seventh. For her, the test of growth in the mystical life was love of neighbor. Although she was profoundly contemplative, she led an active life not only as a reformer of Carmelite life, but also as an adviser to and correspondent with countless people of every station in life.

Teresa died on October 4, 1582, at the convent of Alba de Torres, while on her way back to Ávila from Burgos, where she had made her last foundation. The nuns who were present at her death testified that a luscious, paradisiacal scent emanated from her body, and later, when one of her confessors ordered her grave there to be opened, her body was still intact and redolent of lilies. The confessor severed various parts of her body to be distributed among her powerful admirers, and her cult spread rapidly throughout Spain. One of her hands ended up with Generalissimo Franco, leader of Spain, who kept it by his bed until his death in 1975. The most famous artistic representation of her is a sculpture by Bernini (1598–1680) in the church of Santa Maria della Vittoria in Rome.

Teresa of Ávila was beatified in 1614 and canonized in 1622 (along with Ignatius of Loyola [July 31], Francis Xavier [December 3], and Philip Neri [May 26]), and was one of the first two women to be named a Doctor of the Church, by Pope Paul VI in 1970 in recognition of her outstanding contribution to mystical theology and Christian spirituality. Her feast, which was extended to the universal Church in 1688, is on the General Roman Calendar and is also celebrated by the Church of England and the Episcopal Church in the USA. Ordinarily, the feast day would correspond with her day of death, October 4, but in 1582, on the very day after her death, the Gregorian reform of the calendar was adopted and ten days were omitted from the month of October.

BIBLIOGRAPHY

Ahlgren, Gillian T. W. *Teresa of Avila and the Politics of Sanctity.* Ithaca, NY: Cornell University Press, 1996.

Medwick, Cathleen. *Teresa of Avila: The Progress of a Soul.* New York: Knopf, 1999.

Slade, Carole. *St. Teresa of Avila: Author of a Heroic Life.* Berkeley: University of California Press, 1995.

16 Hedwig, religious; Margaret Mary Alacoque, virgin; Longinus, centurion; Gall, monk; Gerard Majella, religious

Hedwig (ca. 1174–1243), or Jadwiga, mother of seven children, entered a Cistercian convent after the death of her husband, the duke of Silesia. She is patron saint of Silesia. Born at Andechs (Bavaria), the daughter of a count, she lived as a child in a monastery and then, at age twelve, married the future duke of Salesia, who was then eighteen years old. She and her husband helped to found several religious houses, including the first (Cistercian) convent of women in Silesia, as well as hospitals and a house for lepers. After the birth of their seventh child in 1209, she and her husband took a vow of chastity in the presence of the local bishop and lived as brother and sister thereafter. Following her husband's death in 1238, she took the habit of a Cistercian nun, but did not take religious vows so that she would still be free to administer her property for the benefit of the poor. Hedwig was said to have known of the death of one of her sons in battle three days before she received the news and to have foretold her own death at the convent in Trebnitz (Trzebnica), near Breslau (in the Wroclaw province of modern-day Poland), in October 1243. She was canonized in 1267 and her feast was extended to the universal Latin calendar in 1706. Her feast is on the General Roman Calendar.

Margaret Mary Alacoque (1647–90) was the principal founder of devotion to the Sacred Heart of Jesus. Born Margaret Alacoque in a small town in Burgundy (she took the name Mary at her Confirmation), she was only eight when she was sent away to school with the Poor Clares after the death of her father. Having for a long time been attracted to the life of a nun, she entered the Visitation convent of Paray-le-Monial in 1671, at age twenty, making her profession the following year. From 1673 to 1675 she is said to have experienced a series of visions of Christ, revealing to her the love and mercy of God for all people—a point that had been obscured not only by the widespread secularism of France in the seventeenth century, but also by the prevailing influence of Jansenism, a largely French spiritual movement that exaggerated human sinfulness and unworthiness. The visions urged her to persuade church authorities to have a special feast established on the Friday after the Octave of Corpus Christi (which is now celebrated on the Sunday after Trinity Sunday), to urge Catholics to receive Holy Communion on the first Friday of each month in reparation for sins, and to spend an hour in prayer every Thursday night in remembrance of the Lord's agony in the Garden of Gethsemane. (The devotion of the First Fridays was later specified to consist of attending Mass and receiving Communion on nine consecutive first Fridays of the month, with the attached promise that one who had "made the nine First Fridays" would be saved. This devotion was especially popular in the Catholic Church prior to the Second Vatican Council [1962–65].)

When Margaret Mary tried to carry out these directives, she encountered great opposition and suspicion within her own religious community and from theologians who were asked to review her claims. She was supported and encouraged, however, by her spiritual director, Claude La Colombière (also Claude de la Colombière) [February 15], who became one of her first disciples in spreading devotion to the Sacred Heart. His writings and those of John Eudes [August 19], who composed a Mass and Office of the Sacred Heart, were important elements in this process. The devotion itself consists of veneration of the physical heart of Jesus, united to his divinity, as the symbol of his redemptive love for all. The feast of the Sacred Heart was first celebrated in Visitation convents, and then in 1765 Pope Clement XIII officially recognized and approved the devotion and granted permission to the bishops of Poland to celebrate the feast. That was extended to the universal Church in 1856. One hundred years later, Pope Pius XII wrote an encyclical, *Haurietis aquas* (Lat., "You draw waters"), that gave the theological foundation of this devotion. Margaret May Alacoque died at age forty-three, on October 17, 1690, while being anointed. She was canonized in 1920, and her feast is on the General Roman Calendar.

On this day the Greek and Russian Orthodox Churches celebrate the feast of *Longinus* (first century), traditionally regarded as the centurion at the Crucifixion who acknowledged Jesus to be the Son of God (Matt. 27:54; Mark 15:39; Luke 23:47).

October 16 is also the feast of *Gall* (ca. 560–ca. 630), an Irish monk who, after being exiled from France with Columban [November 23], settled in Switzerland, where he became a hermit and an itinerant preacher. He is patron saint of that country.

Finally, it is the feast day of *Gerard Majella* (1725–55), a Redemptorist lay brother who spent his brief adult life as a porter, tailor, and gardener, but with the reputation as the most famous miracle worker of the eighteenth century. He was canonized in 1904 and is patron saint of lay brothers, mothers, and expectant mothers.

17 Ignatius of Antioch, bishop and martyr

Ignatius of Antioch (ca. 35–ca. 107) is the Apostolic Father whose letters to the various churches in the ancient Christian world serve as a major source of information regarding the life, faith, and structure of the early Church in Asia Minor and Rome. He was also the first writer to use the term "Catholic Church" as a collective designation for Christians and among the first to attest to the monoepiscopacy, that is, the governance of a diocese by one bishop. He also used the name Theophoros (Gk., "bearer of God"). He was probably born in Syria of pagan parents, but the facts of his early life are largely unknown. He is thought to have been a disciple of John the Evangelist [December 27]. He became bishop of Antioch ca. 69 and was condemned to death during Trajan's persecution of Christians. He was taken to Rome (perhaps because he was a Roman citizen) under a military guard of ten soldiers, and during this journey wrote six letters to six churches and one separate letter to Polycarp [February 23], the bishop of Smyrna, whom he met en route. The letters to the churches at Ephesus, Magnesia, Tralles, and Rome were all written from Smyrna, and the letters to the churches of Philadelphia and Smyrna and the one to Polycarp were all written from Troas. The letters stress the divinity and the humanity of Jesus Christ, his bodily death and resurrection, the central importance of the Eucharist and the bishop for church unity, and the special reverence owed to the church of Rome as the one founded by Peter and Paul [June 29]. In his letter to Rome he had begged the Christians there not to intervene with Roman authorities to prevent his martyrdom. (Significantly, there is no mention of any bishop of Rome in his letter to the Romans, even though he made mention of the bishops of the other five cities to which he had written.)

Upon reaching Rome, he was taken to the Colosseum and thrown to the lions, dying almost immediately. In his letter to the Romans, he had described himself as "the wheat of God [to] be ground by the teeth of wild beasts to become pure bread." He believed that his own discipleship was grounded in his imitation of the sufferings of Christ. For that reason, he welcomed martyrdom. Ignatius of Antioch has frequently been depicted in art: in the sixth-century mosaics in Santa Sophia, Constantinople (now Istanbul), the Chartres statues, the baptistery in Florence, Botticelli's painting in the Uffizi in Florence, and Fra Angelico's [February 18] in the National Gallery, London.

From the beginning, Antioch kept his feast on October 17. The Church of the West had observed it on February 1 until 1969, when it transferred it to October 17 in order to bring the date into line with Antioch. The Eastern churches, including the Greek and Russian Orthodox Churches, continue to celebrate it on December 20. The Church of England, the Episcopal Church in the USA, and the Evangelical Lutheran Church in America also observe the feast on this day, October 17. On this same day the Greek and Russian Orthodox Churches celebrate the feast of *Andrew of Crete* (which they also celebrate on July 4) and of the Old Testament prophet *Hosea.*

18 Luke, Evangelist

Luke (first century) is the traditional author of the Third Gospel and was a companion of Paul [June 29]. Because he was considered to be a physician, he is the patron saint of physicians. Because he was also thought to have painted an icon of the Blessed Mother in the basilica of St. Mary Major in Rome, attributed to him from as early as the sixth century, he is the patron saint of artists. And because his emblem as one of the four Evangelists is the ox (perhaps because of the Temple sacrifice mentioned in Luke's account of the Nativity), he is also regarded as the patron saint of butchers. According to a reliable tradition, Luke was a Syrian physician from Antioch who wrote his Gospel in Achaea (Greece) and lived as a celibate to the age of eighty-four, when he died in Boeotia. The *Muratorian Canon,* a list of New Testament books probably from the late second century, identifies Luke as the author of the Third Gospel. Irenaeus [June 28] attributes both the Gospel and Acts of the Apostles to Luke, arguing that Luke is the person intended by the first-person references in Acts. The opening of Acts refers to the Gospel and is dedicated to the same person, Theophilus. He is thought to have accompanied Paul on his second missionary journey from Troas to Philippi (Acts 16: 10–17) and on the third from Philippi to Jerusalem (Acts 20:5–24). He also accompanied Paul to Rome, where he stayed during Paul's captivity (Col. 4:14; 2 Tim. 4:11; Philem. 24). Paul specifically mentions Luke as his "fellow worker" in Philemon 24. He is called "beloved physician" in Colossians 4:14 and Paul's sole companion in 2 Timothy 4:11. Some have also identified Luke with the Lucius mentioned in Acts 13:1 and Romans 16:21, but Scripture scholars consider that unlikely.

The basic point of Luke's New Testament writings is to underscore the love and compassion of Christ and his concern for the poor. Some of the most moving and memorable parables emphasizing these themes are in Luke's Gospel, for example, the Prodigal Son (15:11–32) and the Rich Man (Dives) and Lazarus (16:19–31). Women also figure more prominently in his Gospel than in any other, for example, Mary (the whole Nativity account in the first two chapters), Elizabeth [November 5] (1:5–66), the widow of Nain (7:11–17), the woman who was a sinner (7:36–50), Mary Magdalene [July 22] and several others (8:1–3), and the women of Jerusalem (23:27–31). He also places great emphasis on the Holy Spirit in the life of the Church and of the individual Christian (Acts 2; 11:13; 12:12) and on the importance of prayer (11:1–9; 18:1–8).

In 356–57 Constantius II had Luke's relics transferred from Thebes in Boeotia, where he died, to Constantinople, where they were preserved in the Church of the Apostles, built soon thereafter. His feast is on the General Roman Calendar and is celebrated on this day by all the major Christian Churches, East and West alike.

BIBLIOGRAPHY

Fitzmyer, Joseph A. *Luke the Theologian.* New York: Paulist Press, 1989.
Karris, Robert J. *Luke: Artist and Theologian.* New York: Paulist Press, 1985.

19 Isaac Jogues, John de Brébeuf, and companions, martyrs; Paul of the Cross, priest

Isaac Jogues (1607–46), *John de Brébeuf* (1593–1649), and their companions are known collectively as the North American Martyrs and are patron saints of North America. Isaac Jogues was born in Orléans, France, became a Jesuit in 1624, and was ordained a priest in early 1636. In April of that year he was sent to Canada, or the New France, to preach the gospel to the Hurons. After some limited success at Sainte-Marie, he returned to Quebec to ask for more missionaries to convert the whole Huron nation. Since there were no Jesuits available, he was given the services of *René Goupil,* a lay assistant devoted to the Jesuit mission and trained in medicine. During their return trip to Sainte-Marie, they were attacked by Mohawks, who bit off Jogues's fingernails or chewed his forefingers. Goupil was similarly abused. They were taken captive and brought to the Mohawk village. On the way, Jogues accepted Goupil's vows as a Jesuit. During a pause in the journey, however, they were stripped and forced to run the gauntlet up a rocky hill. When they reached the village (located in present-day Auriesville, New York) on the bank of the Mohawk River, they were again forced to run the gauntlet, after which a squaw cut off Jogues's left thumb with a jagged shell. The men were then taken to a building where they were stretched out and tied to the ground while children dropped hot coals on their naked bodies. After three days of torture, they were handed over to the chief to act as his personal slaves.

A few weeks later, Goupil was tomahawked to death for making the sign of the cross on a child. His martyrdom was on September 29, 1642. (He is patron saint of anesthetists.) Jogues, however, endured his months of slavery, during which he was treated as no more than a beast of burden. However, the Christian Hurons who were also held captive with him looked upon him as their priest, and he continued to offer them spiritual consolation. In September 1643 he accompanied the Mohawks on a trading trip to a Dutch settlement in present-day Albany. When the Dutch were unsuccessful in their attempt to ransom him, they hid him in one of their ships until the Mohawks' anger subsided (after six weeks) and then took him to New Amsterdam (present-day New York City) and then back to France in time for Christmas.

The following April he left again for New France, arriving in June. He attended a lengthy peace conference between the French and the Iroquois federation. It was agreed that the Mohawks would also have to give their approval, and Jogues was chosen to go to the Mohawks to secure it. He was accompanied by two Algonquins and four Mohawks. On the way, the group stopped at Fort Orange, where Jogues had met his Dutch liberators. He repaid the ransom they had given the Mohawks at the time of his escape. When they arrived at the Mohawk village, the Indians were amazed to see their former slave acting as the envoy of the powerful French nation. He offered them gifts (including a black chest containing Mass vestments, books, and other religious articles) and explained the terms of the treaty, which they accepted. He returned to Quebec, but asked permission to return to the Mohawks as a missionary once again, now that the treaty had been agreed to. He was accompanied by *John de la Lande,* who was a layman, and several Hurons.

Not many days into the trip they learned that the Mohawks were once again on the warpath. All but one of the Hurons abandoned the group, leaving the two missionaries and one Indian to continue on alone. In the meantime, however, the Mohawks had suffered both a crop failure and an epidemic and were blaming their misfortune on the black chest that Jogues had left there. As they were out searching for Frenchmen on whom to vent their anger, they came upon Jogues and his two companions heading toward the village. They stripped and beat them and dragged them to the village, where they cut strips of flesh from Jogues's neck and arms. The next day, October 18, 1646, he was tomahawked to death as he entered the village lodge, ostensibly to participate in a feast given by a friendlier Mohawk clan. His killer hacked off Jogues's head and dragged his body through the village.

When de la Lande heard the news, he was advised to remain in the lodge, but he did not. When he left the lodge under cover of darkness, he was seized and tomahawked to death. It was the early morning of October 19. When daylight came, the two bodies were thrown into the river and their heads were exposed on the fence surrounding the village. Three years later *John de Brébeuf* and *Gabriel Lalement,* who had worked successfully among the Hurons, were brutally tortured, mutilated, burned, and then eaten when the Hurons' village was attacked by their deadly enemies, the Iroquois. They, along with Isaac Jogues, René Goupil, *Charles Garnier, Anthony Daniel,* and *Noel Chabanel,* were beatified in 1925 and canonized in 1930. Their feast is on the General Roman Calendar.

Paul of the Cross (1694–1775) was the founder of the Congregation of the Passion (Passionists). They were known originally as the Discalced Clerks of the Most Holy Cross and Passion of Our Lord Jesus Christ. Born Paolo Francesco Danei at Ovada near Genoa, Italy, the second of sixteen children, he was deprived of a formal education because of his father's financial difficulties. He served for a year in the Venetian army, hoping to die for the faith in the fight against the Turks. After a lengthy period of prayer and solitude, he decided in 1720, in response to a vision of himself clothed in the habit that would be worn by his Passionists, that he should found a new congregation of priests dedicated to an intense devotion to, and a preaching of, the Passion of Christ. He did so, along with his brother John, at Monte Argentaro, following his own ordination to the priesthood in Rome in 1727. His Rule was approved by Pope Benedict XIV in 1741. Because of the success of the Passionists' ministry to the sick and the dying, in the reconciliation of sinners, and in bringing lapsed Catholics back to the Church, they were soon in demand in many parts of Italy. Their method, derived from Paul of the Cross himself, involved active participation by the laity in processions, vigils, penitential works, hymns, prayers, and other forms of devotion.

Paul was elected superior general in 1747. Final papal approval was granted in 1769, after which Paul resided mainly in Rome next to the basilica of Sts. John and Paul, which Pope Clement XIV had given the congregation after Paul's brother John died in 1765. Under Paul's leadership, there were twelve new foundations, two new provinces, and six general chapters. Near the end of his life, he also founded a convent of enclosed Passionist nuns at Corneto in 1771. He died at age eighty on

October 18, 1775, and was buried in the basilica. He was canonized in 1867. His feast is on the General Roman Calendar on this day, but it is also on the Proper Calendar for the Dioceses of the U.S.A. on October 20.

This is also the feast day (not on the General Roman Calendar) of *Peter of Alcántara* [October 22] (1499–1562), founder of the Franciscans of the Observance of St. Peter of Alcántara, or Alcantarines, and spiritual adviser to Teresa of Ávila [October 15]. The Franciscans celebrate his feast on October 22 (see below).

20 Maria Bertilla Boscardin, nun; Jerzy Popieluszko, priest

Maria Bertilla Boscardin (1888–1922) was a nun and nurse whose life bore a striking spiritual resemblance to that of Theresa of Lisieux [October 1], whose own sanctity was rooted in the faithful performance of the daily, simple duties of her state in life. Born Anna Francesca of a poor family, with an alcoholic and abusive father, at Brendola, near Vicenza in northern Italy, she lacked the advantage of a normal education and was disparaged by many for her seeming lack of intelligence. When, in 1904, she joined the Sisters of St. Dorothy [February 6], she was given the name Maria Bertilla and assigned to work in the kitchen, bakery, and laundry. However, she was also allowed to train to be a nurse and, after her profession three years later, she was transferred to the children's diphtheria ward, where she demonstrated a special gift for relating to ill and disturbed children. With the outbreak of World War I the hospital was taken over by the military for the care of the wounded, and by 1917 it was in the front line of the fighting. Maria Bertilla cared for those patients who could not be moved, even in the face of constant air raids and bombings. She wrote in her spiritual diary: "Here I am, Lord, to do your will whatever comes—be it life, death, or terror."

She and her patients were eventually evacuated from Treviso to another military hospital in a safer area, near Como. Although she proved herself once again an effective and compassionate nurse, her religious superior felt that she was overworked and becoming too closely attached to her patients, so she sent Maria Bertilla back to the laundry. Four months later, however, that directive was countermanded by the mother general of the order, and Maria Bertilla was reassigned to Treviso and placed in charge of the children's isolation ward there. By now the war had ended. During this period she is said to have prayed to Our Lady not for "visions, or revelations, or favors, even spiritual ones," but "to suffer joyfully without any consolation [and] to work hard for you until I die." She had suffered for a number of years from a painful tumor, but in 1922 her health deteriorated sharply. After a failed operation, she died three days later, on October 20. Crowds thronged to her funeral in Vicenza.

A memorial plaque at the hospital in Treviso describes her as a "chosen soul of heroic goodness . . . an angelic alleviator of human suffering in this place." Her tomb at Vicenza became an attraction for pilgrims, and there were reports of miracles. Maria Bertilla Boscardin was beatified in 1952 and canonized in 1961 in the presence of some who had been her patients many years before. At the latter ceremony Pope John XXIII pointed out that the source of Maria Bertilla's "greatness" was her humility, that her sacrifices were "heroic," and that hers was a life of "simplicity arising from an abundant trust in God." Her feast is not on the General Roman Calendar.

This is also the day of death of *Jerzy Popieluszko* (1947–84), a Polish diocesan priest who was murdered by agents of the Communist government in retaliation for his activities in support of the Solidarity movement. He had said that "if we must die it is better to meet death while defending a worthwhile cause than to sit back and let an injustice take place." Five years later, the Communists were voted out of office and replaced by new leaders closely associated with Solidarity.

21 Hilarion, hermit

Hilarion (ca. 291–371), also known as Hilarion the Great, was the founder of monasticism in Palestine and, in the mind of Jerome [September 30], he is the "second Anthony" [January 17]. Born of pagan parents in a village in the south of Gaza in Palestine, Hilarion was educated in Alexandria, where he became a Christian while still in his mid-teen years. For a short time he stayed with Anthony in the Egyptian desert, but left because of the many visitors who came to see the famous master. When he returned to Gaza, he learned that his parents had died. He divided his inheritance among his brothers and the poor and retired to Majuma, between the sea and a swamp, where he lived a life of extreme austerity in imitation of Anthony. He ate very little and slept in a tiny hut. Although he suffered spiritual aridity and various temptations, he persevered in prayer. However, his fame spread after several years, and people began flocking to see him in order to obtain spiritual guidance. A group of disciples also gathered around him against his will, but for their sake he took ownership of household goods and a farm. Eventually, however, he decided to leave his native country in search of a place where he could enjoy complete solitude.

His travels took him to Egypt, Sicily, Dalmatia, and finally Cyprus. He found some solitude in that last place, but he was still disturbed by visitors, including Epiphanius, bishop of Salamis, who wrote about Hilarion to Jerome. When Hilarion died at age eighty, some of the local people wanted to build a shrine for his relics, but his disciple Hesychius (who had become attached to him in Sicily) removed the body secretly and took it back to Majuma. Hilarion's fame derives from the biography written by Jerome sometime between 382 and 396. The work appeared in many versions and translations throughout the East. Hilarion is the patron saint of many villages in Cyprus and is the subject of many icons and mosaics. His feast is not on the General Roman Calendar, but it is celebrated on this day by the Greek and Russian Orthodox Churches.

22 Peter of Alcántara, founder

Peter of Alcántara (1499–1562) was the founder of the Franciscans of the Observance of St. Peter of Alcántara, or Alcantarines, and spiritual adviser to Teresa of Ávila [October 15]. Born Pedro Garavita at Alcántara, Spain, he studied at the University of Salamanca and joined the strict Franciscan Friars of the Observance in 1515. He followed an extremely austere regime of mortification, similar to that of the Desert Fathers, eating sparingly and sleeping as little as possible and then usually in a sitting position. Because of this practice, he was later designated as the patron saint of night watchmen. Ordained a priest in 1524, he became guardian, or superior, of a number of Franciscan houses and was a provincial from 1538 to 1541. In these offices he was known for imposing on the friars as strict a way of life as possible. However, because his efforts at fundamental reform were largely unsuccessful, he received permission at the end of his term to live as a hermit at Arabida, near Lisbon. He found a like-minded group of friars there and soon became their leader. In 1554 he went to Rome to seek permission to found a congregation of friars and also to place himself under the Conventual branch of Franciscans instead of the Observant branch, because the minister general of the latter opposed his plans.

Upon his return to Spain, Peter established a new house at Pedrosa. This was the beginning of the Franciscans of the Observance of St. Peter of Alcántara, or Alcantarines. During this period (ca. 1556), he wrote a widely read book on prayer that was translated into several

European languages. Peter and his friars were formally restored to Observant control in 1561 and recognized as a separate province. They kept their distinct existence until 1897, when Pope Leo XIII united all of the Observant groups. The Alcantarine Rule required that cells be only seven feet in length and that the friars go about barefoot, abstain from meat and wine, practice three hours of mental prayer daily, and subsist on almsgiving. Their communities were also limited to eight friars, and they were forbidden to accept Mass stipends. Peter did not embrace such an austere lifestyle simply for his own spiritual sake or that of his friars, but as a way of helping to reform the Church as a whole. Thus, when others complained about the state of affairs in society and in the Church, he would reply: "The remedy is simple. You and I must first be what we ought to be; then we shall have cured what concerns ourselves. Let each one do the same, and all will be well. The trouble is that we all talk of reforming others without ever reforming ourselves." Needless to say, he encountered much opposition.

The other significant aspect of his life concerned his relationship with Teresa of Ávila [October 15]. They met in 1560, when he was already over the age of sixty, and Teresa was immediately drawn to him. He understood what she was about in her own efforts to reform the Carmelites, and she herself insisted that he did more than anyone else to encourage and support her. Peter died in 1562 and was canonized in 1669, but his cult was never widespread. He was declared patron saint of Brazil in 1826. Although his feast day in the *Roman Martyrology* is October 19 (but is not on the General Roman Calendar), the Franciscans celebrate it on this day.

23 John of Capistrano, priest; James of Jerusalem; Severinus Boethius, martyr

John of Capistrano (1386–1456) was a renowned Franciscan preacher who is the patron saint of military chaplains and jurists. Born at Capistrano in the Abruzzi region of Italy, he studied law at Perugia, married, and became governor of Perugia in 1412. He was imprisoned for a time during a civil war and claimed to have had a vision of St. Francis [October 4] that generated a spiritual conversion. Upon his release, he was determined to become a religious. He separated from his wife, presumably by mutual consent, joined the Franciscans in 1415, and was professed the following year after obtaining a dispensation from the Church. He was ordained a priest four years later, having studied theology under Bernardino of Siena [May 20], one of the greatest preachers of his time. John himself became a successful preacher, attracting large crowds using the same techniques as Bernardino. In 1426, in fact, he effectively defended his former teacher against heresy charges in the presence of Pope Martin V. (After Bernardino's death, John worked successfully for his canonization, which he attended in 1450, and wrote his Life.) In 1429, he and some other friars were themselves charged with heresy for their teaching on the poverty of Christ, but they were acquitted.

John was also deeply involved for several years in efforts to reform, reorganize, and unify the Franciscan Observant friars with the Conventuals as well as the Poor Clares of Perugia. The reform and reorganization efforts met with at least limited success, but the Observants and Conventuals were not reunited. In 1443 he became vicar general of the Cismontaine family of the Observants. John always insisted that efforts at reform should began with oneself. He went about barefoot, wore a hair shirt, and ate and slept little. Contemporaries described him as small, withered, and emaciated in appearance, but with a cheerful and energetic manner.

Because of John's growing reputation, Pope Nicholas V sent him to Austria in 1451 at the request of the emperor for help against the Hussites (followers of John Hus, whose views on the Eucharist and church reform would not be regarded as heretical today). Although he was warmly greeted by the local Catholic community there, historians have been critical of his undue zeal against the group. The next year he was appointed commissary, or commissioner general, for Austria, Hungary, and Bohemia. After Constantinople fell to the Turks in 1453, Pope Pius II called upon John to preach a new crusade against the Turks. It met with little support except in Hungary, which was under direct threat of attack. John's moral support and help in raising an army was credited in part with the victory of the Hungarian forces in defense of Belgrade. However, thousands of bodies were left unburied for too long and disease was rampant. John himself succumbed to it and died at Ilok (or Villach), Austria, on October 23, 1456. The Franciscans were permitted to observe his cult in 1622, and he was canonized in 1690. (Two sources give the year of canonization as 1724.) His feast was extended to the calendar of the universal Church in 1890 (one source says 1880) and is on the General Roman Calendar today.

The Greek and Russian Orthodox Churches, the Episcopal Church in the USA, and the Evangelical Lutheran Church in America celebrate the feast of *James of Jerusalem* (d. ca. 62), "the brother of the Lord" (Gal. 1:19), who played an important role in the church of Jerusalem, presiding at the famous council that decided that Gentile converts would not have to be circumcised or observe Jewish dietary laws (Acts 15). Although this James is sometimes called James the Less [May 3], he is not to be confused with that particular saint. His other name, James the Just, is more appropriate. One ancient source indicates that he was put to death by the Sanhedrin. The Catholic Church does not observe any feast in honor of James of Jerusalem.

This is also the feast day of *Severinus Boethius* (ca. 480–524), author of *The Consolation of Philosophy*, a philosophical discussion of the problem of evil that was written in prison at the end of his life. He was executed for treason by the Arian emperor Theodoric for having defended in court Albinus, a senator and ex-consul. He was also accused of "studies for impious purposes." He was regarded as a martyr and his cult was confirmed in 1883. His feast is observed on this day in Pavia, where he is buried, as well as in some churches in Rome. It is not, however, on the General Roman Calendar.

24 Anthony Claret, bishop

Anthony Claret (1807–70) was the founder of the congregation of the Missionary Sons of the Immaculate Heart of Mary, better known as the Claretians. Born Antonio Juan Claret i Clará at Sallent in northern Spain, he worked at his father's trade of weaving and learned printing before studying for the priesthood. Ordained a diocesan priest in 1835, he went to Rome to offer his services as a missionary and became a Jesuit novice. Because of health problems, however, he had to return to Spain, where for ten years he gave retreats and missions and engaged in other forms of pastoral work in Catalonia. During this period he collaborated with Joachima of Vedruna [May 22] in establishing the Carmelites of Charity, who were devoted to the care of the sick and to teaching, and founded in 1849 the congregation of the Missionary Sons of the Immaculate Heart of Mary (the Claretians). He also drew upon his expertise in printing, publishing some two hundred books and pamphlets, and was the main inspiration in the founding of the Religious Library, which produced thousands of books and other publications between 1848 and 1866.

In 1850 he was appointed archbishop of Santiago, Cuba, a diocese that had been vacant for fourteen years, where he encountered much opposition from powerful anti-Christian groups, including even an assassination attempt. At his consecration he took the name Mary because he regarded her as his mother, protector, and teacher, second only to Jesus. After seven years of dedicated pastoral ministry of every kind, including the cofounding, with Mother Antonia Paris, of the Claretian Sisters, he resigned in 1857 and returned to Spain to become confessor to Queen Isabella II. Although he traveled throughout the country with the queen and was able to preach during these trips, he regarded life in the court as "a continuous martyrdom." Nevertheless, he was able to use his influence to launch new projects, such as a science laboratory, a museum of natural history, schools of music and languages, and an association of writers and artists. Nor did he neglect his own spiritual life. He fasted and wore a hair shirt three days a week, took the discipline (self-flagellation) on two, and spent long periods before the Blessed Sacrament each day. During the revolution of 1868 he accompanied the queen into exile, went to Rome, where he spoke on behalf of the dogma of papal infallibility, then under consideration by the First Vatican Council (1869–70), and died on October 24, 1870, at the Cistercian monastery at Fontfroide, near Narbonne in southern France. Buried in Vic (Vich), near Barcelona, Anthony Mary Claret was beatified in 1934 and canonized in 1950. He is the patron saint of savings banks and weavers. His feast is on the General Roman Calendar.

25 Forty Martyrs of England and Wales; Crispin and Crispinian, martyrs

This feast celebrates the martyrdoms of forty English and Welsh Catholics executed for their faith between 1535 and 1679. Their names were selected by Pope Paul VI in 1970 from a list of some two hundred martyrs already beatified by previous popes. There were four laywomen, three laymen, thirteen diocesan priests, ten Jesuits, three Benedictines, three Carthusian monks, one Brigittine nun, two Franciscans, and one Augustinian friar. The forty include those who were executed for refusing to take the Oath of Supremacy, simply being priests, or harboring priests. Among those also having separate feast days are Alexander Briant [December 1], Edmund Campion [December 1], Margaret Clitherow [March 25], Edward Gennings [December 10], John Jones [July 12], Cuthbert Mayne [November 30], Nicholas Owen [March 22], Polydore Plasden [December 10], John Roberts [December 10], Ralph Sherwin [December 1], Robert Southwell [December 1], John Wall [July 12], Margaret Ward [August 30], Swithin Wells [December 10], and Eustace White [December 10].

The first of these martyrs were executed in 1535 for refusing to recognize Henry VIII as supreme head of the Church in England. There were no executions of Catholics during the reign of Edward VI (1547–53) or Mary I (1553–58), but in the latter's reign some 280 Protestants were put to death. The succession of Elizabeth I in 1558 brought a return to Protestantism, but there was little active persecution of Catholics for the first twelve years of her reign. The change came after the Northern Rebellion of 1569, the excommunication of the queen by Pope Pius V in 1570, and the Ridolfi Plot of 1571 to depose the queen. Twenty of the Forty Martyrs suffered under the legislation that followed the papal action. Altogether about 190 were martyred between 1570 and Elizabeth's death in 1603.

In 1895 Pope Leo XIII beatified 63 of these martyrs and in 1929 Pope Pius XI beatified another 136. It was from these two groups that the Forty Martyrs were chosen for canonization in 1970. The criteria were that they should have been previously beatified, well known, and already the object of devotion on the part of English Catholics. With the new ecumenical spirit brought about by Pope John XXIII (1958–63) and the Second Vatican Council (1962–65), devotion to the Forty Martyrs has waned. There is a growing realization that many on both sides suffered needlessly and that the Roman Catholic Church and the Church of England are sister churches, united by faith, Baptism, and a common commitment to the gospel of Jesus Christ. This substantial change in the relationship of the two churches has been amply demonstrated by the historic meetings and joint prayers that have occurred since 1987 between the Bishop of Rome and the archbishops of Canterbury (Robert Runcie and George Carey), both in Rome and in England. The feast is not on the General Roman Calendar.

This is also the feast day of *Crispin* and *Crispinian* (d. ca. 285), two martyrs of Roman origin who were thought to have preached in Gaul and worked as shoemakers to avoid living off the alms of the faithful. They are patron saints of shoemakers.

26 Cedd, bishop; Alfred the Great, king

Cedd (d. 664) was the bishop of the East Saxons and the brother of Chad of Lichfield [March 2]. Educated at Lindisfarne by Aidan [August 31], he became a monk there and was ordained a priest. He and three other priests were invited in 653 by the newly converted king of Mercia to evangelize his people. Then the king of the East

Saxons, also a recent convert, extended the same invitation with respect to his people in Essex. Cedd was consecrated bishop of the East Saxons at Lindisfarne. As bishop he founded two monasteries in the region, and then another in North Yorkshire at Lastingham in 658. He fasted for forty days before consecrating a monastery, a custom followed at Lindisfarne from the time of Columba [June 9]. However, all three monasteries were later destroyed by the Danes. Soon after the Synod of Whitby (664), where he acted as a mediator between those favoring the Roman system for the dating of Easter and those favoring the Celtic, Cedd died of the plague at Lastingham, where he was buried, on October 26. The ecclesiastical historian the Venerable Bede [May 25] informs us that thirty of Cedd's brethren from Essex, on hearing of his death, traveled north to be near him. They too caught the plague and died there. His cult spread more slowly than that of his brother, Chad, but by the eleventh century his relics were venerated at Lichfield alongside those of Chad's. His feast is not on the General Roman Calendar, but it is commemorated on this day by the Church of England.

Also on this day the Church of England and the Episcopal Church in the USA celebrate the feast of *Alfred the Great* (849–99), king of Wessex from 871 and one of the most successful Christian leaders in English history. His defeat of the Danes stabilized Christianity in England. He also promoted church reform and learning, gathering a team around himself to translate a number of popular Latin works. He himself was mainly responsible for translating Gregory the Great's [September 3] classic *Pastoral Care,* Boethius's [October 23] *The Consolation of Philosophy,* some works of Augustine [August 28], and the first fifty psalms of the Psalter. He founded monastic communities, promoted the education of the clergy and nobles, and served as a model of a Christian king. He has no feast day in the Catholic Church.

27 Blessed Bartholomew of Vicenza, friar

Bartholomew of Vicenza (ca. 1200–1271) was a Dominican friar. Born Bartholomew Breganza in Venice, he was educated at Padua, entered the Dominicans ca. 1220, and served as prior of several Dominican houses. In 1233, with John of Vicenza, he founded the *Fratres Gaudentes* (Lat., "Joyful Brothers"), a military order, for the purpose of keeping the civil peace in Bologna. The order spread to towns all over Italy. As a form of exile promoted by the antipapal, pro-imperial

Ghibellines, Bartholomew was appointed bishop of Nimesia in Cyprus in 1248, became a friend of King Louis IX of France [August 25], and was papal legate to King Henry II of England. In 1256 he was transferred back from his see in Cyprus to Vicenza, where he came into conflict once again with the leader of Ghibellines. Nevertheless, he worked hard to rebuild his diocese and left a legacy of sermons, biblical commentaries, and a treatise on one of the writings of Dionysius the Areopagite. He died on July 1, 1271. Bartholomew was beatified in 1793. His feast is not on the General Roman Calendar, but it is celebrated on this day by the Dominicans.

This is also the former feast of Frumentius [July 20], who introduced Christianity to Ethiopia after being shipwrecked there and serving as secretary to the king. He helped rule the country after the king's death, but left when the king's son came of age. He was sent back as a missionary bishop by Athanasius [May 2], and is patron saint of the country.

28 Simon and Jude, apostles

Simon (first century) was one of the twelve apostles. His nickname was the "Cananaean" (Matt. 10:4; Mark 3:18), Aramaic for "Zealot," and it is used in Luke 6:15 and Acts 1:13. He is often called Simon the Less to distinguish him from Simon Peter [June 29]. His zeal may have been on behalf of Israel's independence or for the law. According to tradition, he engaged in missions to Egypt and Persia, where he and Jude were martyred together on the same day. Their relics were said to have been brought to St. Peter's Basilica in Rome in the seventh or eighth century, but both Reims and Toulouse in France have also claimed to have some of their relics.

Jude (first century) was also one of the twelve apostles, best known as the patron saint of hopeless causes as well as of hospitals. There are only three brief mentions of him in the New Testament: Luke 6:16, John 14:22 (where the author is careful to distinguish him from Judas Iscariot), and Acts 1:13. Two lists of apostles do not contain his name but mention a certain Thaddeus (Mark 3:16–17; Matt. 10:2–4). These few texts imply that, like Simon, Jude was an obscure figure who is often confused with others with the same name. Sometimes he is thought to have a double name, Jude Thaddeus, because Thaddeus replaces Jude in the apostolic lists in Mark and Matthew. Sometimes he is confused with Jude, the brother of the Lord (Mark 6:3). Ancient legends mention his missionary work in Mesopotamia and Persia. Only in the twentieth century did he become known as the patron saint of hopeless causes. It may be that no one wanted to pray to him because his that of name was so close to that of Judas, the one who betrayed Jesus, and that people turned to Jude only after all other intercessors had apparently failed. He is not the author of the Letter of Jude in the New Testament.

Their feast day is on the General Roman Calendar and is observed also by the Church of England, the Episcopal Church in the USA, and the Evangelical Lutheran Church in America. In the Greek and Russian Orthodox Churches they have separate feast days: Simon's on May 10, and Jude's on June 19.

29 Narcissus of Jerusalem, bishop

Narcissus of Jerusalem (d. 215) was a venerable figure in second- and third-century Jerusalem, thought to have been 160 years old at the time of his death. A Greek by birth, he became bishop of Jerusalem ca. 190 and is reported to have performed many miracles, including the changing of water into oil for the church lamps on the Easter Vigil when the deacons forgot to provide the oil. Despite his reputation for holiness, he was often attacked by people who resented the rigor with which he imposed church discipline. He was also criticized by some for supporting the Roman system for the dating of Easter at a council in Palestine. Seizing one of those episodes as an occasion to resign his office, he retired to a life of solitude for several years. Since many had assumed that he had died (or at the very least his retreat could not be found), several bishops in succession were appointed in his place. When Narcissus eventually reappeared, he was persuaded to resume his office. To assist him in his advanced age, a bishop by the name of Alexander was moved from his diocese in Cappadocia to become coadjutor bishop in Jerusalem—the first recorded instance of such a move. In a letter written soon after in 212, Alexander refers to Narcissus as still alive at the age of 116. There are no details of his death, and his feast is not on the General Roman Calendar.

30 Blessed Benvenuta of Cividale, virgin

Benvenuta of Cividale (1254–92) was a Dominican tertiary. Born Benvenuta Boiani at Cividale in Fruili, Italy, of well-to-do parents, she derived her Christian name from her father's remark upon learning that he had a daughter rather than a hoped for son, "She is welcome

(It. *benvenuta*) all the same!" Drawn to a contemplative rather than an active spiritual life, she took a vow of lifelong chastity at a young age and joined the third order of St. Dominic [August 8]. She went to excess, however, in some of her ascetical practices, sometimes using the discipline (self-flagellation) on herself three times a night or tying a rope around her waist so tightly that it dug into her flesh and gave her great pain. Her confessor ordered her to mitigate her austerities and not to initiate new ones without his permission. She was confined to bed a great deal because of asthma, but claims to have been suddenly cured on the feast of the Annunciation [March 25] after making a vow to visit the shrine of St. Dominic at Bologna if she recovered. She died on October 30, 1292, and was buried in the church of St. Dominic, which was demolished in 1807. A popular cult developed quickly and was approved in 1765. Her feast is not on the General Roman Calendar, but it is celebrated on this day by the Dominicans.

31 Alphonsus Rodríguez, religious; Reformation Day

Alphonsus Rodríguez (1533–1617), a Spanish Jesuit lay brother, was the subject of one of the poems of Gerard Manley Hopkins [June 8]. Born in Segovia, Spain, of a well-to-do wool merchant, Alphonsus inherited his father's business when he was twenty-three. Within the space of three years, his wife, daughter, and mother died. He began to think of what God expected of him in this life. He sold his business and retired with his young son to live with his two unmarried sisters, living a life of prayer and austerity. When his son died some years later, he decided to join the Jesuits, but was rejected for lack of education. He applied a second time and was accepted as a lay brother in 1571. For forty-five years he served as the doorkeeper at the Jesuit College of Montesión in Majorca, integrating a life of prayer and self-mortification with his daily responsibilities. He was allowed to take his final vows in 1585. His reputation for holiness grew and soon people came to him for spiritual guidance. Peter Claver [September 9] became one of his advisees while he was a student at the college. It was Alphonsus who inspired Peter to become a missionary in the New World. Toward the end of his life, Alphonsus suffered from bad health and considerable physical pain. Just after midnight on October 31, 1617, he kissed the crucifix, uttered the name of Jesus in a loud voice, and died. In 1633 he was declared patron saint of Majorca and was canonized in 1888, fittingly in the same ceremony as Peter Claver.

The Jesuit poet Gerard Manley Hopkins (1844–89) memorialized him with these verses:

> Yet God (that hews mountain and continent,
> Earth, all, out; who, with trickling increment,
> Veins violets and tall trees makes more and more)
> Could crowd career with conquest while there went
> Those years and years by without event
> That in Majorca Alfonso watched the door.

Alphonsus's feast is not on the General Roman Calendar, but it is celebrated by the Jesuits on this day.

This is also Reformation Day, commemorating the anniversary of Martin Luther's posting of his Ninety-Five Theses on the door of the castle church in Wittenberg, questioning abuses in the sale of indulgences. That date, October 31, 1517, is traditionally recognized as the beginning of the Protestant Reformation. To be sure, the Evangelical Lutheran Church in America observes this day, but *Martin Luther* (1483–1546) is also liturgically commemorated today by the Church of England.

NOVEMBER

1 All Saints

The feast of *All Saints* celebrates the triumph of Christ's grace in every person who now enjoys the eternal vision of God in heaven. The scope of this feast includes those who have officially been recognized by the Church as saints; those whose lives of sanctity were known only to their families, friends, and associates or to members of their parish, diocese, or other religious community; and those, like Pope John XXIII (1881–1963) [June 3] or Dorothy Day (1897–1980) [November 29], who enjoyed an international reputation for holiness but whose causes for canonization have not yet been completed.

There is some evidence that, from as early as the fourth century, the Church in the East had a collective celebration of martyrs (who were originally the only individuals recognized as saints). One such feast seems to have been celebrated in Syria on May 13 and another on the Friday of Easter week. Chaldean-rite Catholics still celebrate this feast on that day. Byzantine churches as well as the Russian and Greek Orthodox Churches celebrate the feast of All Saints on the Sunday after Pentecost. The origins of the feast in the West are even more obscure. It possibly began there in the sixth century, when the Pantheon in Rome was given over to the Church by the emperor Phocas and dedicated to St. Mary and all the martyrs. A seventh-century German lectionary referred to a feast of all the saints, celebrated on a Sunday. In the eighth century a chapel in St. Peter's Basilica was dedicated to Christ, the Blessed Virgin Mary, and all the saints.

The first explicit mention of November 1 as the day for observing such a feast seems to come from England, where the feast was introduced during the first quarter of the eighth century, probably by Egbert of York. In 799 Alcuin of York, then abbot of Tours, wrote to his friend, Arno, bishop of Salzburg, and mentioned a feast of All Saints on November 1, preceded by a three-day fast. A ninth-century liturgical calendar from the north of England lists All Saints as a major feast on November 1. Rome may have very well adopted the English-Gallican practice rather than vice-versa. It is said that Pope Gregory IV (828–44) transferred the feast from May to November because Rome could not accommodate the number of pilgrims who came for the feast in late spring. By the twelfth century, November 1 was securely established as the date of the celebration. In England and Ireland this feast was formerly known as All Hallows. This explains the name for the secular celebration of Halloween, on the "eve" of the feast itself (thus, Hallowe'en, or Hallow evening).

The theology underlying this feast is well expressed in the Second Vatican Council's Dogmatic Constitution on the Church (*Lumen gentium*, Lat., "Light of nations"): "In the lives of those companions of ours who are more perfectly transformed into the image of Christ (see 2 Corinthians 3:18) God shows, vividly, to humanity his presence and his face. He speaks to us in them and offers us a sign of his Kingdom, to which we are powerfully attracted, so great a cloud of witnesses are we given (see Hebrews 12:1) and such an affirmation of the truth of the Gospel. . . . Our communion with the saints joins us to Christ, from whom as from its fountain and head flow all grace and life of the people of God itself" (n. 50). This feast is on the General Roman Calendar with the rank of a Solemnity. It is also celebrated on this day by the Church of England, the Episcopal Church in the USA, and the Evangelical Lutheran Church in America. The Greek and Russian Orthodox Churches celebrate the feast of *Cosmas* and *Damian* [September 26] on this day.

2 All Souls

The feast of *All Souls,* also known as the Commemoration of All the Faithful Departed, is a celebration of the lives of loved ones who have gone before us in death, but who may still be in need of the Church's prayers of petition for their deliverance from purgatory into heaven. Unlike the ecumenical feast of All Saints [November 1], this feast is theologically rooted in the distinctively Catholic doctrine of purgatory, an after-death state of purification from the temporal punishment still due to sins that have already been forgiven, sacramentally (i.e., in the Sacrament of Reconciliation, or Penance) or through a personal act of contrition. Although in the past the period of purgation was measured in days, months, and years, it would not be inconsistent with Catholic doctrine for one to hold that the purgative process is instantaneous rather than prolonged. When faced at the moment of particular judgment with the stark reality of one's life on earth, the deceased may see in an instant how far that life had fallen from the standard of the gospel. That perception would, in turn, generate an instantaneous act of self-reproach that would be purgatively painful in varying degrees of intensity.

There is no real biblical basis for this doctrine, although the classic text that is always cited is 2 Maccabees 12:38–46: "For if he were not expecting the fallen to rise again, it would have been useless and foolish to pray for them in death. . . . Thus he made atonement for the dead that they might be freed from sin" (12:44, 46). It was not until the twelfth century that the doctrine of purgatory emerged in the West. Eastern Christians rejected the West's juridical approach and stressed instead the more mystical nature of the purgative state as a process of maturation and spiritual growth. They denied that the Beatific Vision of God in heaven is available to anyone, including the just, before the general resurrection and the final judgment. The traditional doctrine of purgatory was enunciated by the Second Council of Lyons (1274), Pope Benedict XII's *Benedictus Deus* (Lat., "Blessed God") in 1336, and especially the Council of Florence's *Decree for the Greeks* (1439), which tried to strike a balance between the Western concept of satisfaction and expiation and the Eastern emphasis on purification. Out of consideration for Eastern Christians, the council deliberately omitted all reference to fire and avoided any language that would lead to a concept of purgatory as a place. When the Reformers rejected this doctrine totally, the Council of Trent defined the existence of purgatory and insisted that the souls detained there are helped by acts of intercession of the faithful and especially by the sacrifice of the Mass (*Decree on Purgatory*, 1563). The doctrine is assumed in Vatican II's Dogmatic Constitution on the Church (n. 51) and is reaffirmed in the *Catechism of the Catholic Church* (nn. 1030–32), originally published in 1992.

The first evidence of this feast is in seventh-century Spain, from the time of Isidore of Seville [April 4]. The date assigned to the feast was the Monday after Pentecost. By the first half of the ninth century, monasteries were formally commemorating their own deceased monks and benefactors, but with no fixed date. Amalarius of Metz (ca. 775–ca. 850), a distinguished liturgist and archbishop, made a connection between the feast of All Saints and the commemoration of All Souls: "After the office of the saints I have inserted the office for the dead; for many pass out of this world without at once being admitted into the company of the blessed." Two centuries later, in 988, Odilo [May 11], abbot of Cluny, directed his community to observe November 2 as a day of prayer for the dead. From Cluny the practice spread rapidly and widely, but it was not for another two or three centuries that the feast was commonly found on November 2 in liturgical calendars and martyrologies.

The practice of an individual priest's celebrating three Masses on this day seems to have originated at the Dominican priory in Valencia, early in the fifteenth century and in response to local demands for special Masses for deceased loved ones. In 1748 Pope Benedict XIV approved the feast for Spain, but not until 1915 was it extended to the whole Church, by Benedict XV, because of the number who had already died in World War I and also because of the increasing number of funded Masses for the dead. (The first Mass is for a particular intention; the second, for all the faithful departed; and the third, for the intentions of the pope.) The most famous dedication is All Souls College, Oxford, founded by Archbishop Henry Chichele in 1437. The Commemoration of All the Faithful Departed is on the General Roman Calendar and is also celebrated on this day by the Church of England and the Episcopal Church in the USA. The month of November, and especially this day, is a traditional time for visiting the graves of loved ones.

3 Martin de Porres, religious; Malachy, bishop; Hubert, bishop

Martin de Porres (1579–1639) is the patron saint of race relations and of social justice. He was born out of wedlock in Lima, Peru, to a Spanish knight and a freed slave from Panama. To his father's disappointment,

Saint Martin de Porres

Martin inherited his mother's features and complexion. At his baptism, he was registered as the "son of an unknown father" and was considered "illegitimate," a category that would place him at a considerable social and economic disadvantage in life. In his early years, Martin served as an apprentice to a barber-surgeon. Already a Dominican tertiary, in 1595 he entered a Dominican convent in Lima as a lay helper, in return for room and board, and in 1603 was invited to become a lay brother, devoting himself to the care of the sick and the poor, regardless of race, and to menial tasks of barbering, gardening, and the like within his monastery. He gained a reputation for spiritual insight and for the power of healing. His Dominican confreres called him "father of charity," but Martin referred to himself as "mulatto dog." Because his desire to become a foreign missionary and suffer martyrdom was thwarted, he committed himself instead to a life of prayer and rigorous penances. During his lifetime he befriended Rose of Lima [August 23]. His cult sprang up immediately after his death by a violent fever on November 3, 1639, at age sixty. He was beatified in 1837 and canonized by Pope John XXIII in 1962. His feast is on the General Roman Calendar.

This is also the feast day of *Malachy* (ca. 1094–1148), the bishop of Armagh who reformed the Church in Ireland in accordance with Roman practices and also introduced the Cistercians into the country. He is best known, however, for the "prophecies" about popes that have been falsely attributed to him since the late sixteenth century. It is also the feast day of *Hubert* (d. 727), a Belgian bishop who was thought to have been converted while hunting on Good Friday. He is said to have seen an image of the crucified Christ between the antlers of a stag. Thus, he is patron saint of hunters as well as victims of rabies.

BIBLIOGRAPHY

García-Rivera, Alex. *St. Martín de Porres: The "Little Stories" and the Semiotics of Culture.* Maryknoll, NY: Orbis Books, 1995.

4 Charles Borromeo, bishop

Charles Borromeo (1538–84) was one of the most important bishops in the history of the Church and one of the outstanding figures in the Catholic Reformation. He is the patron saint of bishops, catechists, and seminarians. Born of an aristocratic and wealthy family in a castle on Lake Maggiore, Carlo Borromeo was educated in Milan and then in Pavia, where he earned a doctorate in civil and canon law. He had received tonsure (entrance into the clerical state) at age twelve. His uncle, Cardinal Gian Angelo de' Medici (no relation to the famous Medici family of Florence), became Pope Pius IV in 1559 and the following year heaped honors and responsibilities upon his nephew, including the administration of the diocese of Milan, then under Spanish rule, and a cardinal's hat. In addition, Charles served as the new pope's secretary of state, which required residency in Rome. The duties of Milan were delegated to others. He was a vigorous supporter of his uncle's decision to reopen the Council of Trent in January 1562 (it had been suspended since 1552) for its third and final period and was himself an active participant in the council's business, drafting its Catechism and contributing to the reform of liturgical books and church music.

Saint Charles Borromeo

Profoundly affected by the death of his older brother that same year, he became determined to live an even holier life. Not long after, he was ordained a priest in 1563 and, two months later, was consecrated a bishop. (It is a matter of pastoral significance that Borromeo, like many others at this time, was given a diocese to administer without having been ordained a priest, much less a bishop.) As papal legate for all of Italy, he convened a provincial council at Milan, which promulgated the reforms of the Council of Trent. After his uncle Pius IV died in 1565, Charles obtained from his uncle's successor, Pius V, permission to reside in his diocese. He became the first resident archbishop of Milan in eighty years.

Charles adopted a simple standard of living for himself and gave away to the poor much of his substantial revenue. He held other councils and synods, made regular visits to his parishes, reorganized the diocesan administration, established seminaries for the education of future priests, enforced standards of morality for his clergy, and founded a confraternity to teach Christian doctrine to children. His reforms were so energetic and far-reaching that some disgruntled members of the Humiliati, a lay movement originally founded to serve the poor and that had grown rich and lax itself, hired someone to assassinate him in 1569. Charles was only slightly wounded, but the group was later suppressed. In 1570 and again in 1576 he organized and took a personal role in the feeding of thousands during a famine and the nursing of many others during a plague. When in 1578 his cathedral canons refused to cooperate with some of his reform programs, Charles founded a society of diocesan priests, the Oblates of St. Ambrose [December 7], to carry out his wishes. The society still exists as the Society of St. Ambrose and St. Charles (Ambrosians). In 1583 he was appointed apostolic visitor in Switzerland, where he had to confront witchcraft and sorcery as well as Calvinism and Zwingliism. These and other strenuous pastoral efforts on behalf of the renewal and reform of the Church eventually wore him down. He died in Milan on November 3, 1584, at age forty-six, and was buried in the cathedral. A cult developed immediately and he was canonized in 1610.

Pope John XXIII (1958–63) [June 3] had a special devotion to Charles Borromeo. The newly elected pope picked Borromeo's feast day for his own coronation even though it occurred on a Wednesday in 1958 (traditionally, papal coronations were held on Sunday). Thirty-four years earlier, he had been consecrated a bishop in the church of San Carlo alla Corso in Rome, where the saint's heart is preserved for veneration, and he had spent most of his scholarly life as a historian editing a five-volume collection of Borromeo's writings connected with his pastoral visitations to Bergamo (John XXIII's home diocese). Charles Borromeo's feast is on the General Roman Calendar.

5 Zechariah and Elizabeth

Zechariah and *Elizabeth* (first century) were the parents of John the Baptist [June 24, August 29]. According to Luke 1:5–25, 57–80, while performing his priestly duties in the Temple, *Zechariah* learned of John's forthcoming birth from the angel Gabriel [September 29]. When he expressed doubt about the news and requested a sign, he was struck speechless. After John was born, Zechariah was still unable to speak until the eighth day, when an argument arose about his name. Relatives wanted him to be named after his father, but Elizabeth insisted that his name would be John. Zechariah asked for a writing tablet and wrote: "His name is John." At that moment he recovered his power of speech, whereupon he pronounced the prophetic oracle known as the Benedictus (Lat., "Blessed"), beginning with the words: "Blessed be the Lord, the God of Israel; he has come to his people and set them free. He has raised up for us a mighty savior, born of the house of his servant David." The verses that apply directly to his son, John the Baptist, read: "You, my child, shall be called the prophet of the Most High, for you will go before the Lord to prepare his way, to give his people knowledge of salvation by the forgiveness of their sins." Some of the Fathers of the Church believed that Zechariah died a martyr, but there is no historical evidence of that nor any mention of his martyrdom in the *Roman Martyrology.* Nevertheless, he has been venerated throughout the East and his alleged relics were taken to Constantinople in 415.

Elizabeth, the wife of Zechariah and mother of John the Baptist, was aged and barren when she conceived her son. At her cousin Mary's visit, Elizabeth pronounced the second verse of the Hail Mary prayer: "Blessed are you among women and blessed is the fruit of your womb" (Luke 1:42). Her greeting elicited from Mary another classic prayer, the Magnificat (Lat., "[My soul] magnifies [the Lord]"), which begins with the words: "My soul proclaims the greatness of the Lord, my spirit rejoices in God my Savior for he has looked with favor on his lowly servant." Unlike her husband Zechariah's feast, Elizabeth's has never been celebrated on its own. Their joint feast is not on the General Roman Calendar.

6 Paul of Constantinople, bishop

Paul of Constantinople (ca. 300–ca. 350) was a strong defender of the teaching of the Council of Nicaea (325) against the Arians (who denied that Jesus Christ was equal in divinity to God the Father). Born in Thessalonica, Paul succeeded Alexander in the see of Constantinople ca. 336. But he himself was soon displaced by an Arian, Eusebius of Nicomedia, who had the support of the emperor Constantius. After Eusebius's death, Paul was reelected, but encountered resistance from the Arians. This, in turn, provoked a popular rebellion in support of Paul in 342, during which the emperor's representative was killed in a skirmish. As a result, Paul was exiled to Pontus. He went subsequently to Rome to seek the support of Pope Julius I, as well as of Athanasius

[May 2], who was himself in exile at the time, and of the Western emperor Constans I. Under pressure from the West, Paul was reinstated in Constantinople, but after the death of Constans in 350 Paul was accused of complicity in the deposition of his predecessor and was exiled, first to Mesopotamia, then to Emesa, and finally to Cucusus in Armenia, where he was strangled to death—according to legend—by the Arians. The cult of Paul developed by the fifth century as a Constantinopolitan counterpart to the cult of Athanasius in Alexandria. His feast is not on the General Roman Calendar, but it is celebrated on this day by the Greek and Russian Orthodox Churches.

7 Willibrord, bishop

Willibrord (658–739) was the "apostle of Frisia" and archbishop of Utrecht, and is patron saint of the Netherlands (Holland) and Luxembourg. Born in Northumbria, England, he was educated by Wilfrid [October 12] at Ripon Abbey and went to Ireland at age twenty for further study, but also in protest against the division of his mentor Wilfrid's diocese of Northumbria without consulting him. Willibrord stayed in Ireland for twelve years and at some point was ordained a priest. He returned to England in 690 and, under the inspiration of the monastic leader Egbert, he went with twelve companions as a missionary to Frisia, along the coast of what is now the Netherlands. With the support of the Frankish ruler Pepin II and then of Pope Sergius I, Willibrord's mission prospered. In 695 he was consecrated archbishop of the Frisians by the pope and given the additional name of Clement. He was sent back to his mission territory with a papal mandate to establish a metropolitan diocese with its center at Utrecht and with suffragan dioceses surrounding it, in keeping with the organizational pattern of Canterbury. Willibrord built churches and monasteries and consecrated bishops for the new dioceses. He was joined for three years by Boniface [June 5], whom he hoped would be his successor, but Boniface moved south into Germany in response to his own mandate from Pope Gregory II.

In 698 Willibrord founded his largest monastery, at Echternach (in modern-day Luxembourg), where he died more than forty years later, on November 7, 739, at age eighty-one. Willibrord's cult began almost immediately after his death, and Echternach became an important pilgrimage center. Every Tuesday after Pentecost there is an observance there known as *Springende Heiligen* (Ger., "Dancing Saints"), with origins at least as early as the sixteenth century, which includes a procession of bishops, clergy, and laity in the form of a dance that crosses a bridge over the River Sure and enters St. Willibrord's shrine, where the ceremony ends with benediction of the Blessed Sacrament. Willibrord's feast is not on the General Roman Calendar.

8 Blessed John Duns Scotus, friar

John Duns Scotus (ca. 1265–1308) was a Franciscan philosopher and theologian known as the "Subtle Doctor" and the "Marian Doctor." Born John of Duns, in Duns, Scotland (thus, the name "Scotus"), he became a Franciscan at age fifteen and went to study at Oxford. He was ordained a priest in 1291. After ordination he studied for an advanced degree in Paris, where he remained until 1296. The next year he went back to Oxford and then to Cambridge, where he lectured on the *Sentences* of Peter Lombard. He returned to Paris in 1302, but had to leave again the following year when he refused to support the king's plan to convene a general council against Pope Boniface VIII. He went back to Paris a third time, but now with a letter of recommendation from the minister general of the order, citing his "praiseworthy life" and his "most subtle genius" (thus, the title "Subtle Doctor"). He completed his work for the master's degree at the University of Paris in 1305 and spent the next two years lecturing there. At the end of 1307 he publicly defended the view, controversial at the time, that Mary was conceived free from original sin (a forerunner of the dogma of the Immaculate Conception [December 8]) in anticipation of her role as Mother of God [January 1]. He did not claim, as others did, that Mary had no need of the redemption, but rather than she was its first beneficiary. Because of the vehemently negative reaction to his defense of the Immaculate Conception, Scotus was moved to the University of Cologne, where he lectured and defended the Catholic faith against various dissident groups. He died in Cologne on November 8, 1308, at age forty-three, and was buried in the local Franciscan church. He was venerated almost immediately as a saint. After three previous attempts at beatifying him, his cult was confirmed for the Order of Friars Minor in 1906. In 1993 Pope John Paul II declared that he should be honored with the title Blessed, not by the Franciscans only, but by the universal Church. His feast is not on the General Roman Calendar.

Duns Scotus's dogged attempts to work out every implication of his main insights can be extremely wearing on someone who attempts to emulate him, and seen, ultimately, as irrelevant. The word "dunce" is a later play on his name. The Jesuit poet Gerard Manley Hopkins (1844–89) memorialized him in a sonnet: "He . . . who of all men most sways my spirit to peace." On this day, the Russian and Greek Orthodox Churches celebrate the feast of the archangels, including *Michael, Gabriel,* and *Raphael* [September 29].

9 Dedication of St. John Lateran; Benen of Armagh, bishop

The oldest of the four major basilicas of Rome, *St. John Lateran* (whose official title is the Patriarchal Basilica of the Most Holy Savior and St. John the Baptist at the Lateran) stands on the site of an ancient palace on the Celian Hill, which formerly belonged to the Laterani family. The Lateran Basilica (not St. Peter's), originally known as the Church of the Savior, is the pope's cathedral church in his primary role as Bishop of Rome. It is considered "the mother and head of all churches of Rome and the world." Five ecumenical councils were held there (in 1123, 1139, 1179, 1215, and 1512–17). The emperor Constantine [May 21] received the palace as part of his wife's dowry and then donated it to the Church ca. 312. Thereafter, it was the official residence, or *patriarchum,* of the popes until their departure for Avignon, France, in 1309.

The first basilica was probably an adaptation of the great hall of the palace. During the intervening period the basilica and palace suffered from earthquakes (in 443 and 896) and barbarian attacks (in 455 and the 700s). They were regularly rebuilt, and in 905 the basilica was rededicated to St. John the Baptist [June 24; August 29]. Fire destroyed the buildings in 1308 and again in 1360, and each time they were at least partly rebuilt. However, during the Avignon papacy (1309–77) most of the basilica remained in a state of disrepair. Under Urban V (1362–70) and Gregory XI (1371–78) a new north façade was constructed, and in 1425 Martin V installed the cosmatesque pavement that still survives. A complete Baroque renovation was initiated by Clement VIII (1592–1605) and completed by Innocent X (1644–55). The main façade dates from 1735. This feast, which commemorates the original dedication of the basilica by Pope Sylvester I on November 9, 324, is on the General Roman Calendar.

This is also the feast day of *Benen of Armagh* (d. 467), also known as Benignus, the disciple and successor of Patrick [March 17] in the see of Armagh, the "apostle of Kerry and Clare," and the patron saint of

Connacht. Born in Meath, the son of a chieftain, Benen met Patrick when the famous missionary stayed for a few days at the family's house. He was so impressed with Patrick that he begged to assist him in his ministry. Patrick agreed to take him and gave him the baptismal name Benen, or Benignus, because of the young man's gentle disposition. Benen became Patrick's closest disciple and eventual successor. He is said to have resigned his office in 460 and retired to Glastonbury to live as a hermit until his death in 467. His relics were moved in 1091 to Glastonbury Abbey. Benen's feast is not on the General Roman Calendar.

10 Leo the Great, pope and Doctor of the Church

Leo the Great (d. 461; pope 440–61) is one of only two popes given the title "the Great" (the other being Gregory the Great [September 3]). Born in Rome of Tuscan parents at the end of the fourth century, he served as an adviser to Celestine I (422–32) and Sixtus III (432–40). He was elected to the papacy while still only a deacon and while away in Gaul (modern-day France) on a diplomatic mission. As pope, he proved to be a strong advocate of papal authority and of the teachings of the Council of Chalcedon (451) on the humanity and divinity of Jesus Christ. So forcefully articulated were Leo's claims for the pope's universal and supreme authority over the Church, in fact, that his own pontificate constituted a major turning point in the history of the papacy. He was the first pope to claim to be Peter's heir, which, according to Roman law, meant that all the rights and duties associated with Peter [June 29] lived on in Leo. Previous popes had spoken of their succession to Peter's Chair [February 22] or appealed to his martyrdom and burial in Rome as the basis of their authority. Thereafter, the popes increasingly regarded themselves as standing in the place of Peter, exercising authority not only over all of the faithful, but over all of the other bishops as well.

Indeed, Leo himself exercised firm control over the bishops of Italy, including Milan and the northern region, enforcing uniformity of pastoral practice, correcting abuses, and resolving disputes. In replying to appeals from the bishops of Spain to help in their fight against Priscillianism, a heresy that regarded the human body as evil, he laid down precise instructions for action. Although ecclesiastical Africa was traditionally jealous of its pastoral autonomy, especially against any encroachments upon it by Rome, Leo's rulings on irregularities in African elections and other regional conflicts were eagerly sought after and embraced. When Hilary of Arles (d. 449) began acting as if his diocese in southern Gaul still possessed the special authority over other local churches in the region granted to it by Pope Zosimus (417–18), but revoked by his successor Boniface I (418–22), Leo ordered that Hilary confine his pastoral activities to his own diocese. Specifically, he was to stop interfering in the appointment of bishops of other dioceses. Bishops were to be elected by the local clergy and leading laity, and the election was to be ratified by the people generally. Leo's electoral principle is still quoted, but unfortunately has not been in force for centuries: "He who is in charge of all should be chosen by all" *(Letter 10).*

The East, however, was much less disposed than the West to accept Leo's papal claims. In June of 449, for example, he sent an important letter *(Letter 28),* or *Tome,* to Bishop Flavian of Constantinople, condemning the Monophysite teaching that in Christ there is only a divine nature, Christ's human nature having been absorbed by the divine. The emperor Theodosius II called a council at Ephesus in August (not to be confused with the ecumenical Council of Ephesus, held in 431). Pope Leo was represented by three delegates who had with them a copy of the *Tome,* which Leo expected to be read out and approved. But the council disregarded it, condemned Bishop Flavian, and rehabilitated the monk Eutyches, who had been censured by Flavian for his Monophysite views. Leo refused to recognize the council, referring to it as a *latrocinium,* or "robber council." Two years later another ecumenical council was convened—at the call of the emperor, not the pope!—at Chalcedon, on the eastern shore of the Bosphorus strait, which separates modern-day European and Asian Turkey. That council reversed the decisions taken at the "robber council" of Ephesus and endorsed the Christological teaching of Leo and others; namely, that in Jesus Christ there are two natures, one divine and one human, which are hypostatically united in one divine Person. Leo's *Tome* was respectfully received and approved as a standard of orthodoxy and as an expression of "the voice of Peter." "Peter has spoken through Leo" was one of seventeen affirmative acclamations recorded in the minutes of the council.

Leo is also celebrated for his courageous personal confrontation with Attila the Hun near Mantua in 452, when the warrior was laying waste to northern Italy and preparing to move south toward Rome. Heading a delegation from the Roman Senate, Leo persuaded Attila to withdraw beyond the Danube. In 455 he also met the Vandal king

Gaiseric (or Genseric) outside the walls of Rome. Although Leo failed to persuade Gaiseric to withdraw, he succeeded at least in preventing the torching of the city and the massacring of its people.

Upon his death on November 10, 461, Leo was buried in the portico, or porch, of St. Peter's. His body was moved to the interior of the basilica in 688, and he was declared a Doctor of the Church in 1754. His feast is on the General Roman Calendar and is celebrated by the Russian Orthodox Church on February 18.

11 Martin of Tours, bishop; Theodore the Studite, monk; Mennas, martyr

Martin of Tours (ca. 316–97) is a patron saint of France and was the founder of monasticism in Gaul (present-day France). He was born in Sabaria, in a territory that is now part of Hungary (either ca. 316 as implied in his own writings or ca. 336 as implied in his biography). His father was a pagan officer in the Roman army, and Martin was pressured to serve in the military as well. While still a catechumen, he refused any further military service as a matter of conscience and was imprisoned and then discharged in 357. It is in this period of his life that the legendary episode, so often depicted by artists, was said to have occurred at Amiens. After he cut his cloak in half to clothe a naked beggar, he is said to have seen Christ in a dream wearing the same cloak. In 360 Hilary of Poitiers [January 13] gave Martin land at Ligugé on which to live as a hermit. Disciples soon joined him there, forming the first monastery in all of Gaul and the first known monastic foundation north of the Alps.

Martin was popularly acclaimed bishop of Tours in 372, but continued to live as a monk, first in a cell near the cathedral and then at the monastery of Marmoutier. He founded other monasteries to assist in his evangelization of rural areas. Martin visited the outlying areas of his diocese on foot, by donkey, or by boat. He destroyed pagan shrines and idols and replaced them with churches. His twenty-five-year reign was marked by healings as well as the ordinary pastoral activities of a bishop. He died on November 8, 397, at Candes, in a remote part of his diocese, and was buried at Tours on November 11. His cult spread rapidly, not only because of his reputation for miracles, but also because of a biography written by a historian, Sulpicius Severus, that became one of the most popular Lives of a saint in the Middle Ages. Likewise, his tomb became one of the most popular attractions for pilgrims (until 1652, when it was vandalized by Huguenots), and churches were dedicated to him throughout Europe, including the oldest existing church in England, outside the eastern walls of Canterbury. His feast is on the General Roman Calendar and is also celebrated on this day by the Church of England and the Episcopal Church in the USA.

The Greek and Russian Orthodox Churches celebrate the feast of a cluster of saints, including *Theodore the Studite* (759–826), a Byzantine monastic reformer and opponent of iconoclasm who influenced the formation of the Byzantine rite, and *Mennas* (d. ca. 300), or Minas or Menas, an Egyptian martyr to whose intercession the Orthodox patriarch of Alexandria attributed the defeat of General Rommel's army at El Alamein during World War II.

12 Josephat, bishop and martyr

Josephat (1580–1623) was the first Eastern saint to be formally canonized by the Catholic Church. Born Ioann Kuncevyč (also Kuncevych) in Volodymyr Volyns'kyj (modern-day Vladimir-Volynski) in Ukraine, he entered the Holy Trinity monastery in Vilna in 1604 and soon thereafter (probably 1609) was ordained to the diaconate and the priesthood. When he did so, he took the name Josephat. He became a popular preacher, especially in support of extending the union with Rome to the province of Kiev, and gained a reputation for asceticism. He and a monastic colleague initiated a movement in Ruthenian monasticism that eventually developed into the Order of St. Basil [January 2]. In 1614 he became abbot of Holy Trinity and three years later was named bishop of Vitebsk, with the right of succession to the archbishop of Polock (Polotsk), whom he did succeed a few months later.

As archbishop of Polock he was tireless in preaching and other pastoral activities. He also promoted adherence to the Union of Brest (1596), an agreement that brought the Orthodox metropolitan province of Kiev into full communion with the Catholic Church (at least until the expansion of Orthodox Russia into the area). Moreover, Josephat reduced the interference of local landowners in the internal affairs of the Church, held synods, reformed clerical life, published catechisms, and was energetic in fulfilling his many other pastoral responsibilities. In 1620, however, a rival hierarchy was established, one with little or no sympathy for Rome. Josephat stood firm in support of union with Rome, while insisting at the same time on the preservation of

Byzantine customs, such as a married clergy and the election of bishops. He was murdered by supporters of the rival bishop in Vitebsk on November 12, 1623, and his body was thrown into the Dnieper River. His remains were recovered and interred at Biala, in Podlesie. Josephat was beatified in 1643 and canonized in 1867. His feast is on the General Roman Calendar.

The Benedictines and Cistercians celebrate, in addition, the feast of *Theodore the Studite* [November 11] on this day.

13 Frances Xavier Cabrini, virgin; Stanislaus Kostka, religious; Homobonus, layman; Joseph Bernardin, bishop

Frances Xavier Cabrini (1850–1917), better known as Mother Cabrini, was the first U.S. citizen canonized by the Catholic Church and is the patron saint of immigrants and hospital administrators. Born Maria Francesca Cabrini near Pavia, Italy, the youngest of thirteen children, she tried twice to enter a convent, but was refused by both communities for health reasons. She became a schoolteacher and took a private vow of virginity. When the local bishop encouraged her to become a missionary, she founded a small community of sisters in 1880, establishing convents in Grumello, Milan, and Rome. After receiving papal approval for her Missionary Sisters of the Sacred Heart in 1887, she sought an audience with the pope to explain her plans to embark on a mission to China. Leo XIII listened in silence and then said that her mission was to be "not to the East, but to the West." He and the bishop of Piacenza, Giovanni Battista Scalabrini, who was beatified in 1999, urged her instead to minister to Italian immigrants in the United States. She arrived in New York in 1889, where there were some fifty thousand Italian immigrants living for the most part in poverty and apart from the Church. Archbishop Michael Corrigan was unwelcoming. He felt the nature of the work was not suitable for women and suggested that she and her sisters return to Italy. She cited her letters from the pope and stayed.

Although she received no support from the diocese, she began work among the Italian immigrants, teaching their children, visiting the sick, and feeding the hungry. As the sisters' reputation grew, local shopkeepers donated whatever they could for their work. Mother Cabrini eventually established an orphanage, then a novitiate and a house for her congregation. Additional foundations were made in Chicago, New Orleans, and other U.S. cities. During an epidemic in New York, she founded a hospital named after Christopher Columbus, because the year was 1892, the four-hundredth anniversary of his discovery of America. Similar hospitals were established in other cities. She made nine voyages back to Italy to organize training programs for her sisters and to solidify support for her work on the part of the hierarchy. She eventually extended her missionary outreach to Central and South America, contracting yellow fever after a trip through the Nicaraguan jungles.

Her Rule was finally approved in 1907, the same year she became a naturalized citizen of the United States. By this time there were foundations in France and Spain as well as Italy and the Americas. In 1916, with her work nearly done, she went on a six-month retreat. While wrapping Christmas presents for Italian parochial-school children in Chicago on December 21, 1917, she collapsed and died the next day. Her body rests in Mother Cabrini High School in New York. She was canonized in 1946. There are representations of her in the Immigration Museum at the foot of the Statue of Liberty in New York harbor, on the bronze doors of St. Patrick's Cathedral, New York, in the National Shrine of the Immaculate Conception in Washington, D.C., and by a statue in St. Peter's Basilica in Rome. Her feast is on the Proper Calendar for the Dioceses of the U.S.A. and is also celebrated on this day by the Franciscans. It is not on the General Roman Calendar.

On this day the Jesuits celebrate the feast of *Stanislaus Kostka* (1550–68), a Jesuit novice, born of a politically significant family at Rostkovo, Poland, who walked 350 miles from Vienna (where the Jesuit provincial had refused to accept him) to Rome to plead his case before the superior general of the order. On his way to Rome, he met Peter Canisius [December 21], who encouraged him but also tested his vocation by assigning him menial tasks. The general, Francis Borgia [October 10], did accept him, but Stanislaus died after only nine months in the Society of Jesus. He was canonized in 1726 along with another Jesuit novice, Aloysius Gonzaga [June 21], and is a patron saint of Poland.

The Greek and Russian Orthodox Churches celebrate the feast of *John Chrysostom* [September 13] today.

It is also the feast day of *Homobonus* (ca. 1120–97), a tailor and cloth merchant of Cremona who was so generous to the poor that he was called the "Father of the Poor." He was a middle-class married layman who was canonized only two years after his death, at a time when almost all canonizations were of bishops, monks, martyrs, and royal figures. He is the patron saint of tailors, shoemakers, garment workers, merchants, and business people.

This is also the day of death of *Joseph Bernardin* (1928–96), the cardinal-archbishop of Chicago who moved and inspired a nation and the world with the courageous manner in which he faced, and even welcomed, his impending death from pancreatic cancer. His dying illuminated his whole life as one dedicated to bridge building and peacemaking.

14 Lawrence O'Toole, bishop; Nicholas Tavelic and companions, martyrs; Joseph Pignatelli, religious; Gregory Palamas, bishop

Lawrence O'Toole (1128–80) was one of the most important archbishops of Dublin. Born Lorcán Ua Tuathail in County Kildare, the product of a marriage between the O'Toole and O'Byrne royal clans, he was taken hostage, at age ten, for two years by a local king, but was eventually released to the custody of the bishop of Glendalough. When Lawrence's father came to take him home, Lawrence told him of his wish to become a monk. He was left in the care of the bishop, became a monk at Glendalough abbey, and was elected its abbot in 1153 at age twenty-five. He avoided becoming bishop by pointing out the canonical requirement that a bishop must be at least thirty years of age. However, less than ten years later, in 1162, he was elected archbishop of Dublin.

One of his first acts as archbishop was to import some Augustinian Canons of Arrouaise into the principal churches of the diocese, and he himself donned their religious habit, observed their Rule of life, and imposed it on his own cathedral canons as well. He also gained a reputation for his commitment to the poor, his tireless preaching, and the quality of his liturgical celebrations. When the English invaded Ireland in 1170, he served as a peacemaker, and two years later as a mediator between the king of England and Irish leaders at the synod of Cashel. In 1175 he traveled to Windsor and negotiated a treaty between King Henry II and the Irish high king, Rory O'Connor. On the same occasion, he narrowly escaped death at the hands of a crazed person while visiting the shrine of Thomas Becket [December 29] at Canterbury. He suffered a blow on the head and temporary unconsciousness, but otherwise survived the attack. Lawrence intervened successfully on behalf of his assailant when the king ordered the man hanged.

In 1179 he and five other Irish bishops attended the Third Lateran Council in Rome, at which time he gave Pope Alexander III a full report on the state of the Church in Ireland and was appointed papal legate for the country. The same year he presided over a council at Clonfert, which deposed seven "lay bishops," prohibited the sons of bishops and priests from receiving Holy Orders, and forbade laymen from having any role in the governance of the Church. The growing influence of Dublin was shown in 1180 when Lawrence promoted a Connacht bishop to the primatial see of Armagh. Later that year he pursued King Henry II to Normandy on behalf of Rory O'Connor, but Lawrence died on November 14, 1180, in the abbey at Eu (Seine-Inférieure), while on his way back to Ireland. When the abbot asked him if he had made out a will, Lawrence replied: "God knows I have not a penny in the world." He was buried in the crypt of the church of Our Lady at Eu and was canonized in 1225. His remains were brought back to Dublin the following year. His feast is not on the General Roman Calendar, but it is observed in Ireland and by the Canons Regular of the Lateran.

On this day the Franciscans celebrate the feast of *Nicholas Tavelic and companions* (d. 1391). Nicholas, the first Croatian saint, was a Franciscan, born in Dalmatia, who spent twenty years as a missionary in Bosnia. In 1391 he and three companions—*Déodat de Rodez, Pierre de Narbonne,* and *Stefano da Cuneo*—went to Jerusalem, then under Muslim control, to preach the gospel. All four were killed on the same day, November 14, as a gesture of contempt for Christianity. They were beatified in 1889 and canonized in 1970 as the first martyrs of the Custody of the Holy Land.

On this same day the Jesuits celebrate the feast of *Joseph Pignatelli* (1737–1811), who played a vital part in sustaining the Society of Jesus between the time of its suppression in 1773 and that of its restoration in 1814. Born in Saragossa, Spain, of noble Italian and Spanish parents, he pronounced his vows as a Jesuit in 1755 and was ordained in 1762. When the king of Spain expelled the Jesuits in 1767 (some five thousand in all), Pignatelli left with his confreres on an arduous journey that took them by ship to several different ports, not all of which were hospitable. With the suppression of the Jesuits on July 21, 1773, twenty-three thousand Jesuits, including Joseph Pignatelli, were no longer under vows. He moved to Bologna, where he continued to live the life of a Jesuit as best he could.

When he learned that Catherine the Great refused to enforce the suppression in Russia, he wrote to the superior of the Jesuits there and asked for readmission. He renewed his vows on July 6, 1797, and in

1799 became master of novices at Colorno, the only Jesuit novitiate in Western Europe at that time. Two years later the Jesuit superior in Russia appointed him provincial of Italy, with eventual headquarters in Naples. Another two years after that, Pignatelli and about fifty non-Neapolitan Jesuits were forced out of Naples to Rome, where they were welcomed by Pope Pius VII. The Jesuits found a home at St. Pantaleon's [July 27] near the Colosseum, and within six months they were teaching in six different diocesan seminaries and had opened a novitiate in Orvieto. Joseph Pignatelli died on November 15, 1811, and was buried in the church of Our Lady of Good Counsel. Three years later, Pius VII restored the Society of Jesus throughout the world. Joseph Pignatelli was beatified in 1933 and canonized in 1954. Neither his feast nor that of Nicholas Tavelic and companions is on the General Roman Calendar.

The Russian and Greek Orthodox Churches celebrate the feast of *Philip the Apostle* [May 3] on this day and also commemorate *Gregory of Palamas* (ca. 1296–1359), one of the greatest theologians of the Greek Orthodox tradition, who emphasized our divinization by the grace of God. He became archbishop of Thessalonica in 1347 and was canonized by the Orthodox Church in 1368. His feast is also celebrated on the Second Sunday of Lent.

15 Albert the Great, bishop and Doctor of the Church; Leopold III, duke

Albert the Great (1200–1280), also known by his Latin name, Albertus Magnus, was Thomas Aquinas's [January 28] teacher and is the patron saint of scientists and medical technicians. Born in Swabia, near Ulm, he joined the Dominicans while studying at the University of Padua in 1223 and taught at Hildesheim, Regensburg, and other cities, as well as Cologne, where Aquinas was his student. Albert became Master at Paris in 1248 and in the same year organized the Dominican house of studies at Cologne. He served as prior provincial of Germany for three years (1254–57), during which time he also served as Master of the Sacred Palace (the pope's personal theologian), a post traditionally held by a Dominican. Against his will, he was appointed bishop of Regensburg in 1260. Because of his inability to deal with the serious problems in the diocese, he resigned his see in 1262 to devote his time and energy once again to teaching and writing in Cologne. He participated in the Second Council of Lyons in 1274, despite the shock of

Thomas Aquinas's death on his own way to the council, and publicly defended his former student against attacks on his orthodoxy. Albert's own work, while less systematic than Aquinas's, fills thirty-eight volumes and covers subjects ranging from astronomy and chemistry to geography and physiology. Like his student, he also wrote a *Summa* and a commentary on the *Sentences* of Peter Lombard. Albert's activity as a teacher also influenced a second, more mystical theological school represented by two fellow Dominicans, Meister Eckhart (ca. 1260–ca. 1328) and Johannes Tauler (d. 1361). His contemporaries gave him the title "the Great" and also referred to him as the "Universal Doctor."

Albert's health began to fail him in 1278 as he lapsed into a form of dementia today called Alzheimer's disease. He died on November 15, 1280, and was buried in the Dominican church in Cologne. He was beatified in 1622 and canonized and declared a Doctor of the Church and patron saint of students of the natural sciences in 1931. Albert the Great's feast is on the General Roman Calendar.

November 15 is also the feast day of *Leopold III* (1075–1136), duke and patron saint of Austria. A fair-minded and kindly leader of his people, he founded or reformed several monasteries and was canonized in 1485. His feast day is a national holiday in Austria.

16 Margaret of Scotland, queen; Gertrude, virgin

Detail from *Saint Margaret of Scotland* by Guercino (1591–1666)

Margaret of Scotland (1046–93) is the patron saint of Scotland. Born probably in Hungary, where her father had taken refuge from the Danish rule in England and married the sister of the Hungarian king, Margaret was educated in Hungary and then returned to England with her parents just before the Norman Conquest in 1066. As one of the few surviving members of the Anglo-Saxon royal family, she was unsafe in England and went with her mother, brother, and sister to Scotland, where she was welcomed at the court of King Malcolm III. Malcolm married her ca. 1070, and they had six sons and two daughters. Margaret used her influence at court to promote the reform of the Church in Scotland, bringing various liturgical practices into conformity with those observed in

Rome. She founded monasteries, restored the famous abbey of Iona, and provided lodgings for pilgrims. She was devoted to her children and to the poor, but also found time for a rich prayer life. She died on November 16, 1093, and was buried at Dunfermline next to her husband, who had been killed in battle just before her own death. Her cult developed immediately, but she was not canonized until 1250. When Dunfermline was sacked in 1560, her relics were taken to a chapel in the Escorial, outside Madrid, but her head is preserved by the Jesuits at Douai. Her feast is on the General Roman Calendar, one of the few saints of Scotland so honored. She is also commemorated by the Church of England and the Episcopal Church in the USA.

Gertrude (1256–1302), also known as Gertrude the Great, was a German Benedictine nun and mystic who is the patron saint of the West Indies. Nothing is known of her parents or place of origin, but from age five she lived at the convent of Helfta in Thuringia, where she later recorded her mystical experiences in her *Revelations* and *Spiritual Exercises*. Her spirituality was rooted in the liturgy and Sacred Scripture and focused on the humanity of Christ. Indeed, she is considered a pioneer of the devotion to the Sacred Heart of Jesus. However, she was not the author of the book of prayers attributed to her. Although she was never formally canonized, her name was added to the *Roman Martyrology* in 1677, and in 1738, at the request of the king of Poland and the duke of Saxony, her feast (then on November 15) was extended to all countries. Her feast is on the General Roman Calendar.

17 Elizabeth of Hungary, religious; Gregory Thaumaturgus, bishop; Hugh of Lincoln, bishop; Gregory of Tours, bishop

Elizabeth of Hungary (1207–31) was the queen of Hungary and is the patron saint of Franciscan tertiaries and of Catholic charities. Born in Bratislava, the daughter of the king of Hungary, she was betrothed at age four to the eldest son of the duke of Thuringia, with whom she was raised until he reached the age of twenty-one (and she, fourteen), when they were married. Their brief marriage was a happy one and yielded three children. Elizabeth devoted herself to a life of prayer and almsgiving, at one time giving away so much that she incurred the wrath of others at court. She built a hospital in the basement of their castle, and she regularly fed and nursed the patients. The poor lined up at her door every day, and she provided them food, money, and work.

Saint Elizabeth of Hungary by Simone Martini (1284–1344)

In September 1227 her husband, Ludwig, died of plague on the way to join the Crusade in the Holy Land. Elizabeth heard the news the following month and was completely devastated.

It is not clear whether she left Wartburg voluntarily or under pressure from her brother-in-law, acting as regent for her infant son. In any event, she did go to Bamberg, where her uncle Eckbert was bishop. He expected her to remarry, but she and her husband had vowed not to remarry if one or the other died. Instead she received the habit and cord of a Franciscan tertiary in 1228 and settled just outside Marburg, where, out of the resources of her inheritance, she established a hospice for the sick, the aged, and the poor. She also placed herself under the spiritual guidance of a scholarly ascetic, Konrad of Marburg, who was known not only for his austerity of life, but also for his severity as an inquisitor against heretics. He demanded unconditional subjection from her, reinforced on occasion by physical punishment. On the other hand, he provided invaluable assistance in the administration of her charitable institutions and in the distribution of her funds for the poor. At this time, care of the sick was something that only men performed. Elizabeth is said to have retained her good humor and to have continued in her work on behalf of the needy, carving out new paths for the future of this ministry, but her health was broken within two years, and she was just twenty-four years of age when she died on November 17, 1231. She was canonized only four years later.

In 1236 her remains were taken to the church of St. Elizabeth in Marburg, which became a popular attraction for pilgrims until the Lutheran duke of Hesse had her relics removed to a still unknown place. She remains, however, a significant spiritual presence in that city even to this day. Elizabeth has been portrayed in many paintings as a queen or Franciscan tertiary by such artists as Fra Angelico [February 18], Pinacoteca, and van Eyck. Her feast is on the General Roman Calendar and is celebrated by the Church of England on November 18 and by the Episcopal Church in the USA on November 19.

The Greek and Russian Orthodox Churches celebrate on this day the feast of *Gregory Thaumaturgus* (ca. 213–ca. 270), also known as the

"Wonder-worker." Bishop of his native city, Neocaesarea, in Pontus, he was a disciple of Origen and the teacher of Macrina the Elder, grandmother of Basil [January 2] and Gregory of Nyssa [January 10]. He is a patron saint of desperate causes.

The Church of England and the Episcopal Church in the USA celebrate the feast of *Hugh of Lincoln* (ca. 1140–1200), a Carthusian monk and bishop of Lincoln, who established the first Carthusian house in England at the request of King Henry II. A defender of church liberties, he was renowned for his charity to the poor, and his tomb became an important pilgrimage site. He was canonized in 1220, the first Carthusian to be so honored.

Finally, this is also the feast day of *Gregory of Tours* (538–94), the bishop of Tours who is famous for his *History of the Franks,* which covers events from creation itself to 591. Without this work, the early history of France could not have been written.

18 Dedication of the Churches of Peter and Paul; Rose Philippine Duchesne, religious; Odo of Cluny, abbot

This feast celebrates the anniversaries of the *dedications of St. Peter's Basilica and St. Paul's Outside the Walls,* two of the four major basilicas in Rome. St. Peter's is built on Vatican Hill, over the site where the Apostle Peter [June 29] is thought to have been buried. The original building, in basilica style with a large courtyard (atrium) at its entrance, was constructed ca. 330, during the reign of the emperor Constantine (d. 337) [May 21]. The present church was begun in 1506 under the direction of a succession of architects (Bramante, Raphael, Peuzzi, and Sangallo), but its final shape derives from Michelangelo (d. 1564), who did not live to see the erection of the great dome. The long nave and façade, designed by Carlo Maderno, was added in the seventeenth century. Over the main entrance Maderno installed a loggia for public blessings. The basilica was dedicated by Pope Urban VIII on November 18, 1626. Gianlorenzo Bernini (d. 1680) further decorated its interior with the famous baldachino over the main altar, and the Baroque "altar of the chair" was added. He also designed the piazza in front of the basilica. Excavations in the twentieth century showed that the church is built over a large Roman cemetery. Peter's grave is thought to be under the main altar. The crypts and altars of the basilica contain the burial places of over 130 popes.

St. Paul's Outside the Walls derives its name from its location on the Via Ostia, outside the walls of the city. It was first built over the relics of the Apostle Paul [June 29] by Constantine in the fourth century and was later enlarged. The basilica burned to the ground in 1823 and was rededicated, after a complete rebuilding, on December 10, 1854. The church has been maintained over the centuries by Benedictine monks, who live in an adjacent monastery. The feast of the dedication of these two basilicas is on the General Roman Calendar.

This is also the feast day of *Rose Philippine Duchesne* (1769–1852), French missionary and educator who was a member of the Congregation of the Religious of the Sacred Heart (now the Society of the Sacred Heart). She established the first convent of her congregation in the United States at St. Charles, Missouri, in 1818 and founded many schools and orphanages. Her ministry to the Potawatomi tribe at Sugar Creek, Kansas, won for her the name "Woman Who Prays Always." She died on November 18, 1852, and was buried in the chapel of the convent in St. Charles. She was beatified in 1940 and canonized in 1988. Her feast is not on the General Roman Calendar.

This is also the feast day of *Odo of Cluny* (879–942), second abbot of the famous monastery of Cluny, who raised it to its place of importance in Europe, and who was author of hymns and moral treatises. He died on November 18, 942, at the monastery of Saint-Julien in Tours, while on his way back to Cluny from Rome. His feast is not on the General Roman Calendar.

19 Mechthilde of Magdeburg, abbess; Hilda of Whitby, abbess; Agnes of Assisi, abbess

Mechthilde of Magdeburg (ca. 1207–82), also Mechtild, descended from a noble family in Saxony, was a mystic who left home to become a Beguine (a member of a nonmonastic community of women) at Magdeburg under the spiritual guidance of Dominicans. She recorded her mystical experiences in a book of revelations entitled *Flowing Light of the Divinity*, which contains dialogues with the Lord, bridal mysticism, and some trinitarian theology and eschatology. She suffered from illnesses, personal threats, and much disapproval from official sources. During the 1260s when opposition to the Beguines became intense, she returned home to her family for a time. Then, ca. 1270, she became a nun at the convent at Helfta, where she came into contact with two other visionary women, namely, Mechthilde (also Mechtild) of Hackenborn (with whom she is sometimes confused) and Gertrude the Great [November 16]. Her revelations are considered among the most forceful and poetic examples of women's writings to have survived from the Middle Ages. Her feast is celebrated on this day by the Benedictines and Cistercians and is commemorated by the Church of England, but it is not on the General Roman Calendar. She was never formally canonized.

Hilda of Whitby (614–80) became abbess of Whitby (called Streaneshalch at the time), a double monastery of men and women, in which liturgies were in common but everything else was done separately. She encouraged the reading and study of the Bible as well as the Latin language and literature and established a library. It was probably because of her reputation as well as the suitability of the place that the famous Synod of Whitby was held at her abbey in 664 to choose between the Roman and Celtic systems for the dating of Easter. Given their Celtic Rule, Hilda and her community supported the Celtic method. However, when the synod decided in favor of the Roman practice, she fully accepted the decision. Hilda suffered from a chronic illness for the last seven years of her life. She died on November 17, 680. The abbey was destroyed by the Danes in 800, and it is not clear where her relics were taken. Both Glastonbury and Gloucester have claimed to have them. Her cult was strongest in northern England. The abbey was refounded in the eleventh century. Her feast is celebrated by the Church of England on this day, but is not on the General Roman Calendar. The Episcopal Church in the USA celebrates her feast on November 18.

Agnes of Assisi (d. 1253) was the younger sister of Clare of Assisi [August 11], the foundress of the Poor Clares and the close associate of Francis of Assisi [October 4]. Born Caterina Offreduccio, she was only about fifteen when she followed Clare into the convent. Her relatives used every means, including physical force, to induce her to return home. They failed, however, and Caterina received the habit from Francis, who gave her the name Agnes. In 1220 Francis sent her to Monticelli, outside Florence, to become abbess of a new convent of Poor Clares. She also supervised the foundation of other convents in Mantua, Padua, and Venice. Her sister Clare preceded her in death by only two months. Agnes died on November 16, 1253, and was buried initially at San Damiano, but in 1260 her remains were laid alongside her sister in the newly built church of Santa Chiara in Assisi. In 1752 the Franciscans received permission from the pope to celebrate her feast. They continue to do so today, although it is not on the General Roman Calendar.

20 Edmund, king and martyr

Edmund (841–69) was the king of East Anglia. Born of Saxon stock, he was raised a Christian and became king of the East Angles sometime before 865. During the great war with the Vikings in 869–70, he was defeated and captured. He refused to renounce his Christian faith or to rule as the Viking king's vassal. He was then killed at Hellesden (Suffolk), whether by being scourged, shot with arrows, and beheaded, as the traditional account has it, or by being spread-eagled as an offering to the Viking gods. His body was buried in a small wooden chapel nearby, was found incorrupt ca. 915, and was removed to a place near Bedricsworth (later Bury St. Edmunds). In 925 King Athelstan founded a community of two priests and four deacons to care for the shrine. In 1020 King Cnut ordered a stone church to be built at Bury, with a reformed Benedictine community. Bury soon became one of the most important of the English Benedictine abbeys. By the eleventh century Edmund's feast held a prominent place in monastic calendars in southern England. His remains were lost during the Reformation, but Toulouse attributed its deliverance from a plague ca. 1630 to his relics, and his cult flourished there for over two hundred and fifty years. His feast is not on the General Roman Calendar.

21 Presentation of Mary

The feast of the *Presentation of Mary* commemorates an event not described in the New Testament. According to the apocryphal *Protevangelium of James,* when the Blessed Virgin Mary was three years old, her parents took her to the Temple in Jerusalem and left her there to be educated. The priest received her with a kiss, saying: "The Lord has magnified thy name in all generations. In thee, on the last of days, the Lord will manifest his redemption to the sons of Israel." Then the priest set Mary on the third step of the altar, and the Lord sent grace upon her; she danced and "all the house of Israel loved her." Nowhere in the Roman liturgy, however, is there any indication that this is the event commemorated in this feast.

Because the feast is also celebrated on this day in the East, it is thought that it originated there, probably in the eighth century. It is known there as the Entry of the Most Holy Mother of God (Gk. *Theotokos*) into the Temple and was probably connected with the commemoration of the dedication of the basilica of St. Mary the New in Jerusalem in 543. In the East it is one of the Twelve Great Feasts (along with the Epiphany, the Presentation of Christ in the Temple [February 2], the Annunciation [March 25], Palm Sunday, Ascension Day, Pentecost, the Transfiguration [August 6], the Dormition of the Blessed Virgin Mary, the Nativity of the Blessed Virgin Mary [September 8], Holy Cross [September 14], and Christmas Day [December 25]. Easter is considered the "Feast of Feasts" and is in a class by itself). The feast of the Presentation of Mary was celebrated in the West sporadically from 1372, when a French knight who had returned from the East lobbied hard for its adoption. In 1585 Pope Sixtus V placed it on the universal calendar. The Presentation of Mary in the Temple has been a popular subject of artists such as Giotto, Titian, and others. This feast is on the General Roman Calendar and is celebrated on this day by the Greek and Russian Orthodox Churches.

A religious congregation known as the Sisters of Mary of the Presentation was founded in France in 1828 to educate people in the faith following the suppressions of religious orders in the French Revolution and to care for the poor, the sick, and the needy. Health care and education continue to be the sisters' chief areas of ministry.

22 Cecilia, virgin and martyr; Philemon and Onesimus

Cecilia (third century) was a Roman martyr of whom almost nothing is known for certain. She is the patron saint of musicians, singers, and poets. Her popularity is rooted in a fifth-century legend, according to which she refused to consummate a marriage because of her vow of virginity, and when she also refused to sacrifice to the gods, an attempt was made unsuccessfully to suffocate her. Then a solider was sent to behead her, but three blows to the head failed to kill her. She survived half dead for three days. However, there is no mention of Cecilia in any of the near contemporary martyrologies. A church in the Trastevere section of Rome founded by a Roman matron named Cecilia is probably at the base of the legend. Her supposed relics were transferred to this church ca. 820, and when the church was rebuilt in 1599, the body was found incorrupt (although it quickly disintegrated when exposed to the air). The traditional account of her life is famous as the Second Nun's Tale in Chaucer's *Canterbury Tales*.

The origin of Cecilia's association with music seems to be found in a line taken from her Acts: "as the organs [at her wedding feast] were playing, Cecilia sung [in her heart] to the Lord, saying: may my heart remain unsullied, so that I be not confounded." At the foundation of the Academy of Music in Rome in 1584, she was chosen as its patron saint. Her feast is on the General Roman Calendar and is commemorated on this day by the Church of England.

The Greek and Russian Orthodox Churches celebrate today the feast of *Philemon,* a convert of Paul [June 29] and a recipient of a Letter from him, and of *Onesimus,* his slave who ran away to Ephesus and served Paul during his imprisonment (Philem. 13). Paul sent Onesimus back to Philemon and urged the latter to receive him no longer as a slave but as a beloved brother (v. 16).

23 Clement I, pope and martyr; Columban, abbot; Blessed Michael Pro

Clement I (d. ca. 101; pope ca. 91–ca. 101), also known as Clement of Rome, is best known for his likely authorship of the letter referred to as *1 Clement,* the most important first-century Christian document outside the New Testament and treated by some in the ancient Church as if it were, in fact, part of the New Testament canon. A second letter attributed to him *(2 Clement)* is not authentic. The Roman community at this time was probably divided into a number of small house churches scattered throughout the city and its neighboring districts, each presided over by a presbyter (and possibly more than one). There would have been no united and coordinated leadership within the city's Christian community as a whole, but it was otherwise the case in the community's relations with the Christian communities of other cities. One presbyter (and Clement was specifically mentioned in *The Shepherd of Hermas*) was charged with corresponding with these other communities and probably also with dispensing aid to those in need. As such, Clement and others in his position would have functioned as a kind of foreign minister of the Roman church rather than as its monarchical bishop, or pope in the modern sense of the word.

This first letter of Clement was sent ca. 96 from the church in Rome to the church in Corinth, instructing the Corinthians to reinstate elders (presbyters, or senior priests) who had been improperly deposed and to exile the younger persons who had instigated the rebellion. Significantly, Clement offered no defense for his intervening in the pastoral affairs of the Corinthian church (he had not been invited to do so by the Corinthians), but neither did he appeal to any special Roman privilege. The form of Clement's intervention seems to have been modeled on the relations of the imperial capital of Rome (its senate and emperor) with its outlying provinces. In accordance with the practice of the imperial government, Clement sent with his letter three witnesses to observe and to report on the restoration of peace. His recommendation of exile for the offending parties also mirrored secular Roman practice, in which exile was an escape from trial. Indeed, the letter is marked throughout by a laudatory attitude toward the Roman state. It praises the Roman military as a model of obedience and calls upon Christians to be similarly "obedient . . . to our rulers and governors on earth," to whom God has given the sovereignty. Underlying these words is the conviction that the empire and its rulers have been established by God as the earthly counterpart of the heavenly kingdom. As such, the Roman political system—which is at once imperial and hierarchical—is worthy of being emulated by the Church itself. The influence of the existing Roman political system on the evolving Roman ecclesiastical system, therefore, cannot be discounted.

There is an unverified tradition, attested nonetheless by Tertullian (d. ca. 225) and Jerome [September 30] (d. ca. 420), that Clement was consecrated by Peter himself [June 29] as his immediate successor. If that were true, Linus (ca. 66–ca. 78) and Anacletus (ca. 79–ca. 91) would have to be somehow displaced from, or rearranged on, the list of popes. Third- and fourth-century writers, such as Origen (d. ca. 254), Eusebius of Caesarea (d. ca. 339), and Jerome, equated him with the Clement whom Paul [June 29] mentions as a co-worker who "struggled at [his] side in promoting the gospel" and whose name is "in the book of life" (Phil. 4:3), which is a kind of registry of God's chosen people (Exod. 32:32–33; Pss. 69:28; 139:16).

There is no historical evidence to support the claim that Clement died a martyr or that he was banished to Crimea, where he is said to have preached the gospel while doing forced labor in the mines and was later drowned in the Black Sea with an anchor around his neck. In the ninth century Cyril and Methodius [February 14] claimed to have recovered his relics along with the anchor. The relics were taken to Rome and buried in the church of San Clemente, which, according to tradition, stands on the site of Clement's house. He is mentioned in the

Eucharistic Prayer between Cletus (Anacletus) and Sixtus (d. 258 [August 7]). His feast is on the General Roman Calendar and is also celebrated on this day by the Church of England and the Episcopal Church in the USA. He is commemorated by the Greek Orthodox Church on November 24 and by the Russian Orthodox Church on November 25. He is the patron saint of marbleworkers and stonecutters.

Saint Columban

Columban (ca. 543–615), also Columbanus, was one of the greatest Irish missionary monks of the sixth and seventh centuries. Born in Leinster, he was well educated in Latin literature and the Bible. He became a monk first on an island in Lough Erne and then at Bangor, where he remained many years. Not until 590 or thereabouts did he set sail with twelve companions for Gaul. It was a relatively common occurrence in the Celtic Church at the time for individuals to go into a kind of voluntary exile to spread the gospel. They found the Gallic Church in a depressed state. But Columban and his monks refused to be discouraged and began their work with energy and enthusiasm. Their reputation soon reached the king of Burgundy, who gave Columban a plot of land with an abandoned Roman fort in which to found a monastery. The success of the first led quickly to the founding of a second and a third. The essence of his Rule was love of God and love of neighbor. It also prescribed harsh penances for every conceivable fault, however slight.

After twelve years of ministry, however, Columban and his monks began to sense hostility from the local Frankish bishops, who resented their independence and their Celtic (as opposed to Roman) ways, especially regarding the dating of Easter. When the bishops requested his presence at a synod, Columban refused to attend, asking to be left in peace to do his work. The bishops kept pressing from time to time, and Columban appealed to at least two popes for support. The matter continued to fester without resolution. However, Columban found himself in difficulty on yet another front. He had reproached the king of Burgundy for keeping concubines, refused to baptize his illegitimate children, and prevented his grandmother from entering his monastery at Luxeuil (indeed, he refused entry to any woman or layman). In 610 the king ordered Columban and his Irish monks to leave the country.

Almost immediately their ship ran into a storm, and they had to return to port. Avoiding Burgundy, they went to the court of the Austrasian king at Metz and were well received there, but not by the people, who found them too severe. When the king was defeated in a war with Burgundy, Columban, by now about seventy years old, moved yet again, walking across the Alps to Milan, where he and his monks were also well received. With a donated piece of land, Columban made his final monastic foundation, at Bobbio, between Genoa and Piacenza. He died on November 23, 615, and was buried in Bobbio. His feast is on the General Roman Calendar. St. Columban's Foreign Missionary Society, popularly known as the Columbans, originated in Ireland in 1916 and chose Columban as its patron saint.

The dioceses of the Catholic Church in the United States also commemorate on this day *Michael Pro* (1891–1927), a Mexican Jesuit priest who was executed by a firing squad on November 23, 1927, at the order of the violently anticlerical government. Twenty thousand people attended his burial, and he became one of the best known martyrs of the twentieth century. He was beatified in 1988. On May 21, 2000, Pope John Paul II canonized twenty-seven other Mexicans as saints, all but two of whom were martyred in the 1920s and 1930s during the civil war and most of whom were priests.

24 Andrew Dung-Lac and companions, martyrs; Chrysogonus, martyr

Andrew Dung-Lac (d. 1839), a Vietnamese diocesan priest, was one of 117 martyrs, also known as the Martyrs of Tonkin, who were canonized in 1988. Catholicism was first introduced into Vietnam in 1533, but did not take hold until early in the next century when Jesuits established roots there. By 1639 there were some one hundred thousand Catholics in the country. The first two native priests were ordained in 1668. Severe persecution broke out in 1698, then three more times in the eighteenth century, and again in the nineteenth. Between one hundred thousand and three hundred thousand Catholics suffered in some way during the fifty years before 1833, when the French moved in and secured religious freedom for Catholics. Most of the 117 martyrs—among whom there were eight bishops, fifty priests and religious (especially Dominicans), and fifty-nine laypersons—were put to death (mostly by beheading) during this fifty-year period, especially in the reign of the Annamite kings Minh-Mang (1820–40) and Tu Duc (1847–83). Their feast is on the General Roman Calendar.

This is also the feast day of *Chrysogonus* (d. ca. 304), one of the martyrs mentioned in the First Eucharistic Prayer, but about whom almost nothing at all is known. He seems to have been martyred at Aquileia and was venerated in northern Italy. His cult developed in Rome, where the titular church of San Crisogono in Trastevere is first mentioned in 499.

25 Moses of Rome, martyr; Catherine of Alexandria, martyr; Mercurius, martyr

Moses of Rome (d. 251) was a member of the Roman clergy who was a leading candidate for the papacy at one time and would very likely have been elected if he were not in prison and eventually martyred under the emperor Decius. Possibly of Jewish origin, Moses and his fellow priest-prisoners exchanged regular letters of encouragement with Cyprian [September 16], bishop of Carthage, and formed a united front against Novatian, who was the leader of a group that opposed reconciliation with those who had apostatized under pressure during the persecution. The previous pope, Fabian [January 20], had died more than a year earlier, and the election of a successor was delayed because of the persecution and because the leading candidate, Moses, was in prison. During the spring of 251 the emperor left Rome to fight the Goths and the persecution subsided. By this time, however, Moses had died in prison and was immediately proclaimed a martyr. It is not clear why his feast was placed in November in the *Roman Martyrology.* His feast is not on the General Roman Calendar.

The Greek Orthodox Church and the Church of England commemorate *Catherine of Alexandria* on this day. (The Russian Orthodox Church commemorates her on November 24.) According to tradition, she was a virgin who had been martyred in the early fourth century. However, there is no evidence that she ever existed, even though she is regarded as the patron saint of philosophers, young unmarried women, preachers, nurses, and craftsmen and is one of the Fourteen Holy Helpers, a group of saints notable for their answering of prayers, especially for cures from disease and at the hour of death (see Glossary). She has been venerated in the East since the ninth century. Indeed, Joan of Arc [May 30] claimed to have heard Catherine's voice. Upon Catherine's alleged death by beheading, after a wheel of torture (known as "Catherine's wheel") broke, her body was supposedly carried by angels to Mount Sinai. Her feast was dropped from the liturgical calendar of the Roman Catholic Church in 1969.

The Greek Orthodox Church celebrates the feast of *Mercurius* (third century) on this day. He is one of the so-called warrior saints who have been popular in the East. Much of his biography is shrouded in legend, however. According to the legend, he was a military officer who, after leading a great victory over the Goths, refused to sacrifice to the gods in celebration. The emperor Decius was afraid to punish him in Rome, where Mercurius was popular, so he had him taken to Caesarea in Cappadocia, where he was tortured and beheaded. He was invoked by Basil the Great [January 2] for assistance against Julian the Apostate (361–63), whom he is credited with slaying with his sword, and he was also thought to have appeared to the Crusaders at Antioch, with Sts. George [April 23] and Demetrius. His feast is not on the General Roman Calendar. It is celebrated by the Russian Orthodox Church on November 24.

26 Leonard of Port Maurice, friar; Sylvester Gozzolini, founder; John Berchmans, religious

Leonard of Port Maurice (1676–1751) was a Franciscan priest who was an indefatigable preacher and a vigorous promoter of devotion to the Stations of the Cross. Born Paulo Girolamo Casanova in Liguria, Italy, he joined the Franciscans, was ordained a priest in 1702, and became guardian (superior) of a Florentine friary, then of St. Bonaventure's [July 15] in Rome in 1730. He established some five hundred Stations of the Cross in Italy, including a set in the Colosseum in Rome during the Jubilee year of 1750. After preaching extensively in Lucca the following year, his health failed and he died in Rome on November 26, 1751. He was beatified in 1796 and canonized in 1867. He is patron saint of parish missions. His feast is not on the General Roman Calendar, but is celebrated on this day by the Franciscans.

Sylvester Gozzolini (1177–1267) was the founder of the Silvestrine Benedictines, known as the Blue Benedictines because of the color of their habit. Born of a noble family in Osimo, Italy, he studied law at Bologna and Padua before switching to theology and Sacred Scripture. He was ordained and became a canon at Osimo. However, after he criticized his bishop for the quality of his life, Sylvester was forced to resign his canonry, at age fifty, and he became a hermit near Osimo. Directed by an alleged vision of St. Benedict [July 11], he organized his disciples into a monastery at Monte Fano near Fabriano in 1231. This group became the Silvestrine Benedictines. The congregation was approved in 1247, and Sylvester ruled it for thirty-seven years until his death at Fabriano. He was declared a saint (but not formally canonized) by Pope Clement VIII in 1598. His feast is not on the General Roman Calendar, but is celebrated on this day by the Benedictines.

John Berchmans (1599–1621) was a Belgian Jesuit seminarian who died in Rome of fever and dysentery on August 13, 1621. Given his reputation as a person of prayer and obedience to the will of God, he was beatified in 1865 and canonized in 1888. His remains are in the church of San Ignazio in Rome, but his heart was taken to the Jesuit church in Louvain. He is the patron saint of altar servers and youth. His feast is celebrated on this day by the Jesuits, but it is not on the General Roman Calendar.

27 James the Persian, martyr

James the Persian (d. ca. 421), or James Intercisus (Lat., "cut to pieces"), was the best-known victim of the second great persecution in Persia, beginning ca. 420. According to the largely legendary account of his martyrdom, James was a friend of the pagan king. Because he did not want to lose the king's friendship, he abandoned his faith after the local bishop had provoked the king into a declaration of war on Christians. His apostasy greatly distressed James's wife and mother. When the king died, they wrote to James to reproach him. He was greatly moved by their letter, repented, renounced his position at court, and publicly declared himself a Christian. He was summoned by the new king and condemned to death. His body was stretched, limb by limb, and then cut to pieces. James is said to have remained cheerful throughout the agonizing process, until his executioner finally severed his head from his body. A Greek Orthodox source says that he died on November 27, 389. His feast is celebrated by the Greek and Russian Orthodox Churches on this day, but is not on the General Roman Calendar.

28 Catherine Labouré, virgin; Stephen the Younger, martyr

Catherine Labouré (1806–76) was a French Sister of Charity whose reported visions of the Blessed Virgin Mary gave rise to devotion to the

Miraculous Medal, which depicts Mary standing on a globe with shafts of light coming from her hands. Born Zoë Labouré in the Côte D'Or of France, she joined the Sisters of Charity of St. Vincent de Paul [September 27] in 1830. She took the religious name Catherine. After her period of postulancy, she was sent to Paris, where she had the first of her claimed visions in the convent chapel on the Rue de Bac. The Blessed Virgin was said to have appeared to her standing on a globe with shafts of light streaming from her hands and the words "O Mary, conceived without sin, pray for us who have recourse to thee" surrounding the image. When Our Lady turned around, Catherine said that she saw a capital *M* with a cross above it and below it two hearts, one crowned with thorns, the other pierced with a sword. Catherine also claimed to have heard a voice urging her to reproduce on a medal what she had seen in the vision and promising great spiritual benefits to those who would wear the medal. The visions were said to have continued until September 1831.

Saint Catherine Labouré

The archbishop of Paris gave permission to have the medal struck, and the first fifteen hundred, issued in June 1832, came to be known as the "Miraculous Medal" because of its origin. A tribunal convened by the archbishop in 1836 ruled in favor of Catherine's claims, although Catherine refused to participate lest her anonymity be lost. From 1831 until her death on December 31, 1876, Catherine lived a quiet life out of the public eye. It was her confessor who promoted the devotion to the Miraculous Medal. There was a great measure of veneration toward her on the occasion of her funeral, and cures were reported at her tomb in the chapel of the convent. She was beatified in 1933 and canonized in 1947. Her feast is not on the General Roman Calendar.

The Greek and Russian Orthodox Churches celebrate on this day the feast of *Stephen the Younger* (d. 764), one of the most famous martyrs during the iconoclast persecution. An abbot in Bithynia, he was summoned by the emperor Constantine V to support his war against the use of images and holy pictures. When Stephen refused, he was imprisoned, beaten, and exiled. Two years later he was brought back to a prison in Constantinople and then arraigned before the emperor, who asked him if trampling on an image of Christ was equivalent to trampling on Christ himself. Stephen said, "No." But then he produced a coin with the emperor's image on it and asked the emperor if trampling on that coin would be tantamount to trampling on the emperor himself. The emperor became indignant and commanded that Stephen be scourged. When this failed to kill him, the emperor was heard to say: "Will no one rid me of this monk?"—a plea that anticipated King Henry II's regarding Thomas Becket [December 29]. Those who overheard the remark seized Stephen, dragged him through the streets, and clubbed him to death. His feast is not on the General Roman Calendar.

The Episcopal Church in the USA celebrates the feast of *Kamehameha* (d. 1863) and *Emma* (d. 1885), king and queen of Hawaii, on this day.

29 Saturninus of Toulouse, bishop and martyr; Dorothy Day, foundress

Saturninus of Toulouse (third century), also known as Sernin, was the first bishop of Toulouse. Little is known of him before he became a bishop, but his name suggests that he was an African. He was sent as a missionary from Rome to the area of the Pyrenees Mountains, encompassing northern Spain and southern France. After becoming bishop of Toulouse, he vigorously opposed idol worship there, for which he was dragged by the pagan temple priests into the temple and warned that he must sacrifice to the offended gods or satisfy their wrath with the shedding of his own blood. Saturninus insisted that he worshiped only the one true God and that their gods were evil. Enraged, the priests tied his feet to a bull which then dragged him to his death. His relics were eventually enshrined in what is now the basilica of Saint-Sernin, along with those of his successors. His cult seems to have been widespread in southern France and northern Spain from the third century,

Dorothy Day, 1916

and there are several churches dedicated to him along the route taken by pilgrims to Compostela. His feast is observed in the Mozarabic Rite and also in parts of France, but it is not on the General Roman Calendar.

This is also the day of death of *Dorothy Day* (1897–1980), cofoundress of the Catholic Worker movement, a community of laypeople. Her whole life was dedicated to the service of the poor, the hungry, and the homeless and to peace. Her cause for canonization was formally introduced early in 2000, upon the request of Cardinal John J. O'Connor (d. 2000), archbishop of New York, who considered her, among other things, a model for women who have had or are considering an abortion (Day once had an abortion and later regretted it).

30 Andrew, apostle; Cuthbert Mayne, martyr

Andrew (d. ca. 70) was one of Jesus' first disciples and one of the twelve apostles. Indeed, his name is prominent on all lists of the apostles (Matt. 10:2; Mark 3:18; Luke 6:14; Acts 1:13). His Greek name means "manly." (Philip [May 3] is the only other member of the Twelve with a Greek name.) He is the patron saint of Scotland, Russia, and Greece and also of fishermen and sailors. Born in Bethsaida, on the northeast shore of the Sea of Galilee (John 1:44), he was the brother of Simon Peter [June 29]. Both were residents of Capernaum (Mark 1:29), where they worked as fishermen (Mark 1:16). Andrew learned of Jesus through John the Baptist [June 24; August 29], whose disciple he was. Andrew then introduced Jesus to Peter (John 1:40). Before the feeding of the multitude, Andrew notices the boy with the loaves and fish (John 6:8). With Philip he conveys to Jesus the request of the Greeks to see him (John 12:22). With Peter, James [July 25], and John [December 27], he asks Jesus about Jerusalem's fate (Mark 13:3).

Second-century apocryphal literature recounts Andrew's missionary ventures. The *Acts of Andrew and Matthias* tells us of Andrew's rescue of Matthias [May 14] from cannibals. The *Acts of Andrew*, which survives in a Latin translation by Gregory of Tours (d. 594) [November 17] and in Greek fragments, reports miracles performed in Greece and Asia Minor. The account of Andrew's crucifixion at Patras, Greece, on an X-shaped cross (called St. Andrew's Cross), also circulated independently of these documents. (The cross is incorporated into the Union Jack to represent Scotland.) According to a later legend, Andrew's bones were taken to St. Andrew's, Scotland. Andrew's head, which had been in Constantinople and was then brought to Rome from Amalfi by Crusaders in 1461, was returned to Constantinople by Pope Paul VI in 1964. His feast is on the General Roman Calendar and is also celebrated on this day by the Greek and Russian Orthodox Churches, by the Church of England and the Episcopal Church in the USA, and by the Evangelical Lutheran Church in America.

Cuthbert Mayne (1543–77) was one of the Forty Martyrs of England and Wales [October 25], canonized in 1970. Raised and ordained in the Church of England, he was influenced by Edmund Campion [December 1] to become a Catholic. In 1575 he was ordained to the Catholic priesthood at Douai, the site of the English Catholic college in northern France, and was later sent back to England to minister to Catholic recusants (those who refused to accept the queen as head of the Church) in Cornwall, disguising himself as a domestic steward. He was discovered, arrested, tried, and executed on November 30, 1577, after refusing to acknowledge the ecclesiastical supremacy of the queen.

DECEMBER

1 Edmund Campion, Ralph Sherwin, Alexander Briant, and Robert Southwell, martyrs; Charles de Foucauld, hermit; Eligius, bishop

Edmund Campion (1540–81) was the first Jesuit martyr in Elizabethan England. Born in London, the son of a bookseller, he was a brilliant student at Oxford who was selected as university orator to welcome Queen Elizabeth on her visit there in 1566. Sir Robert Cecil called him "one of the diamonds of England." He was ordained a deacon in the Church of England in 1569 and in the same year took the Oath of Supremacy. But having grown up under the Catholic Queen Mary (1553–58), he was having personal doubts about the newly reopened breach between England and the pope, so he left home for Ireland, where he helped to revive the university in Dublin (later Trinity College) and wrote a history of the country. He returned to England in 1571, a year after Pope Pius V [April 30] issued a bull excommunicating Queen Elizabeth and formally deposing her from the throne. Soon thereafter Edmund crossed the Channel to the (Catholic) English

College at Douai, where he joined the Roman Catholic Church in 1573. After being ordained a subdeacon, he left for Rome to join the Society of Jesus.

In 1578 he was ordained a priest in Prague, where he had been teaching in a Jesuit school. The following year he and Robert Persons were chosen to inaugurate a Jesuit mission in England. He stopped off in Milan to consult with its archbishop, Cardinal Charles Borromeo [November 4], and then entered England disguised as a jewel merchant. Not even all Catholics welcomed them with open arms, for fear that their activities would further upset an already delicate political situation. Campion ministered to Catholic prisoners in London and wrote a challenge to the Privy Council entitled "Campion's Brag," in which he described his mission to England as one of rescuing his fellow countrymen from "foul vice and proud ignorance." Campion's eloquence, learning, and personality, as well as his effective use of the printing press, made him a formidable presence the government could not ignore. As he continued to evade the government's scrutiny by his mobility and effective disguises, he published his most famous work, *Decem Rationes* (Lat., "Ten Reasons"), a defense of Catholicism and a challenge to Protestants to debate him. Four hundred copies were distributed at St. Mary's University Church, Oxford, and a few weeks later he was arrested and imprisoned in the Tower of London. No amount of bribes (from the queen herself), torture (by racking), or theological argument could induce him to conform.

On November 14 he was indicted with others in Westminster Hall on the charge of having plotted rebellion abroad (in Rome and Reims) and of coming to England to carry out the plot. In spite of his typically eloquent defense at trial, Campion was found guilty and condemned to death. On the occasion he said: "In condemning us you condemn all your own ancestors, all the ancient bishops and kings, all that was once the glory of England. . . . Posterity's judgment is not liable to corruption as that of those who are now going to sentence us to death." On December 1, 1581, he, along with *Alexander Briant* and *Ralph Sherwin,* was hanged, drawn, and quartered at Tyburn. On the scaffold he prayed for the queen: "Your queen and my queen, unto whom I wish a long reign with all prosperity." He was beatified in 1588 and then canonized in 1970 as one of the Forty Martyrs of England and Wales [October 25]. Edmund Campion's feast is not on the General Roman Calendar, but it is observed on this day by the Jesuits.

On this day the Jesuits also observe the feast of Ralph Sherwin, Alexander Briant, and Robert Southwell. *Ralph Sherwin* (1549–81) was the first to volunteer for the mission to England, accompanying Campion and Robert Persons as far as Reims in 1580. Sherwin set out from there by himself and was arrested soon after his arrival while preaching in a private home. Like Campion, he was severely tortured on the rack and bribed with a bishopric if he would conform. After more than a year's imprisonment, he was brought to trial with Campion and others and was convicted on the same charge of inciting rebellion against the queen. He protested his innocence of the charge of treason to the end, offering prayers for the queen on the scaffold. He was beatified and canonized with Campion as one of the Forty Martyrs of England and Wales. He is considered the protomartyr (first martyr) of the English College in Rome.

Alexander Briant (1556–81) was a young diocesan priest who had been ordained at the English College at Douai and who returned to England to carry out a mission in the West Country. He was arrested and tortured in the Tower of London by the use of needles under his fingernails, as well as by starvation and the rack, the last being unusually severe in intensity. In a letter from the Tower to Jesuits in England, he reflected on his plight and asked to be admitted to the order. Consequently, he is numbered among the martyrs of the Society of Jesus. He was beatified and canonized as one of the Forty Martyrs of England and Wales.

Robert Southwell (ca. 1561–95), an accomplished poet, was ordained a Jesuit priest in 1584 and returned to England from the English College at Douai, where he was prefect of studies. He carried on his secret ministry for six years under the protection of Anne Dacre, the countess of Arundel and Surrey, who helped him publish his *An Epistle of Comfort,* directed to persecuted and imprisoned Catholics. In 1591 he composed his *Humble Supplication to Her Majesty,* refuting the government's claim that there was no persecution on the grounds of religion alone. As in the case of the other Jesuit missionaries, Southwell's goal was not the conversion of Protestants, but the reconciliation of lapsed Catholics to the Church, especially those in the aristocracy and intellectual community. Like so many others, Southwell was eventually betrayed, imprisoned, brutally tortured, and then, three years later, condemned, hanged, drawn, and quartered at Tyburn. He too prayed for the queen and for the country from the scaffold. He was beatified in 1929 and canonized, with the others, in 1970.

On this day the Church of England commemorates *Charles de Foucauld* (1858–1916), who lived as a hermit in the Sahara (as a witness in the midst of non-Christians) and whose private writings, discovered after his death, inspired the founding of the Little Brothers of Jesus in 1933 and the Little Sisters of Jesus in 1936. He has not been beatified or canonized.

The Greek and Russian Orthodox Churches celebrate the feast of *Nahum*, a minor prophet who was the father of another minor prophet, Amos.

It is also the feast of *Eligius* (ca. 588–660), the bishop of Noyon and the founder of three monasteries in northern France. He had been a goldsmith by trade and is the patron saint of goldsmiths and jewelers.

2 Chromatius, bishop; Maura Clarke, Ita Ford, Dorothy Kazel, and Jean Donovan, martyrs

Chromatius (d. 407) was one of the most distinguished bishops of his time. Born in Aquileia, near Trieste, he participated in the anti-Arian council of Aquileia in 381 while still a presbyter. He was elected bishop of his hometown in 388. He was a friend and correspondent of Jerome [September 30], whom he had met while Jerome was residing in Milan and who dedicated several of his works to him, and of Ambrose [December 7], archbishop of Milan. Chromatius was also a vigorous supporter of John Chrysostom [September 13], who suffered persecution as patriarch of Constantinople under the emperor Honorius. Chromatius also encouraged Rufinus to translate Eusebius's *Ecclesiastical History* and helped with the financing of Jerome's translation of the Bible. He was himself an able commentator on Sacred Scripture, especially Matthew's Gospel. His feast is not on the General Roman Calendar.

On this day the Greek and Russian Orthodox Churches celebrate the feast of *Habakkuk*, a minor prophet who probably lived in the latter part of the seventh century before the Christian era.

December 2 is also the day on which four missionaries were raped and murdered in El Salvador in 1980: *Maura Clarke* and *Ita Ford*, both Maryknoll sisters, and *Dorothy Kazel*, an Ursuline sister, and *Jean Donovan*, a lay missioner, both from Cleveland, Ohio. All four had been profoundly touched by the example of Oscar Romero [March 24], archbishop of San Salvador, who had been assassinated nine months earlier, because of his commitment to human rights and the Church's "preferential option for the poor."

3 Francis Xavier, priest

Francis Xavier (1506–52) was one of the greatest missionaries in the history of the Church and is patron saint of the foreign missions. He is also known as the "apostle of the Indies and of Japan." He is the patron saint of India, Japan, Pakistan, the East Indies, Outer Mongolia, and Borneo. Born at the castle of Xavier (Javier) in Navarre, Spain, he was educated at the University of Paris, where he met Ignatius of Loyola [July 31) and became one of the original group of seven Jesuits who took their vows at Montmartre in 1534 and were ordained priests in Venice three years later. In 1540 he joined Simon Rodriguez at Lisbon and, after several months, sailed on April 7, 1541, to Goa, India, an arduous journey of thirteen months, to evangelize the East Indies. Francis was named papal nuncio in the East.

He enjoyed extraordinary success over the remaining ten years of his life. He shamed the Portuguese Catholics in Goa into a more humane treatment of slaves and a concern for the poor. He also insisted that the Portuguese men take responsibility for the care of their concubines and the children they had with them. He spent the mornings visiting prisons and hospitals, and in the afternoons summoned children and slaves to catechism class with a bell. He also celebrated Mass for lepers every Sunday. In addition to his preaching, he reached the people through religious verses set to popular tunes. He also worked in southern India among the low-caste Paravas and in Ceylon, Malacca, the Molucca islands (the Spice Islands of modern-day Indonesia), and the Malay peninsula. He ministered as a poor man to the poor, sleeping on the ground in a hut and subsisting mainly on rice and water. Although he met with much success among the lower castes, he made almost no impact at all on the Brahmins.

Saint Francis of Xavier
by Giuseppe Laudati,
late 17th C. – early 18th C.

In 1549 Francis Xavier went to Japan, where he made a hundred converts in a year at Kagoshima. He also had limited success in other locations and concluded that he would not be taken seriously as a poor man. He changed into fine robes and brought presents of clocks, eyeglasses, and a music box to the local ruler as a representative of the king of Portugal. As a result, he secured the leader's protection and the use of an empty Buddhist monastery. By the time he left Japan, there were some two thousand Japanese Christians. Within fifty years they resisted fierce persecution and even death. In 1552 Francis was again at Goa, but left after a few months for China. He fell ill on the way and died almost alone on the island of Shang-chwan (Sancian), six miles off the coast of mainland China and about a hundred miles southwest of Hong Kong, on December 3. He was forty-six years old.

His body was placed in quicklime and brought eventually to Goa, where it became an object of popular devotion in the church of the Good Jesus. His right arm was detached in 1615 and is preserved in the church of the Gesú in Rome. Francis Xavier was canonized in 1622, along with Ignatius of Loyola, Teresa of Ávila [October 15], and Philip Neri [May 26] and was declared patron saint of the foreign missions in 1927. There are religious congregations named after him as well as many churches and colleges. His feast is on the General Roman Calendar and is also commemorated by the Evangelical Lutheran Church in America. The Greek and Russian Orthodox Churches celebrate the feast of *Zephaniah,* a seventh-century B.C. minor prophet who may have been a cousin of the major prophet Jeremiah.

4 John Damascene, priest and Doctor of the Church; Barbara, martyr

John Damascene (ca. 657–ca. 749), also John of Damascus and John Chrysorrhoas (Gk., "Golden Speaker"), was one of the most influential Greek theologians in the medieval West; his thought impacted the work of Thomas Aquinas [January 28], Peter Lombard, and others. Born in Damascus, Syria, of a wealthy Christian family, he was well educated by a Sicilian monk (who had been brought back from Sicily as a captive) in science and theology. John succeeded his father briefly as chief of revenue, but ca. 700, after a shift in policy toward Christians, he resigned his office, divided his wealth among his relatives, the Church, and the poor and became a monk and later a priest at the *laura* (Gk., "street") of St. Sabas [December 5], near

Jerusalem. (A *laura,* or *lavra,* was a monastery in which the monks lived in separate cells or huts and in complete solitude, except for liturgies in the monastery church.) John invested his time, energy, and considerable intellectual gifts in the composition of hymns and theological works, the most important of which was his *Fount of Wisdom,* which was divided into three parts: philosophy, heresies, and the Orthodox faith. The last was a summary of the teachings of the Greek Fathers on the main elements of the Christian faith: the Trinity, creation, the Incarnation, the Church, the sacraments, Mary (he held the doctrines of the divine maternity, the Immaculate Conception [December 8], and the Assumption [August 15]), and the Second Coming of Christ.

John had a quintessentially Catholic sacramental vision. "The one who seeks God continually will find him," he wrote, "for God is in everything." He also wrote three tracts against the iconoclasts (those who destroyed icons, statues, and any other representation of Christ, Mary, and the other saints), which brought him the disfavor of the pro-iconoclastic Christian emperors. However, they were unable to take any action against John Damascene, as they had against other anti-iconoclasts, because, ironically, John lived under protective Muslim rule. He died at Mar Saba ca. 749, and his cult developed soon thereafter. He was declared a Doctor of the Church in 1890. His feast is on the General Roman Calendar, and it is also commemorated today by the Greek and Russian Orthodox Churches, and by the Church of England and the Episcopal Church in the USA.

The Greek and Russian Orthodox Churches also commemorate *Barbara* (probably fourth century) on this day. She was thought to have been martyred ca. 303 under Maximian. Her cult was popular in the later Middle Ages, especially in France. According to her legend, after her father killed her for becoming a Christian, he was struck dead by lightning—which is why she is the patron saint of those in danger of sudden death by lightning. She is also the patron saint of firefighters, artillerymen, stonemasons, architects, and builders (the last two because she is said to have lived for a time in a tower). Moreover, she is one of the Fourteen Holy Helpers, a group of saints who were popular in the Rhineland from the fourteenth century and later in the rest of Germany, Hungary, and Sweden until the sixteenth century. Their intercession was considered especially powerful at the hour of death.

5 Sabas, abbot

Sabas (439–532) was the founder of the large monastery of Mar Saba, near Jerusalem, and was the superior of all the hermits in contemporary Palestine. Born in Cappadocia, the son of an army officer, he entered a monastery near his hometown of Mutalaska when only eight years of age. He later became a hermit, at one stage of his life spending four years alone in the wilderness, subsisting on wild herbs and water from a brook. The local people began to bring him bread, cheese, and dates, and disciples were also attracted to him. He eventually consented to their entreaties to found a *laura* (a monastic community consisting of hermit's cells, or huts, clustered around a church). His disciples grew to 150. Since none of the hermits was a priest, some of the monks appealed to the patriarch of Jerusalem, who insisted in 491 that Sabas should be ordained. Upon Sabas's father's death, his mother came to live at the monastery and provided funds for the erection of two buildings, a hostel for pilgrims and a hospital, as well as a second hospital in Jericho and a new monastery near the original one.

In 493 the patriarch appointed Sabas archimandrite over all the monks of Palestine who lived a semi-eremetical life. Sabas also preached in opposition to the heresy of Monophysitism, which posited only a divine nature in Christ, while denying that he also had a human nature. At age ninety-one he asked the emperor Justinian to build a hostel for pilgrims in Jerusalem and a fortress to protect monks and hermits from raiders. The emperor granted these and other requests. Sabas died in his *laura* on December 5, 532, at age ninety-four. His relics were returned to the monastery in 1965 by Pope Paul VI. Sabas's feast is not on the General Roman Calendar, but is observed on this day by the Greek and Russian Orthodox Churches and by the Benedictines and Cistercians.

6 Nicholas of Myra, bishop

Nicholas (fourth century) was the bishop of Myra who is the basis of the legend of Santa Claus (St. Nicholas). He is a patron saint of Russia, Greece, and Sicily, and of many other cities and dioceses, as well as of several categories of people (e.g., children) and occupations (e.g., pawnbrokers). Said to have been born at Patara in Lycia (southwestern Turkey), a province in Asia Minor, he became bishop of Myra, the province's capital, where he enjoyed a reputation for piety and pastoral zeal. He was imprisoned during the Diocletian persecution (303–5) and was later present at the Council of Nicaea (325), where he joined in the condemnation of Arianism, the heresy that denied the full divinity of Christ. The accounts are unanimous that, by whatever means, Nicholas died at Myra, and there was a basilica built in his honor in Constantinople by the emperor Justinian. His alleged relics were secretly removed from Muslim control in 1087 and taken to Bari. (For that reason, he is also known as Nicholas of Bari.) A new church was built to house the relics, and Pope Urban II was present for the solemn opening of the shrine in 1095, while in Bari for a council. From that time forward Nicholas's cult became almost universal in the West. He also has had an important place in the Byzantine liturgical tradition. He is thought to have been the most frequently represented saintly bishop for several centuries.

Saint Nicholas of Myra, 9th C.

The practice of giving gifts to children on his feast began in the Low Countries and became popular in North America through the Dutch settlers of New Amsterdam. The Dutch also combined with the gift giving the Nordic legend of a magician who punished naughty children and rewarded good ones with presents. His patronage of pawnbrokers is linked with yet another legend about Nicholas's throwing three bags of gold through a window to be used as dowries for three young women who would otherwise have been given over to a life of prostitution. The legend is said to be the origin of the pawnbroker's three golden balls, which were adopted from the coat of arms of the Medici family. Nicholas's feast is on the General Roman Calendar and is also observed by the Greek and Russian Orthodox Churches, the Church of England and the Episcopal Church in the USA, and the Evangelical Lutheran Church in America.

7 Ambrose of Milan, bishop and Doctor of the Church

Ambrose (339–97) was the bishop of Milan whose sermons influenced Augustine's [August 28] decision to become a Christian. He baptized Augustine on Easter Sunday, 386. Born in Trier, the son of the pretorian prefect of Gaul, he studied Greek, rhetoric, and poetry and became a successful lawyer. In 370 he was appointed governor of Aemilia and Liguria, with his residence in Milan, the administrative capital of the Western Empire. Upon the death of Auxentius, the Arian bishop of Milan, in 374 there was street fighting between Arians (who held that Christ was the greatest of creatures, but not equal to God the Father) and orthodox Catholics loyal to the teaching of the Council of Nicaea (325). Ambrose appealed for peace between the two sides at the assembly convened to elect a successor. During his speech, a voice (usually identified with that of a child) was heard to say: "Ambrose for bishop." The whole crowd, Arians and orthodox alike, took up the chant—an astonishing development given the fact that Ambrose, although a professed Christian, had not yet been baptized! He pleaded with the crowd in vain. Within a week he was baptized and consecrated the bishop of Milan, with the approval of the other bishops of the province and the emperor. Ambrose gave his personal wealth to the poor and his estates to the Church and at once devoted himself to the study of Sacred Scripture and the writings of the Fathers of the Church, especially Origen (ca. 185–ca. 254), Basil [January 2], Athanasius [May 2], and Cyril of Jerusalem [March 18]. Ambrose became an advocate of their thought in the West and also encouraged monasticism (himself following a quasi-monastic style of life within his episcopal household) and the cult of martyrs. He also proved to be a committed pastor who was always accessible to his people.

Likewise, he emerged as an important political figure, warning the young emperor Gratian about Arianism, which Gratian's uncle Valens was protecting in the East. When the Goths invaded the Roman provinces and swept along the Adriatic and across Greece in 378, Ambrose ransomed captives and melted down golden sacred vessels to raise more money. When criticized for doing so, he replied: "If the Church possesses gold, it is in order to use it for the needy, not to keep it." He also prevented the restoration of the Altar of Victory, a pagan cult, in the Roman Senate, and refused to hand over a church just outside Milan for the use of Arians at court. During Holy Week he and his congregation occupied another church, surrounded by imperial troops, in protest against its conversion by law to exclusive Arian use.

After the murder of Gratian, he reminded Gratian's successor, Valentinian, that the emperor is in the Church, not above it. But when the usurper Maximus threatened to attack Valentinian, Ambrose went to Trier and persuaded Maximus to confine his claims to Gaul, Spain, and Britain. When Theodosius, emperor of the East, defeated and killed Maximus and extended his power over the Western Empire as well, Ambrose chastised and excommunicated him for the massacre in 390 of thousands of men, women, and children at Thessalonica in reprisal for the death of the local governor. Theodosius did public penance. However, Ambrose had also reproached the emperor for ordering the rebuilding of a synagogue that had been destroyed by a Christian mob in Callinicum in 388. He argued that no taxes should be used for the erection of a building to be used for false worship. The emperor gave in to him in this instance as well. Ambrose preached at the emperor's funeral in 395.

Ambrose was a prolific, if not original, writer on a wide range of theological and pastoral topics, including the sacraments, the priesthood (clerical ethics), and the Gospel of Luke. Like many, if not most, writer-saints, he borrowed heavily from earlier writers. He was, however, the first of the Fathers and Doctors of the Church to address the question of Church-state relations, stressing the supremacy of the Church in its own domain and as the guardian of morality.

He died on Good Friday, April 4, 397, having lain for several hours throughout the day with his hands outstretched in the form of a cross while constantly moving his lips in prayer. His cult was immediate and widespread, and his remains were placed under the high altar of the church of Sant'Ambrogio in Milan in 835. He was named one of the four Latin Doctors of the Church, alongside Augustine, Jerome [September 30], and Gregory the Great [September 3] in 1298. His feast day, which is on the General Roman Calendar, commemorates not the day of his death, but of his consecration as a bishop. His feast is also celebrated on this day by the Greek and Russian Orthodox Churches, the Church of England and the Episcopal Church in the USA, and the Evangelical Lutheran Church in America. He is the patron saint of bishops and of learning.

BIBLIOGRAPHY

McLynn, Neil B. *Ambrose of Milan: Church and Court in a Christian Capital.* Berkeley: University of California Press, 1994.

Ramsey, Boniface. *Ambrose.* London: Routledge, 1997.

Williams Daniel H. *Ambrose of Milan and the End of the Nicean-Arian Conflicts.* Oxford: Oxford University Press, 1995.

8 Immaculate Conception

The feast of the *Immaculate Conception* of the Blessed Virgin Mary celebrates the conception of Mary in her mother's womb without the stain of original sin. In Pope Pius IX's bull *Ineffabilis Deus* (Lat., "Ineffable God"), issued on December 8, 1854, Mary's preservation from original sin was a "singular grace and privilege" given her by God "in view of the merits of Jesus Christ" as the Savior of the human race. Like every other human being, Mary was in need of the redemptive work of Christ, but, in anticipation of what God did for all in Christ, she alone was preserved from original sin "from the first moment of her conception."

Mary's "singular grace and privilege" was easier to understand when it was the common opinion among theologians that original sin was indeed a "stain" on the soul of every human being from the moment of conception. However, inspired in part by the Second Vatican Council's characterization of sin as also social and structural (Pastoral Constitution on the Church in the Modern World, n. 25), original sin has increasingly been regarded as a human "condition" that everyone encounters in the world from the moment of birth. This approach has given rise to new questions: How could Mary have escaped the universal "condition" of human existence itself? Did her immaculate conception mean that she was conceived in the fullness of grace, that is, in the state of closest possible union with God, in view of her future role as the Mother of God?

Madonna and Child with Angels by Duccio da Buoninsegna (fl. 1278–1318)

This feast was known as early as the seventh century in Palestine as the Conception by St. Anne [July 26] of the Theotokos (Gk., "Mother of God"), celebrated on December 9, but the doctrine itself has never been accepted in the East because of Eastern Christianity's different theological understanding of original sin. (For the East, humans share in the guilt of Adam's and Eve's sin only insofar as they willingly imitate the first parents by sinning.

Adam's and Eve's sin is a model or prototype only.) The observance of the feast spread from Constantinople to the West, where, still called the Conception of St. Anne and celebrated on December 9, it was attested in Naples in the ninth century, in English monasteries in the first half of the eleventh century, when it was called the feast of the Conception of Our Lady, and in France in the middle of the twelfth.

Upon the introduction of the feast in France, Bernard of Clairvaux [August 20] opposed it, launching in the process a controversy that would last for three centuries. Most of the Scholastics, including Anselm of Canterbury [April 21], Thomas Aquinas [January 28], Albert the Great [November 15], and Bonaventure [July 15], opposed it on the grounds that it detracted from the universality of the redemption, while it was defended by John Duns Scotus [November 8] and the Franciscans, who adopted the feast in 1263. The opponents granted that Mary was sanctified in her mother's womb, but argued that she had to be touched by original sin for at least one instant. Scotus resolved these objections by arguing that Christ can save in two ways: in the first, he rescues from sin those already fallen; in the second, he preserves someone from being touched by sin even for an instant.

The Council of Basel (1439) affirmed the belief and ten years later the Sorbonne required all its candidates to pledge an oath to defend it. In 1476 Pope Sixtus IV approved the feast with its own Mass and Office, and in 1708 Pope Clement XI extended it to the universal Church and made it a holy day of obligation. The Council of Trent (1545–63) explicitly declared that its teaching on the universality of original sin did not include the Blessed Virgin Mary. From this time the belief became general and was defended not only by the Franciscans, but also by the Carmelites, by many Dominicans, and especially by the Jesuits. At the First Council of Baltimore in 1846 the U.S. Catholic bishops chose Mary under her title of the Immaculate Conception as the patron saint of their country. The apparition of Mary to Catherine Labouré [November 28] in Paris in 1830 also promoted the devotion. The definition of 1854 was the culmination of this development. Four years later Mary is thought to have appeared to Bernadette Soubirous [April 16] in Lourdes, France, saying to the young Bernadette: "I am the Immaculate Conception." Five years after that, in 1863, a new Mass and Office were prescribed. This feast (now called the Immaculate Conception of the Blessed Virgin Mary) is on the General Roman Calendar and is also celebrated as the Conception of the Blessed Virgin Mary (without reference to its "immaculate" nature) by the Church of England. The feast of the Conception by St. Anne of the Most Holy Theotokos is observed by the Greek and Russian Orthodox Churches on December 9. The date of the feast in the West is nine months before the feast of the Birth of Mary [September 8].

9 Juan Diego (Cuatitlatoatzin), hermit; Peter Fourier, founder

In 1531 the Blessed Virgin Mary is believed to have appeared four times to *Juan Diego Cuatitlatoatzin* ("the talking eagle") at Tepeyac, a hill near Mexico City, and to have instructed him, in the Nahuatl language, to tell the local bishop of her wish that a church be built on that site. She also left a life-size figure of herself on the peasant's mantle. The first appearance is said to have occurred on December 9. An Amerindian of the Chichimeca tribe, Juan Diego subsequently devoted himself to the pilgrims who came to see this miraculous image of Mary imprinted on his cloak. It is now preserved and enshrined in the Basilica of Our Lady of Guadalupe at Tepeyac. Juan Diego was beatified in 1990 by Pope John Paul II in Mexico City. He was canonized there in 2002. His feast is not on the General Roman Calendar. The feast of Our Lady of Guadalupe is celebrated on December 12.

This is also the feast day of *Peter Fourier* (1565–1640), founder of the Canonesses Regular of St. Augustine [August 28] of the Congregation of Our Lady for the education of young girls. He was also the first superior general of the Congregation of Our Savior, whose educational ministry was with young boys. He died on December 9, 1640, and was canonized in 1897.

10 Mennas, Hermogenes, and Eugraphus, martyrs; Edward Gennings, Polydore Plasden, John Roberts, Swithin Wells, and Eustace White, martyrs; Eulalia, martyr; Thomas Merton, monk

Mennas (third century), also known as Kallikelados (Gk., "sweet and beautiful voice"), was a gifted orator who gave his life in defense of the faith. He was a civil servant in Rome who kept his Christian faith secret and rose eventually to high office under the emperor Maximian. Mennas's friend and secretary was *Eugraphus,* also a Christian. It was not until he was assigned to Alexandria that Mennas revealed himself to be a Christian. He did so by lashing out publicly at critics of

Christianity. Word got back to Rome about the defection of one of its officials. At first the emperor did not believe the report, but decided finally to send one of his magistrates, *Hermogenes,* an Athenian, to investigate. Mennas learned he was coming, but did not try to escape. When his trial began, he spoke at length in his own defense. Although the spectators were moved by his eloquence, the magistrate was not. Hermogenes ordered Mennas to be tortured and his tongue cut out. After a time both Mennas and his secretary, Eugraphus, were summoned before Hermogenes. When the tongueless Mennas spoke in a "sweet and beautiful voice," Hermogenes fell to his knees in acceptance of Christ. All three were beheaded at the command of the Roman governor. Their feast is not on the General Roman Calendar, but it is celebrated on this day by the Greek and Russian Orthodox Churches.

Edward Gennings (1567–91), *Polydore Plasden* (1563–91), *John Roberts* (ca. 1576–1610), *Swithin Wells* (1536–91), and *Eustace White* (d. 1591) are among the Forty Martyrs of England and Wales [October 25], canonized in 1970. Four of the five were executed on December 10, 1591, and one, John Roberts, was put to death on December 10, 1610. Edward Gennings was seized, along with another priest, Polydore Plasden, after celebrating Mass in the house of an elderly schoolmaster, Swithin Wells. Gennings was hanged, drawn, and quartered at Gray's Inn Fields, near Wells's house, and Wells was hanged with him. Plasden and another priest, Eustace White, were executed on the same day at Tyburn. Wells's wife, Margaret, was also sentenced to death, but reprieved. She died in prison eleven years later. John Roberts, a Benedictine monk who had distinguished himself for his ministry to the plague-stricken in London, was arrested four times and banished from the country twice in seven years. While in exile, he helped found the Benedictine monastery of St. Gregory [September 3] at Douai, in northern France. (The monks were expelled from Douai during the French Revolution and eventually reestablished their monastery at Downside in England. Downside Abbey is today the premier house of the English Benedictines and one of the centers of Catholic life in England.) Roberts returned to England in 1610 and was arrested in early December while celebrating Mass. When accused at trial of being a "seducer of the people," he replied: "If I am, then our ancestors were deceived by St. Augustine [May 27], the apostle of the English, who was sent here by the pope of Rome, St. Gregory the Great. . . . I am sent here by the same apostolic see that sent him before me." After being found guilty and sentenced to death, Roberts was hanged, drawn, and quartered at Tyburn.

December 10 is also the feast day of *Eulalia* (d. ca. 304), who was burned at the stake in Mérida, Spain, at age twelve for denouncing a judge who was attempting to persuade Christians to renounce their faith.

And this is the day of death of *Thomas Merton* (1915–68), a Trappist monk and activist in the cause of world peace, social justice, and interfaith harmony, who influenced millions of people of all faiths and of no faith with his spiritual writings, especially his autobiographical classic, *The Seven Storey Mountain* (1949).

Thomas Merton

11 Damasus I, pope; Daniel the Stylite, hermit

Damasus I (ca. 304–384; pope 366–84) was one of the most aggressive advocates of the primacy of Rome in the early Church. Born in Rome, the son of a priest, Damasus was ordained a deacon and accompanied Pope Liberius into exile in 355. He soon returned to Rome, however, and was in the service for a time of the antipope Felix II, in defiance of the oath taken by the Roman clergy not to recognize anyone else as Bishop of Rome while Liberius was still alive. This was a remarkably significant lapse in one who, later as pope, would argue vigorously on behalf of the supremacy of the papacy. It is a lapse that those who cite Damasus in support of papal primacy do not mention.

After Liberius was allowed to return from exile (having himself made some substantial compromises), Damasus became reconciled with him. When Liberius died, a bitter and violent controversy erupted over the choice of a successor. There is a curious discrepancy in two accounts of the election, however. According to the more reliable account, a faction that had been consistently loyal to Liberius met immediately in the Julian basilica of Santa Maria in Trastevere, elected the deacon Ursinus, and had him consecrated Bishop of Rome by the bishop of Tibur (Tivoli). Another, larger faction loyal to Felix met in the church of San Lorenzo in Lucina and elected the deacon Damasus, who hired a gang of thugs to storm the Julian basilica, routing the Ursinians in a three-day massacre. Damasus was consecrated by the bishop of Ostia in the Lateran basilica on October 1, after his supporters had seized the church. Following his consecration, however, bloody fighting continued in the streets of Rome. In a wholly unprecedented act, Damasus asked for help from the city prefect, who, with the support of the emperor, sent Ursinus and two of his deacons into exile. But the violence continued, and Damasus dispatched his own forces to attack Ursinus's supporters, who had taken refuge in the Liberian basilica (now St. Mary Major). A contemporary historian reported that 137 died in the battle. The bishops of Italy were dismayed by the pope's use of violence. When they were gathered in a synod in honor of Damasus's birthday in 368, the pope asked them to approve what he had done and to condemn Ursinus. Their reply was curt: "*Nos ad natale convenimus, non ut inauditum damnemus*" ("We came together to celebrate a birthday, not to condemn someone without a hearing"). The conflict between Damasus and the partisans of Ursinus continued throughout his entire pontificate.

Damasus enjoyed much favor with the court and the aristocracy, especially women of wealth. Roman gossips nicknamed him "the matrons' ear-tickler." His grand lifestyle and lavish hospitality endeared him to the upper-class pagan families. At the same time, he was harsh in his repression of Arianism and achieved condemnations of Apollinarianism (which denied that Jesus had a human soul) and Macedonianism (which denied the divinity of the Holy Spirit) at successive Roman synods. However, like most of his fellow Western bishops, he failed to grasp the meaning of developments in the East. Thus, when there were two rivals for the see of Antioch, Damasus threw his support behind Paulinus, described by one papal historian as "an unrepresentative leader of a reactionary group," instead of Melitius, on whom rested most hopes for unity in the East, including those of Basil the Great [January 2], bishop of Caesarea, who described the pope as impossibly arrogant. When Melitius died in 381, Damasus refused to enter into communion with his successor, Flavian.

Significantly, although few popes in history have made such vigorous, uncompromising claims on behalf of papal primacy, Damasus himself took no part in the ecumenical council of Constantinople in 381, which defined the divinity of the Holy Spirit and whose third canon placed the bishop of Constantinople, "the new Rome," second only to the Bishop of Rome. Damasus was tireless, in fact, in promoting the primacy of Rome, referring to it frequently as "the apostolic see" and insisting that the test of a creed's orthodoxy is papal approval. While the claims of Constantinople were based on synodal decisions and political considerations ("the new Rome"), Damasus's claims for the Roman primacy were based exclusively on his being the direct successor of Peter and the rightful heir of Christ's promises given in Matthew 16:18 ("You are Peter . . ."). He confirmed this in the Roman synod of 381. He had also seen to it that the Roman see, with the approval of the state, was established as the court of appeal for the entire Western episcopate (but, again, not for the entire Catholic Church).

He organized the papal archives, established Latin as the principal liturgical language in Rome, and commissioned his secretary Jerome [September 30] to revise existing translations of the New Testament on the basis of the original Greek. He also composed epigrams in honor of martyrs and popes and had them inscribed on marble slabs. He himself was buried in a church he had built on the Via Ardeatina, but his body was later moved to another of his churches, that of San Lorenzo in Damaso. Damasus is the patron saint of archaeologists, and his feast is on the General Roman Calendar.

The Greek and Russian Orthodox Churches celebrate the feast of *Daniel the Stylite* (409–93) on this day. Daniel, a Syrian, was a disciple of Simeon Stylites the Elder [September 1], Daniel first "pillar saint." Renowned for his sanctity and spiritual insights, Daniel lived on a pillar in Constantinople for the last thirty-three years of his life and was buried in an oratory at its foot.

12 Our Lady of Guadalupe; Jane Frances de Chantal, religious; Spiridion, bishop

The *Blessed Virgin Mary* is believed to have appeared four times (between December 9 and December 12) in 1531 to an Amerindian, Juan Diego [December 9], on Tepeyac hill outside of Mexico City, ten years after the bloody defeat of the Aztec Empire at the hands of the Spanish (Iberian) conquerors. A painted, life-size figure of the Virgin as a young, dark-skinned American Indian woman with the face of a mestizo was imprinted on Juan Diego's cloak. The image gave Indians the assurance that Christianity was not only the faith of their European conquerors, but a faith for them also; indeed, that Mary, the Mother of God, was loving and compassionate toward them. Whatever the origin and authenticity of the story of Juan Diego, it became a powerful spiritual and cultural force in the history of Mexico and Central and South America. In 1754 Pope Benedict XIV authorized a Mass and Office to be celebrated on December 12 under the title of Our Lady of

Guadalupe, and he named Mary as patron saint of New Spain. She was designated patron saint of all of Latin America in 1910, and as "Queen of Mexico and Empress of the Americas" in 1945. In more recent years, her devotion has inspired Latin American liberation theologians, who have portrayed her as an advocate for the oppressed, the poor, and the powerless. The feast is observed throughout Latin America and by the Franciscans, and is also on the Proper Calendar for the Dioceses of the U.S.A. It is not on the General Roman Calendar, but in 1999 the Congregation for Divine Worship and the Discipline of the Sacraments raised it to the rank of feast for all the countries of the Americas.

Our Lady of Guadalupe

This is also the feast day of *Jane Frances de Chantal* (1572–1641), a close friend and spiritual associate of Francis de Sales [January 24] and cofoundress with him of the Visitation Sisters. Born Jeanne Frémyot in Dijon, the daughter of the president of the parliament of Burgundy, she took the additional name Françoise at her Confirmation. Her marriage to the Baron de Chantal when she was about twenty years of age was at first a happy one, but her three eldest children died soon after birth and her husband was killed in a shooting accident in 1601. After his death, Jane took a vow of chastity and lived for a time with her three surviving children at the home of her own father in Dijon, where in 1604 she heard Francis de Sales preach and persuaded him to become her spiritual director. His advice to her was always practical. She should be attentive to the needs of her children before all else, and then to the poor, the sick, and the dying in her neighborhood.

In 1607, when she informed Francis of her desire to enter the cloister, he advised against it and proposed instead that they establish a religious community for women who were prevented from entering the enclosed religious orders for reasons of health. This community would not be enclosed and would devote itself to the needs of society. It would be called the Congregation of the Visitation of the Virgin Mary, and its members would imitate the virtues exemplified in Mary's visit to Elizabeth [November 5] as well as engage in works of mercy toward the poor and the sick. Francis de Sales wrote his work *On the Love of God* specifically for the institute's first members, who gathered as a community at Anneçy in 1610. He insisted on the importance of meekness and humility over bodily austerities. Because of opposition to the idea of non-enclosure, however, Francis de Sales had to modify the Rule in 1613, but without completely sacrificing flexibility. Jane Frances was able to attend to her children, settled the affairs of her deceased father, and founded new convents in various cities in France. In 1618 the institute was raised to the dignity of a religious order.

In 1619 she established a new house in Paris in spite of much opposition and behind-the-scenes maneuvering against it. At the request of Francis de Sales, Vincent de Paul [September 27] served as its director. Vincent described Jane Frances de Chantal as "one of the holiest souls I have ever met." She was personally devastated, however, by the death of Francis de Sales in 1622, and then in 1627 by the death of her only son. The following year a terrible plague hit France, and Jane Frances made her convent available for the sick. She suffered still more from the deaths of a son-in-law and of Francis de Sales's confessor, who was also a devoted friend and supporter of the congregation. Because of these emotional crises, Jane Frances underwent a period of spiritual aridity, reflected in several of her letters. In 1641 she was invited to Paris to meet with the Queen of Austria. Contrary to her wishes, Jane Frances was treated with great deference and showered with much praise for her work. On her way home, she became seriously ill near her convent at Moulins and died there on December 13, 1641. Her body was taken to Anneçy and buried next to Francis de Sales. She was beatified in 1751 and canonized in 1767. Her feast is on the General Roman Calendar.

The Russian and Greek Orthodox Churches celebrate the feast of *Spiridion,* or Spyridon, a fourth-century shepherd who became bishop of a small and remote area northeast of Cyprus. He is patron saint of Corfu, Zakythos, and Kephalonia, and his cult is strong in his native Cyprus.

13 Lucy, virgin and martyr; Odilia, abbess

Lucy (d. ca. 304) is the patron saint of those suffering from diseases of the eye and is traditionally portrayed carrying a tray containing two eyes. She is thought to have been born in Syracuse, Sicily, of noble and wealthy parents, and she is the patron saint of that city. Intending to give her fortune to the poor, she was the victim of an attempted rape during the Diocletian persecution. When she resisted, she was denounced as a Christian, arrested, tortured, and killed. She was honored in Rome in the sixth century as one of the Church's most illustrious virgin martyrs and her name was included in the Canon of the Mass of both the Roman and Ambrosian Rites by Pope Gregory the Great [September 3]. Churches were dedicated to her in Rome, Naples, and Venice, and her name occurs in some of the oldest liturgical books, Latin and Greek alike. Many legends were associated with her name (which is derived from the Latin word *lux,* for "light"). One story is that she tore out her own eyes rather than yield to the rapist and is sometimes depicted offering her eyes to him. Her feast is celebrated in Sweden as a festival of light. The popular song "Santa Lucia" commemorates her. Her feast is on the General Roman Calendar and is also celebrated on this day by the Church of England.

This is also the feast of *Odilia* (660–720), or Odile, an abbess who is the patron saint of the sightless because of the legend that she herself was born without sight. She is said to have been given her sight at baptism. Her cult was popular in Germany, France, and Holland, partly because of her patronage of those who had lost all or some of their sight—a numerous group before the invention of eyeglasses.

14 John of the Cross, priest and Doctor of the Church; Venantius Fortunatus, bishop

John of the Cross (1542–91) was a mystic who founded the Discalced Carmelite friars. Born Juan de Yepes y Alvárez in Fontiveros, between Ávila and Salamanca, in conditions of poverty, he was sent to an orphanage and at age fourteen was apprenticed to a carpenter, a wood sculptor, and a printer, but displayed no skill in any of these trades. Eventually he found work as a nurse's assistant in a hospital for those with venereal diseases. John developed a love for the sick and the poor and a capacity to handle the most menial and unpleasant tasks. His joyful and kind demeanor toward his patients and toward everyone he met is constantly mentioned in his biographies. The hospital administrator sent him to the Jesuit College when he was seventeen in the hope that he would study for the priesthood and return as chaplain to the hospital. But John felt drawn to the monastic life and asked for admittance into the Carmelites. He was accepted in 1563 and took the name

John of Matthias. He was sent to the University of Salamanca, where he proved to be a gifted and hard-working student of theology. He was ordained a priest in 1567.

While at home to celebrate his first Mass, he met Teresa of Ávila [October 15], who was involved in the reform of Carmelite nuns and was trying to effect a similar reform of Carmelite friars. She urged him to join in her efforts. At the time John was thinking of transferring to the Carthusians in order to find a more austere and contemplative rule of life, so he was open to her challenge. After his final year of theological studies, John embraced the Primitive Rule, adopted the Discalced habit, and changed his name to Juan de la Cruz (Sp., "John of the Cross"). In 1570 he was appointed rector of a house of studies at Alcalá, where he suffered from spiritual darkness and temptations. The following year Teresa became prioress of an unreformed convent in Ávila and sent for John to be its spiritual director and confessor. Despite his youth and small stature, John exerted his priestly authority over the headstrong Teresa. However, because of continued opposition from other Carmelites against the Discalced movement, John was seized and imprisoned by the order in Medina in 1575 and was freed the following year only because of direct instructions from the papal nuncio. When the nuncio died, John was arrested and imprisoned again, this time in the Carmelite priory in Toledo.

He spent most of his nine months in prison in total darkness. He was able to pray the Divine Office only when a ray of sunlight penetrated through the tiny slit window high on the wall. The cell was bitterly cold in winter and stifling in summer. The jailer was mean, and John was half starved, covered with vermin, and flogged to induce him to leave the Discalced. Only later did a more compassionate jailer offer him writing materials and a candle, and he was able to write some of his greatest poetry there. In August 1578 he managed to escape by loosening the lock on his cell door and making a rope out of two small rugs. He eventually staggered barefoot and exhausted to the house of the Discalced nuns who had just come out of chapel. The nuns admitted him into the house, tended to his wounds, and fed him what little he could eat. When the friars and constables came looking for him, the nuns refused to let them in. They searched the church and outer part of the cloister, but did not dare to violate the enclosure. The next morning he was taken under the protection of one of the cathedral canons.

When John was safely out of Toledo and had recovered from his ordeal, he was sent as prior of the house of El Calvario, near Baeza, as confessor to the Discalced nuns. He continued to write his poetry there. Although he was given other administrative posts against his will, he fulfilled his duties conscientiously—establishing new friaries and teaching and rendering pastoral care to his friars and nuns. He served as rector of the Carmelite college in Baeza from 1579 to 1582. In 1588 he was elected a councilor (then called a definitor), with membership on the new governing body of the Discalced Carmelites. During this period he composed his famous works, which are usually commentaries on his poems: *The Ascent of Mount Carmel, The Dark Night of the Soul, The Spiritual Canticle,* and *The Living Flame of Love.* For John of the Cross the person proceeds to greater union with God through stages of purification and contemplation.

After Teresa died in 1582, John found himself faced with increased opposition from both sides, the Carmelites of the Ancient Observance and the Discalced alike. He opposed his vicar general's plan to abandon jurisdiction over the Discalced nuns and to expel a favorite confessor of Teresa's from the order. He was elected to no office in the chapter of 1591 and was sent to a remote friary in southern Spain to live as a simple friar. When he became ill there, having heard the news of efforts to expel him from the order, he was taken to the friary at Ubeda, where he endured hostile treatment by the prior. At the time of his death on December 14, 1591, John of the Cross physically bore the marks of his sufferings. It was an effort for him even to speak. He was beatified in 1675, canonized in 1726, and declared a Doctor of the Church in 1926. His feast is on the General Roman Calendar and is celebrated by the Church of England and the Evangelical Lutheran Church in America. He is patron saint of mystics and poets.

This is also the feast day of *Venantius Fortunatus* (ca. 530–ca. 610), bishop of Poitiers and author of a number of hymns that are sung even to this day, such as "*Vexilla regis prodeunt*" (Lat., "Abroad the regal banners fly") and "*Pange lingua gloriosi*" ("Sing, my tongue, the Savior's glory"), which was later adapted by Thomas Aquinas [January 28] as a Corpus Christi hymn.

BIBLIOGRAPHY

Collins, Ross. *John of the Cross.* Collegeville, MN: Liturgical Press, 1990.

15 Mary di Rosa, foundress; Blessed Frances Schervier, foundress

Mary di Rosa (1813–55) was the foundress of the Handmaids of Charity. Born Paula di Rosa in Brescia, Italy, she devoted her early years to social work, particularly the welfare of the young girls who worked in her father's factory. She attended to the sick during a cholera epidemic in 1836 and, after the disease had run its course, directed a house for poor and abandoned girls. After a dispute with its trustees over her practice of allowing the girls to remain in the house overnight, she left to form a school for hearing- and speech-impaired girls, which she later handed over to the Canossian Sisters. She then cofounded the congregation of the Handmaids of Charity, devoted to the care of the sick. Her father gave them a large house and their provisional Rule was approved by the local bishop in 1843. During the political upheavals in Italy, she set up a military hospital to care for the military and civilian wounded. In 1850 the constitutions of her congregation were given papal approval and in the summer of 1852 Paula and twenty-five sisters pronounced their vows. Paula took the name Maria Crocifissa (It., "Mary of the Crucified"). She collapsed from physical exhaustion in Mantua and died three weeks later in her native Brescia at age forty-two. She was canonized in 1954. Her feast is not on the General Roman Calendar.

Frances Schervier (1819–76) was the foundress of the Sisters of the Poor of St. Francis [October 4]. Born in Aachen, Germany, she was the daughter of a successful businessman and goddaughter of the Austrian emperor. After her mother's death she had to assume responsibility for the care of the household. She was generous to the poor and particularly concerned for the sick and abandoned children. In 1844 she became a Franciscan tertiary and in the following year, after the death of her father, she began to live a community life with four other women. When their numbers increased to twenty-three in 1851, they received the religious habit with the approval of the archbishop of Cologne and became the Sisters of the Poor of St. Francis. The congregation consisted of two "families," one devoted to the contemplative life and the other to the active apostolate. In 1858 Frances visited the United States during the Civil War and joined her sisters there in ministering to the wounded and the homeless. She was with them again in the Franco-Prussian War. In 1871 the empress of Austria awarded her the Cross of Merit, but she refused it, insisting that she wanted no personal reward.

She was beatified in 1974. Her feast is not on the General Roman Calendar, but it is celebrated on this day by the Franciscans.

16 Adelaide of Burgundy, nun

Adelaide (931–99) was the foundress of many monasteries of monks and nuns. The daughter of Rudolph II of Upper Burgundy, she was betrothed at age two and was married at age sixteen to Lothair, who was by that time at least nominally the king of Italy. Lothair was poisoned three years later by the father of one of Adelaide's disappointed suitors. She was imprisoned in a castle and was either freed by the German king, Otto the Great, or escaped on her own. On Christmas Day, 951, she married Otto at Pavia. The marriage consolidated his authority in northern Italy, and in 962 he was crowned emperor in Rome. Their marriage ended after twenty-two years with the death of Otto. Her eldest son, Otto II, treated her badly, and she left the court. The abbot of Cluny brought about a reconciliation, and Otto asked pardon on his knees for his behavior toward his mother. Adelaide sent gifts to the shrine of Martin of Tours [November 11] in thanksgiving.

When Otto II died ten years later, he was succeeded by his infant son Otto III, for whom Theophano, his mother, became regent. The Byzantine princess was hostile to Adelaide, who left court once again, this time for eight years. She returned only upon Theophano's sudden death and to act herself as Otto III's regent. Following the advice of saintly men of the Church, she devoted herself to peacemaking and generosity to the poor. She founded and restored many monasteries and worked for the conversion of the Slavs, whose movements on the imperial frontier troubled her final years before her return to Burgundy. She died at a monastery she had founded at Seltz, on the Rhine near Strasbourg, on December 16, 999. She was canonized ca. 1097. Her feast is not on the General Roman Calendar.

17 John of Matha, founder; Lazarus

John of Matha (d. 1213) was the founder of the Order of the Most Holy Trinity, popularly known as the Trinitarians. Born at Faucon in Provence of a well-to-do family, he retired to a hermitage after his schooling was completed. When he found that his privacy was often disturbed, he went to study theology in Paris, received a doctorate, and was ordained a priest. It is said that, during the celebration of his first

Mass (probably just after the Second Crusade of 1147–49), he felt an inspiration to devote his life to the ransoming of Christian slaves from the Muslims. At this time there were many thousands held captive by the Saracens and the Moors. He traveled to Rome to secure papal approval for his venture. Innocent III was so impressed that he ordered the bishop of Paris and the abbot of the monastery of St. Victor to draw up a Rule, and he approved the foundation of the Order of the Most Holy Trinity in 1198. They were given a white habit with a red and blue cross on the breast. A foundation was made in Paris on the site of a chapel dedicated to St. Mathurin (a fourth-century Gallic missionary priest), so the order became known in France as the Mathurins. Members of the order went to Morocco, Tunis, and Spain, and several hundred captives were said to have been released. John spent his last two years in Rome and died there on December 17, 1213. His cult (along with that of his supposed collaborator, Felix of Valois, who never existed) was approved by the Congregation of Rites in 1666. His feast is not on the General Roman Calendar.

This is also the feast day of *Lazarus* (first century), the brother of Martha [July 29] and Mary and a close friend of Jesus, who raised him from the dead (John 11:1–44). According to an Eastern tradition, Lazarus, with his two sisters, was put into a leaking boat by the Jews, but they were miraculously saved and landed on Cyprus, where he was made bishop of Kition. In 890 his supposed relics were taken to Constantinople, where a church was built in his honor. An eleventh-century Western legend maintained that Lazarus had been the bishop of Marseilles. Devotion to Lazarus was widespread in the early Church. The Saturday before Palm Sunday was referred to as Lazarus Saturday because of the procession on that day to the church erected over his tomb in Bethany. He is commemorated in the East on May 4. His feast is not on the General Roman Calendar.

On this day the Greek and Russian Orthodox Churches celebrate the feast of the prophet *Daniel* and his three young companions who were miraculously released from the fiery furnace.

18 Flannan of Killaloe, bishop; Gatian, bishop; Winnibald, abbot; Samthann, abbot

Flannan (seventh century) was the bishop of Killaloe in Ireland. He is thought to have been the son of a chieftain named Turlough in the west of Ireland. According to an Irish legend, he was the disciple of

Molua, the founder of the monastery at Killaloe, and made a pilgrimage to Rome floating on a millstone. Actually, the millstones that accompanied the Celtic saints on their journeys were small in size and were used as altars for Mass. In Rome Flannan is said to have been consecrated a bishop by Pope John IV (640–42) and then to have returned to his father's district as abbot-bishop of Killaloe. Flannan's example motivated his father to become a monk in his old age. According to Turlough's biography, written in 1162, Flannan asked his own abbot, Colman of Kilmacduagh, for a special blessing on his family because three of his sons had been killed. Colman is said to have taken seven steps and prophesied: "From you shall seven kings spring." Turlough's descendants included seven kings, all named Brian. As for Flannan, it seems that, like other Irish monks of the period, he was an itinerant preacher. The cathedral at Killaloe housed his relics, and the remote Flannan Islands off the coast of Scotland are named after him. They have long been a center of religious devotion. On one island, where there is a lighthouse, there are the remains of a tiny chapel called the chapel of Flannan. There are cults of this saint in both Ireland and Scotland. His feast is not on the General Roman Calendar.

The Russian Orthodox Church commemorates the feast of *Sebastian* [January 20] and his fellow deacon-martyrs on this day. It is also the feast day of *Gatian* (d. 301 or 307), first bishop of Tours, who was one of the six missionary bishops who accompanied Denis [October 9] to Gaul sometime in the third century; of *Winnibald* (d. 761), the brother of Willibald [June 7] and Walburga [February 25], who assisted Boniface [June 5] in the founding of the Church in Germany and who also founded, with his sister Walburga, a double monastery (for men and women) at Heidenheim; and of *Samthann* (d. 739), the founder of Clonbroney Abbey in Longfield, Ireland, who is remembered for her practical wisdom. When a monk asked her the most appropriate posture for prayer, she said that every position was appropriate, whether sitting, standing, kneeling, or lying down. When another monk informed her that he intended to give up study to spend more time in prayer, she told him that he could never be able to fix his mind on prayer if he neglected study. And when a third monk said that he was embarking on a pilgrimage, she said that the Kingdom of Heaven can be reached without crossing the sea because God is near to all who call upon him. None of these feasts are on the General Roman Calendar.

19 Anastasius I, pope; Blessed Urban V, pope

Anastasius I (d. 401; pope 399–401) is best known for his condemnation of the great third-century theologian Origen (d. ca. 254), with whose writings he was not even familiar. He did little else that was memorable in his very brief pontificate, except perhaps fathering his own successor, Innocent I. Those who disliked his predecessor Siricius approved of him; namely, Jerome [September 30], who still had a circle of influential friends in Rome, and Paulinus of Nola [June 22], both of whom thought Anastasius more sympathetic than Siricius to the practice of strict asceticism in the Church. When the African bishops, for example, asked the pope to relax the ban on Donatist clergy returning to the Church because of the shortage of priests, Anastasius wrote to the Council of Carthage (401) and urged the bishops to continue their struggle against the heresy (which held that those baptized by heretics and schismatics must be rebaptized upon entering the Catholic Church). Jerome even suggested that the Anastasius's pontificate had been cut short because Rome did not deserve so fine a bishop. Anastasius was buried in the cemetery of Pontian on the Via Portuensis. His feast is not on the General Roman Calendar.

This is also the feast day of *Urban V* (1310–70; pope 1362–70), the sixth—and probably the best—of the Avignon popes. He restored the papacy to Rome for three years, returning to Avignon just before his death. Born Guillaume de Grimoard, he was a Benedictine monk, a canon lawyer, abbot of Saint-Victor in Marseilles, and papal legate in Italy—but not a cardinal—when elected pope in Avignon on September 28, 1362. During the conclave he was actually on a diplomatic mission in Naples. The cardinals at first elected the brother of Pope Clement VI (1342–52), but he declined. When they could not agree on one of their own number, they turned to the deeply spiritual Abbot Grimoard and elected him unanimously. His enthronement and coronation were done without the usual pomp. Retaining his black Benedictine habit and rule of life, Urban V continued his predecessor's reformist agenda. He reduced even further the luxury of the papal court and combated the holding of more than one benefice (income-producing ecclesiastical office) at a time, while cutting the rate of tithes in half. However, he also exhausted the papal treasury by his generous support of impoverished students, colleges, and artists and architects. He founded new universities in Orange (southern France), Kraków, and Vienna.

He failed to achieve one of the main goals of his pontificate, the reunion with the East and the liberation of the holy places in Palestine from Turkish control. At the same time, he sincerely hoped to return the papacy once and for all to Rome and was encouraged by the emperor Charles IV to do so. The city was in chaos and the Vatican was uninhabitable. On April 30, 1367, against the strong objections of the French cardinals and the Curia, Urban V left Avignon and landed at Corneto (now Tarquinia) on June 3. After a brief stay in Viterbo, he entered Rome with an impressive military escort on October 16. He is said to have wept at the condition of the city. All the great churches were almost in ruins and the Lateran Palace was in such disarray that he took up residence in the Vatican, which had been sufficiently restored before his arrival. He remained there for three years, living simply and frugally, but moving in the summer to Viterbo and Montefiascone to escape the intense Roman heat. While in Rome, the pope directed the repairs and refurbishing of churches and other buildings and completely rebuilt the basilica of St. John Lateran [November 9], which had burned down in 1360.

By the end of his pontificate, Urban V seriously contemplated moving back to Avignon. The situation in Italy was unsettled. In the spring of 1370 the Romans joined forces with rebels in Perugia (now under papal interdict), and the pope's adversary in Milan, Bernabò Visconti, was massing his troops in Tuscany. The pope fled Rome for the walled city of Viterbo and then to Montefiascone. In spite of the pleas of the Romans and the warning of the saintly Bridget of Sweden [July 23] that he would suffer an early death if he returned to Avignon, Urban V left Montefiascone. Less than two months after his arrival in Avignon, he fell gravely ill and died. He was buried in the Avignon cathedral (Notre-Dame-des-Doms) at first, but his brother, Cardinal Angelico, transferred his remains on June 5, 1372, to the abbey of Saint-Victor in Marseilles, where the pope served as abbot at the time of his election to the papacy. His tomb became the center of a cult. Urban V was beatified by Pope Pius IX in 1870. His feast is not on the General Roman Calendar.

20 Dominic of Silos, abbot

Dominic of Silos (ca. 1000–73) is especially venerated by the Dominicans because, nearly a century after his death, Joan of Aza [August 2] made a pilgrimage to his tomb, where she had a vision in which

Dominic of Silos promised that she would bear another son. She named the child Dominic [August 8], and he became the founder of the Order of Preachers. Born in Navarre, Spain, of a peasant family, Dominic of Silos worked on the family farm for several years before becoming a monk at San Millán de la Cogolla. He was ordained a priest and became novice master and then prior of the monastery. After a dispute with the king of Navarre over property rights, Dominic and two companions were sent into exile. The ruler of Old Castile welcomed them and in 1041 gave them the run-down monastery of St. Sebastian at Silos, near Burgos. Dominic, chosen its abbot, rebuilt the church, planned the cloisters, and established a renowned scriptorium. Dominic's reputation for holiness, learning, generosity to the poor, and healings grew. The *Roman Martyrology* refers to a belief that three hundred Christian captives were liberated from the Moors when they called upon God in Dominic's name. Three years after his death in 1073, his remains were moved into the church, which was the equivalent of local canonization. Churches and monasteries were later dedicated to him.

Because of the story associated with the mother of Dominic, the founder of the Dominicans, Dominic of Silos's pastoral staff was used until 1931, and the coming of the republic, to bless queens of Spain, and it remained by their bedside until they had a safe delivery. The monastery itself was revived in the nineteenth century and is still active today. It is known especially for its double Romanesque cloisters, its extensive library, and its recordings of Gregorian chant. A painting of Dominic in gold cope and miter, seated in an episcopal chair, is in the Prado Museum in Madrid. His feast is not on the General Roman Calendar. The Russian and Greek Orthodox Churches commemorate *Ignatius of Antioch* [October 17] on this day.

21 Peter Canisius, priest and Doctor of the Church

Peter Canisius (1521–97) was called by Leo XIII (1878–1903) the "second apostle of Germany," after Boniface [June 5], and is generally regarded as one of the principal theologians of the Counter-Reformation. Born of an aristocratic family in Nijmegen, the Netherlands, which was then within the archdiocese of Cologne, he was educated at the universities in Cologne and Louvain, where he studied canon law. He decided to set aside a legal career and marriage and returned to Cologne to study theology. He joined the Jesuits in 1543 after attending an Ignatian retreat in Mainz given by Peter Favre, one of the first companions of Ignatius of Loyola [July 31]. Peter spent his novitiate in Cologne, studying, teaching, and caring for the sick. After ordination to the priesthood, he became a prominent preacher, attended two sessions of the Council of Trent as the theological consultant to the cardinal-bishop of Augsburg, and was recalled to Rome to work with Ignatius for five months. After a year of teaching at the first Jesuit school in Messina, he returned to Rome and made his solemn profession as a Jesuit on September 4, 1549, the eighth Jesuit to be so professed. He was sent back to Germany, where, against his will, he became rector and vice-chancellor of the university at Ingoldstadt and earned a reputation for preaching and catechizing.

In 1552 Ignatius sent him to Vienna to help reenergize a moribund church. There were many parishes without priests and there had been no ordinations for twenty years. Monasteries were deserted and many Catholics no longer practiced their faith. Peter displayed extraordinary pastoral energy and won the admiration of the Viennese people by his ministry to the poor, the sick, and prisoners. He worked tirelessly during a plague in the fall of 1551. The king and papal nuncio invited him to become archbishop of Vienna, but he agreed only to administer the diocese for a year.

In 1555, at the request of the king, he published his famous Catechism, entitled *Summa Doctrinae Christianae* (Lat., "Synthesis of Christian Doctrine"), which was translated from the original Latin into fifteen languages during Peter's lifetime. It was in question-and-answer format (211 in all) and consisted of five chapters, on faith, hope, charity, the sacraments, and justice (including a treatment of sin, good works, the cardinal virtues, and the gifts of the Holy Spirit). Three years later he produced a *Smaller Catechism,* translated into German for schoolchildren and the general public. It also contained pictures and prayers. Later he produced the *Shortest Catechism,* which was written at an even simpler level. In 1556 he was appointed provincial, also against his will, of a new Jesuit province for Austria, Bavaria, and Bohemia, with his residence in Prague. He established a college there (and others in Augsburg, Munich, and Innsbruck), to which even Protestants were happy to send their sons, and then, from 1559 to 1565, he resided in Augsburg, where he again established a reputation for reclaiming lapsed Catholics and converting Protestants. From 1562 until 1569, after his province was divided, he became provincial for southern Germany.

In his formal discussions with Lutherans, he was always courteous and tried to stress common elements of faith rather than differences. He continued to insist on the importance of schools and publications (the printing press was now in full use) and took a leading role in the founding of several Jesuit colleges in northern German provinces and of the University of Fribourg as well. He had been transferred to Switzerland after a dispute with a fellow Jesuit, Paul Hoffaeus, over a number of issues, including the morality of collecting interest on loans (which Peter stubbornly opposed). During his eight years in Switzerland, he preached throughout the canton and is said to have played a large part in keeping it Catholic during a critical period of its history. In 1591 he suffered a stroke that left him partially paralyzed for the remainder of his life, but he took part in the daily domestic duties of the community and continued his writing with the aid of a secretary until his death in Fribourg on December 21, 1597. He is buried in the church of St. Michael in Fribourg. Peter Canisius was beatified in 1864 and canonized and declared a Doctor of the Church in the same ceremony in 1925, the first such instance in history. His feast is on the General Roman Calendar.

On this day the Episcopal Church in the USA and the Evangelical Lutheran Church in America commemorate *Thomas the Apostle* [July 3].

22 Anastasia, martyr

Anastasia (d. ca. 304) was a martyr venerated in Rome since the fifth century and is mentioned in the Canon of the Roman Mass. In the Roman Catholic liturgical calendar her feast shares December 25 with Christmas and by tradition the second Mass (of three) on Christmas commemorates her. Popes in the past sang their second Christmas Mass in the Roman church under her title.

The legend of Anastasia indicates that she was the daughter of a noble Roman and had Chrysogonus [November 24] as her spiritual director. She is said to have married a pagan and also to have cared for Christians who were in prison during the persecution of Diocletian. After her husband's death, she went to Aquileia to minister to suffering Christians there. For this reason, she is known by the Greeks as Anastasia the healer, or medicine woman (Gk. *pharmakolytia*). She herself was eventually arrested and executed. Her name was included in the Roman Canon in the fifth century. A more credible account is that she was not born in Rome and never lived there. Her cult originated in

Sirmium, where it is more likely she was martyred during the Diocletian persecution (303–5). Her relics were later transferred from Sirmium to Constantinople, during the patriarchate of Gennadius (458–71), and interred in the church of the *Anastasis* (Gk., "Resurrection"), founded by Gregory Nazianzen [January 2], where a significant cult of hers developed.

The tradition that the second Mass of Christmas (at dawn) commemorates Anastasia can be traced to the liturgical practice of the church in Jerusalem in the fourth century. The Nativity of Our Lord was not celebrated there as a separate feast, but was folded into the celebration of the Epiphany on January 6. On the vigil of the Epiphany the bishop, clergy, monks, and laity of Jerusalem went to nearby Bethlehem for a ceremony at the cave where Christ was believed to have been born. At midnight they formed a procession and returned to Jerusalem, where they sang the morning Office just before dawn. The dawn Mass was in honor of Anastasia of Sirmium. In the sixth century the liturgy of Jerusalem was imitated in Rome on Christmas Day. At dawn the pope celebrated Mass in the basilica of St. Mary Major (to which the reputed relics of the wooden crib were brought in the seventh century), and from there celebrated a second Mass at the church of St. Anastasia, just below the Palatine Hill, near the Circus Maximus. Finally, there was a procession to St. Peter's, where the pope sang a third Mass. This practice continued through the medieval period. The church of St. Anastasia itself was thought to have been founded as the royal chapel of Byzantine court officials and served as the central place of worship for Greeks living in Rome. It was originally called the *Anastasis* basilica, like the one in Constantinople, which, in turn, was a copy of the one in Jerusalem. The Roman basilica was later dedicated to Anastasia of Sirmium, whose cult, as noted above, was strong in Constantinople.

Another theory is that the church of St. Anastasia in Rome is older than that, having been founded well before the time of Pope Damasus I [December 11], who died in 384. A small part of the building can be dated back to the time of the emperor Constantine [May 21], who resided in Rome from 312 until 324, when he moved the imperial capital to Constantinople. He had a sister named Anastasia, who married Bassianus Caesar, to whom Constantine entrusted the rule of Italy. This older church may then have acquired the dedication to Anastasia of Sirmium because of the connection with the emperor's sister or because of the similarity of the name with the *Anastasis* basilica in

Constantinople. A third theory is that the church simply acquired the name of its founder. The feast of Anastasia is not on the General Roman Calendar, but it is celebrated on this day in the East.

23 John of Kanty, priest; Mary Margaret d'Youville, foundress; Thorlac of Skalholt, bishop

John of Kanty (1390–1473), also Kanti or Cantius, is a patron saint of Lithuania. Born of a well-to-do family at Kanti, near Oswiecim (Auschwitz) in Poland, he was educated at the University of Kraków and was ordained a priest soon after completing his courses. He was appointed a lecturer there and was said to have been effective as both a teacher and a preacher. For some unknown reason, perhaps an expression of envy at his success, he was later removed from his teaching position and assigned to a parish in Olkusz. His parish ministry was less than successful, and after a few years he was recalled to occupy a chair of theology at the university. He was renowned not only for his teaching, but also for the austerity of his life (he slept on the floor and never ate meat) as well as his generosity to the poor. He urged his students to oppose false opinions with moderation and courtesy, and he himself was held in such high esteem that his academic gown was used to vest each new doctor of the university. He died on December 24, 1473, and was canonized in 1767. His feast is on the General Roman Calendar.

This is also the feast day of *Mary Margaret d'Youville* (1701–71), foundress of the Grey Nuns, or the Sisters of Charity of the General Hospital, and the first native-born Canadian saint. Born Marguérite Dufroste de Lajemmerais at Varennes, Quebec, she was married for eight years and had six children, only two of whom survived. After her husband's death (he was a Youville), she and some companions devoted themselves to the care of poor, sick, and aged women in Montreal in 1737. Because of the types of people they nursed, their work aroused opposition in the neighborhood, even inspiring a mob scene with stone throwing and angry shouts of "Down with the *soeurs grises* (Fr., "tipsy nuns")!" Although *gris* also means "grey" in French, the allegation here was that the four women were drunk and that the widow d'Youville was carrying on her husband's liquor trade with the Indians. When the four attended Mass, they were refused Communion because of the charges. Eventually, the people were won over by the nature and quality of their work, for which the sisters adopted a simple

Rule. They embraced the title given them by the crowd and transformed it by adopting a grey habit and calling themselves Grey Nuns.

In 1745, after their house was destroyed by fire, they signed a collective declaration of total renunciation and self-dedication known as the Original Commitment (Fr. *engagements primitifs*), which is signed by Grey Nuns on the day of their profession. A wealthy merchant offered them another house rent free and their work continued. Mary Margaret was appointed director of the General Hospital in Montreal in 1747 and the sisters were officially designated as the Sisters of Charity of the General Hospital. She preferred the older name, the Grey Nuns, because it reminded her of the insults at the beginning and would keep her and her sisters humble. In 1755 the bishop of Quebec formally confirmed the Rule, with Mary Margaret as superior.

During the war between the English and the French, she and her sisters nursed the wounded of both sides, as well as civilian casualties. There developed a saying in Montreal: "Go to the Grey Nuns; they never refused anybody, or any honest work." Later they developed schools and orphanages and worked with prisoners, slaves, Indians, the mentally ill, epileptics, and prostitutes. The hospital was destroyed by fire in 1765, but rebuilt with the help of the government, other religious orders, and the Indians they had helped in the past. When Mary Margaret d'Youville was beatified in 1959, Pope John XXIII called her "the mother of universal charity." She was canonized in 1990. Her feast is not on the General Roman Calendar, but is celebrated in Canada.

Finally, it is the feast day of *Thorlac of Skalholt* (1133–93), the pastorally effective bishop of Skalholt, one of Iceland's two dioceses, and before that the founding abbot of a community of Augustinian Canons. He was a strong advocate of the reforms initiated by Gregory VII [May 25]. He was canonized by the bishops of Iceland in 1198 and is patron saint of Iceland.

24 Sharbel Makhlouf, hermit; Abraham Joshua Heschel, rabbi

Sharbel Makhlouf (1828–98) was a Lebanese hermit. Born Joseph Makhlouf of a poor family in a remote village in Lebanon, near the great cedars, he was a shepherd in his early years and spent time in a cave praying and meditating. He often visited a hermitage where two of his uncles were monks, and in 1851 entered the Maronite monastery of Our Lady of Maifouk, taking the name Sharbel, after a second-century Syrian martyr. Following a period of novitiate, he was sent to the great monastery of St. Maro (a fifth-century Syrian hermit) at Annaya, where he took solemn vows in 1853, and then to the neighboring monastery of St. Cyprian of Kñfan, to study philosophy and theology. He was ordained a priest in 1859 and returned to Annaya, where he lived austerely until 1866 when, following the example of the Desert Fathers, he moved to a small hermitage owned by the monastery consisting of four tiny cells and a chapel. Food was brought to him once a day from the monastery.

Sharbel lived in the hermitage for more than twenty-three years, with the Eucharist at the center of his daily spiritual life. He meditated for hours until late morning, when he would celebrate Mass, and then spent most of the afternoon and evening in prayer before the tabernacle. He slept on the floor, on a mattress stuffed with leaves, with a block of wood wrapped in an old habit as his pillow. He had no heating in the winter. His reputation for wisdom and sanctity brought many visitors seeking spiritual guidance and healing. In 1898 he suffered a stroke while celebrating Mass. He died eight days later, on Christmas Eve night. He was buried in a nearby cemetery, which became an attraction for thousands of pilgrims. He was beatified at the Second Vatican Council in 1965 and was canonized in 1977. His feast is not on the General Roman Calendar.

This is also the day of death of *Abraham Joshua Heschel* (1907–72), a Polish-born Hasidic rabbi who was a strong supporter of the civil rights and peace movements in the United States. He once said that "indifference to evil is worse than evil itself." An official observer at the Second Vatican Council, he wrote works that recalled Christians to their Jewish roots, and his appreciation for the Catholic principle of sacramentality was reflected in his sense of "the holy dimension of all existence."

25 The Nativity of Our Lord; Peter Nolasco, founder

The feast of the *Nativity of Our Lord,* or Christmas, is second in importance only to Easter. It celebrates the incarnation of the Son of God in Jesus of Nazareth, who was virginally conceived by Mary, his mother. The Christmas season begins on December 24 with Evening Prayer I, or First Vespers, and the evening vigil Mass and concludes on the Sunday after Epiphany, the feast of the Baptism of the Lord. The Christmas season is preceded by a four-week period of vigil and preparation known as Advent, which begins on the fourth Sunday before December 25.

Although the actual date of Christ's birth is unknown, this date was selected for the celebration of the event by the early fourth century in Rome. There is no evidence of a celebration of the Nativity of Our Lord before this time. It has been commonly believed that the date was chosen to counteract the pagan feast of the sun god, the Sun of Righteousness, which the emperor Aurelian established in 274. Christ was portrayed as the true "sun of justice." Another theory holds that the cult of the sun was particularly strong in Rome and that the symbolism of Christ-as-sun was deeply rooted in Christian consciousness. There was also a popular belief that John the Baptist [June 24; August 29] was conceived on the autumn equinox and born on the summer solstice, on June 24. Since Luke 1:26 indicates that Christ was conceived six months after John, he must have been conceived on the spring equinox, on March 25 (which is the feast of the Annunciation), and born nine months later on December 25. Whatever the explanation, the old pagan feast provided a convenient day to celebrate the birth of Christ. In the East January 6 was celebrated as the feast of the Epiphany, which focused on both the Nativity and the Baptism of the Lord. (The focus of the Epiphany in the West was on the visit of the Magi.)

Christmas is traditionally celebrated in the West by three Masses: one at midnight, one at dawn, and the third during the day, which have been thought to symbolize the threefold birth of Christ: in the bosom of the Father, from the womb of the Blessed Virgin Mary, and mystically in the souls of the faithful. The religious as well as secular customs (for example, the Christmas tree and the singing of carols) associated with this day were a much later development in Germany, which were then imported into nineteenth-century England by the prince consort and through the influence of the novelist Charles Dickens (1812–70). This solemn feast is on the General Roman Calendar.

This is also the feast of *Anastasia* [December 22] and *Peter Nolasco* (d. ca. 1182–ca. 1256), the reputed founder of the Mercedarian order (Order of Our Lady of Mercy) in Spain, an order dedicated originally to offering its own members in exchange for slaves taken by the Moors, and later, to helping the sick and the imprisoned. (Dominicans have claimed Raymond of Peñafort [January 7] as the main founder of the Mercedarians. Raymond did obtain papal confirmation of its foundation and Rule in 1235.) Many of the details of Peter's life, including the year and place of his birth and the year of his death, are difficult to establish. He was canonized in 1628. Neither his feast nor that of Anastasia is on the General Roman Calendar.

26 Stephen, first martyr

Stephen (d. ca. 35) was the first Christian martyr and one of the seven chosen by the twelve apostles to serve tables, to look after the distribution of alms, especially to widows, and to assist in the ministry of preaching (Acts 6–7). He is the patron saint of deacons, and in the Middle Ages was invoked against headaches. A Greek-speaking Jew living in Jerusalem, he was converted to Christ and became a leader of the Hellenist Christians. The Hellenists, who had their own synagogues, where the Scriptures were read in Greek, argued that the new faith could not develop except by separating itself from Judaism and in particular by placing distance between itself and the Temple and the Mosaic law. The Hellenists also urged the expansion of the Church's mission to the Gentiles. The elders of certain synagogues opposed Stephen and the other Hellenists on every count and charged him with blasphemy for saying that the Temple would be destroyed and that Jesus had set aside the Mosaic law. When given permission to speak before the Sanhedrin, Stephen made an eloquent defense (Acts 7:2–53) in which he accused his accusers of resisting the Holy Spirit, of persecuting the prophets, and of betraying and murdering Jesus, "the righteous one." Then he looked up to heaven and began to describe a vision he was having of the Son of Man standing at the right hand of God. The members of the council shouted out, covered their ears, and ordered him to be dragged outside the city and stoned to death, apparently without any formal trial. Before he died, Stephen asked God to forgive his attackers. The witnesses to his martyrdom placed their cloaks at the feet of Saul (afterward Paul), who consented to Stephen's death, but was later converted while on the road to Damascus [January 25].

The Martydom of Saint Stephen by Ludovico Cigoli, 1597

Stephen's feast has been kept in both East and West at least from the fourth century. His cult was spread even more widely by the discovery in 415 of his alleged tomb. Indeed, he became one of the most popular saints on the Continent in the Middle Ages. A church containing his relics and dedicated to him was built outside the Damascus Gate in Jerusalem in 439 and completed by 460. Its ruins were discovered by Dominicans in 1882, and a new church was erected on the site. His dismembered relics were taken to Constantinople and then to Rome, along with some of the stones thought to have been used in his martyrdom. There are many artistic depictions of him, including one by Fra Angelico [February 18] in the Vatican. His feast is on the General Roman Calendar and is celebrated on this day by the Church of England, the Episcopal Church in the USA, and the Evangelical Lutheran Church in America. The Russian and Greek Orthodox Churches observe his feast on December 27. Stephen's name is included in the Canon (Eucharistic Prayer I) of the Roman Mass.

27 John, apostle and Evangelist

Saint John the Evangelist by Berto di Giovanni, 1461–62

John the Evangelist (d. ca. 101), the son of Zebedee, was one of the twelve apostles and considered to be the author of the Fourth Gospel. Like his brother James [July 25], he was a fisherman and among Jesus' first disciples (Matt. 4:21; Mark 1:19; Luke 5:10). According to Mark 3:17, Jesus gave John and James the nickname "sons of thunder." They may have been cousins of Jesus through their mother, who may have been, in turn, the sister of the Blessed Virgin Mary (cf. Matthew 27:56; Mark 15:40; John 19:25). With Peter [June 29] and James, John was one of the three closest disciples of Christ. They accompanied him at the raising of the daughter of Jairus (Mark 5:37; Luke 8:51) and at the Transfiguration [August 6] (Matt. 17:1; Mark 9:2; Luke 9:28). They questioned Jesus about the end time (Mark 13:3) and failed him in Gethsemane (Matt. 26:37; Mark 14:33). John and his brother James asked Jesus whether he would call down fire on the Samaritans for rejecting him (Luke 9:53) and also requested seats of honor on his right and left in the heavenly kingdom (Mark 10:35–37; but Matt. 20:20–21 attributes the request to their mother). Jesus asked them if they were also ready to drink the cup that he was going to drink. They answered confidently that they could, and Jesus promised that they would do so. In Luke 22:8 John went with Peter to prepare the Passover supper.

John also played a leading role in the first Christian community in Jerusalem (Gal. 2:9) and is listed in the Acts of the Apostles as second to Peter in the upper room (Acts 1:13). He accompanied Peter to preach in the Temple, where they were both arrested (Acts 3–4), and he traveled with Peter to Samaria to examine the new converts there (Acts 8:14–25).

John is traditionally regarded as the author of five New Testament books: the Fourth Gospel, the book of Revelation, and three Letters, or catholic Epistles. He is usually identified with the Beloved Disciple of the Fourth Gospel, who reclined at Jesus' bosom at the Last Supper (John 13:23), to whom Jesus entrusted his mother at the foot of the cross (John 19:26), who ran with Peter to the tomb on Easter morning, arriving there ahead of Peter but allowing him to enter first (John 20:2–8), and who recognized the Risen Lord at the Sea of Tiberias (John 21:7, 20). A man named John wrote the book of Revelation from the island of Patmos (Rev. 1:4, 9), and he was identified with John the Apostle as early as Justin [June 1], a second-century martyr. 1 John 1:1–5 implies that its author was an eyewitness of Jesus, but the author remains anonymous. The second and third Letters of John were written by a prominent "elder," but he too is anonymous.

The New Testament reports the martyrdom of John's brother James (Acts 12:1–2), but says nothing of John's death. Second-century traditions (Irenaeus [June 28] and Polycarp [February 23]) indicate that John was active in Ephesus in Asia Minor, and other sources are cited by the church historian Eusebius of Caesarea (ca. 260–ca. 339). At the end of the second century Tertullian (ca. 160–ca. 225) reported that, during the reign of Domitian (81–96), John went to Rome, where he was dipped unscathed into boiling oil before the Latin Gate. John is thought to have died a natural death in Ephesus in about the third year of the reign of Trajan (98–117), when he was around ninety-four years of age. Jerome [September 30] reported a tradition that, when age and weakness made it impossible for John to preach, he would be carried to the assembly and would say only: "My little children, love one another." When asked why he always used the same words, he is said to have replied: "Because it is the word of the Lord, and if you keep it, you do enough."

John is represented with an eagle, symbolizing the heavenly, or soaring, quality of his Gospel. Many churches are dedicated to him, the most famous of which is the Lateran basilica in Rome (along with John the Baptist [June 24; August 29]). He is also the patron saint of Asia Minor and Turkey. His feast is on the General Roman Calendar and is celebrated on this day by the Church of England, the Episcopal Church in the USA, and by the Evangelical Lutheran Church in America. It is celebrated by the Russian and Greek Orthodox Churches on May 8 and September 26.

On this day the Russian Orthodox Church celebrates the feast of *Joseph* [March 19], *James the Apostle,* brother of the Lord [May 3], and *King David* (d. 970 B.C.). There is a commemoration of *Stephen* [December 26], the first martyr.

BIBLIOGRAPHY

Brown, Raymond E. *The Community of the Beloved Disciple.* New York: Paulist Press, 1979.

28 Holy Innocents, martyrs; Gaspar del Bufalo, founder

The *Holy Innocents* (first century) were put to death by King Herod in an effort to destroy the One who was to be born king of the Jews out of fear for his own throne (Matt. 2:16–18). They are venerated as martyrs who died not *because* of Christ, but *instead* of Christ. When Herod learned that wise men were coming from the East to pay homage to the new king, he called together the chief priests and scribes and asked them where the prophet foretold that the Messiah would be born. They told him that it would be in Bethlehem in Judea (Mic. 5:1). Then he sent for the Magi and questioned them about their movements and plans, ordering them to return and tell him where the child could be found, so that he too could go and worship him. According to the Scriptures, the Magi were warned in a dream to return home by a different route. Then Joseph [March 19], fearing for the child, took Mary and the infant Jesus into Egypt, where they remained until Herod was dead (Matt. 2:12–15). When Herod, who was cruel and suspicious man, realized that the wise men had ignored his command, he ordered all male children under the age of two in the Bethlehem district to be killed, thereby fulfilling the prophecy of Jeremiah regarding "Rachel weeping for her children" (Jer. 31:15). Their number has been estimated at between six and twenty-five. Matthew's account of the slaughter of the innocents was intended as a parallel of the Pharaoh's slaughter of Hebrew children when Moses was born (Exod. 1:13–22).

The feast of the Holy Innocents, who are called simply the Holy Children in the East, has been observed in the Church since the fifth century. The feast has been celebrated on this day in the West since the sixth century. They are depicted in art as children playing around God's heavenly altar with the crowns and palms that are their reward. They are also in a mosaic arch in the basilica of St. Mary Major in Rome. In England their feast was called Childermas. They are the object of special veneration in Bethlehem, where the Franciscans and children of the choir visit their altar under the Church of the Nativity and sing the hymn of Prudentius, the Spanish poet, from the Divine Office. The feast is on the General Roman Calendar and is celebrated also by the Church of England, the Episcopal Church in the USA, and the Evangelical Lutheran Church in America. It is celebrated by the Greek and Russian Orthodox Churches on December 29. On the Russian calendar, the number of slain children is given as fourteen thousand.

This is also the feast day of *Gaspar del Bufalo* (1786–1837), also Gaspare, founder of the Society of the Precious Blood (C.Pp.S.) in 1815, an order of priests and brothers dedicated to parish ministry, particularly parish missions, and other forms of missionary work. It also promotes devotion to the Precious Blood as a sign of Christ's redemptive love for all humanity. The Rule was approved in 1841. (The future Pope Pius IX was an early member of the congregation, and it was his encyclical in 1849 that gave impetus to the devotion.) Gaspar del Bufalo died in Rome on December 28, 1837. He was beatified in 1904 and canonized in 1954. His feast is not on the General Roman Calendar.

29 Thomas Becket, bishop and martyr

Thomas Becket (1118–70), or Thomas of Canterbury, was archbishop of Canterbury when slain in the Canterbury cathedral upon orders from King Henry II. He was the most popular saint in medieval England. Born in London of a wealthy Norman family, he studied at Merton Abbey in Surrey and in Paris. After the death of both of his parents, he had to work as a clerk and then, at age twenty-four, obtained a post in the household of Theobald, archbishop of Canterbury, who conferred minor orders on him and provided him with several benefices. (Until he went to Canterbury, he preferred to be known as Thomas of London. The name Becket he disavowed as something attached to him by his enemies.) Thomas was later ordained a deacon and sent to study law in Bologna and Auxerre. In 1154 he was named archdeacon of Canterbury, second in ecclesiastical dignity only to a bishop and an abbot. At only twenty-one years of age, Henry II was crowned king of England in the same year and appointed Thomas as chancellor of England the following year. Thomas and the king became close friends as well as allies. When Theobald died in 1161, the king wanted to make Thomas the new archbishop, but Thomas strongly resisted, predicting grave political tensions and the eventual end of their friendship. The king paid no heed to Thomas's warnings and pressed forward with the appointment. Thomas continued to resist until urged to accept by the papal legate in 1162. He set out for Canterbury from London and soon after his arrival was ordained a priest and a few days later consecrated a bishop. Soon thereafter he received the pallium (the symbol of an archbishop's office) from the pope, and by the end of the year a notable change occurred in his way of life.

Saint Thomas Becket Enthroned by Gerolamo Santacroce

He wore simple clerical dress and a hair shirt close to his skin. He rose early to read the Bible and celebrated or attended Mass at nine o'clock. He distributed alms to the poor every day at ten o'clock and dined at three in the great hall with many guests and his household. He visited the monastic infirmary and the monks in the cloister at their work. He established a certain monastic regularity in his own household and took particular care in the selection of candidates for the diaconate and priesthood. Conflicts with the king became, as he had predicted, increasingly serious. Thomas refused to pay tax on church lands, and when one of his canons was accused of murder, Thomas refused to turn him over to the royal court, but insisted on judging him in his own. At first Thomas accepted the Constitutions of Clarendon, which codified royal privileges vis-à-vis the Church in 1164, but later repented of his acquiescence when the consequences became clear. The king insisted upon the end of clerical immunity from civil prosecution, the requirement that prelates have his permission to leave the kingdom or appeal to Rome, and the appropriation of revenues from vacant benefices by the crown. Thomas resisted once again. He tried to heal the breach with the king, but the king proved unyielding and vengeful. He refused Thomas an audience and twice prevented him from crossing the English Channel to see the pope.

After a stormy council meeting in Northampton in which barons and prelates loyal to the king attacked him, Thomas left secretly for France and had an audience with the pope at Sens. Thomas offered his resignation, but the pope refused to accept it. Nevertheless, Thomas remained abroad for six years, residing first at the Cistercian abbey at Pontigny and then as guest of the French king at the abbey of Sainte-Colombe, near Sens. He returned to England after the archbishop of York defied his orders and crowned the heir to the throne, Prince Henry. Although the practice of crowning a successor while the incumbent still lived was common on the Continent, it had not been done before in England. Thomas sent papal letters of suspension to the archbishop of York and the six assisting bishops. His farewell words to the bishop of Paris were: "I am going home to England to die."

When he landed at Sandwich on December 1, 1170, the sheriff of Kent tried to prevent him from coming ashore. He received a welcome at Canterbury, but encountered hostility at court. The young Henry, who was his former friend and pupil, refused to see him. On Christmas day, with the backing of the pope, Thomas excommunicated, from the pulpit of Canterbury cathedral, the archbishop of York and the bishops who had assisted at the young prince's coronation. When the king heard the news in France, he asked who would rid him of this turbulent priest, or words to that effect. Four knights took his words as permission to kill the archbishop and set out at once for England. On the afternoon of December 29, they reached Canterbury and confronted the archbishop in his bedroom. The conversation began quietly but became heated and filled with oaths and threats. Thomas retired to the sanctuary of his cathedral, where the monks were singing Vespers.

As Thomas entered the church, he was met by a group of terrified monks who rushed to close the door behind him. Thomas turned around and said, "A church is not a castle," and opened the door himself. The knights rushed in shouting: "Where is Thomas the traitor? Where is the archbishop?" "Here I am," he replied, "no traitor, but archbishop and priest of God." He was hacked to death between the altars of Our Lady and St. Benedict [July 11]. As the knights ran off, they shouted: "The king's men! The king's men!" The cathedral soon filled with people and a thunderstorm broke overhead. As the news of the murder spread and as the horror of the event sank in, there was universal revulsion in England and on the Continent. The pope excommunicated the king, who closed himself off from contact with others, fasting for forty days. The people, however, demanded a more public form of penance, which he performed first in France, where he received absolution from the papal legates, and then at Canterbury in July 1173, eighteen months after Thomas's solemn canonization as a martyr by Pope Alexander III at Segni. Many miracles had been reported at his tomb.

On July 7, 1220, in the presence of the new king, the papal legate, and the archbishop of Reims, Thomas's body was transferred from its resting place in the cathedral crypt to a shrine behind the high altar. The shrine immediately became a major center of pilgrimage until destroyed by Henry VIII's men in 1538. There is a stone carving of Thomas's murder in the cathedral of Chartres. His feast is on the General Roman Calendar and is also celebrated by the Church of England. The Episcopal Church in the USA commemorates him on this day. He was the subject of a film, *Becket,* in 1964.

BIBLIOGRAPHY

Barlow, Frank. *Thomas Becket.* London: Wiedenfeld and Nicolson, 1986.

30 Egwin of Worcester, bishop

Egwin of Worcester (d. 717) was the founder of Evesham, one of the great Benedictine abbeys in medieval England. Born of royal blood, he became bishop of Worcester ca. 693. He was so committed to the reform of the clergy that he evoked the enmity of a faction, which denounced him to the king and the archbishop of Canterbury. As a consequence, Egwin was forced to withdraw from his see for a time. He made a penitential pilgrimage to Rome, where he received papal vindication. On his return to England, with the king of Mercia's help, he founded Evesham Abbey. He undertook a second journey to Rome ca. 709 in the company of two kings, one of Mercia and the other of the East Saxons. In Rome he received a number of privileges for his abbey from Pope Constantine, and it became one of the greatest in medieval England. Egwin died at Evesham and was buried in the monastery. After the Norman Conquest in the late eleventh century, when the cults of many Saxon saints were replaced by Norman ones, Egwin's cult was accepted and the monks of Evesham carried out an extensive fund-raising campaign in southern England to buy wood and stone for a church, using Egwin's relics as a lure. A number of miracles were attributed to the relics. His feast is not on the General Roman Calendar.

31 Sylvester I, pope

The pontificate of *Sylvester I* (d. 335; pope 314–335), also known as Silvester, lasted for nearly twenty-one years, the tenth-longest in history, and overlapped with most of the imperial reign of Constantine (306–37) [May 21]. In spite of the length of his pontificate and the importance of the Constantinian period in which the pope served, Sylvester seems to have made little or no lasting impact on the Church or on the papacy itself. Indeed, it is what he did *not* do as pope that is more significant than what he did do.

Constantine, who occasionally assumed the title "Bishop of External Affairs," called a special council of some 130 bishops at Arles in August 314 to hear another appeal from the Donatists, who were contesting the consecration of Caecilian as bishop of Carthage. (The Donatists were rigorist opponents of readmitting to the Church those who had compromised their faith during the Diocletian persecution.) Significantly, the emperor did not convene the council in Rome or appoint the Bishop of Rome to preside over it, but assigned that responsibility instead to Marinus, the bishop of Arles, and entrusted the general conduct of the council to Chrestus, bishop of Syracuse. Sylvester sent two presbyters and two deacons to represent him. When the council ended, however, it transmitted its decisions to him in a letter that acknowledged his primacy over the West (although not over the whole Church) and asked him to circulate the decisions to the other churches.

Also during Sylvester's pontificate, the first ecumenical council, consisting of some 250 bishops, was held at Nicaea, the emperor's summer residence (in modern northwest Turkey), in July 325. This was the council that first defined the divinity of Jesus Christ, teaching that he is of the same being, or substance (Gk. *homoousios*), with God the Father (against the Arians who held that Jesus Christ was the greatest of creatures, but not equal to God). Significantly, the pope played no part in the proceedings of this ecumenical council. He neither convened the council (the emperor did) nor presided over it

(Ossius [or Hosius], bishop of Cordoba, did). The emperor himself presided over the impressive opening and closing ceremonies, functioning in effect as the council's president. Like other bishops within the empire, Sylvester had been invited to attend the council, but he declined to do so, pleading old age. He did send two presbyters to represent him, but they were given no special status at the assembly other than in signing the acts of the council after the presiding bishop and before the other bishops did.

In spite of Sylvester's lackluster pontificate, the Roman church benefited immensely from Constantine's generosity, which included the building of great churches such as the original St. Peter's Basilica on the Via Ostiensis and the Basilica Constantiniana and its baptistery (later known as San Giovanni in Laterano [St. John Lateran], which still serves as the pope's cathedral church even today). Perhaps because of the pope's unimpressive pontificate, however, a number of legends developed about him a long while after his death. A mid-fifth century biography attributed to him the conversion of Constantine and even of curing the emperor of leprosy. Pious reports circulated in the fifth and sixth centuries that the Council of Nicaea was really convened jointly by the pope and the emperor, not by the emperor alone, and that Ossius presided over the council because the pope had designated him to do so. There was also a growing belief in the authenticity of the so-called Donation of Constantine, an eighth- or ninth-century fabricated document in which the emperor allegedly conferred on Sylvester and his successors the primacy over the great patriarchates, the city of Rome, Italy, and all of the provinces and states of the West. The Donation of Constantine was included in the *False Decretals* (ninth-century forgeries that sought to buttress episcopal independence from lay control) and Gratian's *Decretals* (a twelfth-century unofficial collection of canon law and canonical sources compiled by a monk, John Gratian). By the middle of the fifteenth century, the document's authenticity was questioned by Aeneas Sylvius Piccolomini (later Pope Pius II) and others, but in the meantime this document and the other spurious sources exercised enormous influence on medieval thought.

Sylvester was buried in the private cemetery of St. Priscilla (also known as Prisca) [July 8] on the Via Salaria, but his remains (perhaps only his head) seem to have been moved by Pope Paul I in 762 to the church of San Silvestro in Capite within the city walls. His feast is on the General Roman Calendar.

PART V

EPILOGUE: SAINTS AND THE CHURCH

THE SAINTS ARE HOLY PEOPLE WHO CONVEY IN THEIR LIVES AN example and standard of discipleship that the Church itself strives to emulate and achieve. They remind us that we do not live the gospel in the abstract, but in the concrete circumstances of ordinary human life. As true disciples, the saints incarnate the demands of the gospel in ways that are pertinent to the age and culture in which they live. They reveal new and unexpected understandings of the gospel message and new and deeper meanings of faith in Christ and in the following of Christ.[1] Because of the example of their lives, we are assured that "how we ought to live is grounded in reality itself."[2] In other words, heroically virtuous discipleship is possible, even if difficult, on this earth. And it is possible not only for individual disciples of Christ, but for the Church as a community of disciples.[3]

Whether by popular acclaim as in the first Christian millennium or by a formal canonical process as in most of the second millennium, the making of saints has provided a record of the Church's own evolving understanding of the meaning and requirements of discipleship to Jesus Christ. If, for example, the Church had canonized only the Desert Fathers, a few of whom spent most of their lives sitting atop a pile of rocks, it would have been saying to its members and to the world at large that discipleship demands complete withdrawal from society as we know it and the adoption of a style of life at odds with everything humans know as healthy and normal: love and friendship, sexual intimacy, family relationships, good food, reasonable comfort and security in housing, the ability to move and to communicate from place to place, even over long distances, opportunities to improve the quality of life for others, the enjoyment of art and music and other expressions of the human spirit, and so forth.

By the same token, if the Church had canonized only celibate priests and nuns, it would have excluded the greatest portion of its membership from the realm of sanctity and would, in the process, have demeaned married and family life and the sacrament on which they are spiritually grounded. Fortunately, in the matter of its saints, the Church has been far more catholic than that, occasional lapses notwithstanding.

The purpose of this epilogue is threefold: first, to trace the paths and patterns of canonization, canonical and popular alike, that have been followed and fashioned by the Church over the course of its history; second, to propose categories of saints that, when taken together, reflect and represent the full spectrum of Christian discipleship and indeed of human wholeness itself; and, third, to suggest the names of twenty saints who have had the greatest impact on the life and mission of the Church during its first two millennia of existence.

Paths and Patterns of Sainthood

The first-century Church was a church of missionaries and martyrs, the greatest of whom were Peter and Paul [June 29], the one, apostle to the Jews, and the other, apostle to the Gentiles.[4] Revolutionary in character, the apostolic Church proclaimed, against the contemporary culture, the dignity of the poor and of women. These two foci coalesced in the Blessed Virgin Mary's classic prayer, the Magnificat (Lat., "[My soul] proclaims [the greatness of the Lord]"): "He has thrown down the rulers from their thrones but lifted up the lowly. The hungry he has filled with good things; the rich he has sent away empty" (Luke 1:12–13). Hailed by the Second Vatican Council as the "preeminent" and "wholly unique" member of the Church and "as its exemplar and outstanding model in faith and charity,"[5] the Mother of the Lord is the greatest of all the saints of all time—the disciple par excellence. However, these earliest Christian decades were graced by other women disciples as well, the most prominent of whom was Mary Magdalene

[July 22], one of the first witnesses of the Resurrection (Matt. 28:9–10; John 20:14–18) and, on that basis alone, an "apostle" in her own right (see Acts 1:22). The Church also recognized in these earliest Christian decades that sanctity is more often manifested in less dramatic fashion, that is, in self-effacing fidelity and virtual anonymity. No disciple exemplified this more compellingly than Joseph [March 19], one of the most celebrated saints in all of Christian history and yet one whose biography is among the leanest.

The postapostolic Church of the second century engaged the wider society not only at the level of proclamation, but also of probing intellectual discourse, with both Greek philosophers outside the Church and heretics within. It was the age of the first theologians, such as Justin [June 1], who engaged the educated in serious discussions about the faith, and of theologically sophisticated and pastorally courageous bishops, such as Irenaeus [June 28] and Polycarp [February 23]. Justin and Polycarp, like many of their contemporaries, earned the martyr's crown.

The age of martyrdom continued into the third century, particularly under the Roman emperors Decius (249–51) and Diocletian (284–305). Among the martyr-saints who served as striking reminders of the high cost of Christian discipleship were Pope Sixtus II [August 7], beheaded while presiding at the liturgy in a Christian cemetery, Lawrence [August 10], one of his deacons, Agatha [February 5], a consecrated virgin martyred under Decius in Sicily, Lucy [December 13], a virgin martyred under Diocletian and widely venerated in Rome, and Cyprian of Carthage [September 16], one of the most prominent bishops of the third century.

At the beginning of the fourth century the Church faced its most dangerous and divisive heresy, Arianism, which touched the core of Christian faith, bringing into question the equality of Jesus Christ with God the Father and Creator of the universe. The Council of Nicaea in 325 formulated a definitive response, still proclaimed in the creed today, that the Son is "of the same substance" (Gk. *homoousios*) as the Father. The Nicene dogma, however, did not end the controversy or dissipate its attendant bitterness and violence. The times called for unusual pastoral leadership and the Church was happily blessed with it. This was the century of the great bishop-theologians Athanasius [May 2], the leading figure at Nicaea and the principal promoter of its teaching in the decades that followed, Ambrose [December 7], who converted Augustine [August 28], Martin of Tours [November 11], the founder of monasticism in Gaul (France), Cyril of Jerusalem [March 18],

Hilary of Poitiers [January 13], Gregory Nazianzen [January 2], and Basil the Great [January 2], defenders all of Nicene orthodoxy.

The Church was liberated from persecution in the early years of the century, but it was soon caught in a web of political privilege, thanks to the newly converted emperor Constantine [May 21] and his historic Edict of Milan (313). The Church's new favored status brought with it the temptation to accommodate too easily to the prevailing culture and to sacrifice its prophetic mission in the process. And so the Church also raised up such countercultural saints as Anthony of Egypt [January 17], generally regarded as the founder of monasticism as such, Pachomius [May 9], the founder of communal monasticism, Paul the Hermit [January 15], the first Christian hermit, and Hilarion [October 21], considered by many the "second Anthony."

Doctrinal controversies continued to vex the life of the Church in the fifth century as well, giving rise to two of the most important councils in all of Christian history: Ephesus (431) and Chalcedon (451). It was the age of theological and pastoral giants: Augustine of Hippo, one of the greatest Christian thinkers of all time, Cyril of Alexandria [June 27], who helped shape the teaching of Chalcedon on the divinity and humanity of Christ, John Chrysostom [September 13], the most prolific of the Fathers of the Church, Jerome [September 30], the preeminent biblical scholar, and Pope Leo the Great [November 10], who not only clarified the Church's teaching on Jesus Christ at Chalcedon, but also dramatically addressed the new threat posed by the tribal migrations sweeping across Europe. It was, at the same time, a period of increased missionary activity to the north—to Britain and Ireland in particular, both lands forever linked with the names of Augustine of Canterbury [May 27] and Patrick [March 17], respectively.

In the sixth century monasticism continued to spread and take root, as reflected in the popular acclaim rendered to such saints as Benedict of Nursia [July 11], the founder of Western monasticism as we know it today, his sister Scholastica [February 10], and the great Irish abbots and abbesses Columba of Iona [June 9], Brigid of Kildare [February 1], Ita of Killeedy [January 15], and Columban [November 23]. Looming large over the contemporary hierarchical landscape was the figure of Pope Gregory the Great [September 3], monastic in his spirituality, but an effective pastoral leader and reformer as well. His writings on pastoral care influenced the episcopal ministry of the Church well into the Middle Ages.

In the seventh century the often disruptive and destructive tribal migrations persisted in Europe, while the Muslim invasions pushed the Church out of its traditional bases in North Africa and the Holy Land itself. The task of preserving Christian culture in the face of its threatened dissolution fell initially to such good but not widely influential saints such as Isidore of Seville [April 4], the most learned person of his time, who provided a crucial link between antiquity and the Middle Ages, Benedict Biscop [January 12], who enriched the monasteries of Wearmouth and Jarrow in England with countless books and paintings, and Cuthbert [March 20], the Anglo-Saxon monk and bishop.

In the eighth century the Church regained some of the initiative lost in the Teutonic migrations. In 754 Pepin was crowned king of the Franks and hailed as protector of the Romans. It was the time of Boniface [June 5], who organized the German churches and who was known as the "apostle of Frisia and Germany," Chrodogang of Metz [March 6], reformer of the Frankish Church and of the pastoral life of diocesan priests, and Walburga [February 25], who brought a monastic stability to missionary work as abbess of the double monastery (of men and women) at Heidenheim. The work of preserving and consolidating the treasures of Christian culture fell to scholar-monks such as the Venerable Bede [May 25] in the West and to theologians such as John Damascene [December 4] in the East, whose compilation and synthesis of Greek theology became exceedingly influential in the medieval West.

The ninth century was marked by the Arabs' sacking of Rome and their conquest of Sicily, but also by the inauguration of the Holy Roman Empire under Charlemagne. Christianity began to make inroads in central and eastern Europe. Prince Boris I of Bulgaria embraced the faith ca. 864 and Cyril and Methodius [February 14] became "apostles to the Slavs." At the request of Charlemagne's successor, Pepin III, Benedict of Aniane [February 12] led a reform of Benedictine monasteries throughout France.

The tenth century, sometimes referred to as the "dark ages" of the papacy, witnessed the expansion of Christianity into Hungary, Poland, and Russia through the efforts of Adalbert of Prague [April 23] and Vladimir of Kiev [July 15]. This century also gave rise to the first papally canonized saint in history, Ulrich, bishop of Augsburg [July 4], a good man but not an unusually important figure in the history of the Church or even of his own time.

In the eleventh century the Church consolidated its missionary gains through the episcopal ministry of Stanislaus [April 11], bishop of Kraków and patron saint of Poland, and of Anselm of Canterbury

[April 21], a leading scholar-bishop, and it continued to promote the reform of monastic life through such figures as Bruno [October 6], founder of the Carthusians, and the reform of the Church itself through the efforts of high-ranking pastoral leaders such as Peter Damian [February 21], cardinal-bishop of Ostia, and Pope Gregory VII [May 25] himself. Alas, it was also the century in which the East-West Schism occurred. There were no saints to be found among the main protagonists on either side of that terrible and lasting rupture of unity.

The Church reemerged as a social, political, and religious force in European society in the High Middle Ages through the inspiration and leadership of spiritually heroic figures. The new religious orders, which placed greater emphasis on contemplation than on pastoral activity, but without depreciating the latter, were well represented among the saints of the twelfth century by the Cistercian Bernard of Clairvaux [August 20], prolific spiritual writer and the founding abbot of Clairvaux, which became one of the chief centers of the Cistercian order as well as one of the greatest monasteries in all of Europe, Norbert [June 6], founder of the Premonstratensians (Norbertines), and Hugh of Grenoble [April 1], the Carthusian bishop. But the age of martyrdom was not over, as witnessed by that of Thomas Becket [December 29], the famed archbishop of Canterbury who had been ordered slain for not ceding the rights of the Church to the claims of the king.

A wondrous burst of creative pastoral energy followed in the thirteenth century with the founding of the two major mendicant orders that carried out their mission in the world: the Franciscans, founded by Francis of Assisi [October 4], and the Order of Preachers (Dominicans), founded by Dominic [August 8]. Francis's spiritual associate, Clare of Assisi [August 11], founded the Poor Clares, a contemplative community of women. The new mendicant orders, in turn, produced some of the greatest theologians in the history of the Church: the Dominicans Thomas Aquinas [January 28] and his mentor, Albert the Great [November 15], and the Franciscan Bonaventure [July 15]. They also produced some of the Church's greatest preachers: the Dominican Peter of Verona [April 6] and the Franciscan Anthony of Padua [June 13]. In canonizing them all, four in the thirteenth century and two in the fourteenth,[6] the Church of the High Middle Ages proclaimed itself thereby a community of scholars as well as of preachers, of thinkers as well as of pastoral ministers, a self-critical Church as well as a self-confident one. The thirteenth century also saw the Church's opening of itself to the religious experience of women, exemplified by Mechthilde of Magdeburg [November 19], one of the great mystics of her time.[7] Finally, the thirteenth-century Church's ambivalent relationship with the temporal powers disclosed itself in the patently political canonization of France's late King Louis IX [August 25] in 1297, as part of the negotiated settlement of a dispute between Pope Boniface VIII and King Philip IV over the latter's power to tax the French clergy without papal approval. Louis was also a Crusader.

The fourteenth century was marked by the Avignon papacy (1309–77) and the beginning of the Great Western Schism (1378–1417). Two women devoted themselves indefatigably to the cause of restoring the papacy to Rome and also, in Catherine's case, to ending the schism: Catherine of Siena [April 29], a mystical writer and one of the first two women to be named a Doctor of the Church, and Bridget of Sweden [July 23], also a mystic and foundress of the Brigittines, an order of women and men living in double monasteries with the abbess as superior.[8] The recognition of the sainthood of the abbot and peacemaker Sergius of Radonezh [September 25], the greatest of the Russian saints, venerated by Orthodox and Catholics alike, underscored the reality, often alluded to by Pope John Paul II in the latter part of the twentieth century, that the Church breathes with "two lungs," East and West alike.[9]

The fifteenth century yielded the young warrior-visionary Joan of Arc [May 30] and the evangelically stalwart widow Frances of Rome [March 9], foundress of a community of women without vows to serve the poor.[10] It was also a century in which great preachers such as the Franciscan Bernardino of Siena [May 20] and the Dominican Vincent Ferrer [April 5] were raised up to confront the moral corruption of the time.[11] The latter was also instrumental in facilitating an end to the Great Western Schism by persuading one of the claimants to the papal throne to step aside for the sake of unity.

The sixteenth century was at once turbulent and vibrant, witnessing the rupture of unity between Catholics and Protestants, the emergence of a Catholic Counter-Reformation, and the beginning of the period of Baroque Catholicism, which extended into the nineteenth century and which some nostalgic Catholics continue to equate with the Catholic tradition as such. Among the several characteristics of Baroque Catholicism was an emphasis on the individual spiritual and miraculous exploits of the saints, who served as a principal font of Catholic devotional life. This was also the century of new religious movements, including the Society of Jesus (Jesuits) and the reformed Carmelites. Among these movements' leading saints were Ignatius of

Loyola [July 31], founder of the Jesuits, and Teresa of Ávila [October 15] and John of the Cross [December 14], renowned mystical theologians and leaders of the Carmelite reform.[12] Other founder-saints of this century included Philip Neri [May 26], of the Oratorians, dedicated to the reform of clerical life and ministry; Francis of Paolo [April 2], of a branch of Franciscans known as the Minims, who emphasized humility of life; Camillus de Lellis [July 14], of the Camillians, devoted to the care of the sick and the poor; Anthony Mary Zaccaria [July 5], of the Barnabites, committed to the reform of the clergy; Jerome Emiliani [February 8], of the Somaschi Fathers, dedicated to the care of orphans and the education of the poor; Angela Merici [January 27], of the Ursulines, devoted initially to the education of girls and young women; Peter of Alcántara [October 22], of the Alcantarines, a stricter form of Franciscanism; and John of God [March 8], of the Brothers Hospitallers (Brothers of St. John of God), dedicated to the care of the sick and the poor.[13]

There were two phases to the sixteenth century's Catholic Counter-Reformation. The first tended to be more defensive vis-à-vis the Protestants, a phase represented in part at least by Pope Pius V [April 30], a zealous sponsor of the Roman Inquisition, by Robert Bellarmine [September 17], one of the most accomplished defenders of the faith against the Reformers, and by Peter Canisius [December 21], who defended and reestablished Catholicism in Reformation Germany. The second phase was more pastoral and less polemical in spirit, represented by Charles Borromeo [November 4], one of the greatest reform-minded bishops in the history of the Church.[14] Pius V's hard-line policy toward England, including his excommunication of Queen Elizabeth, provoked a predictable backlash against English Catholics that led to the martyrdoms of such prominent figures as the learned and eloquent layman Thomas More [June 22], Bishop John Fisher [June 22], the Jesuit Edmund Campion [December 1], and many others less well known than they.[15] The sixteenth was also a century of renewed missionary activity in India and the Far East, represented by one of the original Jesuits, Francis Xavier [December 3], regarded by many as the greatest missionary of all time, and by the Japanese Jesuit martyr Paul Miki [February 6] and his companions.[16]

The age of the lay apostolate and of lay spirituality as we know it today had its beginnings in the seventeenth century, particularly through the pioneering efforts of Francis de Sales [January 24], author of the classic *The Introduction to the Devout Life*, which illuminated the relevance of the Church's spiritual tradition for people in various circumstances.[17] Otherwise, the Church continued to equate pastoral vibrancy with the creation of more religious orders, some of which, such as the Vincentians and the Sisters of Charity, touched upon the core of the Christian apostolate: service to the sick and the poor through medical care, evangelization, and education. They also incorporated women into the active ministry of the Church. Others focused their efforts on the spiritual growth of individual members rather than on pastoral and ministerial activities in service to the Church and those in need. Among the founders and foundresses of this century were Vincent de Paul [September 27], of the Vincentians; Louise de Marillac [March 15], foundress (with Vincent de Paul) of the Sisters of Charity; Jane Frances de Chantal [December 12], foundress (with Francis de Sales) of the Visitation Sisters, a congregation of contemplative women with a ministry to the sick in the earliest phase of its existence; John Eudes [August 19], of the Congregation of Jesus and Mary (Eudists), originally dedicated to the education of seminarians; and Joseph Calasanz [August 25], of the Piarists (Order of the Pious Schools), committed to the education of poor children.[18]

The Jesuit martyr Isaac Jogues [October 19] and the Native American Kateri Tekakwitha [July 14] underscored the Church's missionary commitment to North America.[19] The Jesuit Peter Claver [September 9], the Dominican lay brother Martin de Porres [November 3], and the Dominican tertiary Rose of Lima [August 23] highlighted the Church's continued missionary presence in South America.[20]

Finally, this period of Baroque Catholicism was also marked by new devotions, the most popular of which was that to the Sacred Heart of Jesus, based on the visionary experiences of Margaret Mary Alacoque [October 16], a French Visitation nun.[21] The devotion included the reception of Holy Communion on the First Fridays of nine consecutive months in reparation for sins and humanity's indifference to God.

The principal saints of the eighteenth century were also mainly founders and foundresses of new orders with their own spirituality and ministerial focus: Paul of the Cross [October 19], founder of the Passionists, committed to preaching and living in the spirit of the suffering and death of Jesus; Louis Grignion de Montfort [April 28], founder of the Montfort Fathers and the Daughters of Wisdom, rooted in what he called the "True Devotion to Mary"; John Baptist de La Salle [April 7], founder of the Brothers of the Christian Schools, an order of laymen devoted to education; and Alphonsus Liguori [August 1], one of the greatest moral theologians in the history of the Church and founder of the Redemptorists, who dedicated themselves primarily to retreats, parish missions, and missionary work in foreign lands.[22]

The Church continued to raise up the founders and foundresses of religious orders as examples of Christian discipleship in the nineteenth century: Anthony Claret [October 24], of the Claretians (Missionary Sons of the Immaculate Heart of Mary), a congregation of diocesan clergy organized originally to continue the work of catechizing and preaching following the suppression of the Dominicans and Franciscans in Spain; John Bosco [January 31], of the Salesians, dedicated to the education of boys and young men; Elizabeth Ann Seton [January 4], of the Daughters of Charity of St. Joseph, who were devoted to the poor and the sick; Julie Billiart [April 8], of the Sisters of Notre Dame de Namur, devoted originally to the education of poor children; and Peter Julian Eymard [August 2], of the Blessed Sacrament Fathers, dedicated to the perpetual adoration of the Blessed Sacrament.[23]

At the same time, however, the Church of the nineteenth century witnessed the lives of so-called simple saints, those who neither founded new religious communities nor reached great heights of pastoral achievement themselves—as if to underscore the biblical point that God reveals to the "childlike" what is hidden from the "wise and learned" (Luke 10:21). Those saints included, most famously, the young Carmelite nun Theresa of the Child Jesus [October 1], better known as the Little Flower and Thérèse of Lisieux; Bernadette Soubirous [April 16], the French peasant girl to whom the Blessed Virgin Mary is believed to have appeared under the title of the Immaculate Conception at Lourdes; Maria Goretti [July 6], the young Italian girl who resisted unto death the sexual advances of a neighbor; and John Vianney [August 4], the Curé d'Ars, better known for his simple piety than his learning or eloquence. All four came to enjoy enormous spiritual favor with twentieth-century Catholics in the decades before Vatican II.[24]

The nineteenth century was also a time of continued missionary expansion represented, for example, in the martyrs of Korea (Andrew Kim Taegõn and companions [September 20]), of Vietnam (Andrew Dung-Lac and companions [November 24]), and black Africa (Charles Lwanga and companions [June 3]).

The twentieth century was marked by the Church's growing recognition and celebration of the sanctity of women. Among those singled out as examples of Christian discipleship were Frances Xavier Cabrini [November 13], the first American citizen to be canonized and the foundress of the Sisters of the Sacred Heart, a congregation dedicated to the service of the sick, the poor, and of orphans; Katharine Drexel [March 3], American-born foundress of the Sisters of the Blessed Sacrament, a congregation devoted to the service of Native and African Americans; Mary MacKillop [May 25], Australian foundress of the Sisters of St. Joseph of the Sacred Heart, whose ministry is to provide schools for poor children, establish orphanages, and engage in other works of charity; and Teresa Benedicta of the Cross (Edith Stein) [August 9], a convert from Judaism who perished in the Holocaust.[25]

This was also a century of controversial canonizations, including Edith Stein's and those of Maximilian Maria Kolbe [August 14] and of Pope Pius X [August 21].[26] And, finally, it was a century in which many as yet uncanonized saints were raised up to illuminate the Church's path of discipleship in a new age of extraordinary material and scientific progress, but also one of massive violence and cruelty: Dorothy Day [November 29], foundress of the Catholic Worker movement in service to the poor and the homeless; Thomas Merton [December 10], the Trappist monk whose spiritual writings continue to shape the spiritual character of Christians and non-Christians alike; Oscar Arnulfo Romero [March 24], the archbishop of San Salvador who was martyred for his outspoken defense of human rights and social justice; and Blessed John XXIII [June 3], the pope of the Second Vatican Council and of the modern renewal and reform of the Church, to mention only a few.

If this historical survey suggests nothing else, it is that the spectrum of sanctity and Christian discipleship is as broad as it is deep. The next section of this epilogue will flesh out that point in greater detail.

A Spectrum of Saints

The saints, those popularly acclaimed as well as those formally canonized, are as diverse as the community of disciples itself and cover the entire spectrum of its missionary and ministerial activities.[27] In a class by herself, as the disciple par excellence, is the Blessed Virgin Mary, the Mother of the Lord, who has more feast days in her honor in the course of the Church's liturgical year than any other saint by far. Close behind the Blessed Mother in spiritual dignity are the greatest of the apostles: Peter and Paul [June 29], James [July 25] and John [December 27], and Mary Magdalene [July 22], who, though not one of the Twelve, fulfilled the requirements for apostleship in that she was a witness of the Resurrection, indeed the first or at least among the first to see the Risen Lord.

In a second major category are, in fact, the first proclaimed saints, namely, the martyrs (including Peter, Paul, and James), not only those in apostolic and postapostolic times (such as Stephen [December 26], the first martyr, and the two martyr-bishops Ignatius of Antioch [October 17] and Polycarp [February 23]), but also those of later and more recent periods: the Jesuit Paul Miki and his companions in Japan [February 6]; Charles Lwanga and his companions in black Africa [June 3]; Thomas More [June 22], John Fisher [June 22], Thomas Becket [December 29], and so many other English martyrs; Andrew Kim Taegõn and companions [September 20] in Korea; Isaac Jogues and his fellow Jesuit martyrs of North America [October 19]; Andrew Dung-Lac and his companions [November 24] in Vietnam; Boniface [June 5] in Germany; and those from many other lands and cultures, including the martyrs of China [September 28].

A third major category of saints are the missionaries, starting with the Twelve and all of the other earliest disciples who carried the gospel to others beyond Jerusalem: Francis Xavier [December 3], the greatest of all postapostolic missionaries, Peter Claver [September 9], Boniface, Patrick [March 17], Columban [November 23], and the unheralded Turibius of Mongrovejo [March 23]. The last is the patron saint of the bishops of Latin America. An example of a more modern missionary is Frances Xavier Cabrini [November 13], who came to the United States to minister to poor Italian immigrants.

In a fourth category is Francis de Sales [January 24], who, like Vincent de Paul [September 27] and others, incorporated the laity into the ministerial life and activities of the Church, but who also provided them with a distinctive spirituality to inform and nourish their various apostolates.

A fifth category includes those who attained a mystical communion with God, in anticipation of the perfect communion that awaits all the saints at the heavenly banquet table: Teresa of Ávila [October 15], the Church's premier mystic and mystical writer; John of the Cross [December 14], her close associate in the Carmelite reform; Catherine of Siena [April 29]; Hildegard of Bingen [September 17], a twelfth-century abbess; Mary Magdalene de Pazzi [May 25], a sixteenth-century Carmelite who insisted that "God does not germinate in a sad soul"; Mechthilde of Magdeburg [November 19], a thirteenth-century abbess; and Veronica Giuliani [July 10], an eighteenth-century

Franciscan who has been described as the most representative figure of Baroque mysticism. The preponderance of women mystics in this representative sample is worthy of note.

A sixth category is that of the reformer-saints, reformers of the Church in general or of religious communities in particular. Their archetype, as in the case of every category of saints, is Jesus himself, whose own immediate agenda was the reform of contemporary Judaism. The pattern set by Jesus was followed by others such as Anthony of Egypt [January 17], whose flight to the desert was not so much an escape as an act of protest against the increasingly comfortable relationship between the Church and the wider society; Basil the Great [January 2] and the other reform-minded bishops of the fourth and fifth centuries; Isidore of Seville [April 4], at the end of the age of the Fathers of the Church and on the threshold of the so-called Dark Ages; Peter Damian [February 21] and Pope Gregory VII [May 25], leaders of the Gregorian reform of the eleventh century; Catherine of Siena, who directly challenged the popes of the fourteenth century to end both the Avignon "captivity" of the papacy and the Great Western Schism; the great sixteenth-century reformers Philip Neri [May 26], Charles Borromeo [November 4], Teresa of Ávila, John of the Cross, and Peter of Alcántara [October 22], who, when others complained about the state of affairs in the Church, simply said: "The trouble is that we all talk of reforming others without ever reforming ourselves"; and, finally, the twentieth-century reformer Pope John XXIII [June 3].

A seventh category of saints includes Bishops of Rome (popes), other bishops, and bishop-theologians. Gregory the Great [September 3] and Blessed John XXIII stand out in the first subcategory. Outstanding representatives of the second subcategory, other bishops, are Basil the Great and Charles Borromeo, the premier examples, as well as Martin of Tours [November 11], patron saint of France; Thomas of Villanova [September 22], one of the most evangelically inspired bishops in history; Josephat [November 12], the first Eastern saint formally canonized by the Roman Catholic Church and cofounder of the Order of St. Basil; Nicholas [December 6], one of the most legendary bishops in history; and Peter of Tarentaise [May 8], a twelfth-century Cistercian who devoted his whole ministry to the poor and despised praise and honors for himself. The leading bishop-theologians in the third subcategory are Augustine of Hippo [August 28], the premier example, Basil the Great, Isidore of Seville, Athanasius [May 2], Ambrose [December 7], Peter Canisius [December 21], and

Alphonsus Liguori [August 1], one of the greatest moral theologians in all of church history.

An eighth category are the monks of East and West alike. In the East: Theodosius the Cenobiarch [January 11], who created a monastic "city" for the poor, the sick, and the abandoned in sixth-century Cappadocia; John Climacus [March 30], a seventh-century abbot and spiritual writer who, unlike so many others of this type, did not depreciate the body, but rather linked asceticism with works of charity; Pambo [July 18], a fourth-century hermit who insisted that monastic life is not the only or necessarily the best way to God and that what is important is to guard one's conscience toward one's neighbor; and Sergius of Radonezh [September 25], a fourteenth-century Russian who has been acclaimed as the Russian Orthodox Francis of Assisi. In the West: Anthony of Egypt, the founder of monasticism; Benedict of Nursia [July 11], the founder of Western monasticism; the Venerable Bede [May 25], the quintessential scholar-monk; and Bernard of Clairvaux [August 20], one of the great mystical theologians in church history.

In a ninth and closely related category are representative abbesses who exercised unusually effective leadership not only in their monasteries, but in their local and regional churches as well: Ita of Killeedy [January 15], foundress of a monastery, abbess of a double monastery of men and women, and spiritual counselor and perhaps even confessor to many, including future saints; Hilda of Whitby [November 19], abbess of the monastery where the famous Council of Whitby was held in 664 and a leading figure in the contemporary Celtic Church; and Walburga [February 25], assistant to her uncle Boniface [June 5] in his missionary work and then abbess of the double monastery of Heidenheim, established by her brother Winnibald [December 18]. The Council of Trent (1545–63) put an end to most of the special prerogatives enjoyed by abbesses, some of whom wore episcopal regalia, received the homage of local clergy upon their election, and heard the confession of their nuns.

In a tenth category of saints are the foundresses and founders of religious orders, congregations, and institutes: Clare of Assisi [August 11], of the Poor Clares in the thirteenth century; Bridget of Sweden [July 23], of the Brigittines in the fourteenth century; Louise de Marillac [March 15], of the Daughters of Charity in the seventeenth century; Mary Margaret d'Youville [December 23], of the Grey Nuns in the eighteenth century; Magdalen of Canossa [April 10], of the

Canossian Sisters of Charity in nineteenth century; Elizabeth Ann Seton [January 4], of the Daughters of Charity of St. Joseph in the nineteenth century; Blessed Mary MacKillop [May 25], of the Sisters of St. Joseph of the Sacred Heart in the nineteenth century; Katharine Drexel [March 3], of the Sisters of the Blessed Sacrament in service to Native and African Americans in the twentieth century; and Frances Xavier Cabrini, of the Missionary Sisters of the Sacred Heart also in the twentieth century.

Founders include Benedict of Nursia, of the Benedictines in the sixth century; Bruno [October 6], of the Carthusians in the eleventh century; Francis of Assisi [October 4], of the Franciscans in the thirteenth century; Dominic [August 8], of the Dominicans also in the thirteenth century; Ignatius of Loyola [July 31], of the Society of Jesus in the sixteenth century; Philip Neri, of the Oratorians also in the sixteenth century; Vincent de Paul [September 27], of the Vincentians in the seventeenth century; Camillus de Lellis [July 14], of the Camillians also in the seventeenth century; Josephat, of the Order of St. Basil also in the seventeenth century; Alphonsus Liguori, of the Redemptorists in the eighteenth century; John Baptist de La Salle [April 7], of the Brothers of the Christian Schools also in the eighteenth century; and John Bosco [January 31], of the Salesians in the nineteenth century. It should be pointed out that several, perhaps even most, of these foundresses and founders were born into wealthy families and renounced their riches or applied them to the apostolic work of their new religious communities. No gesture could have been more directly responsive to the call of the Lord himself to renounce wealth and possessions, to give the proceeds to the poor, and then to take up the life of a disciple (Luke 18:18–30).

An eleventh category of saints includes those who distinguished themselves as preachers of the Word of God. Two in particular were outstanding: the Franciscans Bernardino of Siena [May 20] and Anthony of Padua [June 13], the latter better known as the patron saint of lost articles. There were, of course, other great and saintly preachers such as the Dominican Vincent Ferrer [April 5], but, as a man of his time (late fourteenth and early fifteenth centuries), he stressed sin and damnation to such an extent that he was known as the "Angel of Judgment," and he had a deeply negative view of Jews. To be sure, Anthony himself preached so strongly in southern France against the Albigensians, who depreciated the goodness of the body, that he was often called the "Hammer of Heretics" there.

A twelfth category is that of royal saints who were devoted to the poor: Edward the Confessor [October 13], an eleventh-century English king; Margaret of Scotland [November 16], an eleventh-century queen of Scotland and patron saint of that country; Elizabeth of Hungary [November 17], a thirteenth-century queen of Hungary; and Louis IX [August 25], who was so personally devout that he became a Franciscan tertiary and is said to have embodied the highest ideals of medieval kingship.

The remaining categories are less easily defined. The thirteenth includes the so-called simple saints, those raised up as a reminder that sanctity does not require great learning or unusual achievement. The two outstanding examples are John Vianney [August 4], the Curé d'Ars, and Theresa of the Child Jesus [October 1], better known as Thérèse of Lisieux and the Little Flower.

A fourteenth category reminds us of the ethnic, cultural, and regional diversity of the saints: Kateri Tekakwitha [July 14], the first Native American to have been beatified; the Peruvian Rose of Lima [August 23], the first saint to be canonized in the Americas; Lawrence Ruiz [September 28], martyred in Japan and the first Filipino to be canonized; Martin de Porres [November 3], a man of mixed racial blood and the patron saint of interracial justice; Mary MacKillop [May 25], foundress of a religious order and soon the first native-born Australian saint; Mary Margaret d'Youville [December 23], foundress of a religious order in Canada and the first native-born Canadian saint; Cyril and Methodius [February 14], "apostles of the Slavs" and co–patron saints of Europe; and, in a kind of special subcategory, Our Lady of Guadalupe [December 12], patron saint of the Americas and of Mexico.

A fifteenth category includes those saints whose canonizations legitimated the new devotions they inspired: Margaret Mary Alacoque [October 16], a seventeenth-century Visitation nun and visionary who initiated the Church's enduring devotion to the Sacred Heart of Jesus; and Catherine Labouré [November 28], a nineteenth-century Sister of Charity and visionary who inspired the devotion to the Miraculous Medal.

A sixteenth category is composed of women who collaborated closely with key male saints in the founding of religious communities and/or in advancement of the Church's missionary and ministerial work. The three most prominent collaborators were Clare of Assisi, with Francis, in the founding of the Poor Clares in the thirteenth century; Louise de Marillac, with Vincent de Paul, in the founding of the

Daughters of Charity in the seventeenth century; and Jane Frances de Chantal [December 12], with Francis de Sales, in the founding of the Visitation Sisters also in the seventeenth century. There were others as well: Macrina the Younger [July 19], who was of great support to her brother Gregory of Nyssa [January 10], assisted him in clarifying his own theological reflections, and inspired his treatise *De anima et resurrectione* (Lat., "On the Soul and the Resurrection"); and Paula [January 26], a wealthy Roman widow who accompanied her close friend Jerome [September 30] to Egypt and the Holy Land, funded a monastery for men and a convent for women along with facilities for pilgrims, and assisted him with her knowledge of Greek.

A closely related seventeenth category is of wives and mothers: Helen [August 18], the mother of the emperor Constantine, who was generous to the poor, reached out to those in prison, and made a pilgrimage to the Holy Land, where she devoted herself to the building of basilicas and shrines, the endowing of convents, the collecting of relics, and the care of the poor, orphans, and prisoners; Monica [August 27], the mother of Augustine [August 28], who assiduously looked after her son's spiritual welfare and supported him in his conversion and baptism; and Margaret of Scotland, wife of King Malcolm III, with whom she had six sons and two daughters, who used her influence at court to promote the reform of the Church in Scotland, founded monasteries, provided lodgings for pilgrims, and served the poor—all while raising her large family.

The eighteenth and final category is that of saints whose cults are larger than themselves, so to speak. In other words, their cults are disproportionate to the limited historical knowledge we have of their lives and/or are promoted more because of what they represent to certain constituencies within the Church (whether based on gender, religious order, or particular devotion) than because of their well-documented spiritual and pastoral achievements. Included in the first subcategory are Joseph [March 19], Jude [October 28], the obscure apostle who is considered the saint of "last resort" for seemingly hopeless causes; Lawrence [August 10], the celebrated third-century Roman martyr; and Nicholas of Myra, the fourth-century bishop who is the basis of the Santa Claus myth. Included in the second subcategory are: Cecilia [November 22]; Agatha [February 5]; Thecla of Iconium [September 23], and Brigid of Kildare [February 1]; Valentine [February 14], Blase [February 2]; Christopher [July 25]; Januarius [September 19], whose preserved blood is said to liquefy three times a year in the Naples cathedral; and Aloysius

Gonzaga [June 21] and Stanislaus Kostka [November 13], two Jesuit novices who were canonized on the same day in 1726.

No single category by itself can convey the breadth and depth of Christian discipleship. Indeed, even when these categories are taken together, that is to say, comprehensively, the reality of Christian holiness remains transcendent to every attempt at description and definition. But in taking the various categories together, one runs far less of a risk of misreading and ultimately distorting the nature of sanctity. It is an all-embracing, all-encompassing, and fully inclusive reality. To choose or to prefer one aspect of it over all others is to lapse into a kind of heresy, which is, in the etymology of the word, a form of "selective perception." In the end, holiness is catholic in content and scope.

Great Saints of History

1. *The Blessed Virgin Mary.* Mary, the Mother of God [January 1], is in a class by herself. Immaculately conceived [December 8], she freely assented to becoming the virgin mother of the Lord [March 25] and, after a life of faithful discipleship, she was taken bodily into heaven [August 15] to enjoy the eternal companionship of her Son. As Vatican II's Dogmatic Constitution on the Church declared: "Mary has by grace been exalted above all angels and humanity to a place after her Son, as the most holy mother of God who was involved in the mysteries of Christ: she is rightly honored with a special cult by the church" (n. 66).[28]

2, 3. *Peter and Paul.* Peter and Paul [June 29] were the two greatest missionaries of the apostolic period. Peter, the chief of the Twelve, was the apostle to the Jews. Together with Paul, he was the foundation on which the church of Rome was established.[29] Paul was the apostle to the Gentiles and undoubtedly the greatest missionary of all time.

4, 5. *James and John.* James [July 25], his brother John [December 27], and Peter were, according to the synoptic Gospels, among Jesus' closest followers. James was also the first apostle to be martyred. John, the traditional author of the Fourth Gospel and the self-described "disciple . . . whom Jesus loved" (John 21:20), is listed in Acts as second to Peter among the disciples in the upper room (1:13), and he stood with Jesus' mother at the foot of the cross, where Jesus commended them to one another (John 19:25–27).

6. *Mary Magdalene.* Mary Magdalene [July 22] is the most prominent female disciple of Jesus in the New Testament, except for the

Blessed Virgin Mary herself. Indeed, Mary Magdalene fulfilled the primary criterion for apostleship, namely, the witnessing of the Resurrection (Acts 1:22). In Matthew (28:1–20), John (20:1–29), and the appendix to Mark's Gospel (16:9–20), she, not Peter, is the primary witness to the Resurrection.

7. *Francis of Assisi.* Francis [October 4] is, like the Blessed Virgin Mary, in a class by himself among the saints. The founder of one of the two great mendicant orders, he is considered by many, including even non-Christians, as the archetypical saint, embodying in his own life and ministry the essence of the gospel of kindness, mercy, and compassion for all of God's creatures and for the whole of creation.

8. *Ignatius of Loyola.* One of the most important elements of the Catholic Counter-Reformation was the founding of the Society of Jesus. Ignatius of Loyola [July 31] amply demonstrated the truth of Thomas Aquinas's insight that action flowing from contemplation is spiritually and pastorally more fruitful than contemplation alone or action alone. Ignatius was a mystic and doer of the highest sort. His company and its many saints stand as his noble legacy.

9. *Dominic.* The founder of one of the two great mendicant orders, Dominic [August 8] initiated a movement that combined a vocation of poverty and of ministry to the poor with that of scholarship and of ministry to students. His dying words listed his bequests to his friars: "Practice charity in common; remain humble; stay poor willingly." His legacy, like that of Ignatius of Loyola, is embodied in his order and in the many great saints it has given to the Church.

10. *Benedict of Nursia.* The growth of monasticism is one of the most important developments in the history of the Church, for which Benedict of Nursia [July 11] deserves the greatest credit. He never became a priest, nor did he intend to found a new religious order. Nevertheless, he influenced not only the flowering of Western monasticism, but of Western civilization itself.

11. *Francis Xavier.* The greatest missionary of the postapostolic period and one of the original Jesuits, Francis Xavier [December 3] carried the gospel in a heroically evangelical manner to India, Japan, and China, where he died off the mainland at the age of forty-six.

12, 13. *Thomas Aquinas* and *Augustine of Hippo.* These are the two greatest Catholic theologians of all time. Thomas Aquinas [January 28] demonstrated in his own life and work that the worlds of scholarship and faith are not incompatible with one another. The theologian of grace par excellence, he also insisted that grace is consistent with nature, building upon it, and bringing it to its fullness. Augustine [August 28] was equally brilliant, though less of a synthesizer than Aquinas. Unlike Aquinas, he was a bishop, who did his theology in a pastoral setting in response to pastoral needs. He also had a greater influence than Aquinas on Protestant theology.

14. *Teresa of Ávila.* One of the greatest mystics in church history and also one of the Church's most courageous reformers, Teresa of Ávila [October 15] was the foundress of the Discalced Carmelites and one of the first two women (with Catherine of Siena) to be named a Doctor of the Church. For her, the test of growth in the mystical life is love of neighbor. Although she was profoundly contemplative, she led an active life, not only as a reformer of Carmelite life, but also as an adviser to and correspondent with countless people of every station in life.

15. *Francis de Sales.* No saint did more to incorporate the laity into the mission and ministries of the Church and then to provide a spirituality to undergird their apostolates than Francis de Sales [January 24]. The central message of his *Introduction to the Devout Life* was a novel one for the times, namely, that the way of spiritual perfection is not for only the elite few and does not require great austerities or withdrawal from the everyday life of the world. Nevertheless, his influence was also felt in the several religious orders that were founded under his patronage, including the Missionaries of St. Francis de Sales, the Oblates of St. Francis de Sales, the Salesians of Don Bosco, and the Sisters of St. Joseph.

16. *Vincent de Paul.* No ministry is more central to the demands of the gospel than the ministry to the poor and the powerless, the sick and the aged, and no saint is more closely identified with that ministry than Vincent de Paul [September 27], founder of the Vincentians and cofounder of the Sisters of Charity. Vincent never allowed forms (enclosure, habit, communal prayer, etc.) to get in the way of substance. He would tell his sisters: "For a cell, your rented room; for your chapel, the parish church; for a cloister, the streets of the city; for enclosure, obedience. . . . Fear of God is your grill, and modesty your veil."

17. *Gregory the Great.* One of the greatest popes in history, Gregory the Great [September 3] was at once an outstanding administrator and visionary pastor. Even in his own lifetime his *Pastoral Care* was translated into Greek and Anglo-Saxon. He set out therein a vision of pastoral care that is adapted to the needs of the people and is rooted in personal example and preaching, with a fine balance between the contemplative and active aspects of all ministry.

18. *Basil the Great.* One of the outstanding bishops in all of church history, Basil [January 2] influenced the development of monasticism in both East and West. Indeed, nearly all of the monks and nuns of the Greek Church to this day follow his longer Rule, which emphasizes community life, liturgical prayer, and manual work. It is sufficiently flexible to allow for almsgiving and for work in hospitals and guest houses, without sacrifice of a strongly contemplative dimension. He was himself an effective preacher, a gifted theologian, and a generous benefactor of the poor.

19. *Catherine of Siena.* A profound and theologically gifted mystic in her own right and an agent of church reform focused principally on the papacy, Catherine of Siena [April 29] was the first layperson and one of the first two women to be named a Doctor of the Church. She also nursed the sick, cared for victims of plague and famine, and preached widely, even as a layperson, calling people to reform and repentance in the spirit of Christ crucified.

20. *Anthony of Egypt.* Generally regarded as the founder of monasticism, Anthony of Egypt [January 17] is revered in the East as the "first master of the desert and the pinnacle of holy monks." He also influenced the Camaldolese monks and the Carthusians, as well as the Little Brothers (and Sisters) of Jesus.

Conclusion

In the final accounting, saints are individuals, not simply types or mental constructs. In their own ways, they incarnate the reality of Jesus Christ in human stories lived by real people, in real places and circumstances, and at particular times in history. In other words, they manifest holiness in the concrete texture of ordinary human existence. They demonstrate that one can be a faithful disciple in this way rather than that, and that there are many paths to sanctity and many expressions of it.

At the same time, these individual saints did not consciously seek to be holy or saintly, but simply to be themselves in the light of the gospel. One is reminded of Dorothy Day's sense of irritation when others referred to her as a saint. "When they call you a saint," she often said, "it means basically that you're not to be taken seriously" or that you are capable of doing just about anything: "Dorothy can do that; she's a saint."[30] The implication was that things come more easily to saints than to ordinary people. But the point is that saints *are* ordinary people who happen to live the gospel in extraordinary ways.

PART VI

TABLES

Feast Days of the Saints

THE LITURGICAL POINT OF REFERENCE IS ALWAYS THE GENERAL ROMAN Calendar. Names in italic are on the General Roman Calendar. Other liturgical calendars, including the Proper Calendar for the (Roman Catholic) Dioceses of the U.S.A., are given in parentheses. If data appears in parentheses immediately after an italic entry, it signifies that the feast is also observed in another Christian tradition or religious order, in addition to the General Roman Calendar. "Orthodox" refers to the Russian and Greek Orthodox Churches in particular, but may include other Orthodox Churches as well. "East" refers to more than the Orthodox Churches. "Anglicans" refers to more than the Church of England. Saintly figures, like Mohandas Gandhi or Dorothy Day, who have not formally been recognized as such by the Catholic Church are not included, even though they are mentioned in the entries for their dates.

January

1. *Solemnity of Mary, Mother of God* (Orthodox, as the Circumcision of Jesus; Anglicans, as the Holy Name of Our Lord Jesus Christ; Lutherans, as the Name of Jesus)
2. *Basil the Great and Gregory Nazianzen, bishops and Doctors of the Church* (Church of England; Episcopal Church, USA, Gregory on May 9; Lutherans, Basil and Gregory on June 14; Orthodox, Basil on Jan. 1 and 30; East, Gregory on Jan. 25 and 30)
3. Geneviève of Paris, virgin
4. Elizabeth Ann Seton, widow and foundress (Proper Calendar for the Dioceses of the U.S.A.)
5. John Nepomucene Neumann, bishop (Proper Calendar for the Dioceses of the U.S.A.)

6. Peter of Canterbury, abbot; Bl. André Bessette, religious (Proper Calendar for the Dioceses of the U.S.A.)
7. *Raymond of Peñafort, priest*
8. Apollinaris the Apologist, bishop; Lawrence Giustiniani, bishop
9. Adrian of Canterbury, abbot
10. Gregory of Nyssa, bishop (East, Benedictines, Cistercians; Lutherans, June 14; Episcopal Church, USA, March 10); William of Bourges, abbot (Cistercians)
11. Theodosius the Cenobiarch (Orthodox)
12. Benedict Biscop, bishop (Church of England); Aelred of Rievaulx, monk (Cistercians, Anglicans)
13. *Hilary of Poitiers, bishop and Doctor of the Church* (Anglicans); Remigius, bishop (Anglicans, Oct. 1)
14. Sava of Serbia, bishop (Orthodox); Bl. Odoric of Pordenone, friar (Franciscans)
15. Paul the Hermit (East); Ita of Killeedy, abbess (Ireland); Maur and Placid (Benedictines)
16. Honoratus of Arles, bishop; Berard and companions, martyrs (Franciscans)
17. *Anthony of Egypt, abbot* (Orthodox, Anglicans)
18. Margaret of Hungary, nun (Dominicans)
19. Wulfstan, bishop (Anglicans); Marguerite Bourgeoys, foundress (Benedictines, Cistercians); Macarius the Elder, monk (East); Henry of Uppsala, bishop (Lutherans)
20. *Fabian, pope and martyr; Sebastian, martyr* (East, Dec. 18); Euthymius the Great, bishop (Orthodox)
21. *Agnes, virgin and martyr;* Meinrad, hermit
22. *Vincent of Saragossa, deacon and martyr;* Vincent Pallotti, founder
23. Ildephonsus of Toledo, bishop; Bl. Henry Suso, mystic (Dominicans)
24. *Francis de Sales, bishop and Doctor of the Church* (Church of England)
25. *Conversion of Paul, apostle* (Anglicans)
26. *Timothy, bishop and martyr, and Titus, bishop* (Anglicans, Lutherans; Orthodox, Timothy on Jan. 22, Titus on Aug. 25); Alberic, Robert of Molesmes, and Stephen Harding, monks (Cistercians, Benedictines); Paula, widow
27. *Angela Merici, virgin*
28. *Thomas Aquinas, priest and Doctor of the Church* (Anglicans)
29. Gildas, abbot

30. Hyacintha Mariscotti, foundress (Franciscans); Bl. Joseph Columba Marmion, abbot
31. *John Bosco, priest* (Church of England)

February

1. Brigid of Kildare, abbess (Ireland, Anglicans)
2. *Presentation of the Lord* (Orthodox, Anglicans, Lutherans); Cornelius the Centurion (Episcopal Church, USA, Feb. 4)
3. *Blase, bishop and martyr* (Russian Orthodox, Feb. 11); *Ansgar, bishop* (Anglicans, Lutherans); Simeon and Anna (Orthodox)
4. Rabanus Maurus, abbot and bishop
5. *Agatha, virgin and martyr* (Orthodox)
6. *Paul Miki and companions, martyrs* (Anglicans, Lutherans); Amand, monk and bishop; Dorothy, martyr
7. Colette, virgin (Franciscans)
8. *Jerome Emiliani, founder*
9. Apollonia, virgin and martyr; Miguel Febres Cordero, religious brother
10. *Scholastica, virgin* (Church of England)
11. *Our Lady of Lourdes*
12. Benedict of Aniane, abbot (Benedictines, Feb. 11)
13. Catherine de' Ricci, virgin (Dominicans, Feb. 4); Bl. Jordan of Saxony, friar (Dominicans)
14. *Cyril, monk, and Methodius, bishop* (Anglicans, Lutherans; East, May 11); Valentine, martyr
15. Sigfrid, bishop (Church of England); Claude La Colombière, priest (Jesuits); Onesimus, bishop (Orthodox)
16. Juliana, virgin and martyr; Maruthas, bishop
17. *Seven Founders of the Order of Servites*
18. Colman of Lindisfarne, bishop (Orthodox); Theotonius, abbot; Bl. John of Fiesole (Fra Angelico), painter (Dominicans)
19. Conrad of Piacenza, hermit (Franciscans)
20. Wulfric, priest and hermit
21. *Peter Damian, bishop and Doctor of the Church*
22. *Chair of Peter, apostle;* Margaret of Cortona, foundress
23. *Polycarp, bishop and martyr* (Orthodox, Anglicans, Lutherans)
24. Ethelbert of Kent, king
25. Walburga, abbess
26. Porphyry of Gaza, bishop (Orthodox)

27. Gabriel Possenti, religious
28. Oswald of Worcester, bishop

March

1. David of Wales, bishop (Anglicans)
2. Chad of Lichfield, abbot and bishop (Anglicans)
3. Katharine Drexel, foundress (Proper Calendar for the Dioceses of the U.S.A.); Cunegund, empress and nun
4. *Casimir, prince*
5. John Joseph of the Cross, religious
6. Chrodegang of Metz, bishop
7. *Perpetua and Felicity, martyrs* (Anglicans, Lutherans)
8. *John of God, religious;* Stephen of Obazine, abbot (Cistercians)
9. *Frances of Rome, religious;* Dominic Savio
10. Forty Martyrs of Sebastea (Orthodox); John Ogilvie, martyr (Jesuits, Oct. 14)
11. Eulogius of Córdoba, martyr
12. Maximilian, martyr
13. Euphrasia of Constantinople, virgin; Ansovinus, bishop; Leander of Seville, bishop
14. Matilda, queen
15. Louise de Marillac, widow and foundress; Clement Mary Hofbauer, religious
16. Abraham Kidunaia, hermit
17. *Patrick, bishop* (Orthodox, Anglicans, Lutherans)
18. *Cyril of Jerusalem, bishop and Doctor of the Church* (Orthodox, Anglicans)
19. *Joseph, husband of Mary* (Anglicans, Lutherans; East, first Sunday after Christmas; Russian Orthodox, Dec. 27)
20. Cuthbert, bishop (Anglicans)
21. Nicholas of Flüe, hermit
22. Nicholas Owen, martyr
23. *Turibius of Mongrovejo, bishop*
24. Catherine of Sweden, abbess
25. *The Annunciation of the Lord* (Orthodox, Anglicans, Lutherans); Dismas, the Good Thief; Margaret Clitherow, martyr; Lucy Filippini, foundress
26. Ludger of Münster, bishop
27. Rupert, bishop

28. Hesychius of Jerusalem, priest (Orthodox)
29. Jonas and Barachisius, martyrs
30. John Climacus, abbot (Orthodox)
31. Stephen of Mar Saba, monk (Orthodox)

April

1. Hugh of Grenoble, bishop; Mary the Egyptian, hermit (Orthodox)
2. *Francis of Paola, hermit*
3. Richard of Chichester, bishop (Episcopal Church, USA; Church of England, June 16)
4. *Isidore of Seville, bishop and Doctor of the Church*
5. *Vincent Ferrer, priest*
6. Peter of Verona, martyr (Dominicans, June 4)
7. *John Baptist de La Salle, priest*
8. Julie Billiart, foundress; Walter of Pontoise, abbot
9. Waldetrude, anchoress
10. Magdalen of Canossa, foundress
11. *Stanislaus, bishop and martyr*
12. Teresa of Los Andes, virgin
13. *Martin I, pope and martyr* (Orthodox, April 14)
14. Bl. Peter González, friar (Dominicans)
15. Bl. Damien de Veuster, priest
16. Bernadette Soubirous, nun
17. Bl. Clare of Pisa, nun (Dominicans); Benedict Joseph Labre, pilgrim (Franciscans)
18. Bl. Mary of the Incarnation, nun
19. Leo IX, pope; Alphege of Canterbury, bishop and martyr (Orthodox, Anglicans)
20. Agnes of Montepulciano, nun (Dominicans)
21. *Anselm of Canterbury, bishop and Doctor of the Church* (Anglicans, Lutherans)
22. Theodore of Sykeon, bishop (Orthodox)
23. *George, martyr* (Orthodox, Church of England); *Adalbert of Prague, bishop and martyr*
24. *Fidelis of Sigmaringen, priest and martyr*
25. *Mark, Evangelist* (Orthodox, Anglicans, Lutherans)
26. Stephen of Perm, bishop (Orthodox)
27. Zita, virgin

28. *Peter Chanel, priest and martyr* (Church of England); *Louis Grignion de Montfort, founder*
29. *Catherine of Siena, virgin and Doctor of the Church* (Anglicans, Lutherans)
30. *Pius V, pope;* Adjutor, monk

May

1. *Joseph the Worker*
2. *Athanasius, bishop and Doctor of the Church* (Orthodox, Anglicans, Lutherans; East, Jan. 18)
3. *Philip and James (the Less), apostles* (Anglicans, Lutherans, May 1; Orthodox, Philip on Nov. 14, James on Oct. 9)
4. Florian, martyr
5. Gotthard of Hildesheim, abbot and bishop; Irene of Thessalonica, martyr (Orthodox)
6. Marian and James, martyrs
7. John of Beverley, bishop
8. Peter of Tarentaise, bishop (Cistercians, Sept. 12); Julian of Norwich, anchoress (Anglicans)
9. Pachomius, abbot (Coptis; Orthodox, Cistercians, May 15); Catherine of Bologna, prioress (Franciscans)
10. John of Ávila, priest
11. Ignatius of Laconi, religious; Odo, Maiolus, Odilo, Hugh, and Peter the Venerable, abbots (Benedictines, Cistercians); Mamertus of Vienne, bishop
12. *Nereus and Achilleus, martyrs; Pancras, martyr*
13. Andrew Fournet, founder; Our Lady of Fátima
14. *Matthias, apostle* (Church of England; Orthodox, Aug. 9); Mary Mazzarello, foundress
15. Isidore the Farmer
16. Andrew Bobola, martyr; Margaret of Cortona, penitent (Franciscans); Simon Stock, friar (Carmelites); Brendan of Clonfert, abbot (Ireland); John Nepomucen, martyr; Peregrine of Auxerre, bishop
17. Paschal Baylon, religious
18. *John I, pope and martyr;* Felix of Cantalice, religious (Franciscans); Eric of Sweden, king (Lutherans)
19. Dunstan of Canterbury, abbot and bishop (Anglicans, Lutherans); Celestine V, pope (Benedictines, Cistercians); Ivo Hélory of Kermartin, priest

20. *Bernardino of Siena, priest*
21. Godric of Finchale, hermit; Constantine, emperor, and Helen (Orthodox)
22. Rita of Cascia, widow and nun; Joachima of Vedruna, foundress (Carmelites)
23. John Baptist Rossi, priest
24. Simeon Stylites the Younger, hermit (Orthodox); Vincent of Lérins, monk
25. *Venerable Bede, priest and Doctor of the Church* (Anglicans); *Gregory VII, pope* (Benedictines, Cistercians, May 26); *Mary Magdalene de Pazzi, virgin* (Benedictines, Cistercians, May 26); Madeleine Sophia Barat, foundress; Bl. Mary MacKillop, foundress (Australia and New Zealand)
26. *Philip Neri, priest* (Anglicans)
27. *Augustine of Canterbury, bishop* (Anglicans, May 26)
28. Germanus of Paris, bishop; Mariana of Jesus de Paredes, mystic (Franciscans); Bl. Lanfranc of Bec, bishop (Anglicans); Bernard of Montjoux, priest
29. Maximinus of Trier, bishop; Theodosia of Constantinople, nun (Orthodox); Bona of Pisa, pilgrim and mystic
30. Joan of Arc, virgin (Church of England); Ferdinand of Castile, king; Isaac of Constantinople, abbot (Orthodox); Dymphna
31. *The Visitation of the Blessed Virgin Mary* (Anglicans, Lutherans)

June

1. *Justin, martyr* (Orthodox, Anglicans, Lutherans)
2. *Marcellinus and Peter, martyrs;* Nicephorus, bishop (Orthodox); Erasmus (Elmo), bishop and martyr
3. *Charles Lwanga and companions, martyrs* (Anglicans); Bl. John XXIII, pope (Lutherans); Kevin, abbot (Ireland)
4. Metrophanes, bishop (Orthodox); Optatus of Milevis, apologist; Francis Caracciolo, founder
5. *Boniface, bishop and martyr* (Orthodox, Anglicans, Lutherans)
6. *Norbert, bishop*
7. Willibald, bishop; Colman of Dromore, abbot; Bl. Anne of St. Bartholomew, nun (Carmelites)
8. William of York, bishop
9. *Ephrem, deacon and Doctor of the Church* (Church of England; Episcopal Church, USA, June 10; Orthodox, Jan. 28); Columba of Iona, abbot (Anglicans, Lutherans)

10. Landericus of Paris, bishop; Ithamar of Rochester, bishop; Bogumilus, bishop; Bl. John Dominici, bishop (Dominicans)
11. *Barnabas, apostle* (Orthodox, Anglicans, Lutherans); Rembert, bishop; Paola Frassinetti, foundress
12. Onouphrios, hermit (Orthodox); Peter of Mount Athos, hermit (Orthodox); Alice, nun (Cistercians)
13. *Anthony of Padua, priest and Doctor of the Church*
14. Methodius of Constantinople, patriarch (Orthodox)
15. Vitus and companions, martyrs
16. Lutgardis, nun (Cistercians)
17. Rainerius of Pisa, hermit; Botulf, abbot
18. Gregory Barbarigo, bishop
19. *Romuald, abbot;* Juliana Falconieri, foundress; Gervase and Protase, martyrs
20. Alban, martyr (Anglicans, June 22)
21. *Aloysius Gonzaga, religious*
22. *Paulinus of Nola, bishop; John Fisher, bishop and martyr* (Church of England, July 6); *Thomas More, martyr* (Church of England, July 6); Eusebius of Samosata, bishop (Orthodox)
23. Etheldreda, abbess (Church of England); Joseph Cafasso, priest; Bl. Innocent V, pope (Dominicans)
24. *Birth of John the Baptist* (Orthodox, Anglicans, Lutherans; Orthodox, also Jan. 6)
25. Prosper of Aquitaine, theologian
26. John and Paul, martyrs; David of Thessalonike, hermit (Orthodox)
27. *Cyril of Alexandria, bishop and Doctor of the Church* (Orthodox, Athanasius and Cyril on Jan. 18, Cyril alone on June 9); Sampson the Hospitable of Constantinople, priest and physician (Orthodox)
28. *Irenaeus, bishop and martyr* (Anglicans, Lutherans; East, Aug. 23)
29. *Peter and Paul, apostles* (East, Anglicans, Lutherans)
30. *First Martyrs of the Church of Rome;* Bl. Raymond Lull, missionary; Theobald of Provins, hermit

July

1. Bl. Junipero Serra, priest (Proper Calendar for the Dioceses of the U.S.A.)
2. Bernardino Realino, Francis Regis, and Francis Jerome, priests (Jesuits)

3. *Thomas, apostle* (Church of England; Orthodox, Oct. 6; Episcopal Church, USA, Lutherans, Dec. 21)
4. *Elizabeth of Portugal, queen;* Ulrich of Augsburg, bishop; Andrew of Crete, bishop (Orthodox)
5. *Anthony Mary Zaccaria, priest*
6. *Maria Goretti, virgin and martyr*
7. Bl. Benedict XI, pope (Dominicans)
8. Aquila and Prisca, martyrs; Procopius, martyr (Orthodox); Bl. Eugenius III, pope (Cistercians); Kilian, bishop
9. Martyrs of Gorkum (Franciscans, Dominicans); Pancratius, martyr (Orthodox)
10. Veronica Giuliani, abbess (Franciscans); Canute, king
11. *Benedict of Nursia, abbot* (Anglicans, Lutherans; Russian Orthodox, March 14; Benedictines, and Cistercians, also March 21); Olga, grand duchess (Orthodox)
12. John Gualbert, abbot (Benedictines, and Cistercians, also March 21); John Jones and John Wall, martyrs (Franciscans)
13. *Henry II, king;* Mildred, abbess
14. *Camillus de Lellis, priest;* Bl. Kateri Tekakwitha, virgin (Proper Calendar for the Dioceses of the U.S.A.)
15. *Bonaventure, bishop and Doctor of the Church* (Church of England); Vladimir of Kiev, prince (Orthodox, Lutherans)
16. *Our Lady of Mount Carmel;* Mary-Magdalen Postel, foundress
17. Hedwig of Poland, queen
18. Pambo, hermit (Orthodox)
19. Macrina the Younger, virgin (Orthodox)
20. Frumentius, bishop (East, Nov. 30). (This is also the former feast day of Margaret of Antioch, martyr, who is still commemorated by the Church of England, but who almost certainly never existed.)
21. *Lawrence of Brindisi, priest and Doctor of the Church*
22. *Mary Magdalene, disciple* (Orthodox, Anglicans, Lutherans)
23. *Bridget of Sweden, religious* (Church of England, Lutherans); John Cassian, monk
24. Declan, bishop
25. *James (the Great), apostle* (Anglicans, Lutherans; Orthodox, Apr. 30); Christopher, martyr
26. *Joachim and Anne, parents of Mary* (Anglicans; Orthodox, Sept. 9)
27. Pantaleon, martyr (Orthodox)
28. Prochorus, Nicanor, Timon, and Parmenas, deacons
29. *Martha, disciple* (Anglicans, Lutherans); Olaf, king (Lutherans)

30. *Peter Chrysologus, bishop and Doctor of the Church*
31. *Ignatius of Loyola, priest* (Anglicans)

August

1. *Alphonsus Liguori, bishop and Doctor of the Church*
2. *Eusebius of Vercelli, bishop; Peter Julian Eymard, priest;* Bl. Joan of Aza (Dominicans)
3. Lydia, disciple
4. *John Vianney, priest* (Church of England)
5. *Dedication of St. Mary Major;* Oswald, king (Church of England)
6. *Transfiguration* (Anglicans, Orthodox); Justus and Pastor, martyrs
7. *Sixtus II, pope, and companions, martyrs; Cajetan, priest;* Albert of Sicily, hermit (Carmelites); Afra, martyr
8. *Dominic, priest* (Anglicans)
9. Teresa Benedicta of the Cross, martyr
10. *Lawrence, deacon and martyr* (Orthodox, Anglicans, Lutherans)
11. *Clare of Assisi, virgin* (Anglicans)
12. Euplus, martyr (Orthodox, Aug. 11)
13. *Pontian, pope and martyr, and Hippolytus, priest and martyr* (East, Jan. 30); Maximus the Confessor, monk (Orthodox, Jan. 21)
14. *Maximilian Maria Kolbe, priest and martyr* (Anglicans)
15. *Assumption of Mary* (Orthodox as "Dormition"; Anglicans and Lutherans as feast of Blessed Virgin Mary); Tarcisius, martyr
16. *Stephen of Hungary, king*
17. Joan of the Cross, foundress; Hyacinth of Poland, friar (Dominicans); Roch, hermit (Franciscans); Myron of Cyzicus, martyr (Orthodox)
18. Helen, empress (East, May 21)
19. *John Eudes, priest;* Bernard Tolomei, abbot (Orthodox, Cistercians); Louis of Anjou, bishop (Franciscans)
20. *Bernard of Clairvaux, abbot and Doctor of the Church* (Anglicans, Lutherans)
21. *Pius X, pope*
22. *Queenship of Mary;* Philip Benizi, founder
23. *Rose of Lima, virgin*
24. *Bartholomew, apostle* (Anglicans, Lutherans; East, June 11)
25. *Louis IX, king; Joseph Calasanz, priest;* Genesius, martyr
26. Elizabeth Bichier des Ages, foundress; Teresa of Jesus, foundress

27. *Monica, widow* (Church of England; Episcopal Church, USA, May 4); Poemen, abbot (Orthodox)
28. *Augustine of Hippo, bishop and Doctor of the Church* (Anglicans, Lutherans)
29. *Beheading of John the Baptist, martyr* (Orthodox, Church of England); Bl. Mary of the Cross, foundress
30. Margaret Ward, martyr; Guérin and Amadeus, bishops (Cistercians); Bl. Ildefonsus Schuster, abbot; Fiacre, hermit (Ireland, France, Sept. 1)
31. Joseph of Arimathea and Nicodemus (Episcopal Church, USA, Joseph of Arimathea on Aug. 1); Aidan, bishop (Anglicans); Raymond Nonnatus, friar

September

1. Giles, abbot (Church of England); Simeon Stylites the Elder, hermit (Orthodox); Teresa Margaret Redi, nun (Carmelites)
2. Mamas, martyr (Orthodox); John the Faster, patriarch (Orthodox)
3. *Gregory the Great, pope and Doctor of the Church* (Church of England; Episcopal Church, USA, Lutherans, March 12)
4. Rose of Viterbo, virgin (Franciscans); Bablyas, bishop (Orthodox)
5. Bertinus, abbot
6. Bl. Bertrand de Garrigues, friar (Dominicans)
7. Sozon, martyr (Orthodox); Regina, martyr; Mark Körösi, Stephen Pongrácz, and Melchior Grodecz, martyrs (Jesuits)
8. *Birth of Mary* (Orthodox, Church of England); Bl. Antoine Frédéric Ozanam, founder
9. Peter Claver, priest (Proper Calendar for the Dioceses of the U.S.A.)
10. Nicholas of Tolentino, friar
11. Protus and Hyacinth, martyrs
12. Ailbe, bishop
13. *John Chrysostom, bishop and Doctor of the Church* (Church of England; Orthodox, Nov. 13)
14. *Triumph of the Cross* (Orthodox, Anglicans, Lutherans)
15. *Our Lady of Sorrows;* Catherine of Genoa, mystic
16. *Cornelius, pope, and Cyprian of Carthage, bishop, martyrs* (Cyprian alone: Church of England, Sept. 15; Episcopal Church, USA, Sept. 13); Ninian, bishop (Anglicans)

17. *Robert Bellarmine, bishop and Doctor of the Church;* Hildegard of Bingen, abbess (Anglicans, Benedictines); Albert of Jerusalem, bishop (Carmelites)
18. Joseph of Cupertino, priest (Franciscans); John Massias, religious (Dominicans)
19. *Januarius, bishop and martyr* (Orthodox, Apr. 21); Theodore of Tarsus, bishop (Anglicans)
20. *Andrew Kim Taegõn, Paul Chõng Hasang, and companions, martyrs;* Francis Mary of Camparosso, religious (Franciscans)
21. *Matthew, apostle and Evangelist* (Anglicans, Lutherans; East, Nov. 16)
22. Thomas of Villanova, bishop; Phocas of Sinope, hermit (Orthodox); Maurice, soldier
23. Thecla of Iconium, virgin (Orthodox, Sept. 24); Adomonán of Iona, abbot
24. Gerard Sagredo, martyr
25. Sergius of Radonezh, abbot (Orthodox, Anglicans, Lutherans); Finnbarr, abbot; Ceolfrith, abbot
26. *Cosmas and Damian, martyrs* (Orthodox, July 1, Nov. 1); Teresa Couderc, foundress
27. *Vincent de Paul, priest* (Church of England)
28. *Wenceslaus, martyr; Lawrence Ruiz and companions, martyrs;* martyrs of China
29. *Michael, Gabriel, and Raphael, archangels* (Anglicans, Lutherans; Orthodox, Nov. 8)
30. *Jerome, priest and Doctor of the Church* (Anglicans, Lutherans); Gregory the Illuminator, bishop (Orthodox; Episcopal Church, USA, March 23)

October

1. *Theresa of the Child Jesus, virgin and Doctor of the Church*
2. *Guardian angels*
3. Francis Borgia, priest (Jesuits); Thomas of Hereford, bishop (Anglicans)
4. *Francis of Assisi, friar* (Anglicans, Lutherans)
5. Bl. Raymond of Capua, priest (Dominicans); Maria Faustina Kowalska, nun
6. *Bruno, priest*; Bl. Mary-Rose Durocher, foundress
7. *Our Lady of the Rosary*

8. Pelagia, virgin (Orthodox)
9. *Denis, bishop, and companions, martyrs* (Church of England); *John Leonardi, priest;* Louis Bertrán, friar (Dominicans)
10. Paulinus of York, bishop
11. Mary Soledad, virgin
12. Wilfrid of York, bishop (Church of England); Seraphin of Montegranaro, religious (Franciscans)
13. Edward the Confessor, king (Church of England)
14. *Callistus I, pope and martyr*
15. *Teresa of Ávila, virgin and Doctor of the Church* (Anglicans)
16. *Hedwig, religious; Margaret Mary Alacoque, virgin;* Longinus, centurion (Orthodox); Gall, monk; Gerard Majella, religious
17. *Ignatius of Antioch, bishop and martyr* (Anglicans, Lutherans; East, Dec. 20)
18. *Luke, Evangelist* (East, Anglicans, Lutherans)
19. *Isaac Jogues, John de Brébeuf, and companions, martyrs; Paul of the Cross, priest* (Proper Calendar for the Dioceses of the U.S.A., Oct. 20)
20. Maria Bertilla Boscardin, nun
21. Hilarion, hermit (Orthodox)
22. Peter of Alcántara, founder (Franciscans)
23. *John of Capistrano, priest;* James of Jerusalem (Orthodox, Episcopal Church, USA, Lutherans); Severinus Boethius, martyr
24. *Anthony Claret, bishop*
25. Forty Martyrs of England and Wales; Crispin and Crispinian, martyrs
26. Cedd, bishop (Church of England); Alfred the Great, king (Anglicans)
27. Bl. Bartholomew of Vicenza, friar (Dominicans); Frumentius, bishop
28. *Simon and Jude, apostles* (Anglicans, Lutherans; Orthodox, Simon, May 10, Jude, June 19)
29. Narcissus of Jerusalem, bishop
30. Bl. Benvenuta of Cividale, virgin (Dominicans)
31. Alphonsus Rodríguez, religious (Jesuits)

November

1. *All Saints* (Anglicans, Lutherans)
2. *All Souls* (Anglicans)
3. *Martin de Porres, religious;* Malachy, bishop; Hubert, bishop

4. *Charles Borromeo, bishop*
5. Zechariah and Elizabeth, parents of John the Baptist (Orthodox, Sept. 15)
6. Paul of Constantinople, bishop (Orthodox)
7. Willibrord, bishop
8. Bl. John Duns Scotus, friar
9. *Dedication of St. John Lateran;* Benen of Armagh, bishop
10. *Leo the Great, pope and Doctor of the Church* (Russian Orthodox, Feb. 18)
11. *Martin of Tours, bishop* (Anglicans); Theodore the Studite, monk (Orthodox; Benedictines, Cistercians, Nov. 12); Mennas, martyr (Orthodox)
12. *Josephat, bishop and martyr*
13. Frances Xavier Cabrini, virgin (Proper Calendar for the Dioceses of the U.S.A., Franciscans); Stanislaus Kostka, religious (Jesuits); Homobonus, layman
14. Lawrence O'Toole, bishop (Ireland); Nicholas Tavelic and companions, martyrs (Franciscans); Joseph Pignatelli, religious (Jesuits); Gregory Palamas, bishop (Orthodox)
15. *Albert the Great, bishop and Doctor of the Church;* Leopold III, duke
16. *Margaret of Scotland, queen* (Anglicans); *Gertrude, virgin*
17. *Elizabeth of Hungary, religious* (Church of England, Nov. 18, Episcopal Church, USA, Nov. 19); Gregory Thaumaturgus, bishop (Orthodox); Hugh of Lincoln, bishop (Anglicans)
18. *Dedication of the Churches of Peter and Paul;* Rose Philippine Duchesne, religious; Odo of Cluny, abbot
19. Mechthilde of Magdeburg, abbess (Benedictines, Cistercians, Church of England); Hilda of Whitby, abbess (Church of England; Episcopal Church, USA, Nov. 18); Agnes of Assisi, abbess (Franciscans)
20. Edmund, king and martyr
21. *Presentation of Mary* (Orthodox)
22. *Cecilia, virgin and martyr* (Church of England); Philemon and Onesimus (Orthodox)
23. *Clement I, pope and martyr* (Anglicans; Greek Orthodox, Nov. 24; Russian Orthodox, Nov. 25); *Columban, abbot;* Bl. Michael Pro (Proper Calendar for the Dioceses of the U.S.A.).
24. *Andrew Dung-Lac and companions, martyrs;* Chrysogonus, martyr
25. Moses of Rome, martyr; Mercurius, martyr (Greek Orthodox;

Russian Orthodox, Nov. 24). (This is also the former feast day of Catherine of Alexandria, martyr, still celebrated by the Orthodox and the Church of England. There is no evidence that she ever existed.)

26. Leonard of Port Maurice, friar (Franciscans); Sylvester Gozzolini, founder (Benedictines); John Berchmans, religious (Jesuits)
27. James the Persian, martyr (Orthodox)
28. Catherine Labouré, virgin; Stephen the Younger, martyr (Orthodox)
29. Saturninus of Toulouse, bishop and martyr (Mozarabic rite, parts of France)
30. *Andrew, apostle* (Orthodox, Anglicans, Lutherans); Cuthbert Mayne, martyr

December

1. Edmund Campion, Ralph Sherwin, Alexander Briant, and Robert Southwell, martyrs (Jesuits); Eligius, bishop
2. Chromatius, bishop
3. *Francis Xavier, priest* (Lutherans)
4. *John Damascene, priest and Doctor of the Church* (Orthodox, Anglicans); Barbara, martyr (Orthodox)
5. Sabas, abbot (Orthodox, Benedictines, Cistercians)
6. *Nicholas of Myra, bishop* (Orthodox, Anglicans, Lutherans)
7. *Ambrose of Milan, bishop and Doctor of the Church* (Orthodox, Anglicans, Lutherans)
8. *Immaculate Conception* (Church of England, as The Conception of the Blessed Virgin Mary; Orthodox, as The Conception by St. Anne of the Most Holy Theotokos, Dec. 9)
9. Bl. Juan Diego (Cuatitlatoatzin), hermit; Peter Fourier, founder
10. Mennas, Hermogenes, and Eugraphus, martyrs (Orthodox); Edward Gennings, Polydore Plasden, John Roberts, Swithin Wells, and Eustace White, martyrs; Eulalia, martyr
11. *Damasus I, pope;* Daniel the Stylite, hermit (Orthodox)
12. Our Lady of Guadalupe (Proper Calendar for the Dioceses of the U.S.A., Franciscans, the Americas); *Jane Frances de Chantal, religious;* Spiridion, bishop (Orthodox)
13. *Lucy, virgin and martyr* (Church of England); Odilia, abbess
14. *John of the Cross, priest and Doctor of the Church* (Church of England, Lutherans); Venantius Fortunatus, bishop

15. Mary di Rosa, foundress; Bl. Frances Schervier, foundress (Franciscans)
16. Adelaide of Burgundy, nun
17. John of Matha, founder; Lazarus (East, May 4)
18. Flannan of Killaloe, bishop; Gatian, bishop; Winnibald, abbot; Samthann, abbot
19. Anastasius I, pope; Bl. Urban V, pope
20. Dominic of Silos, abbot (Dominicans)
21. *Peter Canisius, priest and Doctor of the Church* (Jesuits, Apr. 27)
22. Anastasia, martyr (East)
23. *John of Kanty, priest;* Mary Margaret d'Youville, foundress (Canada); Thorlac of Skalholt, bishop
24. Sharbel Makhlouf, hermit
25. *The Nativity of Our Lord* (Orthodox, Anglicans, Lutherans); Peter Nolasco, founder
26. *Stephen, first martyr* (Anglicans, Lutherans; Orthodox, Dec. 27)
27. *John, apostle and Evangelist* (Anglicans, Lutherans; Orthodox, May 8, Sept. 26)
28. *Holy Innocents, martyrs* (Anglicans, Lutherans; Orthodox, Dec. 29); Gaspar del Bufalo, founder
29. *Thomas Becket, bishop and martyr* (Anglicans)
30. Egwin of Worcester, bishop
31. *Sylvester I, pope* (Orthodox, Jan. 2)

Patron Saints

SAINTS ARE NOT ONLY MODELS OF HOLINESS AND OF CHRISTIAN DIS-cipleship; they are also intercessors with God. For centuries particular saints have been linked in popular devotion with special causes. Some have been designated officially by the Church as the patron saint of a country, occupation, a needy group of people. The existence and wide popularity of this system of heavenly patronage is but one additional indication of the great importance of saints in Catholic life. Unfortunately, it is also an inexact science. Lists of patrons vary from source to source, although the lists are more alike than not.

Adalbert [April 23], Bohemia and Poland
Adjutor [April 30], swimmers and yachtsmen
Agatha [February 5], nurses, firefighters, against earthquakes, volcanic eruptions, and diseases of the breasts
Agnes [January 21], young girls and the Children of Mary
Alban [June 20], refugees
Albert the Great [November 15], scientists and medical technicians
Aloysius Gonzaga [June 21], youth, students in Jesuit colleges and universities
Alphonsus Liguori [August 1], theologians, confessors, and religious vocations
Amand [February 6], innkeepers, wine merchants, and brewers
Ambrose [December 7], bishops, learning, and bees
Anastasius I [December 19], goldsmiths
Andrew [November 30], Russia, Greece, Scotland, fishermen, and sailors
Andrew Bobola [May 16], Poland
Angelico, Fra (John of Fiesole) [February 18], artists

Anne [July 26], Canada, homemakers, widows, women in labor, expectant mothers, childless women, cabinetmakers, miners, and cemeteries
Ansgar [February 3], Denmark, Scandinavia, Germany, and Iceland
Ansovinus [March 13], protector of crops
Anthony Claret [October 24], savings banks and weavers
Anthony of Egypt [January 17], domestic animals, butchers, basket weavers, grave diggers, and those suffering from diseases of the skin
Anthony of Padua [June 13], Brazil, Portugal, searchers of lost articles, travelers, the poor, barren women, and harvests
Apollonia [February 9], dentists and those suffering from toothaches
Augustine of Canterbury [May 27], England
Augustine of Hippo [August 28], theologians, brewers, and printers
Barbara [December 4], architects, builders, stonemasons, prisoners, artillerymen, miners, firefighters, and those in danger of sudden death by lightning and other means
Barnabas [June 11], Cyprus
Bartholomew [August 24], Armenia, tanners, and plasterers
Basil the Great [January 2], Russia and hospital administrators
Bede, the Venerable [May 25], scholars
Benedict Joseph Labre [April 16], the homeless
Benedict of Nursia [July 11], Europe, monks, speleologists, farm workers, and victims of poisoning
Bernard of Clairvaux [August 20], Gibraltar and candle makers
Bernard of Montjoux [May 28], mountain climbers and skiers
Bernardino of Siena [May 20], advertisers, communications personnel, public relations, weavers, fire prevention, and those suffering from hoarseness
Blase [February 3], those with throat ailments and veterinarians
Blessed Virgin Mary (see below)
Bona of Pisa [May 29], flight attendants
Bonaventure [July 15], workers
Boniface [June 5], Germany
Brendan of Clonfort [May 16], sailors and whales
Bridget of Sweden [July 23], Europe, Sweden, and nuns
Brigid of Kildare [February 1], Ireland, scholars, poets, and dairy workers
Bruno [October 6], Ruthenia and the possessed
Camillus de Lellis [July 14], the sick, hospitals, nurses, and nurses associations

Canute [July 10], Denmark
Casimir [March 4], Poland, Lithuania, and Russia
Catherine of Alexandria (Although she is the patroness of many different causes, there is no evidence that she ever existed. Her cult is based entirely on legend. Her feast, formerly on November 25, was suppressed in 1969.)
Catherine of Bologna [May 9], art and artists
Catherine of Siena [April 29], Europe, Italy, and nurses
Catherine of Sweden [March 24], protection against abortion
Cecilia [November 22], musicians, singers, and poets
Celestine V [May 19], bookbinders
Charles Borromeo [November 4], bishops, catechists, and seminarians
Charles Lwanga [June 3], African Catholic youth
Christopher [July 25], travelers, pilgrims, motorists, bus drivers, truck drivers, porters, and sailors
Clare of Assisi [August 11], television, embroiderers, good weather, childbirth, diseases of the eye
Claude La Colombière [February 15], toy makers and sculptors
Clement Mary Hofbauer [March 15], Vienna
Clement of Rome [November 23], marble workers and stonecutters
Columba [June 9], Ireland, Scotland, and poets
Cosmas and Damian [September 26], physicians, surgeons, nurses, dentists, barbers, pharmacists, the sightless, and confectioners
Crispin and Crispinian [October 25], shoemakers
Cunegund [March 3], Lithuania, Poland, and Luxembourg
Cuthbert [March 20], sailors
Cyprian of Carthage [September 16], North Africa and Algeria
Cyril and Methodius [February 14], Europe, Yugoslavia, Moravia, Bohemia, and ecumenists
Damasus I [December 11], archaeologists
David of Wales [March 1], Wales and poets
Denis [October 9], France, the possessed, and those suffering from headaches
Dismas [March 25], prisoners, thieves, and funeral directors
Dominic [August 8], Dominican Republic and astronomers
Dominic Savio [March 9], young boys and choirboys
Dorothy [February 6], gardeners
Dunstan of Canterbury [May 19], goldsmiths, silversmiths, jewelers, locksmiths, and musicians
Dymphna [May 30], the mentally ill and sleepwalkers

Edith Stein (*see* Teresa Benedicta of the Cross)
Edward the Confessor [October 13], England
Eligius [December 1], jewelers, goldsmiths, coin collectors, metalworkers, garage or gas station workers, veterinarians, and horses
Elizabeth of Hungary [November 17], Franciscan tertiaries, Catholic charities, bakers, nurses
Elizabeth of Portugal [July 4], Portugal
Erasmus (Elmo) [June 2], sailors, childbirth, women in labor, and those suffering from stomach and abdominal ailments
Eric of Sweden [May 18], Sweden
Felicity [March 7], barren women
Ferdinand of Castile [May 30], engineers, governors, the poor, and prisoners
Fiacre [August 30], cabdrivers, gardeners, and those suffering from hemorrhoids and venereal disease
Fidelis of Sigmaringen [April 24], lawyers
Florian [May 4], Poland, Austria, and firefighters
Fra Angelico (*see* Angelico, Fra)
Frances of Rome [March 9], motorists and widows
Frances Xavier Cabrini [November 13], hospital administrators and immigrants
Francis Borgia [October 3], Portugal
Francis de Sales [January 24], the Catholic press, writers, journalists, and the hearing impaired
Francis of Assisi [October 4], Italy, Catholic Action, environmentalists, merchants, and animals
Francis of Paola [April 2], naval officers and navigators
Francis Regis [July 2], social workers and marriage
Francis Xavier [December 3], foreign missions, India, Japan, Pakistan, East Indies, Outer Mongolia, and Borneo
Frumentius [July 20], Ethiopia
Gabriel Possenti [February 27], clerics and youth
Gabriel the Archangel [September 29], Argentina, messengers, diplomats, postal employees, radio and television workers, telecommunications workers, and stamp collectors
Gall [October 16], Switzerland and birds
Genesius [August 25], actors, lawyers, secretaries, stenographers, and printers
Geneviève of Paris [January 3], Paris, fever, drought, and rain (excessive)

George [April 23], England, Portugal, Genoa, Venice, soldiers, and Boy Scouts
Gerard Majella [October 16], lay brothers, mothers, and expectant mothers
Germanus of Paris [May 28], Paris
Gertrude [November 16], West Indies
Giles [September 1], the poor, the disabled, lepers, breast-feeding, blacksmiths, and horses
Gregory Thaumaturgus [November 17], desperate causes
Gregory the Great [September 3], England, musicians, singers, popes, teachers, and victims of plague
Gregory the Illuminator [September 30], Armenia
Hedwig [October 16], Silesia
Helen [August 18], converts and the divorced
Henry of Uppsala [January 19], Finland
Hippolytus [August 13], prison guards and horses
Homobonus [November 13], tailors, shoemakers, garment workers, merchants, and businesspeople
Honoratus of Arles [January 16], bakers and cake makers
Hubert [November 3], hunters and victims of rabies
Ignatius of Loyola [July 31], soldiers, retreats, and the scrupulous
Isaac Jogues and companions [October 19], North America
Isidore the Farmer [May 15], farmers, laborers, and Madrid
Ivo Hélory of Kermartin [May 19], lawyers, judges, and abandoned children
James the Great [July 25], Spain, Chile, Guatemala, Nicaragua, pilgrims, laborers, pharmacists, and those suffering from arthritis
James the Less [May 3], the dying
Januarius [September 19], Naples and blood banks
Jerome [September 30], scholars and librarians
Jerome Emiliani [February 8], orphans and abandoned children
Joan of Arc [May 30], France and soldiers
John Baptist de La Salle [April 7], teachers
John Berchmans [November 26], altar servers and youth
John Bosco [January 31], publishers, editors, and young apprentices
John Cassian [July 23], stenographers
John Chrysostom [September 13], preachers and public speakers
John Francis Regis (*see* Francis Regis)
John Nepomucen [May 16], Czech Republic, Bohemia, confessors, those who have been slandered, and bridges

John of Ávila [May 10], Spain and diocesan clergy
John of Capistrano [October 23], military chaplains and jurists
John of God [March 8], the sick, nurses, hospitals, heart patients, alcoholics, printers, booksellers, and bookbinders
John of Kanty (Cantius) [December 23], Lithuania
John of the Cross [December 14], mystics and poets
John the Baptist [June 24, August 29], Jordan, Florence, monks, highways, and spas
John the Evangelist [December 27], Turkey, Asia Minor, friendship, writers, publishers, and victims of poisoning
John Vianney [August 4], parish priests
Joseph [March 19], the universal Church, China, Russia, Canada, Mexico, Peru, Belgium, Korea, Austria, Vietnam, Bohemia, workers, carpenters, fathers of families, social justice, travelers, house hunting, and the dying
Joseph Cafasso [June 23], prisoners and prisons
Joseph Calasanz [August 25], Catholic schools
Joseph of Arimathea [August 31], funeral directors and pallbearers
Joseph of Cupertino [September 18], aviators
Jude [October 28], desperate causes and hospitals
Justin [June 1], philosophers
Justus and Pastor [August 6], Madrid
Kevin [June 3], Dublin
Kilian [July 8], Bavaria
Lawrence [August 10], Sri Lanka, cooks, the poor, and firefighters
Leonard of Port Maurice [November 26], parish missions
Leopold III [November 15], Austria
Louis Bertrán [October 9], Colombia
Louis IX [August 25], France and sculptors
Louise de Marillac [March 15], social workers
Lucy [December 13], those suffering from eye diseases, writers, and Syracuse, Sicily.
Luke [October 18], physicians, surgeons, artists, sculptors, painters, brewers, butchers, notaries, and glassworkers
Margaret of Cortona [February 22], the homeless and single mothers
Margaret of Scotland [November 16], Scotland
Maria Goretti [July 6], Children of Mary and teenage girls
Mark [April 25], Egypt, Venice, notaries, basket weavers, glassworkers, opticians, and cattle breeders

Martha [July 29], cooks, homemakers, hospital dieticians, innkeepers, domestic workers, restaurants, and waiters and waitresses
Martin de Porres [November 3], race relations, social justice, public education, public health service, and barbers
Martin of Tours [November 11], France, soldiers, horses, horse riders, and beggars
Maruthas [February 16], Persia
Mary, Mother of God (see below)
Mary Magdalene [July 22], hairdressers, penitents, and the contemplative life
Matthew [September 21], tax collectors, accountants, bookkeepers, customs officials, security guards, bankers, alcoholics, hospitals, and ships
Matthias [May 14], carpenters
Maurice [September 22], Austria, Sardinia, the papal Swiss Guard, infantrymen, swordsmiths, and weavers
Maurus [January 15], coppersmiths
Maximilian Mary Kolbe [August 14], drug addiction
Michael the Archangel [September 29], Germany, England, Papua New Guinea, Gibraltar, the Solomon Islands, the sick, radiologists, grocers, mariners, police officers, paratroopers, and cemeteries
Monica [August 27], mothers and alcoholics
Nicholas of Flüe [March 21], Switzerland
Nicholas of Myra [December 6], Russia, Greece, Sicily, children, travelers, pilgrims, bakers, brewers, brides, sailors, merchants, sea pilots, perfumers, and pawnbrokers
Nicholas of Tolentino [September 10], babies, mothers, mariners, animals, and the souls in purgatory
Norbert [June 6], Bohemia
Odilia [December 13], Alsace and the sightless
Olaf [July 29], Norway
Pantaleon [July 27], physicians, the medical profession, and endurance
Paschal Baylon [May 17], eucharistic confraternities and congresses, and shepherds
Patrick [March 17], Ireland and Nigeria
Paul [June 29], Greece, Malta, the lay apostolate, and the Cursillo movement
Paula [January 26], widows
Peregrine of Auxerre [May 16], cancer patients

Peter Baptist [February 6], Japan
Peter Canisius [December 21], Germany
Peter Chanel [April 28], Oceania
Peter Claver [September 9], Colombia
Peter of Alcántara [October 22], Brazil, watchmen
Peter the Apostle [June 29], the Church, popes, and fishermen
Philip and James, Apostles [May 3], Uruguay
Philip Neri [May 26], Rome
Phocas of Sinope [September 22], gardeners and sailors
Procopius [July 8], Czech Republic
Rainerius of Pisa [June 7], Pisa
Raphael the Archangel [September 29], physicians, nurses, travelers, lovers, health inspectors, and the sightless
Raymond Nonnatus [August 31], midwives, expectant mothers, and those falsely accused
Raymond of Peñafort [January 7], canon lawyers
Remigius [January 13], France
René Goupil [October 19], anesthetists
Rita of Cascia [May 22], desperate causes and unhappily married women
Robert Bellarmine [September 17], catechists
Roch [August 17], invalids, surgeons, prisoners, victims of contagious diseases and of plagues
Rose of Lima [August 23], South America, Central America, the West Indies, Peru, and the Philippines
Scholastica [February 10], Benedictine nuns and convulsive children
Sebastian [January 20], athletes, soldiers, local police, neighborhood watches, archers, physicians, and victims of contagious diseases and plagues
Sergius of Radonezh [September 25], Russia
Stanislaus [April 11], Poland and Kraków
Stanislaus Kostka [November 13], Poland
Stephen [December 26], deacons, bricklayers, and stonemasons
Stephen of Hungary [August 16], Hungary
Tarcisius [August 15], First Communicants
Teresa Benedicta of the Cross (Edith Stein) [August 9], Europe
Teresa of Ávila [October 15], Spain and those suffering from headaches
Teresa of Jesus [August 26], senior citizens
Theobald of Provins [June 30], janitors

Theresa of the Child Jesus ("Little Flower") [October 1], France, Russia, foreign missions, aviators, and florists
Thomas Aquinas [January 28], Catholic universities, students, Catholic schools, booksellers, and chastity
Thomas More [June 22], lawyers and politicians
Thomas the Apostle [July 3], India, East Indies, Pakistan, architects, surveyors, construction workers, and carpenters
Thorlac of Skalholt [December 23], Iceland
Titus [January 26], Crete
Turibius of Mongrovejo [March 23], Peru
Valentine [February 14], lovers
Venantius Fortunatus [December 14], falling, jumping, and leaping
Vincent de Paul [September 27], charitable organizations, works of charity, hospitals, prisoners, and Madagascar
Vincent Ferrer [April 5], builders and plumbers
Vincent of Saragossa [January 22], Portugal, vine growers, and wine makers
Vincent Pallotti [January 22], missionary priests
Vitus [June 15], Sicily, epileptics, comedians, dancers, those with dog and snake bites, and for protection against lightning and storms
Vladimir of Kiev [July 15], converts
Walter of Pontoise [April 8], those suffering stress
Wenceslaus [September 28], Czech Republic, Slovakia, Bohemia, Moravia, and brewers
Willibrord [November 7], the Netherlands, Luxembourg, and epileptics
Zita [April 27], maids
The *Blessed Virgin Mary* is patroness of many countries under various titles: Albania as Mother of Good Counsel; the Americas and Mexico as Our Lady of Guadalupe [December 12]; Angola as the Immaculate Heart of Mary; Argentina and Paraguay as Our Lady of Lujan; Australia and New Zealand as Our Lady Help of Christians; Bolivia as Our Lady of Copacabana; Brazil, Equatorial Guinea, Corsica, Portugal, Tanzania, the United States of America, and Zaire as the Immaculate Conception [December 8]; Chile as Our Lady of Mount Carmel [July 16]; Costa Rica as Our Lady of the Angels; Cuba as Our Lady of Charity; the Dominican Republic as Our Lady of High Grace; Ecuador as the Most Pure Heart of Mary; El Salvador as Our Lady of Peace; France, India, Jamaica, Malta, Paraguay, and South Africa as Our Lady of the Assumption [August 15]; Haiti as Our Lady of Perpetual Help; Honduras as Our Lady of Suyapa;

Hungary as the Great Lady of Hungary; Korea with her husband Joseph; Luxembourg as Our Lady Comforter of the Afflicted; the Philippines as the Sacred Heart of Mary; Poland as Our Lady of Czestochowa; Puerto Rico as Our Lady of Divine Providence; Slovakia as Our Lady of Sorrows [September 15]; the Solomon Islands as the Most Holy Name of Mary; Uruguay as the Blessed Virgin Mary ("La Virgen de los Treinte y Tres"); and Venezuela as Our Lady of Coromoto.

Places and Their Patron Saints

Albania, Mother of Good Counsel
Algeria, Cyprian of Carthage [September 16]
Alsace, Odilia [December 13]
Americas, the, Our Lady of Guadalupe [December 12]
Angola, Immaculate Heart of Mary
Argentina, Gabriel the Archangel [September 29], Our Lady of Lujan
Armenia, Bartholomew [August 24], Gregory the Illuminator [September 30]
Asia Minor, John the Evangelist [December 27]
Australia, Our Lady Help of Christians
Austria, Florian [May 4], Joseph [March 19], Leopold III [November 15], Maurice [September 22]
Bavaria, Kilian [July 8]
Belgium, Joseph [March 19]
Bohemia, Adalbert of Prague [April 23], Cyril and Methodius [February 14], John Nepomucen [May 16], Joseph [March 19], Norbert [June 6], Wenceslaus [September 28]
Bolivia, Our Lady of Copacabana
Borneo, Francis Xavier [December 3]
Brazil, Anthony of Padua [June 13], Peter of Alcántara [October 22], Immaculate Conception [December 8]
Canada, Anne [July 26], Joseph [March 19]
Central America, Rose of Lima [August 23]
Chile, James the Great [July 25], Our Lady of Mount Carmel [July 16]
China (mission to), Joseph [March 19]
Colombia, Louis Bertrán [October 9], Peter Claver [September 9]
Corsica, Immaculate Conception [December 8]
Costa Rica, Our Lady of the Angels

Crete, Titus [January 26]
Cuba, Our Lady of Charity
Cyprus, Barnabas [June 11]
Czech Republic, John Nepomucen [May 16], Procopius [July 8], Wenceslaus [September 28]
Denmark, Ansgar [February 3], Canute [July 10]
Dominican Republic, Dominic [August 8], Our Lady of High Grace
Dublin, Kevin [June 3]
East Indies, Francis Xavier [December 3], Thomas the Apostle [July 3]
Ecuador, Most Pure Heart of Mary
Egypt, Mark [April 25]
El Salvador, Our Lady of Peace
England, Augustine of Canterbury [May 27], Edward the Confessor [October 13], George [April 23], Gregory the Great [September 3], Michael the Archangel [September 29]
Equatorial Guinea, Immaculate Conception [December 8]
Ethiopia, Frumentius [July 20]
Europe, Benedict of Nursia [July 11], Bridget of Sweden [July 23], Catherine of Siena [April 29], Cyril and Methodius [February 14], Teresa Benedicta of the Cross (Edith Stein) [August 9]
Finland, Henry of Uppsala [January 19]
Florence, John the Baptist [June 24, August 29]
France, Denis [October 9], Joan of Arc [May 30], Louis IX [August 25], Martin of Tours [November 11], Remigius [January 13], Theresa of the Child Jesus ("Little Flower") [October 1], Our Lady of the Assumption [August 15]
Genoa, George [April 23]
Germany, Ansgar [February 3], Boniface [June 5], Michael the Archangel [September 29], Peter Canisius [December 21]
Gibraltar, Bernard of Clairvaux [August 20], Michael the Archangel [September 29]
Greece, Andrew [November 30], Nicholas of Myra [December 6], Paul [June 29]
Guatemala, James the Great [July 25]
Haiti, Our Lady of Perpetual Help
Honduras, Our Lady of Suyapa
Hungary, Stephen of Hungary [August 16], Great Lady of Hungary
Iceland, Ansgar [February 3], Thorlac of Skalholt [December 23]
India, Francis Xavier [December 3], Thomas the Apostle [July 3], Our Lady of the Assumption [December 8]

Ireland, Brigid of Kildare [February 1], Columba [June 9], Patrick [March 17]
Italy, Catherine of Siena [April 29], Francis of Assisi [October 4]
Jamaica, Our Lady of the Assumption [August 15]
Japan, Francis Xavier [December 3], Peter Baptist [February 6]
Jordan, John the Baptist [June 24]
Korea, Joseph [March 19], Blessed Virgin Mary, with her husband Joseph [March 19]
Kraków, Stanislaus [April 11]
Lithuania, Casimir [March 4], Cunegund [March 3], John of Kanty (Cantius) [December 23]
Luxembourg, Cunegund [March 3], Willibrord [November 7], Our Lady Comforter of the Afflicted
Madagascar, Vincent de Paul [September 27]
Madrid, Isidore the Farmer [May 15], Justus and Pastor [August 6]
Malta, Paul [June 29], Our Lady of the Assumption [August 15]
Mexico, Joseph [March 19], Our Lady of Guadalupe [December 12]
Moravia, Cyril and Methodius [February 14], Wenceslaus [September 28]
Naples, Januarius [September 19]
Netherlands, the, Willibrord [November 7]
New Zealand, Our Lady Help of Christians
Nicaragua, James the Great [July 25]
Nigeria, Patrick [March 17]
North Africa, Cyprian of Carthage [September 16]
North America, Isaac Jogues and companions [October 19]
Norway, Olaf [July 29]
Oceania, Peter Chanel [April 28]
Outer Mongolia, Francis Xavier [December 3]
Pakistan, Francis Xavier [December 3], Thomas the Apostle [July 3]
Papua New Guinea, Michael the Archangel [September 29]
Paraguay, Our Lady of Lujan, Our Lady of the Assumption [August 15]
Paris, Geneviève of Paris [January 3], Germanus of Paris [May 28]
Persia, Maruthas [February 16]
Peru, Joseph [March 19], Rose of Lima [August 23], Turibius of Mongrovejo [March 23]
Philippines, Rose of Lima [August 23], Sacred Heart of Mary
Pisa, Rainerius of Pisa [June 7]

Poland, Adalbert [April 23], Andrew Bobola [May 16], Casimir [March 4], Cunegund [March 3], Florian [May 4], Stanislaus [April 11], Stanislaus Kostka [November 13], Our Lady of Czestochowa

Portugal, Anthony of Padua [June 13], Elizabeth of Portugal [July 4], Francis Borgia [October 3], George [April 23], Vincent of Saragossa [January 22], Immaculate Conception [August 15]

Puerto Rico, Our Lady of Divine Providence

Rome, Philip Neri [May 26]

Russia, Andrew [November 30], Basil the Great [January 2], Casimir [March 4], Joseph [March 19], Nicholas of Myra [December 6], Sergius of Radonezh [September 25], Theresa of the Child Jesus ("Little Flower") [October 1]

Ruthenia, Bruno [October 6]

Sardinia, Maurice [September 22]

Scandinavia, Ansgar [February 3]

Scotland, Andrew [November 30], Columba [June 9], Margaret of Scotland [November 16]

Sicily, Lucy [December 13], Nicholas of Myra [December 6], Vitus [June 15]

Silesia, Hedwig [October 16]

Slovakia, Wenceslaus [September 28], Our Lady of Sorrows [September 15]

Solomon Islands, Michael the Archangel [September 29], Most Holy Name of Mary

South Africa, Our Lady of the Assumption [August 15]

South America, Rose of Lima [August 23]

Spain, James the Great [July 25], John of Ávila [May 10], Teresa of Ávila [October 15]

Sri Lanka, Lawrence [August 10]

Sweden, Bridget of Sweden [July 23], Eric of Sweden [May 18]

Switzerland, Gall [October 16], Nicholas of Flüe [March 21]

Syracuse, Lucy [December 13]

Tanzania, Immaculate Conception [December 8]

Turkey, John the Evangelist [December 27]

United States of America, Immaculate Conception [December 8]

Uruguay, Philip and James, Apostles [May 3], Blessed Virgin Mary ("La Virgen de los Treinte y Tres")

Venezuela, Our Lady of Coromoto

Venice, George [April 23], Mark [April 25]

Vienna, Clement Mary Hofbauer [March 15]
Vietnam, Joseph [March 19]
Wales, David of Wales [March 1]
West Indies, Gertrude [November 16], Rose of Lima [August 23]
Yugoslavia, Cyril and Methodius [February 14]
Zaire, Immaculate Conception [December 8]

Groups, Causes, and Their Patron Saints

abortion, protection against, Catherine of Sweden [March 24]
accountants, Matthew [September 21]
actors, Genesius [August 25]
addiction, drug, Maximilian Maria Kolbe [August 14]
advertisers, Bernardino of Siena [May 20]
alcoholics, John of God [March 8], Matthew, [September 21], Monica [August 27]
altar servers, John Berchmans [November 26]
anesthetists, René Goupil [October 19]
animals, Francis of Assisi [October 4], Nicholas of Tolentino [September 10]
animals, domestic, Anthony of Egypt [January 17]
apprentices, young, John Bosco [January 31]
archaeologists, Damasus I [December 11]
archers, Sebastian [January 20]
architects, Barbara [December 4], Thomas the Apostle [July 3]
art, Catherine of Bologna [May 9]
arthritis, James the Great [July 25]
artillerymen, Barbara [December 4]
artists, Angelico, Fra (Blessed John of Fiesole) [February 18], Catherine of Bologna [May 9], Luke [October 18]
astronomers, Dominic [August 8]
athletes, Sebastian [January 20]
aviators, Joseph of Cupertino [September 18], Theresa of the Child Jesus ("Little Flower") [October 1]
babies, Nicholas of Tolentino [September 10]
bakers, Elizabeth of Hungary [November 17], Honoratus of Arles [January 16], Nicholas of Myra [December 6]

bankers, Matthew [September 21]
banks, savings, Anthony Claret [October 24]
barbers, Cosmas and Damian [September 26], Martin de Porres [November 3]
basket weavers, Anthony of Egypt [January 17], Mark [April 25]
bees, Ambrose [December 7]
beggars, Martin of Tours [November 11]
birds, Gall [October 16]
bishops, Ambrose [December 7], Charles Borromeo [November 4]
blind (*see* sightless)
blood banks, Januarius [September 19]
bookbinders, Celestine V [May 19], John of God [March 8]
bookkeepers, Matthew [September 21]
booksellers, John of God [March 8], Thomas Aquinas [January 28]
Boy Scouts, George [April 23]
boys, young, Dominic Savio [March 9]
breast-feeding, Giles [September 1]
breasts, diseases of the, Agatha [February 5]
brewers, Amand [February 6], Augustine of Hippo [August 28], Luke [October 18], Nicholas of Myra [December 6], Wenceslaus [September 28]
bricklayers, Stephen [December 26]
brides, Nicholas of Myra [December 6]
bridges, John Nepomucen [May 16]
brothers, lay, Gerard Majella [October 16]
builders, Barbara [December 4], Vincent Ferrer [April 5]
bus drivers, Christopher [July 25]
businesspeople, Homobonus [November 13]
butchers, Anthony of Egypt [January 17], Luke [October 18]
cabdrivers, Fiacre [August 30]
cabinetmakers, Anne [July 26]
cake makers, Honoratus of Arles [January 16]
cancer patients, Peregrine of Auxerre [May 16]
candle makers, Bernard of Clairvaux [August 20]
canon lawyers, Raymond of Peñafort [January 7]
carpenters, Joseph [March 19], Matthias [May 14], Thomas the Apostle [July 3]
catechists, Charles Borromeo [November 4], Robert Bellarmine [September 17]
Catholic Action, Francis of Assisi [October 4]

Catholic charities, Elizabeth of Hungary [November 17]
Catholic press, Francis de Sales [January 24]
Catholic schools, Joseph Calasanz [August 25], Thomas Aquinas [January 28]
Catholic universities, Thomas Aquinas [January 28]
cattle breeders, Mark [April 25]
cemeteries, Anne [July 26], Michael the Archangel [September 29]
chaplains, military, John of Capistrano [October 23]
charitable organizations, Vincent de Paul [September 27]
charity, works of, Vincent de Paul [September 27]
chastity, Thomas Aquinas [January 28]
childbirth, Clare of Assisi [August 11], Erasmus (Elmo) [June 2]
children, Nicholas of Myra [December 6]
children, abandoned, Ivo Hélory of Kermartin [May 19], Jerome Emiliani [February 8]
children, convulsive, Scholastica [February 10]
Children of Mary, Agnes [January 21], Maria Goretti [July 6]
choirboys, Dominic Savio [March 9]
Church, the, Joseph [March 19], Peter the Apostle [June 29]
clergy, diocesan, John of Ávila [May 10]
clerics, Gabriel Possenti [February 27]
coin collectors, Eligius [December 1]
comedians, Vitus [June 15]
communications personnel, Bernardino of Siena [May 20]
confectioners, Cosmas and Damian [September 26]
confessors, Alphonsus Liguori [August 1], John Nepomucen [May 16]
construction workers, Thomas the Apostle [July 3]
contagious diseases, victims of, Roch [August 17], Sebastian [January 20]
contemplative life, Mary Magdalene [July 22]
converts, Helen [August 18], Vladimir of Kiev [July 15]
cooks, Lawrence [August 10], Martha [July 29]
coppersmiths, Maurus [January 15]
crops, protector of, Ansovinus [March 13]
Cursillo movement, Paul [June 29]
customs officials, Matthew [September 21]
dairy workers, Brigid of Kildare [February 1]
dancers, Vitus [June 15]
deacons, Stephen [December 26]
deaf (*see* hearing impaired)
dentists, Apollonia [February 9], Cosmas and Damian [September 26]

desperate causes, Gregory Thaumaturgus [November 17], Jude [October 28], Rita of Cascia [May 22]
dieticians, hospital, Martha [July 29]
diocesan clergy, John of Ávila [May 10]
diplomats, Gabriel the Archangel [September 29]
disabled, the, Giles [September 1]
divorced, Helen [August 18]
dog bites, Vitus [June 15]
domestic workers, Martha [July 29]
drought, Geneviève of Paris [January 3]
drug addicts, Maximilian Maria Kolbe [August 14]
dying, the, James the Less [May 3], Joseph [March 19]
earthquakes, Agatha [February 5]
ecologists (*see* environmentalists)
ecumenists, Cyril and Methodius [February 14]
editors, John Bosco [January 31]
embroiderers, Clare of Assisi [August 11]
endurance, Pantaleon [July 27]
engineers, Ferdinand of Castile [May 30]
environmentalists, Francis of Assisi [October 4]
epileptics, Vitus [June 15], Willibrord [November 7]
eucharistic confraternities and congresses, Paschal Baylon [May 17]
eye diseases, Clare of Assisi [August 11], Lucy [December 13]
falling, Venantius Fortunatus [December 14]
falsely accused, the, Raymond Nonnatus [August 31]
farmworkers, Benedict of Nursia [July 11]
farmers, Isidore the Farmer [May 15]
fathers of families, Joseph [March 19]
fever, Geneviève of Paris [January 3]
fire prevention, Bernardino of Siena [May 20]
firefighters, Agatha [February 5], Barbara [December 4], Florian [May 4], Lawrence [August 10]
First Communicants, Tarcisius [August 15]
fishermen, Andrew [November 30], Peter the Apostle [June 29]
flight attendants, Bona of Pisa [May 29]
florists, Theresa of the Child Jesus ("Little Flower") [October 1]
foreign missions, Francis Xavier [December 3], Theresa of the Child Jesus ("Little Flower") [October 1]
friendship, John the Evangelist [December 27]
funeral directors, Dismas [March 25], Joseph of Arimathea [August 31]
garage workers, Eligius [December 1]

gardeners, Dorothy [February 6], Fiacre [August 30], Phocas of Sinope [September 22]
garment workers, Homobonus [November 13]
gas station workers, Eligius [December 1]
girls, teenage, Maria Goretti [July 6]
girls, young, Agnes [January 21]
glassworkers, Luke [October 18], Mark [April 25]
goldsmiths, Anastasius I [December 19], Dunstan [May 19], Eligius [December 1]
good weather, Clare of Assisi [August 11]
governors, Ferdinand of Castile [May 30]
grave diggers, Anthony of Egypt [January 17]
grocers, Michael the Archangel [September 29]
hairdressers, Mary Magdalene [July 22]
harvests, Anthony of Padua [June 13]
headaches, Denis [October 9], Teresa of Ávila [October 15]
health inspectors, Raphael the Archangel [September 29]
hearing impaired, Francis de Sales [January 24]
heart patients, John of God [March 8]
hemorrhoids, Fiacre [August 30]
highways, John the Baptist [June 24]
hoarseness, Bernardino of Siena [May 20]
homeless, Benedict Joseph Labre [April 17], Margaret of Cortona [February 22]
homemakers, Anne [July 26], Martha [July 29]
horse riders, Martin of Tours [November 11]
horses, Eligius [December 1], Giles [September 1], Hippolytus [August 13], Martin of Tours [November 11]
hospital administrators, Basil the Great [January 2], Frances Xavier Cabrini [November 13]
hospital dieticians, Martha [July 29]
hospitals, Camillus de Lellis [July 14], John of God [March 8], Jude [October 28], Vincent de Paul [September 27]
house hunters, Joseph [March 19]
hunters, Hubert [November 3]
immigrants, Frances Xavier Cabrini [November 13]
infantrymen, Maurice [September 22]
innkeepers, Amand [February 6], Martha [July 29]
invalids, Roch [August 17]
janitors, Theobald of Provins [June 30]
jewelers, Dunstan [May 19], Eligius [December 1]

journalists, Francis de Sales [January 24]
judges, Ivo Hélory of Kermartin [May 19]
jumping, Venantius Fortunatus [December 14]
jurists, John of Capistrano [October 23]
laborers, Isidore the Farmer [May 15], James the Great [July 25]
lawyers, Fidelis of Sigmaringen [April 24], Genesius [August 25], Ivo Hélory of Kermartin [May 19], Thomas More [June 22]
lawyers, canon, Raymond of Peñafort [January 7]
lay apostolate, Paul [June 29]
lay brothers, Gerard Majella [October 16]
leaping, Venantius Fortunatus [December 14]
learning, Ambrose [December 7]
lepers, Giles [September 1]
librarians, Jerome [September 30]
lightning, protection from, Barbara [December 4], Vitus [June 15]
locksmiths, Dunstan [May 19]
lost articles, searchers of, Anthony of Padua [June 13]
lovers, Raphael the Archangel [September 29], Valentine [February 14]
maids, Zita [April 27]
marble workers, Clement of Rome [November 23]
mariners, Michael the Archangel [September 29], Nicholas of Tolentino [September 10]
marriage, Francis Regis [July 2]
medical profession, Pantaleon [July 27]
medical technicians, Albert the Great [November 15]
mentally ill, Dymphna [May 30]
merchants, Francis of Assisi [October 4], Homobonus [November 13], Nicholas of Myra [December 6]
messengers, Gabriel the Archangel [September 29]
metalworkers, Eligius [December 1]
midwives, Raymond Nonnatus [August 31]
military chaplains, John of Capistrano [October 23]
miners, Anne [July 26], Barbara [December 4]
missionary priests, Vincent Pallotti [January 22]
missions, foreign, Francis Xavier [December 3], Theresa of the Child Jesus ("Little Flower") [October 1]
missions, parish, Leonard of Port Maurice [November 26]
monks, Benedict of Nursia [July 11], John the Baptist [June 24]
mothers, Gerard Majella [October 16], Monica [August 27], Nicholas of Tolentino [September 10]

mothers, expectant, Anne [July 26], Gerard Majella [October 16], Raymond Nonnatus [August 31]
mothers, single, Margaret of Cortona [February 22]
motorists, Christopher [July 25], Frances of Rome [March 9]
mountain climbers, Bernard of Montjoux [May 28]
musicians, Cecilia [November 22], Dunstan [May 19], Gregory the Great [September 3]
mystics, John of the Cross [December 14]
naval officers, Francis of Paola [April 2]
navigators, Francis of Paola [April 2]
neighborhood watches, Sebastian [January 20]
notaries, Luke [October 18], Mark [April 25]
nuns, Bridget of Sweden [July 23]
nuns, Benedictine, Scholastica [February 10]
nurses, Agatha [February 5], Camillus de Lellis [July 14], Catherine of Siena [April 29], Cosmas and Damian [September 26], Elizabeth of Hungary [November 17], John of God [March 8], Raphael the Archangel [September 29]
nurses' associations, Camillus de Lellis [July 14]
opticians, Mark [April 25]
orators, John Chrysostom [September 13]
orphans, Jerome Emiliani [February 8]
painters, Luke [October 18]
pallbearers, Joseph of Arimathea [August 31]
paratroopers, Michael the Archangel [September 29]
parish missions, Leonard of Port Maurice [November 26]
parish priests, John Vianney [August 14]
pawnbrokers, Nicholas of Myra [December 6]
penitents, Mary Magdalene [July 22]
perfumers, Nicholas of Myra [December 6]
pharmacists, Cosmas and Damian [September 26], James the Great [July 25]
philosophers, Justin [June 1]
physicians, Cosmas and Damian [September 26], Luke [October 18], Pantaleon [July 27], Raphael the Archangel [September 29], Sebastian [January 20]
pilgrims, Christopher [July 25], James the Great [July 25], Nicholas of Myra [December 6]
plagues, victims of, Gregory the Great [September 3], Roch [August 17], Sebastian [January 20]

plasterers, Bartholomew [August 24]
plumbers, Vincent Ferrer [April 5]
poets, Cecilia [November 22], Columba [June 9], Brigid of Kildare [February 1], David of Wales [March 1], John of the Cross [December 14]
poisoning, victims of, Benedict of Nursia [July 11], John the Evangelist [December 27]
police, local, Sebastian [January 20]
police officers, Michael the Archangel [September 29]
politicians, Thomas More [June 22]
poor, the, Anthony of Padua [June 13], Ferdinand of Castile [May 30], Giles [September 1], Lawrence [August 10]
popes, Gregory the Great [September 3], Peter the Apostle [June 29]
porters, Christopher [July 25]
possessed, the, Bruno [October 6], Denis [October 9]
postal employees, Gabriel the Archangel [September 29]
preachers, John Chrysostom [September 13]
priests, diocesan, John of Ávila [May 10]
priests, missionary, Vincent Pallotti [January 22]
priests, parish, John Vianney [August 4]
printers, Augustine of Hippo [August 28], Genesius [August 25], John of God [March 8]
prison guards, Hippolytus [August 13]
prisoners, Barbara [December 4], Dismas [March 25], Ferdinand III [May 30], Joseph Cafasso [June 23], Roch [August 17], Vincent de Paul [September 27]
prisons, Joseph Cafasso [June 23]
public education, Martin de Porres [November 3]
public health service, Martin de Porres [November 3]
public relations, Bernardino of Siena [May 20]
public speakers, John Chrysostom [September 13]
publishers, John Bosco [January 31], John the Evangelist [December 27]
purgatory, souls in, Nicholas of Tolentino [September 10]
rabies, victims of, Hubert [November 3]
race relations, Martin de Porres [November 3]
radio workers, Gabriel the Archangel [September 29]
radiologists, Michael the Archangel [September 29]
rain (excessive), Geneviève of Paris [January 3]
refugees, Alban [June 20]

restaurants, Martha [July 29]
retreats, Ignatius of Loyola [July 31]
sailors, Andrew [November 30], Brendan [May 16], Christopher [July 25], Cuthbert [March 20], Erasmus (Elmo) [June 2], Nicholas of Myra [December 6], Phocas of Sinope [September 22]
scholars, the Venerable Bede [May 25], Brigid of Kildare [February 1], Jerome [September 30]
schools, Catholic, Joseph Calasanz [August 25], Thomas Aquinas [January 28]
scientists, Albert the Great [November 15]
scrupulous, the, Ignatius of Loyola [July 31]
sculptors, Claude La Colombière [February 15], Louis IX [August 25], Luke [October 18]
sea pilots, Nicholas of Myra [December 6]
secretaries, Genesius [August 25]
security guards, Matthew [September 21]
seminarians, Charles Borromeo [November 4]
senior citizens, Teresa of Jesus [August 26]
shepherds, Paschal Baylon [May 17]
ships, Matthew [September 21]
shoemakers, Crispin and Crispinian [October 25], Homobonus [November 13]
sick, the, Camillus de Lellis [July 14], John of God [March 8], Michael the Archangel [September 29]
sightless, the, Cosmas and Damian [September 26], Odilia [December 13], Raphael the Archangel [September 29]
silversmiths, Dunstan [May 19]
singers, Cecilia [November 22], Gregory the Great [September 3]
skiers, Bernard of Montjoux [May 28]
skin diseases, victims of, Anthony of Egypt [January 17]
slandered, the, John Nepomucen [May 16]
sleepwalkers, Dymphna [May 30]
snake bites, Vitus [June 15]
social justice, Joseph [March 19], Martin de Porres [November 3]
social workers, Francis Regis [July 2], Louise de Marillac [March 15]
soldiers, George [April 23], Ignatius of Loyola [July 31], Joan of Arc [May 30], Martin of Tours [November 11], Sebastian [January 20]
spas, John the Baptist [June 24]
speleologists, Benedict of Nursia [July 11]
stamp collectors, Gabriel the Archangel [September 29]

stenographers, Genesius [August 25], John Cassian [July 23]
stomach and abdominal ailments, Erasmus (Elmo) [June 2]
stonecutters, Clement of Rome [November 23]
stonemasons, Barbara [December 4], Stephen [December 26]
storms, protection against, Vitus [June 15]
stress, those suffering from, Walter of Pontoise [April 8]
students, Thomas Aquinas [January 28]
students in Jesuit colleges and universities, Aloysius Gonzaga [June 21]
surgeons, Cosmas and Damian [September 26], Luke [October 18], Roch [August 17]
surveyors, Thomas the Apostle [July 3]
swimmers, Adjutor [April 30]
Swiss Guard, papal, Maurice [September 22]
swordsmiths, Maurice [September 22]
tailors, Homobonus [November 13]
tanners, Bartholomew [August 24]
tax collectors, Matthew [September 21]
teachers, Gregory the Great [September 3], John Baptist de La Salle [April 7]
telecommunications workers, Gabriel the Archangel [September 29]
television, Clare of Assisi [August 11]
television workers, Gabriel the Archangel [September 29]
tertiaries, Franciscan, Elizabeth of Hungary [November 17]
theologians, Alphonsus Liguori [August 1], Augustine of Hippo [August 28]
thieves, Dismas [March 25]
throat ailments, Blase [February 3]
toothaches, those suffering from, Apollonia [February 9]
toy makers, Claude La Colombière [February 15]
travelers, Anthony of Padua [June 13], Christopher [July 25], Joseph [March 19], Nicholas of Myra [December 6], Raphael the Archangel [September 29]
truck drivers, Christopher [July 25]
universities, Catholic, Thomas Aquinas [January 28]
venereal diseases, Fiacre [August 30]
veterinarians, Blase [February 3], Eligius [December 1]
vine growers, Vincent of Saragossa [January 22]
vocations, religious, Alphonsus Liguori [August 1]
volcanic eruptions, protection against, Agatha [February 5]
waiters, Martha [July 29]

waitresses, Martha [July 29]
watchmen, Peter of Alcántara [October 22]
weavers, Anthony Claret [October 24], Bernardino of Siena [May 20], Maurice [September 22]
whales, Brendan of Clonfert [May 16]
widows, Anne [July 26], Frances of Rome [March 9], Paula [January 26]
wine makers, Vincent of Saragossa [January 22]
wine merchants, Amand [February 6]
women, barren, Anthony of Padua [June 13], Felicity [March 7]
women, childless, Anne [July 26]
women, unhappily married, Rita of Cascia [May 22]
women in labor, Anne [July 26], Erasmus (Elmo) [June 2]
workers, Bonaventure [July 15], Joseph [March 19]
writers, Francis de Sales [January 24], John the Evangelist [December 27], Lucy [December 13]
yachtsmen, Adjutor [April 30]
young boys, Dominic Savio [March 9]
young girls, Agnes [January 21]
youth, Aloysius Gonzaga [June 21], Gabriel Possenti [February 27], John Berchmans [November 26]
youth, African Catholic, Charles Lwanga [June 3]

Emblems in Art and Iconography

Agatha [February 5], tongs, veil, breasts on dish
Agnes [January 21], lamb
Ambrose [December 7], bees, dove, ox, pen
Andrew [November 30], transverse cross, net
Anne [July 26], door
Anselm [April 21], ship
Anthony of Egypt [January 17], bell, hog
Anthony of Padua [June 13], Christ Child, bread, book, lily, fish
Audrey (*see* Etheldreda)
Apollonia [February 9], hammer, pincers
Augustine of Hippo [August 28], child, dove, pen, shell
Barbara [December 4], cannon, chalice, palm, tower
Barnabas [June 11], ax, lance, stones
Bartholomew [August 24], flayed skin (and holding it), knife
Benedict of Nursia [July 11], bell, broken cup, bush, crosier, raven
Bernard of Clairvaux [August 20], bees, pen, instruments of the Passion
Bernard of Montjoux [May 28], dog, mountaineer's walking stick
Bernardino of Siena [May 20], chrism, sun or tablet inscribed with IHS, three miters
Blase [February 3], iron comb, wax candle, taper
Bonaventure [July 15], Holy Communion, ciborium, cardinal's hat
Boniface [June 5], oak, ax, book, fox, scourge, fountain, raven, sword
Brendan of Clonfert [May 16], whale
Bridget of Sweden [July 23], book, pilgrim's staff
Brigid of Kildare [February 1], cross, candle, flame over her head, cheese, cow
Bruno [October 6], chalice

Catherine de' Ricci [February 13], ring, crown, crucifix
Catherine of Siena [April 29], cross, lily, ring, stigmata
Cecilia [November 22], organ, angel
Charles Borromeo [November 4], Holy Communion, coat of arms with the word "*Humilitas*"
Christopher [July 25], Christ Child on his shoulders, giant, torrent, tree
Clare of Assisi [August 11], monstrance
Clement of Rome [November 23], anchor
Colette [February 7], birds, lamb
Crispin and Crispinian [October 25], shoes
Cosmas and Damian [September 26], box of ointment, vial, surgical instruments
Cyril of Alexandria [June 27], Blessed Virgin Mary holding the Child Jesus, pen
Cyril of Jerusalem [March 18], book, purse
Denis [October 9], head in hands
Dominic [August 8], rosary, star, lily
Dorothy [February 6], flowers, fruit
Edmund [November 20], arrows, sword
Edward the Confessor [October 13], ring
Eligius [December 1], hammer
Elizabeth of Hungary [November 17], alms, the poor, bread, flowers, a pitcher, rose
Erasmus (Elmo) [June 2], intestines
Etheldreda [June 23], necklace
Francis of Assisi [October 4], wolf, birds, deer, fish, skull, stigmata
Francis Xavier [December 3], crucifix, bell, ship
Gall [October 16], bear
Geneviève of Paris [January 3], bread, keys, herd, candle
George [April 23], dragon
Gertrude [November 16], crown, lily, taper
Gervase and Protase [June 19], club, scourge, sword
Giles [September 1], crosier, hermitage, hind, crutch
Gregory the Great [September 3], tiara, crosier, dove
Helen [August 18], cross
Hilary of Poitiers [January 13], child, pen, stick
Ignatius of Loyola [July 31], Holy Communion, book, chasuble, apparition of Jesus
Isidore of Seville [April 4], bees, pen
Isidore the Farmer [May 15], scythe

James the Great [July 25], key, pilgrim's hat and staff, shell, sword
James the Less [May 3], club, halberd, square rule
Januarius [September 19], vial of oil
Jerome [September 30], lion, cardinal's hat, stone
John Berchmans [November 26], cross, rosary, Rule of St. Ignatius
John Cassian [July 23], ladder
John Chrysostom [September 13], bees, dove, pen
John Fisher [June 22], ax
John of God [March 8], alms, a heart, crown of thorns
John the Baptist [June 24, August 29], head on platter, lamb, skin of an animal, ax
John the Evangelist [December 27], eagle, chalice, kettle, armor
Joseph [March 19], Infant Jesus, carpenter's square, lily, plane, rod
Josephat [November 12], chalice, crown, winged deacon
Joseph of Arimathea [August 31], cruets, nails
Jude [October 28], club, square rule, sword
Justin [June 1], ax, sword
Kevin [June 3], blackbird
Lawrence [August 10], book of Gospels, cross, gridiron
Leander of Seville [March 13], pen
Longinus [October 16], lance, armed at the foot of the cross
Louis IX [August 25], crown of thorns, nails, crown, globe
Lucy [December 13], eyes on dish, cord, lantern
Luke [October 18], ox, book, brush, palette, surgical instruments
Margaret of Scotland [November 16], dragon
Mark [April 25], lion, book
Martha [July 29], dragon, holy water sprinkler, broom
Martin of Tours [November 11], cloak
Mary Magdalene [July 22], alabaster box of ointment
Matilda [March 14], purse, alms
Matthew [September 21], winged man, purse, lance, angel
Matthias [May 14], lance
Maurus [January 15], scales, spade, crutch
Meinrad [January 21], two ravens
Mennas [November 11], camels
Michael the Archangel [September 29], sword, dragon, scales, banner
Monica [August 27], girdle, tears
Nicholas of Myra [December 6], anchor, boy in boat, three purses or balls
Nicholas of Tolentino [September 10], basket of bread, star

Norbert [June 6], monstrance
Olaf [July 29], ax, crown, dagger
Odilia [December 13], eyes on book
Patrick [March 17], shamrock, cross, harp, serpent, baptismal font, demons
Paul (Apostle) [June 29], book, scroll, sword
Paul the Hermit [January 15], crow
Peter the Apostle [June 29], keys, boat, cock, net, upside-down cross
Philip the Apostle [May 3], column
Philip Neri [May 26], altar, chasuble, vial
Richard of Chichester [April 3], chalice
Rita of Cascia [May 22], crucifix, rose, thorn
Robert Bellarmine [September 17], cardinal's hat
Roch [August 17], angel, dog, bread
Rose of Lima [August 23], crown of thorns, anchor, city
Sebastian [January 20], arrows, crown
Simon Stock [May 16], scapular
Stephen [December 26], stone
Teresa of Ávila [October 15], arrow, book, heart
Theresa of the Child Jesus ("Little Flower") [October 1], roses entwining a crucifix
Thomas Aquinas [January 28], chalice, dove, monstrance, ox, person trampled under foot, star
Thomas More [June 22], ax
Thomas the Apostle [July 3], ax, lance
Vincent de Paul [September 27], children
Vincent Ferrer [April 5], captives, cardinal's hat, pulpit, trumpet, star
Vincent of Saragossa [January 22], boat, gridiron, cruets, vine
Wenceslaus [September 28], crown, dagger
Zita [April 27], broom

Saintly "Firsts"

1. The first pope to be recognized by the Church as a saint: *Peter* [June 29].
2. The first saint to be formally canonized by a pope (993): *Ulrich of Augsburg* [July 4].
3. The first native-born Australian saint (1995): *Mary MacKillop* [May 25].
4. The first American-born saint (1975): *Elizabeth Ann Seton* [January 4].
5. The first monk to be recognized as a saint: *Anthony of Egypt* [January 17].
6. The first saint to develop a spirituality for lay people: *Francis de Sales* [January 24].
7. The first martyr-saints of the Far East (1862): *Paul Miki and companions* [February 6].
8. The first lay saint (and one of the first two women) to be named a Doctor of the Church (1970): *Catherine of Siena* [April 29].
9. The first martyr-saints of black Africa (1964): *Charles Lwanga and companions* [June 3].
10. The first Native American to have been beatified (1980): *Kateri Tekakwitha* [July 14].
11. The first apostle-saint to be martyred: *James the Great* [July 25].
12. The first canonized saint of the Americas (1671): *Rose of Lima* [August 23].
13. The first Russian mystic-saint: *Sergius of Radonezh* [September 25].
14. The first Filipino saint (1987): *Lawrence Ruiz* [September 28].
15. The first nun (and one of the first two women) to be named a Doctor of the Church (1970): *Teresa of Ávila* [October 15].

16. The first Eastern saint to be formally canonized by the Roman Catholic Church (1867): *Josephat* [November 12].
17. The first U.S. citizen to be canonized (1946): *Frances Xavier Cabrini* [November 13].
18. The first native-born Canadian saint (1990): *Mary Margaret d'Youville* [December 23].
19. The first martyr-saint: *Stephen* [December 26].
20. The first saint of mixed racial blood: *Martin de Porres* [November 3].
21. The first pope to be formally canonized (1313): *Celestine V* [May 19].
22. The first abbess-saint in Ireland: *Brigid of Kildare* [February 1].
23. The first Scottish saint to be canonized (1250): *Margaret of Scotland* [November 16].
24. The first and only pope canonized in the twentieth century (1954): *Pius X* [August 21].
25. The first American saint canonized in the third Christian millennium (2000): *Katharine Drexel* [March 3].
26. The first female saint from Poland (2000): *Maria Faustina Kowalska* [October 5].

Papal Canonizations Chart

THROUGH JUNE 2001, JOHN PAUL II HAS CANONIZED 451 AND beatified 1229. This compares to 303 canonized and 964 beatified by all of his predecessors since Clement VIII (1592–1605) combined.

The 451 canonized by John Paul II include: 156 ordained men, 20 nonordained religious men, 164 laymen, 29 religious women, and 82 laywomen. John Paul II's statistics are greatly influenced by several large "group" canonizations:

The 103 Martyrs of Korea include 11 ordained men, 45 laymen, and 47 laywomen.

The 117 Martyrs of Vietnam include 58 ordained men, 58 laymen, and 1 laywoman.

The 120 Martyrs of China include 58 ordained men, 55 laymen, 7 religious women, and 30 laywomen.

SOURCES: Congregatio Pro Causis Sanctorum (Lat., Congregation for the Causes of Saints); *Index ac Status Causarum* (Città del Vaticano, 1988), plus supplements; the journal *Notitiae,* and *Osservatore Romano.*

Chart on Canonizations by John Paul II and His Predecessors appears on the following page.

Chart on Canonizations by John Paul II and His Predecessors

	John Paul II to June 2001	Paul VI	John XXIII	Pius XII	Clement VIII to Pius XI	Totals
Popes	0	0	0	1	1	2
Cardinals	1	0	1	0	3	5
Archbishops/Bishops	19	3	1	3	9	35
Priests	136	41	3	9	72	261
Nonordained Religious Men	20	3	3	2	23	51
Laymen	164	26	0	1	28	219
Total Men	**340**	**73**	**8**	**16**	**136**	**573**
Religious Women	29	8	2	13	24	76
Laywomen	82	3	0	4	9	98
Total Women	**111**	**11**	**2**	**17**	**33**	**174**
Total Canonized	**451**	**84**	**10**	**33**	**169**	**747**
Total Beatified	1,229	31	4	148	781	2,193
Total Canonized and Beatified	1,680	115	14	181	950	2,940

Notes

PART ONE: WHO IS A SAINT?

1. The date in brackets refers always to the saint's feast day. Readers may go directly to that date in Part IV of the book for the saint's biographical profile.

2. "The Church of the Saints," *Theological Investigations,* vol. 3: *Theology of the Spiritual Life,* trans. Karl-H. and Boniface Kruger (Baltimore: Helicon Press; London: Darton, Longman & Todd, 1967), p. 91. The original article was published in *Stimmen der Zeit* 157 (1955/56): 81–91.

3. *The Meaning of Saints* (San Francisco: Harper & Row, 1980), p. 150. Among those theologians who, in addition to Rahner and Cunningham, were attentive to the theological significance of saints was Hans Urs von Balthasar, for whom the saints constituted "a new interpretation of revelation, an enrichment of doctrine concerning new, until now little noticed features." "The Saints as Theme of Theology," in *The Von Balthasar Reader,* ed. Medard Kehl and Werner Löser, trans. Robert J. Daly and Fred Lawrence (New York: Crossroad, 1982), p. 379.

4. See, for example, Elizabeth A. Johnson, *Friends of God and Prophets: A Feminist Theological Reading of the Communion of Saints* (New York: Continuum, 1998); William Thompson, *Fire and Light: The Saints and Theology* (New York: Paulist Press, 1987); *The One Mediator, the Saints, and Mary: Lutherans and Catholics in Dialogue VIII,* ed. H. George Anderson et al. (Minneapolis, MN: Augsburg Fortress Press, 1992); Gustavo Gutiérrez, *We Drink from Our Own Wells* (Maryknoll, NY: Orbis Books, 1984); and Lawrence S. Cunningham and Keith J. Egan, *Christian Spirituality: Themes from the Tradition* (New York: Paulist Press, 1996). In addition, renewed interest in the lives of the saints and the schools of spirituality associated with them is now being effectively promoted by the Institute for Carmelite Studies in Washington, DC, Cistercian Publications in Kalamazoo, Michigan, the Classics of Western Spirituality series published by Paulist Press since 1978, and the new twelve-volume edition of *Butler's Lives of the Saints* (Collegeville, MN: Liturgical Press, 1998–2000).

5. Lawrence Cunningham makes a similar point in "A Decade of Research on the Saints: 1980–1990," *Theological Studies* 53 (1992): 517. See, for example, Terrence Tilley, *Story Theology* (Wilmington, DE: Michael Glazier, 1985), and Robert A. Krieg, *Story-shaped Christology* (New York: Paulist Press, 1988). On experience as a *locus* of theology, see David Tracy, *The Analogical Imagination: Christian Theology and the Culture of Pluralism* (New York: Crossroad, 1981), pp. 193–229.

6. See the Dogmatic Constitution on the Church *(Lumen gentium),* nn. 39 and 50. The continued insistence on at least one verifiable miracle for canonization perpetuates the notion that the real significance of saints is located in their supernatural power rather than in their person and activities. See again Cunningham, *The Meaning of Saints,* p. 24. Cunningham makes an effective contrast between Padre Pio [September 23], an Italian Capuchin friar known for his stigmata, his alleged power of bilocation, and his allegedly miraculous capacity to read the hearts of human persons, and Cardinal John Henry Newman [see August 11], "one of the truly great spiritual and intellectual Christians of modern times" and "a singular influence for good in modern Catholicism" (pp. 25–26). Indeed, Pope Paul VI once referred to the Second Vatican Council as "Newman's Council." Yet Padre Pio was canonized in 2002, while Newman's cause languishes for lack of a miracle.

7. From the *Enchiridion Militis Christiani* (Lat., "Handbook of the Militant Christian"), in Cunningham, *The Meaning of Saints,* p. 30.

8. See, for example, Francis A. Sullivan, *The Church We Believe In: One, Holy, Catholic and Apostolic* (New York: Paulist Press, 1988), chap. 4, "Marked with a Genuine Though Imperfect Holiness," pp. 66–83; and Lawrence S. Cunningham, "Holiness," in *The New Dictionary of Catholic Spirituality,* ed. Michael Downey (Collegeville, MN: Liturgical Press, 1993), pp. 479–88.

9. Elizabeth Johnson adopts a similarly comprehensive view of the category. See her *Friends of God and Prophets,* pp. 2–3. See also Anderson et al., eds., *The One Mediator, the Saints, and Mary,* p. 51.

10. For a more theologically elaborate background for this paragraph, see Karl Rahner, *Foundations of Christian Faith: An Introduction to the Idea of Christianity,* trans. William V. Dych (New York: Seabury, 1978), pp. 116–37.

11. Elizabeth Johnson points out that the stories of so many of the canonized saints "make them seem too perfect, too miraculous, too otherworldly, too eccentric to have anything useful to say." People today "are more likely to be inspired by unofficial saints such as peacemakers or those with creative charisms who have brought faith to bear on the human dilemma" (*Friends of God and Prophets,* p. 18).

12. On the anniversary of the martyr's death, the local Christian community—especially relatives and friends—would gather for the celebration of the Eucharist over the remains, thereby joining tomb and altar. The belief was that the spirit of the martyr was present in a special way through the remains. As these tombs began to attract pilgrims, churches were built on the site to house the relics. Sometimes the walls of a city were extended to incorporate cemeteries, the most famous example being that of Vatican Hill, once a cemetery outside Rome, where the basilica of St. Peter's was erected over the tomb of the apostle. See Kenneth L. Woodward, *Making Saints: How the Catholic Church Determines Who Becomes a Saint, Who Doesn't, and Why* (New York: Simon & Schuster, Touchstone Books, 1990), pp. 56–57.

13. Elizabeth Johnson notes, as many others have, that the Church's processes of saint-making have been "biased against lay people in general and women in particular, and prejudiced against the full and legitimate use of human sexuality by both women and men" (*Friends of God and Prophets,* p. 102).

14. Because a martyr's death was seen as the perfect sacrifice, made in union with Christ's own sacrifice on the cross, no miracle was required to attest to the martyr's saintliness. In the case of confessors, ascetics, and other holy persons, however, some evidence was required of miracles performed during their lifetimes or after their deaths. The latter kind were usually associated with their tombs or their relics.

15. There was a tradition lasting into the Middle Ages in which individuals would seek to be buried next to, or at least near, the tomb of a saint in order to enjoy the saint's protection at the judgment seat of God. For example, the bishops of Augsburg, Germany, were buried next to the tomb of St. Afra [August 7], a patron saint of the diocese of Augsburg, until the year 1000. Bernard of Clairvaux (d. 1153) asked to be buried with a relic of St. Jude [October 28] so that he would be sure to rise from the grave with the apostle on the Last Day.

16. The council also decreed that no church can be consecrated without the relics of a martyr and indeed that a bishop who consecrates a church without relics should be deposed "as someone who has flouted the ecclesiastical traditions." *Decrees of the Ecumenical Councils,* Vol. 1, ed. Norman P. Tanner (London: Sheed & Ward; Washington, DC: Georgetown University Press, 1990), p. 145.

17. The common use of the word "legend" with reference to the biographies of saints is derived from the Latin *legenda* ("to be read"), referring to this public reading of a proposed saint's life and spiritual achievements.

18. Although this development has to be seen in the light of the growing centralization of power in the papal office, some bishops and their local communities did look upon a papal canonization as lending greater dignity and prestige to their newly proclaimed saints.

19. For an excellent reflection on the Baroque period and its lasting impact on Catholicism, at least until Vatican II, see Thomas F. O'Meara, "Leaving the Baroque: The Fallacy of Restoration in the Postconciliar Era," *America* 174 (February 3, 1996): 10–14, 25–28.

20. See "The Church of the Saints," p. 97. One always has to distinguish, however, between "real" saints and "constructed" saints. The former are those historical persons who had an actual life and played a real part in the history of the Church, either as part of the biblical tradition (e.g., the Blessed Virgin Mary, St. Paul) or in subsequent history (e.g., St. Francis of Assisi, St. Teresa of Ávila); the latter are those who were also real persons but whose religious identity has been constructed through pious embroidery (e.g., the legend of St. Anne, who was the maternal grandmother of Jesus, or that of St. Nicholas) or in response to personal or national needs (e.g., St. Jude, St. George). See Cunningham, "A Decade of Research on the Saints," pp. 520–21. The distinction itself comes from Pierre Delooz, "Towards a Sociological Study of Canonized Saints," in *Saints and Their Cults: Studies in Religious Sociology, Folklore, and History,* ed. Stephen Wilson (London and New York: Cambridge University Press, 1983), pp. 189–216, especially pp. 195–96. Delooz also distinguishes between "real" and "constructed" miracles (pp. 211–12).

21. Rahner, "The Church of the Saints," p. 100. A model, in this instance, is "not merely the plastic representation ('case') of an abstract ideal. . . . The concrete model renders what is represented present for the first time to the others as something genuinely possible. The fact that the model itself is present is the undeniable miracle of the Spirit in the Church" (n. 5). Lawrence Cunningham points out that the saint is "one who in this or that extreme cultural circumstance says, by life and word, that there is a way in which the life of the Gospel can be lived" (*The Meaning of Saints,* p. 171). Similarly, Hans Urs von Balthasar speaks of the saint as one "whose life is a presentation to his [or her] own age of the message that heaven is sending to it, a man [or woman] who is, here and now, the right and relevant interpretation of the Gospel, who is given to this particular age as its way of approach to the perennial truth of Christ." *A Theology of History,* 2d ed. (London and New York: Sheed & Ward, 1963), p. 105.

22. Rahner, "The Church of the Saints," p. 102.

23. I understand Catholicism here as embracing Christian traditions beyond the Roman Catholic, especially the great non-Roman Eastern traditions, Anglicanism, and large sectors of Lutheranism, among others. Sacramentality is by no means exclusively linked with Roman Catholicism, although it is surely central to its theological, doctrinal, and spiritual perspectives.

24. Theologians have, in fact, distinguished between Christ as the primal, or primordial, sacrament and the Church as his fundamental sacrament. See Karl Rahner, *The Church and the Sacraments* (Edinburgh and London: Nelson, 1963), pp. 18–19; and Edward Schillebeeckx, *Christ the Sacrament of Encounter with God* (London and New York: Sheed & Ward, Stagbooks, 1963), pp. 13–47, 55–100.

25. Avery Dulles, for example, has written: "Hardly any practice is so distinctively Catholic as the cult of the saints." *The Catholicity of the Church* (Oxford: Clarendon Press, 1985), p. 85.

26. Those oriental churches, Orthodox and non-Orthodox alike, that add saints to their sanctoral calendars do so by synodal decree, following a period of study. Each church, however, is autonomous and has its own norms. In recent years the Russian Orthodox Church has been canonizing its innumerable martyrs under Communism. In August 2000 Patriarch Aleksy II and the Council of Bishops in Moscow canonized as "passion bearers" Russia's last czar, Nicholas II, and his immediate family, who had been imprisoned and executed by the Bolsheviks in 1918. In the same month the ecumenical patriarch, Bartholomew I of Constantinople, officially "recognized" Stephen of Hungary [August 16] as a saint. Stephen had been canonized by the Catholic Church in 1083. There were claims that this was the first time a Catholic saint had been "canonized" by the Orthodox Church since the East-West Schism of 1054.

In the Church of England and the other churches of the Anglican Communion, "heroes of the faith," as they are often called rather than "saints" as such, are proposed by the particular liturgical commission of that church when revising the calendar for approval or rejection by the legislative body of the church, which in the case of the Church of England is the General Synod. The churches of the Anglican Communion, however, do not canonize saints and do not, by including a name in a liturgical calendar, make any claim about the present heavenly state of the person. The Lutheran sanctoral calendar for the Evangelical Lutheran Church in America and the Evangelical Lutheran Church in Canada was prepared by the Inter-Lutheran Commission on Worship, a group that was disbanded following the approval and publication of the *Lutheran Book of Worship* in 1978.

27. *Origins* 24/24 (November 24, 1994): 412.

28. See "Honoring Contemporary Christian Martyrs and Faith Witnesses," *Origins* 30/1 (May 18, 2000): 6. The sixteen witnesses to faith are listed, with a brief biographical sketch, in several columns accompanying the text of the pope's address at the prayer service. Although the story of the murdered Archbishop Oscar Arnulfo Romero of El Salvador [March 24] was not among the sixteen selected to represent Christian suffering around the world, he was the only person named in the prayer for twentieth-century martyrs of the Americas. The prayer honored "zealous pastors like the unforgettable Oscar Romero, killed at the altar while celebrating the eucharistic sacrifice" in 1980. Of the sixteen witnesses, only two were women: Olga Jafa, a Russian teacher and painter who was sent to a Soviet prison camp in the Solovki Islands from 1929 to 1931, and Margaret Chou, a Chinese Catholic laywoman who was confined in prison and labor camps from 1958 to 1969.

29. See Joseph Goldbrunner, *Holiness Is Wholeness* (Notre Dame, IN: University of Notre Dame Press, 1964).

30. For a fuller development of this broader understanding of virtue, see my *Catholicism: Completely Revised and Updated* (San Francisco: HarperCollins, 1994), pp. 926–52.

31. In acknowledging that the sociologist's description of mental health cannot be the same as the psychiatrist's, Pierre Delooz delivers himself of this understatement: "The lives of the saints over the last two thousand years in a variety of cultures provide exceptionally interesting material for the assessment of what constitutes psychological equilibrium" ("Towards a Sociological Study of Canonized Saints," p. 205).

32. To appreciate the complexity of a genuinely detailed, scientific analysis of the various types, ages, nationalities, etc., of the Church's saints, see Donald Weinstein and Rudolph M. Bell, *Saints and Society: Christendom, 1000–1700* (Chicago: University of Chicago Press, 1982), "Appendix to Part 1: Statistical Profiles of Saints," pp. 121–37.

33. Elisabeth Schüssler Fiorenza, *In Memory of Her: A Feminist Theological Reconstruction of Christian Origins* (New York: Crossroad, 1983).

34. *Friends of God and Prophets,* p. 27. See also Kathleen Jones, *Women Saints: Lives of Faith and Courage* (Maryknoll, NY: Orbis Books, 1999).

35. Elizabeth Johnson points out that before the twelfth century men outnumbered women saints by a seven-to-one margin. In the first eight decades of the twentieth century, the ratio of canonized male saints to canonized female saints was 75 to 25 percent. *Friends of God and Prophets,* p. 27.

36. Michael D. Whalen, "In the Company of Women? The Politics of Memory in the Liturgical Commemoration of Saints—Male and Female," *Worship* 73/6 (November 1999): 489.

37. See Mary Collins, *Contemplative Participation* (Collegeville, MN: Liturgical Press, 1990), pp. 30–31. She points out that the rubric that allows for the abbreviation of the commemorations in the Canon, or First Eucharistic Prayer, for pastoral reasons brackets out some of the men but all of the women. Michael Whalen notes that women are also eclipsed in the Litany of the Saints in which seven women are invoked in comparison with seventeen men ("In the Company of Women," p. 491).

38. *Lesser Feasts and Fasts* (New York: Church Hymnal Corporation, 1997).

39. See Philip H. Pfatteicher, *Festivals and Commemorations: Handbook to the Calendar in the Lutheran Book of Worship* (Minneapolis, MN: Augsburg, 1980).

40. *The Catechism of the Catholic Church* (Mahwah, NJ: Paulist Press, 1994), pp. 247–50, nn. 946–62.

41. Thus, Lawrence Cunningham: "The commemoration of the saints in the liturgy of the Church is not meant simply to honor heroes/heroines who are dead, but to proclaim that they are a pledge of our own hope and faith. We are all part of that community across time and space, who stand in solidarity in the unity of the Spirit" ("A Decade of Research on the Saints," p. 532).

PART TWO: SAINTS AND SPIRITUALITIES

1. For specific entries on each of these (and other) schools of spirituality, see *The New Dictionary of Catholic Spirituality,* ed. Michael Downey, (Collegeville, MN: Liturgical Press, 1993). See also the several entries in *The HarperCollins Encyclopedia of Catholicism,* ed. Richard P. McBrien (San Francisco: HarperCollins, 1995). A sampling of some recent monographs follows. On the Benedictine school: Cyprian Smith, *The Path of Life: Benedictine Spirituality for Monks and Lay People* (Ampleforth, York: Ampleforth Abbey Press, 1995); and Columba Stewart, *Prayer and Community: The Benedictine Tradition* (Maryknoll, NY: Orbis Books, 1998). On the Carmelite school: Wilfrid McGreal, *At the Fountain of Elijah: The Carmelite Tradition* (Maryknoll, NY: Orbis Books, 1999). On the Celtic school: Richard J. Woods, *The Spirituality of the Celtic Saints* (Maryknoll, NY: Orbis Books, 2000). On the Cistercian school: Esther De Waal, *The Way of Simplicity: The Cistercian Tradition* (Maryknoll, NY: Orbis Books, 1998). On the Dominican school: Benedict M. Ashley, *Spiritual Direction in the Dominican Tradition* (New York: Paulist Press, 1995); and Richard Woods, *Mysticism and Prophecy: The Dominican Tradition* (Maryknoll, NY: Orbis Books, 1998). On the Franciscan school: Murray Bodo, *The Way of Francis: The Challenge of Franciscan Spirituality for Everyone* (Cincinnati, OH: St. Anthony Messenger Press, 1995); and William J. Short, *Poverty and Joy: The Franciscan Tradition* (Maryknoll, NY: Orbis Books, 2000). On the Ignatian school: David L. Fleming, ed., *A Spirituality for Contemporary Life: The Jesuit Heritage Today* (St. Louis: Review for Religious, 1991); and John W. O'Malley, John W. Padberg, and Vincent T. O'Keefe, *Jesuit Spirituality: A Now and Future Resource* (Chicago: Loyola University Press, 1990).

2. The theological term for this fourth criterion is "reception," which is the acceptance, assimilation, and implementation of a teaching, a decree, or, as in this instance, the personal example of a holy person by the Church or a significant portion thereof. The act of reception is a confirming witness by the People of God regarding the intrinsic truth and applicability of the teaching, discipline, or personal example. See Herman J. Pottmeyer, "Reception of Doctrine," and Ladislas M. Orsy, "Reception of Law," in *HarperCollins Encyclopedia of Catholicism*, pp. 1081–2, 1082.

3. Saints who have such a profound and far-reaching impact upon the life of the Church that they inspire a school of Christian spirituality are "classics," in the sense that David Tracy uses the term. Classics are not only texts but any extraordinary epiphany of a religious truth that has a pertinence and a depth to offer to later generations. Thus, for Tracy, key saints are also classics; see *The Analogical Imagination: Christian Theology and the Culture of Pluralism* (New York: Crossroad, 1981), p. 147, n. 82; pp. 172–78. There is "one classic event and person which normatively judges and informs all other Christian classics, and which also serves as the classic Christian focus for understanding God, self, others, society, history, nature and the whole Christianly *[sic]:* the event and person of Jesus Christ" (p. 233).

4. This historical survey follows closely the lines laid down in my *Catholicism: Completely Revised and Updated* (San Francisco: HarperCollins, 1994), pp. 1021–51.

5. It should be pointed out here that the Celtic Church and its monastic tradition produced generations of saints and scholars who also led an effort to reconvert Europe following the age of the "invasions." Among the shapers of the Celtic school of spirituality were Columban and Brigid of Kildare.

6. The Victorines were not monks, but canons regular, that is, members of a clerical religious institute as distinct from monastic, mendicant, and apostolic groups. Most of the canons regular adopted the Rule of St. Augustine. They came together for prayer and life in community, but did not generally engage in pastoral ministry.

7. For the original Ignatian text in Latin and a brief commentary on it, see Hugo Rahner, *Ignatius the Theologian* (New York: Herder & Herder, 1968), pp. 25–27; see also Karl Rahner, "The Logic of Concrete Individual Knowledge in Ignatius Loyola," *The Dynamic Element in the Church* (London: Burns & Oates, 1964), pp. 84–170.

8. See her *Autobiography* (New York: Doubleday-Image, 1960); and *The Way of Perfection* (New York: Doubleday-Image, 1964).

9. See *The Collected Works of St. John of the Cross* (Washington, DC: Institute of Carmelite Studies Publications, 1991).

10. See Francis's *Introduction to the Devout Life* (New York: Doubleday-Image, 1972).

11. Cited by E. A. Walsh, "Spirituality, French School of," *New Catholic Encyclopedia*, vol. 13 (New York: McGraw-Hill, 1967), p. 605.

12. *The Spiritual Life* (New York: Desclée, 1930), pp. vii-viii.

13. See *The Three Ages of the Interior Life,* 2 vols. (St. Louis: Herder, 1947–48).

14. *Union with God* (St. Louis: Herder, 1949), p. 40.

15. Ibid., pp. 164–66.

16. See his *Spiritual Autobiography* (New York: P. J. Kenedy, 1964).

17. For an account of this period of his life, see Maritain's *The Peasant of the Garonne* (New York: Holt, Rinehart and Winston, 1968).

18. See *The Divine Milieu* (New York: Harper & Brothers, 1960).

19. *The Inner Search* (New York: Sheed & Ward, 1957), pp. 7, 9. One finds a similar sensitivity to the human dimension of Christian spirituality, but with a more explicitly Thomistic orientation, in the works of Gerald Vann, O.P. (d. 1963), for example, *The Heart of Man* (Garden City, NY: Image Books, 1960), and *The Divine Pity* (Garden City, NY: Image Books, 1962).

20. *The Seven Storey Mountain* (New York: Harcourt, Brace, 1948); *Conjectures of a Guilty Bystander* (New York: Doubleday, 1966).

21. *Life and Holiness* (New York: Image Books, 1964), p. 100.

22. *New Seeds of Contemplation* (New York: New Directions Books, 1961), p. 32.

23. Ibid., pp. 39, 78. For a recent biography of Merton, see Lawrence S. Cunningham, *Thomas Merton and the Monastic Vision* (Grand Rapids, MI: Eerdmans, 1999).

24. *Holiness Is Wholeness and Other Essays* (Notre Dame, IN: University of Notre Dame Press, 1964), p. 1.

25. Ibid., pp. 2, 3.

26. Ibid., p. 14.

27. Ibid., p. 34. For a post–Vatican II development of this approach, see Wilkie Au, *By Way of the Heart: Toward a Holistic Spirituality* (New York: Paulist Press, 1989).

28. For some of the sample references, see note 1 above and Part I, note 4. See also the *Christian Spirituality Bulletin: Journal of the Society for the Study of Christian Spirituality,* which is published biannually at Loyola Marymount University in Los Angeles. It adopted a journal format in 2001.

29. One of the most remarkable developments is the growing number of laywomen, Catholic and non-Catholic alike, who have gained a wide audience for their spiritual writings. For example: Kathleen Norris, *Dakota* (New York: Ticknor & Fields, 1993); *The Cloister Walk* (New York: Riverhead Books, 1996); *Amazing Grace* (New York: Riverhead Books, 1998); *The Quotidian Mysteries* (New York: Paulist Press, 1998); and *Meditations on Mary* (New York: Viking Studio, 1999). Patricia Hampl, *Virgin Time* (New York: Farrar, Straus and Giroux, 1992); and *Burning Bright* (New York: Ballantine Books, 1995). Annie Dillard, *Pilgrim at Tinker Creek* (New York: Harper's Magazine Press, 1974); *Holy the Firm* (New York: Perennial Library, 1988); and *Tickets for a Prayer Wheel* (Columbia: University of Missouri Press, 1987; original, 1974). Finally, the poet Denise Levertov, *The Stream and the Sapphire* (New York: New Directions Books, 1997); and *This Great Unknowing* (New York: New Directions Books, 1999).

30. Aelred Graham, *Contemplative Christianity: An Approach to the Realities of Religion* (New York: Seabury, 1974), p. 74.

31. The writings of William Johnston have a similarly global, and particularly Eastern, orientation, for example, *Christian Zen* (San Francisco: Harper & Row, 1979), *Christian Mysticism Today* (San Francisco: Harper & Row, 1984), and *Being in Love: the Practice of Christian Prayer* (San Francisco: Harper & Row, 1989).

32. See Anne Carr, *Transforming Grace: Christian Tradition and Women's Experience* (San Francisco: HarperCollins, 1988).

33. Gustavo Gutiérrez, *We Drink from Our Own Wells: The Spiritual Journey of a People* (Maryknoll, NY: Orbis Books, 1984); *On Job: God-talk and the Suffering of the Innocent* (Maryknoll, NY: Orbis Books, 1987); and *The God of Life* (Maryknoll, NY: Orbis Books, 1991).

34. Leonardo Boff, *The Maternal Face of God: The Feminine and Its Religious Expressions* (San Francisco: Harper & Row, 1987).

35. Donald Nicholl, *Holiness* (New York: Paulist Press, 1987).

PART THREE: CANONIZATION: PROCESS AND POLITICS

1. Cited by Kenneth Woodward, *Making Saints: How the Catholic Church Determines Who Becomes a Saint, Who Doesn't, and Why* (New York: Simon & Schuster, Touchstone Books, 1990), p. 75. In 1930 Pope Pius XI established a special historical section in the Congregation of Rites to deal with ancient causes. Since eyewitnesses were no longer available, judgments were to be rendered on the basis of historical evidence alone.

2. These are adapted from Woodward, *Making Saints,* pp. 79–86, which mixes outdated with still operative rules and procedures.

3. For an English translation of the full text, see *New Laws for the Causes of Saints,* trans. Robert J. Sarno (Rome: Sacred Congregation for the Causes of Saints, 1983), pp. 3–9.

4. *Divinus perfectionis Magister,* III.13.b. Unfortunately, according to Kenneth Woodward, these biographies "vary widely in quality." In his on-site research for his *Making Saints,* he had "seen important questions not addressed, pious argument in place of solid evidence, and (as in the classic case of Escrivá) contrary evidence not admitted in the tribunals set up to hear from witnesses to the candidate's life and virtue." Moreover, "the Church is not attracting scholars of great competence and commitment to replace the best who have given their lives to this important work." "Slow Up on Saint-making," *The Tablet* 253 (November 13, 1999): 1539.

5. *Divinus perfectionis Magister,* III.15.

6. The pertinent text reads: "We teach and define as a divinely revealed dogma that when the Roman pontiff speaks *ex cathedra,* that is, when, in the exercise of his office as shepherd and teacher of all Christians, in virtue of his supreme apostolic authority, he defines a doctrine concerning faith or morals to be held by the whole church, he possesses, by the divine assistance promised to him in blessed Peter, that infallibility which the divine Redeemer willed his church to enjoy in defining doctrine concerning faith or morals." *Decrees of the Ecumenical Councils,* vol. 2, ed. Norman P. Tanner (London: Sheed & Ward; Washington, DC: Georgetown University Press, 1990), p. 816.

7. Against this view, Jesuit theologian Francis A. Sullivan writes: "It is not clear to me that infallibility on such a question is necessarily required in order for the magisterium to be able to safeguard and explain the deposit of revelation." *Magisterium: Teaching Authority in the Church* (New York: Paulist Press, 1983), p. 136. Questions have also been raised by Peter Chirico, *Infallibility: The Crossroads of Doctrine* (Kansas City, KS: Sheed, Andrews and McMeel, 1977), p. 284.

8. See the Dogmatic Constitution on the Church, n. 25: "This infallibility, however, with which the divine redeemer wished to endow his church in defining doctrine pertaining to faith and morals, *extends just as far as the deposit of revelation,* which must be religiously guarded and faithfully expounded" (my emphasis). And later in the same article: "Furthermore, when the Roman pontiff, or the body of bishops together with him, define a doctrine, they do so *in conformity with revelation itself.*" John T. Ford, C.S.C., a specialist in the theology of infallibility, points out that in "identifying the 'subject-matter' of infallibility with matters of revelation, Vatican II seemingly disowned the position of those theologians who maximalized the scope of infallibility to include practically any type of official papal pronouncement." "Infallibility," in *The New Dictionary of Theology,* ed. Joseph A. Komonchak, Mary Collins, Dermot A. Lane (Wilmington, DE: Michael Glazier, 1987), p. 520.

9. Thus, Francis A. Sullivan writes that, "given the ease of world-wide consultation provided by modern means of communication, a pope could hardly be said in the future to have fulfilled his *grave obligation* to make use of every suitable means available to him in the preparation of an *ex cathedra* definition, if he neglected to consult the episcopal college about the doctrine he contemplated defining" (*Magisterium,* p. 105).

10. Kenneth Woodward has argued that there should be fewer canonizations, "coupled with a greater appreciation for beatification." Canonization, he writes, "should be reserved for those, like Mother Teresa of Calcutta and John XXIII, who have achieved universal recognition. At the same time, beatification ought not to be looked upon as the final step towards something higher. Let it stand, rather, for what it is: exceptional holiness recognized. And let the Blesseds receive their due as regional saints." Canonization should follow only "upon later discernment of the Church as a whole;

that is, only if and when a local saint (Blessed) develops a wider cult" ("Slow Up on Saint-making," pp. 1539–40).

11. And what of the additional problem of approving the cult of someone who never existed? This occurred in the case of Felix of Valois, whom the Trinitarians identified as their cofounder, along with John of Matha. Felix was a fiction created by Trinitarian writers who were attempting to endow their order with luster by claiming as one of their founders a figure with royal blood. There is no documentary evidence he ever existed. In spite of this, his cult and that of John of Matha was approved by the Congregation of Rites in 1666. Innocent XI assigned November 20 as Felix's feast day and in 1694 Innocent XII ordered it to be celebrated by the universal Church, which implied what is known as equipollent (or equivalent) canonization.

12. A point amply demonstrated in my *Lives of the Popes: The Pontiffs from St. Peter to John Paul II* (San Francisco: HarperSanFrancisco, 1997), and in similar works on the history of the papacy.

13. "Saints and Martyrs: Some Contemporary Considerations," *Theological Studies* 60 (1999): 529–30.

14. *Friends of God and Prophets: A Feminist Theological Reading of the Communion of Saints* (New York: Continuum, 1998), p. 101. See also Pierre Delooz, "Towards a Sociological Study of Canonized Saints," in *Saints and Their Cults: Studies in Religious Sociology, Folklore, and History,* ed. Stephen Wilson (London and New York: Cambridge University Press, 1983), pp. 189–216; Peter Hebblethwaite, *In the Vatican: How the Church Is Run—Its Personalities, Traditions and Conflicts* (Bethesda, MD: Adler & Adler, 1986), pp. 105–16; and Woodward, *Making Saints,* pp. 280–335.

15. See, for example, Michael Goodich, "The Politics of Canonization in the Thirteenth Century: Lay and Mendicant Saints," in Wilson, ed., *Saints and Their Cults,* pp. 169–87. In the same volume the introduction by the editor, Stephen Wilson, is particularly useful and illuminating (pp. 1–53).

16. There were at least three other popes who abdicated, and possibly a fourth. See my *Lives of the Popes,* p. 425.

17. See, for example, John Cornwell, *Hitler's Pope: The Secret History of Pius XII* (New York: Viking, 1999).

18. Elizabeth Johnson points out that the *withholding* of canonization has also been employed as a political instrument to ensure conformity with "a narrow definition of doctrinal orthodoxy, thereby largely excluding pioneering thinkers, intellectuals, artists, or anyone with a critical or challenging spirit" (*Friends of God and Prophets,* p. 103).

19. *Making Saints,* p. 385.

20. John Phillips, "Crowds hail Opus Dei's blessed founder," *The Times* (London), May 18, 1992.

21. Kenneth L. Woodward, "A Questionable Saint," *Newsweek* (January 13, 1992): 58. The other dissenting cardinal was Enrique y Tarancón, past president of the Spanish Bishops Conference.

22. Peter Hebblethwaite, "Saint Trying the Church's Patience," *The Guardian* (London), January 10, 1992, p. 19.

23. *Making Saints,* p. 387.

PART V: EPILOGUE: SAINTS AND THE CHURCH

1. See Lawrence S. Cunningham, "Saints and Martyrs: Some Contemporary Considerations," *Theological Studies* 60 (1999): 531, and also "A Decade of Research on the Saints: 1980–1990," *Theological Studies* 53 (1992): 522–24.

2. This is what David Tracy means by a "classic" in his *The Analogical Imagination: Christian Theology and the Culture of Pluralism* (New York: Crossroad, 1981), p. 164.

3. "Being more closely united to Christ, those who dwell in heaven consolidate the holiness of the whole church, add to the nobility of the worship that the church offers to God here on earth, and in many ways help in a greater upbuilding of the church (see 1 Corinthians 12:12–27)." Vatican Council II, Dogmatic Constitution on the Church, n. 49.

4. Some readers will notice the absence of favored saints in the historical survey below. Preference was given to those whose prominence and abiding significance are reflected in the inclusion of their feasts on the General Roman Calendar.

5. Dogmatic Constitution on the Church, n. 54.

6. Francis, Clare, Anthony of Padua, and Peter of Verona were canonized within two years of their deaths (in Anthony's case, less than one year). Dominic was canonized thirteen years after his death, while Thomas Aquinas and Bonaventure were not canonized until the fourteenth century, Bonaventure almost sixty years after Thomas. Albert the Great was beatified in 1622, but not canonized until 1931, at which time he was also declared a Doctor of the Church.

7. Mechthilde, however, was never formally canonized.

8. Bridget was canonized in 1391, but Catherine was not canonized until the following century, in 1461.

9. The date of Sergius's canonization is uncertain, but it was sometime before the Council of Florence's Decree of Union in 1439.

10. Joan of Arc, however, was not canonized until 1921, and then only to reestablish diplomatic relations between the Holy See and France. Frances of Rome was canonized in 1608, early in the century of the laity, heralded by Francis de Sales.

11. Both were canonized at mid-century, in 1450 and 1455, respectively.

12. Ignatius was canonized along with Teresa in 1622. John of the Cross was canonized in 1726.

13. Francis of Paola, who died in 1507, was the only one of these saints canonized in the sixteenth century (1519). Philip Neri was canonized in 1622, Peter of Alcántara in 1669, John of God in 1690, John of the Cross in 1726, Camillus de Lellis in 1746, Jerome Emiliani in 1768, Angela Merici in 1807, and Anthony Mary Zaccaria in 1897.

14. Pius V was beatified in 1672 and canonized in 1712. Robert Bellarmine was not beatified until 1923 and canonized until 1930, because he had supported the view that the pope enjoyed only indirect authority over temporal rulers. Peter Canisius was beatified in 1864 and canonized in 1925.

15. Thomas More and John Fisher were beatified in 1886 and canonized in 1935. Edmund Campion was beatified in 1588, but not canonized until 1970.

16. Francis Xavier was canonized in 1622; Paul Miki, in 1862.

17. Francis de Sales was canonized in 1665.

18. Vincent de Paul was canonized in 1737, Jane Frances de Chantal and Joseph Calasanz in 1767, John Eudes in 1925, and Louise de Marillac in 1934.

19. Isaac Jogues was canonized in 1930. Kateri Tekakwitha was beatified in 1980. She has not yet been canonized.

20. Rose of Lima was canonized in 1671, Peter Claver in 1888, and, although beatified in 1837, Martin de Porres was not canonized until 1962.

21. Margaret Mary Alacoque was canonized in 1920.

22. Alphonsus Liguori was canonized in 1839, Paul of the Cross in 1867, John Baptist de La Salle in 1900, and Louis Grignion de Montfort in 1947. The canonization of

Montfort came at a time when Marian devotions were at their height. His writings and cult were diminished in influence after the Second Vatican Council when Marian devotion became more biblically and liturgically oriented and more firmly Christocentric.

23. Each of these saints was canonized in the twentieth century: John Bosco in 1934, Anthony Claret in 1950, Peter Julian Eymard in 1962, Julie Billiart in 1969, and Elizabeth Ann Seton in 1975. Like Louis Grignion de Montfort's (see note 22 above), Eymard's eucharistic spirituality was outpaced by theological and liturgical developments at the Second Vatican Council.

24. Each of these saints was also canonized in the twentieth century: the Little Flower and John Vianney in 1925, Bernardette Soubirous in 1933, and Maria Goretti in 1950.

25. Mother Cabrini was canonized in 1946, Mary MacKillop in 1995, Edith Stein in 1999, and Katharine Drexel in 2000 (she was beatified, however, in 1988).

26. Pope Pius X was canonized in 1954, and Maximilian Kolbe in 1982. Stein's canonization was controversial because of the sensitivity of the Jewish community, many of whom feel conversion from Judaism is tantamount to apostasy. Kolbe's was controversial because of some evidence of anti-Semitism in his background. And Pius X had a highly unfavorable reputation among Catholic scholars for his persecution of so many of their number in the anti-Modernist campaign.

27. The lists of saints in the various categories that follow are not exhaustive. They are intended to be representative of some of the best of the Church's holiest disciples.

28. Here again the selections are a matter of personal judgment—as, for example, in the case of a century's best athletes or a millennium's most significant figures. Many readers will prefer a list with different names and/or in different order. The ratio of women to men will be especially noticeable. The unfortunate fact is that far more men than women have been canonized, and far more male saints than female saints have had opportunities for exercising leadership in the Church and for making a profound impact on its life and history. That situation has finally—and happily—begun to change, but it will be some time before more recently canonized saints like Louise de Marillac (1934), Frances Xavier Cabrini (1946), Julie Billiart (1969), Elizabeth Ann Seton (1975), Mary MacKillop (1995), Teresa Benedicta of the Cross (Edith Stein) (1999), and Katharine Drexel (2000) will begin to rival in prominence and influence those on the list that follows. However, if this particular list stimulates counterproposals, all the better.

29. See Jean M.-R. Tillard, *The Bishop of Rome*, trans. John de Satgé (Wilmington, DE: Michael Glazier, 1983), pp. 74–86.

30. Cited in Robert Ellsberg, *All Saints: Daily Reflections on Saints, Prophets, and Witnesses for Our Time* (New York: Crossroad, 1997), p. 519.

Glossary

abbess the female leader of a community of nuns. In the Celtic Church of the sixth and seventh centuries, some abbesses exercised authority beyond their monasteries, greater even than that of a bishop, for example, Ita of Killeedy [January 15] and Brigid of Kildare [February 1]. Several abbesses in Ireland and on the Continent also functioned as superiors of double monasteries, that is, of both men and women.

abbot (Aram. *abba,* "father"), the leader of a male monastic community. He is elected by his community and exercises the kind of authority over them that a bishop exercises in his diocese, namely, ordinary jurisdiction.

Albigensianism, a dualist heresy that viewed all reality as an eternal battle between the world of the spirit created by the infinitely good God and the world of the flesh created by the infinitely evil Satan. Its followers regarded themselves as holier than the Church and rejected its authority. The heresy flourished in southern France and northern Italy from the mid-twelfth to the fourteenth century. The Cistercians and Dominicans, led by Dominic [August 8] himself, preached against it, but without success. It was eventually overcome by the Albigensian Crusade (1209–19) and the Inquisition.

anchorite, anchoress, a person dedicated to a life of strict solitude and penance, equivalent to that of a hermit. The person's cell was attached to a church. One of the most celebrated anchoresses was Julian of Norwich [May 8]. The closest approximation of the life of an anchorite today would be that of Carthusian and Camaldolese hermits.

antipope, an individual whose claim to the papacy was rejected by the Church as invalid. There have been thirty-nine antipopes. The first antipope was Hippolytus (217–35) [August 13]; the last was Felix V (1439–49).

Arianism, a fourth-century heresy that denied the divinity of Jesus Christ, regarding him as only the greatest of creatures. It was condemned by the Council of Nicaea in 325, under the theological leadership of Athanasius [May 2], but it continued to divide the empire throughout most of the remainder of the century as it went in and out of favor with successive emperors. The heresy was finally vanquished at the Council of Constantinople in 381, thanks in large part to the careful theological work of the Cappadocian Fathers: Basil the Great [January 2], Gregory Nazianzen [January 2], and Gregory of Nyssa [January 10].

asceticism (Gk. *askesis,* "exercise"), the practice of religious discipline with an emphasis on self-control, self-denial, mortification, penance, and the fostering of virtue. Jesus himself is the model of asceticism. Other New Testament models included John the Baptist [June 24, August 29]. Anthony of Egypt [January 17] and the other Desert Fathers were also classical exemplars of asceticism.

Avignon, a city and archdiocese in southeastern France and the seat of the papacy from 1309 to 1377 (a period also described as the "Babylonian Captivity" of the papacy), and also of rival popes during the Great Western Schism (1378–1417). Catherine of Siena [April 29] was one of the leading advocates of the return of the papacy to Rome.

beatification, the second-to-last step in the official process of proclaiming an individual a saint. Evidence of heroic virtue and of one miracle brought about through the intercession of the candidate (known as the Servant of God) is required. The person beatified is called "Blessed" and may be venerated locally or within a particular religious community.

Bollandists, a group of Jesuit editors of the *Acta Sanctorum* (Lat., "Lives of the Saints"), originally organized by Jean Bolland (1596–1665) in Antwerp, Belgium. Their purpose was to prepare accurate lives of the saints without apocryphal material. Their work continues to be published in the *Analecta Bollandiana,* a journal of hagiographical information.

canonization, the process by which an individual is raised to sainthood in the Catholic Church. Since the word "canon" is derived from a Greek word meaning "rule" or "list," canonization is literally the process of adding someone to the official "list" of saints. The first papal canonization was in 993 by John XV. In 1234 Pope Gregory IX decreed that only the pope has the authority to canonize a saint. Before that, saints were proclaimed locally, usually with the approval of the bishop.

cardinal (Lat. *cardo,* "hinge"), the title given to a member of the College of Cardinals, all of whom are appointed directly by the pope and who serve as his close advisers and as papal electors (if they are under the age of eighty). The title was originally given to members of the Roman clergy who administered certain key ("hinge") churches in Rome. A few of the saints were cardinals, including Charles Borromeo [November 4] and Robert Bellarmine [September 17].

Chalcedon, Council of (451), the ecumenical council that definitively taught (against the Monophysites) that in Jesus Christ there is only one divine Person, but two natures, one divine and one human.

chapter, a meeting of delegates of religious orders for elections and the handling of other important issues that face their community. The term "chapter" is derived from the monastic practice of assembling daily to listen to a reading of a chapter from the Rule. Chapters may be general, that is, affecting the whole order, provincial, or local.

Charlemagne, or Charles the Great (ca. 742–814), Frankish king and from 800 the first emperor of what would eventually become the Holy Roman Empire (in 962). He was the virtual head of the Church in his domains (which included the Holy See); he controlled all episcopal appointments, promulgated monastic and liturgical reforms as well as disciplinary reforms for clergy, and summoned and presided over church councils.

Cluny, French Benedictine monastery founded near Mâcon in Burgundy in 909 and the center of monastic reform during the tenth and eleventh centuries. By the mid-twelfth century there were over one thousand Cluniac monasteries. Cluny was eventually eclipsed by new orders and was finally suppressed by the French Revolution in 1790. Among the abbots of Cluny recognized as saints were Odo, Maiolus, Odilo, Hugh, and Peter the Venerable [all on May 11].

communion of saints, the faithful on earth, in purgatory, and in heaven (the saints, canonized or not), all bound together in one "communion" by the grace of the Holy Spirit. The saints in heaven assist those in purgatory and on earth with their prayers, and those on earth, in turn, pray to the saints to ask them to intercede with God on their behalf.

confessor (Lat. *confiteri,* "to declare openly"), a term applied to those saints of the early Church who suffered for the faith by imprisonment, torture, exile, or the loss of personal property, but who were not actually put to death. They were sometimes known as "white martyrs."

congregation, an alternate term for a religious order or institute. The former distinction between an order and a congregation, based on technical differences related to their vows, is now outdated. Either term applies to a religious community living under a Rule and publicly professing the vows of poverty, chastity, and obedience or their equivalents.

Congregation for the Causes of Saints, the Vatican dicastery, or agency, formerly known as the Sacred Congregation of Rites, responsible for all matters pertaining to the beatification and canonization of saints and the preservation of relics. It also decides on the conferral of the title "Doctor of the Church" on a given saint.

Constantine, Edict of (313), sometimes called the Edict of Milan, a document from Constantine the Great [May 21] granting toleration to all religions, including Christianity. By this act, imperial persecution of Christians came to an end. On the other hand, the privileges that accrued to the Church led to a countercultural revolution of sorts, known as monasticism, under the leadership of such ascetics as Anthony of Egypt [January 17].

Constantinople, the traditional seat of Eastern Christianity. The emperor Constantine transferred the capital of the Roman Empire from Rome to Constantinople in 330, building the new city on the site of the Greek city of Byzantium. It remained the capital of the Eastern, or Byzantine, empire until 1453, when it fell to the Turks.

Counter-Reformation/Catholic Reformation, the renewal and reform of the Catholic Church undertaken after the outbreak of the Protestant Reformation in the early sixteenth century. Among its elements were the Council of Trent (1545–63); the founding of new religious orders, such as the Jesuits (1540), by Ignatius of Loyola [July 31], and the Oratorians, by Philip Neri [May 26]; the reform of existing orders, like the Carmelites, by Teresa of Ávila [October 15] and John of the Cross [December 14]; and the establishment of seminaries for the education and training of future priests. Among the period's leading theologians were Robert Bellarmine [September 17] and Peter Canisius [December 21], and among its leading bishops was Charles Borromeo [November 4].

Crusades, a series of wars fought initially to recover or to defend Christian territory and holy sites in the Holy Land (Palestine), Spain, and Sicily. The First Crusade was called by Urban II in 1095, and the Fifth Crusade ended in 1221. Many of the medieval popes were almost obsessed with the need to launch crusades and push back the Turks from one place or another, including Italy itself. Among the saints who preached on behalf of the Crusades were Bernard of Clairvaux [August 20] and Catherine of Siena [April 29]. Unfortunately, the Crusades were transformed into economic and political enterprises and did much to widen the rift between the Eastern and Western Churches.

cult (Lat. *cultus,* "worship," "reverence"), the public veneration accorded to someone who has been beatified or canonized.

"Devil's Advocate," now called the Promoter of the Faith, an office within the Congregation for the Causes of Saints whose purpose is to investigate thoroughly any objections raised against a cause for beatification and canonization and to safeguard the integrity of the process.

devotions, pious practices not directly connected with the official worship of the Church (liturgy). Examples are the Stations of the Cross (which involve meditation on various aspects of the Passion and death of Jesus, while moving from depiction to depiction, which are usually on the walls of a church), the Rosary, devotion to the Miraculous Medal (popularized by Catherine Labouré [November 28]), and devotion to the Sacred Heart (popularized by Margaret Mary Alacoque [October 16]).

Divine Office, the public prayer of the Church for praising God and sanctifying the day. It is also known as the Liturgy of the Hours. It consists of an Office of

Readings (formerly Matins), Morning and Evening Prayer (formerly Lauds and Vespers), Daytime Prayer (formerly Prime, Terce, Sext, and None), and Night Prayer (formerly Compline). The Psalms constitute many of the prayers. The book containing these readings and prayers is called a breviary. The Divine Office is chanted in common in monasteries and in other similar settings and is recited privately by priests and others who are obliged to do so.

discalced (Lat., "unshod"), the term applied to religious orders or branches of orders whose members do not wear shoes. This practice has its roots in Matthew 10:10 and was taken up by the early Eastern monks, Francis of Assisi [October 4], and the Spanish Discalced Franciscans founded by Peter of Alcántara [October 22]. The name Discalced was used of those reformed Carmelites who became a new order in 1593 after the deaths of their leaders, Teresa of Ávila [October 15] and John of the Cross [December 14].

disciple, discipleship (Lat., "one who learns"), a follower of Christ; the process, life patterns, and matrix of activities involved in the following and imitation of Christ. "Disciple" is the name most frequently given to those around Jesus who accepted him as their Master (Matt. 5:1; Luke 6:17; 10:1; 19:37). "Discipleship" is the primary paradigm for being a dedicated Christian.

Doctors of the Church, canonized saints officially recognized by the pope (or an ecumenical council) as eminent teachers of the faith, among whom are numbered, for example, Augustine of Hippo [August 28], Athanasius [May 2], Basil the Great [January 2], Thomas Aquinas [January 28], Bonaventure [July 15], John of the Cross [December 14], Teresa of Ávila [October 15], and Catherine of Siena [April 29].

dulia (Gk., "service"), the honor given to the saints, recognizing the presence of God in them. It is distinguished from *latria,* which is the worship rendered only to God, and *hyperdulia,* which is the special honor reserved for the Blessed Virgin Mary because of her unique role as the Mother of God.

East-West Schism, the disruption of the bonds of ecclesiastical communion between Rome and Constantinople, beginning already with the Christological controversies of the fifth century but coming to a climax in 1054 with the mutual excommunications by the patriarch of Constantinople, Michael Cerularius, and the Bishop of Rome, Leo IX. The schism was sealed by the Crusades (1095–1291) and the Orthodox rejection of the Decree of Union of the Council of Florence in 1439. Pope Paul VI and Ecumenical Patriarch Athenagoras I mutually lifted the excommunications in 1964 during a meeting in Jerusalem.

Ephesus, Council of (431), the third ecumenical council, which defined (against the Nestorians) that in Christ there is only one divine Person, and that Mary is, therefore, the Mother of God, not only the mother of Jesus.

feast day, a day set aside to honor liturgically the life of a saint. The feast day is almost always the day of the saint's death, since it is regarded as the beginning of a saint's new life in heaven.

Fourteen Holy Helpers, a group of saints known for their favorable response to prayers of petition, especially for recovery from diseases and for spiritual strength at the hour of death. The saints were Acacius, Barbara [December 4], Blase [February 3], Catherine of Alexandria (who almost certainly never existed; see November 25), Christopher [July 25], Cyricus, Denis [October 9], Erasmus [June 2], Eustace, George [April 23], Giles [September 1], Margaret of Antioch (who also probably never existed; see July 20), Pantaleon [July 27], and Vitus [June 15]. The devotion was popular in the Rhineland and then in other parts of Europe (including the rest of Germany, Hungary, and Sweden) from the fourteenth century, but was later discouraged by the Council of Trent in the sixteenth century.

friar (lit., "brother"), the distinctive title of members of mendicant orders, especially the Dominicans, Franciscans, Augustinians, and Carmelites. Friars are distinguished from members of monastic communities who are called monks.

General Roman Calendar, the liturgical calendar, revised in 1969, containing the list of feasts of saints, known as the Sanctorale, celebrated by the Roman Catholic Church worldwide, as well as the Sundays and movable feasts that are associated with the various seasons of the year (Advent, Christmas, Lent, Holy Week, Easter, Ordinary Time), known as the Temporale. The General Roman Calendar is distinguished from the particular calendars of various countries and religious orders, which include additional feasts proper to those countries and religious communities. (*See also* Proper Calendar for the Dioceses of the U.S.A.)

Gregorian reform, the movement of church renewal beginning in the tenth century but linked most directly with its strongest exponent, Gregory VII (1073–85) [May 25]. It included the combating of simony, nepotism, clerical marriage, and lay investiture of church officials.

hagiography (Gk. *hagios,* "holy"; *graphein,* "writing"), biographical narratives of the saints.

halo, a ring or circle of light surrounding the head of a saint to signify a close association with God. Until the fifth century, only Jesus was so depicted. Thereafter, the use of the halo was extended to the Blessed Virgin Mary, the angels, and the other saints.

hermit (Gk. *erēmia,* "desert"), one who embraces a solitary life. Hermits appeared first in the desert (thus, their name) and then as parts of communities of hermits, such as the Carthusians and the Camaldolese. The most famous hermit was Anthony of Egypt [January 17].

heroic virtue, the exemplary practice of Christian virtues so that one becomes a model and ideal of Christian discipleship. There must be evidence of such virtue before anyone can be beatified or canonized a saint.

holiness, a spiritual quality derived from participation in the life of God, who alone is holy (Lev. 19:2). All Christians are called to holiness (Vatican II, Dogmatic Constitution on the Church, chap. 5).

iconoclasm, destruction of religious images ordered by the Byzantine emperors from emperor Leo XIII (717–41) to 843, when their use was restored by the empress Theodora. The controversy between iconoclasts and iconophiles—a replay of the Christological controversies of the fifth through seventh centuries—was bitter and intense. The former insisted that any representation of Christ constituted an assault on his divinity, while the latter maintained that, in keeping with the principle of the Incarnation, the divine is always capable of being embodied, or imaged, in the human or the material.

Inquisition, a now defunct institution established in the Middle Ages for the punishment and eradication of heresy. Sometimes the punishment included torture and death. The Roman Inquisition, established and maintained by the popes, is to be distinguished from the even more infamous Spanish Inquisition, established by Ferdinand and Isabella in 1479. The latter was directed especially against converted Muslims and Jews who had secretly returned to the practice of their respective faiths. It was abolished by royal decree in 1834. The most famous victim of the Roman Inquisition was the Italian astronomer and mathematician Galileo (d. 1642), who was rehabilitated posthumously by John Paul II in 1992. The Roman Congregation of the Inquisition, along with the Holy Office, was renamed and folded into the Congregation for the Doctrine of the Faith by Paul VI in 1965.

institute, religious, a group, approved by competent church authority, whose members live in community and profess the public vows of poverty, chastity, and obedience. It may be of diocesan right (under the local bishop) or of pontifical right (under the direct authority of the Vatican). It may also be clerical or lay, and contemplative or active.

Iona, an important monastery founded ca. 565 by Columba [June 9] on the island of Hy, off the west coast of Scotland. It soon became the center of Irish missionary activity in Scotland and northern England, as well as a channel of communication between Ireland and these areas.

Jansenism, a seventeenth-century Catholic reform movement originating in the Low Countries and France but expanding into the territories of the Hapsburgs and Italy during the eighteenth century. It was pessimistic about human nature and free will and emphasized the need for rigid asceticism, which set it against the Jesuits, who took a more pastorally realistic approach to the moral life. It also opposed the centralizing tendencies of the Counter-Reformation, which set it against the hierarchy of the Church, and the absolutist tendencies of the French government, which set it against the temporal authorities as well. It was condemned by various popes, including Alexander VII (1656 and 1665) and Clement XI (1713) and by saints such as Vincent de Paul [September 27]. Jansenism disappeared in France after the death of a sympathetic archbishop of Paris in 1729, but it produced a schism in Holland in 1723 and survives today as a branch of the Old Catholic Church.

lay brother, a member of a male religious community who is fully incorporated into it but is not ordained. Traditionally, lay brothers had less education than the ordained members and were involved principally in manual labor. Martin de Porres [November 3] was a Dominican lay brother.

martyr (Gk., "witness"), one who has given up his or her life for the faith. The shedding of one's blood was seen as a kind of second baptism in which one's sins were forgiven and salvation assured. No evidence of a miracle is required for the canonization of a martyr.

martyrology, a list of feast days of saints with all applicable names for any given date. The martyrology provides some biographical data, such as place of birth, death, and burial. The *Roman Martyrology* contains the official list of saints venerated by the Church.

mendicants (Lat., "beggars"), also known as friars, religious with the privilege of begging (Lat. *mendicare*) in the dioceses where they have been established. Mendicant orders, first founded at the beginning of the thirteenth century, are vowed to communal and personal poverty. The first mendicant orders were the Franciscans and Dominicans. The Carmelites, Augustinians, Servites, and others were also given the mendicant title and privileges. Unlike traditional monks in the Benedictine tradition, the friars were allowed to work outside of their monastic foundations, engaging in preaching, hearing confessions, and other pastoral and ministerial work.

miracle, an action performed directly by God or through human beings that provokes wonder and amazement. Before a nonmartyr can be beatified, at least one miracle must be directly attributable to his or her intercession with God. A second miracle is necessary for canonization.

mission, parish, a series of sermons and devotional exercises conducted in a parish, over the course of a week or more, for the purpose of renewing its spiritual life and calling people to repentance for their sins. The practice originated during the Catholic Counter-Reformation in the sixteenth century and was promoted by religious orders, especially the Jesuits. The parish mission declined in the eighteenth century, but was revived in the nineteenth and became popular in the United States during the first half of the twentieth century. The practice declined once again after the Second Vatican Council (1962–65).

monasticism (Gk. *monos*, "one, alone"), an institutionalized form of ascetical religious life in which individuals take vows of poverty, chastity, obedience, and (as in the Benedictines) stability, separating themselves from society either singly (eremetic form) or in community (cenobitic form). The individual practitioners are called monks, and their common residence is called a monastery. Anthony of Egypt [January 17] is regarded as the founder of monasticism, and Benedict of Nursia [July 11] as the founder of monasticism as it is known today in the West.

mystic, one whose experience of the presence of God is intense, direct, and transforming, but not necessarily accompanied by extraordinary phenomena. Mystics experience a deep communion of love and of knowledge with God and, in God, with other people and all reality.

Nicaea, First Council of (325), the first ecumenical council of the Church, held at the invitation of the emperor Constantine [May 21], to deal with the problem of Arianism, which taught that Christ was only the greatest of creatures. The council defined the divinity of Christ, declaring him to be "of the same substance" (Gk. *homoousios*) as God the Father. The leading figure at the council and the leading defender of its teachings afterward was Athanasius [May 2].

nun, a woman who is a member of a religious order and who has taken solemn vows of poverty, chastity, and obedience. Nuns observe the papal cloister, which means that they live completely separate from all nonmembers of their community. In the more common usage, nuns are members of a women's religious order who take simple vows and do not observe the cloister. Their usual title is "sister."

patron saint, a saint venerated as a special protector or intercessor in relation to an individual (who took or was given the saint's name at baptism), a city or town, a country, a parish church, a diocese, an occupation, or a particular problem, usually related to health.

Pelagianism, a fifth-century heresy, linked with the name of Pelagius (d. ca. 425), a British monk ministering in Rome, that held that salvation is possible through human effort alone, without the aid of grace. The heresy was vigorously opposed by Augustine of Hippo [August 28].

Propaganda Fide, or Congregation for the Propagation of the Faith, a department of the Roman Curia originally begun by Pius V (1566–72) [April 30] and formally established by Gregory XV (1621–23) to promote the missions to non-Christians in the Orient and later also to Protestants in Europe. It is now called the Congregation for the Evangelization of Peoples.

Proper Calendar for the Dioceses of the U.S.A., the liturgical calendar, supplemental to the General Roman Calendar, containing the feasts of saints that are observed by the Roman Catholic Church in the United States of America.

Quartodecimans (Lat., "fourteenth"), those, especially in Asia Minor, who celebrated Easter on the fourteenth day of the Jewish month of Nisan (what they called Christian Passover), instead of on the following Sunday, in accordance with the practice in Rome and elsewhere in the Church. Victor I (189–98) even threatened to excommunicate them, but he was rebuked by Irenaeus of Lyons [June 28] for making such a threat. The First Council of Nicaea (325) settled on the Sunday celebration of Easter, but the Quartodeciman practice continued until the fifth century.

relics (Lat. *reliquae,* "remains"), in the strict sense, the material remains of the bodies of those who have been canonized or beatified; in a wider sense, any of their personal effects or items used by them in their lifetime. Canon 1237.2 of the Church's Code of Canon Law requires that "the relics of martyrs and others saints [be] kept under a fixed altar."

religious orders and congregations, groups living under a religious Rule and publicly professing the vows of poverty, chastity, and obedience or their equivalents.

Roman Curia, the network of secretariats, congregations, tribunals, councils, offices, commissions, committees, and individuals who assist the pope in his responsibilities as earthly head of the universal Church. Although popes of the early centuries had assistants in their capacity as Bishops of Rome, the Roman Curia as such was first organized by Sixtus V in 1588.

Roman Martyrology, the Catholic Church's official list of saints and their feast days, with basic information about them, such as the date and place of their birth, death, and burial. Compiled by a commission of ten scholars and issued by Pope Gregory XIII in 1584 to replace similar documents in use at the time, it has been revised and updated several times since then.

saint, one who has officially been recognized by the Church as a person who has lived a heroically virtuous life, is now in heaven, and can be venerated publicly by the faithful. There are, of course, more saints than those who have been officially proclaimed as such. Those saints are honored on the feast of All Saints [November 1].

schism (Gk. *schisma,* "tear"), a formal breach of church unity. Unlike heresy, a schism is not directed against orthodoxy of doctrine but against communion. The most famous schisms in the history of the Church have been the East-West Schism (begun in 1054) and the Great Western Schism (1378–1417).

see (Lat. *sedes,* "seat"), another name for a diocese. The Latin word refers to the bishop's chair as symbolic of his episcopal authority.

shrine (Lat. *scrinium,* "coffer"), a container for relics exhibited in a church or chapel; a destination for pilgrims, as, for example, the tomb of a saint.

spirituality, Christian, life in the Holy Spirit, who incorporates the Christian into the ecclesial Body of Jesus Christ, through whom the Christian has access to God the Creator in a life of faith, hope, love, and service.

stigmata (Lat., "marks"), bodily signs borne in commemoration of Christ's Passion, usually in the form of wounds on the hands and feet and in the side. The most famous stigmatic was Francis of Assisi [October 4]. Catherine of Siena [April 29] also claimed to be a stigmatic, but her wounds were not visible.

tertiary. *See* third orders.

third orders, associations of laity (third orders secular) or of religious women and men (third orders regular). Third order has primarily been a category for laypersons who seek to attain holiness by following a way of life in the world, but under the spiritual guidance of a papally approved religious institute, such as the Franciscans and Dominicans. Such members are called tertiaries. Two of the most famous Dominican tertiaries were Catherine of Siena [April 29] and Rose of Lima [August 23].

translation, the transfer, often with much solemnity, of the exhumed body of a deceased holy person from the place of burial to a shrine, where it could be venerated publicly. During the first Christian millennium, translation was tantamount to canonization. Oftentimes, miracles and other prodigies were said to have occurred in connection with the translation, and, in the case of some saints, feast days were calculated according to the day of translation rather than the day of death.

Trent, Council of (1545–63), the Counter-Reformation council, held in three different segments, that defined the seven sacraments, the Real Presence of Christ in the Eucharist, and the role of tradition alongside that of Scripture and decreed the establishment of seminaries for the training of future priests and a catechism for the universal Church. The council shaped Catholic life and worship until the Second Vatican Council (1962–65).

Vatican, the shorthand term for the central headquarters of the Roman Catholic Church, including the pope and the Roman Curia. It takes its name from Vatican Hill, which in classical Rome was located outside the city walls and was the site of Nero's circus and a cemetery. Tradition holds that Peter [June 29] was martyred in Nero's circus and buried in the nearby cemetery. St. Peter's Basilica was built over that site.

Vatican Council I (1869–70), the ecumenical council that defined the dogma of papal infallibility and also taught the doctrine of papal primacy.

Vatican Council II (1962–65), the ecumenical council that ended the Tridentine era (beginning with the Council of Trent in the sixteenth century) and inaugurated a new era of renewal and reform, marked by an emphasis on the Church as the whole People of God, on the collegiality of the bishops (governing the Church in collaboration with, rather than under, the pope), on the social mission of the Church on behalf of the poor and the oppressed, on the participation of the laity in the worship and ministries of the Church, and on the Church's need to dialogue and collaborate with other Christian churches, other religions, and humankind at large.

Venerable, a traditional title given to a deceased person whose holiness is under formal investigation with a view toward beatification and canonization. The title is conferred on those who have been judged to have lived a heroically virtuous life but to whom no miracle has as yet been attributed. Cardinal John Henry Newman

[August 11] was given that title in 1991. The most famous bearer of this title is the Venerable Bede [May 25], who is actually a saint.

virtue (Lat. *virtus,* "power"), the facility, disposition, or attitude that moves one to accomplish moral good and to do it joyfully and perseveringly even against obstacles and at the cost of sacrifice. Virtue exercised to the highest degree is called "heroic."

Select Bibliography

IT IS NOT SURPRISING THAT THE LITERATURE ON THE SAINTS IS voluminous. Since this book is not intended primarily for scholars, but for a general, nonspecialist audience, the listing of titles below is included to provide only a representative sample of scholarly, encyclopedic, and popular works. There are additional references in the notes of the various chapters.

SCHOLARLY SERIES, ENCYCLOPEDIAS, AND DICTIONARIES OF A COMPREHENSIVE NATURE

The work of the Bollandists, a group of Jesuit editors of the multivolume *Acta Sanctorum* (Lat., "Lives of the Saints"), originally organized by Jean Bolland (1596–1665) in Antwerp, Belgium, continues to be published in the *Analecta Bollandiana* (Lat., "Bollandist Collections"), the most reputable journal of hagiographical information, including reviews and bibliographies, in the field. The *Acta* consist of a vast collection of saints' lives, critically edited, with commentary in Latin, and arranged by calendar. Three editions exist: the original begun in Antwerp and continued in Brussels (1643–1940), the incomplete Venice edition (1734–70), and the Paris edition (1863–87).

The *Bibliotheca Sanctorum* is a twelve-volume work (plus an index volume and one appendix volume) published in Rome, between 1961 and 1969, by the Instituto Giovanni XXIII della Pontificia Università Lateranense (It., The John XXIII Institute of the Pontifical Lateran University). David Farmer, one of the most distinguished scholars in the field, refers to this encyclopedia as "the most exhaustive work on the saints extant." Entries are arranged alphabetically and often include extensive bibliographies as well as splendid artwork and iconography.

The new twelve-volume edition of *Butler's Lives of the Saints,* edited by Paul Burns (Collegeville, MN: The Liturgical Press, 1998–2000), is a wholesale revision of an English-language classic. It is the best and most comprehensive source on the saints in English. Entries are arranged according to the calendar (each volume is devoted to one of the twelve months of the year).

Histoire des saints et de la sainteté Chrétienne, edited by Francesco Chiovaro and others (Paris: Hachette, 1986–88), is an excellent eleven-volume collection of lives arranged chronologically. These volumes often take up the theological questions surrounding the saints, accompanied by superb illustrations and color photographs.

Dictionnaire de spiritualité ascetique et mystique, doctrine et histoire, edited by M. Viller and others (Paris: Beauchesne, 1932–95), is published in sixteen volumes (plus an index volume). This excellent French encyclopedia considers many of the saints and provides both a biography and a summary of their thought.

The Roman Martyrology, edited by J. B. O'Connell (Westminster, MD: Newman Press, 1962), is an English translation of the fourth edition following the 1956 typical edition. It contains all the saints recognized to that point by the Catholic Church.

David Farmer's *The Oxford Dictionary of Saints,* 4th ed. (Oxford: Oxford University Press, 1997), is the best one-volume dictionary of its kind in English. The entries are alphabetically arranged, with short bibliographies. The orientation is historical rather than theological, and the bias is toward saints of the British Isles.

Other encyclopedias and dictionaries contain entries on many topics other than saints, but their entries on saints are of great value. This is especially the case with *The Oxford Dictionary of the Christian Church,* 3d ed., edited by Frank L. Cross and Elizabeth A. Livingstone (Oxford: Oxford University Press, 1997); and also *The New Catholic Encyclopedia,* edited by William J. McDonald (Washington, DC: Catholic University of America Press, 1967–), in fourteen volumes (plus an index volume and at least four supplementary volumes). A newly published Jubilee Volume, entitled *The Wojtyla Years,* contains biographical sketches of those whom Pope John Paul II beatified and canonized during his pontificate (pp. 426–637).

The author presumes also to suggest *The HarperCollins Encyclopedia of Catholicism* (San Francisco: HarperCollins, 1995), edited by Richard P. McBrien, which contains a number of entries on individual saints and on various schools of Christian spirituality.

John J. Delaney's one-volume *Dictionary of Saints* (Garden City, NY: Doubleday, 1980) does not pretend to be a work of scholarship, but it is of enduring value because many of its five thousand entries, arranged alphabetically, contain information on saints that can conveniently be found nowhere else.

Special mention should also be made of Robert Ellsberg's *All Saints: Daily Reflections on Saints, Prophets, and Witnesses for Our Time* (New York: Crossroad, 1997), which presents a series of short, yet meaty, meditative essays, arranged according to the calendar, on official saints, saints in the making, and holy persons from other religious traditions.

PRIMARY TEXTS AND COMMENTARIES

The Classics of Western Spirituality (New York: Paulist Press, 1978–) consists of English translations of the writings of many of the most significant saints. The introductions, often by major scholars, usually provide biographical information, historical context, and summaries of the translated texts. Other, similar series include *Traditions of Christianity Spirituality,* edited by Philip Sheldrake (Maryknoll, NY: Orbis Books, 1998–); *The Crossroad Spiritual Legacy Series,* edited by John Farina (New York: Crossroad, 1995–); and *Modern Spiritual Masters Series,* edited by Robert Ellsberg (Maryknoll, NY: Orbis Books, 1998–).

SPECIALIZED STUDIES

Saints are often identified with particular religious orders. Many works highlight the lives of such saints, for example, Marion Alphonse Habig's *The Franciscan Book of Saints* (Chicago: Franciscan Herald Press, 1979), and Joseph N. Tylenda's *Jesuit Saints and Martyrs: Short Biographies of the Saints, Blessed, Venerables, and Servants of God of the Society of Jesus* (Chicago: Loyola University Press, 1984). The Institute for Carmelite Studies in Washington, D.C., has been publishing a series on Carmelite saints and spirituality since 1979, and Cistercian Studies Publications in Kalamazoo, Michigan, has been publishing materials on the Cistercian tradition as well as monastic history and spiritualities since 1970.

Some studies also concentrate on particular periods of church history. One especially excellent work is *Saints and Their Cults: Studies in Religious Sociology, Folklore and History,* edited by Stephen Wilson (Cambridge: Cambridge University Press, 1983). Others include Peter Brown's *The Cult of the Saints: Its Rise and Function in Latin Christianity* (Chicago: University of Chicago Press, 1982); André Vauchez's *Sainthood in the Later Middle Ages,* translated by Jean Birrell (Cambridge: Cambridge University Press, 1997); and *Saints and Society: The Two Worlds of Western Christendom, 1000–1700,* by Donald Weinstein and Rudolph M. Bell (Chicago: University of Chicago Press, 1982).

For broader interfaith and ecumenical perspectives, see, for example, *The One Mediator, the Saints, and Mary: Lutherans and Catholics in Dialogue VIII,* edited by H. George Anderson, et al. (Minneapolis, MN: Augsburg Fortress Press, 1992); *Sainthood: Its Manifestations in World Religions,* edited by Richard Kieckhefer and George D. Bond (Berkeley: University of California Press, 1988); for the tradition of the Anglican Communion and the Episcopal Church in the United States of America particularly, see *Lesser Feasts and Fasts* (New York: Church Hymnal Corporation, 1980; editions are constantly updated); and for the Lutheran tradition, see Philip H. Pfatteicher's *Festivals and Commemorations: Handbook to the Calendar in Lutheran Book of Worship* (Minneapolis, MN: Augsburg, 1980). Unfortunately, the four-volume *Orthodox Saints,* by George Poulos (Brookline, MA: Holy Cross Orthodox Press, 1990–92), arranged by months, is stronger on pious tradition than critical history.

However, the three-volume *Oxford Dictionary of Byzantium,* edited by Alexander P. Kazhdan (New York: Oxford University Press, 1991), contains many fine articles on Eastern saints.

RECENT MONOGRAPHS

My colleague at the University of Notre Dame, Lawrence S. Cunningham, is to my knowledge the leading authority in the United States on the saints and on the literature pertaining to the saints. His delightfully informative little book *The Meaning of Saints* (San Francisco: Harper & Row, 1980) may be dated in parts, but it is a minor classic in the field, cited in just about every recent and current work on the subject. It is still worth reading, at least until he brings out a fuller, more up-to-date version, which he plans to do in time. He also coauthored, with Keith J. Egan, *Christian Spirituality: Themes from the Tradition* (New York: Paulist Press, 1996) and has contributed many articles on the subject in scholarly and popular journals alike.

Kenneth L. Woodward's *Making Saints: How the Catholic Church Determines Who Becomes a Saint, Who Doesn't, and Why* (New York: Simon & Schuster, 1990) is an informative and entertaining account of the canonization process from the perspective of an accomplished journalist. Woodward has been on the staff of *Newsweek* magazine since 1964, where he is senior writer for religion. The quasi-sequel is entitled *The Book of Miracles: The Meaning of the Miracle Stories in Christianity, Judaism, Buddhism, Islam* (New York: Simon & Schuster, 2000).

Even before the Second Vatican Council, two of the leading Catholic theologians of the twentieth century, Karl Rahner and Hans Urs von Balthasar, had devoted monographs or important articles to the theology of sanctity and the role of saints in the Church. Rahner's "The Church of the Saints," in *Theological Investigations,* vol. 3, *Theology of the Spiritual Life,* translated by Karl-H. and Boniface Kruger (Baltimore: Helicon Press; London: Darton, Longman & Todd, 1967, pp. 91–105), is constantly cited. Von Balthasar did various monograph-length studies on figures such as Gregory of Nyssa, Maximus the Confessor, Thérèse of Lisieux, and Elizabeth of the Trinity. Lawrence Cunningham has pointed out that von Balthasar's interest in the saints was part of his larger concern to heal the breach between spirituality and theology, as in his *A*

Theology of History (New York: Sheed and Ward, 1963) or his more recent *Mysterium Paschale,* translated by Aidan Nichols (Edinburgh: T. & T. Clark, 1990).

William M. Thompson made the first systematic attempt to show how the lives of the saints are a locus for the doing of theology. In his *Fire and Light: The Saints and Theology* (New York: Paulist Press, 1987) he pointed out that the lives of the saints remind us that the demands of the gospel are to be fulfilled in the concrete circumstances of ordinary human life rather than in the abstract. The "fire" of saintly experience is always to be tested in the "light" of critical reflection on that experience. The most recent—and best—serious attempt to reflect theologically on the role of the saints is Elizabeth A. Johnson's *Friends of God and Prophets: A Feminist Theological Reading of the Communion of Saints* (New York: Continuum, 1998).

OFFICIAL DOCUMENTS

Pope John Paul II revised the procedures for canonization in 1983. The English translation of his apostolic constitution *Divinus perfectionis Magister* (Lat., "The Divine Master of Perfection") and of the "Norms to Be Observed in Inquiries Made by Bishops in the Causes of Saints" is contained in *New Laws for the Causes of Saints,* translated by Robert J. Sarno (Rome: Sacred Congregation for the Causes of Saints, 1983). The original Latin text of the constitution is in *Acta Apostolicae Sedis* 75 (April 9, 1983): 349–55.

Index of Names

Names of saints and pages of principal entries for saints and blessed are in bold type.

Index of Subjects

Pages of principal entries for feast days are in bold type.

Photographic and Art Credits

Grateful acknowledgment is given to the following individuals and organizations for the photographs and art that appear in this book.

p. 60—Musée du Louvre, Paris, France (Photo: Scala/Art Resource, NY)
p. 66—Photo: © Bettmann/Corbis
p. 78—Photo: Benedict J. Fernandez, National Portrait Gallery, Smithsonian Institution, Washington, D.C., USA/Art Resource, NY
p. 79—Stadtisches Museum Simeonstift Trier, Trier, Germany; Photo: © Archivo Iconografico, S.A..Corbis
p. 85—Museo d'Arte Moderna, Udine, Italy; Photo: © Archivo Iconografico, S.A./Corbis
p. 90—Museo del Prado, Madrid, Spain; Photo: © Archivo Iconografico, S.A./Corbis
p. 93—Photo: © Hulton—Deutsch Collection/Corbis
p. 95—© Bettmann/Corbis
p. 96—Photo: © Andrea Jemolo/Corbis
p. 99—© Bettmann/Corbis
p. 105—Photo: © José F. Poblete/Corbis
p. 122—Photo: © Bettmann/Corbis
p. 126—S. Felicita, Florence, Italy; Photo: Alinari/Art Resource, NY
p. 135—Archbishop's Palace, Ravenna, Italy; Photo: Scala/Art Resource, NY
p. 137—Museo Civico, Padua, Italy; Photo: Cameraphoto/Art Resource, NY
p. 143—Photo: © Bettmann/Corbis
p. 149—Photo: © Catholic News Service
p. 166—Photo: © Corbis
p. 173—Victoria & Albert Museum, London, UK; Photo: © Archivo Iconografico, S.A./Corbis
p. 186—Convento of San Marco, Florence, Italy; Photo: Arte & Immagini srl/Corbis
p. 186—San Marco, Venice, Italy; Photo: Scala/Art Resource, NY
p. 193—© 1998 Lu Bro; image courtesy of Lu Bro. Color reproductions available from Bridge Building Images, Inc., at PO Box 1048, Burlington, VT 05042, 1–800–325–6263 or www.BridgeBuilding.com
p. 207—Photo: © Bettmann/Corbis
p. 208—British Museum, London, UK; Photo: Snark/Art Resource, NY
p. 219—Musée du Louvre, Paris, France; Photo: Giraudon/Art Resource, NY
p. 224—Photo: © Bettmann/Corbis
p. 239—Museo Correr, Venice, Italy; Photo: Scala/Art Resource, NY
p. 251—The Frick Collection, New York, NY, USA; Photo: © Francis G. Mayer/Corbis
p. 256—The State Russian Museum, St. Petersburg, Russia; Photo: © The State Russian Museum/Corbis
p. 262—Photo: © Chris Hellier/Corbis
p. 264—Duomo, Monreale, Italy; Photo: Giraudon/Art Resource, NY
p. 272—© Catholic News Service
p. 276—Photo: © Archivo Iconografico, S.A./Corbis
p. 282—Appartamento Borgia/Vatican Palace, Rome; Photo: Alinari/Art Resource, NY

p. 290—Worcester Art Museum & School, Worcester, MA, USA; Photo: © Burstein Collection/Corbis
p. 292—Photo: © Bettman/Corbis
p. 294—Pinacoteca, Vatican Museums, Vatican State, Italy; Photo: Scala/Art Resource, NY
p. 300—Photo: © Hulton—Deutsch Collection/Corbis
p. 301—from "Historie des Papes" by Maurice Lachatre; Photo: © Leonard de Selva/Corbis
p. 311—© Catholic News Service
p. 317—© National Gallery Collection; by kind permission of the Trustees of the National Gallery, London, UK/Corbis
p. 337—Musée des Beaux—Arts, Tournai, Belgium; Photo: Giraudon/Art Resource, NY
p. 343—Galleria Palatina Palazzo Pitti, Florence, Italy; Photo: © Arte & Immagini srl/Corbis
p. 349—Chiesa di Ognissanti, Florence, Italy; Photo: Alinari/Art Resource, NY
p. 359—Photo: © Bettmann/Corbis
p. 363—Photo: © Bettmann/Corbis
p. 364—Photo: © Bettmann/Corbis
p. 380—Photo: © Bettmann/Corbis
p. 382—Photo: © Bettmann/Corbis
p. 391—Musée de L'Assistance Publique, Paris, France; Photo: Giraudon/Art Resource, NY
p. 395—Benaki Museum, Athens, Greece; Photo: Scala/Art Resource, NY
p. 397—Busch—Reisinger Museum, Cambridge, MA. USA; Photo: © Burnstein Collection/Corbis
p. 399—Bibliothèque Nationale, Paris, France; Photo: Giraudon, Art Resource, NY
p. 404—Basilica of San Francesco, Assisi, Italy; Photo: © Elio Ciol/Corbis
p. 422—Photo: Archivo Iconografico, S.A./Corbis
p. 448—Photo: © Bettmann/Corbis
p. 449—© Catholic News Service
p. 464—S. Pietro in Vincoli, Rome, Italy; Photo: Alinari/Art Resource, NY
p. 466—S. Francesco, Assisi, Italy; Photo: Alinari/Art Resource, NY
p. 474—Photo: © Bettmann/Corbis
p. 479—© George Tanguay/Catholic News Service
p. 480—Photo © Bettmann/Corbis
p. 486—La Galleria Nazionale dell'Umbria, Perugia, Italy; Photo: © Art & Immagini srl/Corbis
p. 490—Photo: © Elio Ciol/Corbis
p. 493—La Galleria Nazionale dell'Umbria, Perugia, Italy; Photo: © Arte & Immagini srl/Corbis
p. 497—Photograph by John Howard Griffin used with permission of the Merton Legacy Trust
p. 500—Mission San Gabriel, Southern California, USA; Photo: © Richard Cummins/Corbis
p. 519—Galleria Palatina, Palazzo Pitti, Florence, Italy; Photo: © Arte & Immagini srl/Corbis
p. 520—La Galleria Nazionale dell' Umbria, Perugia, Italy; Photo: © Arte & Immagini srl/Corbis
p. 524—Silvestro, Venice, Italy; Photo: Cameraphoto/Art Resource, NY